The Diaries of Sir Robert Bruce Lockhart

I: 1915–1938

Books by Sir Robert Bruce Lockhart

MEMOIRS OF A BRITISH AGENT (1932)
RETREAT FROM GLORY (1934)
RETURN TO MALAY (1936)
GUNS OR BUTTER (1938)
COMES THE RECKONING (1947)
MY ROD MY COMFORT (1949)
THE MARINES WERE THERE (1950)
SCOTCH (1957)
JAN MASARYK (1951)
MY EUROPE (1952)
YOUR ENGLAND (1955)
TWO REVOLUTIONS (1957)
FRIENDS, FOE AND FOREIGNERS (1957)
GIANTS CAST LONG SHADOWS (1960)

1. *Sir Robert Bruce Lockhart*

THE DIARIES OF
Sir Robert Bruce Lockhart

VOLUME ONE

1915–1938

Edited by
Kenneth Young

ST. MARTIN'S PRESS
NEW YORK

ST. MARTIN'S PRESS INC
175 Fifth Avenue, New York, N.Y. 10010

Reproduced photolitho in Great Britain by
J. W. Arrowsmith Ltd, Bristol

Library of Congress Catalog Card Number: 73-92618

First published in the United States of America in 1974

AFFILIATED PUBLISHERS: Macmillan London Limited
also at Bombay, Calcutta, Madras and Melbourne

CONTENTS

ILLUSTRATIONS

The publishers are grateful to Robin Bruce Lockhart for providing photographs 1, 2, 3, 4, 5, 6, 9, 12, 13, 17, 18, 21; and to the *Evening Standard* for help with photographs 7, 10, 11, 15, 23, 24, 27, 28, 29 as well as those credited to them below. Bayer, 24; Beaverbrook Foundation, 14; Bertram Park, 1; Camera Press, 27; *Daily Express*, 11; *Evening Standard*, 8, 16, 20, 25, 26; Fox Photos, 23; Keystone, 28; Photopress, 29; Planet, 22; Radio Times Hulton Picture Library, 19; Universal, 7, 10; Vandyk, 15.

INTRODUCTION

The diaries and journals of Sir Robert Bruce Lockhart (1887–1970) consist of nearly two hundred separate volumes, containing an estimated three million words. He began keeping a diary in Moscow in 1915, and for some years had three diaries going simultaneously, using one to jot down his immediate impressions before going to bed – often in the early hours – another, usually written before breakfast, giving a more expansive version of the previous day's events, and a third mainly for appointments, expenditure and addresses or telephone numbers. In addition, he kept special diaries of his trips abroad.

The diaries reflect an extraordinarily diverse career. In Moscow he was Acting Consul-General and returned to Russia after the October 1917 revolution as British representative to the 'provisional' Lenin government. Many of the pre-Communist and Communist leaders he came to know extremely well.

After the 1914–18 war, first as a member of the Legation staff in Prague and then as a banker, he travelled Central Europe and knew kings, politicians, not least the Masaryks and Eduard Beneš, and writers such as Karel Čapek (author of *R.U.R.*). In London his circle of acquaintance was vast: he played golf with the Prince of Wales; he knew H. G. Wells and Arnold Bennett; Lloyd George, Winston Churchill; and his circle expanded when he went to work for Lord Beaverbrook on the *Evening Standard* and became one of his intimates.

The circle increased once again when during the 1939–45 war he became a Deputy Under-Secretary of State for Foreign Affairs; he formed close friendships with Anthony Eden (the Earl of Avon), Brendan Bracken, Whitehall military men such as General Ismay and General Leslie Hollis, and with Sir Orme Sargent, later Permanent Under-Secretary at the Foreign Office. Of these and many more he gives incomparable, speaking likenesses; indeed no one could attempt a life of the Earl of Avon, Lord Beaverbrook or Brendan Bracken without consulting these diaries.

Among many others prominent in the world and in Bruce Lockhart's diaries are the Prince of Wales, King Carol of Rumania, the Webbs, Daisy, Countess of Warwick, Arthur Ransome, G. D. H. Cole, Anthony de Rothschild, Rex Fletcher (Lord Winster), Lord Mountbatten, Austen Chamberlain, Sir Reginald Leeper, Sir Oswald Mosley, Harold Nicolson, Tim Healy, William Gerhardi, Leslie Hore-Belisha, Walter Citrine and Lord Vansittart to whom he paid superb tribute in *Giants Cast Long Shadows* (1960).

It is clear that he began to write consciously for posterity, probably as early as the late 1920s. The diaries, he wrote in the late 1950s, would be an heirloom for his son, Robin. Because he was writing for future readers he felt free to be less than circumspect, and sometimes not quite accurate, in his references to people and events. Many entries could scarcely be printed in his lifetime, nor in the lifetime of some of his contemporaries. His opinions of men and women are often startling in their frankness, though sometimes as he came to know them better he changed his mind. He wrote – sometimes maliciously – of the great men he had known, some intimately; of his friends; and as a spectator of the often bizarre or culpable behaviour of those among whom he found himself, in Lord Beaverbrook's drawing-room, in the offices of government or embassies and at his own various homes.

The inter-war diaries in particular leave an overwhelming impression of the megalomania of many famous men and of the loose morals of them and of the aristocracy – permissiveness was then confined to the rich upper classes; it was not until the affluent 1960s that it seeped down to the lower reaches of society.

Bruce Lockhart himself was no paragon of virtue. Some of the lax behaviour of the rich and famous with whom he associated – partly because of his rôle as gossip writer on the *Evening Standard* – rubbed off on to him; some of his self-indulgence came, however, from his own inherent nature. Of his bad habits he often wrote despairingly, of his anxieties and of his relations with women. He was not for nothing born and bred a Presbyterian.

It must be added that however critically and sometimes erroneously he wrote of the distinguished and powerful, when he was in their company butter would not melt in his mouth. Only afterwards, alone with his diaries, the butter turned rancid indeed.

From the literary point of view it is hard to describe the diaries. He is not exactly a Creevey, for unlike Creevey he had himself a not unimportant part to play in the events he describes; nor exactly a Greville for he had less insight into the course of English politics, though few men knew as much about European politics. Like Pepys he commented on the political and social scene and was equally candid about himself, at least as he saw himself. His disclosures about those in powerful positions in the Second World War will be the stuff of history when the tight-lipped memoirs of some of the leaders themselves are stuffing dustbins.

The diaries are not very like any others known to me. They are much more businesslike, less literary, than those of his friend and colleague, Harold Nicolson; they are far less superficial than those of 'Chips' Channon and wider in scope. Bruce Lockhart was a diplomat by nature, but fortunately indiscreet in his diaries, a fault, if such it is, that must endear him to succeeding generations.

How did he find time to write this mountain of words? He was after all endlessly preoccupied with his day-to-day work as journalist, banker or high government official, writing books, travelling hither and thither, regularly learning new languages, broadcasting, lecturing – in short earning a living. One must conclude that he was a genuine example of the compulsive writer; pen-to-paper became with him as habitual as brushing his teeth. Yet how he was able to write so fully, not least during the last war when he was directing a Political Warfare operation and on call night and day, remains a mystery.

Interspersed with the journals I have edited are some of the more important letters Lockhart received. In both cases, I have sought to explain in footnotes or by textual interpolations who the main personages were; and, by brief connecting sentences or paragraphs, to enable the reader to follow Lockhart's movements against the background of events. I have corrected his spelling of names when I have been able to identify them and have expanded his many contractions.

Some of the diary material that is otiose has been removed; and some has had to be withheld for so-called 'security' reasons – or, more seriously, because living persons might be wounded, defamed or libelled. It has sometimes been necessary to substitute dashes for people's names. Nevertheless what has been allowed to remain gives, in my opinion, an incomparable picture of great men and high events of which Bruce Lockhart's own books are perforce the mere tip of the iceberg.

Robert Hamilton Bruce Lockhart, born on 2 September 1887, in Anstruther, Fifeshire, was a Scot of the Scots. Not a drop of English blood ran in his veins: he never even set foot in England until after he had sailed from Leith to become a student in France and Germany. His father's family were Lowlanders, and the family tree goes back through the Bruces to the Elgins; James Boswell, Johnson's biographer, was a collateral forebear; the ancestry may be traced back to the twelfth century.[1] In the eighteenth and nineteenth centuries some Lockharts had been farmers, others had gone to seek, and sometimes to find, a fortune in the Empire.

R.H.B.L.'s father, Robert Bruce Lockhart, born in Canada, was a schoolmaster, a Cambridge graduate and, at the time of R.H.B.L.'s birth, headmaster of the Waid Academy, Anstruther; later he became head of Spier's School at Beith in Ayrshire. In 1895 he founded Seafield House preparatory school at Broughty Ferry, Forfarshire; and in 1906 he bought another prep school, Eagle House, at Sandhurst, Berkshire, reputed to be the second oldest school of its kind; Disraeli and his brother were among its first pupils.

As Robert Bruce Lockhart was later to point out, the prevalence of the name Robert in his family was 'bewildering both to our friends and to ourselves', though he carried on the tradition by naming his son Robert (known as Robin). R.H.B.L. himself was called 'Bertie' at home but later his friends called him 'Bruce'. As his father also preferred to be called Bruce, this too was confusing. One of his brothers is a near-Robert, General Sir

[1] He seems to have shared a common ancestor, John Reid, who fell at Flodden Field in 1515, with his friend Harold Nicolson, with Bertrand Russell, and General Booth-Tucker of the Salvation Army.

Rob Lockhart. One of his maternal uncles was also Robert. The name 'Bruce Lockhart' was never hyphenated, though some believed it to be.

Robert Bruce Lockhart's mother was a Highlander, a member of the McGregor clan and at his schools he sported the appropriate tartan. Descendants of Rob Roy, they had been crofters until in the early nineteenth century they founded the Balmenach whisky distillery which with Glenlivet ranks as the oldest licensed distillery in Scotland. They made money and spent it and often drank too much of their own product. R.H.B.L.'s grandmother McGregor, a dominating lady to whom he was to be much beholden, had a fortune at her disposal, some of which she invested with at first excellent results in Malayan rubber plantation, whither as a very young man Robert Bruce Lockhart went to work.

He was given at a later date to remark that, inside himself, Lowland and Highland were continually at war; and, he thought, his provident, self-denying Lowland element usually lost the battle to Highland excess and self-indulgence. The journals show how all his adult life he feared the alcoholic disaster of some of his ancestors, even to jotting down in his diaries the number and nature of the alcoholic drinks he had each day, yet his never-ending good resolutions always came to grief; and remorse followed grief. When he was forty-four, he taunted himself in his diary (5 February 1932) with the words: 'Surely by now I have reached the age when other things than drink, self-indulgence and whoring will satisfy me.' Whoring was too strong a word – he seldom if ever frequented prostitutes; but he had many female liaisons, in many classes of society, at home and abroad.

He found it hard to say 'no'; he was generous to a fault partly because, he himself believed, of his 'fatal weakness: I always cultivated my popularity' (*My Scottish Youth*, p. 313). He thought nothing in later years of visiting three night clubs in a night nor of hiring gipsy bands to regale himself and his friends, nor of dancing on the tops of empty champagne bottles. He was usually in debt; and after his sojourn in Central Europe in the 1920s, duns pursued him from Prague to London.

He was without doubt a Highlander in his introspection, his impetuosity, and perhaps, too, in his passion for the romantic past, as well as in his persuasive, diplomatic gifts. He was probably correct in seeing similarities between the Celt and the Slav which gave him insight into, among others, his great friend Jan Masaryk. Yet the Lowlander Bruce Lockhart did assert himself; he was capable of sustained hard work, however punctuated with expensive excesses. It is, indeed, ironical how this introspective man was so largely occupied in such outgoing activities as diplomacy, journalism, writing diaries much more concerned with others than himself and, during the Second World War, in running the most awkward squad any Government had to employ.

When he was a baby, his old nurse recounted: 'He was no exactly an oil painting but my! he was fly!' She was right. He was squat and he had a big head. But he was *sympathique*; many ladies, in and out of Society, fell for his charm.

His early education was at the schools of which his father was headmaster, Spier's School at Beith, and Seafield House. His father was devoted to rugby football and cricket. From the first, R.H.B.L. was keen on games and all forms of sport, above all, angling which he pursued all his life and all over the world and to which he devoted one of the best of his books, *My Rod My Comfort* (1949); 'Of all my books,' he wrote, 'it is my favourite.'

His youth, he says, was dominated by fear; Scottish, and indeed British, education was at that time strictly disciplined. As a prep schoolboy he learned a great deal of Latin, some Greek, committed to memory much Scottish poetry, began to learn the piano and then switched to the violin. The regime was spartan, both at prep school and later at Fettes College, Edinburgh, into which he passed on a scholarship second out of twelve successful candidates in September 1900, and so became a 'Colleger'. At Fettes the daily cold bath and the lack of central heating did not perturb him. He was tough. At Fettes, he made many lifelong friends, not least of whom was K. G. Macleod, his exact contemporary and Scotland's greatest rugger International, and Moir Mackenzie (afterwards active in the Federation of British Industries and knighted), and one of the young masters, subsequently well-known as the novelist Ian Hay. Bruce Lockhart excelled in rugby, becoming a member of the First XV, and in cricket. 'I spent,' he wrote, 'five years in the worship of athleticism.'

I expect this was why, though a 'scholar', he did not blossom out scholastically. He would have liked to have followed his father to Cambridge, but his examination results were not adequate. This, as his subsequent Civil Service examination success showed, was not due to lack of intellect. Nevertheless, 'I was,' he wrote in *Memoirs of a British Agent* (1932), 'a grievous disappointment to my parents.' His younger brothers were luckier or more assiduous in their studies; his next brother, only eighteen months younger, with whom he was exceedingly close in boyhood, J. H. Bruce Lockhart – known from his red hair as Rufus or 'K' (phonetic for carrots) – distinguished himself at Cambridge by obtaining two Blues and a good second in modern languages. He was later headmaster of Sedbergh.

Bruce Lockhart left Fettes school in April 1905. *Faute de mieux* it was decided that he should go to Germany and to France to learn their languages and to prepare himself for a possible future in the overseas Civil Service. In both countries, he greatly distinguished himself in his studies. At the Academy of Professor Tilley (an Australian by birth) in Berlin he earned golden encomia; above all, R.H.B.L. later wrote, 'Tilley showed me how to work – a virtue, in spite of many backslidings, I have never entirely lost. He taught me two other valuable lessons – respect for institutions and customs other than English and the secret of modern languages.' In Paris, he came under 'that good and godly man, Paul Passey', a Calvinist absorbed in linguistic studies. Bruce Lockhart acquired 'an excellent French accent' and a deep knowledge of phonetics which, apart from any other use, proved of value as a kind of code when he was writing his diaries during his imprisonment in Moscow.

He returned, this time to England – where his father was headmaster of Eagle House at Sandhurst, Berkshire – in 1908. Instead, however, of preparing for a Civil Service examination, his McGregor uncle, Ian, home from Malaya with stories of quick fortunes to be made in rubber, fired his imagination. In October 1908, he left with his uncle for Malaya. Before long 'the cloudless Eastern skies, the golden sand with their background of cooling palms and lofty casuarinas' had him in thrall; he came under the influence of the romantic novels of Pierre Loti and of the early Joseph Conrad. From Port Dickson – where he played rugby for the state of Negri Sembilan – he moved into the foothills to open a new rubber estate. The Malay language he studied with success; he wrote short stories and sketches many of which were published under pseudonyms in magazines in Britain; he shot rats and once a cobra with his revolver.

He also fell violently in love with a Malay Princess, Amai, ward of the Sultan of Negri Sembilan. She broke all the rules by living with him in his bungalow. There was a resounding scandal and then, stricken by a most virulent form of the endemic malaria, he left for home via Japan and Canada in October 1910. He believed and indeed stated in *Memoirs of a British Agent* (1932) that he would never see Amai again. But twenty-five years later, when he was forty-eight, he did see her again. In his *Return to Malaya* he described their meeting: it is one of the most moving passages in all his writings.

As in a dream I walked across the primitive river bridge which had separated my bungalow from the rubber estate. The trees on the first clearing were wintering, and in their leafless branches I saw the symbol of my own dead past. Geographical reunion revived a thousand memories, and everywhere I saw ghosts of my youth . . .

Contrary to my expectations I had no difficulty in recognising her. She had changed but not so much as Freddie had led me to believe. As she came forward to meet me, she drew back her head sarong, and I saw that the beautiful oval face of her youth had become broader and more rugged. The skin, too, was darker and slightly weather-beaten. But her eyes, large and lustrous, still looked straight at me. Her figure was erect. There was a fine dignity in her carriage. She was old, but she had worn remarkable well for a Malay woman.

'The Tuan is married?' she asked. 'Yes.' 'The Tuan has a child?' 'Yes.' 'A son?' 'Yes.' 'What does he do?' I told her.

Then Freddie came back with the car.

The brown eyes looked into mine. There was an awkward pause.

For the only time in our lives we shook hands.

'Go in peace,' she said.

'Remain in peace.' I said.

I stepped into the car, and at Freddie's order Kassim drove away at top speed. I looked back only once. She was still standing there by the rice, her arm stretched out like a sign-post. Huge angry clouds had turned the sunset to a fiery orange. Before we reached Seremban the soft tropical rain had fallen. The long drought had come to an end.

Back home in early 1911 at his father's house in Berkshire it was decided that Bruce Lockhart should quit rubber planting for good and seek entry to the Consular Service, at that time distinct from the Diplomatic Service. Examinations for the Service were extremely testing and demanded high standards of learning. So Bruce Lockhart was sent to a crammer. There were, in any case, only four appointments to be had and seventy-nine candidates for them. The subjects were English, French, German, Law, Arithmetic, Geography and Political Economy.

Now the Fettes 'failure' had his revenge. One bright September day – his birthday – in 1911 he heard that he had come first in the tough examination with 1216 marks out of a possible 1600: 'Overnight,' he wrote, 'I had passed from the ranks of the ne'er-do-wells into the Valhalla of heroes.' So he embarked upon his second, but by no means his last, career, and the one that was to bring him to the notice not only of the great ones of the land but of many who never met him.

Sir Edward Grey (later Viscount Grey of Fallodon) was the presiding Foreign Secretary, the head of the Consular Service ('Senior Clerk') was the second Marquess of Dufferin and Ava, temporarily replaced through his illness by a remarkable man, J. D. ('Don') Gregory, later an Assistant Under-Secretary who after a minor scandal withdrew to live at Buckfast, Devon, where he was closely associated with the monks of Buckfast Abbey. Gregory had read and admired some of Bruce Lockhart's stories of the Far East and, as acting head of the Consular Service, took Bruce Lockhart under his wing. They became firm friends.

Three months after his entry into the Foreign Office Bruce Lockhart received a posting. He was to go to Moscow as Vice-Consul. This delighted him. His salary was to be £300 p.a., in those days no despicable sum, and it was to rise by yearly increments of £20 to £500. He was to have a non-pensionable local allowance of £50 p.a. £100 was assigned to him for his outfit. Naturally, the writ ran, 'You are restricted from engaging in commercial pursuits.' But no official provision was made for expenses, and this Bruce Lockhart later found embarrassing.

Before he left for Moscow his parents gave him a farewell party and dance in Berkshire. At one house-party he attended he met a 'beautiful Australian girl', Jean Haslewood Turner who came from Brisbane. Her grandfather had been the richest man in Queensland, but misfortune had later overtaken the estate. Nevertheless she had been accustomed to a life of luxury. 'I succumbed at once. I had only a fortnight in which to press my suit. In ten days we were engaged.' They were married during his first leave from Moscow in 1913.

But when, aged twenty-four, he first arrived in Moscow in January 1912, he was still a bachelor, young and warm-blooded. His chief was Montgomery

Grove, the British Consul-General. Though the Embassy was in those days in St Petersburg, there was plenty in Moscow for the ardent young vice-consul to do and see. He saw and did everything available: 'My first two years in Russia were the happiest in my life,' he wrote forty-five years later (in *The Two Revolutions*, 1957). These years he has described in *Memoirs of a British Agent* and elsewhere. One of the things about the Russians that he found revealing was that shops even in the main streets of St Petersburg and Moscow had, in addition to the names of their owners, painted signs portraying a loaf of bread, a cube of sugar or a ham – with good reason, since rather less than ten per cent of Russians could read or write.

Lockhart liked 'abroad', however often he found it necessary to refresh himself in his native Scotland. He was a natural *boulevardier* and pre-revolutionary Moscow and St Petersburg were a *boulevardier's* natural homes. To a young diplomat it was a paradise of parties, circuses, night clubs, operas, gipsy bands. It was also the land of the 'intelligentsia', a word that Russia gave to the world. As well as great writers, musicians and theatrical producers, it was the country of endless smart talk, much of it politically and morally subversive, paving the way to anarchism from which a Communist dictatorship was the only beneficiary.

To Bruce Lockhart all society was open, nor was it an exclusively Russian society: many business houses and industries were owned and run by Britons, French and Germans. The two brothers Charnock, for instance, were Lancashire businessmen connected with the cotton industry; Harry Charnock was manager of a large cotton mill. Lockhart played soccer for their factory team, the 'Morozovtsi', which won the Moscow League Championship.

The Russian language he quickly learned from Madame Ertel, whose star pupil was Captain Archibald Wavell with whom Lockhart overlapped for two weeks. Field-Marshal Lord Wavell was later a great army commander and subsequently Viceroy of India.

Bruce Lockhart has drawn a disarmingly frank and doubtless accurate picture of his physical self at this time:

> Had I taken stock of myself at that time, I should have seen a young man of twenty-five, broad-shouldered and broken-nosed, with a squat, stumpy figure and a ridiculous gait. The young man's character was a curious mixture of Lockhart caution and asceticism and McGregor recklessness and self-indulgence. Hitherto, the McGregor had held the whip-hand over the Lockhart, and perhaps his chief failing had been an all-too-Celtic tendency to confound licentiousness with romanticism. Such accomplishments as he had –a good memory, a facility for languages, and a capacity for sudden bursts of hard work, were largely nullified by a lazy tolerance, which always sought the easiest way out of any difficulty, and by a fatal disposition to sacrifice the future for the cheap applause of the moment. In short, a still unformed and unattractive young man, whose self-consciousness at moments amounted almost to a disease.

To his career in Russia Lockhart devoted two books, *Memoirs of a British Agent* and *The Two Revolutions*, and parts of several others including *My*

Europe. In addition, his journals begin in Moscow in January 1915. These early Russian diaries are often little more than jottings; they add something, though not a great deal to what he himself later put into print.

Only a brief résumé of events is here necessary. He progressed in the service and earned golden opinions, but his marriage was soon in disrepair. In September 1917, after his wife's second complaint[1] to the ambassador, Sir George Buchanan, about Bruce Lockhart's entanglements with women, he was sent home on 'enforced sick leave . . . it was as a culprit rather than a martyr that I slunk out of Moscow' believing (mistakenly) that he would never return.

Then came the Bolshevik *coup d'état* in October 1917 and Bruce Lockhart in London found himself the centre of enquiries about Russia from politicians, such as A. J. Balfour, Arthur Henderson, Carson, Curzon, Bonar Law, Lord Milner ('about the only one who strikes me as efficient') and the Prime Minister, David Lloyd George. He also met Litvinov, the Bolshevik unofficial ambassador to London ('more sluggish and slower, heavily built with broad forehead, did not strike me as a bad fellow') in, of all places, Lyons corner shop in the Strand.

Before long, such is the whirligig of fate, he was in January 1918 sent – with a letter from Litvinov to Trotsky in his pocket – back to Moscow as head of a special mission to establish unofficial relations with the Bolsheviks. He was thus placed at the eye of the storm between those who believed that no contact was desirable or possible with an illegal régime whose hands were stained with multi-killings – and those who believed that it was essential for contact to be made if only to try to persuade the Bolshevik leaders to continue the war against Germany. And in due course he was involved in another storm: the question whether the Allies should or should not intervene with military forces on the side of the still numerous anti-Bolsheviks.

In Moscow, having almost daily talks with Trotsky, the Bolshevik War Minister, he formed the view that intervention would be madness, and as early as February 1918, sent off telegrams 'recommending conciliatory measures'. When, however, the British Government adopted a contrary policy he loyally supported it, though continuing to point out the dangers. When the Bolsheviks signed the Brest-Litovsk peace with the Germans, he wrote in his diary, 25 March 1918, 'Only policy in this country must be support for any group that will oppose Germans.' But his private diary continued with bitter recriminations against Foreign Secretary Balfour and the British General Staff: 'Our people at home are so incredibly stupid that they will drift into tragedy, almost without knowing it.' Personally he remained in favour of cooperation with the Bolsheviks.

Bruce Lockhart's position with his London superiors became as shaky as

[1] Mrs Bruce Lockhart (now Mrs Loudon McLean) maintains that the complaints were made not by her but by the novelist, Hugh Walpole, who served in Russia and who felt sorry for her. Walpole spent much time in the Bruce Lockharts' company.

with Lenin and Trotsky, particularly after the Allied landings at Murmansk. The Czar and his family were murdered at Ekaterinburg in July 1918; murder indeed became the order of the day – and cholera broke out in Moscow. After the Allied landing at Archangel, Bruce Lockhart's situation was hopeless. On 31 August, there was an attempt on Lenin's life. The consulate was searched by Bolsheviks; the Embassy in Petrograd was sacked and a naval officer was shot. On 3 September 1918 Bruce Lockhart recorded in his diary: 'Papers today full of the most fantastic accounts of an Allied conspiracy of which I am said to be at the head. The account, which reads like a fairy-tale, includes "buying over of Lett troops", "shooting Lenin and Trotsky", "taking Petrograd and Moscow by hunger", "blowing up bridges", and "appointment of dictators".'

Bruce Lockhart, not surprisingly, was arrested on 4 September. He was not ill-treated; and though in danger of his life, retained a remarkable composure. His new friend, Moura Benckendorff, later Baroness Budberg, brought him food and reading matter.

He was released on 1 October, after nearly a month in prison, in exchange for Maxim Litvinov, the unofficial Bolshevik ambassador in London. It took him eighteen days to reach Aberdeen. After his departure, he was condemned to death *in absentia*, and he never returned to Russia. Back in London he was called to the King on 23 October; George V 'was very nice and showed a surprising grasp of the situation; he however did most of the talking and during the forty minutes I was with him I didn't really get much in. He sees pretty well the need for reforms everywhere, and has a wholesome dread of Bolshevism.' He also saw Foreign Secretary Balfour who 'showed far more interest in the philosophy of Bolshevism than in the Russian situation'. But then Balfour was a philosopher!

Not until fourteen years later did Bruce Lockhart's story of these momentous events appear. This account, *Memoirs of a British Agent*,[1] ends with his arrival in Britain.

The tale is taken up again in *Retreat from Glory* (1934). Here the journals give a more explicit account of his shuttlecock existence in the Foreign Office in the months after his return to England, the butt at once of interventionists and non-interventionists. The Foreign Office 'establishment' – Hardinge and Tyrrell[2] – regarded him (in his own words) as 'a hysterical schoolboy who had intrigued with the Prime Minister behind the Foreign Office's back'. His own former Mission members in Russia, however, appreciated him and, with Hugh Walpole present, gave him a dinner on 13 November 1918. A junior member of the Foreign Office, Harold Nicolson – later a close friend and colleague – stopped him on the Foreign Office

[1] 'Agent' not in the sense of secret agent, which Lockhart was not, but as agent or representative of the British Government.

[2] 'The Foreign Office is not in the least interested in my account of things. They prefer the reactionaries who have never even seen Bolshevism. Tyrrell and Hardinge are frankly and avowedly hostile.' As always Milner was 'most sympathetic'.

stairs and firmly observed that Bruce Lockhart's report 'was one of the best that he had ever read'. Bruce Lockhart told his diary that 'Personally, all my sympathies are with Labour but not with Bolshevism' (16 November 1918), and 'I don't like the Bolsheviks, and don't go so far right as Denikin and Co.' (24 October 1918).

Eventually, the war over, he was posted as Commercial Secretary to the British Legation in Prague, the capital of the newly created Czechoslovakia. He had known many Czechs and Slovaks in Russia, indeed had intervened successfully on their behalf, and now began what without exaggeration may be termed his love affair with that country, created by the Versailles peace treaty. With the Czechoslovaks he was to be concerned almost to the end of his long life: he came to admire and to love many of them – President Masaryk and his son, Jan, Eduard Beneš and others less known.

He enjoyed life in Prague and entered fully not to say recklessly into its gay diversions – so fully indeed that his debts soon mounted to about £10,000 and became an incubus which he saw no chance of throwing off as long as he had to exist on the exiguous pay of a Legation Secretary. Moreover his McGregor grandmother, who had frequently helped him with gifts and loans, died in 1922 and in view of the money he had already received he did not figure in her will. He did, however, receive loans from such rich uncles as Tom Macgregor, the Edinburgh stockbroker. A financial crisis in Czechoslovakia increased his Prague bank overdraft overnight from £700 to £2000. He resorted to money-lenders.

To Lockhart at thirty-five his financial outlook seemed hopeless. At this moment help of a sort was at hand. He had been successful as Commercial Secretary at the Prague Legation in smoothing the way for the revival of Central European banks in which the Bank of England was interested. He was offered a post in what was, effectively, a subsidiary of the Bank of England and returned to England at the end of 1922 to be taught the rudiments of another new career. During this period he became friendly with Lady Rosslyn, known as Tommy, the third wife of Harry, 5th Earl of Rosslyn; it was a friendship that lasted for life. Through her, but not entirely because of her, the Presbyterian Bruce Lockhart was received into the Roman Catholic Church on 6 June 1924.

From 1923 to the beginning of 1928, he trekked like a commercial traveller up and down Central Europe on banking business (while also reporting for the Foreign Office). But business, as far as Lockhart's banks were concerned, was retracting. He began to think of yet another career. He had for some time been contributing stories, articles and gossip items to newspapers, particularly to the London *Evening Standard*, whose proprietor, Lord Beaverbrook, he had first met on his return from Russia in 1919. Now Beaverbrook offered him a permanent job as chief diary-writer ('The Londoner') on the *Standard*. Lockhart decided, however, to give himself eight months of freedom before settling down to work in Fleet Street. He set out for Bavaria, Slovenia and

Dalmatia and on his way back visited Switzerland where his wife and small son were then living. He also visited the ex-Kaiser. Though given no audience at that time, he later returned to Doorn, the ex-Kaiser's house of exile in Holland, and had an interview, which was published in the *Standard*. It was the first time since the war that the exiled ex-Kaiser had been willing to talk to a British journalist. The gist of this is given in *Retreat from Glory* (1934) and there are revealing items in the diaries themselves. He also interviewed Gustav Stresemann, the Foreign Minister in the ill-fated German Weimar Government.

From 1929 to 1937, Lockhart was 'nailed to my desk' in London and his visits to Europe were few and brief. It was an immensely busy, bustling life on the *Standard*. He estimated that for Beaverbrook's papers he wrote some 400,000 words a year,[1] as well as other journalism and his own diary; and at last started to write the account of his Moscow years – in 120,000 words. Much of the night – or rather the early hours of the morning – he dissipated in the mushroom *boîtes*, ill-lit and sordid, of the West End of London; sordid yet lures, lairs of the still-rich sprigs of the aristocracy, and the ex-officer would-be aristocracy. Bruce Lockhart was neither; he was a 'personality', but still he had to earn his living. These years are not much dealt with in his books; the diaries, however, cover the gaps, talking in casual journalese about the celebrated people he met in the course of his newspaper activities. He met the Prince of Wales (later, briefly Edward VIII, and for a longer period the Duke of Windsor) and played golf with him on numerous occasions. Through Lady Rosslyn he had the entrée into the highest society. He was an intimate of his employer, Lord Beaverbrook, and for a time became his political aide; he dined with him and his immensely varied circle of acquaintance at Stornoway House, Beaverbrook's London home overlooking Green Park, or spent the weekend at Cherkley, Beaverbrook's country house near Leatherhead in Surrey.

Bruce Lockhart kept up his contacts with the Foreign Office, with the friends of his youth, his banking acquaintance and with old colleagues from Russia and Central Europe. Among newer friends were journalists and authors. Harold Nicolson, whom he had known in the Foreign Office, joined him on the *Evening Standard*, and became a close friend. So, too did John Wheeler-Bennett, the historian, and another historian, Professor Lewis Namier, the spiky, hyper-sensitive Polish Jew. Malcolm Muggeridge, redeemed Communist, Howard Spring and the combative Randolph Churchill were at various periods his assistants on 'The Londoner's Diary'. Lockhart, a personality because of his, however interpreted, Russian exploits, became a remarked-upon figure in London society, a frequent guest of such hostesses as Lady (Sibyl) Colefax at Argyll House, Chelsea, and later at 19 Lord North Street; Lady (Emerald) Cunard at 9 Grosvenor Square; Mrs Ronnie ('Maggie') Greville of Polesden Lacey, whose father was the brewer,

[1] Though he observes that Hilaire Belloc in the 1930s wrote 800,000 words a year.

William McEwan; and of Mrs Muriel Beckett, wife of Rupert Beckett, banker and owner of the *Yorkshire Post*, who lived at Sunningdale. He was, in short, lionised by the frivolous rich gossips.

Himself, he was not happy in the rôle of journalist: 'If I was better paid, I was worse off. For I was much older and had heavier responsibilities.' Bruce Lockhart's home life scarcely existed and when it happened was usually unhappy. The strain of working in Fleet Street all day and writing books by night was ruinous. When his *Memoirs of a British Agent* turned out to be a runaway success – it was filmed with Leslie Howard playing Bruce Lockhart – and his second book, *Retreat from Glory* (1934) did at the time little less well, he took the plunge, left Fleet Street, and lived – or tried to live – by writing books. 'I left Fleet Street – I hope for ever – in 1937,' he wrote in *Guns or Butter* (1938). He toured Europe and Scandinavia, partly to lecture for the British Council, partly to report to Sir Robert Vansittart, then Permanent Under-Secretary at the Foreign Office. In the United States of America he had a triumphant tour as the author of the best-selling *British Agent*. In sober fact the sales of the book enabled him to pay off some, if not all, his debts.

From his first-hand experience of Europe, he became convinced that Nazi Germany must be resisted, rather than appeased, otherwise there would be war. So he found himself opposed to the policies of Chamberlain and the Conservative party as a whole (and at this time Lord Beaverbrook). He was therefore firmly on the side of the dissenters – Eden, Churchill, Lord Cranborne (later Marquess of Salisbury) and Sir Robert Vansittart. If war came, moreover, he with his Foreign Office and Secret Intelligence Service connections was bound to be involved. During the crisis of September 1938 he was summoned to the Foreign Office by his old friend, Reginald (Rex) Leeper, then busy reviving and reorganising the Political Intelligence Department. Leeper told him that, in case of war, there would be work for him in the Department.

In the diaries through Bruce Lockhart's eyes we see the misery of his friend, Jan Masaryk, then Czech Minister in London, as it became clear that his country had been sold down the river. He was summoned, too, by the *Evening Standard*. On the very day, 10 October 1938, that his *Guns or Butter* came out, in which he expressed his hope of never returning to Fleet Street, he returned to the *Standard* though on his proviso of a strictly limited period of three months.

A few days after war broke out in September 1939 he joined the Politica Intelligence Department and dealt with Central Europe and the Balkans. He was also appointed liaison officer to the exiled, provisional Czechoslovak Government led by the former President Eduard Beneš.

Later he became Director-General of the Political Warfare Executive with the rank of a Deputy Under-Secretary of State for Foreign Affairs. As such, he co-ordinated all British propaganda against the enemy, working under such congenial ministers who became personal friends as Foreign Secretary Anthony Eden (now Earl of Avon) and Information Minister Brendan Bracken. His chief colleagues included such military men as Major-General Dallas Brooks and General ('Pug') Ismay; Foreign Office chiefs Sir Orme Sargent and Sir William Strang; and among his staff were Sir John Wheeler-Bennett, Sefton Delmer, R. H. S. Crossman and the late David Bowes-Lyon. Later came such American colleagues as Robert Sherwood and General Bedell Smith.

Bruce Lockhart's task was frustrating. He was seeking to harmonise journalists and dons, stockbrokers and advertising experts and barristers. The strain caused several severe outbreaks of psoriasis; the job, he wrote, 'was my prison and the office was itself my life-sentence'. His ministerial masters treated him with the greatest consideration and kindness. But when the war ended he left speedily, despite offers of an embassy – if he would spend a year organising the Foreign Office's peace-time information services.

Instead he became a gossip writer, broadcaster and lecturer; and he recommenced author. He remarried and moved from one rented accommodation to another, usually managing to spend fishing holidays in his native Scotland, Later still he suffered from depression, his memory became erratic and he had a serious breakdown in health in the mid-1960s. He died in a Hove nursing-home at the age of eighty-two in February 1970.

It is not easy to sum up such a life – as varied in occupation as in geographical situation – in terms of happiness or unhappiness. Bruce Lockhart had a quick brain and considerable gifts of which he was able to make full use, whether in diplomacy, journalism or in the running of a large, difficult war-time department; yet there was something erratic about his conduct of his career.

His first marriage was mainly unhappy, partly because what might have sweetened family life went into social and political contacts, into friendships, or into the surface living of all kinds of clubs. Yet, although he seldom mentions this in the diaries, there were many big family gatherings, usually at his father's house in the 1920s and 1930s, when he was the life and soul of the party, organising games and charades for his son and his many nephews and nieces. Then, full of fun and good humour, he really relaxed and that dark introspection, which fills so many pages in his diaries, was very far away.

Introspective, however, he certainly was. He well knew his own faults of character; he was incapable of eradicating them. He tended to live on his nerves, and to ease tension would plunge into indulgences which he subsequently regretted.

Not all who knew him liked him. Some found in him a smiling slyness, a streak of snobbery, and did not entirely trust him. Others enjoyed his talk and apparent lightheartedness, his public bonhomie. He was easy to get on with, for there was nothing ponderous about him. He was intelligent and amusing. Yet he was easily cast down as the diaries witness. He was immensely well read in several languages; he had great linguistic gifts; he enjoyed reading Russian and Greek, and was a natural scholar who in other circumstances might have done well as a don. He knew reams of poetry by heart. He also had the travel bug, feeling more at home in Europe than in England. It is perhaps significant that his book called *My Europe*, was followed by one called *Your England*. To Scotland he returned again and again for a refreshment of spirit. As he wrote, 'the scent of heather is not a good preparation for city life', and elsewhere (*My Rod My Comfort*) added that 'My heart is in that corner of Invernesshire, Morayshire and Banffshire where the Spey runs at its swiftest.' In his adopted religion, Roman Catholicism, he found solace, despite backsliding, and he prayed regularly.

He wrote a dozen or more books, variable in quality and with one or two exceptions autobiographical. Some, including *Scotch: The Story of Whisky* (1951), still sell well. *British Agent* was a best-seller all over the world. He had the journalist's eye for striking and significant detail; and in such books as *Return to Malaya*, and in his brief study of *Jan Masaryk*, he could touch deeper notes of pathos and regret. Though not great works of literature, they are full of interest for both social and historical reasons. His diaries, now housed in their entirety at the Beaverbrook Library, will continue to be a mine for the historian and an entertainment for those who enjoy reading of men and women, great and less great, of human frailty and folly, and of important events, seen often from the inside.

KENNETH YOUNG

CHAPTER ONE

1915-1917

Lockhart on British Consular Staff, Moscow. Meets Hugh Walpole and Gorky. Russia in wartime. Kiev. The Tsar dissolves the Duma. Made Acting Consul-General. The Revolution of March 1917. Tsar abdicates. Return to England.

The journals of Sir Robert Bruce Lockhart begin on 11 January 1915, when he was twenty-eight and had already spent three years on the British Consular Staff in Moscow. The first words are 'Heard Chaliapin in Boris Godunov'.[1] *This first diary, for 1915–17, is written in a hard-backed journal, purchased in Moscow and without printed dates; it has sporadic entries up to March 1917. The material of this and the next two journals, both for 1918, was in an expanded form the basis of his best-selling* Memoirs of a British Agent, *first published in 1932.*

By the time the journals begin, Lockhart was married and was living with his wife in a Moscow flat. Some of the entries refer to their not altogether happy relationship, resulting partly from his already well-developed party-going habits and partly from his professional work which was far from being a 10-to-6 job. Some of these entries are concealed in his phonetic script or even by writing in Malayan.

Lockhart had always had a literary bent and went on writing short stories and sketches during these years in Moscow. No doubt he was stimulated by his acquaintance with Hugh Walpole, who went to Russia as a Red Cross orderly and later headed the British propaganda bureau in Petrograd.[2]

Monday, 15 February 1915

Reading *War and Peace*. To me this is infinitely Tolstoy's finest work and perhaps the greatest novel in the world. I can hardly tear myself away from it.

Thursday, 18 February 1915

Saw Gorky.[3] He looked very modest and quiet and sat at the back of the

[1] Fedor Ivanovich Chaliapin (1873–1938), born into a Russian peasant family, became a world-renowned bass-singer and actor. Mussorgsky's opera, *Boris Godunov*, provided him with one of his best-known roles.

[2] Hugh Walpole (1884–1941) used his Russian adventures in his novel *The Dark Forest*; he had already published several novels including *Mr Perrin and Mr Traill* and was to become a best-seller. He was godfather to Lockhart's son, Robin.

[3] Maxim Gorky (1868–1936), Russian novelist and playwright; he supported the Bolsheviks and had been in exile until 1914.

hall without making any attempt at publicity. His face is a very expressive one, full of feeling and sympathy, rugged too, except for the softness of his eyes.

Wednesday, 3 March 1915

Hugh Walpole came back. He had seen all the correspondents in Petrograd . . . They all believe in a revolution in Germany and the establishment of a democracy.

Friday, 2 April 1915

Left Moscow for ten days' holiday in Kiev . . . on the way met three trains of Austrian prisoners. They were well enough clothed, poor fellows, and in any case the weather was warm.

Tuesday, 6 April 1915

Went to the Lavra [monastery in Kiev] in the morning . . . When I arrived a service was going on and thousands of soldiers were drawn up in the square. People were picnicking everywhere and I saw one man in a corner of the Cathedral contentedly munching a great loaf of black bread. Unfortunately only a very few of the women were in Russian dress and these were pilgrims from the country.

Sunday, 25 April 1915

New suit came from England per Bowe. It has been made to Father's measure, and is hopeless! At night read Hugh Walpole's *Fortitude*. I like it far the best of all that school – far better than *Carnival* or *Round the Corner*.[1] The writing is a bit uneven, and he has got a horrid habit of putting things in brackets unnecessarily, but the book itself is gold, and the interest in even the smallest and most minor characters never flags.

Sunday, 16 May 1915

Hugh Walpole came down from Petrograd to show us himself in his uniform as a Red Cross Orderly. He has also succeeded in getting himself some sort of military rank as *aide-de-camp* to Guchkov[2] and is full of all that he is going to do for Russia and how he will be more use to Russia than to England. And all the time he is thinking, calculating just how much use Russia is going to be to him. He is really very nice in spite of his extraordinary egoism, and as far as a man of that sort can like anyone, I believe he likes us.

Friday, 4 June 1915

Today I went to see the Gradonachalnik about a naturalised British subject of Austrian origin who had been imprisoned on a charge of espionage. Had

[1] By Compton Mackenzie and Anna Valentine.

[2] Alexander Guchkov was in charge of the Red Cross on the German front.

a long talk with the Gradonachalnik who received me very kindly. He said that the disaster in Galicia was due solely to lack of shells and that until this was cleared up Russia would be in a bad way. He also admitted that there was a great deal of unrest (political) against the Government. It was rather significant that he said that whereas we had put our house in order a hundred and fifty years ago Russia was only beginning to do it now.

Friday, 6 August 1915

This morning's papers brought the news of the evacuation of Warsaw. It will be a bitter blow to the Russians and will go far to shake the already wavering confidence of the people in their government. There is talk of agitation among the Army itself.

Monday, 23 August 1915

Went to the races where we received news of a great Russian naval victory in the Bay of Riga. The crowd did not seem in the least excited about it and there was no cheering.

All day strong rumours emanating apparently from the banks concerning the fall of the Dardanelles. In the evening *Izvestia* brought out a special edition describing the fall of the Dardanelles. There was, of course, a manifestation. People knelt and prayed to thank God for the victory. On the Tverskaya Square near the Skobeliev Monument there was a demonstration against the police and some people were hurt. A disgraceful business to allow the paper to publish false news.

Tuesday, 24 August 1915

Today rumours of a strike at Ivanovo Voznesensk and a shooting, etc. The story is that a party of soldiers fired on the crowd who shouted 'Down with the Government' . . . Fifty casualties reported.

Saturday, 28 August 1915

A policeman arrested two drunkards. One of the latter escaped and then called on the crowd to rescue his comrade. About three thousand people answered the call and attacked the police. There was some revolver shooting. One killed and several wounded. One hundred and three arrests. Twenty policemen wounded, three badly.

Thursday, 9 September 1915

The news of the Emperor's taking over the supreme command from the Grand Duke has been received coolly but quite calmly.

Thursday, 16 September 1915

During the last few days it has become clear that the Duma is to be dissolved. This afternoon it is now an accomplished fact. It is felt, however, that the change in the supreme command and the dissolution of the Duma are all part of the same intrigue and that the Court is responsible for it, some say that it is a pro-German movement to provoke a revolution and thus make peace. Others again say that it is simply a move of the reactionaries to gain time, and to put off the evil day as far as possible. Rumours of strikes and shooting in Petrograd . . . At the final sitting of the Duma there were more scenes. The Progressists and Social Democrats left the room during the reading of the Tsar's ukase. Kerensky,[1] the Trudovik deputy, is said to have cried 'Down with the Government' and even to have raised his voice against the Emperor.

Friday, 17 September 1915

Public feeling is very excited. Today many factories went on strike and at three o'clock the tramway stopped as a protest against the Government's action. The feeling against the Emperor and Goremykin [the prime minister] is very bitter. They say the former is in a very despotic mood and all sorts of rumours are in the air: provocation of a revolution as a pretext for separate peace, Rasputin, assassination of Goremykin, etc., etc. Sent off account to Embassy.

Monday, 27 September 1915

Today a large holiday. There were serious disturbances in the Tverskaya whereby some five people were shot and some ten wounded and numerous others hurt and bruised. The trouble arose over a quarrel between a French soldier and a policeman, the crowd taking the side of the soldier. Cossacks were brought out, and there was a good deal of shooting. Some officers who took the part of the crowd were arrested for drawing their swords on the police. At eleven I went up on to the boulevard and round the side streets of the Tverskaya. The crowd was then thoroughly frightened, but the police too seemed to have lost their heads. The whole thing shows how excited public opinion is here. The people are very angry that the police have not been sent to the war.

Tuesday, 28 September 1915

Saw Chelnokov[2] at his house . . . he too blames the police for its tactlessness yesterday and says they have lost authority. The Emperor seems to have pledged himself to reaction and I dare say we may have trouble of a mild sort.

Friday, 1 October 1915

Countess Robinskaya called today . . . she said the feeling amongst the common people was very strong against the Emperor and that this was far more dangerous than the speeches of a hundred Dumas.

[1] Alexander Kerensky (1881–1970) was to become Menshevik Prime Minister in July 1917, and after the war a regular acquaintance of Lockhart.

[2] Mikhail Chelnokov, Mayor of Moscow, was Lockhart's 'best friend in Russia'.

Saturday, 2 October 1915

At Pokrov, the crowd smashed in windows, shouted for the Duma and against the police and were all drunk.

Sunday, 24 October 1915

Chelnokov said that Khvostov [Home Secretary] had told him that his own position with the Emperor was as follows: 'I have two months in which I shall be his favourite, two months in which he will suspect me, and two months during the course of which he will kick me out. I have roughly until January 1st. I must act quickly.'

Saturday, 18 December 1915

Letter from Bruce[1] enclosing a copy of the Ambassador's despatch about the Moscow office allowance. He says: 'There is scarcely any consular post of the same importance as Moscow at the present moment. It is the industrial and in a certain broad sense the political capital of Russia . . . You will have seen from Mr Lockhart's despatches the excellent work that has been done by that office since Mr C. Clive Bayley's departure.'

Sunday, 26 December 1915

Made my first speech in Russian. Very cold. −26°.

Tuesday, 18 January 1916

Had a long talk with Chelnokov on the internal situation. He is more hopeful but agrees with me that the Russians will require some material successes this summer if they are to go through another winter campaign.

Monday, 31 January 1916

Went to see Chelnokov and had a long talk with him. He was splendidly received by Alexeyev,[2] who is quite well informed as to what is going on, and has evidently no opinion of the ministry. He said to Chelnokov: 'The Emperor is all right but he is surrounded by a lot of ——s.' Chelnokov had fifteen minutes' conversation with the Emperor. Chelnokov had taken down to Alexeyev the resolution of the Duma greeting the army and saying that no peace must be made until complete victory had been obtained. The papers were lying on the Emperor's table. The Emperor asked Chelnokov why the resolution had not been sent direct to him. . . Chelnokov made some remarks about etiquette and said if the Emperor would allow him he would offer him the greeting now. So Chelnokov stood up and in his best official

[1] H. J. ('Benji') Bruce (1880–1951), was Head of Chancery, British Embassy, Moscow, and married to Tamara Karsavina, the great ballerina. Lockhart had been appointed Acting Consul-General.

[2] General Mikhail Alexeyev (1857–1918), ablest of the Tsar's generals, then chief of staff.

manner conveyed Moscow's greetings to the Emperor which pleased the latter greatly. The Emperor then said: 'I agree with everything in the resolution. Peace will not be made until complete victory is obtained and it will be obtained. You are right too in expressing your gratitude to the army. We should all go down on our knees before it for it deserves it.'

The Emperor then asked Chelnokov about things in Moscow. Chelnokov replied that there was no fuel and not enough to eat, as the railways were run so badly. That in those conditions it was not impossible that they would have to reckon with riots, etc. The Emperor replied that if people were cold and had no food and made riots about it one must not be too severe with them. The Emperor then asked if things were really as bad as he said and enquired if he was not greatly exaggerating.

Chelnokov replied: 'No.'

The Emperor then said: 'Everything that I can possibly do will be done.'

Saturday, 5 February 1916 [in Petrograd]

Lunched again with the Ambassador and had a long talk with him. Al Williams[1] told me a good story about Rasputin in which Rasputin is supposed to have said: 'Why has no one from the Left ever approached me, I would do lots of things for them.' . . . Obtained a ticket at the last moment and left for Moscow that night. During my visit Goremykin was dismissed and Stürmer appointed Prime Minister. Sazonov [Foreign Minister] told the Ambassador the new man is not so bad as he is painted.

Thursday, 17 February 1916

'Rout' for the submarine men [from the British Baltic Fleet] at the Duma. Huge crowd there and half Moscow there to meet them. After the 'rout' went to the Altr where the club gave a splendid show for us. Many of the best artists sang, and Novikov and Anderson danced. Cromie [Captain commanding submarines] made a very good speech: 'Gentlemen,' he said, you are all artists, musicians, writers, painters, composers. You are creators. What you create will live long after you. I am only a simple sailor, I destroy, but I can say truthfully that I destroy in order that your works may live.' This made an excellent impression.

Tuesday, 29 February 1916

Novikov and his wife are very nice and very anglified. He was Pavlova's partner in London and after his success there and in America does not like going back to the discipline of the Moscow Ballet Corps.

Saturday, 4 March 1916

Chelnokov also told me about a scandal in Petrograd in which a man called

[1] Harold Williams, correspondent of the *Daily Chronicle*.

Rjevsky was arrested on a charge of plotting against Rasputin's life. Rjevsky when arrested said he had been acting on orders from Khvostov. Bieletsky, the Assistant Minister of the Interior who discovered the thing, has been transferred to Siberia. Chelnokov thinks Khvostov will also go.

Chelnokov showed me a letter from Rasputin.

All the French people I have seen seem quite optimistic.

Walpole says the Foreign Office are very pleased with me and the Embassy too.

Saturday, 18 March 1916

Had a long talk with one of the secret agents of the Military Counter-Espionage Department . . . Hugh Walpole said that Lord Robert Cecil[1] spoke most highly of my work and that the Foreign Office and the Embassy were very pleased with me.

Lockhard let his diary lapse in the summer of 1916. In the spring of 1917 he witnessed the 'first' revolution of March 1917, which brought the moderate Left, and eventually Kerensky, to power.

Sunday, 11 March 1917

Duma dissolved. Rioting in Petrograd. Duma determined not to dissolve in spite of Imperial ukase. Revolution begins. Workmen come out.

Tuesday, 13 March 1917

Revolution in Moscow. Great scenes in front of Town Duma. Workmen and Socialists take the upper hand and encamp in the Duma. Troops all come over. No bloodshed and the crowd on the whole very orderly. No news from Petrograd.

Wednesday, 14 March 1917

News from Petrograd. Temporary Duma committee appointed. Chelnokov appointed commissioner for Moscow. . . Struggle between the moderates and the Socialists as to who is to have the upper hand. Social revolutionaries issuing all sorts of anarchical proclamations. Great masses of troops in the theatre square.

Thursday, 15 March 1917

New Cabinet appointed in Petrograd with Prince Lvov at the head. . .

In Moscow things are gradually straightening out but Chelnokov's position although improved is still very difficult. He is a strong man but not tactful enough with workmen. Still winter weather and very cold. The first

[1] Lord Robert Cecil (1864–1958), later 1st Viscount Cecil of Chelwood, was then Assistant Secretary for Foreign Affairs to Balfour.

stage of the revolution has been a wonderful success. I fear however the subsequent settling down.

Friday, 16 March 1917

Emperor signed Act of Abdication for himself and son in favour of his brother. Latter also refuses throne until the decision of the Constituent Assembly. Struggle now between the Duma Party and the Socialists which may also be referred to as a struggle between the Constitutional Monarchists and the Republicans. Had a long talk with Chelnokov who is improving his position.

Saturday, 17 March 1917

Took part in great review on Red Square. Thirty-three thousand troops took part in the march past, which was most impressive.

Thursday, 22 March 1917

Saw Chelnokov and Oboleshov who has come back from the front. The latter is very pessimistic about the discipline of the army which is the most important thing at the present moment.

Friday, 23 March 1917

Finished a long analysis of the revolutionary movement. Tried to give a fair view but the position is so unclear and so uncertain that any attempt at prophecy is difficult. It seems impossible that the struggle between the bourgeoisie and the Socialist elements or proletariat can pass off without further bloodshed. When this will come no one knows. The outlook for the war is not good.

In this report to London he wrote:

So far the people of Moscow have behaved with exemplary restraint. For the moment, only enthusiasm prevails, and the struggle which is almost bound to ensue between the bourgeoisie and the proletariat has not yet made its bitterness felt. . .

The Socialist Party [is] at present divided into two groups: the Social Democrats and Social Revolutionaries. The activities of the first named are employed almost entirely among the work people, while the Social Revolutionaries work mainly among the peasantry.

The Social Democrats, who are the larger party, are, however, divided into two groups known as the 'Bolsheviki' and the 'Mensheviki'. These names are taken from the movement of 1905 and today have lost their old meaning. The 'Bolsheviki' are the more extreme party. They are at heart anti-war. In Moscow at any rate the 'Mensheviki' represent today the majority and are more favourable to the war. On the other hand both the Social Revolutionaries and the 'Bolsheviki' in Moscow have been carrying on an active propaganda against the existing régime. . .

The chief danger at the present moment lies in the possibility of a reverse on the Russian front. This eventuality would give a very dangerous support to the anti-war party in Russia. . . Even now a considerable portion of the country is undoubtedly tired of the war. . .

Sunday, 25 March 1917

Tremendous Socialist demonstration in Moscow. The order of the crowd was quite exemplary. Fortunately too the anti-war feeling amongst the Socialists seems to be diminishing rather than increasing, although, of course, they all want the war to stop. Still, the majority begin to realise that the war cannot be stopped at once and now admit the necessity of defensive warfare.

Monday, 26 March 1917

Had a meeting with my advisory committee at the Club. Meeting of the Town Duma where the question was raised of democratising still further the present Duma – a further concession to the workmen. This, if accepted, will mean that Chelnokov will not be re-elected Mayor.

In the autumn of 1917 Lockhart returned to England as a result, he plainly says in Memoirs of a British Agent, *of his forming an attachment of which the authorities disapproved. This was to a French Jewess, Madame Vermelle. While he was away the Bolshevik revolution broke out on 7 November, and by 22 December peace negotiations had begun between the Russians and Germans at Brest-Litovsk.*

CHAPTER TWO

1918-1919

Meets Lloyd George and Reginald (Rex) Leeper. Litvinov 'not a bad fellow'. Return to Russia, January 1918 as head ('Agent') of mission to the 'provisional' Communist Government. Meets Trotsky and Lenin. Moscow in a state of siege. Famine in Petrograd. Mirbach murdered. Apathy at the murder of the Tsar. Lenin wounded. Imprisoned in Lubyanka gaol. Other prisoners shot. Moura's visits. Released and returns to England. Armistice. Talks with Lord Milner, the Webbs. Reports to Balfour, Foreign Secretary. Intervention or non-intervention. Lenin's 'criminal face'. Arthur Ransome in difficulties.

In London Lockhart worked for a time as the Russian expert in the new Department of Overseas Trade. He met all the leading politicians. Britain now had no official relations with the Bolsheviks, but Lockhart took the view that it was necessary to have contact with the new Communist Government, and finally the Cabinet agreed. Lloyd George, the Prime Minister, then asked him to head a mission to establish unofficial relations with the Bolsheviks. While arrangements were being made, he met for the first time Reginald Leeper, a young Foreign Office official, with whom he was to work closely in the Second World War.[1]

Friday, 4 January 1918

Saw Cecil at 3.30. At last all the interviews of the past three weeks have borne some fruit, and I am told to clear off as soon as possible. Went over to Admiralty and arranged to go by cruiser which is to meet Sir George [Buchanan, returning from Norway]. During past fortnight I have seen Lloyd George, Milner, Carson, Curzon, Cecil, Hardinge, Buchan, George Clerk, Eric Drummond, Gregory, etc., etc.[2] Milner is about the only one

[1] Reginald (Rex) Leeper (1888–1968) was at this time in the Political Intelligence Department of the Foreign Office. He was later during the Second World War assistant to Lockhart, then Director-General of Political Warfare, and later (as Sir Reginald) became Ambassador to Greece and the Argentine.

[2] Alfred, 1st Viscount Milner (1854–1925), distinguished pro-consul, had been High Commissioner for South Africa, 1897–1905, was now a member of the War Cabinet. Sir Edward Carson (1854–1935), later Lord Carson, was First Lord of the Admiralty. George, 1st Earl Curzon (1859–1925), later 1st Marquess, had been Viceroy of India, 1899–1905, and was then Lord President of the Council. He was to become Foreign Secretary in October 1919. Lord Hardinge of Penshurst (1858–1944), then Permanent

who strikes me as really efficient. Neither he nor Lloyd George think much of the Foreign Office, in particular of Balfour[1] and Hardinge.

Friday, 11 January 1918

At 12 noon met Litvinov, Russia's new Bolshevik Ambassador, with Rothstein[2] and Leeper at Lyons' corner shop in the Strand. Litvinov, more sluggish and slower, heavily built with broad forehead did not strike me as a bad fellow. He does not like German goverment who banished him from Germany. Both men are Jews. Litvinov is married to an Englishwoman.

Saturday, 12 January 1918

Litvinov gave me a very kind letter to Trotsky.[3] Foreign Office tried to establish unofficial relations with Litvinov.

Lockhart left for Russia on 14 January as head, or 'Agent' of the mission to the 'provisional' Communist Government. Other members of the mission travelling with him were Captain William Hicks, Edward Phelan and Edward Birse, several others were already in Moscow.

Monday, 28 January 1918

Came on to Helsingfors[4] as apparently we cannot get across the bridge. Arrived at 11.30 a.m. in Helsingfors to find the town in a state of revolution. No rooms to be had. Met Lednitski[5] and wandered off with him and Hicks to see if he could get us rooms at the Polish priest's. No catch, and as we were on the other side of town we could not get back to the Consulate for the firing. Most unpleasant. Stayed the night in small pension. Met Grove [Consul] and Fawcett, the Vice-Consul, who really runs the show.

Under-Secretary at the Foreign Office; had been Ambassador in St Petersburg, 1904–6, Viceroy of India, 1910–16, and was later Ambassador in Paris, 1920–3. John Buchan (1875–1940) had been Director of Information during the war and was now writing novels and *A History of the Great War*. In 1935 he was to become 1st Baron Tweedsmuir and Governor-General of Canada. Sir George Clerk (1874–1951), Private Secretary to the Acting Foreign Secretary, soon to be appointed British Minister in Prague, where Lockhart was to see much of him. Sir Eric Drummond (1876–1951), later 16th Earl of Perth, was then Private Secretary to the Foreign Secretary, and was to become Secretary-General to the League of Nations, 1919–32, and thereafter British Ambassador in Rome. John Duncan Gregory, one of the pre-war 'brilliant' men of the Foreign Office, was one of Lockhart's early friends in the Foreign Service.

[1] A. J. Balfour (1848–1930), later 1st Earl, had been Prime Minister, 1902–5, and was Foreign Secretary, 1916–19.

[2] F. Rothstein, an official translator in the British War Office; 'an intellectual armchair revolutionary' according to Lockhart. He was later sent out of England and became Bolshevik Minister in Teheran.

[3] Leon Trotsky (1879–1940) was then Commissar for Foreign Affairs and was negotiating the Peace of Brest-Litovsk.

[4] Then in Russian hands.

[5] A Polish lawyer he had known in Moscow.

Wednesday, 30 January 1918

Reached Petrograd 7.30 p.m. Streets in a dreadful state, snow had not been swept away for weeks. Everyone looks depressed and unhappy.

Tuesday, 12 February 1918

Robins[1] and Bruce lunch. Robins: 'Trotsky was poor kind [of] son of a bitch but the greatest Jew since Christ.'

Monday, 18 February 1918

Very little hope of Bolsheviks being able to resist Germans. Our number seems up. Trotsky says that even if Russia cannot resist she will indulge in partisan warfare to the best of her ability.

Thursday, 21 February 1918

Fears of pro-Boche counter-revolution. Events move so rapidly that it is not possible to keep pace with them. Trotsky seems to have re-established his position.

Tuesday, 26 February 1918

Saw Trotsky twice today. Loud in his blame of the French and said the Allies had only helped Germany by their intrigues in Russia. American Embassy left for Vologda with Robins. Sent Ransome down with them. Trouble with Petrov about passport. Determined to stay under all circumstances if Bolsheviks can put up any show.[2]

Wednesday, 27 February 1918

Saw Trotsky again today. Busy all day arranging about passport. . . Had long talk with Petrov. On the whole they have been fairly decent about the passport, but the delays have been terrible and we on our side have been equally indecisive.

I fear the embassies leaving Petrograd in this way will only encourage the Boche to come on.

Saturday, 2 March 1918

Telegram in papers that peace negotiations broken off. Went to see Trotsky. Saw also Lenin. Apparently a mistake as a subsequent telegram is coming to say peace will be signed on Monday on worse conditions.

Sunday, 3 March 1918

News from Helsingfors that Embassy left there tonight for the North. They are not coming back.

[1] Raymond Robins, head of the American Red Cross Mission.

[2] The Germans were advancing on Petrograd, and the remaining embassies were evacuated 350 miles to the eastward to Vologda. Arthur Ransome (1884–1963), now celebrated for his children's books, was then *Manchester Guardian* correspondent in Russia, and known for his life of Oscar Wilde and books on Bohemian life.

Monday, 4 March 1918

Spoke to Trotsky by telephone. He informed me that peace has been signed. Sent off telegram to that effect. Wired Robins. . . In the evening Prince and Princess Obolensky came to supper. Hickie went to doctor and found he had broken a rib.

Monday, 11 March 1918

Went down to see Trotsky who advised me to stay. He is . . . practically dictator for Petrograd. . . Had a most interesting talk. War is now certain. He cursed our ignorance bitterly and said we and France were the only people who did not realise what was happening. We were accusing him with false documents of Germanophilism, while his best friends were running him down for having placed too false hopes on a pro-entente policy.

Tuesday, 12 March 1918

Very depressing telegram from Foreign Office. Sent off long telegram *re* Trotsky. The other day *Pravda* published all the documents against Trotsky and Lenin which they had been able to find, including some of English counter-espionage section! They are sportsmen!

Wednesday, 13 March 1918

Saw Trotsky today and told him about the dangers of Japanese intervention.

Thursday, 14 March 1918

Received long and stupid telegram from Foreign Office. Three numbers are, however, missing. Trotsky appointed president of the Supreme War Council.

Friday, 15 March 1918

We are to leave for Moscow tomorrow. Petrograd looked very beautiful. Trotsky now made War Minister. Sent off a very hot telegram on Japanese situation. Lenin made great speech at Congress to show why peace was necessary. He said: 'One fool can ask more questions than ten wise men can answer.'

Saturday, 16 March 1918

Travelled down with Trotsky in a special train together with seven hundred Letts. The chief supporters of the October Revolution.

Tuesday, 19 March 1918

Hicks left for Siberia together with Webster of American Red Cross.[1]

British and American policy now seems at the different ends of the earth –

[1] To ensure that the Bolsheviks were not arming German and Austrian prisoners of war. They were not.

what we are playing at God alone knows, but one cannot expect much with a Foreign Minister of 74.

Sunday, 31 March 1918

Everything seemed to be going well, when today a bombshell arrived in the shape of a telegram to Washington. It is heart-rending, the stupidity of our General Staff makes me fear for the result of the war.

Tuesday, 9 April 1918

Telegram from Hicks *re* Semenov affair.[1] This looks very serious, worked all day sending off telegrams about the situation. Things are moving towards a crisis. Our people at home are so incredibly stupid that they will drift into tragedy, almost without knowing it. We have done our best and it is difficult to see what more we can do. This stupid affair at Vladivostok has spoilt all the advantages which the German landing at Finland could have given us. Everyone here is against it.. . . [2] Saw Karakhan and Chicherin.[3] They are very upset about the news from China where Semenov is said to have received arms, money and even fifty Japanese artillery men from the Japs.

Friday, 12 April 1918

At 3 o'clock last night the Bolsheviks surrounded and attacked simultaneously the twenty-six headquarters of the Anarchists. The latter were taken completely by surprise, were turned out of the houses they occupied and forced to give up their guns, rifles, ammunition and loot. Over five hundred arrested. Saw Djerjinsky, head of Counter-Revolution Committee who gave us a car to go round and see the results of victory.[4]

Friday, 19 April 1918

Soviet decree about women having the right to divorce a man for a month and the latter not having the right to refuse. Saw Trotsky – fairly satisfactory but hope is not great. In afternoon had long talk with Chicherin and Karakhan on subject of agreement. Overwhelmed with work. We have no staff, and it is impossible to get through half of what we ought to do.

Monday, 29 April 1918

Meeting of military representatives in our rooms. French General Noulens is in favour of intervention without consent and without asking for it. But

[1] A Cossack general, Grigori Semenov, was waging war on the Bolsheviks from behind the Chinese frontier.

[2] The Germans had invaded Finland on 4 April, and the Japanese had occupied Vladivostok on the following day. Balfour said that the Japanese were coming to 'help the Russians' but did not specify which Russians.

[3] L. M. Karakhan, G. V. Chicherin and Karl Radek were the triumvirate now in charge of the Bolshevik Foreign Office.

[4] Felix Djerjinsky, 'a man of correct manners and quiet speech but without a ray of humour in his character', was head of the Secret Police, or Cheka, until his death in 1926.

is unable to produce a single argument in favour of it. Romei, Riggs and I are all in favour of co-operation with the Bolsheviks.[1] Went to see Chicherin and Karakhan. Sadoul came to see me this morning and cursed Noulens upside down. He said he had telegraphed to Albert Thomas about him a few weeks before but now that Noulens had taken away his right of telegraphing.[2]

Wednesday, 1 May 1918

Saw Chicherin and had long talk. Position is certainly not very reassuring. Bad news about the Czechs who are now said to be anti-Bolshevik.

Monday, 6 May 1918

New government in the Ukraine with an Octobrist general at the head of it. First act to restore property to its rightful owners. Great excitement here amongst Bolsheviks who regard this as a direct menace to their government and as an attempt to establish counter-revolutionary centre, not only for Ukraine but for all Russia. American Ambassador arrived in Moscow. Had conference with Allied military representative.

Wednesday, 15 May 1918

Cromie and McAlpine left.[3] Went with Cromie to see Trotsky about the fleet. Trotsky said war was inevitable. I therefore asked if he would accept Allied intervention. He replied that he had already asked the Allies to make a proposition. I then said that if the Allies would come to an agreement on this point, would he give me half an hour to discuss things. He said: 'When the Allies come to an agreement it is not half an hour but a whole day that I will give.'

Saturday, 18 May 1918

More notes from Chicherin . . . with regard to the recognition of the Russian red flag.

Wednesday, 22 May 1918

Articles in the *Times*, *Observer* and *Daily Chronicle* recommending inter-

[1] Noulens was French Ambassador to Russia, General Romei the head of the Italian military mission, and Major Riggs the U.S. military representative.

[2] Captain Jacques Sadoul was a former Socialist deputy who was on the staff of General Lavergne, head of the French military mission. Albert Thomas (1878–1922) had visited Russia in 1917 during the Kerensky régime, when he was French Minister of Munitions, and persuaded Kerensky to launch an offensive against the Germans. Lockhart found him 'a jovial, bearded man, with a sense of humour and a healthy, bourgeois appetite'. He later became first Director of the International Labour Office at Geneva, where Lockhart was to meet him again.

[3] Captain Cromie was Naval attaché and anxious that the Baltic fleet should not fall into German hands. Cromie and McAlpine (a former Treasury official) were based in Petrograd.

vention in a peculiar stupid form. . . Thornhill has arrived at Murmansk, Scale and Poole arrive at Archangel.[1]

Friday, 31 May 1918

After being nearly all day in a train arrived four forty-five at Moscow. Moscow in state of siege. Counter-revolutionary plot discovered and five hundred arrests. Request from Chicherin to use all influence in settling Czech incident. Went up to see Wardrop. During my absence Tamplin managed to burn a cipher by accident.[2] Wonderful carelessness.

Sunday, 2 June 1918

Arrived in Petrograd. Lovely day. Stayed at Petrograd. Rang up Cromie. . . Feeling in Petrograd quite different from Moscow. Altogether quieter and further removed from the struggle. Anti-Bolshevism very strong and hardly concealed. At the cabaret jokes were made at Bolshevik expense which would not be tolerated in Moscow.

Famine pretty severe and grave discontent among the workmen and sailors. Counter-revolution here possible any day.

Tuesday, 4 June 1918

Returned to Moscow. Very worried over the Czech affair which looks bad. Czechs, apparently fed-up with the way they have been treated by the Bolsheviks, have broken into revolt in Siberia. New government said to be formed at Novonikolaevsk. Acting under instructions we all went to Chicherin and Karakhan to inform them that the disarmament of the Czechs or any ill-treatment of them would be considered as an act inspired by Germany and hostile to the Allies. It made a great impression as they thought this a prelude to intervention.

Tuesday, 11 June 1918

Moscow is now very strictly guarded and the Bolshies seem very nervous.

Friday, 21 June 1918

Volodarsky, Petrograd commissar for the press, murdered in Petrograd.

Saturday, 22 June 1918

Disgusting attack on England made by Uritsky, the Petrograd President of the Extraordinary Commission, at the meeting of the Petrograd Soviet on the occasion of Volodarsky's murder. He accuses us of organising Volodarsky's murder. Sent in a fairly stormy note to the Bolsheviks.

[1] Major-General F. C. Poole commanded the small Allied Force in north Russia which included Colonel C. M. Thornhill and Captain J. D. Scale.

[2] Sir Oliver Wardrop, the cautious elderly official who had succeeded to Lockhart's earlier post as Consul-General in Moscow. Tamplin was a young Russian-speaking lieutenant in Lockhart's staff.

Sunday, 23 June 1918

Shastny, Commander-in-Chief of Baltic Fleet, condemned to death and shot within twenty-four hours. Only witness called was Trotsky who finished his speech by saying: 'Gentlemen, I consider before you a very dangerous counter-revolutionary, who should be punished without mercy.'

Thursday, 4 July 1918

Chicherin said it was funny how the military idea had gone to Trotsky's head. A few weeks ago Lenin had to restrain him from declaring war on Germany. Now Lenin's cool brain was trying to restrain him the other way.

Friday, 5 July 1918

Further stormy scenes at the Congress... Lenin is undoubtedly the most imposing figure at the Assembly.

Saturday, 6 July 1918

Mirbach murdered today by two unknown people who came to the Embassy with false documents.[1] Murder took place at three-thirty... We have been moved to a box on the third floor with the Germans opposite... Later the theatre was surrounded by troops and no one was allowed to go out. In night and during afternoon rising by Left Social-Revolutionaries. This speedily squashed. Left Social-Revolutionaries fled.

Sunday, 7 July 1918

Radek came to see me. Mirbach's murderer Blumkin lived in our hotel in room 221. He was a member of the Extraordinary Commission. The Left Social-Revolutionaries during their short revolt arrested Djerjinsky... Their resistance was very weak, but for a time they held the telegraph. This was afterwards retaken by Hungarian war prisoners internationalists. Many of the Social-Revolutionaries have been arrested including Alexandrovich, Vice-President of the Extraordinary Commission. He is to be shot immediately. All papers suppressed. No trains to Petrograd or anywhere, no telegrams to abroad. Yaroslavl said to be in the hands of the counter-revolutionaries.

Tuesday, 9 July 1918

Congress renewed. Trotsky made a great speech, during which after calling the Left Social-Revolutionaries traitors who are trying to drag Russia into the war against the will of the people, he stated that Russia did not want to fight and only wished to keep her neutrality... Spiridonova arrested...[2]

[1] Count Mirbach had been appointed German Ambassador to Russia as soon as the Treaty of Brest-Litovsk was ratified. The object of the assassination was to provoke Germany into restarting the war.

[2] Maria Spiridonova (1886–1918) was the fanatical leader of the Left Social-Revolutionaries.

One of Red Guards dropped bomb by mistake in theatre. Two killed, three wounded.

Sunday, 14 July 1918

Considerable number of Social-Revolutionaries shot for revolt of July 6 and 7 and for Mirbach's murder.

Wednesday, 17 July 1918

Order out by Trotsky that no officers belonging to the British or French are allowed to travel on account of their counter-revolutionary tendencies. . . News that the Emperor had been shot at Ekaterinburg.

Thursday, 18 July 1918

The news that the Emperor has been shot is true – on the night of the 16th. Evidently in connection with the advance of the Czechs who are now nearing Ekaterinburg.

Friday, 19 July 1918

As all bourgeois papers are suppressed, comments on the Emperor's murder are naturally one-sided. Bolshevik press however reviles him as a tyrant and a butcher. States that he made a whorehouse of the throne, etc., and says Government will shortly publish the diaries, etc., which it has in its hand. Rest of people seem to take things indifferently. Their apathy is extraordinary.

Thursday, 25 July 1918

Allied embassies after series of adventures proceeded to Archangel. So here ends the Vologda episode – a thoroughly stupid one at the best.

Tuesday, 30 July 1918

Assassination of General Eichhorn, the German Commander-in-Chief at Kiev. Donskoi, a young Moscow student and a member of the Social-Revolutionary Party, hired a cab and passing Eichhorn, threw a bomb.

Wednesday, 31 July 1918

General Eichhorn dies of wounds. We learn afterwards that at the questioning of Donskoi by the German military authorities, almost the first question asked him was: 'Do you know Lockhart, do you know who I mean?'

Sunday, 4 August 1918

Allies land at Archangel. Great excitement in Moscow, where people imagine we have landed in force.

Monday, 5 August 1918

While in the Consulate, Consulate surrounded by armed band, everything sealed up and everyone arrested except Hicks, Wardrop and me. Our Mission premises on the Lubyanka also raided. Hill, Tamplin and Lingner arrested. This about 3 p.m.

The Consulate visited early in the morning by similar band, acting on authority of Moscow Soviet. Careless of the Secret Service people in Consulate in destroying their documents. . . French Consul-General also arrested.

Tuesday, 6 August 1918

Helfferich leaves Moscow for Berlin with intention of persuading his government to overthrow the Bolsheviks.[1] Panic in Bolshevik camps. Karakhan tells me afterwards that they had taken all measures to blow up Petrograd and to go. . .

Allied representatives go to Chicherin to protest against outrage on French and British Consulates and demand our passports. They are not actually refused, but Chicherin says there is no way out.

Wednesday, 7 August 1918

Nicholas II's diary is now being published in the Soviet papers. It is simple enough and it is difficult to see how such publication will help the Bolsheviks.

Saturday, 31 August 1918

Attempt last night on Lenin's life by two women, a Social-Revolutionary named Kaplan who fired at him point-blank as he was leaving Michelson's factory where he had been speaking at a meeting.

In the night at three-thirty my flat was invaded by a band . . . under [the] command of former Commandant [of] Smolny. A search was made first in our presence and in the presence of the president of the house committee. Protocol was ready, but a second search was made later without witnesses. Hicks and I were taken to the Lubyanka 11.

Sunday, 1 September 1918

After being detained from nine o'clock in the morning on a charge of being mixed up in some plot with the Letts we were discharged. Very wet and beastly. We made our way home. No servants, and the flat all upside down.

Monday, 2 September 1918

Went to see Karakhan about servants and especially about Moura who has also been arrested.[2] He promised to do what he could.

Tuesday, 3 September 1918

Papers today full of the most fantastic accounts of an Allied conspiracy of

[1] Karl Helfferich, former Vice-Chancellor, had been appointed in place of Mirbach, but stayed only a fortnight in Moscow.

[2] Marie Zakrevskaia, daughter of a Russian senator and landowner. She married von Benckendorff in 1911 when he was at the Russian Embassy in London. He was shot by the Bolsheviks and later she married Baron Budberg, whom she divorced a year later. As Moura Budberg she was a lifelong friend of Lockhart.

which I am said to be at the head. The account, which reads like fairy-tale, includes 'buying over of Lett troops', 'shooting Lenin and Trotsky', 'taking Petrograd and Moscow by hunger', 'blowing up bridges', and 'appointment of dictator' not to mention the wildest and most false account of my arrest. *Pravda* in particular excelling itself. Loud appeals for application of severest measures, 'Red Terror' etc.

Wednesday, 4 September 1918

Went again to see Karakhan about servants and Moura. He advised me to go and see Peters, which I did.[1] On arriving there, I found that warrant had already been issued for my re-arrest, so I was detained at Lubyanka No. 11.[2] Kept in a room where the arrested are brought for examination and registration for minor offences... Slept on a sofa. Fed on pea soup and potatoes – the same as the commissars themselves get.

Thursday, 5 September 1918

Most of the commissars seem to be Letts or Russian sailors. Some of them are quite decent and kind; others again are surly and cruel-looking. One or two of the Letts and one Russian in particular were very decent, got tobacco for me and talked with me.

While I was there a bandit was brought in. He made an extraordinary scene; first laughingly assuring his innocence, then weeping and finally cursing and vowing vengeance.

Peters gave me two books to read. *Mr Britling Sees it Through* [by H. G. Wells] which I read again and Lenin's *State and Revolution.*

Friday, 6 September 1918

Papers today contained first foreign comments on alleged 'Allied Plot'. German press is naturally jubilant and terrific in its denunciation of Allied diplomacy.

Bulletins about Lenin are more reassuring and he ought to recover now.

Today, Sheglovitov, Khvostov, Bieletsky and the priest Vostorgov[3] were brought [in]. Saw Peters who said he was sending me to the Kremlin.

[1] Jacob Peters (1886–?1938), who like Litvinov had an English wife, was deputy head of the Bolshevik terrorist-cum-intelligence organisation, the Cheka. He had lived in London, and in 1911 had been tried and acquitted, probably wrongly, for murdering three policemen, with men later involved in the Siege of Sidney Street. See Rumbelow, *The Houndsditch Murders*, 1973.

[2] Part of the real reason for Lockhart's arrest may have been his connection, mainly as paymaster, with Sidney Reilly, the Secret Service spy. But he was not a spy himself in the technical sense. The head of the Secret Intelligence Service in Russia was Commander Ernest Boyce. Reilly's life was written by Lockhart's son Robin in *Ace of Spies* (1967).

[3] The first three were Tsarist ex-ministers and Bishop Vostorgov was a notorious reactionary.

Saturday, 7 September 1918

French and British Notes about the detention of Allied officials and the attack on our Embassies. Russian reply which offers to let us all go in exchange for Litvinov and Co.

Today the ex-ministers and Vostorgov and others were taken out and shot. I saw them all getting into a black prison motor – a huge Black Maria – and a squad of soldiers being brought up, but I did not realise they had been taken away to be shot.

Wet and cold, I had no meat for three days – no wash and no change of clothes.

Sunday, 8 September 1918

Came to Kremlin. Today at six o'clock brought to Kremlin. Placed in apartments in the Kavalariesky Korpus. But instead of being alone as Peters promised I am put in with a Russian(?) called Smidchen who is said to be my agent! Press today full of attacks on Anglo-French [in] which my name figures as the head and evil genius of everything! At a meeting on Friday Krylenko[1] spoke against me and according to the *Mir*, a filthy German rag, stated amidst cries of 'Shoot the scoundrels' that we would be handed over to the Revolutionary Tribunal.

Monday, 9 September 1918

My prison here consists of a small hall, a sitting-room, a diminutive bedroom, a bathroom and a small dressing-room, which I use for my food. The rooms open on both sides on to corridors so that there is no fresh air. I have one sentry one one side and two on the other. They are changed every four hours and as each changes, has to come in to see if I am there. This results in my being woken up at twelve and four in the middle of the night. They are nearly all Letts, but there are also Russians, Poles and Hungarians.

Tuesday, 10 September 1918

Uralsk taken by Red Army. Kazan, evidently on eve of capitulation. The Russian who was with me has been taken to other quarters and I am now alone, thank goodness. Moura has now been released. Today she brought me books, provisions, clothes, etc., for which I was most grateful. I have now an old man who does my room, brings me the papers and fetches hot water for tea. He is presumably an old servant of the Kremlin. My Russian sentry today was most talkative, said he also walked with Bieletsky and comforted me greatly by saying that people said I should not also be shot.

Wednesday, 11 September 1918

Kazan falls to Red Army. Great rejoicing in Bolshevik Press. Flags hoisted

[1] Nikolai V. Krylenko, whom Lockhart described as 'an epileptic degenerate', became the Bolshevik Public Prosecutor and subsequently Minister for Justice.

everywhere and on Kremlin. I went for a walk today around the front of the Kremlin and in the garden of a church, where there is the ikon of 'Our Lady of Unexpected Joy'. The Alexander II monument has been removed as also the cross which marks the spot where fell that arch scoundrel the Grand Duke Sergius.

My sentry today was a Pole who informed me that very few who are brought to the Kremlin ever got out again.

Thursday, 12 September 1918

Success of Allied troops on French front continues satisfactorily. Most of the sentries with whom I go for walks are Letts. They seem mostly pretty decent, sensible lads; in fact I have only struck one really nasty one – a sour-faced looking curmudgeon who swore at England and refused to allow me even to send a message to [the] Commandant. The Letts were much better educated than the Russians, for whom they had a considerable contempt. For instance about the war they state that the Letts always advanced but had to come back because the Ruskies would not support them. They blame too the laziness and dirtiness of the Russians.

Friday, 13 September 1918

Simbirsk taken by Red troops. Lenin on road to recovery – allowed to sit up. Neutral note protesting against Red terror – and fiercely indignant Bolshevik reply.

Not all my sentries are Bolsheviks; they may be divided into three classes: first, the ardent Bolsheviks who convince one by the faith and sincerity in their cause. Of these, among the Letts a goodly number. Secondly, the sheep who go with the crowd – Bolshevik today and Menshevik tomorrow, etc., and thirdly the sceptical who believe in nothing and think that in Russia anything is possible and everything mad.

Monday, 16 September 1918

Spiridonova I see often, although I have not spoken to her. She looks ill and nervous, with great dark lines under her eyes. She is very clumsily and carelessly dressed but might have been quite pretty when younger. She must be about thirty-three now but looks more. With her pince-nez she looks like a board school mistress. She has, however, a most earnest face and evidently lots of courage.

Tuesday, 17 September 1918

Weather wet and muggy. Went for walk. Saw Brusilov who looks haggard, ill and very old.[1] He has a sly foxy face.

[1] General Alexei Brusilov (1853–1926) had commanded the Russian armies in Galicia with considerable success and had been supreme commander under the Menshevik régime.

Thursday, 19 September 1918

Lenin better and allowed to work again – a miraculous escape. During the last few days have read much. Moura has brought me lots of books.

Friday, 20 September 1918

Expected Moura today, but she did not come. Wet again and miserably damp. Moura brings me food galore and dainties of all sorts – also books. I spend the whole day either reading or playing patience. The papers are entirely silent about the Allied 'plot', probably in order to try to incriminate more people. Baku taken by Turks and small Armenian [force] – British force driven out.

Sunday, 22 September 1918

Eighteen days since I was arrested. Today is my fifteenth day in the Kremlin. After the rain and damp of the last four days, today, in contrast, is fine and summerlike. Moura came to see me with Peters. The latter gave me his photograph and behaved very decently. He asked me to take a message to his wife in England. Showed me photos of his wife and child; then said no, he wouldn't trouble me as he was sure as soon as I got out I would blaspheme and curse him as my worst enemy. He does not seem to imagine that any bourgeois can have any feelings of humanity towards the working class. He told me details of his life and adventures; how he became a Socialist at fifteen. He is thirty-two today.

Monday, 23 September 1918

Peters yesterday implied that I shall be allowed to go to England. He said that there would be a trial for certain. This, however, may be bluff. Moura brought very sad news yesterday. I am much upset and wonder how everything will end. Asker[1] came to see me today. He was not allowed to speak about my case but he said everything possible was being done. Poole left Moscow some days ago, but does not appear to have left Russia yet. The English and French are still in the American and Norwegian Consulates. All water cut off and no provisions allowed in. Had a sulky sentry today who refused to allow my note to Moura.

Tuesday, 24 September 1918

Brusilov was released yesterday. In my walk yesterday I noticed on the pillars of the Alexander II monument the following: 'Here the Red Army soldiers of the 9th Lettish Rifles had the pleasure of walking with Brusilov, Lockhart, Spiridonova and Sablin'! Today the *Izvestia* published the letters to Poincaré of one of the French agents, Marchand in which he mentions a meeting at the U.S.A. consulate where the blowing up of bridges and rails was discussed. Although I was not at this meeting and knew nothing about it

[1] Swedish Consul-General, 'a man of great charm and high ideals, who had laboured night and day to secure our release'.

my name is still mentioned as the instigator of everything and arch-criminal. Although the meeting was said to have been presided over by Poole, no mention of the American. For political reasons of course!

Wednesday, 25 September 1918

The press again is full of comments on Marchand's letters, and I am beginning to feel the effects of my being confined to one room without exercise, and my nerves and my sleep are beginning to suffer.

Thursday, 26 September 1918

Karakhan came to see me today and told me I was to be sent to England. There is to be no trial and I am to be set free. Had a long talk with him about our intervention. He has behaved very decently to me, and I will always say so. . . Must take up literary work and journalism now to live. Cold and raining. Went for a walk. Sleeping very badly.

Friday, 27 September 1918

In spite of Karakhan's news last night no meeting with Moura today, as Peters is resting. Hope however, tomorrow everything will be arranged. Read *The Merry Wives of Windsor* and *A Midsummer Night's Dream* – also bits of *Hamlet.* Also most of a book on Japan by Joseph Dautremer translated – and how badly – from the French. Played patience and went for a walk.

Saturday, 28 September 1918

Three years ago yesterday since Norman[1] was killed, and I have not been able to send a telegram home. Last night read *Cyrano* again and wept over the last scenes. It is twelve years last Easter since I saw it at the Porte St Martin with Father. Coquelin has gone since then. . .[2] Peters came in this evening dressed in a leather jacket, khaki trousers and an enormous Mauser pistol with Moura. Told me I would be freed on Tuesday and allowed to go home for two days to pack. He then left us alone. The reunion was wonderful. Although, except just during the first few days before it was clear that Lenin was going to recover I was not really afraid I would be shot, nevertheless, the strain was trying and one never knew what little straw might change everything against us.

Monday, 30 September 1918

Peters told me the other day before Moura that the Americans were the worst compromised in this business and that what they had against me was nothing. And yet not one word has been said against the Yanks! Moura here all day. Litvinov and fifty-four Russians have left England and we are to

[1] A younger brother, killed in France.

[2] Benoît Constant Coquelin (1841–1909) created the title-role in Rostand's *Cyrano de Bergerac.*

be allowed to go as soon as Litvinov gets to Bergen or rather as soon as the Bolsheviks hear he has got to Bergen.

Reading Thucydides . . . also Renan's *Souvenirs d'Enfance et de Jeunesse*. Weather fine but cold. Went for a walk.

Lettish sentry was rather amusing – not very Bolshevik, very proud of his own country and contemptuous of the Russians.

Tuesday, 1 October 1918

Moura came again this morning with a temperature of 39°C. At twelve Karakhan came to say that we were to leave tomorrow. At three I was ordered and taken to my flat but a sentry was posted at the door and I was informed I was under 'house arrest'. Began to pack. Discovered that my pearl studs, my heart pin and gold links, my new waterproof and about a hundred or two hundred thousand roubles have been stolen. The soldiers also drank all our wine, stole our butter and flour.

Madame Malinina came to see me to ask my help to get Hickie released in time to marry her [before he left].[1] Promised to do what I could.

Set free and allowed home to pack under guard of a sentry. . .

Wednesday, 2 October 1918

Asker came to see me and said we were leaving at night. He said at one time I was in serious danger of being shot. Peters sent me a letter apologising for the theft of my things and five hundred roubles for compensation, which I refused. At six the sentry was taken away and at 9.30 Asker came to take me to the station. Hickie got married all right, and by 1.30 the train left accompanied by a guard of Letts.

Asker had a talk with me about the Dutch and Swedish control of British interests. Bulgaria concludes an armistice. Great victories in France, Palestine and Bulgaria.

They reached Stockholm on 9 October.

Friday, 11 October 1918

Very seedy with temperature. Ransome is very worried about his fate and still more about his girl.[2]

Monday, 14 October 1918

Kept half the day at Charlottenburg on the Swedish frontier owing to stupid mistake about Litvinov. Luckily there was a refugee train which came in at 4.30 so I managed to get a message through to Stockholm and got away

[1] Liuba Malinina was a niece of Lockhart's old friend Chelnokov. Captain Hicks was beleaguered in the Norwegian Legation.

[2] Evgenia Petrovna Shelyepina (Genia), Trotsky's secretary. Lockhart illegally gave her a British passport. She married Ransome in 1924.

safely. Otherwise I should have missed the boat. Arrived 10 p.m. at Christiania.

He reached London on 19 October.

Tuesday, 22 October 1918

Dined at Carlton with Jean and went to Alhambra afterwards. My enemies in the Foreign Office are Bob Cecil, Tyrrell,[1] who is back again and fast assuming control, and Hardinge. Bob Cecil has not asked to see me. Hardinge is away with a broken leg and Tyrrell told Leeper he has no use for me. Didn't want to see me and that I was a hysterical schoolboy who had intrigued with the Prime Minister behind the Foreign Office's back. Not much hope in this quarter.

Wednesday, 23 October 1918

Went to 22 Ryder Street. Saw the King... The King was very nice and showed a surprising grasp of the situation; he however did most of the talking and during the forty minutes I was with him I didn't really get much in. He sees pretty well the need for reforms everywhere, and has a wholesome dread of Bolshevism.

Friday, 25 October 1918

After a week at home it is perfectly obvious that apart from the relief of having rescued me from the Bolsheviks the Foreign Office is not in the least interested in my account of things. They prefer the reactionaries who have never even seen Bolshevism. Tyrrell and Hardinge are frankly and avowedly hostile and I may even have difficulty in obtaining another job.

Others were happy to see him, and he was a favourite guest at many dinner-parties. He talked with Sidney Reilly, who had escaped from Russia. He was, too, an object of interest and information to members of the Intelligence services.

Friday and Saturday, 8 and 9 November 1918

Lunched with Sir Samuel Hoare at the Marlborough. The old man was very nice.[2] He is a kind man in his way and by no means a fool – a damned sight more intelligent than some of the old military attachés...

Saw Wardwell[3] again and fixed him up an appointment with Sir George Clerk who thanked him on behalf of His Majesty's Government. Lunched at the Bachelors with Sir Samuel Hoare, Freddy Browning,[4] colonel who does the economic section with 'C',[5] and Wardwell.

[1] W. G. T. (later Lord) Tyrrell (1866–1947), then Head of the Political Intelligence Department at the Foreign Office; later Permanent Under-Secretary at the Foreign Office, 1925–8, British Ambassador in Paris, 1928–34.

[2] He was only 38.

[3] Major Wardwell had been head of the American Red Cross Mission in Russia. Lockhart records that he was 'heroic' in his efforts on behalf of Allied prisoners.

[4] Lieut.-Colonel F. H. Browning (*d.* 1929) had been seconded to the Foreign Office for the Peace Conference which was to open in December; father of Sir Frederick Browning, who was husband of Daphne du Maurier and Comptroller of Prince Philip's Household.

[5] 'C', the head of the Secret Service, was at that time Captain Mansfield Cumming.

Monday, 11 November 1918

Armistice signed. Great rejoicings in London... When I turned up at the Foreign Office at 10.45 there were already crowds before 10 Downing Street. At eleven Lloyd George came out to announce the news. Guns were fired. Cheering, singing, etc. All very orderly.

Thursday, 14 November 1918

Dined with Lord Milner at Brooks's... Milner very nice and sympathetic. Loud in his abuse of the Foreign Office and very bitter on Hardinge. Advised me, however, to hold on and not to give up the government yet. Milner was most sympathetic. He realises the Bolshevik danger but does not think Germany will go Bolshevik. I don't agree. I think Germany, too, will have her Bolshevik phase, although it will be different from the Russian process. What people here seem to me to fail to realise is that Bolshevism in Russia cannot be a lasting success: not because of the inherent faults of Lenin's theories but because an illiterate proletariat and peasantry is not really capable of running itself or understanding its own government.

Saturday, 16 November 1918

Met Archer. Lunched with him, his sisters and the Leepers[1] at the R.A.C. Talked about Bolshevism and decided that it would be difficult to know which side to take if it ever came to a conflict between 'Whites' and 'Reds' in this country. Decided that we should all prefer to remain in bed – the most impossible thing to do in any revolution, as there can be no neutrals in civil war. Personally, all my sympathies are with Labour but not with Bolshevism.

Monday, 18 November 1918

Saw Rothstein and had a long talk with him. He does not believe the story of the Moscow plot. I hope Basil Thomson[2] will not send him out of England. He will be far more dangerous to us there than here.

Wednesday, 20 November 1918

Lunched with the Webbs.[3] Sidney is rather like a Russian Socialist with straggling beard and unkempt hair. She is very charming but a little dogmatic. Talked much about Bolshevism. Gilbert Murray[4] and his wife were there. Webb is convinced Bolshevism must fail economically and thinks Lenin can

[1] Perhaps Lieutenant-Commander N. E. Archer, who had been attached to the Russian Navy during the war and was subsequently in the Commonwealth Office. The second Leeper was either Rex's brother Allen, also in the Foreign Office, or his wife Primrose.

[2] Sir Basil Thomson (1861–1939) was Assistant Commissioner of the Metropolitan Police and Head of the Special Branch.

[3] Sidney Webb (1859–1939), later Lord Passfield, and his wife Beatrice (1859–1947), were Fabian Socialists and admirers of Communism in Russia.

[4] Gilbert Murray (1866–1957), classical scholar and translator, keen supporter of the League of Nations of which he was President, 1923–38.

know nothing of economics! I wish I could feel so even about it as he does.

Saw Sir Eric Drummond. He is quite nice to me, but I see the Foreign Office is a wash-out as far as I am concerned.

Lockhart also composed 'Secret and Confidential' reports, some extracts from which have historic importance:

To A. J. Balfour, the Foreign Secretary and former Prime Minister he had written on 7 November a penetrating analysis of the situation and personalities in Soviet Russia, the probable outcome and the dangers to the rest of the world. He also wrote a memorandum dealing with the vexed question of Allied intervention in Russia:

With the defeat of Germany it is clear that our intervention in Russia has now entered upon a most dangerous phase.

Our victories over Germany have removed our original pretext for intervention, and have at the same time strengthened the position of the Bolsheviks, (I) by raising their hopes for a revolution in Austria and Germany, and (II) by increasing their power in the Ukraine, Poland and the other Russian districts at present occupied by Germany. The Allies have now a choice of three plans:

(1) To abandon our intervention altogether, secure the free and unhindered exit of the Czecho-Slovak troops out of Russia,[1] and come to a working arrangement with the Bolsheviks. (2) To abandon our intervention and secure the free exit of the Czecho-Slovak troops, should they so desire, but at the same time to support with arms and money the anti-Bolshevik organisations in Russia such as the Ufa Government, General Alexeyev's forces etc.,[2] and at the same time to support in the same way a chain of new national States on Russia's Western frontier, such as the Baltic Provinces, Poland, the Ukraine and Roumania, with a view to creating a strong economic barrier against the spread of Bolshevism. (3) To intervene immediately on a proper scale, to strengthen our forces in Siberia and in the North, and at the same time by securing the elimination of Turkey from the war to send an expeditionary force through the Black Sea to join General Alexeyev and march immediately on Moscow in order to strike a blow at the very heart of Bolshevism.

After examining the objections to the first two plans he continued:

Plan No. 3, in spite of its obvious difficulties, still seems to me the best solution of a very difficult problem. Bolshevism, or rather the Bolshevik in Russia can be destroyed, not, however, by gnawing at the outside of Bolshevism, but by digging at the core. The objection to this plan are: (i) a large

[1] There were some 42,000 Czechs, who had originally been fighting alongside the Russians but had turned against the Bolsheviks. At one time they were to control 3000 miles of the Trans-Siberian Railway, Vladivostok and Ufa in the Urals.

[2] General Alexeyev commanded a 'Volunteer Army', later taken over by Denikin on his death in October 1918, against the Red Army.

number of forces will have to be employed not only to destroy the Bolshevik armies, but in order to restore peace and order in Russia. A successful intervention would probably require fifty thousand men in the South via the Black Sea and, at least the same number through Siberia. General Lavergne of the French Mission puts the figure even higher than this, and undoubtedly the more troops we send the more support we will get from the Russians themselves. (ii) To maintain such a force in Russia after the conclusion of more than four years of war may be impossible, probably would be impossible without the co-operation of America. (iii) In the event of this plan being more difficult of attainment than would appear at present, our troops might have to remain in Russia for a considerable period, and might themselves be exposed to Bolshevik propaganda.

The advantages of this plan, however, are far greater than those offered by any other policy. Now that Turkey has concluded an armistice, we have the possibility of acting quickly and of beginning our operations before an armistice is concluded with Germany. Our victory over the Central Empires has probably increased our prestige enormously amongst all anti-Bolshevik Russians who now regard the Allies as the only possible means of salvation. By the time we are in a position to reach Moscow it may be possible to send a relief expedition to Petrograd by sea. With Petrograd and Moscow in our hands we should have no great difficulty in setting up some form of Russian Government which will answer to the needs and wishes of the people.

Finally, in connection with this plan I venture most respectfully to make the following observations:

(1) That our intervention is justified on humanitarian grounds, and that we should do better by proceeding openly against the Bolsheviks, than by trying to suppress them surreptitiously. (2) That for the success of such an intervention American co-operation is essential, and operations should commence at once. This is not possible in the North, but in the South it is quite possible. If America would agree to send the bulk of required troops, it would be possible to secure the necessary complement of French and British troops voluntarily. (3) That whatsoever Government we support should make immediately some declaration which will promise the land to the peasants – not necessarily as a socialistic measure, but as an economic remedy which is long overdue. Without a clear pronouncement on this subject we shall have the peasants against us. (4) That however difficult it may seem, we should proceed cautiously in supporting any one anti-Bolshevik party as against another and, in particular we should beware of a renascence of sentimentalism for the old regime which is already manifest in some sections of the English press. (5) No intervention in Russia can be really successful unless it is accompanied by large supplies of food stuffs and manufactured goods for the starving population, and no economic relief can be given without a military occupation. (6) A successful intervention will give the Allies a predominant economic position in Russia. It will be more than paid for by

economic concessions which will in time repay us for some of the sums we have advanced to Russia.

By restoring order in Russia at once not only are we preventing the spread of Bolshevism as a political danger but we are also saving for the rest of Europe the rich and fertile grain districts of the Ukraine, which in the event of half-measures, or no measures at all, will be rendered sterile by anarchy and revolution. As Europe will require after the war all the grain she can get, the importance of order in South Russia, and in Rumania is one of extreme importance.

Allied intervention is a guarantee of this order. No other policy can promise the same results, or the same security.

Lockhart heard of the official comments on his memoranda:

Friday, 22 November 1918

Lunched with [F. M.] Gunther of the U.S.A. Embassy at White's. He does not take the same point of view as our people about Wilson but thinks that he may now seriously consider intervention. In meantime, our people are dead against it through fear of Labour. Leeper showed me the comments on my report. Hardinge's nil. Cecil's 'very interesting, but' nothing doing. Balfour's: 'a very able document whatever one may think of the conclusions'.

Saturday, 23 November 1918

Saw Wellesley[1] yesterday who informed me that the Foreign Office proposed to offer me the post of assistant commercial attaché at Petrograd with Hodgson[2] as my chief. 'Thank you ever so much!'

Parliament prorogued for new elections. Mr King who has asked a question about me almost every day will, thank God, not be standing again.[3] Harold Nicolson stopped me on the stairs the other day and said my report was one of the best he had ever read.[4]

Wednesday, 27 November 1918

Letter from Milner thanking me for Lenin and Trotsky's photographs and expressing hope that they may be published life-size all over England as the finest anti-Bolshevik propaganda. Milner says he has never seen a more clever criminal face than Lenin's.

Meanwhile Lockhart was meeting such Socialists as G. D. H. Cole and, on 3 January 1919, J. C. Squire, of the New Statesman *('Nice young man with a rather*

[1] Victor Wellesley (1876–1954), Controller of Commercial and Consular Affairs at the Foreign Office, 1916–25.

[2] Robert Hodgson (1874–1956), knighted 1925, commercial counsellor in Russia, 1919–21.

[3] Joseph King, Liberal M.P. for North Somerset.

[4] Harold Nicolson (1886–1968), knighted in 1953, was then in the Diplomatic Service and about to be sent to the Peace Conference. He was later to join Lockhart briefly on the *Evening Standard* and to become a distinguished writer.

milk-and-water Socialism of the bourgeois type – very tolerant in his view and altogether a distinctly attractive type').[1]

Friday, 10 January 1919

Sent for by Foreign Office to discuss question of Raskolnikov's[2] capture by our fleet near Reval. Our operations in the Baltic do not seem to have been of much assistance to the anti-Bolsheviks. Indeed, by encouraging the hopes of the latter, inspiring them to activity and then failing to support them, we are exposing them to needless danger, and increasing the distress of all classes in Russia. No intervention is from every point of view better than half-hearted attempts at intervention which only lower our prestige.

Friday, 24 January 1919

Lunched with Cole and had a long talk on industrial position. He is a cold-blooded logical machine but I liked him. Says he is not a Bolshevik but a Menshevik. That he is opposed to methods of bloodshed, and that he has for that reason lost the confidence of the shop-stewards who are pure Bolsheviks. He is an anti-militarist and therefore anti-interventionist. I told him that our great difficulty with the Bolsheviks during negotiations was that we were always bound by war psychology and war considerations, while Lenin had had no war feelings at all. Cole said nor had he. Told me our government used provocations and that Tyrrell of the Foreign Office had tried to make him come over to the Foreign Office. Left for Bexhill.

Sunday, 9 February 1919

Papers now announce that the four Grand Dukes who were arrested in September after the attempt on Lenin's life were shot on 27 January as reprisal for the shooting of Krylenko who tried to enter the Cossack Army in order to carry on Bolshevik propaganda.

It now appears that both the Tsar and Tsarina and all children have been murdered, also the Grand Duchess Elizabeth and probably the Grand Duke Michael.

Thursday, 2 May 1919

Ransome came down to see me to bespeak my help with the Foreign Office to obtain a visa for Evgenia Petrovna Shelyepina... Had a long talk with Ransome *re* Russia. There is a good deal in what he says and I am inclined to agree that but for our interference and blundering events in Russia would

[1] G. D. H. Cole (1889–1959) was a Fabian Socialist, an economist and, with his wife Margaret, author of detective stories. J. C. Squire (1884–1958), knighted 1933, was acting editor of the *New Statesman* at this time and was poet, parodist and littérateur with a penchant for cricket and the countryside.

[2] Mikhail Raskolnikov was commander of the Soviet Baltic Fleet. He was subsequently Ambassador to Bulgaria and died in 1939.

have shaped themselves differently. Phillips Price[1] and Sadoul have definitely thrown in their lot with the Bolsheviks.

He was offered a post on 20 May 1919:

Steel-Maitland[2] has offered me a post of First Commerical Secretary to Poland. Salary about £2000 – not very keen on accepting.

He lunched with an interesting group on 22 May:

Went up to town to lunch with the Webbs. Arnold Bennett, Tom Jones (L. G.'s secretary), Mrs Bertrand Russell,[3] and Mr and Mrs Sidney Webb. Talked about Bolshevism. There is nothing revolutionary about the Webbs. Tom Jones told a very good story of Curzon reading out a despatch at a Cabinet meeting in connection with the peace celebrations. He came across the word 'beano' which he had never heard before and which he pronounced béano like Italian. Jones as the only man present of humble origin explained the conundrum! Arnold Bennett very stiff and heavy in the general conversation. Speaks in little jerky sentences. One expects something very illuminating, but the mountain rumbles only to bring out a mouse. I liked him very much and went with him from 41 Grosvenor Road to Whitehall. He was much more interesting on literature; said he thought nothing of the *Secret City* and that flattery was not good for Hugh.[4] Very keen on Russian novelists who he said were miles ahead of everyone else. Didn't think much of our younger generation except [D. H.] Lawrence who was a genius spoilt by eroticism. Lawrence is a consumptive. Very amusing on [H. G.] Wells whom he described as a wonder of energy: four novels a year, five mistresses all over the country every year – a regular juggler. Went down to Sonning on Thames.

On 24 October his future was still undecided:

Went up to town to lunch with Sir William Clark[5] at Brooks's. Lindley and Sir Ralph Walter[6] of the *Times* fame also there. Lindley goes on Wednesday

[1] Morgan Phillips Price (*b.* 1885) had been with *Manchester Guardian* and was now *Daily Herald* correspondent. He joined the I.L.P. (rather than the Bolsheviks) in 1919 and was later a Labour M.P.

[2] Sir Arthur Steel-Maitland, Bt, M.P. (1876–1935) was then Joint Parliamentary Secretary, Foreign Office, and Parliamentary Secretary, Board of Trade, where he was responsible for Overseas Trade (Development and Intelligence).

[3] Arnold Bennett (1867–1931), the novelist, was later book critic on the *Evening Standard*, where he was to be a colleague of Lockhart's. Thomas Jones (1870–1955), deputy secretary to the cabinet for many years, and close adviser to Bonar Law and Stanley Baldwin as well as Lloyd George. Russell's first wife Alys (married 1894, divorced 1921).

[4] Hugh Walpole's novel had been published on 17 January 1919. The press had been enthusiastic, Joseph Conrad praised it and it won the James Tait Black prize.

[5] Sir William Clark (1816–1952), then Comptroller-General, Department of Overseas Trade, later High Commissioner in Canada.

[6] Francis Lindley (1872–1950), knighted 1926, had just returned from being Consul-General in Russia. He was later Ambassador to Portugal and Japan. Ralph Walter (1871–1937) was director of *The Times* and one of the family that controlled the newspaper for more than a century.

as High Commissioner to Vienna. Clark suggested I should go at once on a Commercial Mission to South Russia. I think, however, I had better leave Russia for a bit. I don't like the Bolsheviks and I don't go so far right as Denikin and Co.[1] Clark suggested instead Rumania and Czechoslovakia. Lindley was very nice. I told him how I had fallen foul of Hardinge and the Buchanans.[2] He said Hardinge no longer counted. He said Noulens had spoken appreciatively of me. This rather surprises me. Met Hoare, John Buchan, G. M. Young and also Neilson and Thornhill.[3]

He was asked to attend a selection committee at the Overseas Trade Department for a commercial post in Czechoslovakia. He was also to send back regular reports on matters of interest to the Secret Intelligence Service.

[1] General Anton Denikin (1872–1947) was the most active of the anti-Bolshevik leaders.

[2] His difficulty with Buchanan, former Ambassador in Moscow, was over Lockhart's *volte-face* from non-intervention. Buchanan had written to him on 8 January 1919: 'I was much put out at reading your telegram in which you sided completely with the Bolsheviks and did all you could to influence the P.M. to recognise them. Later on you made a complete *volte-face* and used the same arguments in favour of intervention as I have used all along.'

[3] G. M. Young (1882–1959) had been secretary to Arthur Henderson when he visited Russia during the Kerensky revolution and was soon to go with Lindley to Vienna. He later became a distinguished historian and critic and was a fellow of All Souls. Captain John Neilson, like Thornhill, was a comrade from Russian days.

CHAPTER THREE

1920-1924

Commercial Secretary, British Legation, Prague. Begins friendship with Jan Masaryk and Dr Eduard Beneš. Meets Beaverbrook and the Countess of Rosslyn ('Tommy'). Joins Anglo-International Bank. Fears drink and night-clubs. Becomes a Roman Catholic. In Vienna meets Moura again. Heartily dislikes Stravinsky.

Lockhart's journals for 1920, 1921 and 1922 are missing; they may have been among those lost in a fire at Aviemore in the 1950s; or he may not have kept any; or they may have been destroyed for personal or security reasons. Lockhart had accepted the post of Commercial Secretary at the British Legation in Prague, the capital of the new country, Czechoslovakia. Sir George Clerk was the Minister. Here he enjoyed his fishing (as described in My Rod My Comfort, *published in 1949) and came to know President Thomas Garrigue Masaryk; with Masaryk's son, Jan, he began a long and intimate friendship, and he knew Dr Eduard Beneš, a later President of the Czechoslovak Republic. With these and other Czechs, Lockhart's later life was to be bound up in ways he could not have then anticipated.*

During his vacations in Britain, he made new acquaintances and friends. Lord Beaverbrook he had met in the aftermath of his Russian fame, or débâcle as he thought of it. Another new friend was Lady Rosslyn – neé Vera Mary Bayley the third wife of Harry, the 5th Earl of Rosslyn (1869–1939), who came of the ancient Scottish families of Wedderburn and Erskine. When they met in February 1923, Lady Rosslyn – always known as Tommy – had been married since 1908. She had two sons – 'Hamish' (J. A. W. St Clair Erskine) and David – and a daughter – Mary. Her husband had a son – 'Loughie', Lord Loughborough – and a daughter – Rosabelle – by his first wife, Rosslyn, as he himself frankly reveals in My Gamble with Life *(London, 1928) was, in the slang of those days, 'a bit of a rip'. He had a brief brush with politics, the army, became a bankrupt, a lover of horse-racing and an actor. 'I know I have been looked on as a rake and roué,' he wrote; he was frank, too, about his drinking habits, which were for long a torture to his wife and family.*

Lockhart and Lady Rosslyn were to become intimate friends; through her he met royalty, particularly the Prince of Wales (later Duke of Windsor), and many members of the nobility,

During early May 1923 Lockhart was constantly lunching and dining at the Rosslyn's London house, 107 Westbourne Terrace, even when Lord Rosslyn was not present.

He resumed his Legation life in Prague, but next month, June, was on holiday with Lady Rosslyn in Austria. On 5 July she returned to England. In July they were together again. Not surprisingly, he records on 30 July 1923 of his wife Jean:

Jean very ill with complete collapse and severe hysteria. Took her to nursing home at 42 Belgrave Road. Terrible time until doctor arrived when she recovered somewhat.

Hamish returned, and, as I was not allowed to stay with Jean, I dined with Tommy, Captain Maxwell, Dorothy and Hamish and went to *R.U.R.* [by Karel Capek] the Czech play: an interesting idea but not great as a play.

He set off again for Prague via Cologne where he had talks with the British Commercial Secretary at the Consulate. He had meetings with President Masaryk and began to learn Czech. As always he spent much of his evenings in cabarets and was quite capable of hiring gypsy bands to play for him and his friends. As a result his debts grew. He was still writing articles for reviews, but the rewards were slender, compared with his expenditures.

At the end of 1923 he resigned from the Legation and joined the Anglo-International Bank, which, supported by the Bank of England, conducted its business in Central Europe and the Balkans. One reason for so doing was that his grandmother, 'who provided my financial sinews', had recently died.

He was back in England in the early part of 1924, thinking of writing a novel and also of joining the Roman Catholic Church to which Lady Rosslyn adhered. With his wife he went to Charlie Chichester's party,[1] *'a horrid orgy', on 15 February 1924. He received more bills from Prague. On 22 February he received a letter from his father 'very surprised at the idea of my becoming a Catholic. "Their worship is a necromantic rite far removed from the simple worship instituted by Christ."'*

Fishing the Tweed near Kelso on 29 February, he had an extraordinary experience:

Bitterly cold and fierce gale which made the river like a stormy sea. Old Tait, the ghillie who taught Lord Ednam[2] to fish, is seventy years old and had a job to hold the boat in the wind. He carried me across the ford on his back! Fished the junction in the morning without success.

Still feeling tired and lazy – digestion does not seem good.

Back in London he began to fear drink and night-clubs, yet was incapable of resisting; this was to haunt him for many years. On 12 March, he writes:

Broken all my pledges and drank both port and champagne. Arrived 10.30

[1] Charles Chichester (*b.* 1893), great-grandson of 1st Baron Templemore, was a very rich man who was honorary attaché to the British Legations in Bucharest and Prague. In October 1924 he married Pamela Peel. They were divorced in 1928, and in 1934 she married John Wrench. She was to become a close friend of Lockhart, and to die in a motor accident in 1962.

[2] Lord Ednam (1894–1969) succeeded his father as 3rd Earl of Dudley in 1932. His wife, Rosemary Millicent, was the daughter of Millicent Duchess of Sutherland, and thus a niece of Lord Rosslyn.

in London and was dragged round the various night-clubs. Staying at the Metropole.

On 14 March 1924 he writes:

Lunched with Mrs Turner [his mother-in-law] at the Curzon. She was very nice and sympathetic about my becoming an R.C. In evening dined with Jean and Frank at the Ivy. Frank very bitter about women in general and society women in particular.[1]

Pursuing his round of pleasure – over which next day he repined – he went to see Shaw's Saint Joan *on 22 May 1924:*

Colder and wet. In the evening went to *Saint Joan* at the New Theatre by Bernard Shaw. Except for a few Shavian touches, utterly unlike anything else Shaw has written. Intensely interesting, but Sybil Thorndike's Joan was very poor, I though the pert skittishness hopelessly exaggerated.

Letter from Nesbitt's inviting me to write a book.

On 6 June 1924, he was received into the Roman Church by Father Vincent McNabb at St Dominic's Priory; and on 28 June, his last day in London before leaving for Prague:

Last day in London. Went shopping with Tommy in morning. Went to early Mass at the Oratory, breakfasted at 59 Sloane Gardens [Lady Rosslyn's new address]. Lunched at 59 with Jean and Frank. In afternoon went with Tommy to the new [Westminster] Cathedral – Byzantine and not very pretty – and heard vespers and a short benediction service.

In evening dined *en partie carrée* at Kettners. Very tired and depressed.

His function at the Anglo-International Bank was far from clear, he confesses on 1 July 1924:

First day in bank. Am sharing a room with Geduldiger[2] not very satisfactory and have no idea what I am to do or what my future is to be. . .

Had tea with Sir George [Clerk] in the afternoon and had a long talk with him about fishing. Wrote Tommy and Jean.

He continued to be well received at the Legation, partly because of his Secret Intelligence Service connections.

On 15 July he records:

Lunched at the Legation: Delme-Radcliffe, Spencer-Smith, Simon, Clare Sheridan and her brother, Commander Frewen, Greenway and self.[3] I sat

[1] Arthur Francis (Frank) Aveling (1893–1954) served in the Diplomatic Service in Prague, Peking, Warsaw and Brussels. He was a friend of King Leopold of the Belgians, and became an intimate of Jean, Lockhart's wife.

[2] Lockhart described him as 'a local expert . . . who does all the work' in *Retreat from Glory*.

[3] Sir Charles Delme-Radcliffe (1864–1937), had been chief of the British Military

next to the Sheridan woman. She is off to Kiev with her brother on a motor-cycle and then to Odessa – a wild trip for a book and advertisement. She is armed with wonderful letters from the Bolsheviks. She knows nothing about Russia, nor did I like her very much, but she had been rather good-looking. Spencer-Smith and George found her very attractive.

Dined alone at home in the evening. A bad day again – could do no work. Spencer-Smith told me that my doctor in Vienna had told Simon to get me home as quickly as possible.

Lockhart was still writing articles, though a proposed book of fairy tales was turned down by Longmans. He read voraciously books in several languages.

In Vienna in August he again met Moura, his inamorata from Moscow days. On 2–4 August, he noted:

She looks older. Her face is more serious, and she has a few grey hairs. She was not dressed as in old days, but she has not changed. She is making £800–£900 per annum translating Russian into English as Gorky's secretary. She had not changed. The change is in me. I admire her above all other women. Her mind, her genius, her control are all wonderful. But the old feeling has gone. After luncheon at Hickie's villa at Hinterhühl we walked up into the woods and talked. She understood at once...

Did my business with Hickie and in the afternoon talked to Moura. She told me all about her life, about her imprisonment, her escapes, her meeting with Gorky. She despises me for not throwing over everything and taking my courage in both hands, but the truth is that even if everything were favourable and there were no obstacles and no obligations I should not want to do it.

Talked about Russia, the hopeless nonsense talked by the émigrés, and about Lenin. We all agreed more or less... In the evening left for Prague with Moura. We had no sleeper and we travelled up in a carriage with three other people including one of the Soviet representatives in Prague. Moura was a little bitter. Said goodbye to her at the station. She went on to Berlin and is going to Reval to see her children. She will come back to Prague. She has worked very hard; translates six books a year and does 4000 words a day. Her energy is quite marvellous; her translations extraordinarily good. Very tired; indeed, quite exhausted. Peterson came back.[1] He seems very nice. We sat up till eleven talking about Prague. Bought [Georges] Duhamel's *Les Martyres* and Romain Rolland's *Au-dessus de la mêlée*. Moura says I am

---

Mission with the Italian Army during the war, and later in Austria. Michael Spencer-Smith (1882–1946) was a young Director of the Bank of England in overall charge of Anglo-International Bank. Dr Simon was a Viennese Director of the Bank, and Clare Consuelo Sheridan (*d.* 1970) a sculptor, journalist and author, cousin of Winston Churchill. J. D. Greenway was secretary in the Legation at Prague.

[1] Maurice Peterson (1889–1952), career diplomat, was then First Secretary at Prague. He later became a close friend of Lockhart and Ambassador to Iraq, Spain and Turkey. He was knighted in 1947.

a little strong, but not strong enough, a little clever, but not clever enough, and a little weak, but not weak enough.

Lockhart shared the unthinking distaste for Jews that many middle-class Britons of that period professed. On 15 August he wrote:

In the afternoon left . . . for Marienbad: poured with rain all day. Arrived at 9.20 at the Esplanade and did a bummel round the night places. Broke my vows about alcohol and drank too much champagne. A very dull and futile performance. The people at Marienbad are too awful for words – ninety per cent Jews.

The ascension of Mary. Did not go to Mass.

Lockhart was frequently feeling ill or 'seedy'. He complained of rheumatism, sinusitis and a dozen other afflictions. He was always being advised by doctors. His sufferings doubtless were real; they afflicted him for most of his long life of eighty-two years. In Prague, for example, in August 1924, he was plied with 'charcoal made of animals' bones which disinfects the stomach'. He was a classical case of the creaking gate. His young friend, Jan Masaryk, whom he saw much of in Prague, was a similar case, although his end was earlier and of a different character.

On 17 September 1924, he was back in London, dining with Lady Rosslyn at 2 Brick Street, 'and tried to play the ukelele', the craze for which was at its height. With his wife and Lady Rosslyn he went to the theatres and, on Friday, 19 September, saw The Street Singer, *featuring Phyllis Dare. He was back in Prague on 23 September. He went to concerts from time to time, and reported on 13 November:*

In the evening went with Peterson to the Stravinsky concert. The main item in the programme was *The Story of a Soldier.*[1] I do not know if anyone enjoyed it, but a great many people heartily disliked it and left the hall, Peterson and I among them. The Marinetti of music.

But Lockhart was in general unhappy, as he explains on 22 November 1924:

Very tired. Stayed in bed all day. I am in a miserable state just now. Everything seems to be going wrong. My work at the bank is in a most unsatisfactory state. I hope Bark, will do something to improve it.[2] My private life is not much better, and my finances are wrong again.

Tommy, too, seems to have changed, and I seem to be drifting out of her life.

Extraordinarily enough, Prague ran to a St Andrew's Day dinner, as Lockhart records on 30 November 1924:

Abscess on my face. Stayed in bed all day and in evening went to our

[1] Usually known as *The Soldier's Tale*. Emilio Marinetti (1869–1937) was the Italian poet who founded the Futurist movement, glorifying war and the machine age.

[2] Peter Bark (1869–1937), former Tsarist Finance Minister, was then adviser to the Bank of England on Central European affairs, and was knighted in 1929.

dinner for St Andrew's Day. Present: George Clerk, Peterson, self, McKechnie, Douglas and Taylor (in kilt) as Scottish hosts. Guests – Jan Masaryk, Greenway, Hudson, Darton, Oldfield and Adams. Very good show, but the Athole brose was too strong and laid out McKechnie and Douglas, not to mention Darton.

Peterson, I, McKechnie, Adams and Taylor all made speeches, George, Jan Masaryk, Oldfield and Darton replied. Peterson and I also sang a *Vive-la*, and I wrote a poem about Jan Masaryk.

On 20 December, his old chief in Russia, Sir George Buchanan, died. Lockhart was still being dunned in a sometimes embarrassing manner, as he noted on 24 December 1924:

Left at 6.30 a.m. for Joachimsthal. On the Masaryk platform Brousa came up and tried to dun me for money for my car. When I refused, he said he would go to the bank and tell them what kind of a man I was.

CHAPTER FOUR

1925-1927

Manager, Intelligence Department of the Anglo-Austrian Bank. Socialising and night clubs. The Rosslyns' troubles. Beaverbrook. Begins contributing to *Evening Standard.* Visits Yugoslavia, Berlin, Prague. Meets Daisy, Countess of Warwick. Golf with the Prince of Wales. Freda Dudley Ward. In Belgrade. Becomes honorary Austrian Consul in London. Immorality at Eton. Meets Orme Sargent of the Foreign Office.

During 1925 he remained with the Anglo-International Bank in Prague whence he visited Budapest and Belgrade. In June he was in England, his finances 'in a hopeless tangle' and doubtful of his future, since the Bank was cutting down its staff. As extra-mural activity he negotiated with the Czech government on behalf of Baron de Forest, a British subject and M.P. whose pre-war estate in Moravia had been confiscated under the Prague government's Land Reform Act.[1] *He was ultimately successful and received commission of £7400.*

He now became Manager of the Intelligence Department of the Anglo-Austrian Bank which meant six months in London, and six months touring Central Europe. He remained in the post for nearly three years. He began dieting and a long, sometimes successful, fight against the alcohol he believed had ruined some of his maternal ancestors. In London he spent his time equally between Lady Rosslyn (Tommy) and his wife Jean, socialising, visiting new plays, hearing concerts and watching rugby football. He still thought nothing of visiting three night-clubs in a night – as on 17 December 1925, the Café de Paris, Cabaret Club and Little Club. He saw a good deal of his father – head of a prep. school in Berkshire – and his brothers. He visited Lord Beaverbrook.

On 11 February 1926, Lady Rosslyn decided not to see him in future, but they were together two days later. Lord Rosslyn was going bankrupt.

Thursday, 18 March 1926

Tommy came to see me. She is tired out and feeling the strain of the bankruptcy, Harry's return and Loughie's misdeeds. Rose at twelve and went

[1] Arnold Maurice, Baron de Forest (1879–1968), later became Count Bendern and a citizen of Lichtenstein.

to lunch at 7 Charles Street. Rosabelle Brand[1] there and Hamish who has fractured his arm in running in the half-mile at Eton.

Wednesday, 14 April 1926

In evening dined with Tommy at the Hyde Park. She had been all day at Lady Lovat's as the latter is expecting a baby.[2] Tommy has many worries, though her chief worry is past. The Duke of Sutherland is advancing Harry £2000 on Tommy's furniture and will not let Tommy put it into her house! Harry's examination in bankruptcy takes place tomorrow. Tommy came to see me after dinner before returning to Lady Lovat.

Lord Beaverbrook invited him to stay at his country house, Cherkley, near Leatherhead, and so began a series of invitations that lasted for thirty years.

Sunday, 25 April 1926

At seven left for Cherkley Court, Leatherhead, to stay with the Beaverbrooks. Mrs Jean Norton[3] was there. She is very pretty. Beaverbrook in great form. He has an astounding memory, is marvellously well-read in history, and talks well. Blamed me for not having written my memoirs, told me to start at once, and said he would take the serial rights. Fixed me up an appointment with Editor of *Evening Standard*. Bed at twelve. Broke my pledge and drank four or five glasses of champagne

Monday, 26 April 1926

Came back from Cherkley Court. Beaverbrook who sleeps out of doors down there – even in this dreadful weather – received me in his bedroom. Offered to give me a letter to the *Evening Standard*.

On 28 April he saw E. Raymond Thompson, editor of the Evening Standard,[4] *and arranged to contribute articles, and paragraphs for 'The Londoner's Diary'.*

A general strike had begun in Britain:

Walked with Jean to the Tudor Court Hotel and lunched with her mother. Tommy says Birkenhead,[5] who was playing bridge at the Carlton Club till the early hours of the morning told Harry that the government were going to use force to break up the strike. Tommy hopes the govern-

[1] Lady Rosabelle Brand was the Earl of Rosslyn's daughter (*b.* 1891) by his first wife. Her first husband had been killed in the war and she was married to Lieut.-Colonel J. C. Brand.

[2] Laura, wife of Simon, 14th Baron Lovat (1871–1933), who was shortly to become Under-Secretary for the Dominions.

[3] Wife of Richard Norton, later Lord Grantley. She was a very beautiful woman and one of Beaverbrook's dearest friends; she died in 1945.

[4] Thompson (1872–1928) was editor from 1923 to 1928; he wrote biographies under the name of E. T. Raymond.

[5] F. E. Smith, 1st Earl of Birkenhead (1872–1930) had been Lord Chancellor, 1919–22, and was now Secretary of State for India.

ment will win, and then be very magnanimous as after the war, but I fear the employers will jib at the magnanimity.

Dined at club and talked with several members. Sir Thomas Birkett[1] thinks it will be a long struggle.

On 2 May, as part of his bank job, he left for Prague and Central Europe, staying in Prague at the Legation with his old friend, Sir George Clerk.

Thursday, 20 May 1926

Went to see Hotowetz [Czech Minister of Commerce], who is an out-and-out free-trader for Central Europe. Gave me his brochure to read. Says the present system will lead to catastrophe and fears that only a catastrophe will teach the succession states wisdom.

He went to Belgrade and Zagreb, and late in June he was in Berlin:

Monday, 28 June 1926

In afternoon went to the Eden Dachgarten and watched Berlin dance – not a very edifying spectacle. Public mostly Jewish – dancing bad and vulgar – most of the women like men and most of the men like women. At eight went to Scala where I saw a good variety show and some exquisite ballet dancing by Blinova and Worontzov.

Berlin looks quite prosperous but in spite of the fact that it is more modern and more Americanised than London everything looks cheap and vulgar. All Yanks at Adlon.

Back in England the social swim engulfed him:

Sunday, 18 July 1926

Another blazing day. Went down by car with Tommy at eleven to Easton, Daisy Countess of Warwick's place.[2] Drove through Epping Forest. Easton is a hideous house, but a lovely park: herds of deer, St Kilda sheep and rabbits galore. She allows no shooting. The gardens are wonderful – also Stone Lodge, a sanctuary with a lovely garden and an old house, very tiny, with Roman wall. There is a 'friendship border' with flowers planted by King Edward as Prince of Wales. [H. G.] Wells, Philip Guedalla[3] – a real dago – and Basil Dean[4] live on the estate. Had tea with Lady Warwick. She says she

[1] Retired Indian administrator (1871–1957).

[2] Frances Evelyn ('Daisy'), Countess of Warwick (1861–1938), *chère amie* of Edward VII, was one of the earliest aristocratic converts to socialism. She offered her house, Easton Lodge, as a Fabian conference and weekend centre. She had intended it as a Labour college, but the T.U.C. got cold feet.

[3] Philip Guedalla (1889–1944), biographer and historian, was a Liberal rather than a Fabian.

[4] Basil Dean, was a theatrical manager and playwright; he later founded E.N.S.A.

is more 'left' than G. D. H. Cole, who was down with the Workers' Educational Association summer school. The I.L.P. come later, with Kirkwood[1] as Chairman. Lunched and dined at Bishops Stortford.

Saturday, 14 August 1926

Went in with Tommy to Beaufort[2] where we had tea. Met Ronnie Knox, Maurice Baring, Venetia Montagu and Katharine Asquith (Raymond's wife).[3] After tea walked up with Tommy to the falls and saw lots of salmon and sea-trout. The castle is in red sandstone and is new and ugly, but the grounds – and the famous gardens – are really beautiful.

He became friendly, through Lady Rosslyn and golf, with the Prince of Wales, then thirty-two.

Saturday, 28 August 1926

Went to bank for an hour in morning. Felt rotten. Went down to Sandwich by the 11.30. Tommy met me at the Ramsgate Station. There was no room for me at the 'Fourth Green' so I was going to stay at the Granville when the Prince of Wales asked me to stay with him at Smalldown. I slept in his dressing-room. In afternoon Tommy and I played against the Prince and Freda.[4] We played about ten holes and halved. He played quite well and has some good shots. In evening dined with Tommy, Freda and Michael Herbert[5] and then went to bed at eleven-thirty. The Prince expected me to see him, but I did not like to disturb him. Glorious weather. Jean at Bexhill.

Sunday, 29 August 1926

Rose early and went to Mass at Ramsgate. Tommy mistook the time, so we arrived too early and had to wait till nine, when we had a sermon which nearly made me late for golf with the Prince. We played a three-ball at Prince's. I played very badly: could not putt at all. Gave him a half and finished all square. In afternoon we played seven holes: he and Freda *v.*

[1] David Kirkwood (1872–1955), Scottish Independent Labour Party M.P. and shipbuilding trade unionist, later 1st Baron Kirkwood. The I.L.P. was affiliated to the Labour Party—though often in disagreement with it—until 1932.

[2] The Scottish seat of Lord Lovat at Beauly, Inverness.

[3] Ronald Knox (1888–1957), Catholic chaplain to Oxford University, theologian, essayist and wit; Maurice Baring (1874–1946) had been a diplomat, war correspondent and officer in the Royal Flying Corps, he was a poet, travel writer and novelist. Venetia Montagu was the widow of Edwin Montagu (1879–1924), Secretary of State for India, 1917–22; she was an intimate of Asquith and died in 1948. Katherine Asquith was also a widow, Herbert Asquith's eldest son, Raymond, having been killed in 1916.

[4] Freda was Winifred, daughter of Col. Charles Birkin, who in 1913 had married William Dudley Ward (1877–1946), M.P. for Southampton, and Vice-Chamberlain of the Royal Household, 1917–22. They were divorced in 1931 and she later married the Marquis of Casa Maury.

[5] Michael Herbert (1893–1932), younger brother of Sidney Herbert, M.P., who was Private Secretary to the Prime Minister.

Tommy and me: we won two up. Then we played four holes level, and the Prince won two up: played well too! He was delighted. Dined with him in evening: Harry Rosslyn, Tommy, Freda, Michael, Roddie Ward, General Trotter, Greenacre and myself.[1] Sat up till two and talked to him about Russia and Central Europe. He wanted me to stay till Monday evening. Jean's birthday.

Monday, 30 August 1926

Rose at seven and caught the eight o'clock to London. Tommy drove me to the station. Nothing much doing here and I could easily have stayed. Bought Jean a clock and sent Tommy a cigarette box, and some birds for the children. Wrote my bread-and-butter letter to the Prince. He is very simple in a way and terribly modest about himself. He has an inferiority complex! Dinner last night: two cocktails, melon, soup, lobster, cutlets, cold grouse, ice and savoury: sherry, champagne, port and brandy – and whisky!

Dined in evening with Jean and Frank: Jean's birthday dinner, and did myself too well again.

Wednesday, 1 September 1926

Letter from Tommy saying that the Prince of Wales was delighted with me and 'could not like me more'.

Wednesday, 15 September 1926

Last day at Sandwich. Played golf in morning. Tommy and I versus Freda and Riviere. We were badly beaten, both Tommy and I playing very badly. In afternoon went for a walk with Tommy. The Prince of Wales arrived in the evening from Calais after a very rough crossing. We all dined together. He played the ukulele and was very nice. He has sprained his thumb playing golf and says he now plays better through not holding too tight with his right hand. Said he would rather play golf than shoot, but that his father was a wonderful shot both with gun and with rifle.

Thursday, 16 September 1926

Came back to London. Jean ill in bed with sore throat and nervous attack. The Prince of Wales wanted me to stay to play golf.

Towards the end of 1926 his bank – the Anglo-Austrian – took over the British Trade Corporation. This was followed by the news that the Belgrade branch of the B.T.C. had lost some £100,000 through the fraud of their Serbian manager. Much of Lockhart's efforts in the next twelve months were involved in trying to recoup the loss.

[1] Roderick Ward (*b.* 1902), second son of 2nd Earl of Dudley. Brigadier-General G. F. Trotter (1871–1945), Groom-in-Waiting to the Prince of Wales. W. D. Greenacre (*b.* 1900), Equerry to the Prince of Wales.

His rackety night life continued. He was learning the 'charleston', a new dance craze, with a new girl friend, Jill. With Lady Rosslyn he dined and danced at the Piccadilly Hotel where he saw the Prince of Wales on 24 January 1927.

Wednesday, 16 March 1927

Prince of Wales won his race at the Grenadier Guards point-to-point at Bicester. Prince George[1] who had his fortune told by a new palmist, was told to warn his brother not to ride in a race on March 16th, as he would have a serious fall! The Prince of Wales paid no attention.

In April he became, through the influence of his Bank, honorary Austrian Consul in London.

Lady Rosslyn had continuous problems:

Lunched with Tommy at the Savoy. She left at 4.20 for Horsham. She is worried about Hamish's friends at Eton. One of the boys he brought to stay at Freda's had a rouge pot and a powder puff. Freda's maid discovered them and told everybody!

Sunday, 14 August 1927

Dined with Tommy, Hamish, Jean Massereene[2] and Twiston. After dinner talked to the two boys who made my hair curl with stories about immorality and drinking at Eton and Oxford. The modern youth seems to grow up much more quickly than in my day.

He had frequent discussions with the Foreign Office, and on 20 September 1927, the name of one who was to become an intimate appears for the first time: Orme Sargent (1884–1962) – known to his friends as Moley – who was to become head of the Foreign Office in 1946.

Lunched with Tommy at the Berkeley Grill. She was feeling rather ill, having pains in the place where she had her operation. Went to see Harvey, Bateman,[3] and Sargent at the Foreign Office. Discussed Hungary, Yugoslavia and Greece. Later went to Karlovic, the Serb Chargé d'Affaires. In the evening went to hear Professor [Joseph] Redlich, former Austrian Finance Minister and later Professor of Harvard University, lecture on Austria. Very interesting, although he said little that I did not know already.

Lockhart was no mean descriptive writer. On 14 October 1927, he wrote of Trieste and Venice:

Arrived at Trieste at 9.30, raced through the customs and caught the 10.50

[1] Prince George (1902–42), fourth and youngest son of King George V, created Duke of Kent in 1934.

[2] Second wife of the 12th Viscount Massereene, Parliamentary Secretary to the Prime Minister of Northern Ireland. She died in 1937.

[3] Oliver Harvey, later 1st Baron Harvey of Tasburgh (1893–1968), was a young Foreign Office First Secretary; Charles Bateman (*b.* 1892) was also an official there, later Ambassador to Mexico and Poland, knighted in 1954.

to Venice. At Trieste it was cold and damp, and, although the sun came out at Venice, it was not the warmth of Dubrovnik. Goodbye summer. On arriving at Venice, deposited our things at the Grand and went off by gondola to see the Church of the Madonna dei Miracoli – a very fine specimen of Renaissance architecture by Pietro Lombardi with a magnificently carved interior. The altar is on a raised platform to which one ascends by a splendidly carved staircase. Then to St Mark's. We dined at Florian's and then went down to the Rialto bridge in a gondola. The *serenata* was still in full force, but there was a chillness in the air which was not of summer and which spoke of winter and the sadness of farewells.

CHAPTER FIVE

1928

Bad debts. Meets Lord Castlerosse and Lady Bridget Paget. Tour of Europe. His mother dies. More golf with the Prince of Wales. Becomes editor of 'The Londoner's Diary' on the *Evening Standard.* Beaverbrook thinks war in Europe inevitable. Liberal Party is collapsing. Beaverbrook's exercises. Visit to the Kaiser. The King's illness. Winston's bad judgement. Lloyd George on the Kaiser.

By the beginning of 1928 Lockhart's hopes of a future in banking were receding. His managing director Spencer-Smith was killed, aged forty-six, in a motor accident; his successor was Peter Bark, former Tsarist Minister of Finance, who had always been friendly to Lockhart. But retrenchment was the order of the day. Lockhart's debts, meanwhile, had grown again. His thoughts turned to journalism, to which as an outsider he had made considerable contributions, not least to Beaverbrook's Evening Standard.

Tuesday, 21 February 1928

In the evening dined with Beaverbrook at the Vineyard[1] – very interesting. He offered me a job beginning with £2000 a year as leader-writer for the *Standard* and *Express.* He also showed some interest in Continental shares. He is going to Russia and has telegraphed to ask Chicherin[2] if he can take me. Drank some champagne. Late night.

Tuesday, 28 February 1928

In the evening went to see Beaverbrook at the vineyard and got an order for Polyphon shares out of him.[3]

Friday, 2 March 1928

Beaverbrook's shares have gone up to 270. Saw Sharp of the *New Statesman.*[4] He very strongly advises me not to join Beaverbrook.

In tight financial hole. Have no money in bank.

[1] Beaverbrook's tiny Tudor house in Hurlingham Road, Fulham.

[2] Soviet Commissar for Foreign Affairs; Lockhart had known him well in Moscow.

[3] Presumably Lockhart was getting commission for such orders from his uncle, Tom Macgregor, a wealthy Edinburgh stockbroker.

[4] Clifford Sharp (1883–1935) was editor of the *New Statesman* from its foundation in 1913 until it amalgamated with the *Nation* in 1931.

Sunday, 4 March 1928

Went down to [Cherkley Court] Leatherhead to stay with Beaverbrook. Arnold Bennett, Castlerosse, the Pagets,[1] and Jean Norton there. Very amusing conversation, although Beaverbrook himself was not very fit.

Monday, 5 March 1928

Lunched with Beaverbrook and then came up to London with Jean Norton by car...

In evening dined with Hugh Walpole at Arnold Bennett's house, 75 Cadogan Square. Arnold Bennett very kind about my book.[2] Michael Arlen,[3] T. S. Eliot, the poet and editor of the *Criterion*, E. Knoblock,[4] also there.

Yesterday and today broke my pledge.

Wednesday, 14 March 1928

Went to see Beaverbrook and asked him to give me £10,000 as discretionary client.

Tuesday, 20 March 1928

This is the beginning of a critical week, as I must raise at least £750 in order to meet my debts.

Saturday, 7 April 1928

Went over to Cherkley Court in the evening to stay with Beaverbrook. He offered me the job of financial editor of all his papers. Bridget there, also a Canadian called [Frank P.] Jones who was head of Beaverbrook's Canadian Cement Co and who introduced the first dumping laws into Canada.

Monday, 23 April 1928

Tom bought £2000 Polyphons and Beaverbrook £5000.

Lockhart accepted Beaverbrook's offer which was to be editor of 'The Londoner's Diary' with the proviso that he should have some months of freedom before joining; the bank gave him a year's salary, and he set off again for Europe.

He wrote to Beaverbrook, then staying in Newmarket, on 9 May 1928:

[1] Valentine, Viscount Castlerosse (1891–1943), later Earl of Kenmare, an Irish peer and columnist who wrote the 'Londoner's Log' in the *Sunday Express*. Lord Victor Paget (1889–1952), brother of the 6th Marquess of Anglesey, and his second wife, Bridget, whom he married in 1922 and divorced in 1932.

[2] Perhaps the manuscript of a novel that Lockhart was writing at this time, but was never published.

[3] Michael Arlen (1895–1956), Armenian naturalised in Britain, whose best-seller, *The Green Hat*, epitomised the spirit of the twenties.

[4] Edward Knoblock (1874–1945), American playwright, who also wrote plays in collaboration with Arnold Bennett. Lockhart misspells both his name and T. S. Eliot's.

I am seeing Wilson and Gilliat[1] tomorrow, today being inconvenient for all of us, but I should like to thank you now, more warmly than I did in yesterday's hurried interview, for your kindness and for the interest you have always taken in my doings.

In 1918, when I was on the crest of the wave, there were many people who were only too glad to make much of me, but I should like you to know how much I appreciated the interest you took in me after the collapse of Russia and my own partial failure in that country.

I hope that now I am going to work for you, you will never have any cause to regret the offer you have made me.

I expect you know as much as and more of my record as you want, but I shall send you in a few days my curriculum vitae in case you may find amongst my many defects some virtues of which you are not yet aware!

He soon returned to England, where he received bad news:

Monday, 14 May 1928

I was walking in the garden at Hunger Hill[2] with Tommy when William [the butler] came up to tell me there was bad news for me on the telephone. Mother had died, almost in Dad's arms, while she was doing a cross-word with him in the nursing-home. The doctors say it was a clot of blood on the heart. Returned to London immediately. Went with Dad to see her in her last sleep. She looked calm and at peace, but oh! so far away. Spent the evening with Dad. He is a sad and broken old man.

(*Footnote: Friday, 6 July 1928:*) I wish now Mother had been buried here [on Speyside]. I would far rather have come here to see her grave than go down to Sandhurst. She *was* Scottish, and this was her country.)

Immediately after the funeral he went abroad again, returning to Scotland in July, and England in September.

Wednesday, 23 May 1928

Letter from Tommy in which she says that Lady Ednam had told her that Beaverbrook had said that I was one of the most brilliant men of this generation! Arnold Bennett had also spoken to Bridget Paget in the same sense.

Saturday, 1 September 1928

Played golf at Worthing. Tommy and I played against Freda and the Prince of Wales and were beaten by two up and one. The Prince does not

[1] J. B. Wilson (1878–1968), News Editor of the *Daily Express*, 1912–40; George Gilliat, Editor of the *Evening Standard*, 1928–33.

[2] The Rosslyns' home at Coolham, Sussex.

like Beaverbrook, says he wants to get everyone under his thumb and, if he cannot get them, he tries to down them.

Monday, 3 September 1928

In afternoon went over to Worthing and played a round with the Prince of Wales. Glorious day, and we had a great match. I gave him four bisques, and, after I had been four up at the ninth, he got me down to all square with three bisques left and four to go. With the aid of his bisques he made himself closing two, and I had a four and a three and won the last two holes. He had an 81 against Braid[1] in the morning.

(*Footnote: 6 September 1928:* Wrote some paras on P.o.W. for *E.S.*)

Monday, 10 September 1928

In the evening packed my traps and came down to the Bear at Hungerford, partly in order to fish once again before I become a Beaverbrook slave, and partly to escape from London and the fumes of alcohol in which I have lived for the past fortnight.

Saturday, 15 September 1928

Humble[2] tells me that our British optical glass is now the best in the world and that our air-force photography and our air cameras are unbeatable.

He has, in his flight, officers of every class of life from Etonians to Board School boys, and he says if he has a job to give to some one he can trust he never takes a public school boy! He praised the Scots boys from schools like Herriot's.

Lockhart had few friends in London except the Rosslyn family and numerous acquaintances made during his official career. At first he lived in dingy lodgings in Bryanston street; the Evening Standard *building he found 'ramshackle and comfortless'. Among his colleagues were Edward Shanks, poet and literary adviser to Beaverbrook, David Low the cartoonist, Stella Gibbons the novelist and Arnold Bennett, who wrote a weekly book column.*

Lonely as he said he was in these autumn months in 1928, he soon came to know, through his job, most of the personalities then adorning – or disgracing – London life.

Monday, 17 September 1928

First day in [*Evening Standard* building in] Shoe Lane. The street by which I enter my office is St Andrew's Street – patron saint of Scotland, and I hope a good omen.

Went to Foreign Office and had a long talk with Bateman, Harvey and Sargent on Bulgaria, Austria and Yugoslavia – also with Bateman on Chile.

[1] James Braid (1870–1950), Scottish golfer, five times Open Champion – most recently in 1910.

[2] Probably Thomas O. Humble, R.A.F. officer who retired as Group Captain in 1941.

Tuesday, 18 September 1928

I am enjoying my new life. My hours are from 9.30 to 1.15 during which time I am working at full pressure. The afternoons and evenings I use for ferreting out information. Tonight I went to the Chilean Independence Day dinner: all the nitrate kings there: Lord Hunsdon, Sir Arthur Goldfinch, and R. J. Hore, Lord Inverforth, Lionel Rothschild, etc.

Went on to [the] Piccadilly to see Jill.

Sunday, 23 September 1928

Had a long talk with Lord Beaverbrook this morning about foreign politics. He is very anti-League [of Nations,] thinks that war in Europe is inevitable, and that, if we stay out, a European war might be as advantageous to us as the last war was to America. Therefore, we must pull out of the League. I think he is wrong. The way to get war is to say it is coming, and I doubt if we could keep out of a big European war.

Friday, 28 September 1928

[Talking with a Scottish skipper from Aberdeenshire who had come to the Liberal Conference at Yarmouth]. He used to be on the local executive committee of Liberal Party; says it is collapsing now, and men are joining Tories or Labour – a fact which he deplores – now so do I.

Saturday, 29 September 1928

'Labour and Tory are the parties of the bosses. Liberalism was the little man's creed.'

Monday, 1 October 1928

In the evening had an hour's talk with Beaverbrook. He is a full-blooded Imperial Preference man, but an anti-safeguarder. Very interesting about the Liberals. He says they should go to the elections on an anti-safeguarding cry, anti-totalisator and prohibition – a return to the old Presbyterian Liberalism.

Thursday, 18 October 1928

[A Lancashire Liberal M.P., W. M. Wiggins, told him a story]: about Lady Diana and Ellen Wilkinson[1] and latter denouncing Diana for dressing up as a workman. 'Do you think in London she eats chips with her fingers? – No, you silly gorman, she eats with her mouth.'

Friday, 19 October 1928

Lloyd George's day.[2] Great speech in morning on tactics of party and great

[1] Lady Diana Cooper, a famous beauty, daughter of 8th Duke of Rutland, wife of Alfred Duff Cooper, then Financial Secretary to the War Office, later in many other posts and finally 1st Viscount Norwich. Ellen Wilkinson (*d.* 1947), known as 'Red Ellen', had been a Communist, was then Labour M.P. for Middlesbrough East and later for Jarrow, a centre of unemployment in the thirties.

[2] Lloyd George, who had ceased to be Prime Minister when Bonar Law's Conserva-

speech at night on foreign policy. Latter was very dramatic. He came down to hall, armed with a copy of the treaty of Versailles, said we ourselves went to war for a scrap of paper, and now we had not kept our own word with Germany.

L.G. is still the greatest dynamic force in British politics. He gave a wonderful imitation of a racehorse – the Liberal outsider – coming up the straight. Said he was going to a race-meeting for first time. I had the news to London first.

Monday, 29 October 1928

Came up from Hunger Hill. Had a talk with Beaverbrook about House.[1] He looks on House as rather a little 'tick' who has tried by insidious ways to make himself out the big man and Wilson the small man.

It is a great sight to see Max doing his exercises, lying on the floor and expanding and contracting his tummy muscles!

In November 1928 Lockhart went via Germany to see the Kaiser, Wilhelm II, then living in exile near Doorn in Holland. En route *he heard that the Crown Prince was also going to Doorn:*

Monday, 5 November 1928

Crown Prince has gone to Doorn. Heard very good story on Mussolini and Crown Prince. Latter had been to Tripoli and his father asked him what he thought of the natives. He replied, 'I prefer dealing with the black men in white shirts than the white men in black shirts.'

Thursday, 22 November 1928

Telegram from Nowak[2] asking me to meet him at Utrecht. Had a very busy day making my preparations and felt rather excited. Saw Beaverbrook who is not at all antagonistic to the Kaiser, says he is a fine figure in history, and we must do him well.

Friday, 23 November 1928

Arrived at Utrecht at 8 a.m. and found Nowak and Princess Kropotkina.[3] I am *not* to see the Kaiser this time, but I am to be taken to Doorn. Terrible weather: rain and wind and a very low barometer. At 3.45 set out in the

---

tives took over in 1922, had become leader of the Liberal Party in 1926 and was making a determined – though unsuccessful – effort to regain office.

[1] Colonel Edward Mandell House (1858–1938) was principal adviser to President Woodrow Wilson, 1914–17, and, between 1926 and 1928, published *The Intimate Papers of Colonel House*.

[2] Karl Friedrich Nowak, an Austrian Jew, was the Kaiser's secretary and aide. He became his literary counsellor and executor and wrote a history of his reign.

[3] Sasha Kropotkina, daughter of Prince Kropotkin, the Russian anarchist, was Nowak's secretary.

Kaiser's motor for Doorn. Raining when I arrived. At the gateway I was met by Herr Nitz, the President of the Kaiser's household, and taken round the park and gardens. The Kaiser's big Alsatian accompanied us. Then all over the house. The Kaiser is very frightened of journalists. He is very angry over the Ponsonby letters[1] and also over the journalist (one of ours) who climbed into his garden. Everyone was terrified. Nowak took up one or two questions for me and brought back the answers, but I was not allowed to see him. I was not even allowed to ask him which modern English authors he preferred in case it should arouse jealousy – and not a word about German authors. In evening dined with Nowak who told me excellent stories about the Tsar, [Archduke] Ferdinand, Franz Josef and the Emperor Karl. The Kaiser's book is to appear on January 30. He will receive ten copies on his birthday January 27 – and he will present a copy to the Kaiserin which will be a surprise to her. The Kaiser is very hurt that no one in the English royal family sent him a word of sympathy on the death of the Kaiserin.[2] Long talk with Nitz, from which it is clear that the Kaiser believes in his return, i.e., that the Germans will demand his return. There will be no adventures.

Sunday, 25 November 1928

Nowak agrees with me that Lenin was a great man and that history may yet regard him as one of the prophets.

Yesterday Nowak brought back my article with a few alterations which the Kaiser had made himself, and also two pictures of the Kaiser with his dog.

Monday, 26 November 1928

Nowak also told me of General Auffenberg-Komarow's[3] scheme to create a South Slav kingdom after the death or rather murder of King Alexander I. Nowak thinks that England and Germany were secondary factors in start of war. The real cause was the conflict between Russia and Austria. Russia to blame for her adventurous campaign in Balkans and Hungary, for her intransigence in South Slav question.

Some of Lockhart's reflections written at Utrecht on 23 November 1928 – with corrections in the Kaiser's handwriting (here printed in italics), have interest:

Doorn lies some twenty miles from Utrecht, and, as the Imperial motor-

[1] Sir Frederick Ponsonby (1867–1935), later 1st Baron Sysonby, had been Private Secretary to Queen Victoria, Edward VII and George V. In 1929 he was to publish an edition of the letters of the Empress Frederick, the Kaiser's mother, without the Kaiser's permission.

[2] The Kaiser's first wife, Augusta Victoria, died in April 1921, and he remarried, to Princess Hermine of Reuss, in November 1922. The Kaiser's book was *Meine Vorfahren* (*My Ancestors*).

[3] Moritz, Freiherr von Auffenberg-Komarow (1852–1928), Austrian general, protégé of Archduke Ferdinand and victor of the battle of Komarow over the Russians in 1914.

car bore me along the narrow, muddy road, I thought of my Scottish forefathers who had accompanied the Stuarts into exile in this flat, deserted, waterlogged country, where the rain never ceases.

The Kaiser's residence is a small country house, surrounded by a moat and set in a park, of which the chief attraction is an alley of magnificent [poplars] *beechtrees*, forming a vaulted path like the nave of a cathedral. The main entrance is through the gateway of the [Tower] *Porch*-house, a kind of large lodge, of which the windows are fitted with neat, red and white shutters. At the gate there are two Dutch warders – half guards of honour, half detectives. Otherwise, in his exile the former ruler of the greatest army the world has ever seen is unguarded. His relations with the local inhabitants are of the friendliest, and one end of the estate, which has been converted into a Rosarium, planted by his own hand, has been thrown open to the public as a pleasure park.

When the Kaiser came to Doorn, the park was a wilderness and the house itself was shut in by trees. With characteristic Prussian energy this gloom has been partially relieved. *About 3000* trees have been felled – many by the Kaiser's own hand – and gardens laid out. The Kaiser is a great horticulturalist, who plans *with his Dutch headgardener*, and plants everything himself. The Doorn gardeners say that he has the lucky hand. He is very fond of roses and rhododendrons, and the Doorn gardens show a profusion of both. As I was shown round the park, including the two new rose-gardens named after the late Kaiserin Augusta Victoria and the present Kaiserin Hermine, we were accompanied by Arno, a truly magnificent [Alsatian] *Doberman* and the Kaiser's best friend, who greets him every morning by jumping up and placing both paws on the Imperial shoulders.

Life at Doorn has few amusements. There is no shooting and no riding and the Kaiser spends much time with his dogs, of whom Widu, the small dachshund, forms a strange contrast to the splendidly built [Alsatian] *German*. Whatever may be the general opinion of the Kaiser, he is worshipped by his personal attendants, who cannot speak too highly of his thoughtfulness and consideration for others. Of these qualities I saw a concrete proof in the wooden shed where the logs felled by the Kaiser are sawn up into small bundles of firewood to be presented at Christmas to the poor families in the village, *as well as to his servants and their families*.

Doorn itself used to be a country seat of the [bishops] *deans* of Utrecht *Cathedral* and dates from the XIVth century. It was completely rebuilt however in 1770, since when there have been few alterations.

I had always understood that the Kaiser lived in a kind of Siegesallee surrounded by gold furniture and marble statues. At Doorn I was struck by the comparative simplicity and good taste of the decoration scheme. How far the present Kaiserin, who is a cultured and extremely intelligent woman, is responsible for the interior of Doorn I cannot say, but some of the rooms, including the little salon where I had tea, are not only exquisitely furnished, but are very comfortable living rooms. The reception rooms are small. Downstairs there is a fine entrance hall with a small bronze model of [Ranch's] *Jerome's* statue of Frederick the Great, a moderate-sized dining room with a striking portrait of the Kaiser painted only [last year] *a few years ago*, three small reception and audience rooms, and the Kaiser's smoking room. Upstairs are the bedrooms, the Kaiserin's private rooms, and in the main tower the Kaiser's study, a simply furnished room with well filled bookcases and a bust of Moltke. There are one or two fine pictures and some excellent French prints in the house. To me however the most pathetic sight was a glasscase containing cigarette cases, snuff boxes, miniatures – presents to the former ruler of Germany from former European Monarchs. There was a box from King Edward with his miniature set in brilliants, and an almost identical box with a miniature of the late Tsar of Russia, *as well as one with a splendid miniature of Queen Victoria.*

In spite of the frequent rumours to the contrary, I was able to verify that life at Doorn is distinguished by its extreme simplicity. Every morning the Kaiser is up *before* 7 and dressed by 8 o'clock, when he goes for a vigorous walk. At [8.55] *8.45* there are family prayers at which he himself reads a chapter from the Bible. Breakfast, which is his principal repast, is at 9 and may be described as a typically English meal. From 9.30 to 11.30 the Kaiser works in his garden. Indeed, this is now his only form of physical exercise. From 12 to 1 he receives the reports of his secretaries, discusses the newspapers, and attends to the business of the day. Luncheon is at 1 and is an extremely simple meal, consisting generally of two courses. After a short rest the Kaiser retires to his study, where he works till tea time. After tea, which is generally the occasion for a lively [discussion] *conversation* with the Kaiserin about the affairs of the day, he again returns to his study, where he reads or writes till dinner. Dinner is at 8 and is also a frugal meal. The Kaiser indeed is very temperate in all his habits. He eats sparingly, and the only alcohol he drinks is a glass of [champagne] *claret mousseux* with water at luncheon and dinner. He is a normal smoker and likes Turkish cigarettes and an occasional light cigar. After dinner the [household] *gentlemen on service* assemble in the smoking room, where the Kaiser reads aloud for an hour. The books he prefers are travel descriptions, memoirs, and historical novels. He is at all time a voracious reader. In English literature he passes the Baldwin test, for his favourite English authors are Dickens, Scott and Marryat, all of whom indeed he has read and loved from his childhood days. At 10.30 the day is ended, and the Kaiser retires to bed.

It is impossible to visit Doorn without some feeling of melancholy and sympathy, and involuntarily my thoughts turned to the fate of the Stuarts and our own Royal Exiles in foreign countries. There is, however, little of the dejection of Charles Edward in the Kaiser's outlook. His vigour, his cheerfulness, his mental and physical energy, are astounding. Of all his suite the Kaiser himself is the one man whose health seems unaffected by the depressing gloom of Doorn. If Hindenburg is a young man for 80, the Kaiser himself is a schoolboy for 70!

Some day soon I hope to be able to tell what the Kaiser thinks and feels. At present he is a little frightened of journalists, especially of foreign journalists, by whom he indeed has not always been fairly treated. I think I may say, without indiscretion, however, that Daisy, Princess of Pless's statement that 'the Kaiser is a very sad man, feeling terribly hurt by the one foreign country that he loved – England' is a true estimate of the Kaiser's attitude, that he regarded England as his second fatherland, that he did his best to keep peace, and that he [regrets] *is deeply wounded by* the English point of view, which attributes to him the responsibility for the war.

We have not yet had the true picture of the Kaiser. Indeed, the extraordinary manysidedness of his own character makes the task supremely difficult, and to draw a correct balance between his virtues and his faults is almost impossible. If I had to make an aphorism on the Kaiser, I should say that he was too gifted intellectually to make a completely successful Monarch. In my opinion, however, one thing is certain. Sooner or later history will have to revise the verdict, passed by Germany's enemies during the war, on the Kaiser's character.

Monday, 10 December 1928

Tommy told me that Winston [Churchill] had told Simon Lovat that, if the King died,[1] it would mean a Socialist Government and the end of the Monarchy. What rot! Shows how bad Winston's judgement is. [G. D. H.] Cole told me at the *New Statesman* dinner that if the King died the exploitation of loyalty and the Prince's popularity would cost Labour fifty seats. Lloyd George agrees more with Cole's than with Winston's point of view.

Wednesday, 12 December 1928

Saw Lloyd George and had an hour's talk with him. Discussed Jix's bet of two hats to one on the Conservatives winning the election with Lord Rothermere.[2] L.G. prepared to lay two to one against a Labour or a Conservative absolute majority. L.G. told me his experience with the Kaiser. Kaiser got so interested talking to him that King Edward had to pull him away. L.G. said he discovered he was a good listener. L. G. was then the youngest minister. He also told me of [Lord] Coleridge's remark on Henry James 'almost a

[1] The King had fallen seriously ill with pleurisy on 23 November and there was still considerable anxiety about his condition.

[2] Sir William Joynson-Hicks ('Jix') (1865–1932), later Lord Brentford, was Home Secretary, 1924–9, and an active, if slightly ridiculous, crusader against London's vice. Harold Harmsworth, 1st Viscount Rothermere (1868–1940), owner of the *Daily Mail*, and Beaverbrook's chief rival press lord. Parliament was in its last year, and the General Election was to be held on 30 May 1929.

lawyer, almost a statesman, almost a gentleman.'[1] L.G. knew or pretended he knew nothing of the Kühlmann-Smuts negotiations.[2] Saw Beaverbrook.

[1] 1st Baron James of Hereford (1828–1911), lawyer who became Attorney-General in 1873.

[2] Richard von Kühlmann (1873–1948), German Foreign Minister, sought peace negotiations in 1917. Smuts (then a member of the War Cabinet) had negotiated with Count von Mensdorff, the former Austro-Hungarian envoy in London, in Switzerland in December 1917.

CHAPTER SIX

1929

Winston 'in the wrong place' and 'badly dressed'. Visit to Berlin. Lenin at a death-bed. Stresemann shrunk and ill. General Spears on Pétain. Gregory and the Arcos raid. 'The Odd Volumes'. Belloc 'more and more prejudiced'. Banking friends. Snobbish working-class. Empire Day celebrations. Author of *The Wandering Jew*. Election Day: Beaverbrook elated at Baldwin's failure. Nijinsky 'now quite mad'. Millicent, Duchess of Sutherland, very pro-French. Fishing in Yugoslavia. Lady Theo's 'hairy legs'. International Labour Office, Geneva. Paul Robeson and Pola Negri. Bowra 'not very exciting'. Sir Oswald Mosley 'intends to be Prime Minister'. Nicolson and the Diary. Loughie's suicide. Sir Austen Chamberlain rather vain and very garrulous. Bernard Shaw hissed at a boxing match. Prince of Wales eats prunes and drinks water. The Kaiser again.

Lockhart was still pleased with his journalistic post on the Evening Standard *at the beginning of 1929. His acquaintance with men and women of influence and interest constantly increased, and* 'The Londoner's Diary' *was soon established as the gossip column of the day. Nevertheless his fears for his health and his constant dining out – and night-clubbing – worried him. So did his financial affairs*

Thursday, 3 January *1929*

Tommy came to London prior to her departure for the West Indies. Dined with her at Boulestin's. She is very unwilling to go. She told me a good story about Lady Algernon Gordon-Lennox and the Iveaghs.[1] Blanchie is organising a charity exhibition of *objets d'art* at Lansdowne House. She wanted some tapestries from the Iveaghs, but the latter – owing to a rule of the late Lord Iveagh – refuse to allow any *objet d'art* to leave their house. Blanchie got the Queen to intervene – and with success. It was while duck shooting at the Iveaghs that the King contracted the chill which was the beginning of his present illness.

Wednesday, 9 January 1929

Lunched with Bridget who said that Lord Beaverbrook was angry with her and that she had not seen him for three weeks. She has been seeing much of the Prince of Wales, who told her that he liked me muchly. The Prince has

[1] Blanche (*d.* 1945), widow of Lord Algernon Gordon-Lennox, made a Dame in 1919, was an indefatigable organiser of charities. Rupert, 2nd Earl of Iveagh (1874–1967), who had succeeded his father in 1927, owed his family fortune to the Guinness breweries.

a new hobby now: house decorating and furnishing and spends much of his time in antique shops. He has given up the idea of moving into Marlborough House.

Tuesday, 5 March 1929

Saw Lloyd George at Queen Street. He was in great form and seemed full of life. We discussed British foreign policy and damned Chamberlain[1] thoroughly. L.G. said Winston was very angry over the way the Conservatives had treated him over the debate on the compensation for the Irish loyalists. He said the Conservative leaders were the biggest collection of political duds that English history had ever known. Then he added quickly – 'with the exception of Winston, and of course he's in the wrong place'.[2] L.G. put this in more Parliamentary language into *Can We Conquer Unemployment?* and had a footnote exempting Winston from the stigma.

In the evening went to see Winston at the Treasury; had an hour with him, and we discussed his book especially with regard to Russia. Worthington-Evans[3] was there. Winston introduced me to Baldwin. Winston was very funny, when he heard I was 'Londoner'. 'So you're the man,' he said, 'who wrote that I was the worst-dressed man in London and that I was tired the other night (he was referring to the Worcestershire dinner at which the Prime Minister spoke). Awful rot you write sometimes! But I always read it, and the other night you were quite right. I was in poor form!'

I told him what L.G. had said about the Conservatives and about his being in the wrong place. Winston replied with a wry smile: 'They only put me here to keep me safe.'

Friday, 22 March 1929

Saw Lloyd George for an hour this morning. He was in great form and prophesied a victory for the Liberal at the Boston (Spalding) by-election. It came off all right. He was rather sarcastic about Baldwin and said if latter had wanted to make a speech to suit the Liberals he could hardly have done better. Lunched at the Savoy with Bernstorff.[4] Bernstorff confirmed truth of the Kühlmann peace negotiations in May 1918. Falkenhayn was a real adventurer. Mackensen was merely a *Hofgeneral*.[5] Bernstorff informed me that Clifford Sharp was drinking himself to death.[6]

Miss Stevenson, L.G.'s secretary, has 'flu.[7]

[1] Austen Chamberlain (1863–1937) was Foreign Secretary, 1924–9.

[2] Churchill was Chancellor of the Exchequer, and Baldwin Prime Minister. The last volume of Churchill's *The World Crisis* was published in 1929.

[3] Sir Laming Worthington-Evans (1868–1931), Secretary of State for War, 1921–2, 1924–9.

[4] Albrecht Bernstorff, Counsellor at the German Embassy, fat, witty, Oxford Rhodes scholar.

[5] General Erich von Falkenhayn (1861–1922), commanded the German invasion of Rumania, 1916–17. Field-Marshal August von Mackensen (1849–1945) also commanded on the Eastern Front.

[6] Sharp, Editor of the *New Statesman*, survived till 1935.

[7] Frances Stevenson married Lloyd George in 1943 and died in 1972.

2. *Jean, Lockhart's first wife*

3. *Freda, his sister*

4. *Moura Budberg*

5. *Jacob Peters*

6. *Eduard Beneš*

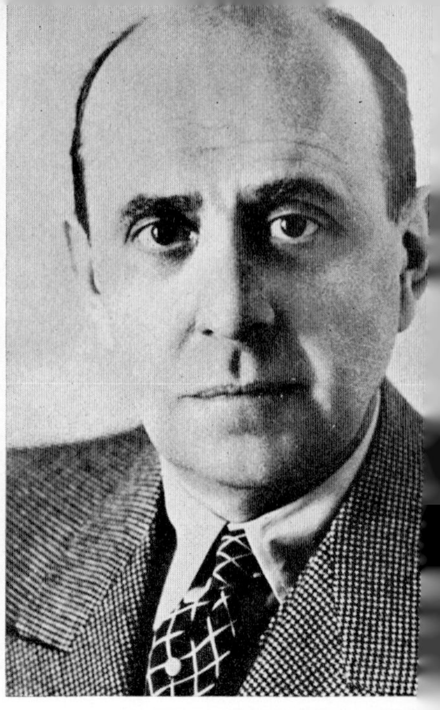

7. *Jan Masaryk*

8. *Maxim Litvinov and Ivan Maisky*

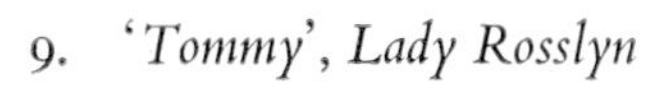

9. *'Tommy', Lady Rosslyn*

10. *Harry, 5th Earl of Rosslyn*

11. *Millicent Duchess of Sutherland*

12. *Pamela Chichester*

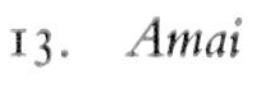

13. *Amai*

14. *Deauville, 1925. Viscount Castlerosse, Max and Peter Aitken, Lord Beaverbrook*

15. *Ramsay MacDonald and Stanley Baldwin*

16. *Winston Churchill*

17. *Lloyd George and Richard Tauber*

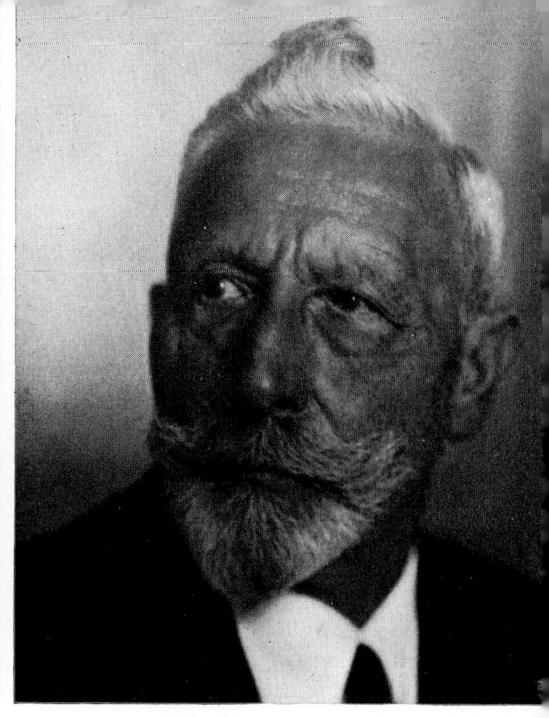

18. *Kaiser Wilhelm II*

Oswald and Lady Cynthia Mosley, 1922

20. *Harold Nicolson*

21. *Leslie Howard and Robert Bruce Lockhart*

22. *Mr Meyrick the 43 celebrate release fr gaol*

23. *The Prince of Wales*

24. *Mrs Wallis Simpson*

25. *Lady Cunard*

26. *Randolph Churchill*

27. *Sir Reginald Leeper*

28. *Sir Maurice Peterson*

29. *Somerset Maugham and his wife*

Tuesday, 26 March 1929

Took Beaverbrook my article on War Reputations.[1] He was quite flattering about it. He made one good remark. 'We are all Presbyterians. It is a damned disgrace that a man with a name like Lockhart should be a Catholic. There's only one redeeming feature about you. It would be a damned sight bigger disgrace if you were an Episcopalian.'

He made me put in a reference to Asquith's private letters to Venetia Montagu during the war – a second Swift and Stella.

Wednesday, 27 March 1929

Feeling rather seedy after last night. I hate and detest this perpetual dining-out. Lunched with Ustinov, an ex-German airman, who is married to Benois's daughter.[2] He is the author of the brilliant expression: 'There will be no peace until men learn that it is a nobler and harder task to live for their country than to die for it.' . . .

Dined with Beaverbrook. I had to take him my article for revision (on War Reputations). Robertson, Wardell, young Max and Peter there.[3] Dead silence when I came in. Max whispered his father was in a rage. The *Evening News* had had a telephone conversation with Captain Randall of the *I'm Alone*.[4] Everything had gone wrong. His papers were the worst in London. Young Max, who had come down for Easter, was packed off to Glasgow. It was after twelve before I could get a word out of him.

Lockhart visited Berlin in April.

Tuesday, 9 April 1929

Moura in Berlin. Lunched with her and Lincoln. Moura is leaving Gorky [while he visits Russia]. Latter is leaving Sorrento and returns to Moscow on May 10th. He has gone right over to the Bolsheviks; having finished his big trilogy, he will do no more literary work. He has started a newspaper, *Our Achievements*, in which he writes leading articles on the Bolsheviks' achievements in electrification and industrialisation. Now 62 years old. Thinks very highly of Voroshilov [Defence Commissar]. Since his come-back has sold 2,800,000 works in Russia alone. Hailed like a god by the people. Only time he was able to see anything for himself was when he was in disguise. He put on a beard!

[1] 'Who are the Men who will Live?', a review in the *Evening Standard* of a book about Sir Henry Wilson, Colonel House and T. E. Lawrence.

[2] Parents of Peter Ustinov.

[3] E. J. Robertson, Managing Director of Beaverbrook Newspapers; Michael Wardell, General Manager of the *Evening Standard*. Young Max and Peter were Beaverbrook's sons, then aged 19 and 17.

[4] A Canadian rum-runner sunk by a U.S. revenue cutter, the U.S.A. being prohibitionist.

Thursday, 11 April 1929

Priceless story of Lenin and the death of his mother-in-law (Krupskaya's mother). Krupskaya tired of watching at death-bed asked Lenin to sit by her mother while she slept. He was to call her if her mother wanted anything. Lenin took a book and began to read. Two hours later Krupskaya came back. Her mother was dead. Lenin was still reading. Krupskaya blamed him: 'Why did you not let me know.' Lenin replied: 'But your mother never called me!' Still Lenin was not inhuman.

Saturday, 13 April 1929

This morning, after much trouble and telephone messages to the Embassy, I was received by Stresemann.[1] I am the first person he has seen for so long for months. I must have pleased him, because he asked me to come back, saying that he would get rid of the Spanish Minister quickly. He has shrunk and looks ill, but his energy is still very impressive. He thinks there is no need for any reform of the constitution. The President and the Chancellor have sufficient power under the present constitution. The problem is one of personalities, and the manner of approaching political problems. German Ministers have more expert knowledge than English, but they are more hide-bound and conventional. Two illustrations: During the war Stresemann begged Delbrück, who was then Food Minister, to get in huge stores of coffee, cocoa, etc., from Italy, before latter entered the war. Delbrück replied: 'What will happen to my stores and to me if the war ends too soon?' Similarly, to a demand from Stresemann to build more U-boats, the Minister of Marine said: 'What would happen after the war to the extra 1st lieutenants and commanders who would have to be created!' Stresemann also told me the Marne was lost through colossal cowardice on Germany's part. Moltke was totally unfit to command. The order to retreat was given by a Lieutenant-Colonel Hentsch.[2] Stresemann said, if he had known then what he knows now, he would have demanded the court-martial of both.

Stresemann said his son had just come back from two terms at Cambridge and was astounded at the lack of knowledge of the undergraduates. Their only question about Germany was: when is the ex-Kaiser coming back, which must have angered Stresemann, as he likes the Kaiser. After a long discussion on internal politics, in which he said he was not afraid of the Stahlhelm[3] or the Communists, he passed on to foreign politics. (German workmen are free-thinkers as regards religion and marriage. In practice, however, they are

[1] Gustav Stresemann (1878–1929) had been German Chancellor in 1923 and thereafter until his death was Foreign Minister. He had negotiated the Locarno Pact with Austen Chamberlain and Briand in 1925.

[2] Helmuth von Moltke (1848–1916), nephew of the great field-marshal, commanded the German forces which made a dramatic advance on the Marne in September 1914. But they failed to sustain the advance and were driven back within two weeks. Moltke was replaced by Falkenhayn in December.

[3] The Stahlhelm (= Steel Helmet) League was the German Nationalist ex-service organisation.

faithful and would break a pot over their wife's head if she were unfaithful. *Deutsch-nationale* stand politically for religion and the sanctity of marriage and deceive their wives daily). Stresemann is very bitter about Austen Chamberlain. Stresemann had succeeded in winning 80 per cent of Germany for his policy of understanding. Austen Chamberlain had played France's game through and through and had given Stresemann no cards to play with. He was especially bitter about the occupation. If we had given him a point there, it would have made reparations and everything else much easier. He admitted Sir Austen meant well and shrugged his shoulders and asked if we were now so weak that we had to do what France told us. He worked himself up into a great excitement over Poland: the cloacine language of their statesmen, etc., and said that 'no country can work down except partly through its own fault.' No German would fight for Alsace – though any Germany had a certain amount of *Schadenfreude* over France's troubles – but no German – Communist to Kaiser – would ever accept the Polish frontier. With a rectification on the Polish front Europe could have peace for a hundred years. . . Said goodbye to Harold [Nicolson] who wants new foreign policy – understanding with America, balance of power in Europe, cessation of following Quai d'Orsay, and a new minister who does not speak French and who will stay at home. Says Englishmen know nothing about foreign politics their facts are always wrong, and their instincts generally right, and their instincts will support their policy. Left 9.47 for London.

Tuesday, 16 April 1929

Lunched with General Spears.[1] Met MacDonogh, Commander Fletcher, and the First Secretary of the French Embassy.[2] MacDonogh was rather nice. We discussed General Haig. Spears told us the story of Pétain and L.G. The latter who had been growing more and more alarmed over the stalemate and heavy losses in Passchendaele went to see Pétain and ask him his opinion. Pétain said: 'M. le Ministre, vous pouvez battre les Boches; vous pouvez battre la boue, mais on ne peut pas battre les Boches et la boue.'

Monday, 22 April 1929

Feeling much better after my week-end. In the evening dined with Gregory at his mother's flat at 40A Hyde Park Gate. He does not seem very depressed.[3] He told me that Austen was the most useless Foreign Minister we have ever had; that at the time of the Arcos raid no one in the Foreign Office knew

[1] Major-General Sir Edward Spears (*b.* 1886) had headed the British Military Mission in Paris 1917–20, and was later an M.P.

[2] Lieutenant-General Sir George MacDonogh (1865–1942), Director of Military Intelligence, 1916–18. Commander Reginald (Rex) Thomas Herbert Fletcher (1885–1961), at that time in the Secret Intelligence Service, was later a Labour M.P., and, as Lord Winster, Governor-General of Cyprus. Jacques Truelle was First Secretary at the French Embassy.

[3] By this time J. D. Gregory had been dismissed from the Foreign Office for financial misdemeanours.

anything about it. Gregory himself first heard about it from Sinclair, the head of the Secret Service. Latter walked in and said: 'I suppose this means the end.' Gregory replied: 'What end?' Sinclair then told him about Arcos. Gregory rushed off in a great state to tell Austen. He was afraid for Hodgson and the others. Austen quite unconcerned and not realising the significance of the raid said: 'Oh yes! I believe Jix did say something to me about it last night.'[1]

Tuesday, 23 April 1929

After lunch had Turkish Bath and in the evening went to dine with Low at the Savoy. I was his guest at the Odd Volumes dinner.[2] Very interesting show: Arbuthnot Lane, Sir George Milne, Sir Walter Braithwaite, Sir Warren Hastings Anderson, Mitchell Banks, Maurice Healy (a nephew of Tim) and 'Khaki' Roberts. Also met my namesake, J. G. Lockhart, who wrote a book on the young men of today and signed it 'Janitor'. Maurice Healy has all his uncle's gift of oratory and repartee. Mitchell Banks told a story of how Maurice and he were on opposite sides in a libel case. Maurice was prosecuting for a young girl who had sued for libel against detectives who had sent her a card offering to guard her presence and prosecute inquiries for infidelities on husband's part. She sued for defamation. Banks said this was merely a usual phrase on the card and part of stock-in-trade. Healy said phrases had various interpretations according to the time and place they were made. For instance, if he and Banks went for a walk in summer, and Banks said, 'This is a dusty day', that would mean nothing. But, if every time they stopped, Banks said, 'This is a very dusty day' that would have quite a different meaning.

Thursday, 2 May 1929

Mike Wardell came back from Berlin with a new camera which takes beautiful photos and can almost go into the waistcoat pocket. I foresee the journalist of the future armed with his flying wings and small pocket engine, his pocket telephone, and his pocket cinema!

In afternoon (6.20) came down to Coolham with Tommy, Loughie and Pam. Countryside is still very backward and the night air is cold. Tommy has swollen gland from the vaccination. Harry very toxi-boo!

Sunday, 12 May 1929

Rained all day. No golf. Played contract most of the afternoon and the

[1] On 13 May 1927, when Gregory was an Assistant Under-Secretary at the Foreign Office, Arcos Ltd in Moorgate, which housed the Russian Trade Delegation, was raided by 150 police and searched by the Special Branch with Foreign Office interpreters. Nothing incriminating was found. Admiral Hugh Sinclair (*d.* 1939) was head of the Secret Intelligence Service. Sir Robert Hodgson (1874–1950) was Chargé d'Affaires in Moscow.

[2] 'Ye Sette of Odd Volumes' was a dining club, which also undertook the occasional publication of odd volumes on esoteric subjects. Lane was a surgeon, Milne, Braithwaite and Anderson soldiers, and the rest of those mentioned were K.C.s.

evening. Belloc came over to tea, with his son and daughter-in-law. He is getting more and more prejudiced in his old age,[1] and was very indignant that H. A. L. Fisher,[2] who had asked him to stay with him when he came to Oxford, was not at Magdalen when Belloc came. Mrs Fisher and the Warden had gone away, merely leaving a note for Belloc. Belloc considered that this was a sign that he was only 'small beer', and that the Fishers would not have done this to Shaw, Kipling, etc.

Monday, 13 May 1929

Lunched with Bark, Porters, and Gordon Leith[3] at the Savoy. Gordon Leith and Richard Norton are partners. Gordon Leith and Sasha Kropotkina are friends. He was the banker whom she received in her pyjamas. I, not knowing Gordon Leith was the man I was lunching with, began to tell the story! Porters gave me an account of his work in Belgrade for the Rothschild group (Rothschild's, Hambros, Barings). He hopes the new government-aided Agricultural Bank will improve the financial situation and will relieve agriculture and cheapen credits. He told me that when the news of Chamberlain's interview with Mussolini reached Belgrade Zivkovitch came into Sverljuga's[4] room and asked the Minister of Finance how much more the country could afford to spend on armaments. Porters was also dining at Sverljuga's when the news of Schlegel's murder was received by telephone. Schlegel was a Zagreb editor who supported the new régime. The other ministers went white, but Zivkovitch never turned a hair and went on eating his dinner as if nothing had happened.

Dined with Beaverbrook, Jean Norton, Lady Weymouth and her mother[5] at the Splendide. Freddy Guest[6] came, furious because today Lloyd George has sent a letter – the official letter of the party – to support the rival Liberal candidate at Bristol. Freddy Guest in a frantic state and talking of turning Labour – anything to get back into Parliament. He is entirely dependent or nearly so on his rich American wife. As M.P. he is someone in America. Without those two initials he is merely a do-nothing. Certainly, he has been hardly treated. He was the man who raised L.G.'s fund and now it is being

[1] Hilaire Belloc, former Liberal M.P., poet and historian, was at this time 58. He died in 1953 at the age of 82.

[2] H. A. L. Fisher (1865–1940), statesman and historian, was in fact at this time Warden of New College, Oxford, 1925–40.

[3] R. H. Porters was a professional banker Lockhart had known in Austria, and Gordon Leith (1879–1941) was a very successful merchant banker.

[4] Pera Zivkovitch was Serbian Prime Minister, and Stanko Sverljuga Minister of Finance and friend of Lockhart.

[5] Daphne, Viscountess Weymouth, wife of the future 6th Marquess of Bath (they were divorced in 1953 and she married Xan Fielding) and Barbara, first wife of Lord Vivian.

[6] Frederick Guest (1875–1937) was a cousin of Winston Churchill, and had been his private secretary. He was defending his seat as a Liberal at Bristol North in the Election due on 30 May. He lost, joined the Conservative Party in 1930, and was re-elected as a Conservative in 1931.

used against him. As Valentine says, L.G. is letting in the gate-crasher before the guest!

Beaverbrook raced back from the Splendide to Stornoway to see L.G. We came on later. Valentine as a South of Ireland loyalist said he would not come. Nothing would induce him to meet L.G. Finally he came. Beaverbrook was in great form, introduced Valentine to L.G. and said: 'Valentine, you must give L.G. a write-up in your Log next Sunday'. Valentine turned his back – he was rather tight – took two steps to the left – for an instant we all thought he was about to insult L.G. – then pirouetting like a fat ballet-master he made a low bow to L.G. 'For me to write up the man who won the war,' he said with sublime sycophancy, 'would be, to use a Catholic simile, like the village curé venturing to write up the Pope.' L.G. in great form – when Valentine allowed him a word – and full of optimism for the election. After L.G. and Miss Stevenson left, Valentine entertained(!) us all for hours with the most salacious descriptions of his life. I have never heard such unlicensed conversation before young women. Valentine should have lived during the Restoration.

Monday, 20 May 1929

Watched the cricket at Lord's: Middlesex *v.* Sussex and then went to the Zoo. Very hot day. Large crowds at both places, especially at the Zoo. The English working-class is snobbish to the core. Everyone in their Sunday best, and bourgeois manners very much to the fore. It is our great safeguard against Bolshevism.

Wednesday, 22 May 1929

Went on to Beaverbrook's afterwards. He was in great form. Having used one of my titbits for a *Daily Express* leader, he gave me a good story for the *Standard.* During one of the elections in Canada when Sir John Macdonald was Prime Minister,[1] the Conservative Press, as in this campaign in England, was not quite supporting the party. The Tory diehards invented a parody on Lady Dufferin's 'I'm sitting by the stile, Mary' which was sung to the Conservative editors and ran as follows:

> I'm sitting on the fence, Johnny,
> And there I mean to sit,
> Till I see who gets the boodle,
> The Tory or the Grit (Canadian for Liberal).

I told him everyone would say it was his own attitude. 'Never mind,' says he. 'Put it in!'

Thursday, 23 May 1929

Dined with Wavey and a merchant captain who told me a curious fishing

[1] Sir John Alexander Macdonald (1815–91) was Conservative Prime Minister of Canada, 1856–73, 1878–91.

story about Japan. There the fishermen train young cormorants to fish for them. They take them out at night, tie a string to their legs, put a ring round their necks to prevent them swallowing the fish and then with lanterns to attract the fish set them free from the boat. The queer thing is that the fisherman seems to know by the feel of the string whether the bird has its fill of fish or not. In this way they can fill a boat with fish in a night.

Friday, 24 May 1929

Empire Day. Hot and sultry and menace of thunderstorm. Rain came down at five-thirty and threatened to spoil the *Express's* Empire Day ceremony which was held in Hyde Park. It was a most impressive performance. One corner of the park had been fitted up like a Greek amphitheatre. In the arena itself were assembled representatives of all the Imperial units of the Empire: Chelsea Pensioners, Boys' Brigade, Boy and Girl Scouts, Navy, Legion of Frontiersmen, Colonial troops, and members of the British Legion. When they had taken their allotted places, there was a most dignified procession of all the churches, followed by the breaking of the various Empire Flags and a religious service. The singing was very fine: 'O God our Help' and 'Abide With Me' being particularly well sung. The only jarring note was the community singing beforehand. It was not good and was out of place. Sat next Harry Brittain[1] who was very optimistic about his re-election at Acton (he was defeated) and full of bounce. Baldwin gave an address on Empire, finishing with the admonition 'of him to whom much is given much shall be expected'.

Saturday, 25 May 1929

Beaverbrook's birthday – he gave a large party to all his old friends of fifteen years' standing and a cheque for £250 to each guest. There was also a lottery with numerous prizes amounting to £500 for the servants.

Monday, 27 May 1929

Went to Stornoway at five and was present at Beaverbrook's interview with George Sylvester Viereck, an American journalist, who wrote *The Wandering Jew*[2] and who has made a name for himself as an interviewer of celebrities. Viereck is of German-Jewish origin. His father was a Socialist member of the Reichstag. During the war he was pro-German – at least until America came in – and he is the only foreign allied journalist who has interviewed the Kaiser. He really wrote the Princess Hermine's book. . . He knows a good deal about philosophy and is certainly a 'live wire'. The

[1] Sir Harry Brittain (*b.* 1873), never again an M.P., enthusiastic imperialist and friend of America.

[2] *My First Two Thousand Years; the Autobiography of the Wandering Jew*, just published.

interview was very amusing, as Beaverbrook was in great form – real Puckish.

Viereck. 'Why and for what motives did you take up journalism?'

Beaverbrook. 'To escape boredom.'

During the interview Beaverbrook gave him his three books: *Success*, *Politicians and the War*, and *Politicians and the Press*. He then signed his name in each, and, as Viereck was leaving, Viereck asked him what his motto in life was. Beaverbrook replied, 'Act justly, love money, and walk humbly'. Then taking his three books and handing them to Viereck, he said, 'Mr Viereck, if you will read *Success*, which is my book on how to succeed in business, you will see that I believe in acting justly. If you will read *Politicians and the War* and notice how lightly I have treated these self-seekers you will see that I love money, and if you will read *Politicians and the Press* you will see that I do *not* walk humbly!'

Beaverbrook also told a good story of Otto Kahn.[1] Latter who was born in Frankfurt wanted to become a naturalised British subject, before he became an American subject. About 1912 he even wanted to become an M.P. Beaverbrook offered to help and to introduce him to the Gorton Division. Kahn went down to Gorton to address his prospective constituents. Beaverbrook was in the chair. The speech was good, but the accent was a bit too much for the Lancashire constituents. The chairman of the local committee said as much to Beaverbrook, who had therefore to save the situation. 'Gentlemen,' he said, 'you have heard a splendid speech. Like me you have perhaps noticed one failing: the un-English accent of the speaker. I myself have suffered from the same drawback, but I can assure you that in a few weeks we French-Canadians soon lose all trace of our overseas accent!'

Dined at Stornoway. Richard and Jean Norton there. Manzi-Fe of the British-Italian Corporation has had to resign.[2] There have been big scandals in the Bank in Rome. I never liked him.

Thursday, 30 May 1929

Election Day. Dined with Harry, 'Gertie' Brand, Mrs and Miss Robertson (Jim Robertson's wife [and daughter]) at the Carlton Club and went into the hall afterwards to hear and see the results announced. Place crammed with men and women. A big screen on which the results (and sometimes pictures of ministers) were projected, loudspeakers, and Harry who was in great form roaring out 'all we want is no change'. At first the results were fairly favourable to the Conservatives; but, when the long list of Labour gains came in, depression reigned supreme. Went off to Beaverbrook's at twelve-thirty: huge party, the Mackenzies, Birkenhead, very drunk and bad-tempered,

[1] Otto Kahn (1867–1934), banker, actually born in Mannheim.

[2] Ignazio G. Manzi-Fe, chairman of Banco Italo-Britannica, was later arrested for misappropriation of funds. Lockhart had once had to apologise to him for an error in an advertisement and had taken a strong dislike to him.

Lady Milbanke, the Nortons, Valentine, the Brownlows, etc., etc. Venetia Montagu came in later from Selfridge's party, and I went down with her to Trafalgar Square to see the crowd: no disorder, but Labour gains loudly cheered. Back again to Beaverbrook, who was clearly elated at Baldwin's failure. He has a butler called 'Stanley'. He at once began calling him 'Oliver' – Baldwin's son, who has been returned as a Labour member.[1]

Lunched today with Cynthia Cheetham;[2] was quarter of an hour late. Eleanor Charter (Toye)[3] there, Lady Annesley, Sargent and another man. Had a great gossip. Sargent says the last sentence in Gregory's book is a bitter hit at Tyrrell – very cleverly done.[4]

Saturday, 1 June 1929

Went down to Horsham to stay with Harry and Loughie. Played three-handed contract and golf-croquet.

Angela Forbes rang up. She has had a nervous breakdown, apparently because Hugo Wemyss has fallen in love with his hospital nurse and has left her in the lurch![5]

Monday, 3 June 1929

Today Beaverbrook asked me to come to Stornoway at four-thirty, as he wanted to see me. When I arrived, he said I had had a very strenuous time, had worked very well, and was going on my holiday. Then he said suddenly: 'here is something towards your expenses' and handed me a cheque for £100. Very endearing of him.

Spent the afternoon buying fishing-tackle and other gear for my holiday.

Beaverbrook said the Conservatives had run their campaign very badly. If he had been manager of the Central Organisation, things would have been different.

In high spirits Lockhart set off for his holiday – naturally for him to Europe.

Thursday, 6 June 1929

Arrived at Havre at six-thirty, had coffee at the station and then caught the

[1] The Conservatives had fallen from 400 to 260, Labour increased from 162 to 288 and the Liberals from 46 to 59. Baldwin's government fell and Ramsay MacDonald formed a Labour administration.

[2] Wife of Sir Milne Cheetham (1869–1938), retired diplomat.

[3] Eleanor Toye had been Sidney Reilly's secretary. Charter was her married name at this time. She later married G. J. Bishop.

[4] J. D. Gregory's book, *On the Edge of Diplomacy*, just published, ends '. . . no one who knows him will doubt that Sir Ronald Lindsay will worthily carry on the traditions of Eyre Crowe.' I.e. not those of Tyrrell, who had recently left the Foreign Office to become Ambassador to France.

[5] Lady Angela Forbes (1876–1950), sister of the Earl of Rosslyn, had conducted her own divorce from Colonel J. S. Forbes in 1906, the first woman to do so in Scotland. She reverted to her maiden name of St Clair Erskine in 1929. Hugo Wemyss (1857–1937) was the 11th Earl of Wemyss.

train to Paris. Met Tommy at the Majestic and went to luncheon with Lady Michelham[1] at the Ritz. She was a sister of Bryd Capel...

She told us a good story of Nijinsky. Latter is now quite mad and is either in a state of coma or is trying to fly like a bird. Mme Nijinsky, a Hungarian, came to Lady Michelham with a beautiful Sargent portrait of Nijinsky in the *Spectre de la Rose* and asked her to buy it. It is a gem of a picture – Duveen says it's worth anything. It was given to Nijinsky by Lady de Grey ... Nijinsky, however, is now ruined and ought to be at home, and his wife is struggling to keep the home together. Lady Michelham refused to buy the picture, but gave them money to get medical advice from the great Freiburg doctor.[2] Latter came, says Nijinsky's foot has the bone formation of a bird and that he can never get well, as he is now more bird than man. Nijinsky went mad through fear in the war.

Friday, 7 June 1929

We arrived at Angers last night at 10 and drove out to Juigné where Millicent, Duchess of Sutherland,[3] now lives. The house is an old monastery house, lies alongside the village church, and has an exquisite Italian garden at the foot of which is a charming pond full of perch, pike, carp, tench and catfish. Although it rained all day, the place is too lovely for words. She herself of course has really made it. The house is exquisitely furnished, and the garden is a glory.

We had an excellent egg and fish luncheon (it being Friday) and then fished all afternoon in the wet with no success. Caught one catfish. At night dined – again an excellent dinner and an excellent burgundy – and talked politics. Lady Millicent is very pro-French and believes that the Germans are plotting a terrible revenge against us.

Thursday, 13 June 1929

Early morning in Ljubljana and a lovely day. Two *contretemps* in the morning before we left. Kobal was away for the day – he has been very ill with influenza, nasal and oral complications... – and my letter of credit from Glyn, Mills could not be cashed because the Bohemian Industrial Bank (Glyn, Mills' correspondent in Ljubljana) had received no renewal form from London for two years. As I expressly asked Glyn, Mills before leaving if they had a correspondent at Ljubljana, this was poor work. The Wagon-Lit Agency also was quite idiotic and had no idea how to issue or to order our tickets for the return journey. Saw Papež, Kobal's assistant. He says Slovenes are content with new régime and prefer it to old. Government, business

[1] Berthe, wife of Herman Stern, 2nd Baron Michelham.

[2] Vaslav Nijinsky (1890–1950), who had been mad since 1917, had consulted many doctors, including Freud and Jung, but none apparently in Freiburg. Lord Duveen (1869–1939) was the great art-dealer.

[3] Sister of the Earl of Rosslyn, she was the first wife of the 4th Duke of Sutherland. They were divorced and she was twice remarried. She died in 1955.

people and industry are also content; Government politicians less so, but they are harmless. Chief danger to new régime comes from disgruntled Serbs. Mussolini very unpopular here – especially his support of Hungarian irredentist claims when his own treatment of the Slovene and German minorities in the Tyrol is a scandal. Arrived at Kika at one o'clock. The inn has been reconstructed and is much more comfortable. The innkeeper Rebol and Peškur, the old fisherman, were there to welcome us, and the countryside looked as beautiful as ever. In the terrible winter, which seized the country this year, the old father died. Although the winter made everything a month late in spring, unlike in England the crops all are now a month ahead. It would seem as if in this part of the world a severe winter is favourable to a good harvest.

In the afternoon went downstream from second mill. Water very low, and we caught no big fish. Evening rise by the bridge pool. Lots of fly on the water, but no big fish moving. Thunderstorm in the middle of the night.

Monday, 17 June 1929

Tommy told me two good stories: one about Juliet Duff and one about Lady Theo Acheson.[1] Former who is very tall had a tremendous success with all the young people in Berlin. All the young men pursued her. No one could understand her *succès* until it was discovered that the Berlin *jeunesse dorée* thought she was a man masquerading as a woman.

Lady Theo Acheson had wonderful hair of which she was very proud. In her passport form under the sub-heading 'any peculiarities' she put in 'hair below the knees'. In the passport this was abbreviated by the passport officer to 'hairy legs'!

Friday, 21 June 1929

Rose at six-thirty and went for the day to Geneva. Saw Phelan[2] and had a long talk with him about his Russian visit. The International Labour Conference was sitting, and he took me into the Bâtiment Electoral where Bureau International de Travail holds its conferences. It was interesting to see all the fifty-five nations represented. Each seat has a set of earphones, and the speeches are translated simultaneously into four languages, while they are being made. The interpreters are seated in kinds of confession-boxes. Had a long talk with [Albert] Thomas. He is only fifty-two. He is all in favour of a resumption of relations with Russa. His reasons being much the same as my own. Told me an amusing story about his reception. Stalin and Rykov[3] did

[1] Lady Juliet Duff (1881–1965) was the widow of Sir Robert Duff (killed in 1914) and daughter of 4th Earl of Lonsdale. Lady Theodosia Acheson, daughter of 4th Earl of Gosford, had been married to Alexander Cadogan since 1912.

[2] Edward Phelan (1888–1967) had been a young Irish official in the Ministry of Labour before joining Lockhart's staff in Russia in 1918. He eventually became Director of the International Labour Office, which was an organ of the League of Nations.

[3] Alexei Rykov had succeeded Lenin as president of the supreme council. He was killed in the purge of 1938.

not see him, but at the seventh of November celebrations they were perched up on the seats of honour on Lenin's tomb, and during the procession Stalin and Rykov stepped down to have a good look at the *socialiste-traître*! Thomas was not guarded in Moscow. Phelan and he both say that the mentality of the diplomats has not changed since 1918. They still say the régime will not last another month! Thomas, who gave evidence in favour of Sadoul at his trial, agrees with me that Sadoul was goaded into Communism by Noulens's stupidities. Thomas still thinks of returning to politics, but he will not desert the B.I.T. except for a *grande nécessité*. He is still a member of the Socialist party. Saw the Café Landolt at the corner of the Rue de Candolle and the Rue du Conseil-General, where Lenin used to sit. Lunched at the Café du Nord. In the afternoon drove out to the Parc des Eaux-Vives, where we gave tea to Biel Duval and her father and a very intelligent and anti-German Polish diplomat called Giradowski. Latter says England has nothing to gain by not recognising the Bolsheviks and perhaps something to lose.

Saw Humbert Wolfe – an attractive personality.[1] He says Gerhardi[2] is being ruined by Beaverbrook or rather is killing himself. He also rates Shanks as a failure. A man who wishes to write must sweat in blood and work. Also met Sanders, the former Secretary of the Fabian Society, whom I had not seen since he came out to Russia in 1917 with Jim O'Grady and Will Thorne. He won Battersea from Saklatvala.[3] He refused to shake hands with latter. Saklatvala gave him a good excuse by blaming him for joining the army. Sanders turned that into an insult not to himself but to the million dead. He also scored off Saklatvala over his attacks on the Labour Party for going to Buckingham Palace. Saklatvala himself, however, took part in two delegations: one to Denmark and one to Berlin. In Copenhagen he met the King and shook hands with him. In Berlin he went to the dinner given by the British Ambassador and, when everybody expected an outburst, lo! 'all was quiet on the dinner front' and Saklatvala drank the King's health like a guardsman!

Returned to Montreux at nine.

Tuesday, 25 June 1929

First day in London. Dined with Lord Beaverbrook. He informs me that he has a new job for me and that I must look out for someone to take my place on the Diary.

[1] Georgian poet and civil servant (1885–1940).

[2] William Gerhardi (*b.* 1895), novelist, now Gerhardie, worked like Edward Shanks, poet and essayist, for Beaverbrook.

[3] Captain W. S. Sanders (1871–1941), shortly to become Financial Secretary to the War Office. Jim O'Grady (1866–1934), trade-unionist Labour M.P., had become Sir James and Governor of Tasmania; Will Thorne (1857–1946) was still a Labour M.P.; S. Saklatvala (1874–1936), son of a Bombay Parsee merchant, was Communist M.P. for Battersea from 1924 until Sanders defeated him in 1929.

The new job, which he later thought had been 'impossible from the start', was to be constantly with Beaverbrook, to be his liaison with the Daily Express, *to write leaders on Saturdays for the* Sunday Express *– and still to write for the* Evening Standard *'Londoner's Diary'. As for a successor to himself on the Diary he approached his old Foreign Office acquaintance, Harold Nicolson, then forty-two, and Counsellor – second-ranking officer – at the British Embassy in Berlin. Lockhart visited him in Berlin and found Nicolson interested in the job – with many provisos. In July negotiations continued and came to fruition.*

Wednesday, 26 June 1929

Dined again at Stornoway. Kenworthy, Venetia Montagu, Mrs Norton and Mike [Wardell] at dinner. Had long talk with Kenworthy, who is probably going as British Ambassador to Moscow.[1] He wants the Prince of Wales to become Head of the Buffaloes – a kind of working-man's lodge. King Edward was head of it at one time. I gather it was Tory in those days. Today, it is mainly Labour. At twelve a strange Egyptian (Mikarius) arrived who is part proprietor of a newspaper in Cairo. He was very amusing and talked incessantly. Ran down Lloyd and said we had made a dreadful mess in Egypt.[2] Lord Beaverbrook referred to my new job. Mike tells me he thinks it has something to do with the *Express.*

The Egyptian told us an amusing story of an Italian countess he had loved for nineteen years. After a long search he found her again – still beautiful but divorced and poor. The great romance, however, terminated. She had changed. How had she changed? Her nose had changed!

Thursday, 27 June 1929

Went with Philip Page to see Hubert Griffith's play at the Arts Theatre Club.[3] He gave me dinner first at the Union Club. The play *Red Sunday* was very ambitious. Lenin, Trotsky, Rasputin and Yusupoff are on the stage. The murder of Rasputin was not bad, but Lenin and Trotsky were poor. Page said the play was more hysterical than historical. It was really a series of episodes – epi*sodic* in fact. According to Philip Page, the highbrow stage in England is full of homosexuals. Met Alan Parsons and James Agate.[4]

[1] Lieutenant-Commander J. M. Kenworthy (1886–1953), Labour M.P., became 10th Baron Strabolgi in 1934. He did not go to Moscow. Sir Esmond Ovey (1879–1963) was appointed Ambassador on 7 December, resuming diplomatic relations which had been broken off in 1927.

[2] George, 1st Baron Lloyd (1879–1941), was High Commissioner for Egypt and the Sudan, 1925–9.

[3] Philip Page was a Beaverbrook Press dramatic critic. Hubert Griffith (1896–1953) was *Evening Standard* dramatic critic, 1926–9, wrote a number of plays and books about Russia.

[4] Alan Parsons was a civil servant and had been private secretary to McKenna and Edwin Montagu, but his chief interest was in the stage, and his wife Viola was the daughter of Sir Herbert Tree. James Agate (1877–1947) had been dramatic critic of the *Sunday Times* since 1923. He was a homosexual.

Friday, 28 June 1929

Lunched with [Sir Peter] Bark. He is very pleased with his G.C.V.O. In the evening Lord Beaverbrook gave a party: the Nortons, the Brownlows, the Campbells, the Johnstones, Paul Robeson and his wife and Pola Negri[1] and my Egyptian friend of two nights ago. I sat next Pola Negri and had rather a boring time. However, we spoke Russian which greatly impressed the other guests. Paul Robeson is a pleasant Negro whose ambition is to play Othello in straight drama. He danced with all the white women. Pola Negri told me a long story about all the men who had proposed to her. Only that morning she had received a letter from a young man who was only twenty, who had never had a sexual connection, and who therefore thought himself an ideal husband for her. . .

More late nights. Too much to eat and too much to drink. This life is hell!

Tuesday, 2 July 1929

Lunched with Bateman at the Wellington [Club]. He told me a good story about a Yugoslav colonel who was complaining to him that all Yugoslavia's neighbours were hostile to her. Yugoslavia, he said, must make friends with Bulgaria, because the Bulgarian is the best fighter. 'The Hungarians we can manage. The Greeks you only have to blow on and they run away. On the Italians you do not even need to blow! But the Bulgarians are different.' Further, he pointed out that Bulgaria suffered fewer losses in manpower than Serbia and that her birth-rate in 1914 and 1915, etc., did not fall like Serbia's.

Bateman's rooms on the top-floor of the Foreign Office have the finest view in London.

Thursday, 4 July 1929

Lunched with Commander Fletcher at the Carlton. Jowitt, the new Labour Attorney-General, Sir Godfrey Collins, who is a publisher and the uncle of the tennis player, Archie Sinclair, Kenworthy, Commander Bellairs, Ammon and myself.[2] Fletcher put Archie Sinclair and Jowitt together so that they might make their quarrel up. Archie has not forgiven Jowitt for deserting the Liberals in the way he did. Jowitt is another of the *carriéristes*

[1] Paul Robeson (*b.* 1898), bass singer and actor, played Othello at the Savoy in the following year. Pola Negri (*b.* 1894) was a Polish film actress, 'all slink and mink', whose career was chiefly in Poland and Hollywood. She made one film in England in 1929.

[2] William Jowitt (1885–1957), later 1st Earl, was elected in the General Election as a Liberal, but immediately afterwards joined the Labour Party to become Attorney-General. He re-fought Preston as a Labour candidate and won. Sir Archibald Sinclair (1890–1970), shortly to become chief Liberal Whip and eventually leader of the Liberal Party and 1st Viscount Thurso, found this hard to forgive. Sir Godfrey Collins (1875–1932) was an earlier chief Liberal Whip; he was the head of Collins the publishers, and his nephew I. G. Collins was one of the best tennis doubles players of the time. Commander Carlyon Bellairs (1871–1955) was the eccentric Unionist M.P. for Maidstone, and Charles Ammon (*d.* 1960), later 1st Baron, was Labour M.P. and Parliamentary Secretary to the Admiralty in the new government.

who did not go to the war. Fletcher himself has joined the Labour Party, chiefly owing to the way he was treated by the Liberals over Tavistock.[1]

Saturday, 6 July 1929

Came down to Hunger Hill... Lovely weather. Did nothing all day. Mr Bowra, the Dean of Wadham, here – not very exciting and he has an irritatingly affected laugh.[2] I should not care to send Robin to Oxford just now.

Sunday, 7 July 1929

Numerous Oxford friends of Hamish came over for tea: Robert Byron, Evelyn Waugh, Nancy Mitford,[3] and a Guinness girl and several others whose names I did not catch. Strange young men with long hair and an aesthetic pose and a strong predilection for cocktails. I am very worried about Hamish and do not think he will do much good.

In the evening went to Cherkley for dinner. Young Max, Peter, Mike Wardell, and Jean Norton there.

Beaverbrook has had a fair amount of success with his Empire Free Trade scheme, but it will be a long crusade, and there will be great difficulties in the Dominions.

Tuesday, 9 July 1929

Lunched with Tom Mosley, Lord De La Warr, Mike, and Blum at the Carlton.[4] Tom Mosley was very friendly; expatiated at great length on the impossibility of becoming a statesman today without constant hard work on such subjects as finance, etc. He said the Labour Party must do something for the underdogs and that if he could have another sixpence on to the income-tax he could keep Maxton[5] and the Clydesiders quiet for ten years. Tom Mosley intends to be Prime Minister of England. I was assured to hear him say that Russia was now a question of secondary importance. I do not think that the Left wing of Labour will let it remain so. De La Warr is a quiet rather pleasant man of about 32.

[1] Fletcher had stood as a Liberal in a by-election at Tavistock in 1928. The president of the local association and other influential Liberals quarrelled with headquarters over Lloyd George's land policy and urged Liberals to vote Conservative. Fletcher was beaten by the Tory.

[2] C. M. (later Sir Maurice) Bowra (1898–1971), classical and Russian scholar, then Tutor of Wadham.

[3] Robert Byron (1905–41), unprepossessing but talented travel-writer and aesthete, killed at sea in the war. Evelyn Waugh was 26 and Nancy Mitford 25; he had published *Decline and Fall*, she nothing as yet.

[4] Sir Oswald Mosley, Bart (*b.* 1896) was always known as Tom. At this time he was Chancellor of the Duchy of Lancaster in the Labour Government with responsibility for tackling unemployment. The 9th Earl De La Warr (*b.* 1900), sometimes known as 'Buck', was Parliamentary Under-Secretary, War Office. Blum was R. D. Blumenfeld (1864–1948), editor-in-chief and chairman of London Express Newspaper Co.

[5] James Maxton (1885–1946), chairman of the Independent Labour Party from 1926, passionate pacifist and spokesman for the Clydeside unemployed.

In the evening went to a cocktail party at the Trotters at the Warren Gallery. They were having a commiseration party for the confiscation of the Lawrence pictures.[1]

Wednesday, 10 July 1929

Met Colonel George Berry, the president of the American International Pressmen's Union (i.e. head of the printing machine manager's union). He is a big man in American labour, which is developing on its own lines and is only international as far as the American continent is concerned. I asked him if the U.S.A. was afraid of its Communists. 'Why, Mr Lockhart,' he said, 'we have a few short-haired women and long-haired bums, but they don't amount to anything.' Berry himself is a Democrat and was only defeated by Bryan by three votes for the Democratic vice-presidency. He has the same self-possession and slow manner of speech as Walter Harper whom he rather resembles. At present he is trying to get the American Legion's draft through Congress and through the Federation of Labour. This draft provides that in the event of war the U.S.A. Government mobilises everything and everybody: men, factories, profits, etc.

Friday, 12 July 1929

Went to Rupert's birthday party and met a large number of actresses and singers and strange young people drinking gin and cocktails and whisky. Pip sang – and sang well, but looked ill and tired. Freda may be going to America with a company in one of Drinkwater's plays.[2] At two a.m. went home and sat up all night writing a big review article of Ludwig's *July 1914*.

(This should be Friday 5th July.) My memory is becoming appalling. I cannot remember what I did the day before yesterday!

Saturday, 13 July 1929

At Hunger Hill for week-end. Hamish, Nancy Mitford. Ba [Cecil] Beaton, and Count Bismarck here. The latter lives in Rome. He is a grandson of the famous Bismarck and hates the Kaiser. The family has obviously never forgiven the latter for 'dropping the pilot'. Bismarck is a peculiar-looking young man – very aesthetic. He says Fascism is on the decline and is definitely unpopular and that the good relations between the Vatican and Mussolini would not last. Army is definitely anti-Fascist.

Monday, 15 July 1929

Gout much better. Went to dinner at 8b Little College Street where Spears had assembled a large gathering to meet [Louis] Wiley, the editor of

[1] On 5 July the police made a raid and removed thirteen paintings by D. H. Lawrence from the Warren Gallery which was run by Dorothy Warren and her husband Philip Trotter.

[2] Rupert ('Pip') was Lockhart's youngest brother: Freda was his sister.

the *New York Times*. Did not see much of latter. He is a fat podgy little Jew of about sixty. Guests were Archie Sinclair, Freddie Guest, Selfridge, 'Jix', Blum, Wickham Steed, Lord Burnham and self.[1] I sat next to Archie Sinclair and Freddie Guest and then over port with Jix. Archie is optimistic about the Liberals. Freddie Guest thinks they are ruined; cursed L.G. and said he could never keep a friend. Jix thinks Beaverbrook's Empire Free Trade will split the Conservative party and that there may be changes in the leadership. Wickham Steed bored us all afterwards by never keeping his mouth shut. We wanted to hear Wiley on Anglo-American relations. Instead we heard Steed's gramophone with its Northcliffe records!

Tuesday, 16 July 1929

Dined with Fletcher at the St James's. He gave me a lot of information about our secret service. The head of it now is Admiral Sinclair, a terrific anti-Bolshevik, who has succeeded the old 'C.', Mansfield Cumming. The new 'C.' is hard up for men for Russia. Incidentally, discovered that Kenworthy has a bad war-record. During the war he was in command of a destroyer in the North Sea and ran into a merchantman. He was the first man to abandon his ship. The gunner, however, and some of the crew succeeded in patching up the leak, and Kenworthy came back. Kenworthy was relieved of his command – but not by court-martial – and was sent to Gibraltar. During war, too, Kenworthy also attended a revolutionary luncheon at which toasts were drunk to the English Republic. Basil Thomson's man reported this to Admiralty. Beatty and 'Rosie' Wemyss[2] were furious and went to L.G. Latter, however, refused to act. Kenworthy has also made a considerable packet of money out of his deals with Russia. Not a good candidate... Late to bed. Went on to club afterwards.

Wednesday, 17 July 1929

Lunched with Gregory at the Savoy. He was to have been appointed editor of the *Fortnightly*, but a Canadian millionaire has just bought it. He told me some very interesting stories about Ramsay MacDonald and Tyrrell. The latter has not given up his drinking habits; has not done a stroke of work for years, and has sometimes been so drunk that J. D. Gregory had to smuggle him out of the office. He shielded him for seven years and then Tyrrell did not raise a finger to help him. Ramsay is very vain, where women are concerned. Lady Margaret Sackville[3] wanted or wants to marry him. J. D. G. said Ramsay once kept him waiting three-quarters of an hour because he had

[1] Gordon Selfridge (1856–1947), of the Oxford Street emporium, had journalistic aspirations and had once tried to buy *The Times*, Henry Wickham Steed (1871–1956), editor of *The Times*, 1919–22, during Northcliffe's ownership. Harry Lawson, 1st Viscount Burnham (1862–1933), proprietor of the *Daily Telegraph*.

[2] Earl Beatty (1871–1936) was commander of the Grand Fleet, 1916–19, and Sir Rosslyn Wemyss, later 1st Baron Wester Wemyss (1864–1933) was First Sea Lord, 1917–1919.

[3] Sister of 'Buck', Earl De La Warr, she died in 1963.

something very important to do. He was writing a letter to Lady Margaret. After he had addressed the envelope and closed it up, he took good care to let J.D. see!

Thursday, 18 July 1929.

Went down with Jill to Sonning to dinner. Played billiards and sat up very late. Full of financial worries. I have my income-tax to pay. Freeman will have to be paid something a month. Jock Anderson is pressing me, and I have over £100 to pay in insurance premiums. Jean, too, is in debt and requires an extra £35.

Friday, 19 July 1929

Very tired after last night. Lunched at Ustinov's to meet Raumer, a former German Finance Minister and a member of Stresemann's party. Raumer is now a big public utility man. He has come over here to learn English and has taken a cottage at St Ives for two months. He is going to live there alone with his English teacher (a female spinster from a London school!). Ustinov says if anyone asks him where the Minister is he will reply: '*Raumer ist in der kleinsten Hütte.*' The quotation is from Schiller and continues '*für ein glücklich Lieblingspaar.*'[1] Bernstorff, Constable, Arthur Willert, Feine, and Count Posziwik the other guests. Bernstorff says the young Bismarck is a most peculiar character; keeps an antique depot in Rome... Had a very heavy meal. Then had to work all evening writing an article on the Red Army! Instead of going to bed, sat up all night playing billiards. Very hot.

Tuesday, 23 July 1929

In the evening went to the Egyptian Legation to the party given by the Egyptian Prime Minister, Mahmoud Pasha. Saw Lord Reading and Amery there.[2] Amery said he could not understand all the fuss that was being made about Twickenham.[3] Empire Free Trade could not come in one flash; it would have to be built up by a series of slow processes. The leadership of the Conservative Party would resolve itself into a struggle between the Free-Traders and the Tariff-Reformers.

Wednesday, 24 July 1929

Lunched with Tommy at the Wellington and argued about class warfare and class prejudice. I said latter had existed from all times and had been invented by the upper classes as a weapon to keep the underdog down.

[1] 'Raumer is in the smallest hut for a happy pair of lovers.'

[2] Rufus Isaacs, 1st Marquess of Reading (1860–1935), had been Viceroy of India, 1921–6. L. S. Amery (1873–1955) had been Colonial and Dominion Secretary until the 1929 election.

[3] Beaverbrook was sponsoring Sir John Ferguson as an Empire Free Trade candidate in the by-election due at Twickenham on 8 August.

Now, however, that the lower classes are beginning to realise what class war is, the upper classes are frightened.

There is considerable indignation in Labour and Liberal circles that Trotsky has been refused the right of asylum in this country.

Although the Bolsheviks are commencing negotiations with us next week for the renewal of relations, the Moscow Press continues to attack the British Labour Government most vehemently. Today, there was a cartoon in the *Pravda* of Jim Thomas reclining in an arm-chair surrounded by footmen: J.H.T. says: 'At last I can do something for the unemployed.' Salary: £5000.[1]

Earlier Beaverbrook and Lockhart had discussed an eventual replacement for him as 'Londoner' in view of Beaverbrook's proposal of a new job for Lockhart, but Nicolson was not easily to be engaged. He was, after all, giving up a Foreign Office career begun in 1909; he had written biographies of Verlaine, Tennyson and Byron. His wife was the poet and novelist, Vita Sackville-West. Was journalism for him? He explained his attitude in a letter to Lockhart dated 22 July 1929:

The offer which you make to me is flattering in the extreme. It is also tempting. I long to get back to London and into the whirl of real life again. Being Counsellor in Berlin is very like being First Secretary at Stockholm. I am a stepney wheel of a car that is seldom taken out of the garage.

In principle, therefore, I am prepared gratefully to consider the proposal. Before I commit myself an inch further than that, there are certain questions I must ask, and certain reservations I must make. The latter may decide Lord Beaverbrook to withdraw the suggestion. Your answer to the former may decide me not to proceed any further.

(1) I should want some index of the salary, etc. I could not accept anything less than I should get at the Foreign Office.

(2) Hours of work. Would I get weekends? Would I be expected to keep late hours at the office – I mean night-hours? Would I ever be given a holiday and if so for how long?

(3) Contract. Would I have to commit myself for any definite period? If so, how long?

So much for my preliminary questions. Now come the reservations:

(1) I do not want Lord Beaverbrook to be under any misconceptions. It would be a mistake, for instance, to suppose that my long connection with the Foreign Office would give me special sources of information. The F.O. would be annoyed at my leaving them, and would cold shoulder me. If anything I should get less and not more information out of them than a man who had never been in the service. In the second place I am by politics and conviction a left-liberal or right-labour. On the one hand I am a pacifist and believe strongly in good relations with America at any sacrifice. On the

[1] J. H. Thomas (1874–1949), originally a railway worker, was at this time Lord Privy Seal to the Labour Government with a special mandate to deal with unemployment. The cartoon was reprinted in the *Evening Standard*.

other hand I am an Imperialist in the modern sense of the term, and I am by no means a passionate free-trader. I could not agree to express opinions which conflicted with these principles. Ethics apart, I fully realise that whatever career I might later make for myself in politics would be based not on push and snap but on consistency and knowledge. I should not wish to prejudice my ultimate prospects by association with opinions opposed to my own radical opinions. I put this forward as I do not wish, even at the outset of our discussion, that I should sail under a false flag.

Let me know about these points and I shall consider the thing further. If you wish to telephone I am here (Zentrum 703) from 9.30 till 1.0 every morning.

Lockhart phoned him and on 26 July Nicolson replied by letter:

I confirm our telephone conversation as follows:

(1) Your people might, if anything comes of all this, offer me a job at £3000 a year on let us say a two years contract as from 1 October next.

(2) This job would be to write and edit a page in the *Evening Standard* upon Politics, Life and Literature. It would occupy me for five days in the week, and I should get probably one month's holiday irrespective of such journeys as I might make abroad on the service of the paper.

(3) I should not be expected to write under my own name anything which conflicted with my own political convictions. I should within reasonable limits (and subject to eventual castigation by Lord Beaverbrook) be allowed to write in my own name opinions which were not necessarily those of the paper. I undertake, of course, to exercise not only my habitual discretion but my inhabitual loyalty in this respect.

(4) I should not be allowed to write for any other paper in the United Kingdom subject to such contracts and engagements as I have already assumed. As a matter of fact these contracts and engagements cover only, I think, three articles – two in *Nash's Magazine* and one in the Christmas supplement of the *Graphic*.

(5) I am to let Lord Beaverbrook know in principle before 10 August. I am to come over some time in the first fortnight of September and discuss further details with him. It will only be after that conversation that either of us will be pledged.

My reply to this is:

(1) In principle I am anxious to continue the negotiations.

(2) I cannot give my consent definitely until I have discussed the matter with my wife. Considerations of domestic finance and convenience have got to be taken into account. I am meeting my wife on 2 August. I hope on 3 August to be able to send you a definite decision, as far as anything at this stage can be definite.

(3) I am very grateful to Lord Beaverbrook and yourself for having put such a proposal to me.

Meanwhile Lockhart passed the hopeful news on to Beaverbrook.

Thursday, 25 July 1929

Lord Lloyd resigns the High Commissionership of Egypt: not really unexpected after Labour's advent to power, as he was almost too Right and too autocratic for Baldwin's Government, but it came at an unexpected moment, and there was great excitement in both the Lords and the Commons. We supported Lloyd in the paper against my advice. Valentine Castlerosse's comment on Lloyd is good: Egypt in the past has stood an Alexander the Great. She could stand a Ptolemy. She could stand a Julius Caesar, but she could not stand all three rolled into one.

Went down to Cherkley for the night. Lord Beaverbrook is delighted that Harold Nicolson is willing to join him. He has said no more about my job. I hope all will be well. He is not taking me to Russia; says the Bolsheviks do not want me. E. F. Wise, the Labour man, will pilot him round.[1] I expect E. F. Wise has put a spoke in my wheel. He probably wants to have the honour and glory of showing Lord Beaverbrook round himself. Graustein[2] there again. It was amusing to see Graustein and Beaverbrook play demon patience against each other. They went on for hours!

Friday, 26 July 1929

Valentine Castlerosse came in. He looked very fat and is off to Baden-Baden for a cure. He told me some good stories. There are great changes pending. Valentine is leaving the *Express*. Baxter has been offered the editorship-in-chief of all Harrison's papers.[3] Dined at the club and sat up till one playing billiards and drinking.

Sunday, 28 July 1929

Rose late and wrote up my diary. Feeling a little better after my liver pill. Went for a walk with Tommy round the fields. The poor woman has a thousand troubles: some she can't tell me and others she did. Pam Chichester is one source of worry. She has become a Catholic through Tommy, and the latter took her to her confirmation sacrament at great sacrifice to herself. Pam did not go to confession before in the morning. On the way to London their car ran over a woman, so they were all rather upset. At confirmation itself Pam made a mistake in the ritual, became flustered, and whispered violently: 'I cannot go on with this puppet mummery!' Poor Tommy is now

[1] E. F. Wise (1885–1933), Labour M.P., had been responsible for supplies to Russia during the war and was now economic adviser on foreign trade to the Russian Union of Consumers' Cooperative Societies.

[2] A. R. Graustein, Canadian paper magnate.

[3] Beverley Baxter (1891–1964) was then editor-in-chief and director of the *Daily Express*. He was later Conservative M.P. and dramatic critic, knighted in 1954. Henry Harrison's chief paper was the *Daily Chronicle*, later merged with the *Daily News* to become the *News Chronicle*.

agitated. Should she tell the priest? Is the sacrament null and void? Rained all afternoon. In the evening went over to Cherkley. Quite useless as far as I was concerned. Graustein was there, and Beaverbrook's whole attention was taken up with him. Most of the evening they played demon patience against each other. It was amusing to see these two enormously rich men behaving like schoolchildren. Bed one-thirty. No alcohol. No cigarettes.

Monday, 29 July 1929

In the afternoon went to see Beaverbrook. He had [R. J.] Thompson with him. The latter was suggesting changes in the paper: less Diary and more news. Beaverbrook then had me alone for half-an-hour – leader was bad. Diary was rotten. I told him I had another letter from Harold Nicolson, and that it looked as if he were agreeable to our offer. Beaverbrook seemed delighted. Later he informed me that I had no chance of becoming an editor unless I went to a sub's table first and that owing to circumstances the job he had in view for me had fallen through. A cheerful prospect. It seems that in getting Harold I have made a silken rope wherewith to hang myself. Bed 11.45. One small Pimms'. No cigarettes. Read Scott's *Journal*. He was a courageous man and is very fortifying when like me one is depressed.

Tuesday, 30 July 1929

In the evening dined at Stornoway. Beaverbrook, Allan Aitken,[1] Robertson, and Wardell there. Beaverbrook says he wants me either to be his assistant or to become an editor. This may entail going as sub-editor to the *Daily Express* – an uncongenial and risky job at my time of life. In any case he promised me a substantial increase at the end of my first year. I am getting less now than I was in 1918 and really less than I was getting at the bank. And after all I joined him in order to make money. I must sell my Russian book [*Memoirs of a British Agent*] before December.

Wednesday, 31 July 1929

Lunched with Rex Leeper who is now second in command of the Press Department at the Foreign Office. He tells me Percy Loraine is certain to get Cairo.[2] He is in favour of professional diplomats, for the reason that, if you give too many posts to amateur diplomats, you will drive all the good men out of the service. He is now very anti-Tyrrell and told me how Tyrrell boasted of having led me up the garden! Rex also said Litvinov bore him no malice and that before the last meeting of the Preparatory Disarmaments Committee at Geneva he sent a message to Litvinov giving him his love. Litvinov sent back another message asking Rex if he remembered their

[1] Beaverbrook's youngest brother.

[2] Sir Percy Loraine, Bart (1880–1961) became High Commissioner for Egypt and the Sudan, 1929–33, He was later Ambassador to Turkey and to Italy.

conversation on the train when Rex took him to Aberdeen in 1918 to send him out of the country. Rex said he'd be back in England inside ten years as ambassador. Litvinov sent back a message to say he seemed to have lost his return ticket.

Thursday, 1 August 1929

Today I am pledged to begin my book! But alas! it is not begun.

Friday, 2 August 1929

August 2nd and still my book is not begun. Tired today after sitting up so late last night over my film article. Lunched at the Bell, went in by tube to Piccadilly, had a hair-cut, collected my golf-clubs at the Carlton Club, and then went to bed till seven. In the evening went with Jill to the Victoria Palace to see Gracie Fields in *The Show's the Thing*. Gracie herself is a Lancashire factory lass with a voice which is elastic enough to make the highest notes, is almost good enough for a second-class opera company, and which by making fun of she makes the most of. Her brother [Tommy Fields] is quite a clever comedian. Had supper at the Monico. Quarter of a bottle of white wine: one cigar. Tommy rang up. It does not look as though Harry were going away.

Sunday, 4 August 1929

As we were feeding, the telephone rang. It was Tommy who rang up to tell me that on Saturday night Loughie had committed suicide by throwing himself from a window in a house in Holland Road. He had been terribly hurt in the arms and legs. The tragedy took place at 12.30 a.m. and he lived till seven-thirty. He was taken to the casualty ward of St Mary Abbot's Hospital where the doctors amputated his foot. His agony and his screams were terrible, but Harry never knew, and it was left to Tommy to sit beside him. He recovered consciousness or semi-consciousness and said to Tommy: 'A coward and chicken-hearted to the end. I made a mess even of this.'

Telephoned to Beaverbrook and asked him to keep Loughie's name out of the *Express*. Alas! in vain.

Monday, 5 August 1929

I feel decidedly better and I have done my exercises every day. On the other hand, I have *not* started my book.

Nicolson wrote again on 1 August:

I have today written to Lord Beaverbrook, telling him that I have been in communication with you (I gave no details of what you said) and that I am in principle prepared to agree.

I have however, after going into the matter carefully with my wife, asked for an increase on the salary which you mentioned. It may be that he will think I am asking for too much. The fact is however that my mother-in-law has decided to suspend our settlements, and dares us to prosecute her in the courts. We are naturally averse from doing this, and the present offer provides a marvellous chance of being completely independent. Only, as our settlement is £2400 pounds a year. I cannot surrender that without getting more from the *Evening Standard.* If Beaverbrook refuses, I shall then have to stick to the career and prosecute Lady Sackville. But it is the chance of being able to avoid this galling alternative which tempts me to sacrifice my prospects for the glories and ardours of independence.

If all goes wrong, I shall still remain grateful to you for having suggested me.

The deal was made in mid-September

Tuesday, 6 August 1929

Letter from Harold Nicolson. He wants more than £3000 and Beaverbrook thinks it is too much. Dined at Stornoway. Robertson, myself, young Max, and Mike there.

In the afternoon went with Harry to the inquest of Loughie at the Kensington Town Hall. There were a good many people there including the woman whom he had been living with. It was a coroner's court, but there was a jury – an extraordinary collection of witless-looking people. It was obvious from the beginning that the coroner thought it was suicide, and he more or less indicated his view to the jury who returned a verdict of suicide during temporary depression. Harry behaved fairly well, although he was disappointed that the verdict was not death by misadventure.

No alcohol. No cigarettes. Reading rather a dull book [edited] by Michael Joseph: *The Autobiography of a Journalist.* A poor effort for such a fascinating subject. On the other hand, it does show that without never-flagging energy and very hard work it is impossible for a man without influence and without private means to arrive anywhere.

Wednesday, 7 August 1929

Tommy came up to London on her way to Loughie's funeral which is to be held at Rosslyn tomorrow. She looks a complete wreck and I fear another nervous breakdown. Lunched with her at the Wellington, then went on to the Foreign Office where, I had a long talk with Rex Leeper and with Sargent. Esmond Ovey has been appointed British Ambassador to Brazil.[1] Several people refused it, but even so he has been passed over the heads of some fifteen senior ministers. . .

In the evening dined with Harry and Tommy at Sorrani's. Harry was quite

[1] Actually Ovey went to Russia.

drunk and talked about nothing else except Loughie which nearly drove Tommy mad. They left at ten forty-five for Scotland.

Beaverbrook is very savage against the proposed new Anglo-Egyptian treaty.

Friday, 9 August 1929

At eleven p.m. went round to see Beaverbrook. He raised my salary £1000.

This raise in salary was in part because Lockhart had become Beaverbrook's chief lieutenant in his Empire Free Trade campaign and was so to remain for two years. On the previous day, the first Empire Free Trade parliamentary candidate, Sir John Ferguson, won the by-election at Twickenham.

Saturday, 10 August 1929

Beaverbrook, Arnold Bennett, Jean Norton, Mike Wardell, Lady Louis Mountbatten, and Venetia Montagu left for Russia. Low did a great cartoon of Beaverbrook and Bennett in the *Standard* on the lines of Meissonier's *The Retreat from Moscow*. Sent Beaverbrook Priestley's *The Good Companions*, Blake's *The Path of Glory*, and bought Tommy a copy of Priestley's *Good Companions*. Both are first editions. Not feeling quite so well today – rather livery.

Cashed £12 today, and have now only £7 10*s* 6*d* left. Books cost me £1 15*s*, taxis 5*s*, ticket to Horsham 12*s* 6*d*, car from Horsham to Coolham £1 5*s*, luncheon 4*s* 6*d*, valet 2*s* 6*d*, porters and papers 2*s* 6*d*, tobacco 2*s* 7*d*, collection in church 2*s* = 31*s* 7*d*.

Came down to Horsham by the 3.20. Went for a walk with Tommy who still looks very ill and on the verge of a nervous breakdown. Harry, who was maudlin, does nothing but talk about Loughie from morning till night.

The Duchess of Bedford returned safely from her flight to India and back in a week. She is 63![1]

Tuesday, 27 August 1929

Lunched with Wheeler-Bennett in Albany.[2] Wheeler-Bennett . . . runs an Intelligence Section [for the Institute of International Affairs] at his own expense. He is writing a book on the foreign policy of the Soviet Government. He was intended for the diplomatic service, but during the war he was in a very bad air raid in London, was nearly killed, and has had a terrible stammer ever since.

[1] Mary Duchess of Bedford, grandmother of the present Duke, had learned to fly in 1928 at the age of 62. She continued her intrepid career until she died in a snowstorm over the North Sea in 1937.

[2] The first mention of a man who became a close friend of Lockhart. Now Sir John Wheeler-Bennett (*b.* 1902), he wrote, among many other books, the official life of King George VI.

Friday, 30 August 1929

In the evening dined with Jill at Scott's, went to [Noël Coward's] *Bitter Sweet* and then went on to the Kitcat and danced – first time I had danced for months and months. Incidentally, the Kitcat is called after the famous literary club of that name which existed in the eighteenth century and of which Addison, Steele, Pope, Congreve and Hogarth were members. I did not like *Bitter Sweet* quite so well as the first time.

Saturday, 31 August 1929

Beaverbrook returned. This morning we had a letter criticising the Diary, and at one o'clock I had a telephone message asking me to come to see him. I am going over tomorrow night. Very hot in London and temperature highest of the year.

Sunday, 1 September 1929

In the evening drove from Camberley to Cherkley to dine with Beaverbrook. He has returned from Russia with no good impressions. The whole thing seems to have depressed him. Mike Wardell says it is because the Bolshies did not make enough of him, but he saw Stalin, and Litvinov lived in his pocket, and he was given special cars, etc. He seems to have been more impressed by the religious revival than by anything else. Told me a very good story about the office for marriage and divorce, which costs nil. In the office there is anti-religious and anti-syphilitic propaganda.

After dinner played ping-pong. I was beaten by Max but beat Peter.

Friday, 6 September 1929

Went down in the evening to stay with Beaverbrook at Cherkley. He was all alone and was very nice. He talked about his boys, was not satisfied with their work, and informed me that he himself would far rather be working than playing golf!

Tommy arrived from Dunrobin.[1] Gave her luncheon at the Maison Basque. She tells me the Prince of Wales turned up in the Casino at Le Touquet the other night quite drunk and quite incapable of standing.

Saturday, 7 September 1929

Tommy told me a very good story about an airman called Jack Scott and Lord Birkenhead. They were in Germany. Scott had been too attentive to someone else's wife and was challenged to a duel. Everyone was in wine. Asked to name his second, he pointed to Lord Birkenhead. Latter, when approached, looked very astonished, pulled himself together, and then said briskly: my choice of weapons, I believe. I choose airplanes and machine-guns!

Harry made a good remark about the famous hymn 'For ever with the Lord' – suggested last line should be 'a day's march nearer Rome'.

[1] The Scottish home of the Duke of Sutherland.

Thursday, 12 September 1929

Dined with Nowak at Taglioni's. Princess Kropotkina, Countess Seidl, and Professor Ogden there. After dinner we went on to Ogden's flat in Frith Street and met Hatfield, another English scientist, who has invented the Mechanical Man. Ogden is a great expert on speech and has invented a language of 500 words (English) in which one can express anything.[1] Both men complained bitterly that no one in England was interested in scientists and that they had to go to Germany to get their stuff taken.

Monday, 16 September 1929

Harold Nicolson arrived. He is to see Beaverbrook tomorrow or Wednesday. I think the deal will come off, in which case what will happen to me?

Very busy translating Nowak's book.

The Nicolson deal is fixed up. It was settled last Thursday. He is coming to us for £3000 a year: three-year contract, etc., etc.

Nicolson, by now at his home near Sevenoaks, wrote to Lockhart on 19 September:

I have searched among my archives and can find no photograph earlier than 1917 – which would give an unauthoritative look to the new member of your staff. I shall therefore wait until I am up in London and then look in at Shoe Lane. I shall give you warning of my coming.

I am so amused at Hardinge having written! What an odd thing for him to do! By the way, if you see Lord B. could you mention to him that I forgot to warn him that he will probably receive from my mother-in-law a letter asking for a statement of my exact salary, etc.? The letter will also, in all probability, inform him that I have twice been in a lunatic asylum, that I have acute kleptomania, that I was mixed up in the Crippen murder case, that Vita has been in prison (anonymously) for theft, that Stresemann has frequently written to her begging her as an old friend to prevent my cheating at cards, and that I am secretly married both to Lady Astor and Miss Susan Lawrence. Lord B. will perhaps wish to ignore these letters.

Tuesday, 24 September 1929

Feeling very seedy. Stayed in bed all day. Saint [his doctor] came to see me and advised more washing-out treatment and strict dieting. In the evening had my first wash-out. The nurse said I needed it very badly.

Went to Dunn's and raised £100 which I need very badly. He told me he knew Hatry and Daniels well, so I imagine they had been to him.[2]

[1] C. K. Ogden, founder of the Orthological Institute at Cambridge and inventor of Basic English. H. S. Hatfield, author of *Automaton, or the Future of the Mechanical Man* (1928).

[2] Clarence Hatry and Edmund Daniels were notoriously crooked financiers who had just been charged with fraud. On 24 January 1930 Hatry was sentenced to 14 years' penal servitude and Daniels to 7.

Sunday, 29 September 1929

Tommy told me that young Bloggs Baldwin[1] had told her that her father could not bring himself to work with Beaverbrook and that he regarded him as one of the most corrupting influences in the country.

Lockhart went down to the Labour Party Conference in Brighton.

Wednesday, 2 October 1929

I lunched with the Mosleys at the Royal Crescent [Brighton] and met a host of weird people: [William] Mellor, the editor of the *Daily Herald*, Mrs Baker, Frazier Hunt, and several agents and Labour journalists whose names I did not catch. The journalists told some good stories of [J. H.] Thomas: one about his visit to the King after the railway trouble in 1921. The King says to Thomas: 'Now, Mr Thomas, tell me in confidence what sort of a fellow is this man Bromley?'[2] 'Between ourselves, Your Majesty, I think 'e's a 'ell of a 'ound!'

Talked to Henderson and congratulated him. He brought Selby down to the conference with him.[3]

Friday, 4 October 1929

In evening went to see [J. M. Barrie's] *Dear Brutus* at the Playhouse. Gerald du Maurier and Mary Casson (Sybil Thorndike's daughter) were the two stars. Very charming and very Barriesque. Later, went on to Café Anglais where Rex Evans excelled himself in innuendos. Ethel Baird did some good imitations. Bed 1.30 a.m.

Tuesday, 8 October 1929

Dinner party at Beaverbrook's: Mrs Norton, Venetia Montagu, Lady Louis Mountbatten, Aga Khan, Mr and Mrs Hopkinson, [William] Barkley, Peterson and self. Michael Arlen, looking more opulent and conceited than ever, came in later. The Aga told a good story of the business abilities of Englishmen, Frenchmen, Germans and Americans. He said he had seen and studied all their methods in every corner of the globe. The Englishman was far the most practical of them all. He could afford to give the others one hour start but not the three hours' extra work which the German did every day. Went on with Maurice to the Melton Club, where we spent a dismal and drinkless hour. London by night is dead just now. Drank like a buffalo and smoked like a chimney.

[1] Betty Baldwin, daughter of the Leader of the Conservative Party.

[2] John Bromley (1876–1945), general secretary of A.S.L.E.F., the railway union, 1914–36.

[3] Arthur Henderson (1863–1935), whom Lockhart had met in Russia, had become Foreign Secretary in the new Labour Government. Sir Walford Selby (1881–1965) was his principal private secretary.

Lunched Harold Nicolson at the Wellington and fixed up his permission to broadcast.

Saturday, 23 November 1929

At Cherkley. Sir Austen and Lady Chamberlain there. Austen very pleasant and easy to get on with. He is old, however, rather vain, and very garrulous. He told some good stories about his early days. After he left Cambridge he went to Germany. He had a letter to Bismarck who asked him to dinner. Bismarck pressed him to drink. Austen refused or at any rate drank very little. Bismarck then asked him about the habits of the young men at Cambridge. Austen replied that there was very little drinking and that the undergraduates were very abstemious. Bismarck broke in: 'Ah, I see. Your young men are just like our young men in Germany. They will never do anything. They cannot drink.' . . .

Austen told me all about Locarno; defended his policy strongly; said he knew all about France's desires and that it was nonsense to say he was in France's pocket. His view was that it is easier to get concessions from the French by conciliatory methods than by denunciation.

Sunday, 24 November 1929

Last night Max – *i.e.* Max senior – was bored by the Chamberlains. He therefore spent the evening making fiendish noises on his wireless instrument. The oscillations made a noise like thunder, and at every clap poor Austen, in the middle of Locarno, jumped about four feet in the air.

The Chamberlains left in the afternoon and were replaced by the Amerys. Latter is a clever little man with an encyclopaedic knowledge, but he has no personality and lacks all charm.

Thursday, 28 November 1929

Dined at Lady Islington's[1] to meet the Prince of Wales and to go on to her charity boxing entertainment at the Holborn. Lady Eleanor Smith, whom I sat next to, Freda [Dudley Ward], the Ronald Trees, Lord Knebworth and one or two others.[2] Discussed journalism with Lady Eleanor. She is vivacious and easy to talk to. She is writing a novel on circus-life. She told me she had libelled Tallulah [Bankhead] once by mistake. She wrote that Tallulah was an anglophobe when she meant to say anglophile. Tallulah sued the *Sunday Dispatch*. Latter said they would pay, but in future Tallulah's name would never be mentioned in any Rothermere paper. Tallulah withdrew her claim.

Not a very big crowd at the Holborn Stadium.[3] I sat behind the Prince.

[1] Anne, wife of 1st Baron Islington, a former governor of New Zealand.

[2] Eleanor Smith, daughter of 1st Lord Birkenhead, later a novelist and author of books on circus and ballet. Ronald Tree, Joint Master of the Pytchley Hounds, later a Conservative M.P. and junior minister. Lord Knebworth was heir to the 2nd Earl of Lytton.

[3] It was an Amateur Boxing Tournament in aid of the Pro Patria Day Nurseries.

Primo Carnera[1] was late in appearing, there being some fuss about his kit. Apparently, at the Stadium boxers must appear in full kit and not in drawers only. He boxed three amateurs. There was some good amateur boxing. George Bernard Shaw and Lady Avery were there. G.B.S. was asked by Anne [Lady Islington] to give the prizes away. He refused, and, as he left, someone hissed. Prince of Wales very nice to me and asked me to play golf.

Saturday, 30 November 1929

Very wet day. Played golf with the Prince at Walton Heath. He drove me down in his new super-Rolls. Only the chauffeur with us. All the way down he discussed the Press; begged me to use my influence with Beaverbrook to have his name kept out of the papers. He described to me what he had to endure. Last year, when his father was so ill, he went up to Leicestershire with the doctor's permission for a day's hunting. Naturally, he did not want it known. When he arrived, he found a band of journalists. He sent for them, explained the circumstances, promised to receive them another time, and begged them to say nothing. They agreed. Hardly had he gone a hundred yards on his horse, when he saw one of them snapping him from behind a tree. He rode up to him towering with passion and made him destroy the plate! Also told me that the *Star* article 'Should the Prince Fly?' had caused untold trouble. Thousands of old ladies had written to the Queen. Played nine holes in the morning – halved. In afternoon he beat me level by three and two. A year ago I used to give him a half. He now plays really well and hits the ball as far as anyone. Lunched in the club. He ate some prunes and drank water. In the afternoon it came on to rain cats and dogs, but he insisted on finishing the round.

He told me that he would have to receive Sokolnikov, the Russian Ambassador, as his father refused to do so. He himself did not care; he hardly remembered the Tsar, but the latter was his father's first cousin, and he could quite understand his attitude.

The Prince said I looked rotten and he was going to drag me out to play golf when he returned from South Africa.

Sunday, 15 December 1929

This morning at eleven-thirty set out for Doorn. Dull and damp, but no rain. Drove through a plain of depressing flatness through an *allee* of poplars. Arrived at Doorn after twelve. On passing through the *Turenhaus* met the ex-Kaiser in the drive. He was wearing a Homburg hat with a chamois beard in the back, and a loose black cape. He carried a stick. His alsatian, Arno, was with him. We got out of our car. I was introduced. His Imperial Highness immediately took me by the arm, welcomed me to Doorn, and thanked me profusely for my help in the matter of the Ponsonby letters. He at once began to talk of Ponsonby's behaviour and how glad he had been to

[1] Primo Caruero (1906–67), Italian heavyweight, was world champion, 1933–4.

receive letters from English friends criticising that behaviour. On entering the house, he went upstairs to change and wash, and then in a few minutes I was summoned to an audience in his *cabinet de travail* upstairs. Quite a small room overloaded with knick-knacks. He offered me a cigarette – very long with a long mouthpiece. I refused, but he insisted, saying that cigarette-smoking helped conversation. He spoke English very well. Then he told me the story of the Englishwoman (in the days when Englishwomen could not speak French) who asked her neighbour at a dinner-party: *Êtes-vous un fumier?*[1] Nowak was present at this interview, and the conversation was half in German, half in English. I had brought a list of questions with me and I handed them to the ex-Kaiser. He read them through. With regard to the one on religion he replied: 'Here is a question on which I can say *eine Menge* [a lot].' Then, turning back to the one: 'Who is the greatest modern democrat?' he said: 'Here is one I can answer at once. Bernard Shaw. Have you read his *Kaiser of America* [*The Apple Cart*]? The Crown Prince has seen it seven times.' He then told me the story of Shaw and Isadora Duncan and their child. 'Yes,' says Shaw, 'but fancy if it were born with my beauty and your brains.'[2] More conversation about Russia, Mexico, Mrs Alec Tweedie,[3] books – English books (he loves Warwick Deeping's *Roper's Row*) and Queen Victoria. He shows me his miniatures and his photographs as a boy in kilts, in a sailor-suit, at Balmoral and Cowes, and as a tiny child of two in skirts, painted by Queen Victoria. Very methodical, energetic, and the voice of a young man. A secretary or gentleman of the household comes into the room. – 'Quarter to one, *Majestät*.' 'All right,' says the Kaiser, 'I haven't committed any indiscretions yet!' He gives me a magnificent photograph of himself, signed and with the inscription: 'Nothing is ended finally until it is ended rightly.' It is a fine portrait, but he himself is a fine-looking man. We go off to our respective quarters to wash our hands. Nowak and I are then ushered into the ante-room where we meet the gentlemen of the Household: Count Finckelstein, Count Hamilton, a Swede-Scot, the Princess Hermine and her daughter, and wait for the ex-Kaiser. He comes down, having changed his coat for a short black coat, a butterfly collar, a striped tie with a large tie-pin holding a miniature of Queen Victoria (this in my honour) striped trousers, and black shoes and spats (very German with little mother-of-pearl buttons right down to the point of the spat!) There is little formality. The Princess goes in first, followed by the ex-Kaiser who holds the hand of his step-daughter and romps in with her. I sit on the Empress's right hand.

When he gave me his photo the Emperor said: 'Put it away in some corner. It may compromise you.' Another feat of which he is very proud was accomplished the day I was there. That morning he had felled his twenty-

[1] A *fumier* is not a smoker but a dunghill.

[2] Shaw and Isadora Duncan, the dancer, had no child. The story was that she had suggested that if they were to have a child it would have her beauty and his brains.

[3] Author of *Thirteen Years of a Busy Woman's Life* and a host of other travel books, including one on Russia and two on Mexico.

thousandth tree since his exile. Nowak said: 'Don't put that in the paper or Wolff, the editor of the *Tageblatt* will say: "What are 20,000 trees compared to 2,000,000 German lives?".'

Luncheon was a simple meal. The ex-Kaiser drank a glass of sparkling burgundy and talked the whole time. His versatility and his range of subjects are amazing. He discussed naval history; said he was probably the only sailor who had read James's *Naval History* through from beginning to end.[1] After luncheon we went into the smoking-room. The ex-Kaiser again engaged me in private conversation. He asked why our great families were selling their places and their treasures: I replied that taxation was driving them out of existence. He said it was just the same in Germany. I said: 'Yes, but you Germans work and we don't.' He replied: 'What is the good of working when every penny of profit goes to pay those damned Yankees?' 'I beg your pardon,' he said, 'I ought not to have said that.' He asked about the Prince of Wales and inquired whether he was still falling off his horse. Then we discussed religion. He expects a great religious revival especially in England and Germany. After some twenty minutes' conversation his little step-daughter came up to him and said: 'Mama says, would you like to go upstairs?' The ex-Kaiser smiled, made his goodbyes, and went off holding his step-daughter's hand. He took my questions with him. Nowak and I went for a walk round the rather mournful park. The garden is very neatly kept. Every rose-bush, every flower, planted by the Kaiser has a little tin ticket 'Planted by S.M.' and the date. After tea the questions were returned to me with the answers in his own handwriting. He had given up his 'siesta' in order to do them. At six left again for Utrecht. Nowak and the Princess left that evening for Berlin.

I left on Monday morning for the Hague.[2]

Tuesday, 31 December 1929

Went down to Cherkley for New Year's Eve. Pam and I motored down with Jean Norton. Shanks, Mike Wardell and Senator Gogarty, an Irish poet and a crashing bore,[3] the other guests. A very boring evening. Senator Gogarty never stopped talking.

[1] A standard history, first published in 1822–4, usually in five or six volumes, though Lockhart credited it with sixteen in the *Evening Standard*.

[2] Lockhart's interview with the Kaiser, in a much less intimate form, made front-page news in the *Evening Standard* on 19 December – 'first allied journalist who has obtained an interview'.

[3] Oliver St John Gogarty (1878–1957), author of *As I was Going Down Sackville Street*, Senator, 1922–36. Yeats called him 'Ireland's chief wit', and Lockhart had better evidence of this later (see page 274).

CHAPTER SEVEN

1930

Beaverbrook and Empire Free Trade, Baldwin and Churchill. How Balfour put Baldwin in. Meets Randolph Churchill, 'gramophone to his father'. Beaverbrook's belief in hell. His 'hallelujah' at Fulham by-election success. Mosley resigns. Harold Macmillan wants Baldwin to go. Nancy Mitford's first novel. Lord Ednam's curse. Hitler. Airship disaster. Lockhart owes £10,000. His friendship with Pamela Chichester. Castlerosse's marriage and his affairs. Lockhart's bad health, enters nursing home. Northcliffe's last illness. Lord Melchett a dirty feeder.

Wednesday, 8 January 1930

Saw Arnold Bennett yesterday at the Savoy. He was lunching with Roberts, the manager of the *New Statesman*.[1] Arnold Bennett is very dissatisfied with Sharp who, he says, is drinking terribly. He is looking for a new editor, and, possibly, for a purchaser of the paper.

Thursday, 16 January 1930

Tommy went back to Coolham. Went to the Eccentric Club dinner to the Lord Mayor. Heard three good stories:

(1) One about the bad American golfer who never swore but everywhere he spat the grass never grew again.

(2) A 'soccer' story about the Spurs: 'Have you seen them play lately'? 'No.' 'Why not?' 'Well, they never came to see me when I was bad!'

(3) About the Gloucestershire farmer with a basket of plums outside Buckingham Palace: 'Well, we had a little show down our way, and they sang "Send him victorious" – so I'm bringing him some.'

Tuesday, 21 January 1930

Dined Stornoway in evening: Winston, Valentine and self. Beaverbrook tried to convert Winston to Empire Free Trade. Winston drunk but unconvinced. He gave Beaverbrook some encouragement, however.

Thursday, 23 January 1930

Afterwards, went on to Stornoway where Winston, Beaverbrook,

[1] Bennett was on the board of the *New Statesman*.

Harold Nicolson and Pat Hannon[1] had been dining. Beaverbrook made another eloquent effort to persuade Winston to take up Empire Free Trade programme. Winston is very depressed about his position, but I doubt if he will take up Empire Free Trade.[2]

Monday, 3 February 1930

Came up from Cherkley. Had a very satisfactory talk with [E. J.] Robertson. Saw Beaverbrook in evening. He went to see Baldwin at six p.m. Baldwin spoke to him for over an hour, read his speech to him, but did not ask for any comment. In evening went to *New Statesman* dinner. Clifford Sharp has completely broken down with drink and is going away for four months. Had a long talk with Cole and Bensusan[3] who are both not unsympathetic to Empire trade. Cole pooh-poohs Empire Free Trade, but is in favour of limited partnerships. Drank alcohol and smoked cigarettes to my detriment.

Friday, 7 February 1930

Beaverbrook told me story of Robertson's rise. In 1913 he was a bell-hop in the Queen's hotel in Toronto.[4] When Beaverbrook offered him a tip, he said he would rather have a job. He is now general manager of *Daily Express*. Came back to Stornoway in evening. Major Hacking,[5] who is the political head of the motor-industry and has great influence with Morris, is not prepared to come all out for Empire Free Trade.

Saturday, 8 February 1930

Trouble between Tom Mosley, Tom Johnston and Lansbury – and Thomas.[6] *Sunday Express* has rather wild story of Mosley leading the disgruntled. Ireland beat England at rugger in Dublin – 4–3. Did two leaders for *Sunday Express* on Keynes and on 'putting the clock back'. Saw Pam, who is

[1] Patrick Hannon (*d.* 1963), Conservative M.P. since 1921, later knighted, was a big businessman in the Birmingham Small Arms Company, who interested himself in everything from the Public Morality Council to Aston Villa Football Club.

[2] Churchill, who had been Chancellor of the Exchequer in the Conservative Government defeated in 1929, was now out of office, having been a minister for most of twenty years. He did not return to office until the outbreak of war in 1939.

[3] S. L. Bensusan (1872–1958), ex-editor of the *Jewish World*, journalist and prolific writer, especially of one-act plays and popular education.

[4] This was a Beaverbrook myth (see below, page 257), though Robertson did work in the hotel industry in a much less humble capacity.

[5] Douglas Hacking (1884–1950), later 1st Baron, Conservative ex-minister, Vice-Chairman Conservative and Unionist Association, 1930–2, later Chairman of the Party organisation.

[6] Tom Johnston (1881–1965), Scottish Labour M.P., then Parliamentary Under-Secretary for Scotland, later Secretary of State for Scotland. George Lansbury (1859–1950) was then 1st Commissioner of Wales in the Labour Government and leader of the Labour Party, 1931–5. The four ministers mentioned were all concerned with unemployment. Thomas was supposed to be in charge, but was totally out of his depth, and Mosley in particular was very frustrated.

in bed with 'flu'. Mrs Howard (Baldwin's daughter) came to her yesterday, said her father could have nothing to do with a man like Beaverbrook, that Canada would have nothing to do with him or his scheme. Came down to Cherkley.

Wednesday, 12 February 1930

In the evening dined alone with Beaverbrook. He had indigestion and was in an irritable mood. He had seen Baldwin for an hour and a half that morning. He will not go our way [*i.e.* towards Empire Free Trade]. Baldwin said, 'I am a simple and straightforward man.' 'Believe me,' said Beaverbrook, 'I am neither simple nor straightforward, but I am more so than you!' Beaverbrook will not take advice. He thinks he understands position better than anyone and is all for hard-hitting. Went to club, got drunk, and then to 43.[1]

Friday, 14 February 1930

In evening saw Lord Beaverbrook who will announce his New Party on Monday, provided Rothermere comes out in favour of food-taxes. It is a big venture. He has already £70,000 promised towards his £100,000 fighting fund.

Tuesday, 18 February 1930

New Party – the United Empire Party – launched by Lord Beaverbrook. Leader by me in *Evening Standard* on the new party. *Evening Standard* makes a very poor show of the new event, the staff being too much engaged on the Jonesco case which is going badly for us. Lawyers and Birkett, too, have handled case badly for us.[2] Anglo-German Association formed. Went round to Stornoway in evening. Sir Thomas Horder[3] there – rather a common-looking little man – Pat Hannon, Castlerosse and Father Ryan.

Thursday, 20 February 1930

Appeal of New Party for Fighting Fund launched in *Express* and *Standard*. Lord Rothermere's papers are in full cry in supporting the Party. Lord Beaverbrook spoke at the Cattle Association dinner. He looks very tired and must be careful not to wear himself out. I wrote the leader yesterday for the *Evening Standard* on Lord Rothermere.

[1] The chief night-club run by Mrs Kate Meyrick, who was constantly in trouble with the police and later imprisoned for bribing Sergeant Goddard.

[2] Barbu Jonesco had brought a libel action against the *Evening Standard* because 'The Londoner's Diary' had said he was not really a Rumanian but a Polish Jew originally called Moritz Leiba. He won his case and £12,000 damages. Norman Birkett, K.C. (1883–1962), later 1st Baron, appeared for the *Standard*.

[3] Horder (1871–1955), later 1st Baron, Physician to the Prince of Wales and later to King George VI.

Friday, 21 February 1930

A very hectic day. Lunched with the Solomons and Mrs Snowden.[1] Latter said Labour did not take new party very seriously. She is opposed to any action regarding Bolshevik presentation of religion, as its effects are likely to be contrary to those expected. She is a bitter opponent of Sir John Reith on the B.B.C.[2] A woolly-headed tyrant!

In the evening wrote a leader for the *Sunday Express* and one for the *Evening Standard*. Did not leave the *Express* office till twelve.

Great support for the New Party and money pouring in fast. J. C. C. Davidson is trying to stop Lord Beaverbrook's broadcast.[3]

Monday, 10 March 1930

Yesterday Lord Beaverbrook told us the reason of his leaving Canada. He bought the Montreal Rolling Mills. They were to be paid for on 1st July. They were bought in April from McMaster, who said 'Today I have the little Napoleon in a cleft stick.' There was a dispute between the various steel-works. Finally it was decided they should amalgamate. Lord Beaverbrook insisted on a valuation. He borrowed the money to pay for the mills from Parr's Bank in London. When the valuation was made it was found that the price he was to get was several million dollars higher than what he gave. He thus made over £1,000,000 sterling by selling his mill before he paid for it. The Bank of Montreal were furious – called his action an offence against public morality![4]

Friday, 14 March 1930

Very tired and run-down. Whelan is ill and has been away for five days. The little man will have us all in our graves before he has finished.[5]

Tuesday, 18 March 1930

Went down to Cherkley in evening with Harold Nicolson. Valentine also there. Discussed Balfour, who is not expected to live through the night.[6] Beaverbrook is not a great admirer of Balfour. It was Balfour who put Baldwin in. When Bonar Law was dying the King sent for Salisbury and Balfour to ask their advice. Salisbury, who was a friend of Curzon, was away from London and was slow in returning. So was Balfour, but he came

[1] Mrs Ethel Snowden (1881–1951), wife of the Labour Chancellor of the Exchequer, member of the first Board of Governors of the B.B.C., 1927–33.

[2] Later Lord Reith (1889–1971), first Director-General of the B.B.C.

[3] J. C. C. Davidson (1889–1970), then Chairman of the Conservative Party, who received a viscountcy when Baldwin retired in 1937, and Beaverbrook were friends. They split over Beaverbrook's challenge to Baldwin but were later reconciled.

[4] For the full and accurate story see A. J. P. Taylor, *Beaverbrook*, page 41.

[5] 'Tich' Whelan, who had been private secretary to Lord D'Abernon in Berlin, was Beaverbrook's majordomo. 'The little man' was Beaverbrook himself.

[6] Balfour died on the following day.

at once and advised Baldwin. Otherwise Curzon would have been prime minister.

Wednesday, 19 March 1930

Wrote some paragraphs about his [Balfour's] golf and his tennis. He was rather a bad loser, and always gave himself the benefit of any doubt about a ball being in or out.

Friday, 21 March 1930

Beaverbrook thinks Harold Nicolson is depressed because he is not a great journalist. Gilliat took Harold's *Lord Carnock* [a biography of his father] to Bennett. Latter would not review it and suggested me as most suitable reviewer.

Saturday, 22 March 1930

A glorious morning. Wrote paragraphs and leaders for Beaverbrook on Neville Chamberlain's speech which is pro-Empire and on T. J. O'Connor's[1] which is anti. Beaverbrook in a difficult mood. Thought for a moment I should not get away. Stayed for luncheon. Venetia and young Max there. Young Max scolded for going off to Hoylake to see Oxford play Cambridge. Went to *Sunday Express*. Gordon[2] told me two stories of Beaverbrook in Russia. He told Stalin we were all interested in trade, not in politics – in fact, 'in selling cooking-pots to cannibals'. When shown the Cheka he said one day that office will renounce Stalin – put someone else in his place. Fancy a country where Lord Byng[3] is stronger than the Prime Minister!

Monday, 31 March 1930

Back to London from Stornoway. The chief is very restive about Baldwin and is always saying we must break – we must break. Such a policy would be stupid and a second journey into the wilderness sheer madness.

Thursday, 3 April 1930

Lunched with George Clerk at the Savoy and discussed Harold Nicolson and Empire Free Trade. George Clerk does not think Harold Nicolson will ever be a journalist. Harold's book appeared: a lead-story in every paper except the *Express*.

Sunday, 13 April 1930

Met Randolph Churchill – Winston's son. He is a good-looking boy with fair hair and distinguished features rather marred by a spotty complexion. Talks nineteen to the dozen and is a kind of gramophone to his father.

[1] O'Connor (1891–1940), Conservative M.P. for Nottingham, knighted 1936.

[2] John Rutherford Gordon (*b.* 1890), then editor of the *Sunday Express*, now editor-in-chief and trustee of Beaverbrook Foundation.

[3] Viscount Byng of Vimy (1862–1935), a general in the First World War, was chief commissioner of Metropolitan Police, 1928–31.

Very egocentric and conceited and therefore very unpopular. I rather liked him. Very anti-Beaverbrook and Rothermere. Says Lord Beaverbrook pays Hannon £2000 a year, that he bribes people to come to his meetings, etc. etc., and more in same strain; that he has put Conservative Party out of power for seven years (Conservatives have ruined themselves by their hatred of L.G.). (This is pure Winston.) Above all, that Baldwin has sold him a pup. Says his father may retire from politics.

Thursday, 17 April 1930

Lunched at Boulestin's with Pam. She is very docile and agreeable to anything, but she had been up till 4 a.m. the night before and seems as weak as water.

Friday, 18 April 1930

Started Greek again. Have forgotten almost everything. Went to church at West Grinstead. Bitterly cold. Adoration of the Cross. (Must get Daily Missal) . . .

Reggie Nicholson here to luncheon.[1] He has seen a good deal of Baldwin and Rothermere lately. He told Tommy that Rothermere was going the same way as Northcliffe. Rothermere was very upset at Beaverbrook's pact with Baldwin. Baldwin told him he hated Rothermere but that he thought Beaverbrook was quite sincere. Reggie thinks Beaverbrook will win if he plays his cards well. Reggie told me the story of the *Daily Mirror* and *Times*. *Daily Mirror* not only failed as a woman's paper but failed at beginning as fiction paper. Reggie put in as manager. Insisted on free hand. One year later, success. Sent to *Times*. Success till war when Northcliffe again interfered. Reggie resigned. *Times* would not stand Northcliffe's interference. Reggie told us interesting story of Spring-Rice.[2] Reggie and Spring-Rice's brother were farming together near Regina about 40 years ago. Spring-Rice, the ambassador, then an attaché at Washington, came to see his brother, went out shooting, came into shack with his gun loaded, and by accident shot another man in shack. Before man died, he cursed Spring-Rice with his last breath. Incident had profound effect on Spring-Rice's life.

Monday, 21 April 1930

Bridges, the Poet Laureate, died. Controversy revived regarding desirability of continuing the post.

Thursday, 24 April 1930

Lunched with Pam at the Wellington. She had been at some party . . . the night before and had passed out. According to her own story, she had been drugged.

[1] Reginald Nicholson (1869–1946) had been Manager of *The Times*, 1911–15.

[2] Sir Cecil Spring-Rice (1859–1918), Ambassador to the United States, 1913–18, and author of 'I Vow to Thee, my Country'.

Lord Beaverbrook peculiarly difficult and impossible to see. Worried me incessantly and kept me at end of telephone line all day. In evening dined with Pam at the Splendide and then went round to Stornoway at eleven. Beaverbrook had gone to bed.

Friday, 25 April 1930

Very hard day's work at the office. Lord Beaverbrook in a violently restless mood. Wrote scores of propaganda literature for him; also the political notes for the *Sunday Express*. Lovely day. Lunched with Tommy at the Wellington. Worked all afternoon and had long talk with Robertson about Beaverbrook. Robertson says one must stand up to him on occasions. Otherwise life ceases and becomes slavery. In evening dined with Pam at the Basque. Then went on to Stornoway, where Beaverbrook had a large party including Winston, Duff Cooper, Mrs Randolph Hearst, Lord Ashfield, McKenna, Bob Boothby, etc.[1] Winston very disgruntled and predicting nothing but disaster for the Conservatives. Boothby who has just returned from Scotland says his constituency is all for policy of action and has no use for Baldwin. Went on to club and then to 43.

Saturday, 26 April 1930

Went to the 43 last night, spent ten pounds on filthy liquor, met Norrie Hamilton, and never went to bed at all. My account is £100 overdrawn and I am on my last legs. A hectic day in the *Express* office. Wrote the *Sunday Express* leaders and also the descriptive notice for Beaverbrook's speech at Dorchester. In the evening came down to Cherkley. Played snooker with Allan Aitken and Peter. Did not go to bed till one. Ill, depressed and miserable. Covent Garden opens tomorrow – I have a ticket but may not be able to go because of the Fulham by-election.[2]

Sunday, 27 April 1930

In the evening Beaverbrook gave us a dissertation on [John] Knox; says there is no good life of Knox, who was a physical coward with a vast amount of moral courage. Knox was a galley-slave. He was the first Scottish hot-gospeller. Beaverbrook is still a Wee Free man and believes that unbaptised children go to hell and also in the real punishment of hell. Played snooker. Bed 11 p.m.

[1] Mrs Randolph Hearst, wife of the American newspaper magnate. Lord Ashfield (1874–1948), formerly A. H. Stanley, chairman of the London Underground Railway. Reginald McKenna (1863–1943) had been Chancellor of the Exchequer and was at this time Chairman of the Midland Bank. Robert – now Lord – Boothby (*b.* 1900) had been Conservative M.P. for East Aberdeenshire since 1926 and Parliamentary Private Secretary to Churchill in the previous government.

[2] In the West Fulham by-election, due on 6 May, Sir Cyril Cobb, the Conservative, was a keen Empire Free Trader and was fighting, with strong Beaverbrook support, to capture the seat from Labour.

Tuesday, 29 April 1930

Interesting facts about Beaverbrook and Northcliffe. Beaverbrook met Northcliffe [first in 1910] when he was standing for Ashton-under-Lyne as a food-taxer. Northcliffe was then against food-taxes. They met at dinner. Northcliffe asked Beaverbrook to come to dine with him, was obviously interested in the young man. Asked him how much he had made. Told him if he would drop the food-tax, he would go far. Tried to persuade Beaverbrook to persuade Bonar Law to drop it. Today Beaverbrook has made Rothermere swallow the food-tax.

1916: Beaverbrook also went to Northcliffe when he wanted to buy the *Daily Express*. Northcliffe said: 'How much have you made?' Beaverbrook gave the answer. It was more than in 1910. Northcliffe said: 'You will lose it all in Fleet Street.'

Tuesday, 6 May 1930

Polling day at Fulham. In evening dined with Pam and went out to the constituency. A cold evening with a continuous drizzle. We stood in front of the Town Hall and waited until after midnight. Very exciting. Crowd seemed predominantly Labour. Then a man slipped out of the main door. 'Cobb's in,' he said, 'by 315.' The rumour spread, and, although I did not believe it, the Labour spirits fell. When we were sure, we rushed round to the Vineyard. Beaverbrook was in the seventh heaven of delight. The Press Association rang up to ask for a message. 'Glory, Hallelujah!' said the chief, and 'Glory, Hallelujah!' it was.

Saturday, 10 May 1930

In the evening came down to Cherkley... I am very tired and thoroughly run-down. Woke up in the night with palpitations.

Sunday, 11 May 1930

Sir Robert Horne[1] here: he looks ill, but is very deferential to Max. He does not strike me as a future Prime Minister. He is canny enough, but has neither character nor great ability. In afternoon played golf with Peter at Walton Heath. Pam went out riding, and her horse ran away with her. Before we came back, she was in the drawing-room with Lord Beaverbrook, Horne, Paddy Hannon, Ashfield, Elibank, and Lord Beaverbrook let himself go about Baldwin. The man must go. We shall get rid of him, etc., etc. I wonder if he is wise enough to make these indiscreet boasts and how many of his so-called friends can be relied on.

Monday, 12 May 1930

Price of raw materials is very low – rubber, tin, and now copper are at

[1] Sir Robert Horne (1871–1940), later 1st Viscount, had been Chancellor of the Exchequer, 1921–2, but out of office thereafter. Beaverbrook hoped he might lead the Empire Free Trade Crusade.

rock-bottom prices. Bonar Law, who was a metal merchant, used to say: always buy copper when it falls to £60, you will be bound to make money. He always followed this rule himself. Today it is £40. If he had bought a warrant for 5000 tons at £60 – not an unreasonable amount for a speculation – he would have lost £100,000, a risk he would never have dreamt of taking.

When he was dying, he asked Beaverbrook to buy copper for him. His mind was wandering. He wanted to see the warrants. To keep him quiet, Beaverbrook did – and made some money.

Tuesday, 13 May 1930

Lunched with Tom Mosley and Mike at the Carlton Grill. Tom Mosley thinks that Labour will be ousted within two years, and that the next winter will see an increase in unemployment. He says only some madness on the part of the Tories can save them. The Tory's best friend has been Churchill, who by thoroughly bad budgeting was able to reduce income-tax by raiding every available fund. The orthodox Snowden has been carefully building the repairs, and by the time the Tories are back in power they will have another nest-egg to play with! Tom will probably resign next week.

Saturday, 17 May 1930

Went down to Cherkley after a busy afternoon at the *Daily Express* writing leaders for the Sunday. The jealousy between the *Daily Express* and the *Sunday Express* is absurd and very damaging to the interests of the paper. Lunched with Pam at the Carlton Grill. Betty Baldwin there. She told Pam that her father would resign tomorrow, but that he could not let the country down, as there was no one else to take his place.

Tuesday, 20 May 1930

Beaverbrook annoyed with me this morning because I did not turn up at Stornoway to see him. Tom Mosley resigns his post as Chancellor of the Duchy of Lancaster. He has been meditating this step for weeks. He says the Government have done nothing for unemployment, feels they will be beaten at the next election, and thinks his own action will strengthen his position in the Party as against the old Radical Free-Traders like Snowden and MacDonald.

Harold Nicolson is rather fed up with his position on the Diary. None of his paras is published – or very few.[1] Dined at Sports Club. Drunk.

Monday, 26 May 1930

Back from Hunger Hill. Still no word from Beaverbrook. He now rings

[1] Nicolson, according to an unpublished manuscript by Lockhart which was to have been called *End of an Epoch*, was an 'ideal colleague, lightning worker. Rather depressing. What we thought good never went in.' At this period Lockhart was not editing 'The Londoner's Diary' but acting as journalistic and Crusade factotum to Beaverbrook.

up Gilliat every day. On Friday Baxter asked me to find out if the Chief wanted the appeal for the *Sunday Express*. I put the message through, received no answer, so rang up later to find out what had happened. Beaverbrook's secretary replied that the Chief had already answered Baxter and wanted to know what business of mine it was to interfere!

Wednesday, 28 May 1930

Mike Wardell came to see me this morning, said that Beaverbrook had been complaining that I was neglecting him, and advised me to go to see him. Which indeed I did. He was very nice, made no reference to the past four days, but, when I asked if I should come the next day, he said, 'Certainly,' but 'Mind you come.' This gave the opportunity to say: 'I think I owe you an explanation,' and then I proceeded to explain that I thought I had lost his confidence. He blew up at once by saying, he had done nothing, didn't I know him, and the difference between anger and nervous exaltation. He then proceeded to blame the secretary who repeated Baxter's message to me last Friday!

Friday, 6 June 1930

Lunched with Harold Macmillan at the Savoy.[1] He is very bitter about the Conservative leadership, wants Baldwin to go, and is prepared to make a speech in his own constituency to that effect. Moore-Brabazon[2] and he run a Conservative Candidates' Association. He wants this body to pass a resolution in favour of Empire Free Trade.

Moore-Brabazon told Robertson that Horne, who is *soi-disant* our man, is telling everyone, or rather Moore-Brabazon, that he must remain loyal to Baldwin. Which shows how oily Horne is. He is indeed a second-rate man.

Thursday, 12 June 1930

The Chief is very near a break with Baldwin. Baldwin, I think, now wants to get away from food-taxes altogether. Harold Nicolson tells me that the Chief is being severely criticised for dropping the Referendum [on food taxes] – not because people like that dangerous instrument, but because he has broken his pledge with Baldwin. 'What would his papers have said if Baldwin had done what he has done?' is the usual remark. Still, Baldwin or rather Central Office, has not carried out the spirit of the pact with him.

Friday, 20 June 1930

Had an amusing para on Harry Rosslyn and his cricket grace: 'For

[1] Harold Macmillan (*b.* 1894), the future Prime Minister, was at this time out of the Commons. He was returned for his old constituency, Stockton-on-Tees, in 1931.

[2] J. T. C. Moore-Brabazon (1884–1969), later Lord Brabazon of Tara, was, like Macmillan, a Conservative M.P. temporarily out of the Commons; he was a pioneer motorist and aviator, and later Minister of Transport and of Aircraft Production.

what we are about to receive, God help us. My wife has changed the menu.'[1]

Wednesday, 25 June 1930

I have had five cheques returned and am now down and out and will have to appeal to Max.

Max's party at Queen's Hall.[2] I was his chief stand-by and M.C. Was there from 7.30 p.m. till 2. Met Jim Thomas, Lloyd George, Robert Horne and various other politicians. Horne said he relied on me more than anyone to keep the bridge open between Conservatives and Max. Arnold Bennett offered me the editorship of the *New Statesman*. Danced with Pam for first time for months.

Thursday, 26 June 1930

If he [Horne] became Prime Minister, he would have no hesitation (in spite of opposition to Press proprietors) of giving Max Dominion and Colonial Secretaryship.

Friday, 27 June 1930

Went to see —— the money-lender. He is sticky and will not reduce beneath 60 per cent.

Wednesday, 2 July 1930

Nancy Mitford has just sold her book and is said to have received the highest price ever for a first novel.[3]

Wednesday, 23 July 1930

Dined at Stornoway: Winston, Lady Beatrice Pole-Carew, her daughter, Harold and myself to dinner. Beaverbrook in good form, ragging Winston, who said: 'Give me a big navy, and I'll swallow your food-taxes.' After dinner a private cinema show to which came Perry Brownlow, Lionel Beaumont-Thomas, Bertie Cayzer,[4] and Paddy Hannon. Sat up till 2 a.m. in the most boring conversation I have ever listened to. Harold Nicolson agreed that it was soul-killing and that he would die rather than do my job. Beaverbrook praised Wells's new book very much: *The Autocracy of Mr Parham*.

[1] Rosslyn was presiding at a dinner at Horsham cricket week, and his interrupted grace was prompted by the presence of a cricketing parson.

[2] A 'non-political' party with 1500 guests in honour of the Empire Press delegates.

[3] *Highland Fling*, published by Thornton Butterworth in 1931.

[4] Peregrine, 6th Baron Brownlow (*b.* 1899), close friend of the Prince of Wales, later to be Parliamentary Private Secretary to Beaverbrook in the Ministry of Aircraft Production; Lionel Beaumont-Thomas (1893–1942) and Sir Herbert Cayzer (1881–1958) were Conservative M.P.s.

Friday, 25 July 1930

This has been an expensive week. Telegram from Jean wanting more money. My debts hang round my neck like a millstone, and I am so tired that I can hardly struggle against them. Max makes no effort to understand his staff. He is kind in his way, but so self-centred that he can appreciate none of the finer feelings in others. His one method is to drive – drive – drive, and in the end the willing horse goes to the slaughter-house.

Saturday, 2 August 1930

Twenty employees of *Evening Standard* given notice. The poor fellows will have an almost impossible chance of finding new jobs with the present unemployment in Fleet Street. Long talk with Gilliat who is alarmed about his own position and talks of resigning. Saw Blum at the *Sunday Express*. He is disgruntled, because Max never consults him about the political situation.

Sunday, 3 August 1930

I am out of favour with Beaverbrook at present: probably on account of my debts, which are now becoming a menace as well as a worry. I have sent in my accounts to Millar.[1]

Tuesday, 5 August 1930

The economic campaign in the *Standard* continues. Everyone is in a state of nervous tension, and both Wilson and Gilliat are cracking under the strain. Gilliat is too immersed in detail to be a great editor. He wilts, too, in a crisis.

Shanks is, like me, in financial trouble and wants a loan of £400 from Beaverbrook.

Thursday, 7 August 1930

Eric Ednam is now upset about the Rosicrucian curse. When he and Rosie were in Egypt last year, Eric had a row at Luxor with the Rosicrucian Society who were holding a celebration. They were angry with him. Rosie made a great after-dinner story out of it. Then Jeremy was killed in the street at Cheyne Walk. Eric got paratyphoid – Rosie was killed in the air disaster. Now Eric has had to get off at Cherbourg on his way to Canada because Billie has a temperature of 102. Even he is beginning to feel queer about the curse. The King's first question to Millie was: 'What about this curse?' Not very tactful.[2]

[1] A. G. Millar, Beaverbrook's assistant and later head of his private office.

[2] Lord Ednam's second son, John Jeremy, died in December 1929 at the age of seven. His wife, Rosemary, died when a small airliner crashed at Meopham on 21 July 1930, killing six people including the Marquess of Dufferin and Ava. Billie was his elder son, then aged ten; and Millie his mother-in-law, Millicent Duchess of Sutherland.

Sunday, 10 August 1930

Furneaux [later second Earl of Birkenhead] struck me as a nice boy – self-possessed, dignified, modest and intelligent. He is very down on young Randolph Churchill and thinks he will do no good. Winston was always a worker. Randolph does not know what work means. Came up from Cherkley after dinner.

At a by-election in Bromley in August, Rothermere, formerly in alliance with Beaverbrook, put up his own free trade candidate. Rothermere had never accepted the pledge of a referendum on food-taxes to which Beaverbrook had agreed with Baldwin (mainly through their go-between Neville Chamberlain, later Chancellor of the Exchequer and Prime Minister). Rothermere's aims extended to a general political campaign; Beaverbrook's aims were confined to taxes on foreign trade and Empire Free Trade.

Meanwhile Beaverbrook took Lockhart and others for a Channel cruise on his steam yacht, the Medusa. *Beaverbrook was distressed at the near-break of his relations with Baldwin. On 31 August Lockhart 'made a mistake'; he left the yacht and went to London for his birthday. Meanwhile Beaverbrook was suffering from paratyphoid which in turn caused irritable depression.*

Wednesday, 10 September 1930

Max still sour with all of us including Robertson – but, most of all, with Jean Norton, Mike and me. 'I thought I had two friends I could rely on – Jean and you. I expected nothing from Mike, but you two let me down.' He went to Cherkley today.

Monday, 15 September 1930

Came up from Cherkley by the nine-thirty. Max more friendly this morning and gave me some stuff for the diary.

'Object of biography is to fortify self-confidence,' said Asquith; 'object of obituary notices is to increase caution.' German Election results: large victories for Hitler who has increased his representation from twelve seats to 105.

English Press full of ridiculous stories, etc., etc., of Hitler (who is 41): how he fought in Boer War.

Thursday, 25 September 1930

Dined tonight at Stornoway. Tom Mosley there. He and Max discussed the growth of feeling against Parliamentary government in this country. Tom says Parliament must be reformed, but neither he nor Max was in favour of Fascist methods. General opinion was that so far feeling is against the professional politicians, but not against Parliamentary traditions.

Friday, 26 September 1930

Tommy showed me some amazing correspondence between Mary[1] and

[1] Tommy's daughter, then only 18.

Ramsay MacDonald. Mary met him at the Londonderrys' at Choire and started a correspondence. Ramsay's letters were very long – full of the trials of a prime minister. Letters reveal his vanity and his snobbishness – one says 'his [the P.M.'s] real address is 10 Downing Street'. He used the above (Chequers) for weekends in order to prevent the Labour Party from driving him into a lunatic asylum. Tommy says Millie is still very distressed over Rosie's death: almost suicidal – takes sleeping drugs, etc. Millie thinks Eric will marry Bridget.[1] This year's Northern Hospital Ball will be used to dedicate Rosemary Ednam ward.

Saturday, 27 September 1930

Hamish came back. He has been staying with Lord Shaftesbury at Abergeldie and went to the ghillie's ball at Balmoral. Queen [Mary] danced all the dances including the Paul Jones and the Flirtation Polka (in which anyone changes partners). She was encased in iron stays and dances very badly. Hamish danced with her. She said: 'They hoped to have another little hop next week.' King said to Hamish: 'I have not seen your father since we were at the opening of the Forth Bridge [in 1890].' He [Lord Rosslyn] had quarter-of-a-million then and £25,000 a year. Things are different.

Friday, 3 October 1930

Sir Herbert Lidiard, the Conservative candidate [at the forthcoming South Paddington by-election], is to hold another meeting of the association on Monday: rather looks as if he were going to rat again. Wrote him a letter for Max tonight putting the case to him very plainly. He has three possible courses (1) he can rat on Empire Free Trade and knuckle under to Central Office. He must be the complete coward and a figure of fun to do this. (2) He can withdraw from the contest altogether, in which case we shall probably capture the association, and (3) he can stand by his declaration and ask the association to re-endorse his candidature. This last would be the honest course and the bold course. I imagine he will try to ride two horses and compromise. I understand the majority of the local association is with us.

Max very interesting on Birkenhead.[2] Says he hated him at first for his faults, but in the end he liked him best because of his faults. The man had talent in profusion, but he never had any character. He was not even loyal to his friends. While they were his friends, he stood up for them, it is true, but his quarrels were frequent, and London was strewn with the fragments of his broken friendships. He died in the arms of his best friend, Redmond McGrath, but he was a recent friend and about twentieth on the long roll of Birkenhead's friends.

Saturday, 4 October 1930

Lunched with Moura at the Savoy. She leaves today for Genoa and then

[1] Ednam did not remarry till 1943.

[2] Who had just died on 30 September.

Berlin, where her address is Koburgerstrasse 1, Berlin-Schoeneberg. Discussed Arnold Bennett's new book *The Imperial Palace*. H. G. Wells agrees with Max that it is rotten. Moura says Arnold Bennett is bored with Dorothy Cheston, his actress-wife . . . and has lost his inspiration since she made him give up wearing shirts with myosotis flowers on them!

Discussed Gorky: now . . . poor, has given all his money away, makes about £300 a year, cannot get foreign currency from Russia now, sells 2,700,000 copies a year . . . Gorky is too emotional to be a critic. Famous supper party in New York before the war – Wells, Mark Twain present. Gorky asked his opinion about English writers – not much, but Hall Caine was great.

Max was very eloquent tonight on Presbyterianism: cursed me for being a Catholic and denying John Knox. Gave us a series of vivid pen-pictures of Chalmers, the Free Church leader, William Henry Drummond, the orator, who was offered a Glasgow seat as a Liberal but refused (Gladstone, Balfour and Curzon were all admirers of his evangelism), Smith, the brilliant Aberdeen professor – who died at 27. (Drummond died in the forties). Faithful Boy who prosecuted him for heresy – 410 ministers walked out of their manses and churches in the Free Church revolt which was a movement for democratic control and no state interference. Seems trivial today, but the conviction of the men and their readiness to suffer for their beliefs were immense.

Sunday, 5 October 1930

Thomas Chalmers, the Free Church preacher and orator, was born in my native village of Anstruther. Smith, apparently did not die at twenty-seven, but at forty-seven. There seems to be some confusion which Smith Max means.[1]

Terrible disaster to the [airship] R.101. She crashed in the gale at Beauvais near Paris and burst into flames. Only eight saved out of fifty-five. Lord Thomson [Secretary of State for Air], Sefton Brancker [Air Vice-Marshal, Director of Civil Aviation] and Major Scott, the man who flew R.34 to America in 1919, among the killed. The *Sunday Express* people sat up all night and remained on duty all day Sunday producing extra special editions.

L.G. and Macquisten[2] to luncheon. Had some talk with Macquisten before luncheon. He showed me some very fierce anti-Baldwin letters from his constituents in Argyllshire and a typical Baldwin chairman of association reply from Sir Ian Malcolm to whom he sent them. Macquisten and L.G. addressed each other in Gaelic or rather Celtic, as L.G speaks Welsh and

[1] Smith was William Robertson Smith (1846–94) and Chalmers was Thomas Chalmers (1780–1847), founder of the Free Church. But there does seem to be some confusion about Drummond.

[2] Frederick Alexander Macquisten (1870–1940), K.C., Conservative M.P. for Argyllshire.

Macquisten Gaelic. L.G., however, is perfectly at home in Welsh, while Macquisten's Gaelic is very sketchy. Although they disagree on almost every subject, they are good friends. They went abroad together – or rather met on the same ship on a trip to South America two or three years ago. L.G. was very nice to Macquisten, took him with him everywhere to his official shows, and said we are two Britons who at home disagree on every subject but who abroad stand shoulder to shoulder. In return Macquisten taught L.G. how to swim. L.G. said he was in no hurry to put Labour out in order to put Baldwin in!

I had a few minutes alone with L.G. during which he discussed Harold Nicolson's *Lord Carnock* in connection with Grey.[1] L.G., who is very bitter with Grey, said Grey's hesitations, concealments and vacillations were responsible for the war. He showed the same indecision during the Agadir incident when (according to L.G.) it was L.G. who persuaded the cabinet to take a firm line. If Grey had shown firmness and decision, if he had explained the position boldly to the cabinet at the very beginning, there would have been no war. L.G. has done nothing on his memoirs yet, has made no progress at all. He is looking for an intelligent young man to devil for him. He will have to hurry up or he will be too late. He has aged a lot this last year.

Tim Healy[2] to dinner. He is getting infirm and rather feeble on his feet, but he was in great form, did full justice to the liquor, had been to the dinner at Buckingham Palace to the Imperial Conference delegates, and was full of the glories of British royalty and of the British Empire. He told stories until far on into the night. Tim says Irish delegation, who are raising question of their status at the Imperial Conference, are not really interested in the question at all and are not in the least desirous of leaving the British Empire. Whole business is a question of internal politics and is intended to do De Valera down. At last week's Dublin municipal elections (Dublin has been also made into a Greater Dublin) De Valera put up a candidate in each of the thirty-five wards. He won only five. Hero of these elections from point of view of Congress Party was Mr Batt O'Connor, the friend of Michael Collins[3] and today one of the most honoured and trusted men in the country. Batt O'Connor was a bricklayer, laid too many bricks and was chivvied out by the trade unions. Went to America, saved some money and came back to Ireland and set up as a builder. Owns considerable property in Dublin and is one of the party organisers. Michael Collins was his god. His building came in useful. He was able to build houses with secret passages to enable Michael Collins to escape or hide.

[1] Viscount Grey of Fallodon (1862–1937) was Foreign Secretary in the Asquith Government, 1905–16; Lord Carnock, Nicolson's father, was Permanent Under-Secretary of Foreign Affairs, 1910–16.

[2] Timothy Michael Healy (1855–1931), Irish M.P., Governor-General of the Irish Free State, 1922–8.

[3] Irish revolutionary leader (1890–1922), largely responsible for treaty with Britain of 1921.

Tuesday, 7 October 1930

Harold Nicolson lunched at Chequers on Sunday. Ishbel MacDonald [Prime Minister MacDonald's daughter] told him that the night before Bennett, the Canadian Prime Minister, had dined there. Seven guests were present, and Bennett said: 'Well, that's a lucky number.' Ramsey MacDonald then replied: 'I don't know. Tomorrow is October 6th which is the Labour Party's unlucky day.' Three or four hours later R.101 had crashed at Beauvais with Thomson, his dearest friend on board. Harold says Ramsay MacDonald is breaking up rapidly. He does not think he will last long.

Edward Marjoribanks[1] to dinner at Cherkley. Max decides to do a leader attacking Baldwin's leadership. Marjoribanks told me afterwards he was against it. He says Neville Chamberlain and Hailsham[2] are all for the scheme of Empire Free Trade, but they are now angry with Max for his tactics.

Marjoribanks's life of Marshall Hall[3] sold 30,000 copies in America, 12,000 in England. Gross profits without counting cheap edition: £5000. Serial rights: £3000 England, £3500 America. Marjoribanks gave half his receipts to Lady Marshall Hall and to the clubs.

Discussed barristers. Nobody today makes as much as Simon[4] and Hogg did just after the war, when they were supposed to be making £50,000 to £80,000. Today Jowitt and Birkett may have the making of £30,000. Most promising young barrister is Frederick Van Den Berg, a South African, who came over here without a penny and now makes £10,000 a year at commercial bar: first-class brain. Pupil of Theo Mathew. Got his start by Mathew handing Ford, a rich professional litigant, over to him. Ford gave him six really big cases including the famous case of Ford *v.* the Attorney-General on the Riot Damages Act. After the war some soldiers jollifying set fire to a haystack in Ford's field at Basingstoke. Ford sued the crown for immense damages! One day Van Den Berg received a summons to come to Ford's rooms. Ford apologised and said: 'I've just had a very serious operation. Doctor has been very negligent. We must bring an action.' He died before he could bring the action. Van Den Berg stood for Parliament at the last election. Fearnley-Whittingstall . . . is also a promising young barrister.

Compare Van Den Berg with Douglas Hogg whose father took him away from Eton at the age of eighteen and sent him to his sugar estates in the West Indies for two years. Hogg – son of Quintin Hogg – good footballer – captain of the Oppidans. Came back for South African war – had great difficulty in getting accepted on account of his eyesight. In 1901, at age of thirty, decided to go to bar. Did brilliantly. His knowledge of sugar stood him in

[1] Edward Marjoribanks (1900–32), Conservative M.P. for Eastbourne, 1929–32, one of the most brilliant young men of his generation, wrote a biography of Carson, as well as of Marshall Hall; he was cousin and heir-presumptive to 3rd Baron Tweedmouth.

[2] Douglas Hogg, 1st Viscount Hailsham (1872–1950), Conservative Lord Chancellor, 1928–9 and in 1938.

[3] Sir Edward Marshall Hall (1858–1927), a powerful advocate and M.P., 1900–6, 1910–1916.

[4] Sir John Simon (1873–1954), later 1st Viscount, lawyer and politician.

good stead. In a few years he was making £15,000 a year as a junior at commercial bar. One of the only two barristers who were given silk during the war.

Friday, 10 October 1930

Valentine returned from U.S.A. full of stories of American corruption, inebriety and immorality. He says he did not meet a single man or woman whom he would care to see again. Lunched with him at Savoy. He was not so amusing as usual. Told us a story of a columnist called [Walter] Winchell who gets over $200,000 a year for writing. At present moment the popular song in New York is 'I'm dancing with tears in my eyes' – Winchell and Valentine were at the Casino (the New York Embassy) and saw a very short man dancing with a tall woman. 'That fellow ought to alter the song', said Winchell. 'He ought to sing "I'm dancing with tits in my eyes!"'

Baldwin accepts Bennett's proposal in principle, knowing quite well that Bennett's thing is almost exactly what Max means by Empire Free Trade with the Dominions, Baldwin goes out of his way to damn Empire Free Trade. It is not clear, however, that he will accept food-taxes. Indeed, it seems almost certain that he will not and that he will advocate the quota. He is a pretty cunning, not to say, slippery customer – Mr honest Stanley Baldwin!

This has been a very trying time for me. Max as difficult as a sick child. Money worries all round me. Overworked. No time for rest or reflection. Ruined health and a complete lack of ambition and power to work – perpetual headaches and perpetual tiredness – mainly the result of perpetual indulgence which in itself is the result of perpetual boredom.

Came down to Coolham for twenty-four hours. Unfortunately, Lord Queenborough,[1] and Harry here: result more boredom, more drink, bridge ad nauseam, and more bad health!

Sunday, 12 October 1930

Went to Mass today. During the sermon learnt the Lord's prayer in Latin: 'Pater noster, qui es in caelis. Sanctificetur nomen tuum. Adveniat regnum tuum. Fiat voluntas tua, sicut in caelo, et in terra. Panem nostrum quotidianum da nobis hodie. Et dimitte nobis debita nostra, sicut et nos dimittimus debitoribus nostris et ne nos inducat in tentationem; sed libera nos a malo.'

'Be ye not drunk with wine, wherein is luxury, but be ye filled with the holy Spirit . . . for if ye live according to the flesh, ye shall die, but if by the spirit ye shall mortify the deeds of the flesh, ye shall live.'

My weekend was not a success. At Coolham I had to play bridge all the time. Harry and Lord Queenborough were excessively boring, and I had much too much to eat and much too much to drink – a folly which I repeated on arriving at Cherkley on this Sunday evening.

Max had had a very busy day: Ferguson, the Ottawa Prime Minister,

[1] Lord Queenborough (1861–1949), Conservative Provincial Parliamentary Whip.

Tom Mosley, Amery (who thinks Baldwin will accept food-taxes), Pat Hannon, Admiral Taylor[1] and Elibank all here. He looks tired and, if he is not careful, will break down altogether.

Monday, 13 October 1930

Spent the morning writing a letter for Max to Howard Ferguson, the Ottawa Prime Minister, in connection with the Bennett incident. The object of the letter is to persuade Bennett to undo the effect of his 'Empire Free Trade is neither desirable nor acceptable' speech. The whole story is a mystery which is not to be explained by Bennett's pique at Max's flirtations with Mackenzie King[2] over the Dunning Budget at the time of the Canadian elections. On Max's own admission he and Bennett have been friends for forty years. Bennett owes a large part of his fortune to his collaboration with Max, and hitherto, every time Bennett has come to London Max has put his car at his disposal and made much of him.

Now at this critical moment in the E.F.T. campaign Max ignores Bennett and Bennett goes out of his way to damage Max by declaring that E.F.T. is no good to Canada although he knows that Max's conception of E.F.T. for Canada – i.e. a limited partnership – is the same thing as his own plan. There must be something more – something personal – behind all this. Max had rather a ridiculous 'Blast' (taken from Knox's *First Blast v. the original wickedness of women*) in the *Express* today. Language very undignified. In the evening Max depressed and silent. Questioned Mike for some time about the supplies of pulp and mechanical pulp. Mike in a difficult position as he has to shield Robertson who has concealed from the Chief that he has bought nearly all the papers' requirements for next year. Max thinks we have bought nothing.

Saturday, 18 October 1930

Marjoribanks had been for a walk that afternoon with Baldwin – latter talked of Max, said he had much of the feminine in his character, was not unfriendly, but said that Max had spoilt his chances by linking himself with Rothermere. Marjoribanks told us a good story about the famous Lord Tweedmouth. Latter had been a great old rip. . . He made a funeral oration on Sir Henry Campbell-Bannerman[3] in the House of Lords and praised him for his fidelity to his wife 'which was all the more remarkable as she was not a woman of any particular attraction' (v. *Hansard*), What he really said *sotto voce* was: 'who was an ugly old bitch'.

Sunday was a typical Cherkley Sunday – work and looking after Max's guests. My job is that of a menial who has no soul of his own.

[1] Vice-Admiral A. E. Taylor, who had been adopted by the local South Paddington Conservative Association, when Liddiard refused to be disloyal to Baldwin.

[2] W. L. Mackenzie King (1874–1950) was the Canadian Liberal leader, who had lost the election to R. D. Bennett's Conservatives in August. He was Prime Minister 1921–30, 1935–48.

[3] Tweedmouth (1849–1909) was First Lord of the Admiralty, 1905–8, Lord President of the Council, 1908. Sir Henry Campbell-Bannerman, Liberal Prime Minister, 1905–8, died in 1908.

Wednesday, 22 October 1930

Stayed down at Cherkley till twelve-thirty writing a new draft of Max's reply. He intends to answer not by letter but by a speech on the platform on Thursday evening. He is now all out for a blunt refusal. He even suggests a two-line answer: 'Dear Mr Baldwin, Stop this fooling: give us duties on foreign foodstuffs – or fight.'

Shanks and I lunch at Stornoway. After luncheon Shanks writes four more drafts. Mine are more conciliatory, but Max inclines for Shanks. At three-thirty Winston arrives, stays an hour-and-a-half, reads all the drafts and plumps for Shanks's most brusque one. Amazing performance. Here is Winston – an ex-colleague of Baldwin in the last Government and still a member of his Shadow Cabinet – advising Max how to counter Baldwin's letter. Shanks and I could spring a bombshell which would ruin Winston's and Max's career. In the evening L.G. came to dinner and gave similar advice to Max; told him he had Baldwin cornered and advised, 'No surrender'. Max says to me privately: 'This time we've got him on the spot!' Max suspects collusion between Baldwin and Bennett. The latter sent for Max this afternoon and tried to urge him to accept Baldwin's offer. Max refused.

Thursday, 23 October 1930

Max's big meeting at the Porchester Hall. Crowded hall, and Max in his very best and most exalted form. He spoke for over an hour and then answered questions for over half-an-hour. He carried the whole meeting with him. Very good at answering questions including such rude ones as: do you think you as a journalist have the right to criticise Baldwin a politician? Max gave a lightning account of his political career, his work as a minister, etc., etc., and wound up by saying, 'You call that being a journalist.' Back to Stornoway afterwards.

Tuesday, 28 October 1930

Wrote a parody of Lovelace's 'Going to the Wars' lampooning Mond.[1]

Tell me not, Max, I am unkind
If from the wizardry
Of your all-too-persuasive mind
To Baldwin's arms I flee.

Though my third mistress now I chase,
To no false shame I yield.
Just see how well I state my case
When pen-and-ink I wield.

[1] Alfred Mond, 1st Baron Melchett (1868–1930), had begun by supporting Empire Free Trade, but then urged Beaverbrook to make peace with Baldwin and accept quotas instead of food taxes.

For my inconstancy is such
As sets by profit store.
I never care for honour much
When ratting pays me more.

Thursday, 30 October 1930

Lunched at Stornoway where I met Brendan Bracken[1] who talked the whole time against Baldwin: said Baldwin was the astutest, cunningest tactician Conservatives had ever had, and the Press would never beat him. Said Baldwin had complained to him: What would Disraeli have been able to do with men like Beaverbrook and Rothermere? Max at once replied: 'Squared it.'

Saturday, 1 November 1930

In evening came down to Cherkley: the Dunns, Hore-Belisha, Mike and Janet here.[2] We sat very long at dinner. Max very good in conversation or rather in monologue... He was annoyed with me for supporting Hore-Belisha's contention that the two rivers of Damascus were Atana and Pharpar and not Phorpar. Also contradicted me about Pitt's age. All very characteristic of his desire to show off. But he was very good as raconteur. Told us how Gladstone had sent Tim Healy to square Crawford who was citing Dilke as co-respondent in his wife's divorce case.[3] Crawford wanted a high court judgeship. Healy was shocked and for two days said nothing to Gladstone. When latter heard, he was prepared to give it. Healy was sent off post-haste to Monte Carlo, but it was too late. Crawford had already sent the papers in.

Thursday, 6 November 1930

He [Beaverbrook] also told good story of L.G. coming back late at night from Criccieth. L.G.'s car broke down outside Horton Asylum. Knocked up porter. 'Who are you?' 'Oh, I'm the Prime Minister.' 'Come inside. We've seven here already.'

After dinner went to Taglioni where we had the gypsy band in private room. Champagne like water. The usual performance. I sang Russian songs, stood on champagne bottles, and paid £30 for my vanity and folly.

[1] The first reference in these diaries to Brendan Bracken (1901–58), later Viscount Bracken, who was to play a large part in Lockhart's life, particularly during the Second World War. He was at this time M.P. for North Paddington, a financier and newspaper proprietor, an intimate and supporter of Churchill.

[2] Leslie, later Lord, Hore-Belisha (*d.* 1957) was Liberal National M.P. for Devonport, 1923–42 (Independent 1942–5), a barrister and journalist, Secretary of State for War, 1937–40. He and Lockhart were right about Pharpar. The Dunns were Sir James Dunn (1875–1956), Canadian steel magnate and business associate of Beaverbrook, and his second wife Irene. Janet was Beaverbrook's daughter.

[3] Sir Charles Dilke (1843–1911) might have been Gladstone's successor but for the scandal of his divorce case involving the wife of Donald Crawford, a Scottish lawyer.

Friday, 7 November 1930

Pam's mother has discovered everything. Tommy likewise, and my life is hell without escape.

Wednesday, 12 November 1930

Retired to bed with a pain in my stomach and a feeling of complete collapse. Probably the result of weeks of this idiotic life with Max: no exercise, no fresh air, no relaxation, no intercourse with my own friends – and on the other side of the balance too late hours, too little sleep, too much food and too much drink.

Spent the whole day in bed in a state of mild coma. Slept a little and dozed most of the day. Read Fr. Rolfe's *Hadrian VII*. It is a story of an Englishman who, after years of persecution by his brother Catholics, becomes Pope. His election is due to the fact that the Cardinals cannot agree. The description of a Papal election is excellent. (A two-thirds vote is required, and many ballots are necessary.) Pope introduces many reforms. In the end he is assassinated by an English Lib.-Lab.

Pam came to see me. Otherwise no news from outer world. My 'tummy' is very upset, and I blow up like a balloon as soon as I try to eat anything. I have a recurrence of the rheumatic pain in the back of my neck.

No cigarettes – no alcohol.

Pam tells me her father saw Lord Wolmer[1] today. Latter said Max had tried to effect an understanding with Baldwin but 'Thank God Stanley had turned him down.'

Thursday, 13 November 1930

In bed all day. Birley,[2] who treated me six years ago, came to overhaul me. He is shocked at my appearance; says if I go on like this I shall not live three years. He wants to write to Max about me. He thinks that my troubles – apart from the unhealthy life I lead with Max – are due to the fact that I am unhappy in my work. He suggests a holiday before I try a fresh start. Very good advice but incapable of fulfilment. Here am I with £10,000 worth of debts. Income-tax people on my door. Freeman pressing for his money. Complications with Pam, Tommy and Jean. A sick wife and child. No wonder my nerves are shattered. However, a fresh start must be made – and it can only be done with iron discipline.

Tuesday, 18 November 1930

First day back at work. Lunched with Pam and had a stupid quarrel with her. Her temper is ungovernable. In the afternoon went over to the *Express*

[1] Viscount Wolmer (*b.* 1887), Conservative M.P., 1910–40, held various ministerial posts, succeeded as 3rd Earl of Selborne in 1942.

[2] Dr James Leatham Birley (1884–1934), consultant physician St Thomas's Hospital, and director of Neurological Department.

and saw Baxter and Mike. Gave Beaverbrook the story of Dina Erroll's wedding.[1] Mike gave me an amusing account of his weekend at Cherkley. Max, Miss Macer-Wright and he went out riding. Mike was told to keep his horse away from Max. Unfortunately, Miss Macer-Wright also lagged behind, and both she and Mike lost contact with Max. Half-an-hour later Mike came up with Max at the bottom of a valley. He was livid with rage and was declaiming to Janet: Damn the fellow, blast the fellow, I cannot see what these women see in him! etc., etc. Mike had not even spoken to the girl!

Friday, 21 November 1930

Harold Nicolson wants to leave Fleet Street. He would like to do his literary article in the *Daily Express* but would like to abandon the Diary. What my own position will be I do not know.

Dina is to be married tomorrow. Donald made a good remark yesterday: 'On Saturday,' he said, 'I go fourth to meet the bride.'

Saturday, 22 November 1930

Winston's remarks to Harold on Max. Harold had a long talk with Winston on Wednesday night. They discussed Max. Winston thinks he is a neurotic; said it was a thousand pities that, when there are so many second-rate people in politics, this man, who with his wonderful dynamic force, his boundless vitality and energy could do so much for the country in its hour of need, was spending all his strength in disruptive enterprises merely out of vanity or boredom.

Wednesday, 3 December 1930

My dinner at Angela [Forbes]'s . . . was not so bad. I talked mostly with Jack and Gwen Churchill. Former is Winston's brother. Latter was with Admiral and Lady Beatty in Russia in July 1914. She told me about Ralph Seymour's death – suicide at Beachy Head. It was Lady Beatty who would not let him marry her niece. As she herself married Beatty – a man with less money and less family name, her attitude was a little extraordinary. Jack Churchill says it is impossible to win a seat in the North or in Scotland on food-taxes, that Winston likes Max, but resents the way in which, through his power in the Press, he digs his friends in the back. It is extraordinary how many people regard newspaper proprietors as megalomaniacs.

Thursday, 4 December 1930

MacDonald announces that an Electoral Reform Bill will be introduced before Christmas. This is the concrete evidence of the pact, which we have been announcing in the *Evening Standard*, between Liberals and Labour.

[1] Idina, divorced wife of the 22nd Earl of Erroll and sister of Buck De La Warr, was to marry her fourth husband, Donald Haldeman, in four days' time.

The *Evening Standard* gets a scoop on the announcement of the Mosley manifesto demanding (1) a Council of Five instead of a Cabinet with power to carry through an emergency policy, (2) a national planning organisation for development of new industries, (3) import control board for foodstuffs, (4) board for control of imported manufactures, (5) trade agreements with Dominions – insulation against foreigner, and (6) some postponement, until reconstruction, of war debt.

Saturday, 6 December 1930

Hugo – very fussy and punctilious – wanted to go to Edwin Montagu's funeral.[1] Came down from Scotland. Everything in order – Clothes immaculate. No top-hat. Thought: well no matter. I can take my bowler. No one will notice once I'm in the church. Arrived at synagogue. Crowded with ministers, all sorts of 'smart people' – all in top-hats, which of course had to be kept on during the Jewish service. And in the middle of this sea of toppers poor old Hugo's bowler was very conspicuous.

Hugo as a young man (as an old one too) was very passionate: loved the former Duchess of Leinster. When she married the old Duke, Hugo made a wax effigy of him and stuck a pin into him every day. The Duke died very soon, but as the Duchess died within a year of him Hugo had no chance of trying to marry her.

Monday, 8 December 1930

Came up from Cherkley by the 9.45. Max very excited this morning. Got on to me on the telephone at about 12.20. 'Take this down for your diary,' and off he went on the new Electoral Reform Bill which is to be introduced before Christmas and which will contain a clause restricting the use of motor-cars at the polls to the physically disabled. I could not understand at first – could not hear very well, and said so. 'God damn, don't you understand?' 'No,' I said. 'Well, goodbye to you,' and down went the telephone in a rage. Ten minutes later he came on again, and, although he made no apology, he was as gentle as a ring-dove. He told me his negotiations with Neville Chamberlain have broken down.

Tuesday, 9 December 1930

Tonight I was at Stornoway from 8 to 8.45. We discussed the *Standard* and the book supplement. He [Beaverbrook] gave me an amplification of our book talk of yesterday. He knows now that I keep a diary and is rather shy[2] about it! He gave me an interesting comparison between Rothermere and Northcliffe. Northcliffe had more charm when he liked to use it, but Rothermere had far more heart – has far more heart than Northcliffe ever had. 'The trouble about Rothermere is that he's a shifty fellow,' he went on. 'I

[1] Hugo, 11th Earl of Wemyss (1857–1937). Edwin Montagu died in 1924.
[2] 'frightened' in the other version of the diary.

suppose,' I said, 'that's why you always go on stressing his constancy and his loyalty.' Then Max said: 'My God, you're going to put all this into your diary.' Which, indeed, is true, as here it is.

Wednesday, 10 December 1930

In the evening met Pam who was in a state of hysteria and tears. My weakness and my terrible fear of hurting anyone cause me to behave with a cruelty which is far worse than calculated cruelty.

Thursday, 11 December 1930

After my escapades of the last two nights was very ill this morning and had to stay in bed all day.

Pam came to see me. She is very unhappy and looks ill. She says she loves me and was looking forward to a 'suburban villa and suburban children', but it is all so hopeless. Harold said to me yesterday that I would never settle down until I had a home, but my liabilities hang round my neck like a halter, and Pam herself is the last person to be happy for long on a beggar's salary.

Sunday, 14 December 1930

Yesterday, Angela told me interesting story about Balfour and Baldwin's appointment as Prime Minister [in 1922]. Angela, Balfour, Hugo, Evan Charteris and various other guests were spending Whitsun at West Runton, Sheringham. Conversation was about successor to Bonar Law. Everyone attacked Curzon – impossible superior person, etc. Only man who defended him was Balfour. On the Sunday or the Saturday, Balfour was telegraphed for by the King. He went for a walk with Hugo in the garden, went over the Baldwin–Curzon argument again, Hugo arguing for Baldwin and Balfour for Curzon. Finally Balfour said, 'Well, I'm afraid it will have to be Baldwin,' and left that night for London to see the King first thing next morning. Lord Salisbury, who was also telegraphed for and who was for Curzon, did not come up till the Monday morning and Balfour was in first.

Monday, 15 December 1930

Last night Max told us some very witty stories of Castlerosse. On Saturday Castlerosse had been lunching with Jimmie Dunn and Disgusting John (Augustus John). They consumed (Dunn drinking nothing) a glass of sherry each, one bottle Rhine wine, four bottles champagne (beginning with Moët 1900 and finishing with a 'no vintage' wine!) and a bottle of brandy. Left Jimmie Dunn's both drunk about five! During this time Castlerosse was wanted at the *Sunday Express*, which he had left at twelve in order to take an important paper to the Aga Khan (it was the proof of his article about the ill-treatment of the Indian Princes by the Lord Mayor, Air Force, etc.). Gordon rang up Max at five and asked if he could help. Max told Gordon where Castlerosse was. Eventually, Castlerosse rang up Max to apologise, inventing some fabulous excuse that the Aga had told him to wait at Jimmie's until he telephoned! According to Jimmie the conversation after luncheon was marvellous, being about how great artists should treat ordinary mortals and Valentine saying to John: 'We artists this and we artists that.'

South Paddington meeting is tomorrow. The Central Office are putting up Hebert Williams. This will be the break, although Neville Chamberlain has written to Max saying that he hopes it will not ruin the neutrality.

Tuesday, 16 December 1930

Max's account of Valentine's marriage on Sunday was very amusing.[1] When Max broke the news to Lady Kenmare [Castlerosse's mother], she asked: 'Were they married in a church?' Max said: 'No.' 'Thank God,' said Lady Kenmare. Then, shortly afterwards, Max had to go to Ireland to buy yearlings. He meets Tim Healy and tells him the news. 'Is she a Catholic?' says Tim excitedly, 'Yes,' says Max. 'Thank God,' says Tim.

Later Max's advice is asked: Shall the wedding be announced or not? The parties discuss whether it should be kept quiet and a divorce arranged immediately or whether it should be announced publicly. Max advises a small notice in the *Express*. Then the other papers will not copy it. Discussion then takes place on form of announcement. Valentine wants 'a marriage was solemnised'. Lady Kenmare says 'solemnise' can only be used of a church ceremony. Valentine is sent off to get the dictionary and returns triumphantly to prove that he is right.

Valentine was once in love with ——'s daughter by his French wife (the chocolate king's daughter). The girl would have nothing to do with him. In despair Valentine tries to get at the daughter through the stepmother's influence . . . He does not soften the girl's heart, but he softens the mother's. Has a long liaison with her. 'Why did you break it off to marry [Doris]?' says Max. 'I didn't,' says Valentine. 'She did.' 'How was that?' says Max. 'Oh, I taught her French practices,' says Valentine, 'and once, while she was engaged in them, she looked up and found me reading the *Evening Standard*.'

Lunched with Harold at Boulestin's. He is red-hot that I should write my book telling the whole story – leaving Max if necessary to do it. He says I shall make £15,000 out of it. I could do it, but for all this burden of debt which is on my shoulders.

Dined with Pam at Sorrani's. She was miserable, and I was miserable. We ate nothing. I drank champagne. She drank *café diablé*. We went to Taglioni's and were bored with everything and everyone, because we wanted to be alone together. She said if only I would put my affairs in order, get my divorce, she would wait two years for me. And I, who ought to settle down, who ought to take decisions, who like her, but who am afraid of hurting

[1] It was Max's account, not the marriage, that was on Sunday. Castlerosse had married Doris de Lavigne in May 1928.

Jean and Tommy, know that it is all useless. After I had run her home, went out by myself to drink, finished up at the 43 where I met Peter. Home at 6.30 a.m. – a nervous and physical wreck.

Thursday, 18 December 1930

Went into nursing home today on Birley's advice – 61 Beaumont Street (Miss Karlin). Miss Karlin is a stout old lady who has had many patients on her hands: Northcliffe, Hatry, Albert de Courville.[1] She is impressed by the fact that money or rather the making of money does not bring happiness. Max used to come here to see Albert de Courville, who made one of the most amazing recoveries in history. Northcliffe had a thyroid operation here about a year before he died. He had two rooms: one for himself and one for secretary. Also had a pianist to play for him in the evening. After operation Miss Karlin found him in chair, out of bed, and exhausted. He had made his valet move him and felt very ill and wanted sympathy. Miss Karlin scolded him properly and to distract his attention asked if she could pick up the telegrams which strewed his bed – telegrams of congratulation from all over the world. She said: 'I don't see one from Lloyd George here.' 'No,' said Northcliffe angrily, 'he hasn't sent one, he hasn't sent one.' He used to be quite irritated if any day during his illness there was no message from the King to ask how he was. On Armistice Day he protested against Miss Karlin's hanging out banners. 'It is not a peace at all,' he said. He wanted to go on to Berlin, I suppose. When he left, he gave all the nurses, including Miss Karlin, rings which he insisted on presenting himself.

Friday, 19 December 1930

In his attitude [Benjamin Constant's, the nineteenth-century French novelist] to women I see a great resemblance to myself. At the present moment I am in love with Pam, cannot bear the thought of letting her go, need her physical companionship, and am torturing her and myself. At the same time I love and adore Tommy, could not hurt her for worlds, and know that in my present circumstances my liaison with Pam can bring nothing but harm to both of us. Like Benjamin Constant, *J'ai lutté pour l'indépendance toute ma vie, mais en vérité j'ai besoin de charmes.*

Again, *On n'est jamais ni tout à fait sincère, ni tout à fait de mauvaise foi.*

Miss Karlin says that most people are at their best in a nursing home – natural, generous and without frills.

Slept well last night. Today, Miss Karlin and Birley regaled me with more stories about Northcliffe. Miss Karlin said that, when Northcliff was having his operation here, a pale-faced secretary used to come to read to him. Secretary looked and indeed was very ill. One day he fainted on the stairs.

[1] Albert de Courville (1887–1960), theatrical and film producer, who started life as a journalist.

When he came to, his first request was: 'Please don't tell Northcliffe.' The poor devil was afraid of losing his job. Miss Karlin, who is no respecter of persons, tackled Northcliffe firmly. He was touched and sent the secretary away for a long holiday abroad.

Birley, who brought Northcliffe home from Evian in his last illness, had an exciting time. He was sent for by Lady Northcliffe, who was at Evian with Sir Robert Hudson.[1] When he arrived, no other doctor there. French doctor would not come near Northcliffe, who sat with a loaded revolver by his side, waiting for the Germans. He would not let Birley examine him. Birley, however, succeeded in humouring him a bit by pretending that he was an expert on digitalis poisoning. Northcliffe imagined he had been poisoned by the Germans. Birley was paid £500 for the job, which was dangerous both to him personally and also to Northcliffe, because there was a real risk of the French clapping him into an asylum. The hotel proprietor of the Royal was already complaining that he was losing clients through the *tapage*. The next day, Price, Northcliffe's home doctor, also arrived. Between them they managed to get Northcliffe into the train: (1) by putting morphia in his champagne; and (2) by humouring his desire to go to Versailles to make his will. (His will had to be made in Versailles!) At Calais Northcliffe made a great effort, dressed and walked unaided on to the boat receiving his salutes of the officials. Birley succeeded in stopping his telegrams from Evian. There was one to Wickham Steed which cost £70 and which was mainly about the necessity of his getting some new clothes, as his grey suit was too shabby for the Editor of *The Times*...

Northcliffe did *not* die of G.P.I., nor was death caused by insanity. He had had heart trouble for some time. There was a faulty valve, and that was the cause of death. He had also general poisoning which may or may not have been responsible for his insanity. But insane he was – according to Birley – raving mad with megalomania.

Sunday, 21 December 1930

Miss Karlin tells me that Hatry, who was a patient here, was another victim of megalomania. He talked not in thousands or hundreds of thousands but in millions. Letters from Tommy and Pam. Eric Ednam is going out with the Prince as A.D.C. He is taking Hugh Thomas, and Piers Legh joins them later.[2] Wrote a long poem.

Monday, 22 December 1930

Did not sleep very well. Birley came in to see me and had a long talk.

[1] Whom she married in April 1923, six months after Northcliffe's death. He died in 1927.

[2] The Prince of Wales set off for a tour of South America on 17 January 1931. Hugh Lloyd Thomas (1888–1938) went as Assistant Private Secretary, and Piers Legh (1890–1955) as Equerry.

He wants me to go away tomorrow to the country and to avoid Beaverbrook and the office. The main thing is to get my health back and my self-confidence. He also insists that I shall get out of my present quarters. With this I agree.

Left the home at four, did such Christmas shopping as I was able to do, spent a lot of money for nothing, and in the evening, in a dense fog went to the Vaudeville with Pam to see *The Breadwinner* – an amusing skit on the modern generation by Somerset Maugham. The first two acts are quite amusing. The last is too long and drags. Somerset Maugham must have made biggish money, and yet his plays are very slight.

Pam was tired and ill. She is disgruntled and unhappy, is heavily in debt, and at the same time is prepared to marry me or to be my mistress provided I give up Tommy and abandon Jean and Robin. And if I were to do it, not only should we be without a penny in a week, but she would be the first to say that the position was impossible. She blames me for lack of courage, for not making up my mind. And she is right. And yet we are both deceiving ourselves and each other. If I were to examine my own conscience and be absolutely honest with myself, I should say: I cannot abandon Jean and Robin, I have no intention of giving up Tommy and *my* friends. In my present circumstances – and, indeed, for ages to come – I cannot marry anyone. I ought to give Pam up. Yet she is fatally attractive to me. I see all her faults, her extravagance, her useless life and her still more useless and vulgar friends, but I do not want to give her up; I have grown used to her and at the same time I am infatuated by her. I therefore cling to her, strive to keep her, and encourage her to believe that I love her passionately – which is indeed true as far as the passion is concerned. It is more, too, than passion. I am full of pity for her, and I feel guilty and responsible. And yet what my conduct really amounts is that she should accept the position of being clandestinely my mistress.

She, on the other hand, says: give up Max – you must get away from him. Go bankrupt, tell Tommy you love me, and I'll stick to you, live with you, if you like, until you can marry me. Which may be honest and genuine, but is hardly practical. If I were to leave Max and go bankrupt, I should find it very hard to make £1000 a year. Pam would admit that I must give Jean and Robin £500 of that. Would she come to me on £500 a year? How long would it last with her habits and her nerves and my habits and my nerves? She says: Write your book and then you will have money. I shall wait for you, but do, do these things first. But would she wait and at the end of the waiting would she accept poverty? The whole outlook is almost hopeless – especially from her point of view. I may be doing her an injustice. Perhaps she means what she says. Probably she thinks she means what she says, which is not quite the same thing. As Fauconnier[1] says, 'Sometimes the English think that they are thinking.'

[1] Probably Henri Fauconnier, whose book on Malaya Lockhart admired.

He had a sympathetic letter from his Evening Standard *colleague, Harold Nicolson, dated 22 December 1930:*

I am terribly sorry to hear that you have broken down– but feel that it is probably a good thing. A real holiday will put you straight...

I was down at Cherkley on Saturday. A ghastly evening. Paul Cravath,[1] Kay Norton, and about six silent soccer blues from Cambridge. Beaverbrook was in good form as far as that goes – but the atmosphere is that of the waiting room to a mortuary. He fired questions at Cravath like a Napoleonic pea-shooter.

He came to my room afterwards and talked about you. He seemed really distressed. He spoke of you with the utmost affection and confidence – and quite agreed that you needed a real rest. He seemed perfectly human and sympathetic about it all and not a bit puckish.

Cheer up, get well, and write your book.

Friday, 26 December 1930

Raymond Oppenheimer and Nigel Seely came to luncheon. Oppenheimer, who is the old Oxford golfer, is the son of the great diamond merchant. His firm are the chief people in the big combine which controls the output. Things are very bad in the diamond trade at present. Almost nothing is sold, and the dealers are carrying something like £14,000,000 worth of stock. He was interesting about golf. The Yankees catch their golfers young, do not allow them to play until they have mastered the one swing and the one shot from right to left. In afternoon went shooting – killed a pheasant. In evening came up to London with Harry who went into a nursing home. Bed 2 a.m.

Saturday, 27 December 1930

Melchett died today... Melchett's death will be a big blow to Imperial Chemicals. I met him three or four times at Beaverbrook's – mostly at luncheon. In outward appearance he was a most unpleasant type ... – vain beyond words and with cruel hard lips and a singularly unpleasant manner of speaking. He was without exception the dirtiest feeder I have ever seen.

Tuesday, 30 December 1930

Discussed 'youth' with my mother-in-law at luncheon. She will not hear a word against youth. I agree in principle, but I pointed out that our English youth had not the same ambition, the same drive, or the same will to work as German and French or even Russian youth. The youth of these countries are maintaining their own civilisation; they are combatting the American civilisation; we are succumbing to it.

[1] American lawyer (1861–1940), member of Colonel House's mission in 1917.

CHAPTER EIGHT

1931

Switzerland. His wife's illness. Hilaire Belloc bitter about England. Beaverbrook and Lockhart's sex life. Harold Nicolson joins Mosley. End of Sidney Reilly, the spy. The Willingdons and India. Masaryk's divorce. East Islington and St George's – a very dirty campaign. Arnold Bennett dies. Kingsley Martin. King Alfonso abdicates. H. G. Wells's sales, and falsetto voice. Shaw on *St Joan*. Kipling's fortune. Hailsham and the leadership in the Lords. King Alfonso's 'best girls'. Castlerosse and the Baptists. Mosley and Hitlerism. At Churt with Lloyd George. Gandhi prays in the House of Commons. Churchill 'nearly always slightly the worse for drink'. Aga Khan on Tolstoy and Gandhi. The King and J. H. Thomas's 'guts'. Aneurin Bevan's drink and good living. Sultan of Johore's scandals. J. H. Thomas the biggest 'bluffer'. Losses on *Action*, the Mosley weekly. James Joyce's drunken bouts and obscenity.

Thursday, 1 January 1931

At the Hôtel du Parc, Château d'Oex [Switzerland], trying to recover my shattered health. My fifteenth day without alcohol. Began again my morning exercises. Indigestion and distention still present. Memory and mental exhaustion still bad. Nerves are better. Self-control better.

Here the New Year began badly with a thaw which has destroyed nearly all the snow, made winter sports impossible, and taken away all the exhilaration from the mountain air. Celebrated the day by beginning my book. Wrote 750 words and after the first paragraph did not find the work too difficult. If I keep up anything like this rate of progress, I shall be finished in six months. Otherwise, I spent a very quiet day with all too little fresh air and exercise. Jean still in bed.

Friday, 2 January 1931

Two letters from Tommy who says she will not be able to come to Juigné at the end of my stay here. This is bad news as Millie intends selling the house, and I may never see it again. No news from Pam since Tuesday. In the afternoon did some more writing. Sent off three paragraphs to the *Evening Standard*. Wrote 500 words of my book. I am dealing now with the Malayan episode in my life and do not find the writing easy. In the *Temps* there is an interesting article on Fascist literature pointing out that Fascism has so far produced no great writer. The best Fascist book is Mussolini's Diary, and that was written before the march to Rome. What I must get hold of is Mussolini's life of Huss. This is very critical of the Catholic Church and was written of course before the Vatican Treaty. The book has been called in and is now very valuable.

Read *The Apple Cart* again. It makes first-rate reading. What dishonest fools Swaffer[1] and the *Express* were to crab this play and to say that Shaw had lost his powers. Although all the evidence at present is to the contrary, I do not believe that dishonesty in journalism pays in the long run.

Saturday, 3 January 1931

Jean got up today for the first time. She is on the verge of a [nervous] breakdown. Robin, who has been making a snow fort and who has been lying in the wet snow in the process, has developed a cold. Last night at dinner we discussed my book. Jean asked me if I were going to put my 'Malay woman' into it. I said: 'Yes, the book was to be absolutely frank and personal or it would not be written at all.' Jean said nothing, but my mother-in-law was shocked. 'How could you think of such a thing when your own son will read the book one day?' I pointed out that, if this consideration were to prevail with every author, many of the world's best books would never have been written. It made little effect. I can see that I shall have great trouble if I write what is really a frank autobiography. There is rather an attractive woman here – a Mrs M., the wife of an officer in the R.F.C. He is in India. Began Constant's *Adolphe*.

Monday, 5 January 1931

In the evening we had the annual Fancy Dress Ball at our hotel – a dreadfully boring affair with a sit-down supper and the usual sequence of gregarious stupidities in which English middle-class colonies indulge. Jean insisted on sitting up, would not dance, and then was annoyed with me because I danced too much with Mrs M. She was annoyed not so much because she was jealous as because she was afraid the accursed English colony would gossip. She was almost rude to Mrs M. in that she took no notice of her. All so terribly stupid and boring – boring because I do not like hurting Jean, boring, because if I had stayed in the ball-room by Jean's side the whole evening I should have died of heat and nervous frustration or irritation, boring, because I was or am attracted by Mrs M. whom I find restful and – vainest of all male vanities – prepared to admire my futile self. Long letter from Tommy full of sound advice. No letter from Pam. Her letters have changed and certainly reveal little interest in me. I think she was piqued because she thought I had plaqué'd[2] her and her pride was hurt. I doubt if she will ever care much for anyone. It is time I was cured of this infatuation.

[1] Hannen Swaffer (1879–1962) was dramatic critic of the *Daily Express*, shortly to join the *Daily Herald*, and a somewhat sensational journalist.

[2] French for jilted.

Tuesday, 6 January 1931

Glorious weather. I was out in the fresh air all day and, in spite of last night, felt marvellously well. On a day like this Switzerland is certainly superb, and the scenery is enchanting. I had a scene with Jean in the afternoon. She is jealous of P.M., or rather she is jealous and depressed because she is out of things and thinks she is not wanted. . . Finished *Adolphe*: it is ultra-sentimental for these materialistic days, but the type of *Adolphe* – the man who cannot break with a woman, partly out of pity, and partly out of vanity – is common enough. The shoe indeed fits myself. The moral is that it is more cruel to the woman one pities not to break and to go on torturing her than to break once and for all. Letter from Moura. . . She writes cheerfully and kindly. She is a big-minded and a big-hearted woman. During the last three days work has suffered severely, and my total production since Saturday is one article on *Malaisie*.[1] Bed 10.30. Not much smoking: two or three pipes, a cigar and two cigarettes – one bottle beer. Did *no* exercises today. Had a skating lesson. If it had not thawed last night, I should have made considerable progress.

Thursday, 8 January 1931

On Tuesday night there was a Russian concert in the hotel or rather a concert by a Russian. The woman was quite good, but no one turned up. As she receives nothing from the hotel, but depends for her earnings on sending the hat round she could have made nothing. Met a young Georgian Prince – aged twenty-six. He was just going to the Corps des Pages when the revolution broke out. He was imprisoned, saw his uncles shot, went to Paris, graduated in law, and is now tubercular. He says this generation of Russians is dead. What is there for him to do or take an interest in. He has lost faith in everything. He does not believe in the émigrés and very little in the Russians. Says even today the Russian émigrés have learnt nothing from the revolution and are squabbling in Paris with the Georgians over the independence of Georgia within a federal Russia. Another lovely day with no work done. Wrote letters in the morning. Skated and 'luged' in the afternoon. At last am beginning to make some progress as a skater. . . Letter from Genia who is full of good advice about my book, says it should have been written five years ago as far as the interest in Russia is concerned (and for the delay I have to thank alcohol and the wasted years in Prague) but that if I can make it personal and dramatic it can still go well. I agree.

Saturday, 10 January 1931

Tommy writes that the cold in England is intense and that skating has begun. Also that Eleanor and Pamela Smith[2] were received into the Church

[1] Henri Fauconnier's book, published in English later in the year as *The Soul of Malaya*.
[2] Daughters of the 1st Earl of Birkenhead.

of Rome four days ago. Pam writes to say that the Freeman-Thomases[1] have invited me for next weekend. Much as I like him, I shall not go.

Then had a fearful and degrading row with Jean about P.M. which ended in my going up to the Grand at half-past eleven with P. We danced only twice (the band was useless) and then sat and talked till two. I find her restful and simple, and her healthy outlook and enthusiasm amuse me. I told her all my iniquities and painted myself in black colours, and then said half-jokingly that in six months' time she would admit (1) that she loved me, and (2) that she cursed the day she met me. Stranger jokes have happened. At present I feel attracted to her and have neglected my work for her. How far this hotel is responsible for the attraction I do not know. Certainly the atmosphere of this English colony here is enough to drive anyone insane.

Thursday, 15 January 1931

My last day at Château d'Oex. Was unable to do anything because of my cold which is very heavy and which now threatens to attack my right antrum. Lovely afternoon.

There is an old Indian Civil Service man here called Le Mesurier whose mother was Scottish. He remembers as a small boy asking if he might bring a boy friend home for the holidays. His mother asked what the boy's name was. On learning it was Campbell, she said 'No. Your grandfather is a Stewart of Appin. He will have no Campbell in his house.'

Left at 7.45 for England. Had to wait two hours at Montreux for my train, which, owing to impossibility of obtaining sleepers on the earlier trains, was the Simplon. Fortunately, it was punctual. Travelled second-class all the way. Slept fairly well in spite of my troublesome antrum.

Saturday, 17 January 1931

Tommy told me some fierce gossip about Lady Sybil Graham[2] and her Italian lover with whom she used to go to a house of assignation. The house was raided. She gave her name. Police refused to accept it and demanded identification. She was identified by her husband! Also some gambling scandals about the St James's Club and a man who cooked the washing-book[3] and an American who announced he could not pay. Valentine has been in trouble, too, with the Committee for hinting about the scandal in the Press. Wrote P.

Sunday, 18 January 1931

Mild and spring-like weather. Stayed in bed till twelve, when I dressed and foolishly went for a short walk with Tommy. Pam and Niggs flew over

[1] The Hon. Inigo 'Nigs' Freeman-Thomas (*b.* 1899), soon to become Viscount Ratendone and eventually 2nd Marquess of Willingdon, and his wife Mary 'Blossom'.

[2] Wife of Sir Ronald Graham (1870–1949), Ambassador to Italy, 1921–33. She died in 1934.

[3] The record of gambling debts.

in an airplane and kept us all waiting for luncheon. By tea-time my head was like a lump of lead, and my antrums were throbbing. Went to bed with temperature of over 100°. Tommy telephoned to Gilliat. Harry left by the 6.50 for London. Belloc came over to tea. He is not well, is suffering from insomnia and high blood-pressure. He has made £350 out of his *More Cautionary Tales*. He was bitter about his history, which is not going at all, and more bitter about the decline of this country: its lack of intelligence, its inability to work, its lack of morals. Said our standard of morals was the lowest in Europe. Blamed Low [the cartoonist] for going to the *Evening Standard* – a prostitution of his talent. There is a little sourness and envy in the old boy's criticism – he cannot forget that Jacques Bainville has sold 80,000 copies of his history in France, while he cannot sell 500 of his in England – but much of what he says is true. Especially when he says he has never felt so hopeless about England before. What is wrong with us is not so much our position as our attitude. Hilaire Belloc astounded me by saying that he can do 8000 words in a day and can finish a novel in a fortnight or three weeks. Perhaps that is why he does not sell well. Took 20 grains of aspirin. Slept well.

Monday, 19 January 1931

Tommy told me a good story of the King. There was a family dinner-party at Buck House. George R. turned to the Duke of York and said: 'Bertie, is David still in love with the lace-manufacturer's daughter?'[1] Since then, Fredd's friends call her: Miss Loom, the weaver's daughter (Happy Families).

Dr Bennett came – a waste of a guinea, but I suppose it was necessary in order to satisfy the sharks of Fleet Street.

Tuesday, 20 January 1931

Hamish, who left for London yesterday, has upset the whole family by failing to keep an important appointment with his father. A notice has also appeared in the *Daily Express* stating that Hamish is working his passage as a steward on the same ship as Harry, will have to serve his father with refreshment and call him 'My Lord'. Long talk with Tommy, who is still shattered by my behaviour about Pam. Her pride and her religion have been injured by the gossip about her two converts.

Still feel very muggy. My mind is a blank, and I have no desire and no capacity for work. The last two years of my life have been barren as far as production is concerned and stagnant, if indeed not retrogressive, as far as progress is concerned. What I must do now is to build up my mind and my memory again by self-control and by increased physical efficiency.

More trouble about my insurance policies from Baillie and Gifford. The matter of my debts will now have to be tackled very seriously. Long talk

[1] Freda Dudley Ward's father, Col. Charles Birkin (1865–1932), was a lace-manufacturer. The Prince of Wales was known as Daird to his family.

with Tommy about my wretched behaviour over Pam. The cause of all my failures is my inherent inability to deny myself anything.

Thursday, 22 January *1931*

Tommy, Harry and Mary left for the West Indies. Saw them off at Paddington for Avonmouth. Tommy looked very seedy. Drove back with Angela Forbes who wants to do some articles for the *Express*. She is very down on Hamish... Bought a wireless on the hire purchase system.

In the evening dined with Pam at the Wellington. She looked ghastly and has obviously been beating it up hard.

Antrums much better, but still feel very run down.

Friday, 23 January 1931

First day back at the office. Harold has been seeing Beaverbrook during my absence, and Gilliat, waiting as usual to see what my position with the chief is to be, is aloof and secretive. It is not a healthy atmosphere...

French Government resigns. Anna Pavlova dies at the age of 45. *New Statesman* and *Nation* agree to amalgamate. Another intellectual paper gone. How different from France! In the evening at half-past six went to see Max. He kept me waiting half-an-hour, as he was closeted with Doidge[1] and a prominent local inhabitant from East Islington. We are on the verge of war to the knife with Baldwin again and are to contest East Islington. When I finally was ushered into the room, Max indulged in his usual habit of reading the paper without taking any notice of me. Finally, after a little desultory talk about politics, he said 'Are you really better?' I answered 'Yes.' 'Well, then,' said Max, 'take a hint from me and cut some of your women out and cut them off the *Evening Standard* exchange.' Then followed accusations of ruining my health through women. I told him he was on the wrong tack and that he ought to see Birley. His answer of course was that he knew more about me than any doctor...

In the evening went with Pam, Nigs and Blossom to the Palace to see Cochran's Varieties – very good show with the four Marxes as the big turn. Had supper with Nigs afterwards at Kettner's. Blossom and he have strong Labour sympathies. They are going to fly to India next year to stay with Nigs's father who will be Viceroy then.

Saturday, 24 January 1931

Much colder. Went round to Max at nine, but had no satisfaction out of him. Harold, whom I suspect of having (probably quite innocently) told him of my telephone conversations, says that Max is conscience-stricken at having over-worked me and is therefore telling everyone in self-defence that I have ruined my health through sexual excesses! Pam left for Scotland.

[1] F. W. Doidge (1884–1954), New Zealand journalist, later High Commissioner for New Zealand, financial secretary of London Express Newspaper Co., then organiser of the Empire Crusade.

Lunched at the Wellington and spent the afternoon in my flat listening to the broadcast of the Franco-Scottish match on my wireless. Scotland won 6 (two penalties) to 4...

Went round to Stornoway in the evening and found Max resting in bed. Winston rang him up on the telephone and indulged in some anti-Baldwin conversation over India. Winston is to speak three times next week. Max gave me the paragraphs on it for the Diary. Then the *Sunday Express* arrived. He praised the leader and the political notes lavishly. Said the *Sunday Express* lot were a clever crowd, that Gordon was the man we wanted for the *Standard* and that Barkley's work was first-rate... Dined with him at Stornoway. Jean, Kitty[1] and Perry Brownlow there.

Broke my pledge last night and drank ¼ bottle white wine for dinner and half a bottle of champagne for supper.

Sunday, 25 January 1931

In the evening dined at Stornoway. Duff and Diana, Kitty and Perry, Jean, the Fitzgeralds, Springman, Lord Amherst, and the McKennas. Likewise Jimmie Dunn who has just returned from Cannes where he has lent his villa to [Augustus] John and is having his portrait painted. John has painted or tried to paint him four times. He is never satisfied; does an admirable portrait the first day, paints it out the next day and so on till the picture is ruined. Stayed till one. Drank nothing. Duff very pro-Baldwin. His idea of the next Conservative Government includes all the old gang except Jix, Bridgeman[2] and perhaps Austen. He gives Irwin as Secretary for Foreign Affairs...[3] Max very interesting on investments and world recovery. Max's advice is: to buy shares of raw material companies. There can be no industrial revival without a raw material revival.

Monday, 26 January 1931

Spoke to Lloyd. He tells me that the amalgamation between the *New Statesman* and the *Nation* is really an absorption of the *Nation* by the *New Statesman* and that except for a few reviewers the *New Statesman* is taking over very few people.

Dined with Max. Only Jean there, and the whole conversation was about Jean's new house which Max is advising her about and presumably furnishing. Jean's star seems in the ascendant again.

Max tells me Bridget's children are being brought up as Cats. Attacked me for saying that I was a Cat. because I thought R.C. religion did more for me. Said only test was: which religion conformed most to teaching of Christ.

Harold Nicolson dined with Tom Mosley. Harold has now abandoned his

[1] Katherine, neé Hariot, Lord Brownlow's first wife (*d.* 1952).

[2] 1st Viscount Bridgeman (1864–1935), had been Home Secretary, 1922–4, 1st Lord of the Admiralty, 1924–9.

[3] Lord Irwin, later Earl of Halifax, at that time Viceroy of India, did not become Foreign Secretary until 1938.

Liberal inclinations and is prepared to stand for Tom as a Mosley candidate.[1] He is convinced Tom will be prime minister one day.

Tuesday, 27 January 1931

Have a fresh infection of cold which is almost as bad as my original cold. Did some paragraphs for Max on Sir Joseph Hood, who died last week. He was a solicitor in Liverpool when he acted for Ogdens [tobacco company]. In this way he came into contact with J. B. Duke, when latter was forming British-American Tobacco. Duke took him to London, put him into Bats and into a fortune. Duke picked out [Sir Hugo] Cunliffe-Owen in much the same way. He was negotiating the purchase of the Imperial Tobacco Company's foreign interests at Bristol. Cunliffe-Owen, then a subordinate and head of the export department, was called in. Duke took a fancy to him and brought him to London. Duke, an eccentric, made his money in tobacco. Had also big hydro-electric interests.

Wednesday, 28 January 1931

Gave luncheon to Benji Bruce and Karsavina at Boulestin's. They told me some good stories. [Emil] Cooper, the famous Moscow conductor, who is now at Riga Opera, was unable to get out of Russia. He tried various ways. At last he went again to the Commissariat for the *n*th time to make his application. He was received by a pale intellectual young man. 'What's your name?' 'Cooper.' 'What's your profession?' 'Artist.' 'Ah! You are Fenimore Cooper? I was brought up on you as a boy.' And Cooper received his application in the name of Fenimore Cooper.

In the spring of 1917, when Henderson was already on his way to Petrograd, the Foreign Office sent a telegram to Buchanan, praising his work and suggesting he would like a rest. In other words, a recall. Benji Bruce went to Sazonov, learnt from him that Tereshchenko would not like Buchanan to go, and telegraphed privately to G.R.C. [Sir George Clerk] that Henderson's appointment would be a disaster. . .[2]

Sazonov, Paléologue [French Ambassador] and Buchanan used to meet daily at ten. One day they began discussing a telegram which Paléologue and Buchanan had just received. Sazonov began the discussion. Paléologue left first, and Sazonov turned to Buchanan. 'Did you notice anything about our discussion this morning?' Buchanan thought and then saw light. 'Yes,' he said. 'You seemed to know all about our telegram before we told you.' Sazonov had had the decipher from his *cabinet noir* long before the Ambassador had received the telegram.

[1] Mosley officially launched what was then called the New Party on 1 March 1931. Nicolson was one of the first to join Mosley, who hoped he could gain the support of the Beaverbrook press. It was only later that Mosley became a Fascist.

[2] Sergius Sazonov had been Tsarist Foreign Minister, and was appointed Ambassador to London by Kerensky, and Tereshchenko became Foreign Minister.

Again, just when Kerensky Government was collapsing, Tereshchenko came to British Embassy: 'For God's sake change your cipher, we've had them for months, and as for the Italians they have been telegraphing home the positions of our troops from headquarters in a cipher which everyone has and the Germans have been making their dispositions accordingly.'

Sunday, 1 February 1931

Max has telephoned every day – or rather his secretary has – to ask how I am. He is a queer man. He demands sympathy in handfuls and gives none, and yet there is something attractive and compelling about him. Harold says he is one of those friends whom one will like better when they are dead.

Thursday, 5 February 1931

The political situation in East Islington is complicated and looks bad for us. Springman has withdrawn his candidature on the ground that Miss Cazalet agrees with him. Max seems to have agreed to the withdrawal and then to have changed his mind. The Crusade has now put up General Critchley, but I fear the shilly-shallying will do Max harm, will strengthen the public's belief in Baldwin as an honest man and in Max as a twister.[1] The whole episode gives the impression that Max is more intent on doing Baldwin down than on getting his policy through.

Telephone message from Flying Corps Hill who wants to see me... He tells me that Reilly's death was more or less as described in *Diplomatische Unterwelt* and that he was in the Cheka's hands almost from the beginning. I must keep this, if possible, for my book.[2]

Sunday, 8 February 1931

In evening dined at Wickham Place, the home of Nigs Freeman-Thomas and his wife. Nigs and Blossom now become Lord and Lady Ratendone, as Lord Willingdon has just been made an Earl.[3] He and his wife were there... Lord Willingdon is a charming old boy, who has been made 'something' by every Prime Minister since Asquith. He is very pro-Canada and likes the Canadians and believes in their future. He puts Mackenzie King[4] much higher than Bennett, whom he regards as a small man because of his vanity and his personal sensitiveness. He thinks Bennett made a mistake in

[1] Miss Thelma Cazalet (later Cazalet-Keir) was in favour of tariffs, but also loyal to Baldwin. Beaverbrook's new candidate was Brigadier-General A. C. Critchley (1890–1963), born in Canada, a director of cement manufacturing companies, the first to build and operate a greyhound racing tack, at Manchester, in 1926.

[2] George Hill – later Brigadier, D.S.O., O.B.E., M.C., had been a British agent and close associate of Reilly.

[3] The Earl – later Marquess – of Willingdon (1866–1941) had served as Governor of Bombay and Madras, been Governor-General of Canada, 1926–30, and at this time was about to become Viceroy of India, where he remained until 1936.

raising his tariffs before he came over, says that his stock in Canada has gone down since the conference and that the farmers are furious with him. It will require a miracle in the way of a world recovery to save him. Lord Willingdon is anxious to meet Max. He is in favour of reform in India, but is prepared to take a strong line with Indians like Gandhi who apparently will not accept our proposals. He is rather upset that the home Government should have released Gandhi and his colleagues before he has had a chance of seeing the situation. Had a long talk with Lady Willingdon. She also wants to meet Max, because she liked Lady Beaverbrook. . . She says that Lord Willingdon and she who are leaving on April 3rd, want to fly there, if they can obtain the King's permission. When they were in China they were suddenly appointed to Canada. They therefore came home by the Siberian railway, travelled in tremendous state to Manchouli, then shared a sleeper and a washing-place with their next-door neighbour. Near Moscow the pass Karakhan had given them flew out of the window, but after fifteen changes they arrived safely at Victoria in fifteen days with 24 boxes and £7000 worth of jewellery. She told me a good story about Dunning, who is now in charge of Canada's winter-sports place 'Lucerne' in Quebec. He took Lady Willingdon down the local Cresta in a 'bob'.

Monday, 9 February 1931

Harold says that everyone he has seen tells him that Max has made a complete fool of himself over East Islington. Lord Willingdon said last night that Max had thrown away a wonderful chance. He (Lord Willingdon) did not like the name Empire Free Trade, but Max, if he had stuck to speaking his gospel, had a wonderful rôle. He (Lord Willingdon) would join any Empire Party, but he hated all this personal abuse. It showed how small the politicians were today.

Tuesday, 10 February 1931

Went round to see Max at 9.15. He gave me some paragraphs to do and was not unfriendly. Spoke to him about Lord Willingdon, but he said: 'What's the good of my seeing these people? I'll see him and be pleasant to him if I come across him, but why should I go out of my way to bother about him!' Went in to *Express* to see Blum. He is very pessimistic about Max, thinks we will crash at East Islington, and that this time the bitterness is far worse than during South Paddington. Harold thinks the same. . . Lunched with Pam at the Wellington. She left afterwards for Portsmouth. She says Critchley is both a cad and a fool and that Sir John Buchanan-Jardine,[1] who is pro-Max on policy, said: how can anyone join Beaverbrook when he is surrounded by cads and men of fifteenth-rate intelligence? Today we were offered Reilly's memoirs for sale. There is a good deal about me in them: some of it lies and some of it unpleasant.

[1] Scottish baronet, sportsman and soldier (1900–69).

Captain Hill (Reilly's friend) came to see me about a job. Bed 12.15. Broke my pledge.

Wednesday, 11 February 1931

Went to see London General Press about Reilly's memoirs. They were quite friendly about omissions. They had already taken out Winston's name. They want him to write a preface. It is quite clear, I think, that Reilly was trapped back into Russia by the Cheka people. Apparently, they got hold of Boyce first. Boyce sent for Reilly, and Reilly was put into touch in Berlin with two agents-provocateurs. Reilly was kept in prison for a time, then taken out in a car outside Moscow one day and stabbed by Artzanov.[1]

Thursday, 12 February 1931

Lunched with [Constant] Huntington of Putnam's at the Athenaeum. Discussed my book. He was not only very interested in having it, but went so far as to suggest an immediate advance in order to enable me to leave Beaverbrook now. Huntington also went to see the Kaiser and received a photograph (the same as mine) with exactly the same Lincoln inscription as mine.

In the afternoon went to see Jan Masaryk, who is divorcing his wife. She is being divorced because she refuses to give up her travels (he has not seen her for about eighteen months) and therefore prejudices his position here as Minister. Jan Masaryk has been t.t. for four months and feels a new man. He is very upset, because he still loves her and also anxious lest anything detrimental to him or her appear in our Press. I told him I thought least said soonest mended. Robertson gives the same advice.

Friday, 13 February 1931

Gave a luncheon party at Boulestin's: Jack and Cornelia Cecil,[2] Pam, Nigs and Blossom – quite a success, but too much to eat and drink. Cornelia Cecil lipsticks the lobes of her ears, which is something new to me. At three went to see Tom Mosley. Met W. J. Brown there.[3] Tackled them on the young man theory. They both talked platitudes about breaking across party lines and party credos, and said the young man's movement could only come through the Labour Party. Certainly, the young men in the Conservative Party are 'dead'. Retired to bed at four and slept till eight.

Dined with Dad at the Royal Societies. He was 73 yesterday. Discussed

[1] Commander Ernest Boyce, R.N., was the head of the Russian section of the Secret Intelligence Service at the time. He had been in Russia with Lockhart. The facts of Reilly's death, as related by Robin Bruce Lockhart in *Ace of Spies*, are much less certain and more complex.

[2] The Hon. John Cecil (1890–1954), diplomat, had been first secretary in Prague in 1921, married Cornelia Vanderbilt in 1924.

[3] Trade union adviser, journalist and author (*d.* 1960), Labour M.P. West Wolverhampton, 1929–31; Independent M.P. Rugby, 1942–50.

schools. He favours Eagle House and Wellington for Robin. Went on to the Chapmans' at ten to pick up Pam. Went to Taglioni's and sat up till one fifteen when Pam suddenly felt faint and we went home. I have been back only a week – or rather a week out of the home. I have not written a line of my book. I am back into my old ways, and already I feel deathly ill. It is hopeless trying to do fifteen different jobs at once. Young Max's 21st birthday. He had a large party at Stornoway. I was not asked.

Saturday, 14 February 1931

Worthington-Evans died in his sleep – of emphysema which is apparently the result of long-standing bronchitis. He, Birkenhead, and Austen Chamberlain were directors of the London and Counties General Trust. As Birkenhead received £15,000 per annum in directors' fees and Worthy £5000, the saving in overhead charges to the company is £20,000. Austen receives £2000.

Monday, 16 February 1931

A cold and snowy day. Talked about East Islington to Harold, who has been staying with Tom Mosley. Latter thinks we have a chance of winning East Islington, but says a victory will do us more harm than defeat. Defeat would be a bore, but the return of an imbecile and a cad and a bounder like Critchley would be a disaster for Max. Harold thinks that Max is now more interested in fighting than in his policy and that his weak point is that when his terms are accepted he puts forward new demands.

This morning, when I showed Max my paragraphs about Worthington-Evans, he found the words 'on his doctor's orders'. 'Take that out,' he said. 'I hope to God when you write my obituary, you will never say anything about doctor's orders to me. Doctors may advise me. They cannot order me.'

Thursday, 19 February 1931

Polling day at Islington. Took voters to the poll all day and evening till nine p.m. Then went to dine at the Quo Vadis, home to rest, and then back to Islington at one to hear the poll declared. [Mrs Leah] Manning, the Labour woman, won by nearly 3000 votes; Critchley was second, 1200 ahead of Thelma Cazalet. Crawfurd, the Liberal, only polled 4000 votes. Less than half the electorate voted (as a matter of fact it was 51%) – this in spite of Max's frantic propaganda. Back to Stornoway at 1.30, Max surrounded by his court (Jean, Alex Kinloch,[1] his wife, Doidge, Janet and Clinton) took his defeat very well. He was quite pleased to have beaten the official Conservative. Very tired and quite exhausted...

Our canvass at Islington was disgraceful. We only canvassed about a quarter of the electorate, and yet we returned about 10,000 promises for Critchley. On this basis Critchley should have received about 40,000 votes!

[1] Younger brother of Jean Norton (*b.* 1902), became 12th baronet in 1944.

Whole streets were returned as 'for Critchley' which had never been canvassed and were definitely Labour.

Tuesday, 24 February 1931

Max came back from Paris in the evening and at once had a dinner-party for Garvin,[1] Paddy Hannon, and another man whose name I did not know. Max is very funny about his dinner-parties. Even I must not know who is dining with him. The other day Valentine, having found out from Whelan who was dining with Max, said to him: 'You have so-and-so dining with you tonight.' 'How do you know?' says Max. 'Whelan told me,' was the reply. The next day Max sends for Whelan, reprimands him, and says: 'In future, if anyone – *anyone*, mind you – asks you who is dining with Lord Beaverbrook, tell them to ask Lord Beaverbrook himself.'

Max has a good story of Hailsham. On the day after the speech (Hailsham's mad-dog speech on Max), Max was going up to Islington. Max, remembering the votes which accrued to Roosevelt after the attempt on his life,[2] said gleefully: 'If I'm shot today, Critchley will get in, and I shall be in a hell of a hole.' 'Yes,' said Valentine (the story was improved later by Edward Marjoribanks, Hailsham's stepson), 'Yes, but there will be a hell of a hole in you, too!'

Saturday, 28 February 1931

Dined with Max in the evening. He gave me a lot of 'dope' on nervous habits and human vanities. Birkenhead's bridge vanity. Valentine's dress vanity. Winston's habit of breaking matches. Lord Ashfield's habit of tapping the table with his fingers. Max was going to the Chaplin film [*City Lights*] that evening; he had made up his mind to dislike it before he went. He thinks far too much fuss has been made of Charlie and hounded Valentine off to write an article against him. Valentine, who liked the film, produced a very funny article.

Monday, 2 March 1931

No man plays up to Max better than Valentine who is the prince of toadies and 'bum-suckers'. Valentine, however, is not the fool people take him for. He has an amazing belief in his own journalistic genius, believes that he can sway millions of people, and that he is an immense power in Fleet Street. He does not write with his tongue in his cheek. Hence his success. To do him justice, he is very loyal to Max and fights his battles for him with a lack of finesse and subtlety which would drive Max frantic if he could hear him.

Wednesday, 4 March 1931

Duff Cooper is to be adopted as Conservative candidate for St George's

[1] J. L. Garvin (1868–1947), editor of the *Observer*, 1908–42.

[2] In 1912 Theodore Roosevelt stood as Progressive Party candidate for President. He was shot on 14 October, but recovered to complete his campaign. Woodrow Wilson was elected.

[Westminster].[1] Harold Nicolson says Duff's reputation for cleverness is a Society fable. Duff is clever in a way, but he has never worked. Never did a stroke at the Foreign Office and was never taken seriously. Was disliked by Lord Curzon. On one occasion Duff was called to luncheon by the Marquess not as a Foreign Office official but as the husband of the beautiful Lady Diana. During pause in conversation the Marquess leant across and said: 'And, Mr Cooper, in the intervals between entertaining your beautiful wife, how do you occupy yourself?' In the Foreign Office the two men who have gone into politics in recent years are Johnny Baird (Lord Stonehaven)[2] and Duff. Duff is lazy. Johnny was an ass. When Duff left, the Office said: 'If Johnny Baird can make a success in politics, Duff may be Prime Minister.' Not very flattering to the politicians. Dined with Max in his bedroom. He has [*word illegible*] – nerves I expect. Jean Norton arrived and stayed till eleven-thirty. We all think Diana will be a more serious candidate than Duff himself.

Friday, 6 March 1931

In the afternoon met Moura at the Wellington. Sat there till 8.30 drinking sherry. Then went on to the Hungaria restaurant where we remained till two a.m. I felt very ill after drinking so much. She – as usual – never turned a hair. Naturally, we discussed Russia the whole evening. Moura thinks we are all wrong about the Russians. She thinks, like Wells, that the capitalist-finance system has broken down and that Russia will succeed with her Five-Year Plan – not necessarily in five years, but in the sense that she will make rapid progress towards becoming an industrial nation like the U.S.A. She saw Gorky a few weeks ago. He is now ultra-Bolshevik, has returned to his own class, believes implicitly in Stalin, and justifies the terror from which formerly he shrank. He and Moura both believe in the danger of foreign intervention. Moura assures me that the recent trials in Moscow were by no means 'faked'.

Tuesday, 10 March 1931

Lunched with Tommy who has been helping Diana Cooper. She says that Diana has a great many society women helping her and that they are very satisfied with their canvass. Tommy dined last night with Duff: Lord Stanley, Margesson, Euan Wallace, etc.[3] They were saying that only people who want

[1] Duff Cooper was the official candidate. The Empire Free Trade candidate was Sir Ernest Petter (1873–1954), a west-country diesel-engine manufacturer.

[2] (1874–1941), chairman of the Conservative Party organisation 1931–6, created 1st Viscount 1938.

[3] Edward, Lord Stanley (1865–1948), eldest son of 16th Earl of Derby and elder brother of Oliver Stanley; Captain David Margesson (1890–1965), Conservative M.P., and later Chief Whip, 1931–40, created 1st Viscount 1942; Captain Euan Wallace (1892–1941), Conservative M.P., 1922–41, had been Assistant Whip 1928–9, and was to hold many ministerial posts.

Baldwin to go are the old men in the party and that the young men are on his side.

Canvassed all afternoon. Dined with Jean Norton and Pam – then to Stornoway and later on to Jimmie Dunn's at Norfolk House. Max told me of Sir James Erskine's negotiations to join us.[1] Erskine said he must first have a letter of support from Rothermere (his negotiations were begun with the United Empire Party). Rothermere gave it. He then wanted £5000 in cash. Rothermere refused. Rothermere, however, offered him a joint promise from Max and himself to help him to get a baronetcy. Max, however, refused to be a party to this deal, and Erskine is standing out. Talked to Jimmie Dunn till after one o'clock. He thinks Max is the greatest man in the world and that he ought to be Prime Minister. As regards his business reputation, the attacks on him were due to jealousy. No man can name a company floated by Max which has not paid the shareholders handsomely.

Friday, 13 March 1931

Last night went to the Caxton Hall with Vivian Peel to hear Max and Malcolm Campbell speak. A huge crowd, which could have filled the hall ten times over, and a marvellous reception for Campbell, who more or less acquitted Duff Cooper of the charge of libel. The other night, at one of his own meetings, Duff lost his temper and practically accused the *Daily Express* of having bought Malcolm Campbell for the St George's campaign. Campbell is a pleasant-looking fellow with an expression of great earnestness. He is a poor speaker, but his sincerity went down with the public.[2]

This has been a very dirty campaign. The *Daily Mail* and Rothermere, who have been incredibly stupid – dragging in the comparison of rich men who can look after their fortunes and those like Baldwin, who cannot, thus giving every newspaper in the country the opportunity of taking the story of Baldwin's gift of War Loan to the nation – may have been the first to start the mud-slinging, but Duff has been a good second. Valentine Castlerosse's contribution has been two jokes: (1) There are two Mrs Baldwins, and one is called Stanley; (2) I'm all for the captain going down with the ship, but I don't see why the ship should go down with the captain.

Wednesday, 18 March 1931

Last day at St George's. Did a certain amount of recanvassing. Everyone very tired and their nerves on edge... General feeling that Duff will win comfortably owing to (1) Petter's mistakes over League of Nations Union and the Education Bill, and (2) the Rothermere campaign of abuse of Baldwin and Duff especially, (3) the attack on Baldwin's private fortune,[3]

[1] Erskine (1863–1944) had been Conservative M.P. for St George's, 1921–9.

[2] Sir Malcolm Campbell (1885–1948) was a famous racing driver, setting up land and water speed records; he was also an insurer of newspapers against libel actions.

[3] 'It is difficult to see how the leader of a party who has lost his own fortune can hope to restore that of anyone else, or of his country,' wrote the *Daily Mail*.

(4) calling Duff a 'softy'. Max sent a letter to the newspaper contradicting Baldwin's statement about the *Daily Express* refusing to print Mrs Baldwin's letter. Dined at the Wellington and went back to Committee Rooms afterwards. Pam hysterical with tiredness and Jean not much better.

Friday, 20 March 1931

Saw Tommy at the Bath Club. She was lunching with 'Bloggs' Baldwin. She says that Duff and Diana were not at all certain of the result[1] till the end and that at the victory party at Lady Stanley's, Edward Stanley proposed Duff's health in a speech in which he made no mention of Baldwin. Apparently, too, during the election Duff wished to make a speech about the press indulging in personalities and lurking for their information in dark passages. Lord Stanley said: 'Duff, as the champion corridor crawler, you had better cut that passage out. Someone in the audience might laugh!' This of course in reference to Duff's pouncing and corridor prowling in private houses at night.

Sunday, 22 March 1931

Dined at Stornoway: present Paddy Hannon, Baxter, Mike, Valentine. Max is furious with the *News Chronicle* for this hypocrisy in attacking us over advertising in America.[2] He wants Baxter to run an anti-Cadbury campaign for being a Quaker, a Friend, and an anti-dancing and anti-gambling fanatic, for boosting of those views in the *News* and for running a racing and tipster evening paper in the *Star*. 'Photograph him every day,' says Max. 'Photograph him on his way to church – in church – coming back from church. Show the old bugger up.' Discussed Woolwich. Max is determined to fight. Wants to adopt Sinn Fein tactics. Paddy tried to restrain him by suggesting that, as the whole crusade was a one-man show dependent on Max, he must think of his health. 'These elections won't kill me,' says Max. 'They're what keep me fit.'

Monday, 23 March 1931

Arnold Bennett and Tim Healy are both dying. Arnold Bennett has had typhoid since shortly after Christmas and, after recovering, has had a severe relapse. He is supposed to have contracted it in France: He went to Paris and Fontainebleau at Xmas time and is supposed to have drunk water. His heart has now given way. He is too weak to have blood transfusions and is being given saline injections instead. Straw has been put down in front of his

[1] Duff Cooper won St George's by 5710 votes.

[2] Baldwin, in a speech on 17 March, attacked the *Mail* and *Express* for advertising themselves in New York as media for selling U.S. goods in Britain while campaigning for Empire Free Trade. The *News Chronicle* attacked the *Mail* – not the *Express* – for not reporting this speech. Laurence Cadbury (*b.* 1889) was the proprietor of the *News Chronicle*.

house.[1] Arnold Bennett keeps a note-book in which he enters up all his personal expenses daily. He has hundreds of them. They will make an interesting record in a hundred years. I know no man who makes better use of his time than Arnold Bennett.

Tim has been operated on for dropsy and is not expected to recover. He is at his home at Chapelizod in Ireland. I have seen him fairly often in recent years – always at Max's and generally drunk. The last time I saw him was at Cherkley about the time of the Imperial Conference. He had been to dine with the King and told us the Irish delegation had been greatly impressed. At Cherkley Tim had a bad leg, so he came down to dinner in a dinner-jacket on the top of his ordinary trousers (grey). He drank and talked a great deal, and I helped him to bed and took off his elastic-sided boots for him. He was devoted to Max, who played a great part in breaking down Bonar Law's resistance to the Irish settlement. He talked to me of Max's policy and expressed his belief not only in the policy but in its ultimate success.

Tuesday, 24 March 1931

Dined with Max in the evening. He informed me that Neville Chamberlain had been to see him and had spent three hours with him. Max said Neville had offered very generous terms. Between them they had drawn up a formula which Neville had taken away for Baldwin's eventual approval and acceptance. It does not go as far as Max's policy but it goes farther than Baldwin has yet gone and extends the free hand to every branch of agriculture.[2] Max said Neville had admitted that, if things continued as they are now, Max would win several by-elections. The Conservatives now regard him as the best platform-speaker in the country. That was why they wanted his co-operation. All of which shows that Neville is not such a bad diplomat as he is thought to be and that he knows his Max. I advised (as far as he listens to anyone's advice) to accept. I think he may, although all evening he kept harking back to Mike and me: 'What about fighting? What about telling them all to go to hell and adopting Sinn Fein tactics?' I said: 'What about the country?'

Sunday, 29 March 1931

Arnold Bennett died yesterday. He was very nice to me always, praised my Birkenhead obituary, and offered me the editorship of the *New Statesman*. He was a little sore about my review of his *Imperial Palace*...

Max has come to terms with the Conservatives and is sore with me for going away at such an important moment.

[1] A custom of some antiquity, presumably to quieten the noise of horses' hooves.

[2] Neville Chamberlain (1869–1940) was then Chairman of the Conservative Party, soon to become Chancellor of the Exchequer and then Prime Minister. This was the so-called Stornoway Pact. It was far from a victory for Beaverbrook; Baldwin's assurances were vague and did not commit the Party – see Taylor, *Beaverbrook*, pages 306–7.

Tuesday, 31 March 1931

Had eight paragraphs in the Diary: on Willingdon's staff, on diplomatic brawls, and on Lord Aberdare.[1] Lunched by myself at the Cheshire Cheese. At three went with Gilliat to the Arnold Bennett Memorial Service at St Clement's in the Strand. The service was conducted by Bishop Russell Wakefield[2] whom I met thirteen years ago after the war at Lairgs. He was fishing the Shin with the Bishop of London. His address was poor, although as usual, I felt emotional. The hymns were 'Jesu, Lover of my Soul' and 'Abide with Me.' The first was Bennett's favourite. Arnold Bennett was cremated. Letter from Millie telling me that Arnold Bennett took her off in *The Card*. She was the Countess of Chell. He had only seen her once.

At 7.15 met Jean and Robin at Victoria. They were both very tired... Having extracted their heavy luggage from the Customs and given them dinner, I went round to Stornoway, where Max was giving a dinner to the *Sunday Express* people. Listened for two hours while Gordon and Christiansen talked hot air about journalism. Christiansen said Robert Sinclair (the man who does our 'Today' column in the *Standard*) is the Arthur Brisbane of England![3]

Thursday, 2 April 1931

Lunched with Mike and his boy at the Savoy... Mike wants the Diary modelled on Harold Nicolson. He intends to make Harold virtually responsible for the Diary. I think this would be a grave mistake. Harold's tastes are not the public's tastes. He is altogether too precious. However, we shall see.

Rained most of the day. Came down with Jean and Robin to St Ronan's by the 4.57 via Wokingham. Spent most of the evening carrying luggage upstairs. Sat up with Dad till after two waiting for Freda who came down by a late train after the theatre. She is playing in *Good Losers* – a play by Michael Arlen and Walter Hackett at the Whitehall Theatre. The Beaverbrook–Chamberlain Pact has had a bad press in the weekly papers. Most papers think it will not last. I do not think it will. Max has no ambition to play second fiddle. I doubt if he will ever enter a Conservative administration.

Tuesday, 7 April 1931

The Diary arrangement made by Wardell has gone through, and Nicolson is not only to sub-edit and 'give a Nicolson twist' to all paragraphs, but is actually to select the paragraphs for the Diary. The arrangement is bad. Harold Nicolson has no experience of day-by-day journalism. In any case his tastes are not those of the average Diary public. Gilliat is now superseded except for his right of veto for libel, etc. He does not like it. Neither do I.

[1] An Italian prince and diplomat had come to blows at a Franco-Italian boxing match. Lord Aberdare had just won the Amateur Rackets Championship at the age of 46.

[2] Henry Russell Wakefield (1854–1933) had been Bishop of Birmingham, 1911–24.

[3] Arthur Christiansen (1904–63), assistant editor *Sunday Express*, 1928–33; editor *Daily Express*, 1933–57. Brisbane (1864–1936) was an American journalist working for Hearst.

The position is humiliating for me. Two years ago, when I recommended Harold, I wrote that I was hanging myself with a silken cord. The noose is now drawn. The curious thing is that all this upset is due to Harold's complaints about his paragraphs not being taken and to his desire to be relieved of the Diary.

Came down to Horsham with Tommy, Mary and David [two of the Rosslyns' children]. Tommy told me a good story about the Baldwins, Lord Beauchamp[1] and Lady Beauchamp. Lady Beauchamp has left him because of his homosexual habits. There was almost an open scandal lately. There was some ceremony at Madresfield, Malvern, lately – the enthronement of a bishop – and the Baldwins went there, staying with Lord Beauchamp. They received a letter of protest from Lady Shaftesbury (Lady Beauchamp's sister) and from the Duke of Westminster (who has given a house to Lady Beauchamp). Lady Beauchamp put a notice in the papers to the effect that although she was living away from Lord Beauchamp, she was quite well.

Thursday, 9 April 1931

Had an unsatisfactory morning in Shoe Lane. Wrote about eight paragraphs, none of which went into the Diary. Gilliat and Toulson are now hopeless. They yield and defer to Harold Nicolson in everything – not because they believe in his judgement – on the contrary – but because they are terrified of offending Beaverbrook and think that Harold Nicolson is Beaverbrook's star. Shanks asked to see me. He would like to resign, but cannot afford to. He says the paper is seething with discontent and blames Max for interfering and messing people about until all confidence is destroyed and Gilliat for not asserting himself. He says the paper is now not only a Soviet but a whole collection of Soviets with Ogpus and spies complete. He says Gilliat has never been the same since the Jonesco affair. Went to bed with a liver attack and did not work on my Yugoslav article.

Friday, 10 April 1931

Spent a profitless day in my office. Wrote about six paragraphs only three of which went into the Diary. The latter had nine paragraphs on art, music and literature. Harold may be a good writer, but he is no judge of popular journalism. On the editorial side Mike is hopeless. Lunched with Kingsley Martin, the new editor of the *New Statesman and Nation*.[2] He says the new paper is doing very well and has now a bigger circulation than the *Spectator*. Discussed Russia. He does not think Western capitalism in its present form will be able to stand if the Five-Year Plan succeeds – and I think it will succeed although not necessarily in five years. He wants me to do an article

[1] 7th Earl of Beauchamp (1872–1938).

[2] Kingsley Martin (1897–1969) had recently joined the *New Statesman* from the *Manchester Guardian*; he remained editor for 30 years.

on this aspect of the problem. In the afternoon wrote an article on Yugoslavia for the bank.

Left my office at 8 p.m. and went to Stornoway to dine. Max had been to a Gipsy Smith, now seventy, evangelist meeting at the Queen's Hall and had been shaken by it – especially, by the statement that a man's guilt shall be measured by the amount of his responsibility. Valentine in great form with the brandy bottle and moderately witty in his cups. Bed midnight. No cigarettes. One sherry, half bottle vin rosé, one glass champagne, one glass port. Kingsley Martin is a member of the 'Loyalist Grouser' group which meets at Easton Hall.[1] They have been very active lately. Hitherto, they have discussed mainly new methods of socialisation and Parliamentary reform. Now they are to have a meeting on International and foreign affairs and one on Empire policy. Noel-Baker[2] has attended a recent meeting.

Saturday, 11 April 1931

When I arrived at Cherkley, I found Max alone and, as usual lately, difficult and uncommunicative. I told him that I had been told that Oliver Baldwin had said that his father knew nothing of the Beaverbrook–Chamberlain Pact until he read it in the papers. Max said: 'I wish that were true. It would show that Neville is giving Baldwin a bad time. But I am afraid it is not true.'

Sunday, 12 April 1931

This afternoon Max telephoned L.G., and they had a long conversation on the terrace in the course of which Max said that Neville was a food-taxer and had said so both to him and to Wright and ten of Wright's colleagues.[3] They had put the question to Neville: 'Is it the intention of the Conservative Party to adopt the policy of duties on foreign foodstuffs?' and Neville had replied: 'That is the intention of the Conservative Party.' This had been said previously to Max and then to Wright and his colleagues, when Max was out of the room. Neville had admitted to Max that they (the food-taxers including himself) might have a rebuff. 'I agree,' said Max. 'Only I'm sure in that case you will never consent to lead the Party.' Max told L.G. he expected a row in about a month's time. He thought that Baldwin would go part of the way, when he came to make his speech in four weeks' time, but that he would not go far enough. He thought that Baldwin's position would be weaker in a month's time. He admitted to L.G. that he thought the *Daily Telegraph* agitation against the Crusade was *not* inspired. In fact, as far as Conservative headquarters were concerned, they were anxious to keep both

[1] Easton Hall was the Countess of Warwick's house, see above, page 63.

[2] Philip Noel-Baker (*b.* 1889), Labour politician, then M.P. for Coventry and Parliamentary Private Secretary to the Foreign Minister.

[3] J. F. Wright had founded the Agricultural Party to advocate food taxes. Beaverbrook had consulted with him, rather than any of his Empire Free Trade colleagues, over the Stornoway Pact.

the *Telegraph* and the *Mail* quiet. Max also said he had consulted Winston before he made his pact, and that Winston had advised him to accept Neville's offer.

Tuesday, 14 April 1931

Great excitement in Spain. At the municipal elections on Sunday – the first Spain has had for nine years – the Republicans were overwhelmingly successful. A crisis of the first magnitude has developed, and, as the Republican wave swelled, there was nothing left for King Alfonso to do except abdicate. This he did late on Tuesday afternoon.

Young Randolph Churchill is determined to marry his American lady in spite of the fact that she has very little money and is a Jewess. She is several years older than he is, and is the daughter of a man called Samuel Halle in Cleveland, Ohio. Mrs Winston has just come back from America. She went there to try to persuade Randolph to come home but without success.

Thursday, 16 April 1931

Max came up to London for Tim Healy's requiem Mass at Westminster Cathedral. He was impressed by the service – thinks it was finer 'than any opera he has ever seen'. Had a long talk with Harold, who is going to stand as a Mosley candidate for Chiswick.

Saturday, 18 April 1931

Max talking increasingly about selling the paper. H. G. [Wells] and Max discussed Arnold Bennett... Arnold Bennett's *Imperial Palace* sold 100,000 copies in America. H.G.'s *History of the World* has sold over 2,000,000 copies. It will beat *All Quiet* [*on the Western Front*]. Last year it sold 500,000 copies at a dollar in America and for a time was beating the Bible. H.G. rather amusing about [Theodore] Roosevelt – whom he hated as a poseur of the first magnitude. The only time he was ever in a brothel was after he had been received at the White House by Roosevelt. He came out disgusted, hailed a cab and said: 'Drive me at once to a gay house.' 'Black or coloured?' said the driver. 'Coloured,' said H.G. He wanted, he said, to readjust his moral values after the hypocrisy of Roosevelt and the White House. Max told a story of Arnold Bennett. When he had finished *Lord Raingo*, he came in and said: 'I've finished my book.' Dorothy Cheston[1] said: 'How relieved and happy you must be.' 'On the contrary,' said Arnold, 'I'm lonely and miserable and depressed, I've killed a friend.'

Sunday, 19 April 1931

Rained all day. Talked alone to H.G. all morning. He is not a very impressive talker. His falsetto is a little irritating and he has a habit of pausing after

[1] Actress, lived with Arnold Bennett from 1923, bore his daughter, took the name Dorothy Cheston Bennett – see her biography of him, 1935.

each sentence with a little 'hum' which seems to mean 'There you are.' But he is very placid and even-tempered and generally has something interesting to say. . .

He chafed at the want of exercise. At his place at Grasse in the South of France he plays badminton and has taught his mistress . . . to play. H.G. believes Russia is going to succeed, that capital individualism is dead or dying because it does nothing to save itself, and that world economic depression is only just beginning. He asks why Max does not take up the international currency question rather than a mad thing like Empire Free Trade. Lord Wargrave,[1] and a friend to luncheon, likewise Jimmie Dunn. In the evening Otto Kahn arrived. He had nothing very new to say: slump in America is not over yet; there may be some more bank smashes, but big banks are sound, and in Kahn's opinion America will be all right. He thinks Europe is in a bad way and that England should do something to persuade France to alter her policy. What is wanted, he said, is a little audacious friendliness to undo the work of the Peace Treaty. When H.G. talked to him about the burden of debts, the necessity for internationalism, etc., and America, Kahn said: 'Oh, America is out of it.'

Kahn is going to France and Italy. He will not go to Germany – a country where half the Press is anti-semitic and 'Where four persons out of five would knock you on the head if they dared.' Kahn is a Jew who was very pro-American in the war. His refusal to go to Germany is half-fear and half-pride.

Monday, 20 April 1931

Came up from Cherkley by the ten forty-five. Had a paragraph about Arnold Bennett's estate. He left only £11,000 plus his manuscripts, first editions and copyrights. Also some valuable books. His first wife gets the income of ⅔ of his estate; his second wife . . . gets the income of ⅓. Position is complicated for Dorothy Cheston Bennett . . . by the fact that first wife gets a special gift of £5000. Dorothy has asked Max to lend her £3500.

Friday, 1 May 1931

Lord Beaverbrook came back by the 6.35. I had to go down to Cherkley with him. He was in a very pleasant mood, liked his German trip and the Germans, thinks that Hitler will do well, only stayed a night in Paris, because he hates the French. Seems pleased with Baldwin's speeches and said, 'If he keeps this up, the ranks will soon be closed.' Thinks Ashton-under-Lyne has done in Tom Mosley.[2] After dinner, although he must have been tired, he played the wireless (with fiendish noises) until 12.30.

[1] 1st Baron (1862–1936), ex-Conservative M.P.

[2] The result of the Ashton-under-Lyne by-election was announced that day; Allan Young, secretary of the New Party, was bottom of the poll.

Monday, 4 May 1931

Today, Harold had a drawing [in 'The Londoner's Diary'] by Gaudier-Brzeska or rather a drawing of Gaudier by the model (Miss [Nina] Hamnett) whom Gaudier had been painting. The fellow threw off his clothes and said 'now you paint me'. The picture was crude, rude and rather suggestive of a man on the cabinet or presenting his backside as an invitation. As I predicted to Gilliat, it produced a storm at Cherkley.

Sunday, 10 May 1931

Lloyd George and Megan [his daughter] came to dinner. Jean Norton, Janet and Valentine and Mike the only guests. L. G. and Max played around with the wireless for a long time. Then we discussed hymns and, especially, funeral hymns in connection with the parson's refusal to allow 'Rule, Britannia' to be played at Glen Kidston's memorial service.[1] L. G. said he loved hymns especially sung in harmony with bass voices predominating. He wants Handel's 'Largo' played at his own funeral.

Monday, 11 May 1931

Last night Max made Valentine read his India article out loud to L.G. The latter was very amused. At dinner Max and L.G. talked about operations. Max, referring to Snowden and Carson, both of whom have had prostate gland operations, declared that after this operation a man was no good either mentally or physically. He instanced R. D. Blumenfeld. L.G. countered with Clemenceau who had the same operation in 1912 when he was 71. He agreed, however, about Rosebery, who was the first famous statesman he could remember to have had this operation. Discussed war – L.G. says that today the Poles would beat the Germans, and music – L.G. is getting the wireless bug.

Tuesday, 12 May 1931

We are having some trouble about our Reilly memoirs which we are now publishing. Reilly's first wife is still alive and declares that she was never properly divorced. She threatens us with an injunction if we continue to refer to Pepita Bobadilla (Reilly's third wife) as Mrs Reilly. Pepita threatens us with blood and thunder – damages – if we do not. Reilly's real name was Rosenblum. So much we have ascertained from the wedding certificate of the first wife.[2]

Wednesday, 13 May 1931

Roy Howard, the head of the Howard-Scripps combine, who own twenty-four evening papers in the U.S.A. and one morning paper, here to dinner: a dapper, unimpressive, unhealthy, nervous little man rather like Poole, the

[1] Glen Kidston, record-breaking pilot and playboy, had died on 5 May when his airplane crashed in South Africa.

[2] For the full story of Reilly's complex marriages – and relations with other women – see Robin Bruce Lockhart's *Ace of Spies* (1967).

American diplomat, wears an eyeglass which he never uses, very neatly dressed (large black-pearl stud at night, a lurid jade tie-pin in the day-time), and wears a ring on each hand. Amusing in his newspaper talk which he understands; boring about world politics which he does not understand. He made two good remarks:

Max. 'Who is editor of the *New York American* (Hearst Press) now?'

Howard. 'I dunno. It's ten days since I left New York.'

Max. 'The *Sun* now (another rival) is an absolutely first-class paper, isn't it?'

Howard. 'It suits me puffectly.'

Thursday, 14 May 1931

Valentine is filing his divorce petition against Doris. I doubt, however, if he will every carry it through. He is so much under her influence, and she will not hesitate to hold him if she can. She has 'guts' and has already informed —— that she will slap her publicly the next time she sees her.

Max's attacks on the League [of Nations] are causing great excitement. The *News Chronicle* are running a daily campaign against him. The little man, however, does not care. I have been in torment the last two days. I see the weaknesses of the League and am quite prepared to attack them. I dare say it may fail, but I cannot help thinking that the proper course is to fight for a real League rather than for its suppression.

Friday, 15 May 1931

A fiendish day. I felt tired and 'nervy'. The truth is that I am worried about Max's anti-League stunt. Many of his criticisms of the League are true. Yet there is something immoral about his wish to destroy it, and, if he wishes, as he says, to put nationalism in its place, I cannot see that we are any better off from the peace point of view. In any case you cannot reduce foreign affairs to a vicious simplification. We had a telephone exchange this afternoon. He rang up three times in ten minutes: (1) to ask why my article against the League was not finished (I told Whelan I had difficulty in attuning my views to his and could not go the whole way), (2) to tell me he did not wish me to sign anything with which I did not agree; we all had free expression in his papers! (3) to tell me to drop the whole thing. He had plenty of sympathisers, who agreed with him and who would write the article. I was a European and he was an Empire man. My day was completely messed up, and in the evening, instead of going to the 1900 dinner to Churchill (which would have been fun) I came down to Cherkley. Jean was here. We had more discussions about the League. I told him his campaign would be very unpopular. He was quite inpenitent, said he would get lots of support, had been through this kind of thing before (probably in 1923 when he attacked France), that the League was no good, and that attack was good for a newspaper anyway.

Sunday, 17 May 1931

Max very funny about Whelan, who apparently gives us all nicknames. I am called – God knows why – 'His Excellency'.

Abe Bailey[1] came to England from the Cape when he was a boy and went into the City at the mature age of fifteen. He began his public life then, for apart from his business he attended evening classes and took an active part every Sunday in the Sermon Lane Mission. He still gives it £25 every year. He used to go to church every Sunday to learn how to speak. Spurgeon[2] was his model. He is anti-League and says the world has been ruined by three men: Wilson with the League, Baldwin with the American settlement, and Norman with the gold standard.[3]

In the afternoon finished my article, then went for a brisk walk with Max and Gordon. He has now taken to calling me a Continental, but is delighted with Garvin. Yet Garvin's anti-League of Nations which is in today's *Observer* is an exact paraphrase of mine. I expect Max used a good bit of my stuff in talking to Garvin. Bed midnight.

Wednesday, 20 May 1931

Max is writing his own life and has already started on it. He began today and in about three hours had dictated four or five thousand words. The idea arose out of the re-sale of the second volume of his *Politicians and the War* to the *Express*. This was to help the *Standard*, who had already given £5000 for them. Mike tried to get £10,000 from Robertson, and it was not till Max had agreed to throw in his early life as well that Robertson agreed. Max's real object, however, is not so much to help the *Standard* as to help the *Express* to reach the 2,000,000 mark before the *Mail*.

Felt very ill after last night. Stayed in bed till luncheon-time, telling office that my father was ill – a shameful and even dangerous proceeding. Did not get up till two, when I went down to Sonning with Pam to play golf. Pam, who had been up late the night before, was in a bad temper, and altogether the day was not a success.

Rarely have I felt so ill in my life after drink. My resolutions of Sunday last have not only broken down. They have never been put into effect.

Thursday, 21 May 1931

Still feeling ill after yesterday. Wrote an obituary of Snowden – mostly a

[1] Mine-owning millionaire and racehorse-owner (1864–1940).

[2] Rev. C. H. Spurgeon (1834–92), famous Baptist preacher.

[3] In 1923 Baldwin as Chancellor of the Exchequer negotiated the terms of the settlement of the American debt at much worse terms than the Cabinet had hoped. Sir Montagu Norman (1871–1950), Governor of the Bank of England, was still clinging to the gold standard to which Britain had returned in 1925, and was to abandon in September 1931.

rehash of a previous article I wrote about him after I interviewed him.[1] When Max entered the House of Commons in 1910, one of the first speakers he heard was Snowden. Snowden was then thirty-six. He spoke with great effect, and Max was impressed.

'Who is that man?' he whispered to Bonar Law.

'Snowden,' said Bonar Law.

'Is he sincere?'

'Certainly,' said Bonar Law. 'If he were in power, he'd hang us all on lamp-posts.' . . .

Went round to see Tommy, who was taken ill at dinner at the Terrell's last night, but was unable to see her. In the evening dined with Max and Janet at the Savoy.

Friday, 22 May 1931

Lunched at 11 Chester Street [Tommy's house] and met Captain Fane, who told me a good story about L.G. and Snowden. L.G. sent Snowden a basket of brown eggs after his operation with the following note: 'From one hen-roost robber to another.'

Saturday, 23 May 1931

Belloc came over to tea. The old 'boy' has not been feeling well, is suffering from high blood-pressure, and has been unable to work. He has been struggling away at his *History of England*, which brings him in about £100 a volume. He has been working so hard that he cannot work on his Cranmer which will bring him an advance of £1500.[2] He is very bitter about English people. In art, business, literature – money is their only test of success. He says he can test his own position among his friends by what he makes. Says Wells has not read a book for thirty years and is a philistine, but has ability in summarising the brains of others.

Tuesday, 26 May 1931

Came up from Coolham by the 9.1. In the afternoon went to see S. of Harley Street for Max. S. is the stone quack who has treated Millicent Hawes[3] and George and Eileen Sutherland. I pretended to have a stone in my own kidney and simulated Max's symptons. S. swore he can cure me (that is Max) without an operation. He struck me as a gas-bag and a liar, but he is certainly a fine specimen physically and, presumably, he has had some successes. . . S. took my water, said my liver was out of order, and that I was inclined to diabetes. Max came back from Paris by the Golden Arrow, and I went to the station to meet him. We went down to Cherkley almost imme-

[1] Philip Snowden (1864–1937), Labour M.P. and Chancellor of the Exchequer, created 1st Viscount, November 1931. He was ill at this time.

[2] Probably Belloc's *Cromwell* (1934); he wrote no book on Cranmer.

[3] Millicent, Duchess of Sutherland's name after marrying her third husband. George and Eileen were her son and daughter-in-law.

diately, and I spent the evening alone with him. We discussed doctors most of the evening. He is worried about his stone and is in rather low spirits. He is inclined to give S. a trial.

Thursday, 28 May 1931

Heavy thunderstorm and an atmosphere like lead. Lunched at Spears's to meet Princess Murat, a lively old girl, who was in Russia in 1917, met Rasputin and painted him. Other guests were Mr and Mrs Bernard Shaw, Lady Annaly, Lord Alastair Innes-Ker, Eddie Marsh,[1] Howard Baker, Harold and a woman, whose name I did not catch.

After luncheon G.B.S. skilfully silenced all conversation and gave us twenty minutes' monologue on St Joan: (1) The first Protestant – she put God before the Church, yet she wanted to go on a Crusade *v.* the Hussites, (2) the first nationalist – she organised war on a nationalist basis instead of on the tournament and ransom basis of the knights and landowners, and (3) she was the first military leader to understand the value of cannon as distinct from mere noisy accompaniment to battle.

In the evening came down to Cherkley. Jimmie and Philip Dunn,[2] Mike and myself only guests. Max up in arms against Winston who has been attacking Low in the *Strand* [magazine] in an article on cartoons. I do not think the attack is very offensive – not more offensive than is justified, but Max wants to go for Winston at any price. Throughout dinner, before it and after it, we had stone *ad nauseam*: reports of Max's doctors, x-ray photographs, long accounts of Pepys's stone troubles and his remedies for them, long account of Calvin, who died of stone at the age of fifty-six. Max talked well – especially good was his suggested article for Valentine on his fortieth birthday. Valentine to become a great man and devote himself to ambition because many great men did not develop their greatness until after forty: Knox, Cromwell and [Edward] Harriman of the Union Pacific. Valentine would have to convert Scotland back to Catholicism by the methods of Knox. He could not be a Knox, because he would have to lead an austere life, and there was Doris. He could not be Cromwell. Cromwell succeeded by his Ironsides. Tom Mosley had pre-empted Cromwell by his organisation of 'Fisticuffers'. Harriman had made fame and fortune by making the 'privy' doors on the Union Pacific all the same size and dimensions – uniformity of design from Frisco to New York – and more in the same vein.

Mike asked Max what he would have done in August 1914, if he had been made commander-in-chief, knowing all he knows now. Max's reply was 'Dig ourselves in, cement our trenches, make them invulnerable, and let the Germans wear themselves out against us.' It was what we ought to have done

[1] Lavinia, wife of 4th Baron Annaly; Lord Alastair Innes-Ker (1880–1936), equerry in ordinary to the King; Edward Marsh (1872–1953), knighted 1937, civil servant (private secretary to Churchill 1917–22, to J. H. Thomas 1929–36), Georgian poet and biographer of Rupert Brooke. Shaw's *St Joan* had appeared in 1923.

[2] (*b.* 1905), son of Sir James, was to marry Lady Rosslyn's daughter, Mary, in 1933.

in 1914, but we were stopped by the soldiers' parrot-cry that the morale of troops declines unless they can take the offensive.

Thursday, 4 June 1931

Down to Cherkley in evening. Travelled down with Valentine. Harold Macmillan, who is Kipling's publisher, had told him at luncheon that Kipling's fortune must be nearly a million, that Kipling spent nothing, and that his Jungle Books alone had brought him in a steady £30,000 a year for years. Clarence Dillon of Dillon, Read to dinner. Tall, clean-shaven, rather ascetic looking man, very abstemious and very lugubrious about America. Max, in his usual way with Americans, very pro-British and very confident about Britain's financial and industrial position. Dillon had stone in the kidney in 1917; rather than wait five weeks to have the stones removed and the kidney drained, he had it out altogether and was back to work in nine days.

Friday, 5 June 1931

Yesterday Max saw Neville Chamberlain. This interview was the reason for his secret visit to London. The Conservatives who have been trying to persuade him to join the Shadow Cabinet for some time, want his opinion on the alternative vote Bill. Hailsham wants the Conservatives in the Lords to throw out the Bill which will then take two years to go through – by which time the Liberals will no longer be dangerous or will have grown tired of waiting. Max thinks Conservatives are unnecessarily afraid of alternative vote. Labour will not give its alternative vote to Liberals. He would amend Bill (i.e. university vote and motor-car restrictions) but not reject it.

Sunday, 7 June 1931

After dinner Max was eloquent about love of power. What an opportunity L.G. threw away in 1918 because he could not abandon his love of power! If he had resigned after the Armistice; if he had said: 'I have done my job; others must make the peace'; above all, if he had had nothing to do with the Peace Treaty, he would have been in a position where not only England but half the world would have clamoured for him to come back. I asked Max if anyone had put this to L.G. at the time. He said that on the Sunday which fell somewhere about December 12th, 1918, he talked at Cherkley with L.G. on this subject from 10 a.m. to 10 p.m., pointing out the advantages of resigning. L.G. listened but was not influenced. . . Talked to Max about Mike's fiancée who has had a difficult weekend. Max now says he approves of her.

Monday, 8 June 1931

Irwin [Viceroy of India] suffers from religious mania and is an Anglo-Catholic of a very advanced and ardent type. Before seeing Gandhi he went into meditation and retreat, consulting and confessing to his favourite priest.

Pam and Jean came up with Max by car from Cherkley. Pam was very indiscreet and told him tales about Harold and me on the telephone: she hated Harold for telling Max she was always telephoning to me and told Max she could never get on to me for Harold being rung up by Jean Massareene.

Tuesday, 9 June 1931

At the Canning and Chatham Club dinner at Oxford last night Lord [David] Cecil told Harold Nicolson how much he admired Beaverbrook. 'I like him,' he said. 'He is a fanatic and so am I.'[1]

Yesterday Jean told me she had met [P.H.B.] Lyon, the new head of Rugby. Lyon had said that he hoped he would not call Mr X., sir. 'Why?' asked Jean. 'Because he was my old house tutor!' Lyon also said that Vaughan[2] had said that on every staff there should be at least one master who was ragged. It was good for the boys.

Wednesday, 10 June 1931

Max kept us waiting two hours for dinner last night. I imagine that he was putting through some finance deal – something connected with Gaumont's and cinemas. He was also doing something else. He was seeing Hailsham, who came to offer him the leadership in the House of Lords, Salisbury having resigned because he is out of tune with the Empire policy. Max, who is now being frequently consulted by the Conservatives, refused, although Hailsham said the only alternative was Bridgeman. Max said: 'What about yourself?' Hailsham said he wished to be Lord Chancellor in the next government. He then asked Max if he (Hailsham) should take it temporarily. Max said: 'No: you are the alternative leader to Baldwin and you cannot be put into the leadership by the anti-Baldwinites if you are Baldwin's lieutenant.' Hailsham said: 'I have thought of that.' Finally, Max agreed that if there was no one better than Bridgeman, Hailsham should take the leadership but only temporarily.[3] Hailsham told Max that he was out of favour with Baldwin, having demanded a more vigorous leadership in Baldwin's presence at a Shadow Cabinet meeting the other day. Neville Chamberlain is seeing Max today. . .

Harold tells me that Jarvie, a city chap, who played a big part in the formation of the Morris Committee, has now joined or is supporting the New Party.[4] McFadyean,[5] the former Reparations expert in Berlin, has also joined.

[1] Lord David Cecil, then aged 29, was in the chair at the dinner and sat between Churchill and Nicolson. He was later Professor of English Literature at Oxford.

[2] W. W. Vaughan (1865–1938), the previous headmaster.

[3] Hailsham did become leader of the House of Lords, 1931–5.

[4] John Gibson Jarvie (1883–1964), founder of the United Dominions Trust hire-purchase empire

[5] Sir Andrew McFadyean (*b.* 1887), Treasury official and later President of the Liberal Party organisation.

Dined with Tommy at 11 Chester Street and went to film afterwards. Hamish came in and told us how Randolph Churchill had his face slapped in America. Randolph said to a woman: 'What lascivious eyes and lecherous lips you have. I hope you live up to what you look.'

Thursday, 11 June 1931

Lunched with Jean Norton and heard much gossip about the King of Spain[1] who is staying with Lord and Lady Louis Mountbatten. The King is very deaf and has been consulting Scott, the English aurist. A Paris aurist told him he would have to be careful and restrict his love-making. Scott tells him his ear can be cured and that he can make love as much as he likes.

The King, who is very emotional and upset by the ingratitude of the Spaniards and especially of the aristocracy, speaks English quite well till he gets excited. He is a broken man and can talk of nothing else but the terrible day. He is poor and has not more than £6000 per annum. He had a large fortune abroad, but took it back to Spain to avoid the charge of being labelled a profiteer in bad times. (Here he is followed by detectives wherever he goes.) His secretary in Madrid, who could have smuggled his securities out of the country, handed them over to the Republicans.

The King was given only half-an-hour to pack. He preferred to use the time for destroying the photos of his best girls – there were 250 of them – and left with only a suitcase. On the ship – a naval cruiser – which took him to Marseilles he tried to take one of the small boat flags as a souvenir (the Republicans had torn up the Royal Flag in order to make a Republican flag out of it). The crew made him pay for it. He was landed at Marseilles at 3.30 a.m. with his suitcase. There was no one to meet him and he had to walk half-a-mile to get a taxi.

Since his departure he has had great difficulty in getting the Republicans to send him his personal effects. In return for a request for clothes the Republican Government sent him six pairs of riding breeches and two pink coats. His second set of false teeth (the first set evidently went wrong during the trouble), for which he had to send, was treated by the Spanish Customs authorities with great suspicion, and he had to pay 2000 pesetas export duty on them. He did, however, succeed in getting his Garter sent to him.

Last night Edwina [Mountbatten] gave a party at which the King was introduced to Marion Davies.[2] He had no idea who she was. She tried to get an interview out of him for her protector William Randolph Hearst. He kept

[1] Alfonso XIII (1886–1941), King of Spain, had been deposed when a republic was established on 14 April, see above page 163.

[2] (1877–1961), mistress of William Randolph Hearst (1863–1951), the American newspaper magnate, who promoted her as a film star in virginal parts, rather than as a comedienne for which she had more talent.

on saying: 'Don't talk about that horrid old man. He's only a newspaper man. You are too young, too beautiful, too blonde!' Later, he asked Jeanie if he could sleep with Marion Davies. 'You'll have all the Hearst Press against you if you do,' said Jeanie. 'Oh! I daren't do that,' said Alfonso.

Hearst is ponderous both in body and speech, has a sallow complexion, large pouches beneath the eyes, and looks unhealthy. He is not aggressive, talks slowly, and follows Marion Davies with his eyes all the time. I had some talk alone with him. He says Wall Street is dead and that the slump may last some time, although industry is beginning to pick up again. Newspapers are also feeling the strain. There may be some failures among provincial newspapers. He agrees entirely with Max's anti-League campaign. He seemed chiefly amused by the interest and news value we have given to our earthquake – which did no damage. It reminded him of the story of the Englishman who was buried in the San Francisco earthquake. The rescuers were digging near him when they heard a voice saying: 'Hi, pick me out first. I'm English. We're not used to this sort of thing.' A Hearst story of the slump. Man engages room in hotel. Reception clerk: 'Do you want it for sleeping sir, or, for jumping off?'

Saturday, 13 June 1931

Angela Forbes there and as offensive as ever. Twitted me all the time about my subservience to Max and asked why I did not stand up to him. The accusation is true, but the advice is difficult to follow.

Came over to Cherkley in the evening. Max in a difficult mood. He has been having trouble with his daughter and his son-in-law. Two days ago Ian,[1] who has been working in the *Evening Standard*, walked out of the office and said he was not coming back. Janet has been having a row with her father about money.

Monday, 15 June 1931

Came up from Cherkley by car with Max. Had two paragraphs in the Diary. On arrival found Harold in a great state of excitement. I had written a paragraph saying that Duleep[2] had just been elected a member of the Garrick Club. Gilliat had asked Harold (who is also a member) to verify it. Harold rang up the Secretary who confirmed it, adding: 'For God's sake don't put this in the paper.' Harold, terrified of being expelled from his club, begged Gilliat to take it out. Which he did.

Lunched with Freda [his sister], Jean [his wife] and Louis de Lorriol.[3] Freda's play has just come off. The child has several hundred pounds' worth of debt and does not know what to do – not a very cheerful outlook for her,

[1] Ian Campbell (1903–73), later 11th Duke of Argyll, married Beaverbrook's daughter, Janet, in 1927. They were divorced in 1934.

[2] Duleepsinhji, the great Indian cricketer, nephew of Ranjitsinhji.

[3] A Genevan businessman and friend of Lockhart's wife.

or for me who require a large guarantee from Dad. This was an unfortunate day. When I arrived at the office Lady Louis Mountbatten had left a message asking me to ring up. Mike at once assumed that this was to arrange an interview for me with the King of Spain. I thought otherwise – and was right. It was to take me to task for my paragraphs about the King of Spain. Jean Norton, of course, had let me down by inventing an excuse which let her out completely and left me in the soup.

Tuesday, 16 June 1931

At luncheon discussed Harold. He wants to get out of his contract with Max in order to edit Tom Mosley's new weekly [*Action*]. He would also get the literary reviewing in the *Daily Telegraph*, for which they are prepared to pay him £3000, renew his broadcasting, and make an income of about £6000 per annum. Last year his wife and he paid income tax on £9000 earned by literary work. She made about £6000 out of *The Edwardians* in America alone. In the afternoon went to see Rex who had been asked by Vansittart[1] to reprove me gently for certain leakages of information in the Diary, too much mention of Foreign Office secrets, etc. Van, who does not like Harold, wanted to make a row. Rex advised diplomacy and seeing me. According to Rex, Harold has many enemies in the Office. Dined with Max and Valentine at Malmaison, the new restaurant which Sorrani has opened in Stratton Street. It was packed to the last table – God knows why! Valentine drank pints of brandy. Max and I were bored. Went on to the Embassy [club] which was even more boring, and which is evidently failing. Then down by car to Cherkley.

Wednesday, 17 June 1931

Not such a good day: too much to eat and wine for both luncheon and dinner. Gave lunch to Kerensky in the Carlton Grill. Max, to my surprise, turned up and took quite an interest in Kerensky. Kerensky, who is forty-nine, looks marvellously well. He had his right kidney out for tuberculosis just before the revolution, and has never had a day's illness since. He has two sons: both in England and both engineers. One is building the new Thames bridge; the other is with a road-making firm in Rugby. Kerensky, Lenin and Protopopov[2] all came from Simbirsk. Kerensky's father was a state official and was Lenin's guardian or trustee. His ancestors were priests. Kerensky never knew either Lenin or Trotsky and had only seen them once or twice in the distance. Max asked Kerensky why he did not shoot Trotsky in 1917. Kerensky replied that Trotsky took no part in the July rebellion of 1917. He also asked him if he was the best orator in Russia. Kerensky replied that he could not say, but that in 1917 there was no meeting, however hostile or

[1] Sir Robert – later Lord – Vansittart (1881–1957) was Permanent Under-Secretary for Foreign Affairs and to be uncompromising opponent of appeasement.

[2] (1864–1918), Tsarist Minister of the Interior.

Bolshevik, which he could not dominate and finally turn by his oratory. . .

What was the reason of his collapse? Kerensky replied that the Germans forced on the Bolshevik rising, because Austria, Bulgaria and Turkey were on the eve of making a separate peace with Russia. The Austrians had decided to ask for a separate peace less than a fortnight before the Revolution.

Max: 'Would you have mastered the Bolsheviks if you had made a separate peace yourselves?'

Kerensky: 'Of course. We should be in Moscow now.'

Max: 'Why didn't you do it then?'

Kerensky: 'We were too naive.'

Kerensky, who after the October revolution was in hiding for nearly eight months, fled to peasants in the Pskov government [i.e. region] to start with. In spite of the price on his head no one ever betrayed him. Last year he came to Oxford to lecture and attacked the Bolsheviks. They obviously complained, for the next time Kerensky went to our Passport Control Office in Paris he was refused a visa unless he gave an undertaking not to talk about Russia. MacDonald and Henderson, pointing out that England, the great home of liberty, had reached a funny stage when it demanded that Kerensky, when asked his opinion about Russia, should say: 'I have one, but the British Labour Government do not allow me to express it.' He received his visa.

Came down to Horsham by the 4.50, watched Sussex *v.* Notts for a few minutes, then took Duleep, Pelham [Warner], and Sir Home Gordon (pronounced Hume) out to Coolham. Duleep – very nice and told us some good stories: how Ranji telegraphs to him when he is not playing well and says: 'Suggest you give up cricket and take to tennis and challenge Betty Nuthall [tennis champion].' Ranji, who arrives on Saturday, will go straight to Ballynahinch. He is fishing mad now. He is still a good shot, but he can no longer play cricket, as he has only one eye [the other] he lost in a shooting accident in 1915.

Monday, 22 June 1931

Max was very amusing about Valentine's early career. He met Valentine shortly after he was wounded [in the First World War]. Valentine was then tall and slim (!) and very good-looking. He was entangled with a French prostitute called F. After his wound, was floating about London looking for a job. All the time was putting up schemes for bringing F. over to London as a hospital nurse or anything. Later, Max gave him a job in the Ministry of Information.[1] Party of Baptist Ministers came over from America to see British effort. They were an important mission and were to be sent to the front. Valentine begged to go. He wished to get back to Paris to see F. He went. Visit a tremendous success. Baptists delighted with Paris and with Valentine. Lord and Lady Kenmare [Castlerosse's parents] came to Max to beg him to send Valentine on no more missions to Paris. Then Max got

[1] Beaverbrook became Minister of Information in February 1918.

Valentine a job with Lancelot Smith.[1] Soon quarrelled. Valentine in debt. Wasting his money on F. Smith and Valentine both went to see Max. Max stormed at Valentine who went up the drive with Smith. 'The little man,' he said, 'was pretty hot in what he said, but I'm sure I'll get my money in the end.' Later, Valentine asked Max to supper at the Savoy one night. There was a private room. Max went in, not knowing what was going to happen. There was Valentine – his face in strips. F. had scratched him till his cheeks were bare of flesh. Valentine then went with Max's help to New York to a finance house. After a year he turned up in London again. What was wrong? Oh, finance did not suit him. What was the trouble? Well, there was a woman whom he had to follow to London. Who was it? It was Mrs Hearst. Max did not believe it, but it was. (Before this, there was an episode when Max went to Deauville to see Lloyd George. There Valentine met —— and at once fell. Soon he had taken up his quarters at ——'s house.) Later, he became Max's travelling companion. They went to Monte Carlo together. Max wanted to write an article on Monte Carlo, so he said to Valentine, 'You go into one room and write an article, and I'll go into another and do the same.' When Valentine came back, Max said: 'Your article goes.' It was a very good one. And that is how Valentine became a journalist.

Tuesday, 23 June 1931

Harold wrote to Max today asking to be released from his contract. Spoke with Max about it in the evening. He said that Harold would not be a serious loss to us. He was too precious. He thought he was a fool hitching his wagon to Tom Mosley's star, but he did not wish to stand in his way. He agreed it would be foolish for Harold to remain in Fleet Street. Harold asked me today where Hearst was. He wanted to approach him for money for a new evening paper which the New Party propose to form. They require £1,500,000.

Wednesday, 24 June 1931

Again nothing on my book. Stayed to luncheon at Cherkley and then drove up to London with Max who is pessimistic about himself, says his life's work is done, and wants to pull out of England altogether. Advised him to take a holiday before deciding anything. Talked to Harold about the Diary – in the event of his going. He says I am the only person to run it and recommends me to get in two young men to go about and collect material.

Friday, 26 June 1931

Pam went over to Paris – nominally by herself to see the Grand Prix. I do not believe it. It is more than time that I rid myself of this entanglement altogether. Letter from Moura exhorting me to pull myself together and saying that I can do something better than act as valet to Max.

[1] (1870–1941), partner in Rowe & Pitman, stockbrokers.

Sunday, 12 July 1931

In the evening Eddie Goulding[1] came to dinner. He is an Englishman who has spent years in Hollywood, is a famous producer, writes songs, and works twenty hours a day. He is very bitter about our films and our failure to grasp the importance of 'information' for the Empire. He would like to revive the Ministry of Information. He sees the American film destroying the Empire. He sees America and civilisation itself being destroyed by the gangster. He invented the 'stand-in' girl – mainly for Greta Garbo who during her menstruation cannot work.

Tuesday, 14 July 1931

At 1.15 went to have my medical test for the London, Liverpool and Globe Insurance people. Two doctors this time, as my policies amount to more than £5000. I was given a better bill of health than three years ago – a first-class life, in fact, which I feel far from possessing. Lunched at the Wellington. In the evening went round to see Tommy. Found Tommy out and the house full of young men to see Mary: John de Forest, who proposed and was rejected that evening, Bill Astor, John Betjeman, Hinchingbrooke, etc.[2] ——, who is Lady Castlerosse's friend, is known amongst the young and irreverent as the 'belching baronet'. Tommy came in late. She is still sore with me about Max's party and his invitation to Mary to help him. However, we dined together at the Carlton Grill and made friends again. Pam, who is in trouble, came back from Portsmouth. I went to see her at ten o'clock and arrived just as she did. Stayed with her till twelve.

Thursday, 16 July 1931

A bad day. Bobby Shaw,[3] who is in the Coldstream or the Grenadiers, has been caught out on a 'buggery' charge and comes up at the Vine Street Police Court tomorrow. There are twenty guardsmen to give evidence against him. Lady Astor came to see Max about it. There will be no publicity. Shaw was given every chance of leaving the country, but his mother did not want him to take it. Valentine Castlerosse, who has been restored to his wife for some time, set an ambush for her last night and waited outside her house himself. Along came . . . the belching baronet, waited for Lady Castlerosse's signal, and, when it came, made for the front door. Valentine set on him and hammered him, the while Lady Castlerosse descended and shrieked 'Murder!' in the street.

[1] Edmund Goulding (*d.* 1959), director of *Grand Hotel, Dark Victory, Claudia.*

[2] John de Forest (*b.* 1907), second son of Arnold Maurice Count Bendern, see above, page 61; Lockhart was to see more of him later; William Waldorf Astor (1907–66), like his parents, a Conservative M.P., succeeded as 3rd Viscount in 1952; John Betjeman (*b.* 1906), soon to become a Beaverbrook journalist, now Poet Laureate; Viscount Hinchingbrooke (*b.* 1906), later Conservative M.P., renounced Earldom of Sandwich, 1964, and became Mr Victor Montagu.

[3] Son of Nancy, Lady Astor by her first marriage (*d.* 1970).

Spent afternoon talking to the National Provincial Bank and to the insurance people. In order to get my overdraft I shall have to leave Glyn's. In evening dined with Tommy and went to *Late Night Final* – a play of the newspaper world – very anti the popular newspaper proprietor. E. V. Lucas[1] was there. His lady friend has just died, and we took him to supper at the Savoy. Although he is very shaky, he drank one and a half bottles of champagne. He said no man nowadays could be a journalist and remain a gentleman – which is more or less true.

Sunday, 19 July 1931

Dined at Stornoway in the evening: the Amerys, Janet, Pam, Jean Norton, and Max and Peter. Big Max very serious about the international crisis, thinks it will last a long time and that, if France stands out, the situation will be very serious for England. Amery said: 'Norman [Governor of the Bank of England] has sacrificed our industry and our production for the sake of a bill-market which may plunge us into disaster at any moment. We have preferred to be moneylenders to being manufacturers.'

Monday, 20 July 1931

Dined at Stornoway: Venetia Montagu, the Wadsworths (Americans who are going to Russia on business), Edward Marjoribanks, Jimmie Dunn, and Driberg.[2] Lots of conversation – mostly about women and the [Geneva disarmament] conference which Max thinks is bound to fail. He has been talking to Snowden. Apparently Snowden and Ramsay are very pro-German. Henderson, however, who has staked everything on disarmament and has therefore to conciliate the French, is playing up to the French.

Wednesday, 22 July 1931

Max is good to people in trouble; notably, Lady Astor, who sent her husband on Friday night to thank Max for the help he had given her over Bobby Shaw's case (Bobby Shaw is Nancy's son by her first husband. He was convicted of 'buggery' and was given five months).

Friday, 24 July 1931

John Strachey and Allan Young resigned today from the New Party.[3] Max, not trusting Harold, told me to get hold of Strachey for the story. I spoke to him on the telephone. He said that the trouble had been coming for some time, that Young and himself felt that Tom was drifting very rapidly back to Toryism. Harold was very sore about my paragraphs. At the

[1] Author and chairman of Methuen, publishers (*d.* 1938).

[2] Tom Driberg (*b.* 1905), joined *Daily Express* 1928, wrote 'Dragoman' column and 'William Hickey' in the *Daily Express*, later a Labour M.P.

[3] John Strachey (1901–63) had been a Labour M.P. since 1927, but had left the party to join Mosley. He returned to the Labour Party and was re-elected in 1945 and became a minister. Allan Young had been secretary of the New Party; he became a friend and confidant of Harold Macmillan.

same time he can hardly expect the paper to be run for his consideration. After telling me for weeks that Young was a brilliant man and the great stand-by of the party, he now says that he is a neurotic and going off his head.

Lunched with Tommy and Harry. They give up 11 Chester Street tomorrow, Harry going to Le Touquet for the weekend today. In the afternoon tidied my desk up at the *Evening Standard. Let us see how long I can keep it neat!* In the evening went with Jean to meet Mrs Turner [his mother-in-law] who arrived from Switzerland. Had another row with Jean – this time about Pam, who cannot keep her tongue behind her teeth. Dined at Stornoway. Rob [his brother] who has just returned from Canada, Gerhardi and self. As Max was interested in having Rob's news, I talked to Gerhardi. Gerhardi quarrelled with Max about two years ago, because Gerhardi was rude to Tim Healy. Now Max, pleased with Gerhardi's portrait of him in *Memoirs of a Polyglot*, has taken him back – but with a proper gulf of offended greatness. He did not say more than two words to Gerhardi all evening.

Sunday, 26 July 1931

In the evening dined with Maurice Peterson at Monseigneur. We made pigs of ourselves and finished up at the 43 in a blaze of bad alcohol – my first lapse since June 5th. Maurice told me two good stories: one about Franco,[1] the Spanish airman, who is behind most of the Communist trouble in Spain. Franco was rescued from the sea (after the failure of his Atlantic flight) by H.M.S. *Eagle*. Spaniards decided to give the officers and crew a silver centrepiece in the form of an eagle to commemorate the occasion. Franco, however, made himself so impossible with the King that during the monarchy the Spaniards did not like to make the gift. Franco has also made himself unpopular with the Republic, and H.M.S. *Eagle* is still without a centre-piece. Franco is no hero. He ran away during his own attempted revolution and left his co-mutineers in the aerodrome to bear the consequences. Even the Portuguese found him revolting. In Lisbon he spent all his time drinking and messing about with women.

Maurice thinks Tyrrell will leave Paris soon owing to the scandal of his daughter's marriage.[2] The first British woman to be married in Notre Dame since Mary Queen of Scots, she is now having her marriage annulled [as unconsummated]. She told Mrs Cavendish-Bentinck about this – long ago. She said, 'Never mind dear. It took Charles nearly a year.'

Monday, 27 July 1931

Met Neville Chamberlain at Stornoway. He had come to see Max before he left for Canada. Neville will never be Prime Minister. He is as cold and 'clammy' as a dead trout.[3]

[1] Ramon Franco, brother of General Franco, later to be shot down over the Mediterranean in December 1936 during the Spanish Civil War.

[2] Tyrrell remained Ambassador to Paris another three years.

[3] Chamberlain became Prime Minister on 28 May 1937.

Tuesday, 28 July 1931

At last after days of uncertainty Valentine is going to Canada after all. Max has been playing hurt feelings. Tonight, however, he told the story to his own credit: how he had told Valentine he could not take him because of his reputation, etc., and how Valentine had besought him to take him, and promised to reform, and in the end had cried. Max had then said, 'I could not resist the tears.' Doris, apparently, also rang Max up and promised to divorce Valentine if only Max would take him to Canada.

Monday, 3 August 1931

Cargilfield [School], which has about 180 boys, has a library.[1] Here are the returns for 1930 and 1929 (in brackets). Total books taken out 1530 in 1930. Natural history books were an easy first. Authors came as follows: Buchan 88 (90), Conan Doyle 81 (62), Kipling 49 (67), Stevenson 39 (77), Dickens 33 (27), Merriman 33, Verne 25, Weyman 21, Anstey 20, Chesterton 14 Haggard 13, Kingsley 11, Scott 9, Dumas 7.

Thursday, 13 August 1931

Millie told us a good story about Lyautey. In 1909 she thought herself in love with Colonel Fitzgerald. They wanted to go to Algeria and Morocco where 'Fitz' knew Lyautey and many of the French.[2] In the circumstances they decided to go as brother and sister. Millie was introduced to Lyautey as Miss Fitzgerald. She was staying with him, when a letter arrived from the Comte de Vogüé (Lyautey's greatest friend) asking him to be especially kind to the Duchess of Sutherland. Lyautey enjoyed the joke immensely.

Friday, 14 August 1931

Bridget Paget arrived [at Juigné] – looking very ill. She is on her way to Biarritz to stay with the Prince [of Wales] and Eric Ednam. Millie thinks she is going to marry Eric and hates her – subconsciously, perhaps, because of Rosie.

Saturday, 15 August 1931

Dined at home. Millie cannot stand Bridget and is obviously full of resentment at the idea of her marrying Eric. . . Harry is also making himself a nuisance by insisting on Tommy going to Le Touquet. Millie is angry and has given Harry a piece of her mind – which will not help Tommy. Altogether it looks as if I shall have to go to Munich alone. We have not been such a happy family since Bridget arrived and to make matters worse the weather has also broken down.

[1] His brother Rufus was Headmaster at this time.

[2] Millicent Duchess of Sutherland married Colonel P. D. Fitzgerald as her second husband in 1914. Louis Lyautey was resident commissary general in Morocco, 1912–25, and became a Marshal. The Marquis de Vogüé was a champagne magnate and President of the Suez Canal Company.

Sunday, 16 August 1931

The Prince who was to have come to Angers by plane tomorrow, telephoned to say he would come to Tours instead. Millie is in a fever lest he should not turn up at all and Bridget will be left on her hands. Bridget is in a bad state of health...

Monday, 17 August 1931

A day of storm and wind. All our plans for doing anything were upset by the Prince of Wales, who postponed his departure from England until tomorrow. Bridget was therefore left on our hands for another day.

Bridget said that the Prince was a fool to let a man like Valentine see him at his private parties, which were harmless enough, but where everyone including the Prince took too much to drink.

Lockhart arrived in Munich on 20 August 1931.

Friday, 21 August 1931

Another cold and unpleasant day. In the morning Captain Droctor, an ex-officer who is now an art-dealer and who is well in with Hitler, came to see me. He said it would not be possible for me to see Hitler today, rang me up again at one and asked me to wait, as it might be possible, rang me up again at two and he would call for me in a car immediately. I was not, however, to see Hitler (he has gone to North Germany for a week) but I was shown round 'Das Braune Haus' by Alfred Rosenberg, who is Hitler's best friend and intellectual adviser.[1] Rosenberg drove me himself in his car to the Nazi headquarters which are now the old Bülow Palace next to the Glyptothek and the Propyläen in the Tierstrasse. The whole place has been reconstructed under Hitler's personal guidance (he began life as a builder). Imposing entrance – two pillars – one with Deutschland Erwacht – swastika, and the entrance hall with Nazi guard. No one – not even Hitler himself – can bring a stranger in without passing the control. Rosenberg tried to bring us and was pulled up. Control, he explained, is necessary on account of Communist 'provokators' and police-spies. Upstairs magnificent committee-rooms including the new cabinet room for the national council. Magnificent leather chairs in tiers round the room: big centre table with two chairs like a throne, big swastika shield on carpet with swastika design: even clock is made in form of swastika.

Back in London, Lockhart saw Mosley:

Thursday, 27 August 1931

In the afternoon saw Tom Mosley who professes to be delighted with his

[1] Alfred Rosenberg (1893–1946), fervent Nazi, at one time Hitler's deputy, edited *Völkischer Beobachter* and was commissioner for East European Affairs during the war; hanged at Nuremberg.

prospects. He claims to have foreseen the crisis.[1] It was its inevitability which made him leave the Labour Party and start his own. There is no more chance of his returning to the Labour Party than flying. They are a rump without a single man of any eminence. The National Government cannot help the situation merely by a policy of cutting down. Circumstances will compel them to remain longer than they intend, and without a constructive policy the revenue situation (which depends on industry) will get steadily worse. That is when the New Party will come in. Tom has been seeing a good deal of Winston. He claims he will get support from Labour and Conservatives and L.G. He is *very* interested in Hitlerism and has made a close study of it. Lastly, he feels sure Max will join up with him – must join him eventually.

Monday, 31 August 1931

Max came back at 3 p.m. – he has shingles – having crossed on the Norddeutscher Lloyd *Europa*. He apparently came back as quickly as he could. He has already made up his mind about the new Government. Baldwin was a fool to go in with Ramsay. He should have formed a government himself – or rather – he should have told the King he would form a government. This in itself would have enabled him to obtain financial support for the pound. He could then have gone to the country on tariffs and he would have come back with 350–400 Conservatives. Instead, in his insane desire to foist the responsibility on the Socialists, he has been left with the baby. The question of tariffs has been shelved, and the Conservatives will have to bear the responsibility of the unpopularity of the present government, the Socialists having slipped out and left only their shell composed of MacDonald, Thomas and Snowden. Max dined alone with Amery. Edward Marjoribanks came in later. He told us Hailsham, who played an active part in the negotiations, is furious with Baldwin. He (Hailsham) was never offered a seat in the cabinet.

Tuesday, 1 September 1931

Went round to see Max at 7.30. He was very busy and rather secretive. He has a hush-hush political dinner tonight. All I know is that Edward Marjoribanks is going. Baldwin, Neville Chamberlain and, I think, Ramsay have asked to see Max. He has told them to go to hell. In his own words to Robertson and me he said: 'It is a matter of intense interest to Mr Baldwin to know what I intend doing during the next three weeks. Well, he won't know.' What he intends doing is spiking Baldwin's guns through the agency of Hailsham. Bernstorff, whom I saw yesterday, tells me that *The Times* had a note saying that 'it was a good thing for the country that at the moment of

[1] The crisis, mainly financial, had resulted in the formation on 25 August of the National Government, basically Conservative, but with the Socialist Ramsay MacDonald remaining as Prime Minister, while the Conservative leader, Stanley Baldwin, became Lord President of the Council. The gold standard was abandoned in September.

crisis most of the people who might have caused mischief were either ill or abroad'. Max and L.G. were envisaged. The paragraph was not passed.

Wednesday, 2 September 1931

Dined at Stornoway: present Sir Richard[1] and Lady Squires, Bridget Paget, Hore-Belisha and, later, Edward Marjoribanks. Hore-Belisha and Edward hate each other. They are both self-seekers. Squires made a good remark. Belisha was telling how Gandhi at his farewell demonstration in Bombay kissed several women but paid no attention to his wife who stood aloof. 'Why,' says Squires, 'he's almost a European.' Marjoribanks refutes the idea that Simon has no human side to him. Simon married very young without a penny. Took a tiny cottage in the country for his wife – bad drains – and in consequence wife died after second baby was born. Simon never forgave himself and took the mother's burdens on his own shoulders. He was a wonderful father to the boys. For twelve years he could talk of nothing but his wife's death.[2]

Thursday, 3 September 1931

Had a long talk with Thornhill about Russia. He also told me that at Archangel the 13th battalion of the Yorkshire Light Infantry revolted and set up a Soviet. Two sergeants were given fifteen years. They should be coming out now. Eleanor Toye told Jean that Reilly used to suffer from severe mental crises amounting to delusions. Once he thought he was Jesus Christ.

Lockhart and Beaverbrook visited Lloyd George at his home.

Saturday, 5 September 1931

Churt is a lovely place – even in the rain it looked lovely. House – built by L.G. himself ten years ago on Lord Ashbourne's estate – quite small. Stands on a height overlooking the plains for miles. Has a porch with pillars, birch-trees, heather all round, and a side garden-wall with roses. L.G.'s library – full of books of statesmen's speeches – Fox, Grattan, Sheil, Pitt, Peel, etc., and lives of statesmen. Glorious view from one window towards Wales and the west. Old Welsh crossbow and an old English ship (model) on walls. On French window – a stained-glass panel of St David with leek and coat-of-arms. I sat in library with Miss Stevenson and the doctor, while Max talked to L.G. Doctor was in Malay States at one time. He said L.G. has made a very good patient – wonderful health for his age – and will be as strong as ever. Must however go slow. He has not been out yet (weather too bad) and has only been allowed to take a very general and limited interest in politics.

[1] (1880–1940), Master of the Supreme Court of Newfoundland.

[2] Sir John Simon (1873–1954), later 1st Viscount, became Foreign Secretary in November.

Max says he looked very frail – hands shrunk – that, in fact, he will not be back in politics for some time. The doctor told me that L.G. had spoken frequently about Max and that he admired him greatly.

On the way down Max talked about himself, said he was paying now for the nervous strain of East Islington and St George's. Said he had a terrible reaction in May and June – especially after he came back from Germany, was unhappy and miserable, worried over trifles... Says he is cured now and well again. During his holiday he went to Newcastle, New Brunswick, his home town, but could not stand it. He lived in a private [railway] car and pulled out to a siding a few miles out. It was no good. He was pursued by men who had known him as a boy, who had been at school with him, wanting to borrow anything from $5 to $5000.

He wants a general election at once and a new Tariff Party formed under Ramsay. This would give the Tariff Party: (1) all the Conservatives, (2) a large MacDonald Labour vote in the constituencies, and (3) a Liberal following under Simon. He thinks – which is obvious – that the Conservatives must rope in some of the other people for their tariff programme. He saw Ramsay on Thursday and put this plan up to him. Ramsay, he said, agreed or at least said he was not opposed to a tariff. Baldwin will be pleased. I told Max that Baldwin's point of view would be: 'Here is this terrible man Beaverbrook stirring up hornets' nests again at a moment when we should all be pulling together. He is thinking only of himself and not of the country, etc.' Max agreed. His comment was: 'At any rate we'll embarrass him.'

Monday, 7 September 1931

Max told a good story about his first meeting with Gerhardi. Gerhardi came at eleven in the morning. Max said: 'Will you have a drink?' 'Yes,' says Gerhardi. 'What'll you have,' says Max. 'Champagne,' says Gerhardi. His one desire was to see H. G. Wells. Max asks him to dinner for that purpose. Gerhardi comes in his same old suit. Wells takes no notice of him whatsoever. Gerhardi is sad. Then, as the men leave the dining-room, Gerhardi draws back deferentially to give place of honour to H.G. But H.G. says: 'No, you first. You are tomorrow. I am yesterday.' Gerhardi is in seventh heaven.

Harold Nicolson, who had joined Oswald Mosley's paper Action, *'The New Weekly of the New Movement,' wrote to Lockhart on 11 September 1931:*

Will you help me in a certain matter?

I want to crib good cartoons from foreign papers. I have arranged for (and can manage) all except the Russian. You, I believe, take in Russian cartoons. Could you be an angel and send me any good ones with a rough translation of the captions?

How shall I repay you for this service? Merely by giving you paragraphs more informative and accurate than the Olivier paragraphs free of charge.

The bore is that what I know is not knowledge in the sense of the *E.S.* I can give you much inside information about the New Party, but for the moment that is no good to you.

Meanwhile here is one point of interest. [Arthur] Henderson admitted (see Hansard) that his economy committee had agreed to economies of 56 million. How were these produced? They simply must have hit the teachers and police if not the unemployed. This is a point on which the National Government have not really tackled him. But Tom will. If you throw out hints in the Diary on this point you will eventually seem to have been very well informed. But this is for your ear only. You understand. I do not mind telling you everything since you can grasp it. I mind telling Gilliat or Shanks anything since they get hold of the wrong end of every stick.

Saturday, 12 September 1931

The Prince of Wales, who is going to stay with Laura at Stronelarig, has been going great guns with Lady (Thelma) Furness[1] at Bayonne. Lord Furness, whom Tommy saw at Le Touquet, is miserable about it. The Schneider Trophy [air] contest put off on account of weather. G. M. Thomson,[2] the Scottish author, joined us temporarily today during Shanks's absence on holiday.

Sunday, 13 September 1931

In the afternoon played golf. In the evening Rudolph de Trafford and his wife, and Simon Rodney and his wife came to dinner.[3] Rudolph de Trafford is a clever fellow. He is with Lee, Higginson. He says we must have an election this year. There will be no confidence in the City until we can get a government which will be in for several years. There has to be an election in two-and-a-half years anyway. He also tells me that last January an American banker wrote to Sir Guy Granet[4] saying that he was afraid of the pound and thought we might have to come off the gold standard. Granet was furious. What the hell could an American know about our situation? Nevertheless, he sent the letter to [Montagu] Norman who was impressed and asked Granet to come to see him. 'This is very interesting', said Norman. 'It's exactly the ammunition I want for the Chancellor.' Rudolph de Trafford also told me that one of his American partners had hit the nail on the head when he said: 'Half the trouble in the world today is due to the fact that the Bank of France is stronger than the Bank of England.' Trafford says the Governor is all right and that rumours of his resignation are nonsense.

[1] Thelma, Lady Furness, mother of 2nd Viscount Furness and daughter of an American diplomat, Harry Hays Morgan, (*d.* 1970).

[2] George Malcolm Thomson (*b.* 1899) became Beaverbrook's personal secretary, and later chief leader writer on the *Daily Express*, wrote many books and was *Evening Standard* book critic.

[3] Rudolph de Trafford (*b.* 1894) was a banker and the Hon. Simon Rodney (*b.* 1895) the brother of the 8th Baron Rodney.

[4] (1867–1943), barrister and chairman of the London, Midland and Scottish Railway.

Thursday, 17 September 1931

Max in a frenzy about two paras in today's Diary on Gandhi's praying in a Committee room in the House of Commons. Yesterday, Gandhi, who had been seeing some Labour members at the House, went into a Committee Room, when seven o'clock came, to pray with Miss Slade. Horrabin[1] and Lansbury were there, and Allison, our Lobby correspondent, slipped in with Barkley. The paragraphs were written on an exalted note,[2] and Max was annoyed at our giving publicity to the 'sly old fox' who was clever enough to use even the House of Commons for his propaganda... 'How I hate the enemies of the Empire!' said Max.

Sunday, 20 September 1931

Arrived at Stornoway with Renate Mueller[3] to find Max, Robertson, Mike, Thomson, Valentine and Sir Matthew Wilson all assembled. There had been a cabinet meeting. On Friday and half day Saturday £37½ millions had been withdrawn from England. In self-defence we had had to abandon the gold standard. Tariffs are dropped for the moment, the Liberals having persuaded the Cabinet that we must restore the confidence of the foreigner at any price, and that the fall of the pound which is inevitable will do everything that tariffs can do. This is the point of view of Winston, who only a few days ago proclaimed himself a tariffist! Winston is very weak these days – like a schoolboy trying to get into the team. He is nearly always slightly the worse for drink. Max went off to see the Prime Minister at nine-thirty. He did no good *re* tariffs. Ramsay talked to him about his wife (Ramsay's). It was a very friendly talk, but for the moment tariffs are shelved, and Max never really got down to tin-tacks. This afternoon Ramsay, Baldwin, Snowden and Samuel[4] received a delegation of editors at 6.30.

Edward Marjoribanks said to Hore-Belisha: 'This is your chance now to make an attack on the Government. It's your big chance to get a name for yourself.' Great fellows – these politicians – always thinking of themselves.

Monday, 21 September 1931

Stock Exchange closed. Unofficial quotations for sterling were approx.: $4.15, 105–110 francs, 18–19 marks. Max, after seeing McKenna and Winston, prophesies that in three months time the pound will be nearer $4.40 than $4. He is delighted at the collapse of the gold standard. He has always opposed it vigorously both in private and in public.

Lunched with Namier and Malcolm MacDonald at the Lombard.[5]

[1] J. F. Horrabin (1884–1962), journalist, cartographer and Labour M.P.

[2] 'Her eyes were closed and her classic features lit up with light of devotion ...'

[3] German film actress, who also appeared in an English film, *Sunshine Susie*.

[4] Sir Herbert Samuel (1970–1963), later 1st Viscount, was Home Secretary and leader of the Liberals in the National Government.

[5] Lewis Namier (1888–1960), historian, knighted 1952; Malcolm MacDonald (*b.* 1901), son of the Prime Minister, was then National Labour M.P. for Bassetlaw.

Malcolm is rather nice – not very prepossessing, but with a nice voice and a nice accent. He is of course pro-Labour, but is supporting his father. He says that until Monday morning (August 24th) his father was convinced that Baldwin was going to form a ministry. When he left Lossiemouth [his home] he said he would be back for good in a few days. The King pressed him to remain – but the real reason was that the Conservatives did not want to form a government, they being obsessed with the idea of landing Labour with the baby. The other point he made was that, while Labour still retains all its genuine old Labour support in the constituencies it has lost the floating vote which put them in last time. He says if there were an election today his father's policy would win easily.

At Stornoway in evening. McKenna and Winston there and, later, Max dined alone with Hailsham. Meeting of 1922 Club [Conservative back-benchers] at which almost unanimous resolution was passed for an immediate election on tariffs under MacDonald. A Baldwin election had almost no appeal. 25 Liberals will support it.

Tuesday, 22 September 1931

Stock Exchange still closed, but will open tomorrow. Max, busy all day telephoning diary, leaders, news stories and city articles to all his papers. He is a news service in himself. I doubt if Northcliffe *contributed* anything like as much to his papers. Lunched with Pam. She may be going to India. Nigs and Blossom and Buck and Diana are all leaving on the 15th October. Nigs is to entertain Gandhi on the 3rd. Apparently, the India Office gave a party for Gandhi on his silence day!

In the evening gave Tommy dinner at the Basque. She saw Freda and Bridget. The Prince rang up. Bridget has just bought pounds' worth of dresses and will of course have to pay more for them. The Prince rang up Peacock who apparently advised her to stay at 110 if she could. The Prince says there will be an election, and that it will be a very good thing. Pamela Smith was to have gone today to Germany to finish her education. She is not going. Her mother has been told that revolution in Germany is a dead 'cert' before Xmas.

Saturday, 26 September 1931

Rothermere has gone to Berlin. Lord Hailsham came in and talked to Max.

These two are very close friends now and are out to torpedo Baldwin. Leslie Hore-Belisha and Edward Marjoribanks had a row, and Edward lost his temper. Leslie – a Jew and a Liberal – had been sticking up for Disraeli, while Edward – a Tory and an aristocrat – was crabbing Dizzy and extolling Gladstone. I don't know what happened – perhaps it was Hore-Belisha's reply to Edward's boast that he had the biggest chest in the House of Commons. 'That comes from blowing your own trumpet so much' – at any rate Edward lost his temper.

Played golf at Addington with Benskin and Drayton. Lunched at Cavalry Club and in the evening dined with Moura at Monseigneur. She had to leave me for an hour to go to Wells's party for Charlie Chaplin at the Eiffel Tower. Wells likes Chaplin – says they are two Cockneys, but thinks Charlie has an overdeveloped sense of publicity and feels awkward and begins to pose if he is not recognised in the streets. Wells walked with him along Tottenham Court Road. Drank too much and finished up at the 43. Spent the best part of £20.

Sunday, 27 September 1931

Dined at Stornoway: Aga Khan, Valentine, Richard Norton, Scatters, and a young American banker who sang divinely. Max had promised the Aga a party with women whom the Aga had never seen. They were: Mrs Hall, Renate Mueller, two Childs' sisters (the other sister married the Portman heir), and Edith Baker, who played for us divinely. Aga told me Gandhi was a complete follower of Tolstoy – the two men never met but corresponded. Tolstoy's *Letters to a Hindu* were written to Gandhi. Richard Norton, who has been seeing much of Charlie Chaplin, says that Charlie has scored most out of his famous interview with Gandhi. He has learnt a perfect imitation stunt of Gandhi and Miss Slade. Richard also told me George Edwardes story of Tolstoy. George Edwardes was on his way to Vienna to buy a play, saw Tolstoy's death in papers, and said: 'Poor old Tolstoy! I liked his "Goodbye" so much.' Edwardes and Tosti were friends.[1]

Monday, 28 September 1931

J. H. Thomas[2] and the King on J.H.T.'s taking office in the new Government: The King. 'A year ago you said to me when I came through my illness: "Sir, it was 'guts' that pulled you through." Now I say to you, Mr Thomas, it was "guts" – magnificent guts – that made you do what you did!'

Dined at Stornoway: Brendan Bracken, Mrs Montagu, Daphne and Henry Weymouth.[3] Daphne and Henry left early, and Mrs Hall, who had been dining at the House of Commons, came in afterwards. Likewise, Lord Londonderry. . . Nothing settled yet about the crisis or the election. Max says the Liberal ministers will sign on the dotted line. I'm not so sure.

Tuesday, 29 September 1931

Max in a very difficult mood this morning. He thinks that the anti-election gang have won the day and that the Empire policy has gone west. He was in a foul temper, got himself tied into knots with his appointments and nearly made me late for the Diary. For all of which I, of course, was

[1] George Edwardes (1852–1915) was a theatrical manager, and Tosti's 'Goodbye' a favourite Victorian drawing-room ballad.

[2] Secretary for the Dominions to both the new and the old governments.

[3] Later 6th Marquess of Bath.

blamed. In the evening dined at Stornoway: Gerhardi and Miss Spilsbury, the daughter of the famous Government pathologist [Sir Bernard Spilsbury], Mrs Hall, Robertson and self. Moura came in afterwards and we listened to H. G. Wells's broadcast on the wireless: 'What I should do if I were world dictator.' Afterwards, H.G. came in with Miss Matheson of the B.B.C.[1] – at Max's special request. In the meantime, Max had been visited by Hore-Belisha, who was inclined to be pessimistic about the prospects of the election. Thereupon, Max was in a fever, took Hore-Belisha into a corner, discussed politics with Hore-Belisha, rushed off to telephone to Winston and paid no attention. H.G. was hurt or rather annoyed. He has just finished his book: *The Work, Wealth and Happiness of Mankind* and is off to America on Wednesday week to be shown round and lionised at the time of publication. His plan to save the world is a kind of grand Council of Fabian Society experts. He thinks only internationalism on a grand big scale can save the capitalist system. Miss Matheson gave me the names of the only two real failures on the B.B.C. The two were Tallulah Bankhead and Kenneth Bell, the history don from Balliol, who insisted on speaking without a manuscript.

Wednesday, 30 September 1931

Gave Pam luncheon at the Jardin des Gourmets. Corrected the proofs of my article on the ex-Kaiser, wrote my paras for the *New Statesman*, and in the evening went round to see Lloyd and Kingsley Martin. The latter has a very poor opinion of Ramsay, who is all things to all men. He says the real reason why Henderson and the Labour cabinet were so angry with Ramsay was that from the moment that the cabinet had decided to resign Ramsay went off, changed his mind, came over on the King's advice to the idea of the National Government, and the next thing the men, who had been his Party colleagues for years, knew was that the National Government had been formed. Ramsay MacDonald had not consulted them at all – and this rankles.

Saturday, 3 October 1931

H.G. talked on the inevitable collapse of capitalism and the coming revolution. Valentine, who was very drunk, argued with him. The result was complete boredom for everyone else. H.G. is not impressive. He is like a board-school teacher who has all his facts marshalled and who produces platitudes with the manner of a great original thinker. H.G.'s great function has been his ability to summarise history, science, education, etc., in a popular manner. I am not surprised that Lenin is reported to have said that H.G. was a 'mutton-headed bourgeois'. Castlerosse told him that he had read this in Trotsky's book. Wells did not like it. . . He is a vain old boy. Wells said: 'Trotsky was one of the greatest soldiers of modern history,' – the kind of statement which may get into text-books and which is sheer bunk. Trotsky had organising ability.

[1] Hilda Matheson, head of the Talks Section, B.B.C.

Sunday, 4 October 1931

Tommy tells me that Simon Lovat has received a cable from the Cape saying South Africa is coming off the gold standard. Tommy also says that the Prince is doing all he can to make Eric marry Bridget.

Tuesday, 6 October 1931

Today was Thomson's first day with Max. In the evening he went off to Scotland to his brother's wedding. Mike seemed to think it an extraordinarily stupid thing to do. In my opinion, it is not so stupid as a man of brains becoming a Beaverbrook slave! Plummer[1] came back from America where he saw the big bankers: Lamont of Morgans, Charles Mitchell of the National City. They are very frightened and expect a terrible winter with unemployed riots and machine-guns. Mitchell said: 'The government will meet the situation by taxing the rich, but they won't get my money.' Eddie Cantor has taken Will Rogers's place as America's leading humorist. He has exploited depression. Here is an example: Talking of depression in hire purchase business, he says: 'Yeah, business is so bad that even those who never meant to pay have stopped buying.'

Brendan Bracken made a good remark at Max's the other night. He said: 'Neville Chamberlain is riding cock-horse on his father's tombstone.' Brendan Bracken has a very poor opinion of the Conservative leaders.

Wednesday, 7 October 1931

Max told a very good story. Scene: Churt. L.G. wakes up and asks his nurse: 'What's the news?' 'The Liberal leaders have thrown in their lot with Ramsay MacDonald.' 'Nothing of the sort,' says L.G. 'I'm the Liberal leader.' Nurse picks up paper and reads: 'Sir Herbert Samuel and Lord Reading, the Liberal leaders, have joined the National Government.' L.G. props himself up in bed and waves an arm towards the West and Wales: 'Christians awake' he ejaculates, then sinks back on his pillow.

Thursday, 8 October 1931

Had a very hard morning's work – Max on the telephone every two minutes. Lunched with Millie and Tommy at the Maison Basque. Millie was staying with the Prince at Bayonne when his father telephoned to him about the money crisis and the need for him (the Prince) to give up £10,000 a year. The Prince was in a night haunt at the time and was furious: 'The King [who is giving up £50,000] and I are being had for a pair of mugs,' he said. Millie and Tommy both say that the Prince is more irresponsible than he was. They blame Lady Furness who has a bad influence on him. Freda, at any rate, kept him under restraint. She could get him back tomorrow if she wanted to, but apparently, she does not want.

[1] Leslie Plummer (1901–63), a Beaverbrook executive, later knighted and a Labour M.P.

Wednesday, 14 October 1931

Afterwards went back to Stornoway to dine. J. D. Cassels, the barrister and the Camberwell candidate, and his wife were there. He was formerly member for Leyton, I think.[1] Cassels has taken Marshall Hall's place at the criminal bar. He has defended various notorious murderers... Nearly all of them were hanged! Cassels looks Jewish, but is, I believe, Canadian. Took Renate Mueller home. She had forgotten her latch-key and could not get the porter to answer the bell. Finally a head appeared at a window and called out in German: '*Bist du da?*' It was a man's voice and I conclude she has someone living with her.

Sunday, 18 October 1931

Came up with a young man called [E. D.] O'Brien by the 6.40. He was with Hamish and Randolph Churchill at Eton and Oxford... Randolph ... is irritating and irrepressible, but has 'guts'. He is very ambitious, goes on the theory that to succeed one must be unpopular.

O'Brien and Freddy Birkenhead once gave Randolph a terrible 'ragging' at Oxford, turned his rooms upside down and turned Randolph over and smacked him hard. The next day Randolph went round Oxford saying that O'Brien and Freddy Birkenhead had tried to 'rag' him, but he had scared them both off.

Wednesday, 21 October 1931

Went to Bracken's meeting at the Porchester Hall, Paddington. Bracken, Esmond Harmsworth [later 2nd Viscount Rothermere], and Winston were the speakers. They were all very cautious and made no mention of food-taxes. Esmond Harmsworth, whom we described in 'The Londoner's Diary' the other day – at Max's bidding of course – as one of the few orators in England, was terrible. He has nothing to say and cannot say it. Had supper at the Savoy afterwards with Bracken, Winston, Jack Churchill, Duke of Marlborough, Randolph, [Weech] the former headmaster of Sedbergh, and Lebbury, the general manager of the Westminster Bank. Randolph was very amusing, dominated most of the conversation, did New Party propaganda, and twitted his father with lack of political courage. Weech, who pretends to know the North and who has worked for years on Northern Conservative associations, says that the National Government majority will not exceed 80. I bet him it would. I, however, bet Bracken £5 that it would not exceed 275.

Thursday, 22 October 1931

Dined with Renate Mueller, the German cinema-star, who is doing the English version of *The Private Secretary* at the Gainsborough Studios. The

[1] Cassels (*b.* 1877), M.P. West Leyton, 1922–9, was contesting North-West Camberwell as a Conservative with Beaverbrook support in the General Election which had been called for 29 October.

English version is to be called *Sunshine Susie*. Renate is the daughter of a former editor of the *Muenchner Neueste Nachrichten*. Her sister is a doctor of psychology. She herself is fair, rather pretty, but inclined to plumpness, works very hard, is not intelligent, but is very nice. She has had numerous affairs of the heart and sleeps with those whom she likes. ..

Dined at Monseigneur, danced – Renate dances a Viennese waltz very well – and went to the Savoy where we were joined by Barbara Din and Deneš, the two stars in *Viktoria and her Hussar*. Deneš is a Budapest Jew of great talent. Barbara is a Russian from Moscow – very vivacious and attractive although not at all pretty. Finished up with champagne and gipsy songs in Barbara's room at the Savoy.

Saturday, 24 October 1931

Max returned from Manchester where he had been speaking at the Free Trade Hall. He is delighted with the article in the *Manchester Guardian* describing his speech at Darwin. The article was written by a man called Howard Spring.[1] The caption was 'The Pedlar of Dreams'. Max was delighted and is busily hunting for an old song, which I believe was called 'Make my Dreams Come True'. I remember Kitty Moran singing it in Prague. She did a 'step-waltz' to it.

Lunched with Bracken and Hinchingbrooke at Bracken's house in [Lord] North Street. It is very nicely furnished. Bracken, who has artistic tastes, owns half [Lord] North Street and was trying to let or sell a house to 'Hinch'.

Wednesday, 11 November 1931

Winston was noticeably drunk. Aneurin Bevan[2] is interesting. He talks well, is entirely self-taught, uses long words which he frequently mispronounces, believes in revolution, etc., differs very little from a Bolshevik except that he thinks himself superior to them and enjoys the good things of life. Drink and good living will do him in.

Wednesday, 18 November 1931

Lunched with McLelland, who told me some good stories of the Sultan of Johore, who today had his Australian widow bride of six months ago enthroned. Sultan was asked once if he knew the Aga Khan. 'Yes,' he replied in his halting English, 'I know him. He and I got drunk together once in Paris.' In his early days he had several scandals in Singapore: (1) when in a selling plate he ran a crack horse and had it painted to disguise it, (2) when to amuse himself he put a soda water bottle (small size) up an Austrian harlot's vagina and could not get it out; and (3) when he was arrested for being drunk

[1] (1889–1965) later a colleague and friend of Lockhart, and a highly successful novelist.
[2] (1897–1960) M.P. Ebbw Vale, 1929–60, Minister of Health 1945–51.

and said he was the Sultan of Johore. 'Git along wid you,' said the Irish inspector. 'Every bloody Malay says that.'

Saturday, 21 November 1931

Then Hailsham came on to the telephone to ask Max what attitude he Hailsham should take towards the first anti-dumping order.[1] Max delighted. Turned to us. 'Cabinet Ministers, when in doubt, no longer consult their colleagues. They telephone to me.' He then had a long talk with Hailsham about Winston, during which he crabbed Winston hard. Then he turned to me: 'We've had enough of Winston's rascality. We can't trust him. He'd sell us tomorrow.' This is possibly true, but the real reason in Max's eyes is that there is no room for two strong men in the Empire movement.

Monday, 23 November 1931

Dined at Stornoway: Jenny Lee[2] who is going on a lecture-tour to the U.S.A. and Canada, Daphne Weymouth, Cudlipp, Andrew Holt,[3] and Mrs Johnstone. Henry Weymouth came in later. Rather a boring evening. Jenny Lee who is a miner's daughter, speaks with an artificially refined Scottish accent. She is very sure of the approaching doom of capitalism. At the end it was rather amusing to see the guests drive off: Andrew Holt, the stolid Canadian millionaire with no brains except for money, in a huge Rolls, and Daphne and Henry Weymouth – the young aristocracy – in a tiny Baby Austin.

Monday, 30 November 1931

Today was the anniversary of Lady Beaverbrook's death, and Max was mournful and lugubrious. He is very observant of all anniversaries. I sat alone with him after dinner. He was silent for long intervals. His only reference to Lady Beaverbrook was at dinner when he said: 'Four years ago today I was sitting in this chair listening to very satisfactory reports from the doctors about my wife's health. The same evening she died. All doctors are frauds anyway.'

Wednesday, 2 December 1931

Went this morning to see Rosenberg who is staying at the Piccadilly. He was very surprised that I had tracked him down. He is here to make contacts. Dined with him in the evening at Boulestin's and went on to the Savoy. He says Hitler is not coming to London just now (the air is full of rumours

[1] Hailsham was now Secretary for War, and in the Cabinet.

[2] Jennie Lee (*b.* 1904) had been elected as Labour M.P. for North Lanark in 1929, but had just lost her seat in the election. She was to marry Bevan in 1934.

[3] Percy Cudlipp (1905–62), later Editor of the *Daily Herald*, was then film critic on the *Evening Standard*. Major Andrew Holt was the son of Sir Herbert Holt, chairman of the Royal Bank of Canada. Beaverbrook had tried and failed to get him a knighthood in 1928–9.

that he is coming at once) and that there will be no coalition with Brüning[1] at the present moment. He gave me a long account of his own career. He took his degree as an architect at Riga, came to Munich from Reval in 1919, and got into touch with Eckhardt, the poet. They began speaking against Marxism during the Eisner régime. Hitler was also engaged on a similar task with a small group of his own. They met and joined up. Hitler's chief amusement is motor-racing. He does not race himself, but knows all the names of the great drivers.

Friday, 4 December 1931

In the evening dined with Mike Wardell at his house: present the Mosleys, Mrs d'Erlanger, the two Wardells and self. Tom Mosley looks pale and tired. He talked a good deal about the necessity for militant organisation against Communism, said that when the crash came the man who could control the streets would win.

He told us of his experiences with Thomas when they were working together on unemployment. Thomas was hopelessly lost. One day he came in triumphantly to Horace Wilson.[2] He had a telephone box in his hand. 'Look 'ere,' he said, 'this is where you fellows go wrong. This little box now is British-made and costs only 5*s*. Your box (pointing to the one on the wall) costs 12*s*.' 'Yes,' said Horace gently: 'But your box is empty and costs 5*s*. It's not the box which costs 12*s*. in our case – it's the things inside it. The shell of our box costs only 3*s*.!' It was a typical example of the ignorant minister up against the expert. Tom said the J.H.T. was the biggest 'bluffer' politics had ever known. He could only exist in a state on the verge of a collapse and was himself a symbol of that collapse.

At eleven Mike took Rosenberg down to the *Express* to show him over the building. While we were there, we watched the presses printing Hitler's pronouncement – no reparations – Treaty revision, etc. – to the Foreign Press correspondents.

Monday, 7 December 1931

Max is jealous of Winston. Yesterday in the *Sunday Express* there was a 'box' with a statement that Winston had travelled to America in a German liner. Now the truth is that Winston, who was leaving on the *Berengaria* on December 2nd or 3rd, put off his trip in order to take part in the India debate. In order to do so, he cancelled his passage on the *Berengaria*, gave up one lecture in America, and lost by his decision several hundred pounds. He took the *Europa* because she was the only boat which could get him to New York in time. Bracken and Randolph were indignant and at once complained to me. I told Max, who made light of the incident. There was too much Winston

[1] Heinrich Brüning was German Chancellor, 1930–2.

[2] Sir Horace Wilson (*b*. 1882), civil servant, chief industrial adviser to the government (1930–9) and Prime Minister Chamberlain's right-hand man.

anyway. He was not to be trusted, etc. He must take his knocks. The story was repeated in the 'Dragoman' column of the *Express* today. My theory is that the insertion in the *Sunday Express* was with Max's approval, but that Monday's was not.

Saturday, 12 December 1931

Went to see Max in the evening. His latest favourite is young Frank Owen – the baby M.P. in the last Parliament.[1] Max now consults him (in his usual way when he is luring another fly into his web) on almost everything.

Wednesday, 16 December 1931

Gave Tommy luncheon at the Basque. She says that people generally are becoming very fed up with the *Daily Express* and Max. Everywhere she goes she hears him being blackguarded and people vowing to boycott the paper.

Tuesday, 22 December 1931

Action, the New Party weekly, is going smash. They will have to close down by December 31st. Tom Mosley's own income has been greatly reduced. His wife is paying her losses and costs in the Leiter case[2] (£8000 a year for three years) out of income. She and Tom have let their houses and are living over a garage. *Action* itself had a fund of £20,000. The Party raided the fund for £5000 after the election. *Action* has spent about £12,000. The Party now require another £2000 to pay election expenses – so *Action* is on the rocks. They have been willing to save their face by amalgamating with the *Saturday* [*Review*]. Bracken has been playing with the idea. Colin Cooper[3] has also been approached. He told Harold that this was the fourth weekly which had approached him for funds in the last four weeks.

Friday, 25 December 1931

Tried to be very nice to Jean, but succeeded only in being foul. Came down here [Bexhill] with the intention of retrenching, changing my whole mode of life, and setting up house with Jean again in order to put my financial house in order, but I fear it will be impossible.

Monday, 28 December 1931

I had a further instance of newspaper dictatorship today. Belloc has written a poem in heroic verse on wine. It is a fine poem and is dedicated to Duff Cooper. It has taken him twenty years to write. I had this as an exclusive

[1] Owen, then aged 26, had been Liberal M.P. for Hereford, 1929–31, was at this time on the *Daily Express*, became Editor of the *Evening Standard*, 1938–41.

[2] Concerning Cynthia Mosley's inheritance from the Leiter family. Her father was Marquess Curzon and her mother was the daughter of Levi Zeigler Leiter, a very rich American.

[3] Major Colin Cooper (1892–1938), successful young banker and businessman with interests in engineering and aircraft.

news story. Had it been by anyone else it would have been well worth a Diary paragraph. There is, however, a ban on Belloc from high quarters, and Gilliat would not risk publishing.

Tuesday, 29 December 1931

Before luncheon Harold came in to see me. *Action* having gone smash, the *Sunday Dispatch* has offered him £2000 a year for a weekly article on the same lines as Castlerosse's 'Londoner's Log' in the *Sunday Express*. Harold would like to accept because of the money; he is, however, a little conscience-sore about Max, as he broke his contract with the *Evening Standard*. I advised him to write to Max. He was afraid lest Max might suggest his returning to us and nothing on earth would induce him to do that. He need not worry. Max is far too proud to ask Harold Nicolson to come back. Harold and Tom are off to Rome tomorrow night: Tom is taking his épées with him and hopes to fence his way into Mussolini's presence. Esmond Harmsworth is to meet them in Rome and will go on with Tom to Berlin.

Wednesday, 30 December 1931

Lunched with Harold and M. R. Gillet, the editor of the *Revue des Deux Mondes* and a well-known French art critic. Gillet brought Harold a letter from James Joyce.[1] Joyce's eyes are very bad again and he will probably have to have an operation. He is about to become a grandfather. His son is up for his audition at the Paris Opéra. Joyce has occasional bouts of very heavy drinking. During these bouts, his family have to leave him not because of his violence, but because of the stream of foul language which issues from his lips.

[1] (1882–1941) Irish author of *Ulysses* (1922) and *Finnegans Wake* (1939); he had been living in Paris since 1920.

CHAPTER NINE

1932

Drinkers: Birkenhead, Churchill, Bracken. Nieland, Nazi M.P., organising London group. Ustinov *père* on Hitler. Randolph Churchill living with Lady Castlerosse. Commander Fletcher on the bad state of the Navy. J. H. Thomas and Lord Passfield's knee-breeches. Harold Nicolson's finances. A. V. Alexander and Mussolini. The Swedish Match King. Edward Marjoribank's suicide. Arnold Bennett's child by Dorothy Cheston. Scandal about Prince George (Duke of Kent). Masaryk unhappy. Lord Dudley's *affaires*. Diana Duff Cooper in *The Miracle* and the King's *faux pas*. Karl Ketchum, journalist, and the Thompson–Bywater murder. Ramsay MacDonald and Lady Londonderry. Attlee 'fierce on Ramsay'. Buchman of the Oxford Movement 'like a bagman'. Mosley wears Fascist badge. Walter Citrine on Russia. Belloc fulminates against Lawrence. Joad's improbable sex stories. Hugh Walpole's praise. *Memoirs of a British Agent* published. Millicent Duchess of Sutherland and her mania about cruelty.

Friday, 1 January 1932

Still very cold, but towards afternoon a rapid thaw set in. Rearranged my room for my new secretary. She will cost me £4 a week. How I am to pay her, I do not know. Letter from Gordon Dadds this morning telling me to make an appointment at once as I must do something about my income tax.

I spent a quite useless and uninteresting day, leaving the office at seven and going straight to the Wellington Club, where I met a number of fellows who were recovering from their last night's celebrations and potations. As a result I myself had too many drinks and sat up late playing bridge.

Altogether a bad opening to a year which is likely to see me made bankrupt and which is bound to be full of financial worries. I am now down to bedrock in all my possible resources: overdrawn by £43 at Glyn, Mills, and nearly down to nothing at the National Provincial. I really must cut out alcohol entirely out of my life. It is the ruin not only of my health but of my mind, and the only thing to do is to ban it completely and utterly.

Saturday, 2 January 1932

Before dinner we discussed Birkenhead and when drink first began to undermine his mind. Max said that even during the period when he was being teetotal for his bet (about 1925) he was drinking secretly. He would even go so far as to ask Max (if they were out at dinner) to have a brandy and to tip it into his (F.E.'s) ginger ale. Winston, I imagine, is going the same way. Brendan, too, drinks far too much: champagne, port, brandy, whisky, etc. Edward Marjoribanks puts Simon as the greatest lawyer of our time; Carson – also a great lawyer – as the greatest advocate. He also thinks very highly of Van den Berg. Latter was left without any money and had a very hard time. Did some reporting for a living.

Sunday, 3 January 1932

In the afternoon Rothermere and Austen Chamberlain arrived [at Cherkley] – separately. Austen came from the Simons' – to escape, as he said, from Lady Simon. Rothermere, as usual, very pessimistic about England's future: no virility, no public opinion. Instead of protesting against the taxation which is ruining us, we pay without thinking. The newspapers are killing themselves through this insurance madness[1] (incidentally, the *Mail* is the instigator of whole business); *Daily Herald* and Berry Bros[2] are going bust; *Daily Mail* and *Daily Express* must amalgamate to save themselves! He looked less revolting than usual and was quite nice with Jeanne, Janet's little girl.

Monday, 4 January 1932

My new secretary, Miss Schapiro, started work. She is an Anglo-Russian Jewess; speaks French, English, Russian and German, and seems very capable. I should have had her two years ago. Had a very busy day – two paragraphs in the Diary – and in the afternoon I tied up and cleared off my arrears of correspondence.

In India Gandhi arrested and Congress declared illegal. Our attitude towards Gandhi is amazing: a year ago he was in prison; then he was released and conferred on equal terms with Irwin, came to England as a delegate to the Round Table Conference, and was received by everyone including the King. He returns to India and has not been five days in the country when he is arrested again and clapped into jail!

Thursday, 7 January 1932

Stayed in bed until three when I dressed and went down to Horsham to stay a night with Tommy before going back to work. Tommy tells me she hears from friends at Liverpool that my sister Freda has been running me down and not only saying that I never did a hand's turn for her but also making disagreeable innuendoes about Tommy and myself. She is a foolish child. Letter from Jean asking again for more money. She is in debt. How it

[1] Giving insurance free to those willing to agree to take the newspaper regularly for a period.

[2] William Ewert Berry (1879–1954) and his brother James Gomer Berry (1883–1968), later Lords Camrose and Kemsley, controlled the *Sunday Times*, the *Daily Telegraph* and a chain of provincial newspapers.

all will end I do not know. But now we are right up against it, and there seems no escape from bankruptcy – none, certainly, from complete drudgery and slavery. I must get my book sold which means I must write it. I must also try to do more outside work: obituaries for *The Times*, etc. I might write a *Criterion Miscellany* for Faber and Faber.

Harry left yesterday for the South of France. Tommy joins him at the end of the month, and they go for a fortnight or three weeks to Morocco (Marrakesh). There is apparently excellent trout-fishing in the Atlas Mountains. I wish I could go with them. The drudgery of Fleet Street is destroying my mind. Only the severest discipline and the strongest effort of will can stand against it. Life would be more endurable if the hygienic conditions of our office were better. For three and half years now I have worked in artificial light.

Friday, 8 January 1932

Numerous small clubs are springing up just now – mainly to provide cheap meals. They are run mainly by ex-officers, etc. I do not believe they can pay. Offered to go down to Cherkley. While I was out, message came back to say: 'Lord Beaverbrook would be delighted, but if there was the slightest risk of more cold I was not to come.' Not quite understanding this cryptic message I rang up Whelan and discovered that Lord Beaverbrook's solicitude was for himself and not for me.

Wednesday, 13 January 1932

This morning Thost[1] came to tell me that he had heard from Rosenberg. I was to go to Munich at once to see Hitler. Made all arrangements to go on Thursday and went off to lunch with Jean, Grannie, Aunt Alice and Robin at Gerland's. After luncheon took Robin to Olympia to see the circus – rather poor. Dashed back at 5.30 to Shoe Lane only to find that Gilliat was against my going tomorrow because he has no one to replace me. Rather absurd – a Hitler interview has some value today. Tomorrow it may be too late.

Thursday, 14 January 1932

Decided this morning that I am not to go to Munich for ten days or so. A new worry is the appearance of —— in the office. He is very hard up and has been told by the committee that he must pay his club debts (about £80) within a month or resign. He came to us with the story of —— who has had to resign the Wellington for the row he made at the staff ball the other night.

Again at the Wellington. Dined with Drayton and Fuller and played snooker. Again too much to drink.

[1] Dr Hans Wilhelm Thost, Nazi newspaperman in London. 'Not unfriendly,' wrote Lockhart in the unpublished *End of an Epoch*, 'but wild and full of crazy notions about England. Afterwards expelled.'

Friday, 15 January 1932

Moura arrived from Germany. Gave luncheon to Thost, the Nazi correspondent here. He is a mild fellow, had been with a girl all night, and was dying for beer. He was with Hitler and Goebbels in the Brown House – sitting on the stairs and joking together – at the time of Stennes row.[1] When they went out, they bought a paper (Jewish *Tageblatt*) with a headline: Hitler holds Goebbels a prisoner in the Brown House! On another occasion, the Jewish Press announced that Streicher, the editor of the Nuremberg *Stürmer* (very anti-Jewish) had been dropped by Hitler and was out of favour. Hitler saw this – stopped at Nuremberg on his way from Munich to Berlin and appeared same evening on Streicher's platform.

Saturday, 16 January 1932

At nine thirty this morning went to see Herr Nieland, the Nazi M.P., who is visiting London in order to organise the local German Nazi group. Nieland, whose headquarters are at Hamburg, is the commander of the Nazis abroad. He tells me there are 20,000,000 Germans abroad and he hopes to do as well as Mussolini who has 800,000 sworn Fascist members at home and 600,000 abroad. Herr Nieland, who is an active, healthy Teuton, is only 31. He thinks Hindenburg may remain as President, but that Brüning will go. Hitler, he says, is bound to [follow] him. The only logical outcome of the German crisis is Hitler or Communism. There is no other issue.

Monday, 18 January 1932

Lunched with Bernstorff at the Carlton Grill Room. The other guests were Ustinov, who has just returned from Berlin, and von Stutterheim, the correspondent of the *Berliner Tageblatt*, who is married to a Beckett, Beatrice Eden's sister.[2] Von Stutterheim is leaving London and going to Rome, and Scheffer, who made a reputation in Russia and who is now in Washington, is taking his place here. The *Tageblatt*, which is owned by Mosse, the advertising people, is retrenching not so much because it is doing badly as because Mosse itself is having a bad time. Ustinov, who has just returned from Berlin, is anti-Hitler and pro-Brüning. He thinks, like Bernstorff, that I have been too pro-Hitler in the *Evening Standard*. All I have done, however, is to give the news and on occasions to give the Hitler version. Ustinov's idea is that Hitler has ruined his chance, that Brüning has stolen his programme and that everyone prefers a programme carried through without civil war to a programme that will almost certainly mean civil war, not because it differs from the Brüning programme but because it will be Hitler's and carried out by Hitler people.

[1] Walter Stennes was a Nazi and influential Storm Trooper who tried, but failed, in 1931 to challenge the leadership of Hitler and Roehm. He was sacked from both Party and S.A., and soon left Germany.

[2] Baron Kurt von Stutterheim's wife Cynthia and Anthony Eden's wife Beatrice were daughters of Sir Gervase Beckett.

I am inclined to think that Hitler has missed *a* chance if not his only chance of seizing the supreme power. I do not believe, however, that his party will dissolve. There is now too much behind it, even if the elements which compose it are diverse.

Friday, 22 January 1932

In the evening dined with Ted Parsons[1] in Pont Street. Lord Plender, who is seventy, a barrister called Thorpe, General Swinton, who wrote *The Green Curve* (Ole Luk-Oie) and was 'Eye-Witness' during the war and helped to invent the tank, were the other guests.[2] Thorpe tells me that on the Sunday in July before his operation, L.G. was at Churt. The whole house-party had to sing hymns: including his favourite: 'Count your many blessings. Name them one by one.' This was also sung after his recovery. Thorpe thinks L.G. will be Prime Minister again – cf. young Randolph Churchill's prediction that the next Parliament will be composed of young men of under forty and L.G. and his father. After dinner went to 43 and then to the Bobbin. Met Nancy Meyrick and spent about £20. Had a long talk with Alec Purves. Got home at 6.30 a.m.!

Wednesday, 27 January 1932

Letter from Huntington [of Putnam's the publishers]. He says the first pages of my book made him cheerful for the day and that he can see this is going to be an important book. I am to hear from him again 'very soon'. So far so good. In the meantime I am having a race with my creditors. I must have money before February 15th or go definitely under. Lunched with Pam who also likes the book. Took her home and then back to office.

Thursday, 28 January 1932

Dined at 33 Cliveden Square with the Gibbses Sir Philip told me one good story about Marie Corelli.[3] When he was literary editor of the *Tribune*, Marie Corelli asked him to let her write an article and to promise that he would not alter a word of it. He promised. She then wrote the article and put it in together with a letter calling Philip 'the only gentleman in Fleet Street'. He cut this out and pinned it on his desk. When he read the article, it libelled every other paper in Fleet Street except the *Tribune*. He could not publish it

[1] E. P. Parsons, a cousin of his wife, and founder of the stockbroking firm of that name (now Castello, Parsons & Co.).

[2] William, 1st Baron Plender (1861–1946), chartered accountant and indomitable committee-man; perhaps J. H. Thorpe (1887–1944), Unionist M.P. for Rusholme, 1919–23, and later a K.C.; General Sir Ernest Swinton (1868–1951) wrote under the pseudonym 'Ole Luk-Oie' and was at this time Professor of Military History at Oxford.

[3] Sir Philip Gibbs (1877–1962) was one of the most famous war correspondents (Balkan War, First World War) of all times, novelist (*The Street of Adventure* and some fifty others), essayist and autobiographer (*The Pageant of the Years*, 1947). Marie Corelli (1855–1924) wrote immensely popular romantic novels.

and told her so. Whereupon he received a letter calling him 'The biggest cad and liar in Fleet Street'. He cut it out and pinned it on his desk.

Friday, 29 January 1932

Lunched with Moura. She showed me a letter from Gorky. He asks her to get all the English books on the history of English caricature. He signs himself: 'Yours sorely grieved, Maxim Gorky – author – over forty, tawny-haired, bad-tempered and overwhelmingly famous.'

He has a great love for animals. When Wells was staying with him in 1919, he had a Great Dane. It went everywhere with Gorky. It was called Diane. It even went for walks with Wells. One day it went for a walk by itself and never came back. It had been eaten by a starving populace. Today, Gorky still loves dogs. He has a pedigree fox-terrier bitch called Piksha (name of coarse Russian fish) and a mongrel whippet. But they are kept at Sorrento! Came down to Cherkley.

Thursday, 4 February 1932

Saw Huntington of Putnam's about my book. After a long conversation I think I shall do fairly well in that I shall get £750 for the English rights. He means to have the book. Today, I published the letter about the subscription list to Winston.[1] I received it from Marjoribanks's secretary. He was rather upset, and I expect that I have mortally offended Bracken and Randolph. In the evening went with Tommy, Miss Reid and Harry to the Hippodrome to see *Bow Bells*. Then to Savoy. Felt very ill.

Friday, 5 February 1932

I have been in trouble over the publication of the Winston testimonial letter. Edward Marjoribanks, in particular, is very upset that I should have used the text of his letter. In the evening dined with Pam at the Escargot. She is going away for the week-end to the Gairdners and is apparently being accompanied by her new American friend Homer Smith. It would be a solution of two-thirds of my difficulties if she would marry him.

Great excitement in the Press today over the *Daily Herald* story of a brothel in Geneva which has been specially brought from Paris for the duration of the Disarmament Conference. The brothel was provided at the request – it is said – of the Japanese delegation.

Have done nothing on my book for three days: must now before Lent make one last strenuous effort to lead an ascetic life. Surely by now I have reached the age when other things than drink, self-indulgence and whoring will satisfy me. How I hate London and the Londoners. They fill me with the same disgust as Holland and the Dutch filled Voltaire:

'*Adieu: canaux, canards, canaille.*'

[1] Lord Burnham, Brendan Bracken and half a dozen others had sent a circular inviting subscriptions to buy a motor-car to give to Churchill to celebrate his recovery from an accident in New York. Charlie Chaplin was a generous contributor.

Saturday, 6 February 1932

I could not go to Coolham, as the Rosslyns were also full up. I was to have gone to them for the day on Sunday. Instead, I got drunk at the club, sat up till two and then went on to the Bobbin, where I spent the best part of £20 and did not return until eight a.m. I had all the three Meyrick girls at my table: Nancy, Bobbie and Kathleen. Altogether a degrading and depressing performance.

Monday, 8 February 1932

My final income-tax assessment is in. I owe approximately £1425 with something to come back on the other years before 1929. How it is to be paid God knows.

Wednesday, 10 February 1932

Edgar Wallace died. His new play (produced by Gerald du Maurier) *The Green Pack* had its first night last night. In one scene four men draw cards to decide who is to commit a murder. The card drawn is the 'Ace of Spades' – the death-card. While this scene was being played, Edgar Wallace was dying in Hollywood.

Thursday, 11 February 1932

Still bitterly cold. Lunched with Randolph and a man called Farrar, who has been at Hollywood, has an island in the South Seas, and has now been given a job by Basil Dean as a scenario writer. He says Hollywood is bankrupt in ideas and in money and that there is now a great chance for England, France or Germany to conquer the film business. He declares that a short time ago Laski[1] tried to commit suicide. Randolph tells me: (1) that Edward Marjoribanks is no use at the bar (St John Hutchinson[2] told him he (Marjoribanks) does not make £800 a year at the bar); (2) that he (Randolph) was living with Doris Castlerosse (i.e. next door). Valentine rang him up and said: 'I hear you're living with my wife.' Randolph replied: 'Yes, I am, and it's more than you have the courtesy to do.' Randolph wants a job as a speaker at the Trocadero and says he has nearly fixed it up. If they give him £100 a week he'll do it. He also said Max had been the worst possible influence on Winston's life. Launched our great story about Raymond de Trafford and Alice de Janzé's wedding in the *Express*.[3] Dined with Pam and afterwards went down to 'vet' the proofs. Letter from Huntington: contract will be

[1] Probably Jesse L. Lasky (*d.* 1958), pioneer American film producer, at that time Vice-President of Paramount – and not Harold Laski (1893–1950), Socialist professor at L.S.E.

[2] (1884–1942) K.C., Recorder of Hastings, and collector of modern paintings.

[3] Five years earlier, in March 1927, Raymond de Trafford and Alice, Countess de Janzé, were both found shot in a first-class compartment at the Gare du Nord, Paris. She had attempted to shoot him and herself. She was given a six months' sentence which was later revoked. They were married on 22 February 1932.

O.K. £500 on signing, and £250 on receipt of the manuscript. Rumours that Max is giving up newspapers and going into films – bunk, I should think.

Monday, 15 February 1932

In the evening went to dine at the Octavian Club at the Carlton Club annexe. The Octavian Club is an international club of eight members – founded to improve Anglo-German relations by a man called Balfour who last year toured Germany with a team of golfers. Guests are always brought to these monthly dinners. I went as Bernstorff's and met Sir Alexander Walker of Johnny Walker,[1] General Hayes, a most amusing American, Webster, the head of the Port of London police, and various other people.

Commander Fletcher (ex-M.P. for Tavistock) of the Secret Service was also there. I heard more stories in an hour than I have heard in the past three years: some of them were very good. Fletcher tells me the Navy is in a very bad state and suggests that I should write a page seven on it entitled 'The Navy Ruined by Sport'. He will give me the dope. In spite of what was a very festive evening I remained teetotal. Had, however, too much to eat and did not get home till one o'clock.

Tuesday, 16 February 1932

Tommy returned from Paris after four or five days with Millie. She has a spite of hate against the selfishness of all the family: Harry has been trying to let Hunger Hill over her head to please himself, Millie is full of her own woes, and the Duke of Sutherland has done nothing about keeping Hélène's grave in order and is letting her mother [Millie], i.e., the grandmother of the future Duchess of Sutherland, more or less starve on £400 a year.[2]

Tommy, who dined at the Embassy, told some good stories of J. H. Thomas, who also dined there on his way to Geneva. King George was very upset about Lord Passfield's not wearing knee-breeches at court and about Mrs Sidney Webb not calling herself Lady Passfield. Did not know whom to consult, so spoke to J. H. Thomas. J.H. said to King confidentially: 'Now, your Majesty, I expect it's really those knee-breeches that worry you.' King said yes. 'Well,' says J.H.T., 'poor Sidney can't put 'em on, because his wife wears 'em.' King was delighted, told everybody. Story got to Lord Passfield's ears and now Lord Passfield wears knee-breeches.[3]

Wednesday, 17 February 1932

Gave luncheon at Boulestin's to Jan Masaryk and Fletcher. . . Jan told some

[1] Walker (1869–1950) had worked for the Ministry of Munitions as well as being a whisky distiller.

[2] The Dowager Duchess of Sutherland's elder son was the 5th Duke (1888–1963). Her second son, Alastair, married Elizabeth Hélène Desmarest. He died in April 1921; and she remarried in June 1931 and died in September 1931. Her 11-year-old daughter Elizabeth was heir presumptive to the Earldom (not the Dukedom) of Sutherland.

[3] Sidney Webb (1859–1947), Socialist and prominent Fabian, Dominion and Colonial Secretary, 1929–31, had been ennobled, much against his will, as Lord Passfield in 1929.

good stories. How Dawes one night invited a largish party to dinner including Austen, Hanbury-Williams, etc.[1] One of the butlers was very drunk, terrified all the old ladies by nearly spilling soup, etc., down their backs. So bad, that even Austen had to say: 'General, you may give *us* nothing to drink, but there seems to be plenty of alcohol in the servants' quarters.' At the end of dinner butler came forward, took off his wig, and said: 'Ladies and gentlemen, I hope you enjoyed your dinner – and my entertainment.' He was a music-hall performer engaged by Dawes. Washington was angry.

Thursday, 18 February 1932

I was asked to luncheon by Will Thorne at the House of Commons. We had a long talk over old days.[2] He will be seventy-five next month. I must get his book: *My Life's Battles*. He knew Karl Marx's daughter Eleanor very well. She committed suicide, because Dr Aveling, the man she lived with, was carrying on with someone else. He, too, killed himself a few weeks later. Thorne's book was written by Brodsky of the *Daily Herald* and was serialised by *Tit-Bits*. He made only £400 out of it. Of this he gave £200 to Brodsky, £100 to another man, and paid income-tax on the whole lot.

Friday, 19 February 1932

Gave luncheon at the Carlton Grill to Kerensky and young Randolph. Kerensky is well, but is getting short-sighted. He believes 1932 will be fatal to Bolsheviks. They are in financial straits. The kolkhozi [collective farms] are unpopular. The harvest will be bad. He also believes there has been a deal between the Bolsheviks and Japan, Russia selling her interests in Manchuria for cash. I doubt it. I agree that Russia cannot go to war. The Bolos [Bolsheviks] dare not. There is already a psychology: the Russo-Japanese War gave the constitution and the Duma, the Great War gave us the land, the next war will rid us of the Bolos.

It was very amusing to hear Randolph and Kerensky (in execrable French) arguing the merits of dictatorship and democracies. Kerensky is still a democrat. He admits, however, that the technique of the Parliamentary machine has not kept pace with the increased speed of modern life. The technique is still that of the horse omnibus in a motor-bus and airplane world. Kerensky says all the young men talk the same today. They do not analyse. Randolph Churchill has been speaking in the New Party Club. He said that castration was a modern remedy for ineffectives in hygienic world of thought. It ought

[1] General Charles Gates Dawes (1865–1951), U.S. Ambassador to Britain, 1929–32, had been Vice-President 1925–9, and before that responsible for the 'Dawes Plan', a scheme of reparations within Germany's capacity to pay. Major-General Sir John Hanbury-Williams (1889–1946), diplomat and soldier, Marshal of the Diplomatic Corps, Extra Equerry to the King, etc.

[2] Will Thorne (1857–1946), Labour M.P., 1905–45, founder and general secretary of the National Union of General and Municipal Workers. He had visited Russia in April 1917 as one of a party of Socialists sent out on a futile mission to encourage the Russians to continue the war. Lockhart found him 'an honest giant'.

to be applied to political ineffectives. It would, however, be unnecessary in case of Baldwin and Ramsay, as they were old women already (loud applause).

Sunday, 21 February 1932

Raymond de Trafford is marrying Alice de Janzé tomorrow. Rudolph has gone over for the wedding. Young Fulke Warwick is engaged to Margaret Whigham. He sent his papers in, but Pilcher, his colonel (Grenadier), refused to take them, saying: 'Really, Fulke, you cannot send in your papers and get engaged every six weeks.' The girl is in Cairo, where Fulke is with his regiment.[1]

Tommy told me a story about Euan Wallace and Lord Reading. Latter has grapefruit from his villa on the sea of Galilee. Also about Sir Alexander Kleinwort, who lives in Sussex,[2] dines in an open car, beard and all, and insists on his chauffeur doing the trip to Lombard Street in 1¼ hours. Chauffeurs always having their licence suspended. He turns them into gardeners!

Monday, 22 February 1932

Gave luncheon to Harold at the Jardin [des Gourmets]. He was very enthusiastic over my book, is prepared to bet that it is a best seller and ever so much better than *Bengal Lancer*,[3] and begs me not to alter the style or to try to make it literary. He himself is worrying about money. He has an offer to do a column for the *Sunday Times* and would like some reviewing for the *Sunday Express*. He says Vita and he have only £300 in the bank, but she has £2000 in the U.S.A., will receive £3000 for her new novel which is almost finished, and they both have capital sunk in their places at Weald and in Kent. In addition, Vita will have about £10,000 a year when her mother dies. I wish that I were so pleasantly worried. Saw Huntington. I am to get more under my contract – there is to be an improvement on the percentages, and I am to receive something in the form of an advance on American and serial rights, even if they are less than the original advance.

Tuesday, 23 February 1932

One of my main troubles is that I cannot avoid getting tied up with engagements. London in this respect is the devil, for, when I do have a free night, I am tired and want to sleep. Today, I had a message from Cherkley asking me to dine tomorrow evening. Today, is the ninth anniversary of my first meeting with Tommy. We met at the Embassy at a dinner given by

[1] Fulke Warwick is the 7th Earl of Warwick (*b.* 1911). He did not in the end marry Margaret Whigham, but the girl he had been engaged to previously.

[2] At Cuckfield. He was a banker (1858–1935).

[3] Francis Yeats-Brown's *Bengal Lancer* was first published in 1930 and at once became a best-seller.

Ashmead-Bartlett: Harry, Tommy, Ashmead, Mona Dunn, and Mrs Norman and myself. Of the party Ashmead and Mona are dead.[1]

Wednesday, 24 February 1932

Leslie Hudson, who used to be our secret service man in Prague, came into my office today. His father cut him off without a penny on account of his various matrimonial troubles, but when the father died the son's brother and sister shared their inheritance with him. In the evening was to have dined with Max, but at the last moment he put me off. Tomorrow, it will be a fortnight, since I last saw him...

Dined alone at the Carlton Grill and then went to 10 Cadogan Gardens to pick up Tommy and take her to see *Dr Jekyll and Mr Hyde*[2] – a poor show but better than *Frankenstein*. The monster idea does not lend itself to film work. Met Miss Halle – the girl Randolph was supposed to be engaged to. Her father was or is the Woolworth of Cleveland.

Sunday, 28 February 1932

Samuel, the conscientious, honest, hard-working man, to Archie Sinclair: 'I'm so tired, and yet I've got to go to speak in Yorkshire tonight. I'd give anything to not to go, and yet I suppose I'll have to.'

Archie. 'Oh, if you're feeling run down, please don't go. We can't have you being knocked up. You can easily say you've another engagement.'

Samuel, touched: 'Well, I'd like to, but I can't do that. You see I haven't another engagement.'

This is the story that Liberals are putting out as pro-Samuel propaganda. As Stresemann once said of himself, 'I have friends in all parties even in my own.'

Monday, 29 February 1932

Another Parliamentary story: there is a member in the House of Commons called [Sir] Percy Harris.[3] He is known as the housemaid because he always empties the chamber. Here, too, is an aphorism of Stalin: 'The Russians stood the Romanovs for 300 years; they'll put up with me till my death.'

Tuesday, 1 March 1932

Lunched with A. V. Alexander, the Co-operative leader and former first Lord of the Admiralty,[4] and Fletcher at the St James. Alexander rather a pleasant, fat and decidedly able man. Slightly vain. Believes in co-operation

[1] Ellis Ashmead-Bartlett (1881–1931), war correspondent, Conservative M.P., North Hammersmith, 1924–6; Mona was the eldest daughter of Sir James Dunn, she died in 1928.

[2] The Reuben Mamoulian version, starring Fredric March, still generally thought to be the best.

[3] (1876–1952) Liberal M.P., later Chief Whip.

[4] (1885–1965) Alexander was again First Lord of the Admiralty, 1940–5, and ended his life as Earl Alexander of Hillsborough.

and thinks England will have to go more than half-way to meet the new industrial revolution (i.e. end of private enterprise) if she is to avoid revolution.

Told me some good stories: how Henderson and he went to see Mussolini about the naval agreement. Henderson was very nervous, for as chairman of the Second International he had unveiled the statue to Matteotti.[1] Mussolini, however, very gracious. He received Alexander, who had brought the proposed figures with him after consultation with the French, alone and cross-examined him for twenty minutes on them. When he saw that Alexander was not to be over-persuaded, he said: 'Well, if you can convince my experts, you will not find me an obstacle.' They did not agree with the Italian experts – Grandi and Ruspoli – who went back to consult Mussolini. That night Mussolini dined with the English ministers at the British Embassy. He agreed to everything, saying: 'I have done this, because I am honoured that England should have sent two such important ministers to see me and because I want peace.' Alexander, who was impressed, believed him on both points.

When Ramsay was making his cabinet in 1929, a newspaper rang up Alexander to know why he was not in the cabinet. Alexander said that he hadn't been asked. A few minutes later he received a message to call on MacDonald at 5.30. He went and found Lansbury and Tom Mosley there. Mosley was with the chief, as Alexander called him. When Mosley came out, Alexander went in. Ramsay began as usual with complaints of his hard life. 'This is the devil of a job. I'm having a very hard time.'

Then he turned to Alexander. 'And what do you want?'

'That's your business and not mine,' said Alexander.

Ramsay looked surprised, then went on: 'I can't give you the Board of Trade – which I should like you to have – because of Willie Graham. Do you think you could manage the Admiralty?'

'I'll try anything you like to give me,' said Alexander.

Again Ramsay was pleased. 'I see you're in a very submissive mood,' he said, 'very different from our friend who has just gone out.'

Alexander also showed me two letters from Snowden to him. The first was written in April 1931. Snowden was then ill and was very afraid that the quota scheme which he hated was going through. He begged Alexander to hold the fort for him in the cabinet. Alexander did. A little later Snowden wrote another letter to thank Alexander and to tell him that the danger was past and that he, Snowden, had a letter from MacDonald saying that while he approved of it in principle, he disliked it in practice, and that on mature reflection he was prepared to wait a bit, etc. Six months later Snowden sent a letter to the Sheffield electors on the eve of the poll telling them not to vote for Alexander, as he could not be trusted.

[1] Henderson signed the Five-Power Naval Disarmament Treaty in Rome in April 1930. Three years earlier he had unveiled a statue in Brussels to Matteotti, the Italian Socialist and Anti-Fascist who was murdered by the Fascists in 1924.

Snowden and Winston had great duels – Snowden generally won. On one occasion, however, Winston scored. Winston hated speaking *before* Snowden. One day he got up first and began to speak. As he warmed up, Snowden took out his pencil and began to sharpen it.

'I see,' said Churchill, 'that the Chancellor of the Exchequer is sharpening his arrows against me.'

'Oh no,' said Snowden, 'I'm only sharpening my pencil in order to take down the pearls of your oratory.'

'In that case,' said Winston, 'I have no objection to casting them before the right honourable gentleman.'

Alexander, incidentally, says he is the only man who has ever called a Minister of the Crown a liar without being called to order. During the naval debate about Invergordon in the Short Parliament Sir Philip Cunliffe-Lister leant across and without rising made some remark, when Alexander was speaking, to the effect that 'You ran away like rabbits.' Alexander said loudly: 'That is a deliberate lie,' and was not called to order. The incident is in Hansard without Cunliffe-Lister's name. . .[1]

After dinner went on to Salzmann's where I met two well-known Germans just back from China, and a German correspondent just back from Russia. Herr Schneider, who has been at Hankow, gave me a most graphic description of Chinese executions [during the invasion by Japan]. They take place in the main streets in the busiest centre of the town (Hankow, for example). A bugle blows. Places are marked out and a square roped off. Bugle blows again, and crowds hurry to spot. Then a large lorry rolls up, say, with ten victims, each guarded by two men. The executioners have a sword and carry a pistol in their hand. The lorry draws up in the arena. The men get out and take their place. There is another rat-ta-tat. The victims sink forward on their knees. Another rat-ta-tat, and the executioners strike. There are one or two one-stroke men – they are the champions who cut the head clean off with one blow. The crowd cheers like madmen. There is another rat-ta-tat on the bugle. 'Heads off.' Those executioners who have failed to sever the head with one blow now saw them off. More cheers. Another rat-ta-tat. The executioners enter their 'lorry' and with pointed pistols (they are afraid the victims may have friends in the crowd) drive off. The crowd rushes forward to examine the spot. Some bring strips of flannel and dip them in the blood. The blood of strong men is good for the weak – and consumptives suck these strips. As an exhibition of blood-lust it is disgusting. The war is a cruel war – there are no prisoners on both sides. All the Germans agree that Japan cannot coerce China (the Chinese put the man who buys Japanese goods in a cage) but that Chinese unity (between Chiang and Feng

[1] The Invergordon mutiny occurred in September 1931 during the brief life of MacDonald's first National Government. Cunliffe-Lister (1884–1972), Unionist M.P., later Lord Swinton, was then President of the Board of Trade, and Alexander a member of the Labour opposition.

for example) will last only as long as the foreign invasion continues. Corruption of young Chinese is terrible – it has destroyed the old traditional honesty. The Chinks who have been in Europe and America have learnt all that is bad in white civilisation and none of the good.

Sunday, 6 March 1932

I worked, while 'Hinch', who is Baldwin's private secretary, sat out in a long chair in the sun. He was wrapped in a thick rug, a cigar hung from his lips, at his side was a gramophone playing a Wagnerian concert all through the morning, and on his knees was a carefully bound folder in which were Stanley Baldwin's Parliamentary papers. Occasionally, 'Hinch' would glance at his papers, then, puffing his cigar, would turn his eyes to Chanctonbury Ring to enjoy the beauty of Nature, while never for a minute was the gramophone allowed to rest. A very soulful and serious young man who sets himself a high standard of rectitude and ambition. . . The Kleinwort boys came over to luncheon: they are about thirty, very alike, very talkative, and rather serious young men. They are inseparable, ride well to hounds, and their horses, too, are inseparable, so that if one rides a Kleinwort horse one is more or less tied to the other Kleinwort for the day.

In the evening 'Hinch', Mary and Pempe Dudley Ward[1] went to the Howards (Baldwin's daughter). They wanted to come to Hunger Hill but would not because of my presence and my connection with Max. They apply this vendetta to anyone associated with Max.

Monday, 7 March 1932

I came back to the office after luncheon to find that Briand [French Foreign Minister] had died very suddenly. He had a stroke after being shaved by his barber in Paris and died soon afterwards. Briand, who was an innkeeper's son, was born at Nantes and went to the bar there. As a young man he was a great fornicator and was once caught copulating with a woman in an open field. She was the wife of the public prosecutor of Nantes. Briand was prosecuted for an '*outrage des mœurs*' and was disbarred for unprofessional conduct. The disbarment was later removed.

Sunday, 13 March 1932

Lovely day. No sooner had I started work than the telephone rang: Lord Beaverbrook to speak. He spoke himself: 'Have you seen your newspapers? Kreuger?' I guessed he'd shot himself, although I had not seen the papers.[2] 'Tomorrow,' said Beaverbrook, dramatising himself, 'you have to tell the story. You must sell thousands and thousands of extra copies. Get

[1] Penelope, daughter of Freda Dudley Ward, was an actress, later married to Sir Carol Reed, film producer.

[2] Ivar Kreuger, financier and 'match king', shot himself when the Swedish Match Trust dropped in value from £180m to £45m.

hold of the woman: the Princess Bismarck, the Swedish minister's wife. The day is short. Go to it.' And there was nothing for it but to pack my bag and return to London. Strangely enough, Rudolph de Trafford, who knew Kreuger better than anyone else, came to Hunger Hill that afternoon. I of course missed him. I *did* see the Swedish Minister – Baron Palmstierna – alone for an hour. I bluffed him into giving me an interview. He liked Kreuger very much, saw him always when he came to London, and dined alone with him here just about Christmas time. Kreuger was obviously worried. He said, 'Swedish Match Co. would pull through if Europe pulled through. If Europe went, the world went.' He blamed the politicians for idling and postponing when the world's need was urgent. He blamed France's policy.

Monday, 14 March 1932

Very busy at office. Max has taken the Kreuger suicide very much to heart. It is of course a big story, but much bigger to him, because he visualises himself in a similar situation, than to our news people who would rather have run their paper on the sweep (Irish sweep draw was today) and even on the German elections. Hindenburg just failed to get through on the first ballot. He obtained nearly 6,000,000 more votes than Hitler, and should win hands down at the second ballot.

Tommy went into retreat today. I wish I could have gone, too. The rush of this senseless newspaper life is killing me. It has neither rhyme nor reason. Went to see Kosteliansky, a Russo-English Jew, whom I met in Prague years ago. He is now head of a large orange business in Palestine and is an ardent Zionist. He is very critical of our administration in Palestine, says that our officials are men from the Colonial Service – mainly, from Africa – that they expect servility, get it from the Arabs and not from the Jews, and are therefore pro-Arab. Says that Wauchope[1] is first-rate, as he understands these nationality problems. Tel Aviv, the new Jewish city is very up-to-date – a kind of mixture of Odessa, Brighton and Coney Island – has its cinemas, theatres, cabarets, motor-buses, etc. Palestine is almost the only country in world just now where there is no economic crisis.

Sunday, 20 March 1932

At Hunger Hill – Archie and Marigold Sinclair, Lord Carlisle, Mrs Cavendish, Rudolph de Trafford, and a man called Stokes. Played bridge before dinner – much against my will – and won £2. 6! . . . Archie told me that five or six years ago [1928], when Baldwin was putting through women's vote, Winston raised a revolt to make age limit twenty-five. Backed by many Liberals including even C. P. Scott.[2] Archie sent him a letter (he had been employed as a kind of canvasser) and to make it quite secret adopted a kind

[1] General Sir Arthur Wauchope (1874–1947), High Commissioner for Palestine and Trans-Jordania, 1931–8.

[2] (1846–1932) great Liberal editor of the *Manchester Guardian.*

of cipher in which he transcribed all names into Chinese forms: Jong Si Mong. Winston glanced at the letter, thought it concerned China, and marked it at once for 'despatch to Sir Austen Chamberlain at the F.O.' Fortunately, Archie came in in time to prevent a disaster.

Thursday, 31 March 1932

Went straight to the office without having been to bed at all. Felt like death. There is only one safe rule for me – complete teetotalism or else escape from London. Here I am – ill again, my nerves shattered, and my digestion and throat affected, and all the result of my own folly and excesses. Spent the whole morning trying to find out if there was any truth in the story of Nancy Meyrick's engagement to Charles Fitzroy (Lord Southampton's son). Obviously the boy, even if he wants to marry her, does not want the Press interfering.

Met George Clerk for a cocktail at the Wellington. Asked him to tell me quite frankly what my position was vis-à-vis the Foreign Office during the years 1914–1917. He said that: (1) I was backed very strongly by Buchanan, and (2) with that backing I was regarded by the cabinet as the man whose opinion of Russia and on Russian affairs counted most. Lunched at the Slocombes[1] to meet Bogomolov, the Russian Counsellor. A very pleasant bourgeois who behaved very tactfully. Mrs Slocombe is a Russian of the intense type – looks like a prophetess – has dark, dark hair, great dark eyes.

Sunday, 3 April 1932

Woke this morning in a depressed mood. Opened my newspapers and was horrified to read that Edward Marjoribanks had committed suicide – shot himself in the heart with a shot-gun which apparently he had fired by working the trigger with a pencil. The last letter I had from him was a request for Kühlmann's address. He wanted to check some statement in connection with his life of Carson. I do not think Edward had it in him to be Prime Minister of England. He lacked balance, and I always felt when he became excited that there was something abnormal about his mentality. I fancy there was insanity in the family. Before I had dressed, young Southam rang up to say that his father had shot himself at Hastings in exactly the same way as Edward on Friday night.

Monday, 4 April 1932

Still very tired and run down. Everyone tells me how ill I look. Spent most of the morning writing paragraphs about poor Edward Marjoribanks. I am sure he was obsessed with the idea that he would go mad. There was insanity in the family. The final blow, however, was another love affair – a woman who had turned him down. He was unfortunate in all his love affairs.

[1] George Slocombe (1894–1963), foreign editor of the *Evening Standard*, and his wife Marie Karlinskaya.

I expect he bored women by his own introspection. He was once devoted to Sally Lindley – once engaged to one of the Becketts. Max at Cherkley and very upset indeed.

Tuesday, 5 April 1932

Still feeling very depressed and run down. My nerves were not relieved by a conversation with Mike who informs me that Max has a new job for me: to write a column under my own name in the *Daily Express* every day. This would mean my leaving the *Standard* and giving up the Diary. Mike says it is a wonderful chance. Possibly. But I see the drawbacks. Apart from the fact that I dislike the connection with the *Daily Express*, I doubt if I can write the stuff they require. Secondly, I doubt if anyone can keep that kind of thing up for months on end. Thirdly, it means complete slavery and no holiday and probably the complete return to Max. The only advantage I can see is that I may have more time for my own writing.

Wednesday, 6 April 1932

Gave luncheon to E. F. Wise at Boulestin's. He seemed rather impressed by the fact that nearly everyone in the room came up to speak to me: Brendan Bracken, Esmond Harmsworth, Rudolph de Trafford, McCaw, Schuster, etc., etc. Its only significance is to remind me of all my failures. Wise very interesting about Russia. He returns there in about four weeks and visits the remoter parts: Turkestan, Siberia, etc. He is quite convinced the economic system of the world is going the Russian way. He thinks that the National Government has saved the Parliamentary system in England. Its rule by Orders in Council will enable the next Labour Government to nationalise the Bank of England, etc., by the same methods. Very many people are going to Russia this year: co-operatives, Labour men and likewise business bourgeois like Rudolph de Trafford and his friend Stokes.

Wednesday, 13 April 1932

Lloyd George in wonderful form – very neatly dressed in new suit, single stick-up collar, tie-pin, long, thin watch chain folded twice across his waist-coat. Miss Stevenson had begged me not to talk too much about his health, so we began on politics: He might go to Clacton [where the Liberals were to hold their party conference]. In certain contingencies he would go. If Liberals at Clacton decided to support National Government, Liberal Party dead. No use in his returning quickly to Parliament – rotten Parliament and bad Government. It had done nothing. There had been no improvement. He would support Government on Irish question. De Valera was sincere, but obstinate and no brains. Government had made a mess abroad. Simon no match for Tardieu. French thought they had him. Yet Simon was an eel. You think they have him and he is away (L.G. illustrated eel slipping away with his hands). He [Lloyd George] had something else to do: he would write a book on disarmament. He had signed the Peace Treaty. It had been broken. It was a duty he owed to the world. Liked writing. It gave him a new amusement. Did most of his writing in bed. Went early to bed – rarely later than ten – a habit he acquired in war and woke early.

Very good conversation, which finished with . . . a caution to Max (Baldwin will do him in yet; he is far cleverer and more cunning than Max).

Friday, 15 April 1932

Last night Sir William Goode[1] told me lots about his life: how he became friendly with Hoover over the Panama–Pacific Exhibition at San Francisco in 1914 and over Belgian Relief Commission. Hoover gave up £50,000 a year to do this job. Goode has a very high opinion of Hoover. He does not like Blackett.[2] He says governor is terribly sensitive to criticism, that Niemeyer stands up to Governor and Governor does not therefore like him as well as he did, that Siepmann is the best of the four Treasury fellows (Blackett, Niemeyer, Leith-Ross and Siepmann) and that the City would pick Siepmann first.

Met Driberg at the 43. He is very unhappy in his job as 'Dragoman'. He writes poetry. He said that if he died now and I had to write his obituary would I ring up Edith Sitwell and she would tell me all about him. He said he *must* get away, go round the world as a steward in a ship – anything. But has he – have any of us? – the courage? I doubt it.

On 18 April 1932, Harold Nicolson wrote to Lockhart from Sissinghurst Castle, Kent.

I am buried here leading the simple life and conditioning myself for the Primus Stove existence which communism will entail upon all of us. I find it easy to do so provided that one does not have to brush one's clothes. It is very cold and very muddy. Like the Great European War. But I take exercise, write my rotten novel, and am perfectly happy if impoverished. I am very glad that I did not take the *Sunday Dispatch* job, or get a job on the *Sunday Express*. Starvation is really better than the smug cynicism of Shoe Lane or Fleet Street.

I sympathise with your misery. My only advice is to stick it. You will, I think, make a great success with your book. You may thereafter write another book equally successful. And then you can lead your own life – free from galling humiliations.

I met Mrs Chichester [Pam] the other day. She accused me of having told

[1] Goode (*d.* 1944) had been a newspaperman, News and Managing Editor *Morning* and *Evening Standard*, 1904–10, and was then Financial Adviser to the Hungarian Government.

[2] Sir Basil Blackett (1882–1935) was a director of the Bank of England, as were Niemeyer, Leith-Ross and Siepmann. The Governor was Sir Montagu Norman, who remained in the post till 1944.

Max that she rang you up. I was somewhat startled (not so much by the accusation – as I may well have said something and Max may well have twisted it into something disagreeable) – but by her evident impression that I had done this in order to supplant you in Max's affections. I *have* a hazy recollection of his saying that you were wasting your substance on drink and lechery – and my saying that not at all, you were merely bothered by your friendships with several different women at the same time. In any case Mrs C. admitted that you, when told by her of the incident, had brushed it aside as unimportant. And I know perfectly well that you would not imagine I should try to put any spokes in your wheel.

Wednesday, 27 April 1932

Duns from the money-lender for interest on my loan and from Mrs Hutchinson for arrears of rent. Also demands from Baillie and Gifford for our £100 on insurance premiums.

Met Moura at the Wellington at seven. She tells me H. G. [Wells] was down at Cherkley for weekend. Max and he had discussed Arnold Bennett's child by Dorothy Cheston. Max said he would have to do something for it. He said he could not stand seeing Arnold Bennett's ghost at his bedside every night shaking an admonishing finger at him.

Thursday, 28 April 1932

Lunched with Neil Chaplin and Trevor Wignall [football writer] at the Savoy Grill. Trevor Wignall told us some tales of journalism twenty-five years ago: the drinking was colossal. Men like Charlie Hands seemed to stand it. Charlie Hands is still living. He is now over seventy, lives at Ventnor, drinks a bottle of sherry and two bottles of port a day. Hands receives a pension of £2500 a year paid to his wife. His great plan as a reporter was always to find the pub where the telegraph operators went. Once he had the telegraph operator lined up, he knew his copy would go off first. [Edgar] Wallace and Hands taught Wignall his job as a reporter. In those days Wallace had a large, flowing moustache.

In the afternoon Randolph Churchill came to see me. He tells me there has been a scandal about Prince George – letters to a young man in Paris. A large sum had to be paid for their recovery. I expect Randolph has been told this by some American journalist. In the evening dined at the St James's with Fletcher, Bernstorff and Jowitt, went to *The Cat and the Fiddle* (rotten) and supped at the Savoy Grill. Except Jowitt, whom I liked, we all drank too much, and there was no good conversation. Bernstorff is confident that there will be no Hitler régime in Germany. He says Hitler is afraid of power and is now being pushed by his lieutenants.

Friday, 29 April 1932

Lunched with Mike at the Savoy. He told me that Max showed him the cutting from *The Times* about my book and said: 'Bruce seems to have plenty of time on his hands.' Mike replied that he thought I had only my diaries to write up and that writing the book did not take up much time! Max then asked if he came into it. Mike said 'No', but that he would figure largely in the second volume, for which I had kept very full diaries. Max said: 'Let 'em all come.'

Saturday, 30 April 1932

A glorious day – warm and summer-like. Caught the 1.40 to Horsham and was met by Tommy at the station. Victor Rothschild[1] and Pempe Dudley Ward staying here. Victor Rothschild is a queer fellow – a kind of Jewish Cunningham-Reid. He is very clever, was a scholar at Harrow, and is now working for a fellowship at Trinity, Cambridge. He is a first-class cricketer, but is giving up his chance for a Blue this year in order to work. He hates the athletic people. He is studying biology. He is shy and suffers from an inferiority-complex – like most people of this nature, he appears bumptious and intolerant. He told me some queer stories about cocktail parties at Cambridge, how they 'doped' the cocktails of a lot of young girls from London and made them pass out. He was also hard on the athletes, but ranked Cambridge far higher than Oxford, morally, intellectually and athletically. Very severe on Harrow. There was, he said, no Harrovian of his time who was proud of having been at Harrow. School was in terrible state when Norwood came. Vice reigned unchecked.

Monday, 16 May 1932

Jan Masaryk is leaving for Prague and will probably go to Belgrade.[2] He has had six years here. He is worried and unhappy. At his party the other night there were about three parties, and a few favoured guests remained till six or seven a.m., while Jan had in the Hungarian gipsies and himself played and sang Slovak songs. He is the greatest contortionist among diplomatists and can put his head between his legs. Sir John Simon, Lady Londonderry, etc., had supper at his table. Lady Londonderry, fresh from Geneva, announced loudly: 'Ah, yes! Beneš can do what he likes there. He has them all in his pocket.' Simon tried to remonstrate. Jan, however, butted in: 'Never mind, Sir John. Everyone knows that Lady Londonderry has had a Hungarian bias for the last two years.' (This refers to her friendship – liaison? – with ——.)

Saturday, 21 May 1932

Elizabeth Belloc and Miss Leveson-Gower came to luncheon. Latter, who was married but who has reverted to her maiden name, is psychic and can get herself back into the past. She has the power, when she is visiting, say, an old monastery or house to visualise it as it was hundreds of years before and

[1] (*b.* 1910) later 3rd Baron Rothschild.
[2] Masaryk remained Czechoslovak Minister to Great Britain until 1938.

to see rooms long since buried and avenues and gates that no longer exist and people, etc.

Sunday, 22 May 1932

Stories about Lord Dudley:[1] his extravagance. When he was Viceroy of Ireland he met a very lovely woman. He asked her to come to a Viceregal Court. She said she had no tiara. 'I'll get you one,' was the reply. And he did. Three years ago or so he was carrying on an affair with an Austrian lady who could speak no English. Lord Dudley wrote to her in French, which he did not speak very well. He wrote letters in English first and then translated them into French. He left two copies of the English originals in his blotter and Gertie Millar (Lady Dudley)[2] found them. There was hell to pay! When Lord Dudley made his collieries into a company and handed them over to Eric Ednam, he had to live three years in order to avoid death duties. They insured him for £25,000 a year. He lived the three years (although he was ill then). He had a fortune of £500,000 a year. In the end he received £5000 p.a., and subsequently £15,000 from Eric.

Sunday, 29 May 1932

In the evening John de Forest came down and told us his life story. First, *re* [golf] championship. He has been out of luck and form lately. Luck changed when at Le Touquet for French Championship. Never gambles, but won £35 with a 100-franc note. Changes again when returned. Thought his brother had entered him. Entry accepted at last minute. Form changed two days before meeting. Had nothing to do. Went to see Bobby Jones in Edinburgh and saw that his hip movement had been wrong. He dreamt he was going to win. The course was a strange one and unlike any golf course, but he was the winner. Tootie, his father,[3] is now claiming all the credit and gave interview to papers in which he said John was no good at work and therefore, he, Tootie, had made him into a golfer. John, who has had his allowance cut off several times, stands to gain financially by winning. Tootie should now pay up handsomely.

When de Forest was twenty-one or so, he walked out on his father and went to earn his own living. He had been in Price Waterhouse [accountants] and could not stand it. (He had never been to public school.) Got a job at Rugby with British Thompson-Houston. Left in charge of power station. Man was to have come at night to switch off extra current. He never came. John tried and blew out side of factory. Went with mate to Coventry, lived in workmen's lodgings above a slaughter-house. Workmen very kind. Raffled his sweater – worth about 5s. – for a pound. Tickets 1*s.* each. Finally,

[1] 2nd Earl of Dudley (1867–1932), had fallen seriously ill in April and was to die on 29 June. He was Lord Lieutenant (not Viceroy) of Ireland, 1902–5. Lord Ednam was his heir.

[2] Actress ('Gaiety Girl') and previously wife of composer, Lionel Monckton (*d* 1952).

[3] Arnold Maurice, Count de Bendern.

got a job as van driver for New Brunswick Company. . . Gets job as Brunswick manager in Paris at £500 a year. Company goes 'bust' – is about to start new panatrope machine[1] with former representative of 'B.T.H.' Returns to his father who at this moment begs him to come to Biarritz. Takes up golf now as more serious object. Father offers him £1000 if he gets through two rounds of amateur.

Friday, 3 June 1932

Tommy picked me up at 6.30 and after a stand-up snack at Scott's we went on to the Lyceum to see *The Miracle*[2] – a very moving performance. I found myself shedding hot tears! Went round to see Lady Diana Cooper afterwards. As the Madonna she stands motionless for over forty-five minutes. She *was* tired. A bug had bitten a huge mark on her shoulder, and she could not scratch it. She had a cold, and she dared not cough. She told us Max had at last come to see *The Miracle*: he missed the first act, which is three-quarters of the play and Diana's great performance. The *Express*, too, never mentioned the King's visit to *The Miracle*, because Max has a feud with Cochran, so childish. Diana told us a good story of the King's visit. He sent for her, of course: 'You played this part twenty-five years ago?' 'No, sir,' says Diana, trying to be polite. 'How's your broken leg? I remember you broke it on our Coronation Day!' 'No, sir, on Peace Day.' The third tactless remark was praise of her performance, with the remark, 'But of course you have no words to say, and talking is three-quarters of acting!'

Saturday, 4 June 1932

Public opinion here still anxious about new German Government, which has had a bad Press over here. Rumours of a reactionary coup d'état, Hindenburg's resignation in favour of Crown Prince, etc. Herr von Papen dissolves the Reichstag.[3] Situation very unclear. Hitler, for the moment, seems to be standing in the background. His reluctance to take action on his own may make him 'catspaw' of reactionaries.

Sunday, 5 June 1932

Still bitterly cold. Great excitement in the Press over the situation in Germany which is described as critical. Rumours that the von Papen Government – the Monocle Cabinet – is to remain in power for a long time and that the ex-Crown Prince is to succeed Hindenburg as President. The *Sunday Express* has played the story up very big. I find it hard to believe that the Junkers, who are not really Hitler's affair and who polled so few votes at the

[1] An early form of electric gramophone.

[2] An enormously popular spectacular play put on by Max Reinhardt and C. B. Cochran.

[3] Von Papen had formed a new ministry on 1 June. This (see next entry) was called the Monocle Cabinet because seven out of nine of its ministers were members of the old nobility.

recent elections, can establish themselves, but there is so much despair and fatalism in Germany that anything is possible. The German Embassy is very upset.

Friday, 10 June 1932

Lunched at the Savoy Grill with Bernstorff, Hallam and Randolph Churchill. Hallam is being transferred immediately to Memel. Conversation monopolised by Randolph, who talked a vast amount of nonsense. He is an attractive boy, but is lazy and has no principles except those of a brigand, who is out to exploit everyone he can. At the same time he is very conceited about his ancestry. To the great amusement of us all, he related how Max had told Winston or Bracken that 'Young Randolph was improving.' Randolph's comment was 'What damned impertinence!' He also complained bitterly of the gossip-writers and said he was trying to form a society to exclude them from parties. He gave us an amusing account of his row with Castlerosse. They met for first time a year ago at a party given by Venetia Montagu. Valentine said Winston had murdered 250,000 men at the Dardanelles. Finished up by saying: 'For two pins I'd hit you.' 'Don't do that,' said Randolph. 'I'm *not* your wife.' Dined at club. Bed midnight.

Thursday, 16 June 1932

Big Max and Little Max are going tonight to the coming-of-age dinner given by Winston to his son Randolph. Practically all the famous sons and fathers in public life are to be there. Freddy Birkenhead is to propose Randolph's health. Spoke to Randolph on the telephone. He gave me most of the information about the dinner himself. What an amazing thing privilege and position still are in England! Here is a boy who, born in a less privileged circle, would have had to work hard and make his own way. As it is, he is lazy, lascivious, impudent and, beyond a certain rollicking bumptiousness, untalented, and everything is open to him. One thing his position has given him is good looks and charm.

Friday, 17 June 1932

In the evening went to L.C.C. reception at the County Hall. Perfect night and a very fine building with a model Parliament hall and a fine terrace. Saw Hugh[1] and Jean Turnbull, who tell me that there is to be another cut in police pay in October; at same time the Corporation has decided not to take a penny off the wages of the corporation dustmen, etc.; likewise Lord Ashfield, Hore-Belisha, Jan Masaryk, who is very pessimistic, Louis Greig,[2] two Sheiks – Mr Montagu Norman, very pontifical and spectacular with his beard. He stood admiring view on terrace. Wore his medals: D.S.O. and South African War medal.

[1] Sir Hugh Turnbull (*b.* 1882), Commissioner of Police for the City of London.

[2] Sir Louis Grieg (1880–1953), Gentleman Usher to the Duke of York.

Saturday, 18 June 1932

General opinion is agreed regarding the excellence of young Lord Birkenhead's speech at the Randolph Churchill dinner on Thursday night. Even Max was full of praise. Winston, Hailsham and Brendan Bracken were enraptured. They declared that the young Freddy was as good as, if not better than, 'F.E.' Someone else said 'more of a gentleman'. This morning I had a shock – a letter from Moura in which she requests me to alter the part in my book referring to her. She wants it made more formal. She wants to be called Mme Benckendorff all through. She is as conventional as a Victorian spinster. And why? Because I said that fourteen years ago she had waving hair – whereas it is 'flat as a Ukrainian's'. Therefore, my description is shallow, false, etc., and this is obviously all that the episode meant to me! Therefore either the full love story or nothing. This will be very difficult. The book, however, will have to be altered. She is the only person who has the right to demand an alteration.

Tuesday, 21 June 1932

Lunched today with Slocombe in his house at Glebe Place. It was formerly Dina Erroll's. Present Freddy Wilson, an ex-*Express* man, who has been editing a newspaper in India for the last four-and-a-half years, Thomas and Leadley, the Canadian publicity man. Wilson is an entertaining scoundrel, who tells a story well. Discussed Ashmead, George Mair, Arnold Ward and all the 'splendid failures'. Max ran a series on them in the *Express* not so long ago. They included Masterman, Gerhardi, etc.[1] Wilson wanted to 'do' Arnold Ward. 'No,' said Max, 'it would be too true.' Mair would have been the same. Most of the splendid failures were collected and exploited by Max. He got 'em cheap.

Wilson told a good story of Winston. At North West Manchester election *v.* Jix he made a wonderful peroration about the heroism of a British regiment during Buller's attempt to relieve Ladysmith. They were stormed by shot and shell. (Immense effect of Winston's military imagery) etc., etc. And who were the heroes who put up this glorious defence? The men of the Lancashire Fusiliers. Tremendous uplift, but Winston was [*word illegible*]. He went on to Dundee. The young Liberal band, which accompanied him, was surprised to hear the same peroration. This time, however the gallant heroes were the men of the Black Watch!

Also discussed Karl Ketchum.[2] He is in a home and apparently has only two months to live. . . Leadley was the man who got him into the home. The doctors told him to make him drunk and dope his drink. Leadley gave a party, doped Ketchum's drink, but the others all got drunk and Ketchum

[1] Arnold Ward (1876–1950) had a brilliant career at Oxford, which, after a spell as a foreign correspondent and an M.P., came to nothing. C. F. G. Masterman (1873–1927), a Liberal politician who seemed to have great promise but held no post after 1915.

[2] Ketchum, a legendary journalist, survived and was still alive in Canada quite recently.

remained sober. Leadley had to knock him out in the end before they could carry him in to the home... Went to see Pam, who is much better, and dined with Moura at the Eiffel Tower.

Wednesday, 22 June 1932

The best story of Karl Ketchum was his start as a journalist on the *Express*. He was sent out to do a story on the funeral of Thompson, the husband of the woman in the Thompson–Bywater murder. Nine o'clock came – no Ketchum. Finally, he arrived just in time. 'Well,' said the chief sub. 'Have you a story?' 'Sure,' said Ketchum, and out of his pocket he produced the wreath cards from the grave. One bore the words: 'To my loving husband – Dorothy Thompson.' Ketchum had waited till everyone had gone; had then climbed over the railings, and stolen the cards. The chief sub, who had been there for years and who was as tough as you make them, was almost shocked. 'That young man will do,' he said. 'He's got initiative.'

Sunday, 26 June 1932

Hamish told me a story of Ramsay MacDonald's visit to Castle Grant, when he (Hamish) was staying there. Ramsay MacDonald was terrible – vain and pompous. Talked all the time about Geordie and Eileen (the Duke and Duchess of Sutherland), referred in his conversation with Hamish to Lady Londonderry as Circe, and complained dreadfully how hard it was for him to be there when he felt all the time that he should be doing his duty in London. Ishbel who was there, was disgusted. 'Thank God,' she said to H., 'father hasn't got three eyes!'

Monday, 27 June 1932

Went to Test match [England *v.* India] for an hour with Moura – it was very slow and uninspiring cricket. Saw Sutcliffe and Holmes scratch 19 indifferent runs in 45 minutes. Ground, however, was crowded. I cannot think how England can afford to idle in this way.

Wednesday, 29 June 1932

Yesterday Brendan Bracken lost his hat in the House of Commons. He left it in Hore-Belisha's room. It was returned to him today with a slip inside it:

'Brendan Bracken has lost his hat,
Which is really nothing to wonder at;
For Brendan's head grows at such a rate
That yesterday's hat won't fit his pate.'

I went on to the club and then on to the '43'. Latter is still open in spite of Mrs Meyrick's promise to the judge not to use place again as a club or to sell drink. Same old waiters, same band, same girls. Norrie Hamilton, an old habituée, said that the old lady was selling drink last Friday. I expect it was on the bottle-party basis. It is rather amazing. This is the kind of thing one might expect from the Russian police. But here it is extraordinary.

Thursday, 30 June 1932

Lunched at the St James's Club with Fletcher, Alexander, the former First Lord and Labour Co-operative leader, and McFarlane, who is in the film world. Alexander was very amusing about Ramsay MacDonald against whom he is very bitter. He described the scene when Ramsay MacDonald came back to his Cabinet and told them his decision to form a National Government. He advised them to follow his advice or they would regret it and told them that 'in high quarters neither L.G. nor Baldwin was trusted!' Actually, what the King did say (and Lady Mar told Tommy) was: 'You've got us into this mess, Mr MacDonald, and you've got to get us out.' Alexander is very sour about the manner in which in the debate on the crisis Ramsay MacDonald made use of secret Cabinet documents to show that Alexander had accepted the cuts. Alexander had protested against the cuts. Asked if they would create disturbances in the fleet, he consulted his technical advisers and reported that, if the rest of the nation had similar cuts, navy would bear its burdens. The other day in the House, Attlee, who got a D.S.O. in the war, was taunted with disloyalty to his chief. He said: 'Some of you have been soldiers, no doubt. You will know then that there is only one occasion when a soldier is justified in disobeying orders. That is when his senior officer goes over to the enemy.' Pretty fierce on Ramsay.

Wednesday, 6 July 1932

Went to a luncheon given at St Ermin's [hotel] by the Oxford Movement.[1] Saw Buchman, the ex-Lutheran American minister, who is the head of the movement. He is a little man, clean-shaven and with closely-cut hair. He has the face of a bird, his keen eyes darting here and there through horn-rimmed spectacles set on a large beak-like nose. He was dressed in grey-striped trousers and the short black coat and waistcoat worn by City men. Looked like a bagman. Many celebrities there: A. V. Alexander, Lord Buxton, Duchess of Atholl, Mrs Snowden, and Mrs Baldwin, Locker-Lampson, James Watt, the Scottish Communist, Hofmeyr, the South African Rhodes scholar. Young men stood up and testified what the movement had done for them. They call themselves the 'life-changers' and the movement consists in dedicating one's life to Christ.

Thursday, 28 July 1932

Dined with Bernstorff and Morsbach, a young German Conservative of thirty-five, who is head of the students' exchange committee in Germany.

[1] Later called Moral Rearmament, founded 1921 by Frank Buchman (1878–1961).

He is a very intelligent young man, thinks that for some time now the party politicians in Germany will be discredited (this includes Brüning, who in his opinion has been too much a party man), and is sure that we shall have non-party Government in Germany for some time. Very pro-Hindenburg. Says, however, that if by any chance Hitler did obtain an absolute majority at the election Hindenburg would send for him. The President would *never* break his oath to the constitution.

Tuesday, 2 August 1932

Hamish, who is great friend of the Lygons, dined with Lord Beauchamp[1] on his last night in England. He says Beauchamp was a grand father and adored by his children, who loathe their mother. Lord Beauchamp informed his children that there was only one way out. He would kill himself. He would go to Wiesbaden, pretend to take a cure, and would take an overdose of sleeping draught on the Friday. He went. First night he put a glass of port to his lips, doctor seized it and said 'no'. This triviality so angered Lord Beauchamp he forgot all about the suicide. His children still fear he will take his life.

Thursday, 4 August 1932

Aldous Huxley's description of the Sitwells: 'Two wiseacres and a cow' – very good.[2]

Beaverbrook is ill again. He has not been in Berlin, but in Paris. I fear I have ruined myself irretrievably by my blunder or my secretary's blunder in sending him my manuscript with two unrevised references to himself.

Sunday, 7 August 1932

Discussed finances with Jean. I don't see how I can get out of my present mess without selling the serial rights of my book or making a contract for a new one. Jean herself is in trouble. Her overdraft has been called up by the Union Bank of Australia. What a fool I have been! We were far better off and happier than now when we had £500 a year in Moscow in 1912. Now I have £3000 a year and am a pauper. I pay £750 to Jean and Robin – £200 to my secretary – £400 in insurance premiums and interest on loans – £1000 is deducted at source for my debt to Beaverbrook and Dad – I owe £800 in tax – in all, £3150 or – £150 before I begin to live.

Monday, 8 August 1932

Came up from Bexhill by 8.13. Met Anthony Mendl, brother of Charles Mendl[3] and now liquidator of the Anglo-International Bank in Rumania, on the train. He says King Carol is unpopular and is not respected. He never goes anywhere without a police-car or two in front of him – never walks in

[1] The Lygons were the children of the 7th Earl Beauchamp (1872–1938).

[2] Osbert, Sacheverell and Edith Sitwell. The reference was to a political cry of earlier years: 'Two acres and a cow.'

[3] Sir Charles Mendl (1871–1958), Press Attaché British Embassy, Paris, 1928–40.

streets. Quite different from his grandfather. Has his woman with him (Lupescu). Has his son completely under his thumb. Maniu,[1] who welcomed his return, now against him because of his treatment of Queen. Has never been crowned – this makes peasantry superstitious about him – say God doesn't want him to be King. Wife, sister of King of Greece. Latter married Carol's sister. Surrounded by sycophants. Lives in his mountain palace two-and-a-half hours from Bucharest. Likes uniforms – restless, loves shooting and fast motoring. Rumanian bankruptcies – very amusing. Three kinds – (1) bankruptcy on petition of creditor; (2) judicial liquidation, whereby bankrupt can present his balance sheet to court and go bankrupt himself. This super plan for crooks – as if order once granted no fear of detection for fraud; (3) the concordat – makes an arrangement to pay his creditors so much in certain time – also from court, but assets must show 60% of liabilities. In each case nothing is ever paid except to the lawyers.

Letter from Beaverbrook, praising my book and saying 'it will be a big success'.

Sunday, 14 August 1932

Still feeling below par – have catarrh and indigestion. Went to mass at Dunmow – tiny church which was crammed full. [Lockhart was staying at Easton, Daisy, Lady Warwick's house.] A newly ordained priest was serving his first Mass. The local priest is Father Field – a fierce old boy who rules his flock with a staff of iron. After a prayer for the harvest he startled us all by saying in stentorian tones three times: 'God Save Russia' followed by a single: 'God Save the Pope'. In afternoon went for a walk with Tommy through the thousand-acre park to the Sanctuary. There is there a little house – fragment of a former monastery destroyed by Henry VIII – with niches for statues, etc., a garden of friendship with flowers planted by Lady Warwick's admirers. Each flower has an iron stake in front of it with a plaque shaped like a heart and an inscription on it: 'Lily of the Valley. Planted by H.R.H. The Prince of Wales, Nov. 15, 1892.' King Edward – then H.R.H. – is almost the only man who figures in this garden. The others are all women. King Edward figures often – most of the flowers he planted are various forms of daisies. The Shakespeare garden contains all the flowers mentioned by Shakespeare with a plaque quoting his remarks about them and the play in which they occur. Old Lady Warwick is remarkable. She gets up at five, sleeps only five-and-a-half hours, feeds her animals (she has an array of dogs, monkeys, and parrots, etc.). She eats like a wolf. (For breakfast she had two sausages, a fish-cake, and bacon), bathes in the sports-pool and altogether is a very live wire.

Saturday, 27 August 1932

Came down to Coolham by the 1.40 – very hot, and I felt wretched. I have

[1] Julius Maniu had been Prime Minister of Rumania, 1928–31.

been drinking very hard for the last six weeks, am overdrawn to the last farthing at the bank, am hopelessly in debt and being dunned by solicitors and money-lenders, and have no more will-power to compete with the situation. Made a fresh vow to start a teetotal and diet régime. Did nothing all afternoon except lie in the garden and rest. In the evening played chess with Harry. Went to bed at ten-thirty and took a liver pill.

Harry, who has just returned from Dr Dengler's at Baden-Baden, paid over £100 on his bill alone for twelve days. He looks much better, but has started drinking again. The cure itself is quite simple: no potatoes, no alcohol, no starchy foods, no sugar, etc., a considerable amount of walking and then massage and water massage. Harry has also been at Le Touquet. Fortunately, he paid expenses and made £50.

Gertie Millar (Lady Dudley) there. She has been left the villa and an allowance of £5000 which Eric can make or not as he likes. She does not expect more than the tax-free portion of £5000. She is sharing her villa with Lord and Lady Furness, talks all the time of Eddie Dudley, has had him photographed when dead, and sends her visitors for rides in Dudley's electric chair (presented to him by Lord Furness). Lord Furness and she get on very well – because they both come from Lancs–Yorks and both are of the people. Lady Dudley (Gertie) is a born raconteuse.

Monday, 29 August 1932

Came up from Horsham by the 9.1. Lunched with Cudlipp at the Wellington Restaurant. He is very jealous of Gilliat and wants to step into his shoes.[1] Gilliat is back today. I spoke to him about my book [i.e. its serialisation]. He has heard nothing from Wardell, who will not be back until the 10th. If they refuse it after all this delay, I shall not be able to place it anywhere else. Gilliat likes it, but thinks that its frankness may subject me or rather 'The Londoner' to attacks. He said to me, 'Now that you are a man in a public position, why do you talk of yourself as being discredited in your book.' I replied: 'Well, am I not discredited? Look at me now!' He was shocked. He thinks a journalist – a successful journalist – is a great man. And even the most successful journalist is a slave or else a victim of his own conscience.

Wednesday, 31 August 1932

Spoke to Gilliat about my book. He now tells me that it is practically certain that the *Evening Standard* will take the serial rights of my book for post-publication serialisation. I shall receive about half of what I should have for pre-publication serialisation. Spent an hour and a half with Putnam's. Huntington is against all the fantasy titles and still clings to *Memoirs of a British Agent*, which nobody likes. I am sick and stale of the whole thing now. And he tells me he does not want me to leave London until the book is out. There

[1] Percy Cudlipp succeeded Gilliat as editor of the *Evening Standard*, 1933–6.

is an immense propaganda to be done. And this is the time my secretary chooses to have her tonsils out!

Thursday, 1 September 1932

In the evening dined with Arnold Benskin and Drayton at the Naval and Military. Arnold Benskin told us a very good story of the British troops at Baku in 1919. Benskin has the finest sturgeon, caviare, etc. One day sergeant-major came to the adjutant: there was trouble with the men!

'What?' said the A.D.C. 'Are they not getting enough exercise?'

'No, sir, it's not that!'

'Good God,' said the A.D.C. 'You don't mean to say they're going "bolshie".'

'No, sir, it's not that? You know 'ow fed up we got in France – plum and apple. Well, sir, the men say they can't stick this 'ere fish jam any longer.'

Friday, 2 September 1932

Spent half the morning at the office trying to ascertain whether Bob Boothby was engaged or not.[1] He was reported to be by Brendan Bracken, but the story is denied by nearly everyone including Bob himself and Tom Mosley who was with him on the Lido. The lady's name is supposed to be Miss Islan or Inslan. A degrading performance.

Lunched with Moura, who has returned. Gorky has been very ill in Berlin – lung trouble again. Attended by Prof. Kraus. Had to have oxygen. Age 64. Was not allowed to go to Holland to attend the anti-war congress. Bolshevik trade union delegation wanted him to go on to Paris. Moura would not let him go [on account of his health].

Wednesday, 14 September 1932

Lunched with Moura. H. G. Wells has returned to England from Grasse to spend a month here and to see his friends. He is taking Moura to Shaw's *Too True to be Good* on Friday night. H.G. will be 66 on Thursday the 22nd. Except for his women he has no real men friends. He takes little interest in the young men and unlike Gorky does not put himself out to encourage them. He has his two legitimate sons whom he likes, but does not allow to interfere with his life. His two sons, by Rebecca West and Amber Reeves he looks after generously. Anthony, the West boy, he used to like. Then . . . H.G. just slipped away. He is an adept at slipping away and never seeing people again. Bennett was probably his only friend, and I doubt if the two men ever unbent very much to each other. Bennett wanted H.G. to have something personal of his and left him two ash-trays. 'I would rather have had Bennett,' said H.G., 'but the trays are very nice.'

[1] Boothby (*b.* 1900), Conservative M.P., 1924–58 (and thereafter Lord Boothby), married Diana Cavendish in 1935.

Thursday, 29 September 1932

Lunched with Tom Mosley and his wife at the Savoy Grill. Tom in a grey shirt with a little gold Fascist badge in his buttonhole. His book comes out tomorrow. It is called *The Greater Britain*. His British Fascism is Mussolini in policy and Hitlerite in organisation: corporate state, Parliament to be elected on occupational franchise with functions restricted to electing government and vote of censure. House of Lords to be replaced by National Corporation which will act as Parliament of Industry. Organisation on Hitler group system. Monthly contributions of 1*s.* per month. Ordinary members to wear grey shirts and flannel trousers. Storm troops: black shirts and grey bags.

Lady Cynthia was rather amusing about Freda Dudley Ward. When she went to her first party in London, nobody knew her. She was terribly dressed. Was taken out by Richard Norton and Ali MacIntosh, who was then in charge of something at Barker's. Ali taught her to dress.

Friday, 30 September 1932

Lunched at the Marlborough Club with Moir Mackenzie and Walter Citrine, the General Secretary of the T.U.C.[1] Citrine, who was with Moir at Ottawa, is a man today between 40 and 50, tall, thin, and slightly angular, red cheeks, clear blue eyes, and grey hair. . . He told us his experiences in Russia.[2] He is not at all pro-Bolshevik, although in favour of trade with Russia. When he went with a colleague (I must look up and see who it was), they dined off gold plate, etc., in the Kremlin. Never had Citrine seen a more sumptuous meal. He could not help contrasting it with some children he saw sleeping under straw in the Theatre Square. The next day it snowed. The invitation to go to Russia came from Tomsky, who wished Citrine to advise them about T.U.C. organisation. Actually, the questions fired at Citrine were about politics.

Bolsheviks: 'Do you consider J. H. Thomas a traitor?'

Citrine: 'No. Tell me anything he's done by word or deed to betray his own people.'

Bolsheviks: 'He writes for the capitalist press.'

Citrine: 'Do you object to his writing for the press or to what he writes? If he writes for his Party, do you object?'

Bolsheviks: 'Don't be silly. Would the capitalist press print anything against themselves?'

Citrine: 'The capitalist press in England will print anything that will sell their papers.'

[1] Moir Mackenzie (1886–1963) had been at Fettes with Lockhart and was then Empire Director of the Federation of British Industries. Walter Citrine (*b.* 1887), knighted 1935, 1st Baron Citrine 1946, was General Secretary of the T.U.C., 1926–46.

[2] Mikhail Tomsky, Chairman of the Soviet Central Council of Trade Unions, attended the T.U.C. conference at Scarborough in 1925 and invited Walter Citrine and George Hicks to visit Russia.

Citrine was then told that Lenin had said this and that, etc. Citrine replied that Lenin had said so many things that, when they were added up, they contradicted each other.

Sunday, 2 October 1932

Glorious morning. Winter time or rather ordinary time started. Went to mass at Belloc's house at Shipley at nine. Mass was celebrated by missionary from Bombay – an English convert. The chapel is a tiny room on upper floor of Belloc's house and can hold about eight people. Old Belloc assisted as server. He is ageing very rapidly and now puffs and blows like a grampus. My last vision of him will be, as we all knelt, of him trying to blow out the candles. Or better still perhaps: downstairs, saying goodbye to us, fulminating against the politicians and running down D. H. Lawrence as filth.

Huntington came to luncheon. He has published Florence Barclay's *The Rosary*. Her books still sell at rate of £100 a week. Florence belonged to Barclay family, married a clergyman in Leytonstone and was a very fine speaker. Her sister was or is Mrs Barrington Booth of Salvation Army fame. Likewise Marie Stopes's *Married Love* which has sold millions. Many people told Putnam's that when they published Marie Stopes's book they would lose Mrs Barclay. Mrs Barclay, when she was about to undergo a severe operation, sent for Huntington and told him how much she liked *Married Love*, what a beautiful book it was, and how she tried to say what it said in her novels. Finally, Huntington published Erich M. Remarque's *All Quiet on the Western Front*, of which in England alone 860,000 were sold in first year. Remarque subjected to every kind of calumny in Germany: that he is a Jew, was never at war, and his name is Kramer (Remark!). All nonsense. Remarque is an injured war soul, has no joy in life, never answers attacks, never allows himself to be fêted, never accepts invitations. No *joie de vivre*. His wife, who is consumptive, has plenty. Hence their frequent attempts to divorce and their reunions. Remarque's great friend is the dog Huntington sent him over by plane to Berlin. Played golf.

Monday, 3 October 1932

Shanks's book [*Queer Street*] which came out last week has had wonderfully good reviews except from [J. B.] Priestley. Shanks and Slocombe, of course, are in the position of being able to arrange for good reviews. . .

Came up with Tommy by the 9.1. Lunched with Cudlipp at the Wellington. He is very self-satisfied. In my opinion, and in Slocombe's, the Diary is becoming very dull. In the afternoon went to see Huntington. Not only did he give me another advance of £200, but he wrote me a letter in which he says that he is fairly confident that 'further substantial profits will be received in addition to the total already advanced'. I have now made or am certain to make at least £1100 out of it. Not bad for a first book. Went to the club and had four drinks.

Tuesday, 4 October 1932

Went to see Tommy off at the station last night. She had come up to see Millie who left last night for Dunrobin. Tommy had been lunching with Bridget. Latter, who is broke, told her that Max had been very good to her about the overdraft he had guaranteed and did not want his money back. Bridget had one great stroke of luck. A friend (a man of course) who heard she was hard up gave her £2000 on condition she never disclosed the name. He said he could not bear to think of her in a state of poverty...

Another bad day and a worse night. Gave a luncheon party at Boulestin's to Randolph Churchill, Montgelas,[1] and Maurice Peterson. Randolph, who has a bad cold, in great form. Talks of starting a London newspaper to be published at 6 a.m. It would have the advantage of being several hours later than the so-called morning papers. Told us that his father was very restless and was trying to go to the Blackpool Conservative Conference after all. When they were away in Germany together, they had a heart-to-heart talk. Winston went for Randolph. 'What are you doing? When I was your age, I was reading five hours a day. You spend most of your time in night-clubs, staving off a vast army of debtors by eking out a precarious living as a hack-journalist.'[2] Randolph very amusing on Bracken whom he describes as God's greatest liar because he does not mind being found out.

Wednesday, 5 October 1932

Lunched with Harold and young Hobhouse[3] at the Jardin. Harold has been a prince of propagandists about my book. His own novel *Public Faces* comes out tomorrow. The lady assistant secretary is a composite picture of Gertrude Bell and Hilda Matheson. Stanley Primmett, the editor, is a composite figure of Gilliat and Reginald Pound of the *Express*. The Secretary for Air is Kitchener. Harold told a good story of Lindemann[4] and Winston. Winston had had a real row with Randolph, who finally had flung out of the room in a furious temper. Winston went to the mantelpiece, turned round an ornament, and then more in sorrow than in anger addressed Lindemann. 'Lindemann,' he said, 'you are a professor of biology and experimental philosophy. Tell me am I as a parent responsible for all the biological and chemical reactions in my son?'

Saturday, 8 October 1932

Lunched with Moura at the Berkeley Grill and had coffee with H. G. Wells, who was lunching with a rather 'sexy' American girl. At 66 H.G.

[1] Count Garnerin de Montgelas, German journalist working in London.

[2] 24 years later Randolph Churchill was awarded £5000 damages because the *People* had called him a 'paid hack'.

[3] Christopher Hobhouse (*d.* 1940), author and close friend of Nicolson, who had started writing for *Action* when still an undergraduate.

[4] Frederick Lindemann (1886–1957), later Lord Cherwell, scientific adviser and personal assistant to Churchill during the war.

looks marvellously young. He has the skin of a man twenty years younger. He is writing his novel on the world a hundred years hence [*The Shape of Things to Come*]. When he writes a book, he writes what he calls the frame first. That is, the introduction and the last chapter. Moura squabbles violently with him about Russia and foreign politics. Joad was dining with them the other night, discussing the reconstruction of the world.[1] Joad was drunk and began relating very improbable sex stories: how young girls (American) offered themselves to him in return for his wasting his valuable time on them in giving advice. This is a common reaction of sexual impotency. The English intellectuals are quite divorced from realities. When they wish to protest in unison against the Simon Note and the hypocritical handling of the disarmament question, they draw up a letter and put birth-control and legalised abortion as their first desiderata and abolition of war as second.

Sunday, 9 October 1932

Elizabeth Belloc came to dinner. She is not my affair, but she has an attractive little face. We discussed Baldwin at dinner. Elizabeth and Tommy were violently pro. This made me rather aggressive. Baldwin would not be where he is, but for the hundreds of thousands of women who think and say that 'Well, Baldwin is an honest man.'

Thursday, 20 October 1932

Luncheon to H.G. at Boulestin. Saw L.G. from 5 to 6.30. Spoke at the Tomorrow Club. Supped with Pam at Savoy.

My luncheon to H.G. was rather tedious. I was quarter of an hour late. Tommy and Harry turned up at Boulestin's to see Moura. My other guests were Bernstorff and Randolph. H.G. rather 'crotchety' because Moura talked to Bernstorff and very anxious to command the conversation. Gave Randolph some good cracks. Randolph asked him what he thought about Gilbert Frankau's attack on the Book Society.[2] 'I know nothing about the Book Society, but I'm against Gilbert Frankau in principle. I'm a man of peace, but if there is ever a pogrom in my Utopia it will be for Gilbert Frankau.'

Bernstorff expressed great surprise that Samuel (stupid vain man) should get so much publicity. Randolph said: 'Quite obvious. He has 5,000,000 Liberal voters behind him.' 'Rot,' says H.G., 'you mean he's got in front of 5,000,000 Liberal voters.'

H.G. was slightly cutting and patronising about my book, but he sat up all night reading it and was gracious enough to say that I'd succeeded in putting myself over as a personality. Said in reference to Beverley Nichols's book on Melba: 'I'm against writing about people when they're alive, but death ends

[1] C. E. M. Joad (1891–1953), loquacious popular philosopher and original member of the B.B.C. Brains Trust.

[2] Gilbert Frankau (1884–1952), annoyed that the Book Society had not chosen any of his novels, attacked it, falsely claiming that it only chose books whose publishers gave a special discount. The row blew over – but no book of Frankau's was ever chosen.

all obligations and ought to do so.'[1] The fictitious decencies mean that today we know nothing about Gladstone, Burton, etc.

Moura left for Paris. H.G. went to station with her. I went back to Mayfair to see Randolph's £8.8 suite of three rooms and bathroom.

Friday, 21 October 1932

L.G.: Re present House of Commons said that in all his career he had never seen a house with such a low level of intelligence. Said there was only one clever parliamentarian in it – only one big political boss. This was Baldwin. Baldwin was a really clever tactician and would always beat Lord Beaverbrook: (1) because he knew how to wait; and (2) because you cannot run a political campaign in this country from Fleet Street.

Monday, 24 October 1932

Sir Abe Bailey in pessimistic mood. He had rather gone back on his Imperialism; says the crisis is a world one and can be solved only by world action; we have till March 1933; if we can carry through till then, things may improve; if not, civilisation may fall. Thinks that *laissez-faire* has come to an end and that individual capitalism is doomed. Full of praise for MacDonald and very critical of Max who he now thinks is doing great harm. Sir Abe, I expect, has lost money!

Tuesday, 25 October 1932

In evening dined with Pam, then went on to the club, played billiards, and went to the Bobbin with Frank Wood. Sat up very late and spent £8. In consequence felt a complete wreck.

The only hope for me is to go completely teetotal. I should think that I have put on nearly a stone in the last six months. My digestion is atrocious and I never feel well. I cannot go on very long like this.

Memoirs of a British Agent, *due to be published on 2 November, was chosen by the Book Society, the chairman of whose selection committee, Lockhart's old friend Hugh Walpole, wrote to him from his home near Keswick, on 25 October 1932:*

I was delighted that you liked my review. I have long wanted to do something in return for all you did for me. But quite determined I was all the same not to influence the Book Society. Nor did I. I said not a word until they themselves were enthusiastic. And in what I've written I've been altogether honest.

You will I think have a great success. You've given it remarkably the impress of your personality. I can see you, hear you, watch you through it all.

[1] Dame Nellie Melba, prima donna, *b.* 1861, had died the previous year. The book was *Evensong*.

Thursday, 27 October 1932

Hugh Walpole has written a most flattering review of my book for the *Book Society News*. It is a handsome tribute. I hope the old fellow will now do the introduction for the U.S.A. edition.

Still feeling very seedy.

Friday, 28 October 1932

In the afternoon wrote letters to Hugh and the Prince of Wales about my book. In the evening met Ransome and Moura at the Wellington. Ransome, who is very fat, has lived on milk for the last three years on account of a duodenal ulcer. He is very upset by a statement in my book saying that, 'I rewarded Evgenia Petrovna by giving her a British passport.' The point is that it was Ransome who wanted to get her out. Evgenia Petrovna knew nothing about it.

Saturday, 29 October 1932

Belloc and his daughter came over in the evening. Belloc looks better. He told us a good story about Lord Denman's brother who married for money a Miss Sutherland, daughter of the P. & O. king. After two or three years, during which Denman collected a good deal of cash, things went wrong, and his wife sued him for nullity suit. Old Sutherland, very upset, did everything he could to patch things up. No good. Finally went to *The Times* to stop publicity. Again no good. *Times* always reported legal cases. Just as he was going away, he had a brain-wave. 'Perhaps you could have a misprint?' The misprint was arranged. Case was reported as Tinman and Southerland! Denman then married a woman from the North and had a large family!

Discussed why London could not produce a cheap restaurant with good cooking. Decided that there were too few people that cared. Went to bed at eleven. Reading *The Coming Struggle For Power* by John Strachey – a former colleague of Tom Mosley's in the New Party and now a Communist. It is interesting. He puts Baldwin in a class by himself among post-war politicians. So does L.G. Learnt some poetry by heart to improve my memory, which is becoming very bad: probably due to alcohol. Have had three days' abstinence and feel better already.

Monday, 31 October 1932

In the evening went to Randolph's dinner-party at the Savoy: young Lord Birkenhead, Lord Dufferin, Michael Berry,[1] Roy Harrod, a Christ Church economist, Patrick Gordon Walker, a history don, and Frank Pakenham.[2] All young men. Pakenham has just been given a job as leader-

[1] 4th Marquess of Dufferin and Ava (*b.* 1909, killed in action 1945); Michael Berry (*b.* 1911), 2nd son of Lord Camrose, later Lord Hartwell and proprietor of the *Daily Telegraph*.

[2] (*b.* 1905), now 7th Earl of Longford.

writer by the *Mail*. Birkenhead and Randolph are both contributing a regular feature to the *Sunday Dispatch*. Dinner was a miniature 'blind' and we all drank too much. Roy Harrod, the economist, thinks Europe must increase its population or perish – especially Western Europe. After dinner women came in: Lady Dufferin, who was Maureen Guinness, Lady Honor Guinness, Mr and Mrs Bryce (latter an Argentine), and a Frenchman and his wife. Went back to Hans Crescent with Lord Dufferin and sat up late talking to him. He was rather drunk...

Wednesday, 2 November 1932

My book came out today. Excellent reviews by Cummings and Ransome in the *News Chronicle* and *Manchester Guardian* respectively. A good review in the *Telegraph*. A vulgar and disgusting review in the *Express*. In the evening dined with Tommy at the Carlton Grill and went to see the new Harold Lloyd 'talkie' next door. Laughed and enjoyed myself.

Rather an anxious period, as it will be several days yet before we can tell if the book is to be a success.

Hear definitely now from Huntington that my book has been taken for January or February by the Book Society in the U.S.A. This will mean $5000 for me.

Thursday, 3 November 1932

Letter from Ramsay MacDonald about my book. He is hurt that he is so little mentioned and that I do not tell the story of his thwarted visit to Russia. I do not know it. I wrote and told him so, saying I was writing another book on Russia – a short history this time and not an autobiography – and should be glad if he would give me the facts. All reviewers of my book lay great stress on its literary qualities, which of course is very much to my advantage as a writer.

Friday, 4 November 1932

More reviews of my book: first class provincial Press, notably *Glasgow Herald*, *Scotsman*, *Birmingham Post*, and first-class weeklies. Harold very good in *New Statesman* and Clennell Wilkinson also very good in *Week-End Review*.

Letter from Max saying he hears nothing but praise on all sides and supposing that 'I shall make a fortune and spend it like Lord Castlerosse and other capitalists.'

Steel-Maitland telephoned to congratulate me and to ask me to luncheon to meet Kerensky. Latter also telephoned. He is hurt by a paragraph which I wrote about him six weeks ago. Again the fault of those infernal editors. They cut down my two paragraphs into one, thereby making the final impression both crude and cruel. What I have suffered from being known as

'The Londoner' and being accused of enormities I have never committed!

Went with Pam and the Duncan Millers to see Bobby Howes in *Tell Her the Truth* – supper afterwards at the Savoy. Not very amusing and everyone rather bored. Saw Fletcher. He tells me that Compton Mackenzie, whose book of memoirs[1] has been banned and who himself has been summoned, gave great offence because when he was head of our Secret Service in Athens he kept a lot of memoranda, which he should have destroyed – obviously for publication afterwards.

Saturday, 5 November 1932

Letter from MacDonald saying story of his thwarted visit to Russia cannot be told yet. Must ask Kerensky if he knows anything about it.

Came down to Horsham by the 1.40 – a dull, bleak day. I feel thoroughly tired out with a sense of impending disaster. My book has gone too well, and everyone is prophesying great success, but . . . Went out shooting, but saw nothing. Shot one rabbit. Elizabeth Belloc to dinner and for the night . . . Played chess with Harry and lost. He has laid me two to one I do not sell 20,000 copies in England before the end of the year.

Sunday, 6 November 1932

Angela St Clair Erskine and Molly Long came to luncheon. Angela full of praise of my book – dealt out with plenty of sly digs and cuts but nevertheless genuinely meant. Quite a good review by Ransome in the *Observer*; also a friendly notice in the *Sunday Express*.

Everyone praises this book for its literary qualities, but Russia was a great background.

Tuesday, 8 November 1932

More letters about my book: from the Prince of Wales, Max, Cromer,[2] Sam Hoare, to people like Moir Mackenzie, Mrs Thompson, and Freda. Max's letter was great. 'Dear Bruce, I had your book in the train last night. Some of the chapters are very fine. The whole book is moving to a degree. It will give you a place in literature. Your ever M.B.'

Jean came in to see me and in five minutes we had a scene. She is very upset about the book and on the least provocation becomes hysterical about it.[3]

Wrote Tommy, Moura and Dad. . .

The Times gave a column of notice to my book today. With the exception of the *Express* all reviews have been first-class.

[1] *Greek Memories*, eventually published in 1940.

[2] 2nd Earl of Cromer (1877–1953), banker and diplomat, was then Lord Chamberlain to the Royal Household.

[3] She disliked his frankness about his relations with other women.

Wednesday, 9 November 1932

Still in bed. This was my black day. After all the praise which has been showered on my book a bombshell arrived today in form of a notice of libel from Mrs Reilly's solicitors. I had – perhaps rather stupidly . . . – referred not to her but to Reilly's 'first' wife.[1] Maplesdon does not think the libel (if any) is serious.

Thursday, 10 November 1932

Two-column review of my book in *The Times Literary Supplement* – also a very flattering one in *Everyman*. We are taking the words 'first wife' out of the second edition which is now being printed.

Did some more work on my synopsis. Wrote Max, Millie and Tommy. Sent off cheques to Kerrison. Pam tells me she has heard from Jean Norton. She says Max is raving about my book.

Friday, 11 November 1932

In the evening dined at the Huntingtons': the Eshers, Lord Gerald Wellesley, Mrs Belloc Lowndes,[2] and the Harry Grahams. Mrs Belloc Lowndes, who is Belloc's sister, was very kind about my book and said I should do very well out of my next: film rights, etc. Betts[3] told me today that I was already being discussed by Universal Pictures. My cheque from the American Book Society has already arrived. It works out at £1390. I am leaving £590 with Huntington as a nucleus for income tax and also a caution for the Reilly libel. The lawyers report favourably on this, but I 'hae ma douts'.

Wednesday, 16 November 1932

Letter from Tom [Macgregor]. It is polite but menacing and bowled me over like a ninepin. Apparently, in November 1926, when he advanced me £1400, I gave him a paper assigning to him all rights in my 'book of Russian memoirs'. Tom says Baillie and Gifford found the document in his papers, implying that he himself had forgotten all about it. He says he is reminding me in case I have forgotten all about it. So far so good. He then goes on to say that Baillie and Gifford have sent the document to Messrs Mayo, Elder and Rutherford to deal with as they think best.

I am uneasy and depressed. My impression is that the document refers to the Czech book I was writing, but I may have signed something stupid. It is hard to believe that Tom will extract his pound of flesh, but one never knows. I may be fated to have a big success and to lose by it. Went into the club at seven a.m. and filled myself up with drink.

[1] For details of Reilly's complex marriages, see Robin Bruce Lockhart's *The Ace of Spies* (1967).

[2] 3rd Viscount Esher (1881–1963), had been in Military Intelligence and was to become an important administrator of the arts; Lord Gerald Wellesley (1885–1972), later 7th Duke of Wellington, ex-diplomat and patron of the arts; Mrs Belloc Lowndes (1868–1947) was almost as prolific a writer as her brother.

[3] Ernest Betts, film critic on the *Evening Standard*.

Thursday, 17 November 1932

Lunched with Wheeler-Bennett in his charming flat in Albany. Present: Mr and Mrs Victor Mallet – son of late Sir Bernard Mallet – General Sir Neill Malcolm and his daughter.[1] Mrs Mallet was born the daughter of a partner in Kleinworts and in her youngest days knew Beaverbrook and the children. Mallet himself is very anti-Beaver. Wheeler-Bennett, who has just returned from Berlin, tells a good story of Hindenburg: Hindenburg has a dream; thinks he is at gates of Heaven. St Peter asks: 'Who are you?' 'Paul Hindenburg.' 'What did you do on earth?' 'I did my duty.' 'Are you sure you did your duty or did you only keep your oath to the constitution?' Before Hindenburg can think of the answer he wakes up.

Saw Tommy and fixed up our trip for Saturday. Saw Moura at 6.30. She says Harold is jealous of my success. She is going with H.G. to Paris and then goes to Sorrento to Gorky. . . She showed me a correspondence card. On it H.G. had written in very small neat handwriting: *Dear Moura! Sweet Moura!* He sends her lots. Gives her presents.

Friday, 18 November 1932

Lunched with Mrs Belloc Lowndes at Boulestin's. She was very kind and promised to do all she could to push my book with the cinema people in America. She advises me to do nothing until she returns. She goes there for six weeks in January. She is very interested in abnormal sex, knows Vita Nicolson very well or rather knew her very well at the time of her passionate friendship with ——. The idea was that —— should marry Hugh Walpole in order to prolong the relationship.

Went to see Huntington in the evening. He is amazed at Tom's behaviour. He does not think the document is valid, but when he received it and saw the name Macgregor in it and I told him it was my uncle he at once jumped to the conclusion that it must be a money-lender. He thought 'uncle' was my politeness for money-lender! Long letter from George Clerk full of praise for my book. He thinks I have been too modest and has indeed said so.

Sunday, 20 November 1932

Millie is ill. She has a bad heart from too many sleeping draughts and is bitter and cruel about everyone. She is the only Erskine who has not been a drunkard. Now she has begun to take little nips of brandy for her heart. I hope it is not the beginning of a family failing.

Friday, 25 November 1932

Lovely morning: warm as English May and bright sunshine. Left Les

[1] Victor Mallet (1893–1969), later knighted, professional diplomat then at the Foreign Office, Ambassador at Madrid and Rome after the war. His wife's father was Herman Andreae. Malcolm (1869–1953) had served on the Military Mission in Berlin, 1919–21, and was to become High Commissioner for German refugees.

Sables [d'Olonne] by car for Nantes at eleven. Millie came with us. We went to her villa Golfe Stream to pick her up. She is definitely mental now; has a mania about cruelty to animals and wishes to arrest every man here who has a horse. At the same time she herself has a curlew or some kind of black gull which she has rescued. She keeps it in her room, calls it the Prince d'Olonne, and feeds it forcibly on oysters, shrimps and cockles!

Monday, 5 December 1932

Siepmann[1] told me: (1) that his B.B.C. brother wants me to broadcast; and (2) that he himself may be in a position to offer me a job in the Bank of England. Francis Ronald is leaving. I am to lunch with him on Monday. Siepmann tells me that the Governor (Montagu Norman) keeps no papers. His desk is bare. But in his left-hand drawer is a book with the entry, date and brief account of every conversation. The Governor keeps a very full diary.

Thursday, 8 December 1932

G.R.C. [Sir George Clerk] told me that Hardinge had done me in for my honour when I returned from Russia. He said it made him furious. Also told me real story of 'fez' incident between Hamza Bey, the Egyptian Minister, and Kemal,[2] at Angora. On October 29, Turkish Republic Day, Kemal gave large dinner for his Cabinet and foreign Heads of Missions. Latter in full uniform. After dinner there was a reception and ball in Angora Palace Hotel. As Kemal was going down the line of ministers, he noticed 'fez' on Hamza's head. He asked him quite politely as a friend to take it off for that night. The 'fez' was part of Hamza's religion and official uniform. He hesitated. Kemal made a sign to a waiter. Hamza then removed the 'fez' which was carried away on a tray by the waiter.

Thursday, 15 December 1932

Lloyd[3] thinks things are rather difficult in Russia just now, especially as regards food. He came back in September. He does not like Kingsley Martin very much and does not think he is a good editor. We discussed Sharp and agreed that in his day he was the best editor of a weekly paper in England. He is near his end now in more senses than one. His wife has left him. He has no money. And he is drinking as badly as ever. Gollancz gave him an advance to write a life of Rhodes. The advance has gone or is going on drink – and of Rhodes not a line has been written. A whisky bottle would be the suitable tombstone for half the brilliant men of Fleet Street.

[1] Harry Siepmann (1889–1963), banker, Adviser to the Governor of the Bank of England, 1926–45. His brother Charles (*b.* 1899) was in the B.B.C. from 1927 until the outbreak of war; he had recently been made director of talks.

[2] Mustafa Kemal Atatürk (1881–1938), dictator of Turkey 1923–38, had abolished the fez, despite riots all over the country, as part of his campaign to modernise Turkey.

[3] C. Mostyn Lloyd, foreign editor of the *New Statesman*.

CHAPTER TEN

1933

The Webbs keen on the Bolshevik experiment. Sprigs of the aristocracy at the funeral of Mrs Meyrick, the night club 'queen'. Beverley Baxter amusing and bumptious. Jim and Amy Mollison, the aviators. General Waters and the Kaiser. Sinclair Lewis drink-sodden. Lunches at Lady Colefax's. Tales of Hitler's hobbies and of Admiral Beatty. Lewis Namier on the German Jews. Sefton Delmer on Berlin. Russia prefers Fascism to 'jelly-bellied democracy'. Kühlmann and Lloyd George on war secrets. Somerset Maugham's Mongolian face and precise manner. 'The English Mystery', British Fascist Society. Prince Louis Ferdinand and Lily Dalmita. Prince of Wales 'quite pro-Hitler'. Leslie Howard to play Lockhart in film. Maisky and the Russian *Hamlet*. Lloyd George's jealousy of his secretary. Douglas Fairbanks flees. Sees television with J. L. Baird, its inventor. Michael Arlen: 'Keep your money'. Randolph Churchill and Lady Astor.

Friday, 6 January 1933

Dined at Mike Wardell's: only guests myself and Colonel and Mrs Johnny Dodge.[1] The latter, a huge genial fellow and a son of Mrs Lionel Guest, is an M.P., was one of the first Englishmen to trade with Russia after the war, and was imprisoned by the Bolsheviks at Batum. He is now interested in Russian–English trade treaty and wants me to join his Parliamentary Committee. Nothing doing of course. After dinner he insisted on taking us to the Hungaria to hear Makarov sing. We drank a whole bottle of vodka and everyone got rather drunk including Ruth Wardell and Mrs Dodge, who is an American, is called Minerva and looks it! I had a great triumph. When Makarov was asked to sing 'Drinking' (*Im tiefen Keller sitz' ich hier*), he said: 'Tonight I shall sing a Russian drinking song in honour of a great friend of Russia, Mr Lockhart, whose book everyone is reading.' He then sang a *charvchka*, and made me drink a glass of champagne without heeltaps. Then Baleiev came on and made a speech, said how most glad of all he was to see the great English friend of Russia, Mr Lockhart. He then kissed me on both cheeks. Huge applause.

Monday, 9 January 1933

Lunched at Savoy with Bark. Present Sir Ian Hamilton Benn – rather an

[1] Lieut.-Colonel John Bigelow Dodge, D.S.O., D.S.C. (*b.* 1894), Unionist Candidate (not Member) for Mile End. He was American by birth, and Mrs Lionel Guest was the daughter of a former U.S. Ambassador to France.

old bore, Admiral Scott Robson, and von Thyssen. Benn, who was very long-winded, became with Max temporary joint secretaries to Bonar Law when Johnny Baird (now Lord Stonehaven) went off to war in August 1914. Benn was associated with Max in business in 1908. He was head of a Canadian trust company over here or rather a trust for floating Canadian loans, and Max, who was then head of Montreal Trust Co., was the source of supply in Canada. Benn helped Max when he first came over here. It was Benn who introduced him to Bonar. Latter was first attracted to Max, because he found him such an extraordinary good wit-sharpener. Yet he was almost disgusted finally with Max – almost at the beginning of their friendship – by Max's antics after and at Aston-under-Lyne.[1]

Wednesday, 11 January 1933

Gave a luncheon to Kerensky at the Carlton Grill. Present: A.F.K., who looked well, Negley Farson, Alexander Woollcott,[2] and George Slocombe. Woollcott, who has just come back from Dublin, is fat and rather Russian-looking. He told two good stories: how in Moscow and Leningrad the young girls and boys ran after him and stared. They had never seen a fat man; and the new international code of gallantry. In New York the *galant* man gives flowers; in Peking fifty pounds of rice. In Moscow Woollcott was kissed by the prettiest girl in the town because he gave her a roll of toilet paper.

Kerensky was full of the horrors of Russia and said Russia would either destroy Stalin or Stalin destroy Russia. He had been lecturing in Berlin – Lunacharsky[3] was present. Kerensky's father, who was a kind of inspector-general of education, was a Conservative. Kerensky himself was interested in politics at the age of six...

Negley Farson gave me two good stories: one, an account of Lord Rothermere's liaison with Stephanie Richter, Princess Hohenlohe-Schillingsfurst published in the French *Aux Ecoutes* of January 7, 1933. Numbers of telegrams (photographed facsimile) are published signed by Rothermere with greetings such as 'I miss your smile, girlie.'

Lockhart received a letter from the Webbs, the Fabian Socialists Lord and Lady Passfield who had recently visited Russia:

'We have been reading your book with delight: what a sale it must have had! I think the Bolsheviks treated you very well. We had a fascinating time in the U.S.S.R.; but to punish me for my old age, I had a breakdown in the middle of our tour which resulted in a most amusing visit to Kislovodsk –

[1] The by-election won by the then Max Aitken in 1910.

[2] Negley Farson (1870–1960), American travel-writer and foreign correspondent; he had been in Russia running an export business at the time of the Revolution. Alexander Woollcott (1877–1943), American journalist, dramatic critic and broadcaster, the original of *The Man Who Came to Dinner*.

[3] Anatoly Lunacharsky (1875–1933), Russian writer, Commissar for Public Instruction, 1917–1929, 'a man of brilliant intellect and wide culture' according to Lockhart.

the Tsarist Aix-les-Bains, where I spent what energy I had in arguing with the holiday-makers and invalids at the 80 Trade Union rest houses. Fortunately, my very intelligent interpreter turned out to be a trained nurse. Was it prevision – a fear of having one of the 'Webbs' dead on their hands?

Wednesday, 18 January 1933

Gave luncheon to Fletcher and Maurice Peterson at Boulestin's. Fletcher very down on Ramsay who is notoriously ungrateful to his friends. Fletcher has been seeing a lot of Jowitt, who stood by Ramsay during the 1931 national government crisis. Ramsay then sacrificed him. He still sends messages to Jowitt saying why has he never been to see him and occasional postcards with such remarks as: 'Lang may your lums reek.' Jowitt says: 'If he wants me to come to see him, why doesn't he ask me?'

In the evening dined with the Webbs at the London School of Economics. Present: Tommy, Eileen Power, who is the authority on medieval history, Meyendorff, Toynbee and his wife.[1] Webbs, especially Mrs Webb, are now very keen on Bolshevik experiment. They see or she sees a force akin to the old Jesuits in the Communists and thinks Communism will be a new religion. She wants to go back to Russia again before she dies and in order to get a final revision on their Russian book which will be the last *magnum opus* of the Webbs.

Friday, 20 January 1933

Feeling very ill after last night. Lunched with Moura at the Jardin des Gourmets. She told me an amusing story about the ex-Kaiser. He has had some English guests staying with him; for example, Lady Ottoline Morrell, who is a half-sister of the Duke of Portland.[2] Lady Morrell says that the ex-Kaiser is well and reads aloud to his family and guests every night. He does this because Napoleon read aloud at St Helena. His favourite author just now is P. G. Wodehouse. Stolid German members, who may not appreciate the humour of P.G.W., never need to fear that they shall not laugh in the right place. All those passages which the ex-Kaiser considers funny he reads out twice!

Slept in the afternoon. In the evening dined at Quaglino's with Mrs Fred Pearson and the Baers. Colonel Baer is American military attaché in Vienna, Prague, Budapest, has had four years there. He is very pro-Hungarian and anti-Czech. Puts the fighting qualities in Central Europe as follows: Serbs first (they have a new .75 – best gun in Europe), Hungarians second. Does

[1] Eileen Power (1889–1940), Professor of Economic History at L.S.E., 1931–40; Alexander Meyendorff (1889–1964), Reader in Russian Institutions and Economics at L.S.E., 1922–34; Arnold Toynbee (*b.* 1889), Research Professor of International History; his wife Rosalind was a daughter of Gilbert Murray.

[2] (1873–1938) wife of Philip Morrell and eccentric patron of Bloomsbury Group and D. H. Lawrence.

not think much of Italians. Czechs have good staff and fair material, but no captains and lieutenants. He was with General McArthur once after war in Dalmatia; they saw a woman carrying petrol tins, sack of flour, a baby and knitting at the same time. Husband with rifle following in lordly manner smoking pipe. American general shocked, asks wife why she does not make her man carry her burdens. 'Why should I be such a fool? He's a soldier. How can he fight for me if he carries these things?'

Monday, 23 January 1933

Mrs Meyrick's funeral was held today; the service was at St Martin-in-the-Fields. Young London was well represented, and there were numerous sprigs of the aristocracy including Lord Ebury and young Percy.[1] I did not go, but spent the afternoon in my office clearing up my arrears of correspondence. Wrote a long letter to Baillie and Gifford about the proposed trust for my affairs.

Question (*à la Daily Express*): How much money have you wasted: (1) in night-clubs and cabarets; and (2) on money-lenders' interest? Answer: Since 1918 about £15,000.

My teetotal repentance did not last long. In the evening went to the Sports Club, dined with Charles Murray and sat up drinking whisky until one o'clock.

Wednesday, 25 January 1933

Feeling very ill after riotous night. This morning the Meyricks rang up about an article in the *Daily Mail* – an interview with their father in which he said: (1) that Mrs Meyrick left a luxurious home in order to start night clubs, (2) that she had a craze for making money for herself, (3) that he himself had then an income of £5000 a year, and (4) that 'the children worshipped the ground he trod on.' Went round to 3 Park Square to get a story. Found Mary, Kathleen, Nancy, Bobbie and Gordon. All very indignant. Truth is: (1) that Dr Meyrick ran through all Mrs Meyrick's money, thus forcing her to work for her children, (2) that Mrs Meyrick never spent a penny on herself, (3) that the father did nothing for them meant nothing to them, and (4) that, until this last Christmas when Mrs Meyrick, who wished for no bitterness, allowed him to come to the house, neither Nancy nor Bobbie had seen him since 1919, and the others only casually and intermittently. When he came into room, the younger daughter did not know who he was. Later in day, Nancy asked me to write the preface for her mother's book. I went round again and found there young Percy, nephew of late Duke of Northumberland. While they dined in dining-room, I wrote the preface![2]

[1] Robert, 6th Baron Ebury, and Hugh, Earl Percy (younger brother to the 9th Duke of Northumberland), both then 18 years old.

[2] *Secrets of the 43*, published later that year, contains the preface drafted by Lockhart, but signed 'Her Children'.

Thursday, 26 January 1933

Lunched at Ciro's with Gladstone Murray of the B.B.C.[1] His party included Baxter, Wardell, Lady Snowden and Rex Palmer who has something to do with gramophone records. Lady Snowden is very upset at losing her place on the board of the B.B.C. and is bitter about Ramsay MacDonald whom she now denounces as the personification of ingratitude. She tells me that Snowden has been accumulating material for his memoirs and is about to begin writing them. He expects to finish soon. He is a quick worker.

Discussed music. Baxter proposed a three years' ban on Wagner to give the works of other musicians a chance. Lady Snowden replied that Wagner was the only safe composer for a Covent Garden success in England. No other composer paid. *Die Zauberflöte* [Mozart] was a failure. [Richard] Strauss was too expensive. Baxter was amusing and bumptious as usual. 'He said: Well, I've killed technocracy. Did you read my leader?' Mike: 'Yes. It was good. The only drawback was that the *Evening Standard* said the same thing five days ago.' Baxter. 'Yes, I know. But you see the public want to know about it.' When Baxter went to see L.G. for the first time, Max shouted to him: 'Don't patronise him, Baxter!'

Wednesday, 1 February 1933

Went to luncheon given by '32' Club in honour of Cramp, the General Secretary of the National Union of Railwaymen. The '32' Club is a light Labour club of which Malone is President and Fletcher (second in our Secret Service and now a Labour candidate) is Treasurer. Dunnico in chair.[2] Cramp is good-natured but pretentious; minces his words, is careful with his aitches, is very neatly dressed and rather dapper. Takes great care of himself. Said nothing about the railwaymen's wages-dispute. No famous guests there except Nathan, the Liberal M.P.[3] Kenworthy arrived at function in top-hat.

Saturday, 4 February 1933

Had a longish talk to Jim Mollison who has more small talk than Amy.[4] Latter spoke well, twitted newspapers, and has obviously poise. She is, however, a highly-strung young woman and takes her whack of champagne and brandy. I asked her if she did not get awfully tired at the end of a long flight by having to pull herself together and talk to crowd, instead of relaxing. She said – and he agreed – that the relief at landing was so great that it gave

[1] Murray (1873–1970), a Canadian, was then Director of Public Relations at the B.B.C.

[2] C. T. Cramp (1876–1933) had been Chairman of the Labour Party in 1925. Lieut.-Colonel L'Estrange Malone (*d.* 1965) and Rev. Herbert Dunnico were Labour M.P.s, Dunnico being Deputy Speaker of the House of Commons.

[3] Colonel Harry Louis Nathan (1889–1963), later 1st Baron Nathan, left the Liberals and joined the Labour Party in 1934.

[4] Jim Mollison (*b.* 1905) and Amy Johnson (*d.* 1941) were two celebrated aviators, who had married in 1932. She was the first woman to fly solo to Australia in 1930, and he broke the England–Australia record in 1931. She was a popular heroine and had songs written about her.

you the necessary kick to carry on with. Jim, who has read Loti, has lived for six months in Tahiti, can amuse himself quite easily by himself with scenery and a gramophone, and would be glad to escape from civilisation. He was in New York during final stages of Jimmie Walker's régime [as Mayor] and had to be given the freedom of city by Jimmie in the Plaza Hotel, as Roosevelt would not allow him [to] use Town Hall until he was cleared of charges against him.

Sunday, 5 February 1933

Lunched with Moura at the Berkeley. Zinovy Pieshkov, the Colonel of the French Legion, who has just married Marie de Briel in Paris, is Gorky's adopted son. His real name was Sverdlov and he was a brother of the great Bolshevist Sverdlov. Gorky adopted him because they were both had up for distributing illegal proclamations. Brought before the police inspector, young Sverdlov swallowed his. This pleased Gorky, who then adopted him. Pieshkov was then a boy of thirteen. He took Gorky's name – Pieshkov – entered army. Did well in war, fought for Kolchak, is now in Foreign Legion. . .

Watched the great Labour demonstration against the Means Test in Hyde Park: very peaceful, large number of old men, respectable, orderly. I saw one badge: it was a dove and below it the inscription: 'Thou Shalt Not Kill.'

Rested again in the afternoon. Went to see our new premises at Ennismore Gardens, but they are too grand and too expensive for us. In the evening went with Pam to the Stoll Kingsway cinema and saw the *Big Broadcast*. Supper at Harry's Bar and then late to bed.

Today cost me nearly £4 in entertaining people. This must stop.

Wednesday, 8 February 1933

Wrote 1200 words on 'Where is Germany Going?'

She is very obviously going Fascist very rapidly and whether or not the von Papen–Hitler–Hindenburg combination wins the election there is little doubt that they will remain in power.[1] It remains to be seen how far the German people will stand for this return to Prussianism. They will stand a good deal, but I shall be surprised if Bavaria and the South-West do not make something more than a vigorous protest.

Discussed my finances with Mike. He will not pay me any more for the serialisation of my book in the *Evening Standard*. This means that he has bought it for £200 – one of the cheapest prices even the *Evening Standard* has ever paid for a serial. The *Sunday Express* paid £1000 for the Marjoribanks *Carson* – a poor book and a poor seller. He will also not reduce or remit the reduction of £10 a week from my salary to repay the Beaverbrook debt. He is not unkind, but like everyone else in that office he is afraid of Max.

[1] Hitler had been appointed Chancellor on 30 January; elections were due on 5 March.

Friday, 10 February 1933

Dead after last night. This has been a bad month for me. Lunched with Moir at the Ivy. His guests were Walter Citrine, the Secretary of the T.U.C., and Dawson, the Economic Adviser to the Colonial Office. Citrine told me a lot about Ramsay. Jimmie Thomas, he said, is Ramsay's best friend and has more influence with him than anyone else. When Snowden left, he wrote Ramsay a letter reproving him for having gone back on all the principles they had agreed on when the National Government was set up. Ramsay's revenge was to sack Lady Snowden from the B.B.C. and put Mary Hamilton in her place.[1] When Swaffer wrote his cad's article in the *People*, saying that he had followed Ramsay one night from Whitehall to a private flat, the flat in question was Mary Hamilton's. A few years ago – 1929, I expect – Ramsay asked Citrine who he thought would be Ramsay's successor in Labour leadership. Citrine said he saw no one but Henderson. Ramsay demurred, pointing out mistakes Henderson had made in Egypt, etc. Ramsay's suggestion was Mosley. Citrine's comment was: ridiculous! At Ottawa[2] Citrine said our civil service was miles on top. Everything was well-prepared. T.U.C. and F.B.I. were in accord. Only Ministers had no plans, and principles. Government wished to make Citrine a knight for Ottawa. It was announced to Citrine by Thomas calling him up by phone: 'I say, Walter, I want to see you. This ruddy Government wants to make you a bloody knight!' Citrine refused.

Friday, 17 February 1933

At five-thirty went to the Savoy to meet the eighteen present and recently past Oxford undergraduates who are bringing out a book on Monday called *Red Rags*: it is a symposium on present-day Oxford. Met Quintin Hogg, Hailsham's son, who has had a very brilliant record.[3] He tells me that the Union pacifist debate is not to be regarded as a joke.[4] It was a serious affair. The Conservative Association resent Randolph's intrusion. They suggested Steel-Maitland as a more suitable person to move the resolution that the offending notion should be removed from the minutes. They apparently sent a deputation to Central Office to consult it regarding their action. Hogg is supporting Randolph. He also tells me that the October Club is quite a flourishing affair; its members are not drawn from the working classes but from the rather rich type, which stays late in bed and, when it misses the modest Labour bus, takes a fresh car to reach its destination.

[1] Mary Agnes Hamilton (*d.* 1966), Labour M.P. for Blackburn, 1929–31, Governor of the B.B.C., 1933–7, biographer of MacDonald.

[2] The Imperial Conference of July–August 1932 to discuss the lowering of trade barriers with the Empire.

[3] Quintin Hogg (*b.* 1907) was, like his father before him, later Lord Hailsham and Lord Chancellor.

[4] On 9 February the Oxford Union passed by 275 to 153 the motion 'that this House will in no circumstances fight for its King and Country'.

Saturday, 18 February 1933

Came down by the 5.30 to Barnton Stacey to stay with General Waters.[1] He is very old, was the man who gave Sir William Robertson his chance by preventing him from being sent to Ireland as garrison instructor, was Military Attaché from 1893–97 in St Petersburg, knew the Emperor and Sir Robert Morier[2] (who asked for him as military attaché), was present at the Emperor's wedding, with the Duke of Connaught . . . smoothed over the row over the Russians taking Port Arthur in 1898 (we had sent an ultimatum saying Russia was not to arm it) by seeing Emperor who said he did not want to fight, but to ask him not to fortify Port Arthur was like asking him to build a strong house and leave the door open for burglars.

Later, from 1901 to 1903 or 4 [Waters] was military attaché in Berlin. In this capacity was great friends with the Kaiser. When the ex-Kaiserin died, General Waters, who had not seen the Kaiser for twenty-five years, wrote his condolences to Doorn. Only four English people wrote – and none of the Royal family. The Kaiser was grateful – I remember his bitterness about this when I was at Doorn – and since then Waters has been in a very privileged position, goes frequently to Doorn and has an amazing collection of letters and books from the ex-Kaiser. He used to be on very good terms with King George. On one occasion they were discussing the Empress of Russia together. The King was very down on her. Waters insisted that she was not pro-German. The King agreed. 'I've known her all my life and I hate her, but I admit she's not pro-German.'

Waters said the real trouble was that the Emperor was the weaker character of the two and was bossed by his wife. The King sat up: 'What a man! Do you suppose that if my wife interfered with me in my work I should pay the slightest attention?' Waters smiled and tried to evade an answer. The King insisted. So Waters said: 'Well, sir, a clever woman can help her husband without his being aware of it.'

Waters was also very much in evidence at the time of King George's visit to Berlin (then Prince of Wales). There had been a tension between the ex-Kaiser and King Edward over a speech of Bülow's in which derogatory references were made to British Army. King Edward wrote a personal letter to Kaiser. Nothing happened. King George then refused to go unless there was an apology. All arrangements had been made, and his refusal would have created grave situation. Ex-Kaiser said he would withdraw his Ambassador from London if Prince of Wales did not come. By this time Lascelles [British Ambassador] had received copy of King Edward's letter. There was memorial service in English Church in Berlin for Queen Victoria's death (anniversary). Kaiser came. Lascelles asked him if he had received the letter. Kaiser said 'No.' Lascelles showed him it. Kaiser took Lascelles home with him. Then

[1] Brigadier-General Wallscourt Hely-Hutchinson Waters (1855–1945).

[2] Robertson (1860–1933) was Chief of the Imperial General Staff, 1915–18. Morier (1826–93) was British Ambassador to Russia, 1884–93.

came himself to Embassy and spent afternoon in framing reply. It arrived at Windsor just in time for George to carry out his programme. He actually left next day. Waters met him at the frontier. Kaiser had said that King Edward's original letter had been mislaid. George said to Waters. 'What do you think? Did the Kaiser get the first letter?' Waters, who liked Kaiser very much, said: 'I think he did, sir.' The King slapped him on the back and said: 'You bet he did.' When Waters had been to Doorn, he wrote to King George and offered to tell him about the situation. The reply through the Private Secretary was not encouraging, and Waters heard later King was furious with him for going to Doorn!

Ex-Kaiser told Waters his part in attempt to rescue the Tsar. Approach was made to ex-Kaiser by English Royal family through Danish Court. Kaiser very naturally pointed out that, as his troops were facing Russian troops, he could not do much. He, however, had a message sent through Stockholm to the Provisional Government warning them that he would hold them responsible with their lives for anything that happened to the Tsar. Later, when arrangements were made for the exit of the Tsar and for his passage to England Kaiser was again approached for a safe conduct as far as submarines and German naval attack was concerned. He gave it willingly. He maintains the only reason why Tsar was not brought out was because L.G. was afraid of Labour repercussions in England. Kerensky agrees with this.

Waters, who is a Welshman and was probably first soldier to join the Labour Party, says ex-Kaiser is splendid with his money. He keeps eighteen royal families and, in all, fifty families including those of loyal officers who were ruined because of their loyalty to him.

Sunday, 19 February 1933

Talked again in afternoon [with General Waters]: stories of ex-Kaiser, King Edward, the Tsar all piled themselves up. Ex-Kaiser told Waters that, if ever he came back to the throne, Waters would be his first ambassador. He would have no one else. Waters has an amazing collection of letters and photographs of the ex-Kaiser. In the letters the ex-Kaiser expresses himself very freely about the King's behaviour over the publication of the Ponsonby letters. Very rightly he asks what would have been the case if the position had been reversed and a German official had smuggled out the Queen of England's letters (the property of the English King) and they had been published in Germany with a disgusting preface and the Kaiser's permission – at a time, too, when the House of Windsor was in trouble!

Waters had lucky career. He was in Russia in 1892 on a visit as major: attracted Morier's attention and next year Morier asked for him as military attaché. He was in Russia from 1893 to 1898. In 1898 he made the trip from Krasnoyarsk to Khabarovsk in mid-winter by sleigh. Dangerous both for snow-drifts and robbers. Crossed Lake Baikal by sleigh: railway not finished then. From 1900 to 1903 he was military attaché in Berlin. From 1907 to 1910 he was in command of British troops of occupation in North China. During Russo-Japanese War he was British representative with the Japanese. He had resigned just before then, but King Edward wanted him to go and he wanted to go himself. War Office were angry, but he went. Almost only pre-war case of an officer whose resignation was cancelled.

Wednesday, 22 February 1933

Geoffrey Holdsworth, a good-looking young man who writes and has been living in Capri, can spout poetry by the yard. He was through the war and had two months' military prison for leaving a fatigue party, because he was ill, without leave. He said it was hell, and the brutality of the sergeants unbelievable. Men who had just been operated on for appendicitis were kicked in the 'tummy'. Complaints were no good. Even if the sergeant was reprimanded, you paid for it afterwards. Still, he would go back if there were a war tomorrow.

Sinclair Lewis was a terrible disappointment.[1] He is tall, reddish, clean-shaven with raw-red skin and blotchy face with eyes almost popping out of his head. He is drink-sodden, his stomach has gone to pieces, and he has shingles. He is just over forty and looks fifty. It is hard to see how he can live long. Apparently, when he works he has long periods during which he does not drink at all. He has certain qualities and a considerable gift for lewdness. He is brimful of self-confidence and talks away merrily as though he were expected to perform.

He gave a wonderful account of his visit to G. K. Chesterton, starting off with a few lines of 'Don John of Austria,'[2] then Chesterton's great stomach heaving and the man himself saying: 'I am very glad to see you, Mr Lewis, in London. I hope you are enjoying your stay.'

'Yes, sir.'

Then more lines of Don John (which Sinclair Lewis admires greatly).

Then Chesterton to Holdsworth. 'And your friend writes too? How interesting!'

Then another chant from Sinclair Lewis roared out with feeling – and finally an outburst: 'God, may I never meet a famous author again?'

Holdsworth is very pessimistic about the world; predicts war within one year between Germany, Austria, Hungary, and Italy *v.* France, Poland, Czechoslovakia, Yugoslavia, and Rumania. Lewis was prepared to agree. I don't. Sinclair Lewis hopes England and America will form an offensive and defensive alliance to keep out and then clean up the mess, but he is afraid of Russia, which he thinks will get hold of the defeated countries. Lewis says one day we shall say, 'Thank God for Russia.' Sinclair Lewis left early,

[1] (1885–1951) American novelist, author of *Main Street* and *Babbitt*, first American to win the Nobel Prize for literature; he was then forty-eight.

[2] Chesterton's rollicking poem *Lepanto*.

feeling as usual suddenly sick. His legs gave way and he had to be helped into the taxi – oh, sad sight.

Thursday, 23 February 1933

Princess [Marthe] Bibesco is rather tall, dark, with large eyes and a broad Slav type of face. She . . . is most certainly a fine conversationalist, speaking perfect French and very good English, and was, I thought, attractive. She was very amusing about Tsar Ferdinand of Bulgaria whom she knew well and who she declared was the complete cynic. He never referred to his people in any other terms than '*mes bufles*' – my buffaloes. Terrible roads in Bulgaria.

Tuesday, 28 February 1933

Met Dr Jinnah, the Muslim champion.[1] He is slim, has beautiful hands, wears a monocle, and is rightly described as the 'Beau Brummel' of the East. Met also Sir Harcourt Butler – now rather old and Jewish-looking – and Sir Reginald Johnston,[2] who was tutor to Pui Yi, the last Emperor of China and now Regent of Manchukuo. Mr Cheng, his brother-in-law, sat two away from me. He is a quiet young man with a small moustache, biggish teeth, and perpetual smile. His wife, Pui Yi's sister, is the first Chinese Princess to land on English soil. She had a baby here – in Johnston's house.

Friday, 3 March 1933

Lunched at Lord Dufferin's at 4 Hans Crescent. Tom Mosley, the only guest. We talked much about Fascism. Tom thinks the clash between Fascism and Communism is inevitable everywhere. It will come here. It has come in Germany. Hitlerism was inevitable. All the talk of Schleichers, etc.,[3] was nonsense. Trouble is in this country that people do not realise what is coming. People like Rothermere do not; otherwise they would be glad to have Mosley's movement as a second string for their safety. Tom admits that Hitler will need a world recovery or at least a slight improvement in world conditions in order to satisfy his followers. Tom, on the other hand, requires continued disaster here to give him a chance. He maintains that England is the country best adapted to Fascism!

Monday, 6 March 1933

Max has been in Berlin. He went, as usual, without telling anyone. When I was writing my paragraphs on the German elections, he came through with his own. They were very derogatory to the Nazis – and to the Jews. The

[1] Mohammed Ali Jinnah (1876–1948), President of the Muslim League, later first Governor-General of Pakistan.

[2] Sir Harcourt Butler (1869–1938) was Governor of Burma, 1923–7; Sir Reginald Johnston (1874–1938) was a professor of Chinese.

[3] General Kurt von Schleicher (1882–1934) had succeeded von Papen as Chancellor but could not prevent Hitler ousting him in January 1933. He was murdered on 30 June 1934.

stories of Jewish persecution are exaggerated. It is true that the Nazis say, when asked what they are collecting money for, 'to build a new railway to Jerusalem', but they are not really worse to Jews than to others – unless they are Communists. Max saw the storm troops and did not think much of them. He said, or made me say, that the cavalry leader could not sit on his horse, that the bands were bad, and that the men, mostly ill-formed lads and dissipated old boys, gave no appearance of a disciplined body. This appeared in the Diary. In the afternoon Thost, the Nazi correspondent here, rang up. He was very angry and, when I was unable to give him any satisfaction, declared that he would communicate with Lord Beaverbrook!

Monday, 13 March 1933

Lunched at Lady Colefax's house in King's Road (Argyll House) – very nice indeed. Present: Mrs Doubleday, Bonnor, an American, Sir Edwin Lutyens, Gielgud, Mrs McLaren, Lord Berners, and Lady Lavery.[1] I sat next to Lady Lavery. She looks now about forty-five and may be more! But she is full of charm and I got on with her easily. She recommends me to do a life of Kevin O'Higgins rather than of Erskine Childers.[2] She knew former very well. She took him once to see Max. O'Higgins could not think why Max wanted to see him and was rather nervous. Had no clothes or rather had forgotten his trousers, and Lady Lavery had to borrow a pair for him. No one else at dinner. Max talked all the time round newspapers. He wanted O'Higgins's support to buy a paper in Ireland. He was finally bored, said straight out: 'We don't want to sell our papers to any outside influence' and took his leave. For a long time Max was down on O'Higgins. After he was killed, he used to talk about how well he knew him! Also talked much about Valentine whom Lady Lavery likes. She thinks Doris is like Max, Ramsay MacDonald. They have gifts of endurance or permanence! They survive everything, rebuffs, unpopularity, plague, etc. Doris is having her portrait painted by Lavery. She wants it for the Academy, and, thinking getting into the Academy is like getting in to Buckingham Palace, she asked Lavery: 'It will get into the Academy, won't it? If I were to be divorced, it wouldn't make any difference?' . . . Aneurin Bevan, she says, thinks he is going to marry Sibell Lygon.

In the evening went to the Book Trade dinner, where I was a guest of

[1] Sibyl Colefax, wife of Sir Arthur Colefax, K.C., was a very active society hostess and lion-hunter. Sir Edwin Lutyens (1869–1944) designed the Cenotaph, Liverpool Cathedral and New Delhi; John Gielgud was then appearing with great success in *Richard of Bordeaux*, Gerald, 14th Baron Berners (1883–1950), composer, painter and writer. Hazel, wife of Sir John Lavery, President of the Society of Portrait Painters; she died in 1935.

[2] Kevin O'Higgins (1892–1927), Irish Sinn Feiner who became Vice-President of the Free State. Robert Erskine Childers (1870–1922), clerk in the House of Commons and author of *The Riddle of the Sands* (1903), a classic spy story which predicted the Great War; he became an ardent Sinn Feiner and was shot by the Free State Government for illegally possessing a firearm.

honour, sat between Miss Elizabeth Collins (Godfrey Collins's daughter) and Mrs John Buchan, and made a speech which went down very well on the whole. Both Collins (Sir Godfrey: the head of the publishing firm) and John Buchan referred very nicely to my book. Rose Macaulay, however, and Beatrice Kean Seymour talked mostly of Tschiffely,[1] who was the other star turn. Lady Oxford [Margot, widow of H. H. Asquith] took me by the arm and said 'I must meet you. I want to congratulate you – not on your book but on your speech – so good.' She speaks in little jerky sentences. Afterwards went to Sports Club and sat up till one.

Thursday, 16 March 1933

Lunched at the Chaplins'. He is a brother of Lady Londonderry. Both Lord and Lady Chaplin worked for Petter in the St George's by-election.[2] Both Lord and Lady Londonderry were very angry and upset. Lady Londonderry loves Ramsay or rather likes him very much. He is quite at home there. Lady Chaplin told me that she has been at Londonderry House. The telephone will go. A message comes: 'The Prime Minister would like to dine at 7.45.' Lady Londonderry may have arranged for 8.45. She alters all her arrangements without even a 'damn'.

Thursday, 23 March 1933

Dined at the Omar Khayyam Club – in their private room at Pagani's Restaurant in Great Portland Street. They always have the same room – a hideous monstrosity with a ghastly portrait of King Edward as a Lifeguardsman. Anthony Hope[3] – frail and leaning on a stick – in chair. He was once President of the Union at Oxford and his father was the first boy entered at Marlborough. The Club drink the toast of the Master – also of Edward FitzGerald. Ralph Straus[4] proposed guests in good speech. Reith (who is a teetotaller), a Canadian called Cobb and I responded. Only claret – the ruby wine of Omar – is drunk. The menu has an original poem – this time by James Laver[5] – and a drawing. Members include Horder, Humbert Wolfe, Straus, Aubrey Hammond, Wyndham Lewis, etc.

Friday, 24 March 1933

Lunched with Thost – the correspondent of the *Völkischer Beobachter*. He was full of stories of Hitler. Latter is now almost complete vegetarian. Started

[1] A. F. Tschiffely (1895–1954) rode 10,000 miles from Buenos Aires to Washington and wrote a best-seller about it.

[2] Petter was the Beaverbrook candidate who stood and failed against Duff Cooper, the official Conservative, see above, page 156.

[3] Sir Anthony Hope Hawkins (1863–1933), author of *The Prisoner of Zenda*. He died three months later.

[4] (1882–1952) novelist, biographer and book-reviewer, interested in limited editions and fine printing.

[5] Laver (*b.* 1879), now best known as a writer on costume and fashion, was a Newdigate poem prizewinner and had written several volumes of poetry and light verse.

about a year ago as a result of indigestion. The indigestion is cured. Hitler is a non-smoker and a teetotaller. Hitler's hobby is motor-cars and motoring. He said recently of the Deutsch-Nationalen: it was a wonderful machine – a super Rolls-Royce, but it is a 1913 model, and a 1913 model won't pull a 1933 weight. Thost tells me that he has been here four years but that he had never been asked even to tea at the [German] Embassy. As soon as Hitler came into office, he was asked to dinner!

In the evening dined with Cynthia Cheetham[1] or rather I gave her dinner at the Berkeley and took her to a cinema to make up for having chucked her party last week. She was rather sore about it, as she had asked a lot of people including Mrs Leo Rothschild to meet me. She says London continues to rave about my book and that she hears I am leaving Max and am going to Hollywood to play in the film of my own book!

Sunday, 26 March 1933

Felt desperately ill and shaky; did not rise till twelve and then only with difficulty. A few more weeks of this and I shall be a complete wreck. My will-power is gone, and the incessant financial worry is driving me insane. . .

Lunched at Berkeley Grill and in a fit of extravagance took a car and motored down to Virginia Water, Ascot, Bracknell, Sonning and home. A glorious day, but not so many signs of spring in the country as there are in London. Here in Ennismore Gardens the daffodils are out, and there are all kinds of almond blossom. In Berlin they say there is no spring. Hitler has suppressed all the *Blätter* [newspapers/leaves].

Dined with Pam at the Basque. She told me a story about Beatty and Jellicoe told to her by a man who was a 'snotty' on the *Iron Duke* at the time. When Beatty superseded Jellicoe, the officers of the *Iron Duke* ordered a twenty-four hours' silence. No one spoke except to give words of command. Next day – a Sunday – Beatty as C.-in-C. had to read lesson. He had previously discovered this and had found out what lesson was. When time came, chaplain went up to him and asked him to read. Beatty walked up to lectern, closed the book, and delivered lesson very dramatically. He had learnt it by heart. His performance captured both officers and men.

Wednesday, 29 March 1933

Lunched at Sir Ian Hamilton's: sat next Lady Leslie, Shane Leslie's mother,[2] and Lady Lloyd, wife of Lord Lloyd, who has just come back from a trip to South Africa. Met also Lady Lavery again, Gerhardi, who asked me why I did not leave Fleet Street now, 'Jerry' Villiers, Goodheart-Mendl,[3] and about

[1] Wife of Sir Milne Cheetham (1869–1939), retired diplomat.

[2] General Sir Ian Hamilton (1853–1947), who led the Gallipoli expedition. Lady Leslie was aunt of Winston Churchill as well as mother of Shane Leslie (*b.* 1884), later 3rd Bart, somewhat eccentric kilt-wearing literary Irishman.

[3] Gerald Villiers (1882–1953); and perhaps a slip for Harry Goodhart-Rendel (1887–1959), Slade Professor of Fine Art.

half-a-dozen others, whose names I did not catch. Gerhardi, who was a kind of office-boy in military uniform to Knox in Russia when I was Consul-General and who came to Max as a beggar, said: 'Get out of Fleet Street and write books. The Press, you know, that leaves a smell.' True, but patronising from Gerhardi, and not so easy for me to get out.

Saturday, 8 April 1933

Lunched with Namier at the Athenaeum and discussed German–Jewish relations. Namier will not even look at German lager. He says this business is serious. The persecution may take on more civilised forms, but what it means is the final liquidation of German Jewry. The Jews will have to prepare now for another flight from Spain. As many as possible will be sent to Palestine. The cruellest part of the persecution is that Jews are not allowed to leave Germany. This is worse than Tsarist Russia. The Nazis cannot have it both ways: they cannot say they want to reduce the number of their Jews and then refuse to allow them to leave the country. Namier says Germans are fools. Everything was going their way. The anti-German front in Europe was breaking down. Now they are reviving the word Hun. How, too, can they talk about the rights of German minorities in other countries?

Wednesday, 19 April 1933

Moscow sentences: Thornton three years, MacDonald two; Monkhouse, Cushny and Nordwall to be deported; Gregory acquitted.[1] Ten of eleven Russians condemned to long terms of imprisonment, one acquitted. No death sentences. On the whole intelligent opinion here holds: that (1) the sentences are lighter than were expected; (2) there was some foundation for the Bolshevist case; and (3) that we mis-handled the case from the beginning. There was certainly no excuse for our original attitude that the men must be innocent because they are British and that the Russians have no right to try them. Nevertheless, today the Privy Council met at Windsor and the King signed a proclamation putting an embargo on the chief Russian goods imported into this country.[2] The *Daily Mail* and *Express*, whose language on the trial has been vituperative, are jubilant. They think that their threats have saved the lives of the Englishmen. Ovey holds the same view and thinks that the high tone he took with Litvinov at the beginning saved the men from being shot. What balls! As the *Daily Herald* says this morning comparing the present hysteria to the war of Jenkins' Ear: today they are ringing their bells, tomorrow they will be wringing their hands (Walpole). Lunched with Bernstorff, Amery and Clifford Sharp. Latter is in bad way: no money and nerves gone. He was drinking again. He is now prepared to go to Berlin to write up Hitler. The German Government will pay.

[1] Six British Metropolitan-Vickers engineers and twelve Russians had been arrested for sabotage and tried, with Vyshinsky as prosecutor.

[2] The Russians replied in kind, but the engineers were released and an Anglo-Soviet trade agreement was negotiated.

Saturday, 22 April 1933

Tommy also knew Sir Henry Royce who died today.[1] In 1914 he had a villa at Le Canadel near Cavalaire. Even then he was a hypochondriac and very fussy about a new set of false teeth which he manipulated badly. One room was given over entirely to plans and models of engines. He used to have all new Rolls cars out to France to test them on the hills of Esterel. Millie knew young Rolls. In 1906 he came to her: 'I have the best engineer in the world, and I am going to make the best car. You must take shares in the company we are forming.' More to please Rolls than from any belief in the future of the Rolls-Royce, she put in a few hundred pounds. This investment repaid her twentyfold. At night played bridge.

Wednesday, 26 April 1933

Lunched at Savoy with Linton Wells, the Hearst man in Moscow. He loves the I.N.S. work, has been there several times, and, although not very good on politics, is a good feature man. He tells me: (1) that Metropol and National Hotel are open again and that first is centre of night life, has champagne, whisky (latter cheaper than here) and five women (latter known as valuta girls), but that Nationalnaya is best hotel to live in; (2) that my old friend Peters is now in Siberia keeping an eye on [Marshal] Blucher, the Bolo general, and that his English wife is now servant and cook to Jessie Lloyd, the daughter of a rich Chicago Socialist. Jessie works on *Moscow Daily News*. Peters divorced his English wife in 1920 or thereabouts. She found him remarried when she returned to Russia. She is of course a Soviet citizen now. There is one daughter of this marriage. She is very lovely and is in the ballet school. Linton Wells thinks famine will be terrible. He says everyone in Moscow including all foreign diplomatists think that we handled our case in trial very badly.

Friday, 28th April 1933

Lunched with or rather gave luncheon to Sefton Delmer,[2] who is over here for a few days. He is quite young, only twenty-seven, speaks English with a slight German accent, is Jewish-looking, and very fat. He knows the Nazis very well and does not like Rosenberg. Goebbels and Goering do most of the Nazi entertaining. Frau Goebbels has a sort of 'salon'. Roehm makes no disguise of his homosexuality. Hitler relies on his advice more than on anyone else's. He knows that it is disinterested. Roehm, on account of his exposure over homosexuality, cannot be promoted! When Papen resigned Chancellorship, Hindenburg gave him a photograph of himself with the inscription on top: '*Ich hatt' einen Kameraden.*' [I had a friend.] There is now a decree for an

[1] (1863–1933) the engineer who, with the Hon. C. S. Rolls (1877–1910), founded Rolls-Royce in 1907.

[2] *Daily Express* Berlin correspondent, born in Berlin 1904, the son of a Tasmanian professor working there. He was later a close colleague of Lockhart in P.W.E.

entirely Aryan Committee for the German Stock-Exchanges. In Berlin Herr Brecker and another German colleague have been rushing round for a week between Government and brokers. So far they have found only two Germans for their committee of thirteen.

Saturday, 29 April 1933

Came down on same train as Harry. He was very drunk and is doing his best to kill himself. As Casanova said of himself, 'I have often observed that for the greatest part of my life, I have been trying to make myself ill, and then, when I had finally achieved this, in trying to get well again.' Casanova was equally successful at both. So used Harry to be. But now no longer.

Thursday, 11 May 1933

Harold very upset about the Nazis, the Press (the *Express* article today),[1] and various other manifestations of the Press Lords. He refused to meet Hearst in America. Went to Rosenberg's reception to Press at Claridge's: rather a poor showing. Had a longish talk with Bismarck.[2] I understand that reason Rosenberg did not see me was Thost, who told him I was not coming! Minor Communist demonstration outside Claridge's, six men and a boy. The whole story grossly exaggerated in the Beaverbrook Press. Scene at Cenotaph: Rosenberg's swastika wreath removed by British ex-captain who is fined 40*s*. Rosenberg did not consult his Embassy *re* this step.

Saturday, 13 May 1933

Lunched with Moura at the Perroquet. She is going with H. G. [Wells] to Salzburg on June 2nd. She has just returned from Berlin and says that the Hitlerist Terror is worse than anything that ever happened in Russia or Italy. Rot – although I admit that this revolution has many mean and pettily spiteful aspects. Moura's stories are always amusing. Definition of a Zionist, or rather of Zionism: 'When two Jews send a third Jew at the expense of a fourth to Palestine.'

The German revolution has had another funny repercussion. The Nazis announced that they had banned *The Star*. The English *Star* [an evening paper], taking on in the Liberal fashion the protection of German citizens in Germany, at once made the most of this, brought out huge posters 'We Should Worry!' and gave great accounts of the special police on the frontier to hold up copies of their paper. Now it turns out that the paper banned is *The Toronto Star*!

Thursday, 18 May 1933

Curious situation in Russia. Russia does not hate Fascism so much as the

[1] 'Europe – the Truth, One Vast Munitions Factory – Germany Defies the Treaty'.

[2] Count Gottfried Bismarck, Nazi deputy for Pomerania, brother of Prince Otto Bismarck who was at the German Embassy in London.

jelly-bellied democracy of Britain. She prefers the Fascist system of government; (1) because the Fascist form of rule justifies and is the same as her own; (2) because the corporate state is more akin to her own ideal and in the event of a change goes over en bloc to Communism; and (3) she understands exactly where she is with Mussolini: trade and no propaganda nonsense. Result is Mussolini is never attacked in Soviet Press. Gorky once wrote something against Musso. It did not go in.

Friday, 19 May 1933

In evening took Kühlmann, who arrived yesterday, down to Cherkley. Only guests besides ourselves were Lloyd George and Miss Stevenson. We talked till twelve, L.G. and Kühlmann holding the floor. L.G. in velvet dinner jacket, large double watch-chain passed through waistcoat buttonhole, a flowing bow-tie and button-boots. His hair now almost snow-white with two rather greyer strands down back of his head. Complexion still rosy and wonderful...

Very interesting discussion on uncleared-up secrets of war...

Kühlmann on Dardanelles. Says we were almost through on first attack. Turks had only fourteen shells per gun. His Ambassador Wangenheim in state of great excitement – very nervy – Kühlmann says: 'Well, let's make best of it. Let's go riding and then in evening we shall see. If Allies get through, we can go off into Asia Minor. (They were all prepared for this.) If we win, we can drink a bottle of champagne.' When they came back, General Liman von Sanders is waving a flag and shouting 'Victory'. They have their champagne.

Kühlmann on interview with Kaiser on Polish frontier during interval in Brest–Litovsk peace. Hindenburg and Ludendorff have made line on military basis. They are thinking in terms of next war with Russia. Kaiser sends for Kühlmann who accepts Hofmann's line. Kaiser retains Kühlmann half-an-hour after time he has appointed for Ludendorff and Hindenburg. They scowl at Kühlmann as he comes out. Kaiser, however, gives way to military pressure. Kühlmann thinks Hofmann was best general in German side. L.G. very down on British generals. Thinks French was the best and got a raw deal.[1]

Kühlmann and [Thomas G.] Masaryk. In his book or in a book President Masaryk, in referring to the shooting of Miss Cavell [British nurse shot by Germans], laid chief blame on Baron Lancken, who was, I think, the civil governor or diplomatic authority in Brussels at the time. Lancken, as a matter of fact, did everything he could to stop the shooting. Kühlmann and Lancken were staying together when they read this. They wrote off at once to the President who replied that he had good evidence for this statement. Kühlmann then wrote back enclosing his own and Lancken's signed statement. Masaryk at once accepted their statement and promised to amend his own

[1] Sir John French (1852–1925) was ousted from the command of the B.E.F. by Haig in 1915, before Lloyd George became Prime Minister.

original statement at once. Later, Poincaré made similar charge in his Memoirs. Again, Kühlmann wrote. Poincaré was stiff and obdurate. It was not until they quoted Masaryk's behaviour that Poincaré agreed to accept the correction.

Kühlmann and Moltke. After Franco-Prussian War the great Moltke said that the next big war in Europe might last for years: it would be another Seven Years' War and perhaps even a Thirty Years' War.

L.G. and Antwerp. Kühlmann said one of the wisest things England could have done was the Antwerp move.[1] The whole British army there right on German flank – could have stopped German advance on Paris. Probably true. L.G. made interesting statement that this was French's original idea. Later, at the Cabinet Council which decided the Antwerp expedition, Winston was against it. Max and Kühlmann, having always given the credit or the blame to Winston for this expedition, challenged L.G. on this, but he was quite definite and quite sure on his point.

Friday, 26 May 1933

Lunched with Moura at Jardin des Gourmets – guests Somerset Maugham, Barbara Back, whom I did not like, Meriel Buchanan,[2] Montgelas. Somerset Maugham has a very Mongolian face, very precise manner, rather short fingers with broad, flat ends. Rather conceited. Hates the English climate. Rises early and likes to sleep in afternoon. Thinks that if he had gone to Russia sooner he would have been able to ginger up the Mensheviks so much as to make Bolshevik *coup d'état* impossible. A great admirer of Savinkov.[3] Thinks *Voyage au bout de la nuit* [by Louis-Ferdinand Céline] greatest book of recent times. Once in America Professor of Dramatic Literature at Harvard said to him: 'You know Mr Maugham, the play of yours I really like best is *The Mollusc.*'[4] Meriel Buchanan told me that, after he had written his memoirs, Sir George Buchanan destroyed all his Russian diaries and private papers.

Tuesday, 30 May 1933

Yesterday at luncheon I met Gordon Beckles[5] and Bill Needham, manager of *Sunday Express*. Bill told me a very good story of Max and [A.V.] Alexander. On one occasion Needham and Gordon were summoned to Stornoway. Max started off: 'He is good boy, that Alexander. You know his story: born

[1] When the Germans besieged Antwerp in 1914, a small British force was sent in, but could not prevent the city falling. Churchill is usually given the credit.

[2] W. Somerset Maugham (1874–1965), novelist and playwright, had been a secret agent in Petrograd. Meriel Buchanan was a daughter of Sir George Buchanan, former British Ambassador in Moscow.

[3] Boris Savinkov, Minister of War under Kerensky, counter-revolutionary schemer who finally returned to Russia in 1924 and was arrested and executed. He impressed Churchill, but Lockhart thoroughly distrusted him.

[4] Actually by H. H. Davies.

[5] Gordon Beckles (1901–54) was on the staff of the *Daily Express*, 1928–38, and later Assistant and Deputy Editor *Daily Mail*.

in the gutter, went to a board school, now keeps his father and mother.'

Gordon: 'I don't think this quite agrees with the facts, sir.'

'Don't you?' Max gets on the telephone. 'Alexander. Good boy.' Then he puts his questions. 'Oh, you were born in a villa, were you? Hm. You were not at a board school! Hm. A grammar school. Your father is not poor! He keeps *you*!' Collapse of Max. This all *à propos* of a story about Robertson being a bell-hop in today's *Express*. Robertson was never a bell-hop in a Toronto hotel, but a reception clerk. All typical of Max's exaggeration.

Monday, 5 June 1933

Had a talk with ——. He is Fascist-mad and thinks we shall have Fascism very soon here. He tells me that Graham Seton Hutchison,[1] the writer and author of *The W Plan*, etc., is Senior Paladin of a British Fascist Society called the English Mystery. Hutchison is a great friend of Hitler. He speaks German well and has been writing up Germany. He has been doing this for some years, wrote a pamphlet on German wrongs in Silesia, and I remember Bernstorff telling me at the time that he was paid by the Germans and asking me if he was worth the money. —— has been unlucky. He sent Clifford Sharp over to Berlin the other day at the expense of the German Government. He cost them over £100 and then could not place an article in any paper.

Tuesday, 6 June 1933

Mary Erskine [Tommy's daughter] is now definitely engaged to Philip Dunn, son of Max's 'Jimmie'. Tommy is trying, as usual, to make the best of things, but I expect that in her heart of hearts she has misgivings. I share them. The boy is, fortunately, not like his father. Bill Aitken,[2] who knows him well, says that he is not a bad fellow, is quite intelligent, but is rather negative. Bill thinks he is too anglicised! He has nice manner, but clammy hands which I do not like. I doubt if he will be able to manage Mary.

Bill told me today that Max's story of his early poverty is greatly exaggerated. His father was a true scholar who was wasted in New Brunswick. His mother was a Noble and came of a rich family. Her brother ran through two fortunes. Mrs Ramsay, Max's sister, took a first in history at one of the Canadian Universities. She knows Max inside out and rather foolishly tackles him when he is romancing about his grandfather being an agricultural labourer, etc.[3]

[1] Lieut.-Colonel Graham Seton Hutchison (1890–1946) founded the Paladin, 1930, and the National Workers' Movement, 1933. Wrote many adventure stories.

[2] William Travers Aitken (1903–64), son of Magnus Aitken. Later Conservative M.P., Manager *Express* News and Features, knighted 1963.

[3] See *Beaverbrook* by A. J. P. Taylor (London, 1972). Beaverbrook's grandfather was a lime-merchant, quarrymaster and property-owner – 'a man of some substance'. Beaverbrook's father received 'the best education Scotland could offer' (Edinburgh University for eight years). He married Jane Noble, daughter of a prosperous storekeeper and farmer.

Friday, 9 June 1933

My dinner last night was a complete humiliation. Went to Guildhall with whose people I am on good terms. Was given a comic and special introduction to the Lord Mayor and the Sheriffs. Did not have to go round in the procession. Then went into the hall almost last and found there was no place for me. The *Evening Standard* had muddled the invitation. I found a young reporter from the City Office in my place. I did not like to turn him out, so I left. Low's[1] party at his Golders Green house was a great Bohemian affair: half Chelsea and Fleet Street. Nice house with garden all lit up. Among celebrities saw Priestley, whom I did not like, Florence Austral (whose husband is a New Zealander and was rather drunk), Marie Ney (also N.Z.), J. B. S. Haldane, Louis Golding, etc.[2]

Friday, 16 June 1933

Wheeler-Bennett saw Brüning. While they were talking at night in his little flat at the Krankenhaus [Hedwiga], some Nazis turned up in the street singing *Horst Wessel Lied*. Brüning rose up, put out the lights quite calmly, and waited until they had passed. Otherwise, they would have made a provocative scene outside his window. Then he resumed his conversation at the exact point where he had broken it off.

Monday, 19 June 1933

Rose at 7 and caught 9.1 to London. Lunched with or rather gave luncheon to Dr Erich Winter and Herr Bené, two Nazi officials at the Conference.[3] Bené is permanently here and is the Nazi group leader here. Winter is a member of the Saxon Government and has to do with the co-operative societies. He was born in London, is an Old Pauline, and speaks English perfectly. He was very interesting on the peasant side of Hitler movement and tells me we should watch Darré, who has organised Hitlerism among the farmers who are his chief support. Darré is in charge of the Nazi Agricultural machine and may be Minister of Agriculture at any moment. He is of Huguenot extraction and was born in the Argentine.

Tuesday, 20 June 1933

In afternoon went to Maurice Peterson's cocktail party. Met Rex Hoare again. He is now Minister at Teheran and confirms story of the Shah's outburst at races before whole diplomatic corps three weeks ago. There was a

[1] David Low (1891–1963), then *Evening Standard* cartoonist, knighted 1963, was a New Zealander.

[2] J. B. Priestley (*b.* 1894), novelist and playwright. Florence Austral (1894–1968) was an Australian soprano and her husband, John Amadio (*d.* 1964) a flautist. Marie Ney, actress, began her career in Australia. J. B. S. Haldane, F.R.S. (1892–1964), biologist, polymath and polemicist. Louis Golding (1895–1968), best-selling novelist.

[3] The World Economic Conference had been opened by the King at the Geological Museum on 12 June.

race in which a young Turkoman boy and a Persian officer provided a thrilling finish in which they rode each other off and slashed each other with their whips, the race ending in a free fight. The Shah sent for boy who was brought before him by two soldiers. Shah then gave him a kick in the stomach and a cosh on head before everyone. Later, he sent the boy the equivalent of £10. Shah has violent temper.

Wednesday, 21 June 1933.

Not sleeping well and feeling thoroughly used up. I am in a sea of trouble. My life is complicated in half a hundred ways. Pam is ill again and is very trying. Moura is back again. Jean is not much better, is still an invalid, still surrounded by nurses and medicine bottles. Tommy is in a state of collapse over Mary's wedding. And I have to listen to all their woes and try to comfort them. At the same time I have to work sixteen hours in Fleet Street and write my books as well.

Wednesday, 5 July 1933

In the afternoon went to call on Prince Louis Ferdinand who has just arrived and who has been recommended to me by General Waters and the Kaiser.[1] He is staying at Brown's where he has a small room like a cubicle on the top floor. His whole luggage for six months in America consists of three suitcases and a cardboard tailor's box plus a dispatch case and a typewriter. His allowance, paid by the ex-Kaiser and not by his father, does not amount to more than £600–700 a year.

Prince Louis is tall – 6ft 1in, dark, with fine forehead and silky black hair brushed back, and a prominent nose. He looks more Latin than German and indeed likes Latin civilisation. His brothers call him 'The Spanish Jew'. He is intelligent and has charm.

Thursday, 6 July 1933

After luncheon drove Prince Louis Ferdinand round to see the sights. Took him to see Godfrey Thomas to arrange about seeing the Prince of Wales.[2] Called on German Ambassador. In the evening dined at the De Trafford's (Rudolph). Present: The Rodneys, the Rosslyns (Harry very drunk!), Lady Alington, Mrs Piers Legh,[3] and Reg Stokes. The Prince drank a good deal, Harry more. Finally, Harry, rather inclined to be quarrelsome, poured a

[1] Prince Louis Ferdinand was a grandson of the Kaiser. In *Potsdam and Doorn* (1935), Waters (see above, page 25) pays great tribute to Lockhart for arranging the visits of Prince Louis Ferdinand – then aged 25 and an employee of the Ford Motor Co. in the United States – and also for keeping the Press away from him. Louis Ferdinand, although the second son of Crown Prince William, was in the direct line of succession because of his elder brother's morganatic marriage in 1933.

[2] Sir Godfrey Thomas, Bart (1889–1968), Private Secretary to the Prince of Wales, 1919–36.

[3] Lady Mary Sibell Cooper, wife of 3rd Baron Alington. Sarah, wife of Piers Legh, Equerry to the Prince of Wales, 1919–36.

large glass of port into the bottle again. Stokes saw him and chaffed him. Harry then turned on Prince. 'I suppose you think this is rather disgusting. What would you have done?' 'Oh!' says Prince quickly. 'If I had been a Scot, I should have saved it for the next time.' Went on to Savoy to dance afterwards. Prince likes dancing. He dances well. Danced with June [de Trafford] and Lady Alington. After all other guests had gone, he received a note from Lily Dalmita, the cinema star whom he nearly married and who was the cause of his going to America. She came over to us and said: 'How have you been.'

Friday, 7 July 1933

Prince Louis met Lily Dalmita in Germany and fell in love with her. He was writing his thesis for his doctor's degree on immigration question and had to go to Argentine to collect necessary material. Lily had gone to America. So Prince Louis persuaded Kaiser to let him go just to U.S.A. on way to Argentine. Bigelow, former American Ambassador and ex-Kaiser's friend, gave him letters to Ford, etc. Louis went to Los Angeles and nearly married Lily. Scandal in papers. Trouble at home and Doorn. A restaurant keeper advises Louis 'not to be a fool'. He wires to Ford to give him job at Los Angeles. Ford recommends him to listen to his grandfather's advice and suggests Buenos Aires. Louis goes to Buenos Aires, passes his degree, works for Ford, and tries to forget Lily. Lily behaves well. . . Last night she was circumspect, never gave her name to hotel, etc., and has now gone away.

Gave luncheon to Prince at Boulestin's. Tommy, Mary and Philip Dunn. Later, took him down to Cherkley. Max alone and in good form. He liked the Prince who, asked what his chances of the throne were, said that, as long as Hitler's popularity lasted, he would be God, Pope and Kaiser for Germany.

Max: 'I am pro-German. I had hoped much from Hitler. But he's a persecutor.'

Prince nervously: 'I think there has been some exaggeration about the Jewish affair.'

'To hell with the Jews!' says Max. 'He's persecuting the Lutheran Church.'

Saturday, 8 July 1933

I am exhausted. Came down with Prince Louis to Horsham by the 1.40. Spent a very boring afternoon and evening. Harry was very drunk and intolerably conversational and almost rude. Tommy worried and nearly distracted. We sat up till one waiting for Penelope Dudley Ward who was to arrive at eleven. She came at two and then talked with Tommy for over an hour. Result – no sleep for me. I fear the Prince must have been bored. The manners and the selfishness of the young generation of so-called English society are incredibly bad. The Prince, who is quite unspoilt, looks very delicate. He takes acidol-pepsin after every meal, does not smoke . . . Harry spent the whole evening trying to persuade him to induce Henry Ford to use

Arcanol, the German paint, which Harry floated into an English company. The Prince says Henry Ford is past his best.[1] He did one great service. He turned the motor-car from a class-dividing into a class-unifying instrument. But he has never had much of an idea since and has not kept pace with his competitors. There is only one man in Ford's who can get drunk. This is ——, a former newspaper man and now Ford's 'brain manager'. —— has bouts, during which he is drunk for days on end. Ford, however, can't do without him.

Sunday, 9 July 1933

In the afternoon motored over to Churt to see Lloyd George. Lovely afternoon. Present: L.G., Dame Lloyd George, Megan, Gwilym[2] and his wife, the Laverys, Frank Pakenham (who is writing a life of De Valera) and General Smuts.[3] Latter spoke very nicely to me and said he remembered my reports very well. He also knew my Dutch uncle Marchant very well. L.G. in very good form. He asked me about the Prince and referred very nicely to the Kaiser. 'The Kaiser', he said, 'had undoubted qualities. If he had not been Kaiser, he would have been a very great man. Kaisers have no chance from the start.' Then Smuts and he took the Prince outside and talked for nearly an hour on Germany, Hitler, etc. L.G. was very pleased. Gwilym is a great fisherman. He tells me that in 1922 or '23 L.G. went out salmon-fishing twice near Gairloch I think. Got a salmon each time in first ten minutes. Motored back to London with the Prince and sat up all night writing article for bank.

Monday, 10 July 1933

In afternoon rested and at six took the Prince to the House of Commons where we had tea with Winston, L.G., Bracken, Boothby, and Norma Shearer and Irving Thalberg.[4] The Prince had a good talk with Winston, who informed him that he was a monarchist and that he hoped the Prince would regain his throne. 'We prefer the Hohenzollerns to the gangsters,' he said. Oliver Stanley and Lady Maureen Stanley also there.

In the evening the Prince took Penelope to dine and dance. He has fallen for her quite a lot and thinks she is very intelligent and full of sex appeal. I meant to go home to bed but met Frank [Aveling] at the nursing home,

[1] Henry Ford (1863–1947) had been producing cars since 1893, and had handed over control of his firm to his son Edsel in 1919.

[2] Dame Margaret Lloyd George, his first wife (*d.* 1941); Megan Lloyd George, his daughter, later a Labour M.P.; Gwilym, his son (*b.* 1894), then a Liberal M.P., later a Conservative minister and then Viscount Tenby.

[3] Jan Christiaan Smuts (1870–1950), South African statesman, was a member of the War Cabinet when Lockhart was British Agent in Moscow.

[4] Thalberg (1899–1936), immensely successful American film producer, production manager of Metro-Goldwyn-Mayer until 1933; he was married to Norma Shearer, film actress.

dined with him, and then played billiards until 1 a.m. Very foolish to tax my health in this way. I have never been so tired out as I am this year...

Tuesday, 11 July 1933

Today we staged a meeting between Miss Brimble, the Prince's old English Governess, and the Prince. They were photographed together at the *Standard* and gave an interview to one man. Afterwards, they lunched together and later joined Bark, Mažuranič and me at our table at Boulestin's. Miss Brimble is rather arch and prim, but quite intelligent. She told me Prince Louis was the naughtiest of the Crown Prince's children, but by far the most original. He was always a good linguist...

Dined alone with the Prince at the Basque. He has a weak 'tummy', suffers from acid or the lack of digestive acid and has to take acidol-pepsin after every meal. Then went on to Max's party which lasted all night. Duke Ellington's Negro band played, and a great many people were tight. The guests included Prince George, Lord and Lady Louis Mountbatten, peeresses, ministers, ex-ministers, journalists, Low and Strube [another cartoonist], cinema stars and demi-mondaines. Prince enjoyed himself, but was at once taken up by Lady Castlerosse! Who of course asked him to her party the next day. I had one awkward moment. The Prince wanted to meet Prince George and asked me if I could arrange it. I spoke to Edwina Mountbatten. She was not exactly rude, but more or less laughed me off by saying 'You had better get hold of my husband; he speaks German,' and did nothing about it. Prince Louis noticed it.

Wednesday, 12 July 1933

Very tired again. Today, the Prince lunched with Randolph who had a private party for him at Quaglino's. I had asked Randolph to ask some young Conservatives. He brought Lord Melchett[1] and a bunch of Jews! However, they all got on very well. In the evening went to Lady Castlerosse's party, after dining at the Savoy with the De Traffords, where I met Mrs Buist[2] a sister of Violet Cripps. She urged me to leave Max and said modern men lacked courage. All sorts and conditions present at Doris Castlerosse's Party from Prince George down... This afternoon, too, we saw the Prince of Wales, who had three-quarters of an hour chat with the Prince and then came out and said a few words to me.

Thursday, 13 July 1933

Prince Louis liked the Prince of Wales very much. They talked Spanish and German as well as English. Prince Louis says the Prince's Spanish is quite good and that he is the only one of his relations with whom he can talk Spanish.

[1] Henry Mond, 2nd Baron Melchett (1898–1949), wealthy businessman, had been a Conservative M.P. until he succeeded to the title in 1930.

[2] Gladys, daughter of Sir William Nelson and wife of Lieut.-Commander Colin Buist.

The Prince [of Wales] was quite pro-Hitler, said it was no business of ours to interfere in Germany's internal affairs either *re* Jews or *re* anything else, and added that dictators were very popular these days and that we might want one in England before long. I expect the Prince of Wales has been influenced regarding Germany by —— and ——, both of whom are ardent Hitlerites. . .

Today we lunched with Esmond Harmsworth and Ward Price[1] at Warwick House and were nearly half an hour late owing to traffic and rain. The Prince was not so good with Esmond, partly because Ward Price talked too much, partly because Esmond was shy, and, partly because Prince himself was tired. His baby name in the family is 'Lulu' . . . In the evening dined quietly off sausage (*Bratwurst*) at Schmidt's. Had tea with the Aga Khan, who said that but for war Germans would have captured trade of the East.

Friday, 14 July 1933

Very tired and exhausted. I have now been 'off the wagon' for a month. June 14 to July 14, and the result is that I feel ghastly. I am, too, a bundle of nerves. Today, at ten minutes to one I had to go to lunch at the German Embassy. Marsh came in to say Wardell wanted a paragraph done on 'bridge'. There was no one there. I had no time. Finally, I went down to the pub to get Shanks, who was rude to me. Whole performance very humiliating.

Luncheon at Embassy: Prince Louis, Prince Gustavus Adolphus of Sweden and his wife, Prince and Princess Bismarck, Lord and Lady Abingdon, Princess Windischgrätz, etc. Dr and Frau Schacht.[2] I sat next Frau Schacht, who is nice and homely. Prince Louis spoke to Schacht, who is confident and optimistic about Germany. Prince Gustav Adolf never said a word to Prince Louis; he [Louis] was rather bitter and commented severely on the jealousies and petty nature of royalties. At 3.30 came down with him to Barnton Stacey to stay the night with General Waters, who came to the station with a temperature of 102° to meet Prince Louis. This is what the ex-Kaiser calls *Pflichtgefühl* [sense of duty]. The ex-Kaiser loves Waters and sends him numerous cuttings, copies of *Kladderdatsch*, etc. – sometimes with caricatures of King George whom he dislikes. Fished on the Waters' water at Middleton. Caught four and all about one pound.

Saturday, 15 July 1933

The Prince [Louis Ferdinand] seemed quite *emotionné* on leaving. He is a little bitter about the snobbishness of royalties, a little sore about Prince George and Beaverbrook's party, angry with Prince Gustav Adolf, who sat next but one to him at luncheon yesterday and did not address a word to

[1] G. Ward Price (*d.* 1961), war correspondent in both wars, later director of Associated Newspapers.

[2] Hjalmar Schacht (1877–1970), then president of the Reichsbank, later Hitler's Economics Minister, was in London as a leading member of the German deputation to the World Economic Conference.

him. In the end he liked Prince George, said he was artistic and effeminate and used a strong perfume, and that this appealed to him. Prince George told him that he had got into trouble with his father for going to Lady Castlerosse's party. . .

Tuesday, 18 July 1933

Lunched at the Carlton with Mrs Belloc Lowndes and Mrs Brown Maloney, the editress of the *Herald Tribune*. Latter is life long friend of Howe (Roosevelt's secretary) and Franklin Roosevelt. She wants me to do some work for her and *The Sunday Magazine* which is to start next January. She advised me very strongly not to let the publishers rush me into finishing my next book before my own time. She told some good stories. Howe has one religion: F. D. Roosevelt. He was for ten years a reporter with Munsey. Then he joined Franklin D., was with him as assistant secretary to the Assistant Secretary of the Navy.[1] Howe always told F.D. that he would be president of the U.S.A. Used to say: mustn't do this, mustn't do that: one day you'll be President. When Roosevelt stood for State Senate, he got typhoid. Howe used to go in to see him every day. 'You're winning in this district – that district, etc.' Finally, Roosevelt won. Howe had stumped the state for him to ensure his candidature. Finally, when Roosevelt was paralysed and everyone said his career was finished, Howe came in and said: 'Well, this makes it quite certain now that you'll be President of the U.S.A.' (Reason: 'Because a good-looking face on a lame body always gets the public sympathy, and because you will now be spared all the political nonsense – handshaking, platform stumping, etc., which ruins a man.') Howe used to golf. Has a weak heart now and has to be careful.

Lockhart wrote to the Kaiser telling him of his grandson's doings in England. The Kaiser replied on 22 July 1933:

Your detailed account of my grandson's, Prince Louis Ferdinand's, visit to England pleased me greatly and I thank you sincerely for it.

My special thanks, however, are for your kind efforts in getting the Prince into touch with members of the Royal Family and with the many and prominent men of your country. I am glad that, in this respect, the Prince's ability, his pleasant and tactful personality, his knowledge attained by serious academic study and his world-wide practical experience made itself felt. This well-guided visit to England will, without doubt, have a good influence on the Prince's character and spirit and it would be particularly agreeable if, through this visit, the German–English relationship is further and better understanding and friendliness reached.

Your countrymen's remarks about me and about Germany in their conversations with the Prince are interesting, if contradictory. Mr Lloyd George,

[1] Roosevelt had been Assistant Secretary to the Navy, 1913–20; and was first elected President in 1932.

who once worked with all energy for my downfall ('Hang the Kaiser!'), now expresses his admiration for me, and the anti-German Mr Winston Churchill wishes for their best and to my advantage to see the setting up again of a Kaiser Throne! The opinion on the German National Socialist movement swings between the cry for an 'English Hitler' and the term 'Bandits'. This points to the fact how unclear in many ways the other side of the Channel is in respect to German affairs. On the other hand the remark of the Prince of Wales, that we have a right to deal with our affairs as we deem it right, shows sound judgement. Prince Louis Ferdinand will no doubt have agreed with him on this point.

I remember with pleasure your visit to Doorn and hope that you will repeat it. At the moment I am reading aloud to my Gentlemen your autobiography which is of great interest to us. Once again many thanks for your kindness and with kind regards.

Wilhelm

To this Lockhart replied on 2 August 1933:

I am deeply grateful to Your Majesty for your commendation of my services to Prince Louis. They were given very willingly. The Prince himself made my task very simple, and without the charm of his own personality no efforts of mine could have succeeded in producing the very favourable impression which he made on everyone.

I was also very flattered to learn that Your Majesty is reading my memoirs. It may interest Your Majesty to know that I have just received a request for an autographed copy for President Roosevelt, who has read the book 'with absorbing pleasure and admiration'.

I am also profoundly moved by Your Majesty's gracious invitation to revisit Doorn. Your Majesty, doubtless, realises that I am now what is known as a newspaperman, and, if it would be possible for me to publish some account of my visit, I should be greatly benefited.

Naturally I realise the necessity for the greatest discretion, and of course anything I wrote would be submitted in advance for Your Majesty's approval.

Should, however, Your Majesty decide that the present moment is inopportune for any kind of publicity, I should still like very much to have the honour of visiting Doorn. Among other matters I should be very glad to have the opportunity of discussing with Your Majesty the position with regard to the third volume of poor Nowak's book, the rights of which have been acquired by my newspaper.

It will be difficult for me to leave London at the present moment, although, if Your Majesty so wishes, I could come during a week-end. If I may be so bold as to make a suggestion, I should prefer, if it suits Your Majesty, to come early in September.

Your Majesty will be relieved to learn that General Waters, who has been ill and who nevertheless insisted on coming to the station to meet Prince Louis with a temperature of over 100°, has now quite recovered.

To Prince Louis, Lockhart wrote on the same day, 2 August 1933:

After I left you on the *Europa*, I was given the chance of ten days' holiday and took it with both hands. I went to Scotland all by myself to fish and to have a rest. How I wish you could have come with me! I could then have shown you my old country, and you could have seen how an internationalist Britisher can turn into a very nationalist Scot.

I sent in a report on your English visit to your august Grandfather. He wrote me a most charming letter, in which he said all kinds of nice things about you and even about me. I expect you must have sung my praises too loudly. In any case, he asked me to renew my visit to Doorn and I am most grateful to you for anything you may have done to help me in this direction.

It was so nice to see you in England and to know, as I have learnt since your departure, what a good impression you made here. If I may offer you any advice, may I say how very wise you have been not to identify yourself with any political party or particular political view in your own country? I am sure that, if you continue to maintain this attitude and to retain that broad sympathy and understanding of human affairs which you already have in a very marked degree, your chance will come sooner or later.

Do write and tell me how you like your new department in Fords.

P.S. I must thank Your Royal Highness very much for the charming frame and photograph which I received on my return from Scotland. It now stands on my table at home, where I hope it will inspire me to make progress with my new book, which is already far behind its schedule. I hope that you managed to struggle through *British Agent* and that you will tell me frankly what you think of it.

P.S.2 I wonder if you would like to do me a great favour and help me by writing an article for my paper on your experiences with Ford. The article should be about 1200 to 1500 words, should be bright and personal, and should give some account of the types of men to be found among Ford's workmen, their lives, their amusements, your own friends amongst them, etc. If suitable we should pay you about £30 or even £40 for it, which I think you will agree is very good remuneration for a short article. Can you send us it as soon as possible?

The letter, incidentally, is addressed to 'Dr Louis Ferdinand' in Detroit.

Wednesday, 2 August 1933

Great excitement in office over rumoured appointment of Hon. Anthony Winn[1] to *Evening Standard*. Shanks and Marsh very agitated. Shanks gave me

[1] (1909–1942) fourth son of 2nd Baron St Oswald. He did join the *Standard*.

luncheon and tried to borrow £100. Poor devil, I told him I was on the verge of bankruptcy myself, as, indeed, I am. My negotiations with ——'s creditors do not go too well. We have offered 25%. They are demanding 75% or immediate bankruptcy proceedings. Meanwhile, Huntington has rather put me in the cart by giving great prominence to his announcements of my book for this autumn. He knew quite well that there is no prospect of its being ready. I am not going to be jumped by any of these fellows.

Tuesday, 8 August 1933

Lunched at Lady Colefax's. Present: Mr and Mrs Lewisohn of the copper and manganese firm (one married Edna May), Lady Cunard, who talked incessantly, Lady Sybil Graham, who told me Sir Ronald was not leaving Rome until October, Harold Nicolson, and Roger Fry.[1] Lady Cunard very aggressive about gossip-writers whom she abhors. I expect she has suffered. She is pro-Hitler and goes to Munich tomorrow. She may come back with changed views. Funny how every revolutionary movement claims Christ for itself. The Bolsheviks shocked the world by putting up posters of Christ as the first Communist. Now Mueller, the new Hitlerian Protestant leader claims Christ as 'the first anti-Semite'. Lady Cunard very amusing about Curzon – most indiscreet of all ministers, came straight from Cabinet meeting, told everything in great detail, and never asked one not to tell.

Thursday, 10 August 1933

At four went out to Royal Northern Hospital to see Tommy who is being operated on tomorrow. Tommy was very brave, but I am more afraid for her mind than for her body. When I left and was downstairs in my taxi she came to the window and called out to say 'goodbye' to me. On the way home I passed an empty bier. Oh God! What life would be without her I cannot think. I pray she may be spared for many years.

Went to dine at Rembrandt with Leslie Howard,[2] a charming and rather shy young man not unliked the Prince of Wales. Wilke, the story buyer of Warner Bros, and Damon also there. Howard I liked very much. He has definite ideas which conform with my own how my part should be played. He means to have them carried out.

Wilke put up typical piece of American hustle. As a new form of publicity he wanted Howard and me to do a film. He 'buzzed' us off to Teddington where a whole 'set' was waiting for us. We were kept there till 11.30. In the end Howard and I did all the dialogue ourselves – most of it by me. We had no make-up – Howard, in any case, uses next to none – and therefore we had

[1] Emerald, Lady Cunard (1872–1948), widow of Sir Bache Cunard, society hostess, intimate friend of Sir Thomas Beecham and George Moore. Roger Fry (1866–1934), artist, art-critic and exponent of the post-impressionists.

[2] Film actor (1893–1943), who was to take the part of Lockhart in the film of *Memoirs of a British Agent*.

to have very powerful lamps. Heat was therefore terrific. Did quite well – so well, in fact, that one of the 'set' hands asked the producer 'who was the guy who was playing the author's part'.

Friday, 11 August 1933

Tommy operated on at 10.30 this morning. All went well. Lunched with Harry who was in terrific form, taking the waiter into his confidence one minute and cursing him the next, sending off telegraphs about the operation and arranging his bets with the telephone operator at the same time. It would have been comic to anyone who does not know the tragedy of Tommy's life. My own behaviour was no better. I joined in Harry's alcoholic celebrations, went from Quaglino's to the Wellington, played billiards there till dinner-time, drank more cocktails before dinner and went back . . . to dine downstairs at Quaglino's. . . Went to bed at twelve sick in mind and body and disgusted with myself.

Thursday, 17 August 1933

Lunched with Namier and discussed Germany or rather listened to him denounce Germany. He will not discuss it. He has recanted all his previous views and now thinks France was right from the first. He is the supreme exponent now of 'once a German always a German'. He thinks Germany will go to pieces, says all trade depends on a ten per cent margin, and that the Jews will be strong enough to deprive Germany of that. He carries his hate so far that, although he suffers badly from insomnia, and there are only two drugs which will help him – one, German and the more effective, and the other, French – he will not touch the German one.

Discussed a project for me to write a life of Beneš for Methuen. Namier thinks I should do this in order to establish a place for myself in the writing of modern biography when my autobiographical work is done. It would bring me in a steady income and would be an escape from Fleet Street. There is something in it, but I do not think I should attempt such a task without the security of a substantial advance.

Went to see Dame Adelaide Livingstone who wished to see me urgently. A gentleman had written to one of the members of the Lytton Commission[1] – presumably, Lord Lytton – a most violent letter and had signed it 'Bruce Lockhart'. Lord Lytton or the member in question had supposed it was me. . . No relation of mine.

Monday, 21 August 1933

Came up from Bexhill by the 9.13. Lunched with Randolph Churchill at the Savoy Grill. He had an article in yesterday's *Sunday Dispatch* saying that Elias, the proprietor of the *Daily Herald*, had been and, as far as he knew, still was a member of a Conservative association, lent his garden for Con-

[1] The League of Nations Commission into the Japanese invasion of Manchuria.

servative fêtes, etc.[1] Today, both *Mail* and *Herald* had a letter from Rothermere saying he had read these 'inaccuracies which he regretted and deplored'. When I arrived at the Savoy, Randolph had heard nothing about it. He was indignant because he had not been consulted. He tells me that his father, L.G., and Austen Chamberlain are concocting a combined letter to the B.B.C. protesting against the political broadcasts which, apparently, are to be confined to the *large* political parties. He also told me that Winston had been annoyed by the reference to him in my book: 'His conversation, like Mr Churchill's, was a monologue', would not read the book, and said, 'I never thought much of that fellow anyway'! Randolph says Winston never bears malice, however.

Wednesday, 23 August 1933

Randolph, who left yesterday for Cannes, told me a good story of Rothermere and Brendan. There was a supper-party at Esmond Harmsworth's. Some big piece of news came in late at night, and Esmond, at Rothermere's request, sent out for a *Daily Mail*. Man came back with one copy. Meanwhile, Brendan Bracken, who was also present, sent out for his *Financial News* and presently man returned with whole bundle and Brendan gave one to each guest, remarking, 'See what we can do – a copy for everyone while the *Mail* can produce only one.' 'Very simple for you, Bracken,' said Rothermere. 'Your man brought a whole edition!'

Friday, 25 August 1933

A bad day. Glorious weather. Went to lunch with Maisky[2] at Harrington House. Found Maisky quite nice. His book on Manchuria and Mongolia written in 1921 has been revised and is to come out in Moscow in two months. It deals with politics, history, economics. Told me he liked my book very much and that it reminded him of a Moscow which even he was almost forgetting. He used to edit *Zvezda* at one time. Russians are playing *Hamlet* – Hamlet as a cynic who is all out to regain his throne; fakes his father's ghost as a propaganda stunt to get supporters. Ophelia is a society girl, loves pleasure, hunting, parties. Bores Hamlet – interferes with his work. Ophelia rides on to stage. Foreign journalists, diplomatic corps – like it. Russians don't. 'It's not Shakespeare,' they say. Story of Stalin and young dramatist; who came to him for help. Couldn't get on.

'Do you work?' says Stalin.

'Yes.'

'How much?'

'Oh, I produce three plays on an average every year.'

[1] Julius Salter Elias (*d.* 1946), later Lord Southwood, had been a member of the Hornsey Conservative Association, contributed to Conservative funds and lent his garden for Conservative fêtes. But after he took over the Labour newspaper, the *Daily Herald*, he scrupulously kept out of politics.

[2] Ivan Maisky (*b.* 1884), Soviet Ambassador to Britain, 1932–43.

'My advice to you is: Go back and write one play in three years.' Met American correspondent Raymond Gram Swing. Says recognition of Russia will be decided by Roosevelt on purely business lines.

Saturday, 26 August 1933

Caught the 2.5 and went down to Ashridge, the Bonar Law College, to lecture to the students (both sexes and all ages) on Lenin. Met by General Hoskins[1] (very nice and broad-minded), Sutton, the Senior Tutor. As I had not prepared my lecture properly, I did not do very well. Dined there, had more drink. After dinner listened to Sir Charles Petrie[2] lecture on Mussolini. He is very pro – also very pro-monarchist. Mussolini's ancestry – family came of better stock – there was a Mussolini Square in a town in the Romagna. Called Benito after Benito Juarez, the Mexican leader [who] shot Maximilian. His novel, *Cardinal's Mistress*, written as a serial for Cesare Battiste in Trentino. Wrote a study of German philosophers. His lady love thought the names were name of girls and tore the manuscript up. Reads one-and-a-half hours every night. Good linguist: French, German, Spanish, English.

Wednesday, 30 August 1933

Lunched with Rex Leeper at Wellington Club. Litvinov, whom Rex saw during Conference, is writing his Memoirs. Rex very bitter on Simon who he says is most unpopular and incompetent Secretary of State in modern times. He is slow, indecisive and afraid. The other day Rex went to Sargent. 'Why don't you write a firm note to Mussolini about this?' 'Well, you see, Ronald Graham is afraid of Musso, and the Secretary of State is afraid of everyone, so what's the use.'

Thursday, 31 August 1933

A wasted day. Lunched at Wheeler-Bennett's. Present: Bartocszy, Villari, Neill Malcolm, Petrie, Vernon Bartlett, and young Hodson.[3] Petrie very critical of Beneš, whom he accuses of trying to make a Central Europe with Prague as capital. Petrie now says that Czechs will have to accept a Habsburg restoration as only means of keeping their own independence. Petrie is a violent monarchist.

Friday, 1 September 1933

Another wasted day. Gave luncheon to Kerensky at the Wellington. Discussed the various secret peace proposals during the war. Kerensky is

[1] Major-General Sir Reginald Hoskins (1871–1942) was Principal of Bonar Law College, 1929–38.

[2] 3rd Bart (*b.* 1895), right-wing journalist and historian.

[3] Vernon Bartlett (*b.* 1894), journalist and broadcaster, had been London Director of the League of Nations and was later an Independent M.P. Harry Hodson (*b.* 1905) became editor of the *Sunday Times* in 1950, and was later Provost of Ditchley.

convinced that had the Germans not known in advance and on that account made a deal with the Bolsheviks, Russia would have made peace with Turkey and Bulgaria in 1917 and Kerensky would still be in power. Kerensky swears that the negotiations were on the point of success. Kerensky also tells me that all the stories of his truculence towards the Emperor are untrue. He says the Empress said to him: 'What a pity we had not known men like you before!' and refers me to a Countess Hendrikova who was Lady-in-Waiting and who now lives at Kensington Palace.

Dined at home. Disturbed by Thost, the Nazi correspondent. After asking him to write an article in reply to the Brown Book on the 'Hitler Terror' we have now turned it down: this is Mike's doing, as Cudlipp had told Thost that he liked it. All very awkward for me, as Thost, who came to my house to see me, accused me of having a Jewish secretary and England of having Jewish watch-dogs in all important posts. Winston, e.g., was anti-German because of his connection with 'Berny' Baruch.[1] I was so bored that to get rid of him I went out to Club. Sat up late talking to Charles Murray, Dr Bruce, etc.

Saturday, 2 September 1933

My birthday – forty-six today and still feebler in character and self-control. Fleet Street is no place for me. With very few exceptions I loathe and despise everyone connected with it, and the exceptions are the failures. Most of the successful ones have trampled over their mother's or their best pal's dead body to lift themselves up. They are dead to decency. Felt rotten after last two days. It is amazing how even a little alcohol turns my stomach, makes me ill, and destroys my will-power.

Wednesday, 6 September 1933

Lunched with Moura. . . Moura tells me that this year Gorky is not coming to Italy but is going to the Crimea. . . Gorky also told Moura that at the opening of the White Sea Canal, Nekrassov, the former Kerensky Minister of Railways and an engineer, wept tears of emotion at the completion of so great an achievement by Russians! He was employed on the construction.

Dined at Montgelas's to meet Werner Krauss[2] and his wife. Krauss, who is said to be the greatest actor in the world, met his present wife four years ago during the performance of Shaw's *Apple-Cart.* (*Der Kaiser von Amerika.*) He played Magnus; she (Maria Bard) the mistress. Krauss who must now be over fifty, fell in love with her. His own wife was so unhappy that she committed suicide. Krauss then married Maria.

[1] Bernard Baruch (1870–1965), American financier, influential friend of Churchill.

[2] Werner Krauss (1884–1959), German actor and film star, was later prominent in Nazi propaganda films, such as *Jew Süss.*

Lockhart wrote to Maisky, the Russian ambassador on 6 September 1933:

I enclose herewith a cutting from the *Moscow Daily News* which may amuse Your Excellency.

I am used to being 'shot at' in the Press. It is the lot of most diplomats – and all journalists.

I do not mind my book being called 'notorious'. I accept the adjective with equanimity. But I am at a loss to understand the reference to 'vilifying the Soviets'?

Maisky replied, rather neatly, on 8 September 1933:

Just on the eve of my departure for holidays, I am writing to you in connection with your letter of September 6th to remind you that as a rule newspaper journalists in all countries do not actually read the books about which they are writing. This is what has happened to the writer in the *Moscow Daily News* to whom you refer in your letter. So don't worry about his comments on your book.

Thursday, 7 September 1933

Lord Grey [of Fallodon] died. Last week, when I dined with L.G. at Churt, I had a premonition that he would die on the same day as L.G.'s book [*War Memoirs*, vol. 1] came out. I told L.G. this at the time. Now it has happened. My article on L.G.'s book had to be transferred from page seven to page eleven.

Lunched with L.G. and Kerensky at the Metropole in the Chinese room. First time the two men had met for fifteen years (since 1918); first time they'd ever had an intimate conversation. Incidentally, I was Kerensky's interpreter in his first conversation with Sir George Buchanan. L.G. made very full notes. He was really pumping Kerensky for his book, the third volume of which comes out next June. Kerensky told him much: the three prophecies of Rasputin [to the Tsar]: (1) 'Don't declare war; if you declare war, it will be bad for you and Alexis'; (2) 'If I am killed, you will lose your throne in six months'; and (3) 'If I am killed, they will burn my body.' All these were correct. When Rasputin was killed, the murderers threw his body in the Neva. It was discovered, taken to Tsarskoe Selo and buried in a special mausoleum. A few days after the February revolution a crowd of revolutionaries went to Tsarskoe, dug up the body and burnt it. His influence was great; almost complete over the Empress, who used to telegraph to the Emperor at the front: 'Let me know the date of the attack at once; our friend must pray first'; or again 'Stop the offensive; harm will come; our friend does not approve.' Very interesting was Kerensky's revelation that on the night of February 26th (Russian Style) there was a meeting of the Left leaders in his flat at St Petersburg. They decided that it was ridiculous even to talk of revolution. The strongest opinion in this sense was expressed by the Bolshevik representative Yurenev – now Ambassador in Japan! Revolution broke out next morning (February 27, R.S.). Protopopofy had dissolved the Duma... Kerensky is of opinion that but for the Kornilov episode there would have been no Bolshevism and the war would have been over by December.[1] Brusilov described Kornilov as a man 'with the heart of a lion and the brains of a sheep'. Kerensky's government was on the verge of making separate peace with Bulgaria and Turkey. Austria was willing to enter into negotiations. Germany heard this and informed Bolshevists who, fearing that peace would cut ground under their feet, launched their revolution. Dined at Sports Club and sat up drinking till one a.m.

Monday, 11 September 1933

Lovely day. Wrote all morning and did 1800 words. Talked to Tommy in the afternoon, shot in the evening, and dined with Tommy at night. Discussed housing problems and made up my mind to look for a furnished house. Tommy tells me: (1) that Harry is going to read the lesson at the broadcast service from Rosslyn Chapel on September 21st; and (2) that she might be able to persuade Grannie Rosslyn to give me her papers. On one occasion Harry dug up the 'twenty barons of Roslin bold', who lie there in their armour. He did the job at dead of night, found the skeletons but no armour. An ancestor had been there before.

Tommy also told me good story of Nurse Cavell: she had sister (Mrs Wainwright, wife of the doctor, who lives at Henley-on-Thames) who is exactly like her. The two sisters were brought up together, trained as nurses at St Thomas's together, and were very great friends. It was to her sister at Henley that Nurse Cavell sent the men whom she assisted to escape. The Wainwrights had some means of communicating with her and tried to warn her. She paid no heed. A week after her execution [by the Germans in October 1915] a man turned up at the Wainwright's house and asked to see the doctor on private business. He was from an American film company. He wanted Mrs Wainwright as she was so like her sister, to play the part of Nurse Cavell in film which his company was about to do. Dr Wainwright kicked him out.

Tuesday, 12 September 1933

Lunched with Ivor Nicholson, who published L.G.'s book. He was with Hearst and also in Ministry of Munitions during war. Knows Beaverbrook and is intimate friend of the Berrys. Is going to suggest me as Editor of the *Sunday Times* to Camrose. Also wants me to write a book for him. Told me curious story about book he is to do by Goering [*Germany Reborn*]. Thing was arranged months ago through an Irishman... The Irishman hardly knew Goering; book was poor. Goering then decided to stop it on nominal grounds that Hitler did not like it. Nicholson had already spent £1400 or so

[1] General Kornilov (1870–1918) attempted to oust Kerensky in a military coup in September 1917, but failed.

on setting it up, insisted that Goering should refund and also give him a real book. He agreed at once, and his lawyer signed contract. The MS. is nearly ready. Strangely enough, Goering has adopted for form of book same style of question and answer as [Emil] Ludwig did with Mussolini! Went to [E.V.] Rieu of Methuen's afterwards and told him I could not do Beneš book. He tells me Nicholson paid £15,000 for L.G.'s book. Incidentally, L.G. was asked to send autograph copy to the King. He sent specially bound copy intended for himself with an inscription referring to King's part in the war.

Wednesday, 13 September 1933

Yesterday, Ivor Nicholson, who is a Welshman, gave me a very full account of L.G.'s life with Frances Stevenson. . . L.G., too, is as jealous of her as Punch. On Sunday Nicholson was motoring back to London. Frances was going. At about eleven Nicholson wanted to go. L.G. took Frances upstairs and kept her an hour. She came down flushed and nervous. She told Nicholson on way up how sorry she was, but L.G. was always the same: very jealous and ready to make a scene over any man! L.G. that night was very good on Gladstone, says he was far and away the most picturesque personality of his lifetime. He would make a first-rate life even today. Gladstone had been poorly done. Morley, who was a dull dog, would be remembered by the fact that he had killed Gladstone (the life).[1]

Lunched at Ritz with Lady Lavery, 'Bogey' Harris, Sibyl Colefax, and Sir Eric Phipps. Poor conversation. Lady Lavery drove me to office. Told me some Tim Healy stories: 'Eight hours work, eight hours play, eight hours in bed with Kitty O'Shea!'[2] Kitty was 'pure as snow' – 'I know that now,' says Tim – 'hoar-frost!' Also excellent story of Senator Gogarty who made a speech defending the trees on an island off Dublin which were to be cut down because they were a shelter for much immorality. Gogarty made a beautiful speech eulogising nature: then appealed to the Senators: 'Gentlemen, you cannot commit this vandalism. I can assure you these trees have been more sinned against than sinning!' The trees remained. Also story of, I think, Lady Cunard or Mrs Greville, who addressed John Drinkwater[3] as Mr Bayswater. He said: 'My name is not Bayswater.' 'I'm so sorry, Mr Bathwater.'

In evening went to Ballet (Russian) with Maurice [Peterson]. Saw *Les Sylphides* (Chopin), *Les Presages* (modern) Tchaikovsky and *Le Beau Danube* (Strauss). Danilova in a class by herself. Krabushinska not dancing.

Supped at Savoy. Maurice told me he was only extra man for Diplomatic; doubtful if he would get in; had only till January 1st of same year to get vacancy. His father pulled every string including Morley[4] who sent for Maurice. Maurice had lost marks, which would have put him on top, for

[1] Lord Morley's life of Gladstone was a vast four-volume work published in 1903.

[2] Parnell's mistress and cause of his political downfall.

[3] (1882–1937) poet and dramatist, not a man to appreciate a mistake of this kind.

[4] Lord Morley (1838–1923) was Lord President of the Council and Grey Foreign Secretary in the Liberal Government when Peterson joined the Foreign Office.

bad handwriting. Morley said: 'What is this, young man? I understand you lost marks for handwriting.' Maurice explained that he had had to write fast and had had to strike out many words. Morley replied: 'You know what Palmerston said about people who erased what they wrote: it showed grave defects of character.' He then wrote a very nice letter to Grey, which did the trick.

Thursday, 28 September 1933

Lunched with Brendan Bracken at his house in [Lord] North Street. He did it up himself and has made it very nice. His study is panelled with inset bookshelves and some fine books including Shakespeare and Casanova. He has a fine Burke by Romney over the fireplace. Brendan is an Irishman himself and I assume takes Burke as his Parliamentary model. We discussed newspapers. Brendan thinks that Max will be the last of his tribe and that the reign of the great Press Lords is coming to an end. He told me that Rothermere does not like Max, but is afraid of him, and that Esmond positively hates him.

Sunday, 1 October 1933

Meanwhile, Harry, who is broke again, is going about with a face as long as death and is making every kind of difficulty about Tommy's going abroad. He is, I suppose, the most selfish man in the world in his actions; yet just because it is entirely unconscious it is perhaps less reprehensible than my own selfishness. . .

Did the round with Tommy after luncheon and in the evening did crosswords. Tommy has had an offer for the house and will probably take it. This fills me with dread, not because it will deprive me of a pleasant weekend haunt, but because Tommy is doing it for Harry's sake, and Harry will drink himself to death more quickly in London than anywhere else, will spend more money, and leave Tommy worse off.

Tuesday, 3 October 1933

Very busy day. Lunched with Moir Mackenzie, who told me that Walter Citrine, who is a great friend of his, is very anxious about the Fascist movement in England. He (Moir) has an immense opinion of the power of Lord Weir who he says was responsible for the change over of Gilmour to the Home Office and Walter Elliot to the Board of Agriculture.[1] Also great admirer of Horace Wilson who is self-made man. Made his career when he was with Lord Askwith[2] at Ministry of Labour. Strikes were always settled Askwith acquired great reputation. Wilson went. Next two strikes went

[1] 1st Viscount Weir (1877–1959), industrialist, had been Air Minister in 1918, and with Mackenzie as Industrial Adviser at the Imperial Conference at Ottawa in 1932. Sir John Gilmour (1876–1940) had left the Ministry of Agriculture in 1932 to become Home Secretary and Walter Elliot (1888–1958) had taken his place.

[2] 1st Baron Askwith (1861–1942), frequent conciliator in industrial disputes.

wrong. L.G. very upset. Q. 'What's wrong with Askwith?' A. 'Nothing, but he's changed his staff.' 'Ah,' said L.G. This was foundation of Wilson's rise. He is an absolutely gold brain.

Dined with Jean at Max's; present: Sibell Lygon, Miss Dawes (a Canadian), Mrs Smith (an American – very in love with Esmond Harmsworth), Esmond, Brendan and self. Brendan very bumptious at dinner. Discussed cartoonists. Max said: 'Strube is the highest paid man in the cartoon line – and he knows Tom Webster gets £10,000.' Low does not get as much, but, as Esmond said, he gets enough to keep him from the *Daily Herald*! I said that Low had a wider world influence than any cartoonist has ever had. Max agreed. Max told – almost with tears in his eyes – story of Christiansen, to whom *Herald* offered £3000. He came to Max and asked if he still wanted him. Max said: 'Of course.' Christiansen: 'All right, I'll stay.' Max then telephoned office to raise his salary to £3000. Christiansen sent money back. Max thinks it's 'too, too wonderful'. In two years' time Christiansen will be drawing £5000! Had long talk with Esmond, who prophesies that in five years' time Tom Mosley and the Fascist Party will be a power in the land.

Wednesday, 4 October 1933

Lunched with Harold at the Jardin des Gourmets. He will probably come back to the *Standard*. The position is at present that he has asked until November 1st to consider his decision. He wants to sell Long Barn. If he can get a good price, he will sell and then nothing will induce him to come to Fleet Street. If not, he will have to take the job for bread and butter. At present Mike's idea (as explained to me!) is that Harold will be the sub-editor and co-ordinator of the Diary and that I will be the 'Londoner'. Harold says Mike has given him a free hand to do what he likes and that I shall be the 'Londoner'. I expect Harold's version is right.

In the upshot, Nicholson did not return to the Evening Standard *and explained why in a letter to Lockhart from Sissinghurst Castle on 31 October 1933:*

I have written to Mike telling him that I cannot accept his offer. The more I came to think of it the more I realised that after having tasted the joys of freedom I could not possibly contemplate going back to an office.

I have not got the taste for journalism and nor do I really enjoy working for the Diary.

When Mike first made the offer to me I was deeply worried by our financial position and felt that I would have to accept. Shortly after my conversation with him we had an offer to buy my house at Sevenoaks and although this offer came to nothing, and although our recent auction of the adjoining farm was not successful, yet the ensuing delay convinced me that it would really not be possible for me to return to Fleet Street. At the same time we found that we had made more money in America than we imagined and that we could collect enough money from various sources to carry us on for at least another year. By the end of that year anything may happen.

I do hope that Mike won't feel aggrieved at my having given him hope that I would accept the proposal and then chucking it at the last moment. I know, however, that I should have entered upon the work with so little enthusiasm that I would not really have been of any value.

Sunday, 8 October 1933

Harry and Tommy's silver-wedding day. What a tragedy! All her own private money (some £12,000) gone – given to Harry. Such a succession of financial crashes that even now, when Harry's claws have been clipped by his Trustees, Hunger Hill will have to be sold and Tommy will have to go back to a nomadic existence or to a flat in London, both of which she hates. . . What a comment on self-sacrifice, duty, etc. Certainly, Tommy has kept her home together, but at a price which was excessive. Harry would be better dead, and without her he would have killed himself years ago. Now, when he does die, Tommy will have literally nothing to live on. She will need her reward in the next world.

Tuesday, 10 October 1933

Arrived at Paris and went to the Continental where we found Millie in a state of great excitement. She was closeted with Douglas Fairbanks and his secretary Tom Geraghty. Douglas Fairbanks had fled for refuge to the Continental. He had read a paragraph in the Paris *Daily Mail* saying that Mary was about to divorce him.[1] As he . . . is terrified that, if he is made a free man, —— will catch him, he fled to Millie . . . who advised him to go to Spain. She first suggested his coming with us to Montreux but he said it was *too* near! He gave us dinner before he left. He looks like a dago and is, I believe, an East End Jew from New York, but he has charm and personality and talks well. He told us how he practised bull-fighting for a film; practised first on a mechanical bull; then on two-year-old bulls. Got some up from Mexico including one or two four-year-olds. One day at rehearsal wanted to show off his prowess as a banderillo. Everyone watching. Lost his nerve. Threw the darts anyhow and bolted. First and last time he has tried with darts. Can manage cape quite well.

Thursday, 12 October 1933

Millie was very amusing at dinner and told us some of her experiences. When she was thirteen, she fell in love with Sir Walter Gilbey, who was then Master of the Essex. He treated her as a child. Millie then went and stole every handkerchief she could and shoved them into her bosom to give her a fine pair of breasts! She knew Lord Rosebery, who was in love with her,

[1] Douglas Fairbanks senior (1885–1939), married Mary Pickford (*b.* 1893) in 1920. They were not divorced till 1935.

very well. She gives him a very bad character: cruel and weak and inordinately vain. He married Hannah Rothschild, whom he treated abominably. She adored him and grovelled before him. Rosebery gambled all his fortune away on turf. Lord Durham or some old boy told him that his only salvation was to marry Hannah Rothschild. Rosebery said nothing would induce him. Within a week he had further losses at Newmarket and was engaged![1]

Tuesday, 31 October 1933

Today, I lunched with Raymond Swing of the [*Washington*] *Post* and Viola Ilma, the founder of 'Modern Youth' and the leader of the youth movement in the U.S.A. Her grandfather was a Swiss Quaker missionary, who went to Abyssinia and married into Abyssinian Royal family. She has an aunt in London called Princess Asfa Y-Ilma. Her grandfather had twelve children. Her father was the youngest, went to America, and married an American. Viola Ilma is twenty-three and pretty. Began with $12 last February: has now 200,000 supporters, and is going back after seeing youth in Germany (and Hitler) to float her show as a company and organise her movement on self-supporting lines like the Nazi Gauleiters. Hopes to start a world movement and plans a world conference in Geneva next year. Her supporters come mainly from points west of Chicago. She has a hundred $15-a-month supporters: they include Professor Warren (Roosevelt's currency man), Tom Lamont, Freddy Warburg, etc.; has support of most millionaire's sons nearly all of whom are Radicals. Has no contributor over thirty or any one on staff. Turned down contribution from many people on this score including Mencken. Made her first speech at Chicago International Congress of Women this summer – 3000 people, Jane Addams in chair.[2] Shook them so much they sent her on tour to Europe! When she started, wrote to Mrs Hoover long letter setting out aims. Got no reply. When Roosevelt came in, said to her typist: 'Bring up the Mrs Hoover letter. Change Hoover to Roosevelt and Republican for Democrat and buzz it off to Mrs Roosevelt. Next day wire from White House to come to see President and Mrs Roosevelt.

Monday, 13 November 1933

At two-thirty went on with Church to 133 Long Acre to see a private demonstration of television by the British Television Co. The general manager of the General Electric, Railing was there. I met also Baird, the television inventor.[3] He is a queer, fair-haired, lumpy, untidy man with a strong Scottish accent. We were put into a small room and faced with a small aperture about the size of a small biscuit tin. A magnifying lens was

[1] 5th Earl of Rosebery (1847–1929), married Hannah, daughter of Baron Meyer de Rothschild, in 1878. He became Prime Minister, 1894–5.

[2] (1860–1935) pacifist, worker for women's rights, Nobel peace prize winner.

[3] John Logie Baird (1888–1946). His system of television had been taken up by the B.B.C. but did not lead to that now in use.

placed before it and here we saw the television film: scenes from *I Was a Spy* and Mickey Mouse. The entertainment is almost good enough for the public now. Inside a year the public will be buying their radio sets complete with television and will put on their radio film in the same way as they tune in. I shall (or should, if I had any) go a bear on cinema theatre shares. England, Germany and America are racing for the supremacy. We are ahead on development at present, but when the thing becomes perfected the Germans and Americans will pour money into it, and we'll lag behind.

Wednesday, 15 November 1933

Last night Michael Arlen discussed books and authors with me. Said he could not work in London. Made up his mind as young man to earn enough by thirty-five to be independent. Worked very hard as young man – always by day, up most of the night. Got t.b. Wrote *The Green Hat* at Southport, where his mother lives. Made stacks of money; took everything; did everything: plays, articles, etc. Now lives in South of France, dictates from nine to twelve, corrects in afternoon from five to seven. Told me not to be bluffed into writing too many books. He does one in two years. His contemporaries like Compton Mackenzie, Stephen McKenna, Gilbert Frankau all have been ruined by turning out too many books. 'Keep your money,' he said. 'Before the war W. J. Locke[1] must have had £250,000. His wife spent it all. He had to go on writing after he had written himself out: killed himself with brandy.'

Monday, 20 November 1933

At luncheon today sat between Sibyl Colefax and Daphne Weymouth. Daphne Weymouth told me a good story of Lord Lloyd who as High Commissioner in Egypt had a private secretary called Dodd Franklin(?). Lloyd, who maintained a viceregal pomp, kept himself quite aloof from his staff. One day he sent for Dodd Franklin and asked him to order his car. Dodd Franklin rushed down the stairs, and, as he passed, one of his secretaries asked him where he was going. 'God wants his chariot!' shouted Dodd Franklin. Lloyd heard him through the open window, was furious, and sent him home. In Wall Street they call Hitler the 'North German Lloyd'.

Sibyl Colefax talked about Simon who she says is unpopular even at the Bar, because he took briefs even when he could not attend to them. She says that for a long time Simon was devoted to Mrs Ronnie Greville and that everyone thought he would marry her. Simon did not marry because he was afraid she might spoil his chances of becoming Prime Minister. He married his first wife's nurse, but is still a good friend of Mrs Ronnie Greville. Talked to Sir Ronald [Graham] who says that Mussolini was very angry at Germany going out of the League without telling him and refused to see German Ambassador.

[1] (1863–1930) Secretary to the R.I.B.A. and author of such best-sellers as *The Beloved Vagabond* (1906).

Wednesday, 22 November 1933

Jan was very funny on Ramsay whom he knows well. At Geneva Ramsay used to go into Lady Londonderry's bedroom every night and talk to her from 11.30 till 2. Beneš and Jan knew, because their detective made a note of the times and of Ramsay's costume. Visits, of course, quite innocent: Ramsay calls her his fairy godmother. In any case she has —— for her physical needs. Jan is great friends with all of them. But it is the most curious triangle in the world. —— is the poodle dog who fetches and carries. Lady Londonderry gets tight. Ramsay loses his head.

Ramsay, who is a little ashamed of his treatment of Jowitt, asked him to dine recently. Jowitt accepted. He came to fetch him and they walked off together. 'Where are we going?' said Jowitt. Ramsay said: 'Londonderry House.' Jowitt refused to go.

Thursday, 23 November 1933

In the evening went to the Canada Expeditionary Force dinner at the Connaught Rooms. Record attendance: 500. President: Sir Henry Burstall (known as Sir 'Premature' Burstall because of bad English shells in first attack), Prince Arthur of Connaught, who is member of C.E.F., always buys his ticket, and pays his drinks, Montgomery-Massingberd, brother of Hubert Montgomery and more like a diplomat than a soldier, Jack Seely masquerading as Lord Mottistone and playing Napoleon with his right hand tucked crosswise in his wasitcoat, a very emotional padre called Wells who was a Lance-Corporal in the 72 Battalion, and Winston, who spoke magnificently against the surrender men after being introduced as a man of 'guts' by Hamilton Gault, who raised Princess Pat's.[1] I spoke to Winston and congratulated him on best speech he had made for long time. He said that it was hard work for him now speaking in the House. In the old days he always had a majority or a strong minority to shout, 'Hear, hear', etc. Now he was alone. Tonight he certainly had the men with him, and they are a difficult audience.

Tuesday, 26 December 1933

Last night: dinner was a gluttonous and boring show with about seven courses. Present: Castlerosse, H. G. Wells, Gerhardi, Murphy, Joe Coyne, Brendan Bracken, Frank Owen, Aneurin Bevan, Mike Wardell and half-a-dozen Canadian and American women of whom I knew only Miss Dawes.

[1] Lieut.-General Sir Henry Burstall (1870–1945), Canadian Artillery Commander; Prince Arthur of Connaught (1883–1938), grandson of Queen Victoria, G.S.O. to the Canadian Corps, 1817–18; General Sir Archibald Montgomery-Massingberd (1817–1947), C.I.G.S.; his brother Hubert (1876–1942), British Minister at The Hague; Major-General John Seely (1868–1947), Deputy Minister of Munitions, 1918, had only been ennobled as Lord Mottistone the previous June; probably Rev. George A. Wells (1877–1964), shortly to become Bishop of Cariboo, and in the Second World War Protestant Chaplain-General to the Canadian Forces; Brigadier A. Hamilton Gault (1882–1958) raised Princess Patricia's Canadian Light Infantry in the Great War and was then a Conservative M.P.

Sat next Aneurin Bevan and a Scottish lady novelist whose name I never learnt. Discussed Maxton – agreed that he would never do anything in England. I said he was a Christ-like Gandhi-like figure. Bevan said he [Maxton] would rather shed his own blood than the blood of his opponents – a martyr-figure who was always wounding himself. The most popular man in House of Commons could not be considered seriously as revolutionary leader. Cursed London as stagnation hole and ruin of young men. Bevan says he is pulling out this year. He knows that it is his ruin. It is ruining him very quickly.

Friday, 29 December 1933

Lunched with Randolph Churchill at Brooks's Club and was amused. Randolph, who drank a large sherry, a pint of beer, and four large glasses of port, was in great form and gave me some amusing hints on the States. He says that Scots are popular in the States because Americans have an inferiority complex with regard to Englishmen which they do not feel in the presence of Scots. There is something in this. Also gave me full account of his father's methods as a writer and of his life generally. Randolph adores his father; does not get on very well with his mother. Told me story of his grandfather Lord Randolph and Lady Astor. Lady Astor saw Randolph smoking when he was seventeen, pulled him out, and asked him if he was not ashamed. Randolph replied that he often smoked cigars. Whereon Lady Astor replied that if he did not take care he would die like his grandfather of debauchery. Randolph was hurt and said nothing. Later, Lady Astor repeated the story in public. Randolph was told and wrote a dignified letter demanding an apology saying that if he were to tell his father he would be very indignant. Lady Astor crawled. Randolph of course had told his father already. Winston had laughed.

CHAPTER ELEVEN

1934

Tour of U.S.A. Lippmann, German-Jewish internationalist. Lindemann, Oxford's best physicist. King Edward and Mrs Keppel. Peter Fleming's activity. Scottish Nationalists and Neil Gunn. Rats at the opera. Prince of Wales at Hammam Turkish baths. MacNeill Weir on Ramsay MacDonald. Beaverbrook on his visit to Stalin. Aldous Huxley's 'wax-like complexion'. Mosley and his adherents. Empire Crusaders. Prince Friedrich of Prussia. Film of his *British Agent*. Sir Thomas Beecham 'fierce hater of politicians'. Bracken in love with Penelope Dudley Ward. Lloyd George's vitality failing. Mrs Ronnie Greville enthusiast for Hitler. Prince George very in love with Princess Marina. Rothermere on what Hitler has done for Germany.

Thursday, 4 January 1934

Much warmer and almost too mild. Lunched with Ted Parsons at the Savoy; present: Lord Lurgan, General Swinton, Sir Albert Stern, Commander Burney,[1] and Mackarness. Swinton is a fine old boy. Tells me that there is a book coming out on Britain's neglect of the air which will make a stir. It is by Groves of the Air League. Swinton has written a preface. Swinton, who is 'Ole Luk-Oie' and was 'Eye-Witness' in the war, is now a don at Oxford. He worked for three years preparing L.G.'s memoirs. L.G. paid him, used very little of the MS, and never even sent Swinton a copy of his book. Swinton says the book is not worthy of the man. Although he thinks L.G. ungrateful, he says he was a very great man. He begged him to confess himself wrong in one or two places – even if he wasn't. L.G. did not take his advice. Swinton was once paid £25 for two words. In 1913(?) an American comedian called Frank Tinley came over, and *Daily Express* offered £25 to best two-word title to describe him. Swinton won with 'The Fun-beam'. Bought a Turkey carpet, gave a luncheon, and lent his £25 to a brother officer plus a quid which he never saw again! Burney rather interesting – thinks whole world will go for planned economy.

In evening saw Bernstorff who is over here. Very bitter against Neurath[2]

[1] 3rd Baron Lurgan (1858–1937), Chairman of Carlton and Ritz Hotels; Lieut.-Colonel Sir Albert Stern (1878–1966), banker and munitions expert, Chairman of the Tank Committee, 1916. Commander Sir Dennistoun Burney, Bart (1888–1968), inventor of the paravane, airship designer, ex-Conservative M.P.

[2] Baron Konstantin von Neurath (1873–1956) had been German Ambassador to London in 1930, became Foreign Minister, 1932–8, and then Nazi 'protector' of Czech territories.

who he says did him in more than Nazis. Neurath took his own son into diplomatic service through back door and has made his son-in-law Mackenzie Minister in Budapest. Bernstorff talks of going into bank here. Dined at home and worked on lectures.

Friday, 12 January 1934

Lunched as guest of American Press Association at Savoy. Luncheon to Elisabeth Bergner.[1] Negley Farson in chair. He was quite good. C. B. Cochran spoke for Bergner who said only one sentence of thanks. Cochran – poor, too much publicity and no personality. Sat next to Gollancz, who tells me that in three or four years he will go into politics (Labour) but will not abandon publishing. He reads detective novels when he is on holiday and won't look at a manuscript. Likes Francis Beeding, who he tells me is really Hilary St George Saunders in collaboration with Geoffrey(?) Palmer.[2] We discussed Sherlock Holmes, and Gollancz said that Sherlock Holmes was still very popular with the young. Mrs Farson said: 'Would you put him among the world's half-dozen best-known characters in fiction?' Gollancz hesitated and said: 'Yes, I'd put him first. Indeed, I'd find it hard to think of five others.' I mentioned Pickwick, Crusoe, Don Quixote. But it would not be an easy list.

Monday, 15 January 1934

Heard from Germany at last after nearly a month's waiting that Hitler is still away and that there is no chance of an appointment this week. So that is that. Miss Schapiro thinks that everything was arranged for last week but that the Nazis did not want me in Berlin then, because of the Van der Lubbe execution.[3]

Lord Rothermere today came out in open support of Tom Mosley and in favour of British Fascism both in the *Mail* and in the *News*. Roosevelt announces his dollar revaluation scheme. As far as I can see, it will not affect the present exchange value of the dollar very much.

Tuesday, 16 January 1934

Lunched with Tolokonsky[4] at Simpson's. He is leaving London. His Foreign Office wants him to go to Washington. He wants to work in Russia. He says no one in Russia wants to live abroad (the times are too exciting and too interesting), and those who do want to live abroad permanently are no use to the Bolsheviks and are therefore not the men to send. Tolokonsky,

[1] Austrian film actress (*b.* 1900), whose greatest successes were in Britain.

[2] Saunders (1898–1951) was at this time on the secretariat of the League of Nations, later he wrote the official account of the Battle of Britain. The 'Francis Beeding' detective novels include *The Six Proud Walkers, Death Walks in Eastrepps*. His collaborator was John Palmer.

[3] Marinus van der Lubbe had burned down the debating chamber of the Reichstag on 27 February 1933, just before the elections; he was executed for the crime on 10 January 1934.

[4] 1st Secretary at the Soviet Embassy.

who was Commissar to the Vth Army in 1918 and took part in the Red Army's triumphant campaign from the Urals to Vladivostok, thinks war in Far East is almost certain. Says much depends on attitude of this country. Will we finance Japan? Japanese victory would not help England. Chief danger is belief in this and other countries that Russia will be easily defeated. Russians today are much stronger in Far East. Japan has – from her own point of view – waited too long. Sokolnikov, former Ambassador here, is now in charge of Far Eastern Affairs.

Tolokonsky also told me that the Bolsheviks have been paid the full £100,000 for the Codex Sinaiticus. He tells me the £10,000 which the public have to subscribe was put up by someone who figured in last honours list.

Wednesday, 17 January 1934

Lunched with Lady Colefax. . . Sat next an old Colefax who is very keen on fishing. He tells me that Stafford Cripps[1] was in his chambers. He is not an ambitious careerist, but really believes all he says. He has money and will have more – his wife's mother is an Eno of Fruit Salt fame!

Thursday, 18 January 1934

Gave luncheon to Harold at Boulestin's. Discussed my lecture tour in the States. Harold and Vita made £3000 and spent £1000. The latter, however, was high, because when the tour was over they took a holiday in the West at their own expense. They had, too, an exchange rate of under $4. On this basis Harold netted about £1500 in three months and spent £500 – net profit £1000. I shall therefore be lucky if I clear £300 net. Harold says I must speak a full hour. Otherwise they will think that they are not getting their money!

In the evening dined at the German Embassy to meet Herr Mejer, the head of the new Deutsches Nachrichts-Bureau. Only men present. Sat next Wassner, the Naval Attaché, and Scherpenberg [Second Secretary]. Wassner told me he was in submarines from 1915 to 1918. In his flotilla there were in this period 94 submarines. At end there were only eleven. He was only officer in this flotilla who remained from first to last. His opinion was Germans shilly-shallied with submarine policy – only half-measures. Result was that England was given time to find counter-measures.

Saturday, 20 January 1934

Still feeling very seedy. Violent quarrel with Jean during which I lost all self-control and behaved like a cad. . . She has a social complex, is interested only in people, and is obsessed with the idea that I have a great social life from which I wilfully exclude her! Ye Gods! Still, there is no reason and,

[1] Cripps (1889–1952) had made a fortune as a patent lawyer. He had been Solicitor-General, 1930–1; and was to be a wartime Ambassador to Russia, and post-war Chancellor of the Exchequer and apostle of austerity.

certainly, no good purpose in my losing my self-control... I gave up my Christmas holiday – my only holiday in the year – to go to Pettings.[1] Because we didn't go away on the Saturday I was caught by Beaverbrook, had to dine with him on the Christmas Day, and spent Boxing Day alone by myself. I have hardly been away since. I slave all week and all night. Yet they both grudged me my week-end, represent themselves to my relations as martyrs, and make me out a spendthrift who deprives them of their just income. The facts are: (1) I pay the rent – nearly £400; (2) I pay all the house books – approximately £750; (3) I pay Robin's outfit and nearly half his fees – £160; (4) my insurance policies and income-tax amount to £100; (5) I pay my secretary £200; and (5) I give Jean an allowance of £400 – in all, leaving me £100 for my own expenses! It means ruin in two or three years.

Sunday, 21 January 1934

Very cold with white frost but brilliant sunshine. Worked all morning on my lecture. The Quentin Gilbeys came to luncheon. He, like George Gilbey, is a racing journalist and makes about £2000 a year. He is one of the Gilbeys, the wine-merchants. It is a family business; the shares are privately held and not quoted; and it has paid 20 to 25 per cent regularly even in the slump. It is admirably organised and depends for its success, not on big hotels, clubs, etc., but on the family grocer. When the off-licence first came in, Gilbeys had previous knowledge and immediately organised agencies with the grocers all over England.[2] That is basis of their business today. Only eldest son is allowed to go into business to prevent it being swamped by family connections. The big business – strangely enough – is not in port and cheap clarets but in spirits – whisky (Spey Royal) and gin.

Monday, 22 January 1934

At five went to see Maisky and had two hours' talk with him. I asked him about my return to Russia. He said that, as there had been a legal decision in my case, the matter would not be quite so simple, as some form of amnesty would be required. He was, however, quite sure that everything could be arranged and was very flattering, etc. He gave me interesting account of Stalin, who, he said, had now established very nearly the same mental superiority over his colleagues as Lenin once enjoyed. In the autumn Maisky made a tour of the kolkhozi [collective farms], admitted frankly that in 1932 there had been great difficulties, and said that situation had been saved by Stalin with his ... motor-tractor centres manned by Communists in the kolkhozi districts. Very worried about situation in Far East,[3] but says Russia is strong, is putting up strategic railways, has munitions factories, etc., in the

[1] Frank Aveling's family home.

[2] In 1860 the Wine and Refreshment Houses Act introduced 'grocers' licences' which were extended to cover spirits in 1861.

[3] Where Russia was threatened by the Japanese invasion of China.

Far East and has extended the double line on the Siberian. He says Russia wants peace for her internal development. She says: 'Leave us alone.'

Tuesday, 23 January 1934

At dinner last night Rex and Connor Green talked volubly on Russian–Japanese situation. Connor Green, who had been in Siberia with the Whites, at our Legation in Peking, and at the Embassy in Tokyo, is convinced that the Japs will fight – not now, because their strategic railways are not ready, but in two years' time. They want to knock Russia before she is too strong and thus gain fifty years respite...

Finished up at office today and said goodbye. [Lockhart was going on his American lecture-tour]. Asked Mike if I could write articles in America. He said I'd better not write on Russia, as my views conflicted with paper's views, and I must remember that Americans will look on me as 'The Londoner' – writer of most famous column in journalism, etc. Mike really seems to believe this – that my journalism has given me a name, etc. The Yanks know me through Russia and through my book. I don't suppose one in a million even knows I am a journalist! Lunched with Moura. In afternoon was to have seen Tom Mosley and went to Fascist headquarters to do so. His phlebitis, however, was so bad that he had had to lie up again. Dined with Tommy at Boulestin's.

Thursday, 25 January 1934

[On the way to United States.] Rather a wasted day. Ate and drank too much. In the morning worked on my lecture and walked. Talked to Raymond Massey, the actor.[1] He is a relation of Massey Harris, the big agricultural implements people, who before the war did a big business in Russia. Massey Harris sold out at very good profit before slump. Young Massey is now spending the money on the theatre. He is opening in Toronto in Keith Winter's new play with Gladys Cooper. Brings it to New York on February 15. Raymond was in Russia with Knox and came out of Siberia just before Kolchak was killed. He did not think much of the Whites...

Met [Jonathan] Cape, who told us a long story about Mary Webb's *Precious Bane*. Hutchinson's had two previous books of Mary Webb's and had right to *Precious Bane* for advance of £300. Mary Webb always wanted money. Hutchinson's would not give it and cancelled it. Cape took it – gave £100 advance – bought the other Webbs from Hutchinson. He sent *Precious Bane* to Tom Jones who gave it to Baldwin. Baldwin 'boosted' it at Literary Fund dinner.[2]

[1] Massey (*b.* 1896), Canadian actor; his brother Vincent became Governor-General. Winter's play, *The Shining Hour*, was an enormous success.

[2] For the full story see *Jonathan Cape, Publisher* by Michael S. Howard (1971). Mary Webb died before Baldwin gave the boost that made the book a best-seller, and Cape did not acquire the other books until afterwards.

Saturday, 27 January 1934

After working hard on my lectures all morning, I received an invitation to take a cocktail with the captain before luncheon. He had Cape, the publisher and an unpleasant man, and Jeffrey Farnol[1] with him. Farnol is 55, has been writing for years, was for some time in New York, and knew O. Henry, Bob Davis, etc. He lives at Brighton and is an idealist and an internationalist. When he sold *The Broad Highway* to Sampson Low, he signed a contract agreeing to give them first refusal of everything he wrote. He forgot – omitted to have a clause retaining film rights for himself, and publishers paid him nothing for film rights. He is now tied to them – more or less for life, I suppose, but is free as far as America is concerned. He is on lecture racket like me.

Sunday, 4 February 1934

Rose at ten-fifteen and went out by car to Tom Lamont's [the banker] place at the Palisades quite close to the Rockefeller estate. There are detectives about. All the Morgan partners are guarded. Went out with Miss Duffield, a niece of Lamont's, who works in Saks store. Lovely place – magnificent view over Hudson – few houses round about like Russian *dachas*. Deepish snow; boys tobogganning. Family party. Mr and Mrs Lamont, Tom junior and his wife with two boys, C. Lamont and his wife Margaret. There is a third son, Austen, who is studying to be a research doctor. Tom junior is in business. . . Also present Mrs van Heusen – a Scottish woman who married an American two years ago. She tells me that both Tom Lamont and his son C. thought there was too much of the book in my Harvard lecture. Went for a walk before luncheon and saw Tom Lamont's swimming pool of which he is very proud and which he uses for exercise in winter: very nice with comfortable verandah, diving board and at back a jiggle board – kind of pole-seat slung on rolling trestles on which Negro 'nannies' used to sit and rock their babies. It has a back and forwards and sideways movement which is grand for liver. Mrs Lamont's wisecrack: '*Every* New York woman is a Sibyl Colefax.' Harold and his wife did not go down *at all* over here. Mrs van Heusen told me that the Lamonts could not stand her.

Sunday, 18 February 1934

At four went round to the Zentays (he is a Hungarian doctor; she has something to do with books) where I met about ten of the highbrows of St Louis, including the well-known Dr Lippmann, a German-Jewish doctor who matriculated at Freiburg. Dr Lippmann, who is an internationalist and a thinker, believes that the U.S.A. is going Fascist, that Roosevelt may be impeached within a year (especially if he yields to the sound money men and cuts short the T.V.A.[2] funds) and that Fascism will be the inevitable prelude

[1] (1878–1952), romantic novelist. *The Broad Highway* (1910) was his first great success.

[2] The Tennessee Valley Authority, a scheme to conserve eroded land and aid the unemployed.

to Communism or state capitalism. He would like to think that Roosevelt could decide, but does not think it possible. He says that until 1929 politics in the U.S.A. were purely childish: an affair of parties, corruption and flap-doodle. Now the native has developed or is developing a social conscience. But the capitalists will not see the red light. They will destroy themselves, because, whereas a man will give up honour, home, wife, parents, children, etc., he will never voluntarily sacrifice money.

Back in England, Lockhart re-started his social round:

Monday, 26 March 1934

Lunched with Randolph at the Savoy Grill. Met Vivian Jackson and Diana Guinness.[1] Vivian Jackson is pro big-business men mainly because they supply the funds and the equipment for research work! Diana Guinness, as the friend and inamorata of Tom Mosley, is for dictators. Professor Lindemann, a tall rather shy man with small moustache, small eyes, and grey hair with baldness on top, was also at luncheon. He is Oxford's best physicist and is a fine thinker. In economics he will have none of the new catchwords, does not believe that there is any fundamental change in production, but holds that things like the dole, legislation, etc., have interfered with the natural migration of labour and with the keeping on of industries which are uneconomic. He was not very convincing on this. He has been in America and has a poor view of American university education. Equipment is good, but in a country where money means much they do not pay their professors.

Wednesday, 4 April 1934

A wet and unpleasant day. Gave luncheon to Anthony Winn and Bill Aitken at Boulestin's. Conversation was rather dull. Bill Aitken talked most of the time. He is a very nice fellow, has ideas, but is inarticulate and unable to express them and has a rather woolly mind. Anthony Winn told a good story about the King and Queen. The Queen was walking in Buckingham Palace gardens and, noticing that her chief detective had been away for two days, asked what was wrong with him. The man had piles, and ——, who was walking with the Queen, stammered a bit and replied that he was suffering from an unfortunate disease. A day or two later the King was walking in the garden with another equerry. The detective was still absent, and the King asked: 'What on earth are we going to do about the detective?' The equerry replied: 'Oh, sir. He'll be back in a day or two. He's only got a bad attack of piles.' 'Oh!' said the King, 'is that all? That fool, ——, told my wife that he had syphilis.'

Sunday, 8 April 1934

On arrival found Robin's report from Dartmouth [he was a naval cadet].

[1] Diana Guinness, *née* Mitford, was the wife of Bryan Guinness (later Lord Moyne); divorced 1934; married Mosley (whose first wife had died in 1933) in 1936.

It is not very good... But then – it is the same type of report as I always was given myself. What is bad in the boy's case is the complete absence of any kind of intellectual conversation in his own home. Here the talk is always about the theatre or the cinema or social gossip. What chance or hope is there for a boy in such an atmosphere?

Sunday, 22 April 1934

Belloc and Vivian Jackson came to tea and we discussed Cromwell, science, the Press and Oxford. The old boy, who has been abroad since Christmas – mostly in Italy – says British public is most ignorant and most uninformed in the world. It is not told about anything that is going on in the world and does not care. He is doing and has nearly finished his *Cromwell* whom he hates; says Cromwell was a very easy man to understand. He had two qualities: he hated the Catholics and he was a good cavalry leader. Held forth at some length on dons whom he rated as small-minded, rusty, gossipy, and lazy people who gave themselves great and ridiculous airs and become moth-eaten. Vivian Jackson told the story of don who complained bitterly that his lectures were nothing like as well attended as they had been twenty years before. 'And I know it's not my fault,' he added pathetically, 'because they are the same lectures.'

Monday, 23 April 1934

Lunched at Sibyl Colefax's. Present: George Clerk, Eddie Marsh, Desmond MacCarthy, André Maurois and his wife, Alfred Beit, McMullen of Vogue, Margerie and his wife of French Embassy, Mrs Sieff, Kitty Rothschild,[1] Lady Oxford. Kitty Rothschild is or was rather Kitty Schoenborn. She sat next me, and we discussed Austrian politics. She says Habsburgs have been disgracefully treated – as lepers – and that they did not make Europe what it is today, but we did. They are the poorest royal family in Europe today, etc., etc. She says, however, that she herself is not a monarchist, but she resents the idea that a new nation like Yugoslavia should be allowed to dictate whether or not Habsburgs shall return! Talked to Margerie, who is intelligent and talks English well. He told me Stresemann told him that at the end he was *hundemüde* – dog-tired! He tells me Maurois's *King Edward* has sold 250,000 copies in three months in French edition! Giraudoux, whose play [*Intermezzo*] was performed here by Stage Society on Sunday night, has just been appointed Inspector of Legations and Consulates – much travelling.

Wednesday, 25 April 1934

Gave a luncheon to Barbara Din, Moura, Albrecht [Bernstorff], Montgelas,

[1] Desmond MacCarthy (1878–1952), literary critic and broadcaster, literary editor of the *New Statesman*; André Maurois (1885–1967), French novelist and biographer, anglophile; Roland de Margerie (*b.* 1899), 1st Secretary French Embassy in London; Mrs Sieff, wife of the future Lord Sieff, head of Marks and Spencer; Countess Kitty Schoenborn-Bucheim, *née* Wolff, married Eugene Daniel Rothschild in 1925.

and young Nikisch, the son of Arthur Nikisch, the famous conductor. Barbara Din, who was here two years ago with Oskar Deneš in *Victoria and Her Hussar*, has now married young Nikisch, who himself is a very fine musician. He is apparently not a Jew, has long sensitive hands and looks very highly strung. As Barbara herself is a bundle of nerves, they make a queer pair. No very good conversation, and, as the show lagged, I had recourse to alcohol to make it go. In consequence did not work in the afternoon. . .

Had a long talk to Allen Leeper on Austria. He does not like the Austrian revolution and thinks, like me, that the so-called Socialist plot was merely an excuse for Fey and Starhemberg to have a go at the Socialists.[1] Allen told me a good story of the transience of human glory. The other day he was dictating a despatch on disarmament to the best typist in the Foreign Office. Curzon's name was referred to several times, Allen just dictating 'Curzon' without any prefix. When the typescript was brought back, Curzon was entered as 'Mr Curzon'. The Marquess would not have liked it.

Thursday, 26 April 1934

Fletcher had me to luncheon today with Alexander, the ex-First Lord of the Admiralty and the Co-operatives' leader, and [H.B.] Lees-Smith [a Labour M.P.]. Alexander was in great form. He is clever, but rather conceited and a little fond of the good things of life and likes coming to the St James's. He has been speaking all over the country, admits that, industrially, things have improved, but is certain that Labour is missing all along the line.

Sunday, 29 April 1934

Had a long talk to Dad in the evening about our family. My great-grandfather and my great-grandmother, between them, must have left nearly £200,000 . . . a very considerable fortune for those days. Uncle Tom – great-grand-uncle Tom – was unmarried. He went out to America in the year of Waterloo (New Orleans) in order to make money to marry the girl of his desire. While he was away, she jilted him. Afterwards, he never had a woman in his house. He lived in Glasgow and had a very fine house. My great-grandfather had three sons, Robert, my grandfather, Tom and Wallace. Wallace died before his father, but the old man decided that his children should inherit. He divided up his estate into three-eighths for my grandfather, three-eighths for uncle Tom, and two-eighths for Wallace's children. As grandpapa had six children – Uncle Tom six, and Wallace only two, the latter benefitted greatly.

Tuesday, 1 May 1934

Knickerbocker gave a luncheon today for Walter Duranty,[2] and I had my

[1] There had been civil war in Austria in February, and the Socialists had been suppressed by Prince Starhemberg and Major Fey, supporters of Dollfuss, the Austrian Chancellor, who had been ruling without Parliament since March 1933.

[2] H. R. Knickerbocker (1898–1949), American journalist and broadcaster, European

first meeting with the King of Reporters. He is certainly attractive – short, with no trace of American accent, speaks goodish French, has a keen, rather ungracious expression when talking with Knickerbocker whom he uses as a whetstone for his ideas, and his hair is thinning rapidly. Talks well – throws out ideas to see how they will digest themselves. Has a swell new job: four months a year in Moscow, eight months free or special work on special pay for his paper. Wants to write his memoirs now. Knickerbocker says he will never do it. 'Knick' and he ran a fiction factory in Moscow; in three weeks wrote six stories; made $4000; one story won the O. Henry Prize; then 'Knick' was transferred to Berlin. Duranty says that distribution is a big problem in Russia; thinks war in Europe almost certain and that everyone who does not think so is a madman...

Good story of King Edward and Mrs Keppel. They had retired for siesta after luncheon on board yacht. Suddenly steps were heard down companion-way.

King Edward: 'Pst, there's someone coming.

Mrs Keppel: 'Well, it's certainly not Your Majesty.

Thursday, 3 May 1934

Robin left for Dartmouth today. Last night I took him to the cinema, and after the cinema and dinner we all played cards. He has improved considerable and has stood a rather difficult holiday in London reasonably well. True, he is very spoilt and, what is worse, encouraged in every form of luxury. He hears far too much about the frivolous side of life – stage, cinema, society gossip, etc. He reads mainly trash, and I am strongly in favour of packing away all trash from children (I mean literary trash) and giving them only the best. It is amazing how people who are anxious to do their best for their child do not realise this.

Lunched with Harry and Tommy and Hamish and in the afternoon drove Tommy to the nursing home. She has aged a great deal and is obviously being very rapidly affected by the strain. But her courage is wonderful. There is, I gather, very little hope for Mary. She has now developed peritonitis and, even if she recovers, will have to undergo yet another major operation for short-circuiting. She can keep no food down, suffers great pain, and has to be relieved by stomach pump. Yet she is full of pluck and fights every inch of the way.

Friday, 4 May 1934

A bad day. Lunched at the Wellington with Conrad Drayton and discussed future of club with Bailey. It is quite clear that the club cannot carry on in its present premises, and the odds are that it will cease to exist altogether.

---

and war correspondent: Walter Duranty (*d.* 1957), foreign correspondent of *New York Times*, 1913–39, was in London for the publication of his book *Russia Reported*.

Its members are likely to be absorbed in other clubs like the Royal Thames Yacht Club, the Junior Carlton and Brooks's. Most of our best members have two clubs already and are not likely to support the various suggestions which have been made for carrying on in smaller premises. It is a sad end for a club which once was of very high standing and which was the first club to run a lady's side. It was also Casement's club and so had the queer distinction of having one of its members shot for treason! Membership, however, has declined from over 1100 to 840 in the last two or three years.

Saturday, 5 May 1934

A cold and squally day with storms of rain. Lunched at 62 Onslow Gardens. Tommy, who has never left Mary's side and sleeps at the nursing home, looks very ill. She is putting far too severe a strain on herself. Mary's illness is such that, if she recovers, she will require weeks and weeks of nursing. It is from Tommy's point of view a ten-mile race and, if Tommy exhausts herself in the first mile, she will be no good for the nine remaining miles. Tommy tells me that Lady Mar and Kellie has written to her saying that her picture – a magnificent Kneller of the wife of 'Bobbing Joan' Mar (1715)[1] (she was the sister of Lady Mary Wortley Montagu) – which she lent to the recent exhibition of British Art at Burlington House, came back with a 7½-inch slash in it. Hamish tells me that when Lord Bath (Henry Weymouth's father) lent a picture (panel) to Philip Sassoon's exhibition it came back cracked, because the room was too cold or too hot.

Slept in afternoon instead of going to the Rugby League Cup Final. In the evening dined with the Buffs. Met the Colonel of Regiment – General Sir Arthur Lynden-Bell – a grand old boy who runs his regimental association marvellously. Buffs are up to full strength – all or 90 per cent Kentish men – and work is done entirely by association which not only finds work for ex-Buffs but supplies regiment with recruits. If every regiment had first-class association, there would be no need for British Legion.

Sunday, 6 May 1934

Mike spoke about the *Standard*, *Express*, etc., on way home. He is a Max-worshipper and denied strenuously: (1) that Baxter had ever made anybody; and (2) that he had nothing to do with the making of H. V. Morton (as he claimed recently). So far from Baxter having a claim on the copyright of Morton's *In Search of England*, *Scotland*, etc., series, because it was his idea, real truth is that Morton was so fed up at being put on idiotic sub-reporter jobs by Baxter that he threatened to resign. Max, who then had an office in Fleet Street, sent for him. Morton told him he was fed up, said he knew he could do good work if he were left alone. Max gave him his chance

[1] Lady Mar and Kellie, wife of 12th Earl of Mar. John, 6th Earl of Mar (1675–1732), changed sides so often that he was known as 'Bobbing Joan', eventually leading a Jacobite rebellion in 1715 which lost him his title, though not his life.

and Morton started with his *In Search of London*. It was huge success for paper. The series has been a gold mine for Morton.[1] Dined at 62 Onslow Gardens. Mary is making a miraculous fight.

Monday, 7 May 1934

Cold and windy. Lunched with Tommy and Harry and Hamish at 62, Onslow Gardens. Mary is holding her own and fighting every inch of the way. There is now a chance that she may live. Dawson of Penn[2] (whom Tommy hates) will not put it at more than a chance. [Bernard] Schlesinger, the surgeon, is more optimistic. After luncheon went to the London General Clinic with Tommy and then for a walk or rather a seat in the park. Tommy is very overwrought and is suffering from strain. Her eyes are bad again, and she is bound to have a breakdown. Her life is like a scene out of a domestic novel. . . Went to London Library and collected some books about Australian poetry. I have to write an article on Lindsay Gordon[3] who (on Friday 11th) will be the first Empire poet to be included in the Poet's Corner in Westminster Abbey. Wrote a long letter to Scott Douglas about finances which are hopeless.

Wednesday, 9 May 1934

More trouble over the Diary which goes from bad to worse. *Telegraph* diary [Peterborough] is now better. It is based on our old Diary. Chief trouble is total lack of co-ordination. No one makes any attempt to organise a Diary. Cudlipp himself has not the Diary mind. Ramsden is ineffectual, and the Fleming[4] experiment has been a complete failure.

Monday, 14 May 1934

Peter Fleming drove me in his car to Boulestin's where I had to lunch with Mazuranič.[5] Peter tells me that he has written his new book on the Far East [*One's Company*] (90,000 words) in less than four months (i.e. since he joined the *Standard*). He works from 1.30 to 6 in the afternoon and does 300 words a day! This, in addition to writing articles for American magazines and doing dramatic criticism for the *Spectator*. His activity puts me to the blush. At Vailima, Stevenson, who was a sick man, wrote half of *Catriona* (I suppose about 40,000 words) in a month. Scott's *Guy Mannering* in three weeks, however, beats the lot! As Stevenson said, what thews and sinews!

Mazuranič was interesting Told me that conditions were not so bad in Yugoslavia. No one had any money, but living was very cheap and food plentiful. Told me sensational story of propaganda schools for agitators and

[1] H. V. Morton (*b.* 1892) has been writing travel books on this pattern ever since.

[2] Lord Dawson of Penn (1864–1945), physician-in-ordinary to four kings.

[3] Adam Lindsay Gordon (1833–70), 'first of Australian poets'.

[4] Peter Fleming (1907–71), who had already published *Brazilian Adventure* (1933), had joined the *Standard* for a while.

[5] Zelimir Mazuranič, Yugoslav minister and delegate to the League of Nations.

assassins run by Italians – out near Bari – where Croat boys are trained and sent over to Yugoslavia to assassinate King Alexander.

Wednesday, 16 May 1934

In the evening meeting of Wellington Club – decided to wind club up, date June 30th. Good deal of opposition from the members and some indignation against the Committee. . .

Saw Duff Cooper and Maurice Baring at White's today. Duff says Baldwin and L.G. are coming close again. Baldwin reads proofs of L.G.'s book. Maurice, asked by me to give me real English translation of Pushkin's lyric, *Ya perezhil svoi zhelania*, produced on back of White's menu-card:

> 'I've lived too long; I'm in the ruck;
> I've drunk too deeply of the cup.
> I cannot spend; I cannot f—k;
> I'm down and out; I'm buggered up.'[1]

Friday, 18 May 1934

Things go from bad to worse, and I see no hope anywhere. Jean makes no attempt to economise or even to do her duty by Robin. . . I am the beast of burden who has to do the work and, above all, to pay. I am always in the wrong whatever happens. When I am nice, the best I can hope for is to be allowed to listen to a lot of senseless chatter about films and theatres and personal gossip. It is a heart-breaking atmosphere.

I want to get out of Fleet Street, but how can I when we are plunging into debt more recklessly, more wilfully, than we have ever done before? . .

Tommy has remained here for Whitsun to be with Mary, Philip having gone to Le Touquet and Harry to Hunger Hill with all the servants! Harry has let Hunger for July and August – just the months when Tommy wished to be there. It is an amazing performance, because the old man means to be kind and, indeed, told me he would not do this ten days ago. Unfortunately, he has started drinking again.

Tuesday, 22 May 1934

The [George Malcolm] Thomsons came to dinner. We had some good conversation about the Scottish National Party. Thomson tells me big man in North is Neil Gunn who is an excise-man; wrote *The Morning Tide*, but is now so keen on politics that he has no time for writing; has a meeting at his house nearly every night. The Party is fairly extreme and even has some arms.

Went on to Sibyl Colefax's supper party: Somerset Maugham, Geoffrey Toye, Moura, G. B. Stern[2] and some others whose names I did not catch:

[1] Lockhart prints another, more decent, version by Baring in *Retreat from Glory* (1934), p. 266.

[2] Edward Geoffrey Toye (1889–1942), composer and conductor, was then Managing Director, Royal Opera, Covent Garden. G. B. Stern (*b.* 1890), prolific authoress of novels and plays.

also Franz Mendelssohn. Not much good conversation – Geoffrey Toye told me how in second act of *Meistersinger* rat ran into Lady Anglesey's box, ran across her lap, then visited Lady Cunard, and disappeared. Rats apparently are bad at Opera, being so close to Covent Garden, and great precautions have to be taken.

Friday, 25 May 1934

In the afternoon came back and meant to work. Jean, however, was out, and before dinner I received three 'duns' for amounts varying from £40 to £50. I therefore went out to kill my boredom and irritation. Drank heavily, played bridge, and sat up till 2 a.m., when I went to the Slip In [nightclub], where I remained till 7 a.m. Found Hamish there, and we went on to the Hammam [Turkish] Baths together. A futile and degrading performance.

Saturday, 26 May 1934

This morning at the Turkish baths ran into the Prince of Wales, who had just come down from Prestwick. He said Wallace was a good fighter.[1] Also saw Maurice Baring, Michael Berry, Lord Carnarvon!

Tuesday, 29 May 1934

At six saw Moura, who tells me that H.G. . . . dined with Roosevelt, was not so impressed as he expected to be, but thinks there is some hope in U.S.A. He now wants to go to Russia to see Stalin.

Dined at Stornoway. Present: Lord Beaverbrook, A. J. Cummings, MacNeill,[2] ex-M.P. and former p.p.s. to Ramsay MacDonald, Frank Owen, and Dr Erich Winter. Much conversation about Ramsay Mac – mostly very anti. MacNeill has written a book on him – a 'debunking' book. Argument between Cummings and MacNeill, as to whether or not Ramsay was a careerist . . . MacNeill said he was and that he faced both ways even in the war. All agreed that he was very vain. Cummings told how he once went to see him. Ramsay had a copy of the *Star* [then the paper for which Cummings worked] in front of him. There was a paragraph about himself saying that he had been in poor health. 'Do you see this?' he asked Cummings. 'That came from Henderson. Don't tell me it didn't. I know it did.' . . .

Winter very eloquent about the dangers of Japanese competition and the necessity for Europe to pull together. Max rather quiet until Russia cropped up. Then he became very dramatic over his account of his interview with

[1] W. Lawson Little (U.S.A.) beat James Wallace (Britain) in the final of the British Amateur Golf Championship at Prestwick that day. Wallace was an Ayrshire sawmill worker.

[2] Cummings (1882–1957), political editor, *New Chronicle*, had recently reported the Metropolitan-Vickers Trial and the Reichstag Fire Trial. MacNeill Weir (*d.* 1939) had been Labour M.P., 1922–31, and Parliamentary Private Secretary to MacDonald, 1924–1931. His book, *The Tragedy of Ramsay MacDonald*, seems not to have been published until 1938.

Stalin. Stalin had started conversation by thanking Beaverbrook for supporting Russia and then by attacking Winston. Max was furious. What made him more furious, he said, was that in crossing the streets in Moscow he had nearly been run down by a huge Rolls-Royce. It was Stalin's!

Wednesday, 30 May 1934

Felt a little better today. Had luncheon at our house for the Bolins[1] and the Petersons. Bolin told us that, while there is no truth in the report that ex-King Alfonso has abdicated, monarchist circles are intriguing that he should do so in favour of Don Juan. He (Bolin) considers this inopportune and premature, although it will probably be necessary some day. There are too many people who might be inclined to accept the monarchical idea again but who would dread the return of Alfonso. Both Peterson and Bolin agreed that it was the Berenguer[2] régime which brought the monarchy down.

Maurice Peterson told a good story of Togo who died yesterday.[3] When he (Maurice Peterson) was in Tokyo, there was a collection for the preservation of Togo's battleship as a national relic. Togo gave five yen – not because he was stingy, but because he was mouse-poor, five yen representing about half a day's retired pay for a Jap admiral.

Thursday, 31 May 1934

Dined at 62 Onslow Gardens. Present: Sir Maurice Bonham Carter and Lady Sinclair (Marigold).[4] Much talk about politics. Marigold down on L.G. and asked how he could get away with all his criticisms about what ought to be done in Europe when he was the man who was responsible for the whole mess by signing the [Versailles] Treaty. Bonham Carter agreed, but gave the answer. No one was in a position to attack L.G. over the treaty. The whole country was demanding an even more violent treaty and was attacking L.G. for being too conciliatory. I should look up the story of the 300 M.P.s who sent a telegram to L.G. asking for sterner reparations.

Friday, 1 June 1934

Wasted half the afternoon waiting for Valentine Castlerosse who promised to turn up at 2.30 and arrived at 3.30! I had to see him about the row between Baring's and the Censor over the *House of Rothschild* film. Story is roughly this: When film was shown, Baring's went and disliked it. Film showed Baring's as a minor concern dependent on Rothschild's and going snivelling

[1] Gustavo Bolin (*b.* 1870) was a retired diplomat who had been British Acting Consu in Malaga.

[2] Dámaso Berenguer (1873–1953), Cuban-born general, nominated by Alfonso to succeed Primo de Rivera as dictator of Spain, January 1930. But he lost control and resigned in February 1931.

[3] Admiral Togo (1847–1934) was the hero of the Russo-Japanese War of 1904–5.

[4] Bonham Carter (1880–1960), husband of Asquith's daughter, Violet; and Marigold, wife of Sir Archibald Sinclair; both in the councils of the Liberal Party.

to Rothschild's for help. Facts were just reverse. Nathan Rothschild, founder of English business, became a British subject only in 1804. When Sir Francis Baring died in 1810, he left £7,000,000 and was described by Erskine as 'the first merchant in Europe'. When Baring's did the great French Reparations Loan after Waterloo, they did it with Hope's of Amsterdam; they had the valuable support of the Duke of Wellington, but they did not bring in Rothschild's because Rothschild's were then not important, big, or classy enough. Baring's protested about film to company who said they thought Baring's approved. Baring's then protested to Film Board of Censors who said they understood Baring's had approved. Typical Hollywood work!

Val told me good story of first Labouchère.[1] Labouchère was a clerk in Hope's Amsterdam and wanted to marry Miss Hope (? or was it other way round) and also to become a partner in Hope's. Went to Hope, to ask for Miss Hope and was turned down. Then Labouchère said would it make any difference if you knew that I am shortly to become a partner in Baring's. Then he went to Baring's, asked to be made a partner, was turned down. Again, he said: 'Would it make any difference if I told you that I was shortly to marry Miss Hope?' He pulled off both!

Friday, 8 June 1934

Cold and dull. Beginning of Test Match. Papers full of repercussions of last night's Mosley meeting at Olympia.[2] In the 'Brown House' of the Mosley Fascists in King's Road, Chelsea, there are three portraits: one of Tom in the middle, with Mussolini on one side and Hitler on the other. Hitler's people are not very keen on Tom. Mussolini, on the other hand, takes lively interest. Grandi [Italian Ambassador], who does not believe in him, has orders to report any development and got into trouble with Mussolini for not reporting some interview Tom had with German Ambassador.

Aldous Huxley told us lovely story of his recent visit to Perugia – saw a squad of Fascists marching, leader was shouting out something to make the step. It was not *uno – duo – uno – duo*, but *Du-ce, Du-ce*. Very typical. Aldous Huxley is pale, very unhealthy-looking, with long tapered fingers and a wax-like complexion. He wears very powerful bifocal glasses which give his eyes a very stereoscopic expression. He is poor, never makes very much out of his books, and has lost his American magazine market.

Saturday, 9 June 1934

Had more talk last night about Mosley meeting. Two 'Sirs' were wearing Black Shirts at the meeting: Sir John Rhodes and Sir George Duckworth-King. Opinion in Wellington Club was very anti. Harry tells me that in Carlton Club opinion is very divided. There are a lot of anti-Baldwin rebels.

[1] Henry Labouchère, Baron Taunton (1798–1869), uncle of his namesake the Radical M.P.

[2] It had ended in violence, and 21 people were arrested.

Friday, 15 June 1934

Very depressed. There is no attempt to economise here, either on food or on anything else. Cocktail parties, theatres, anything except work. . . When I packed my bag tonight, my dress shoes and my golfing shoes had not been brushed since last week. What a life!

Saturday, 16 June 1934

Blazing sunshine and very hot. Began the day with a quarrel with Jean over an unpaid bill. I lost control, and we had an undignified slanging match. I should not mind anything if I could see any sign on her part of even the faintest intention to try to economise and to live within our income and not right up to and over it. I can understand that she has no feeling of duty, affection or any sentiment towards me at all. . .

Bad day on the Diary. No one here. I was to have left at one-forty, but had to remain and do more Diary matter. Caught the 3.30 to Horsham. Very hot in train. Tommy came to meet me, and when we arrived at Hunger Hill we met Rosabelle Brand,[1] a young Coldstream called Campbell Stuart Gray-Phillips. Discussed Mosley and Fascism. He is obviously gaining some converts. In evening went out shooting. Place is overrun with rabbits, but they all scuttle at one shot. Shot seven or eight.

Tuesday, 19 June 1934

Blum has made very little out of his books. His *R.D.B.'s Diary* sold only just over 2000 copies in England which brought him in about £90. He made about £150 out of it in U.S.A. Heinemann's sold remainder to Selfridge's at 1*s*. a copy. Blum was furious. His *All in a Lifetime* did a little better, but not much. His *The Press in My Time* was sold for £70. He managed to serialise it, however, in *Nash's Magazine* for £300; so here he did pretty well. He is also serialising his new one in *Nash's*.

Thursday, 21 June 1934

Gave Reggie luncheon in the Wellington and talked about Rothermere.[2] Reggie does not put Rothermere in same class as Northcliffe, and says that but for Northcliffe none of the Harmsworth brothers would ever have achieved distinction. Rothermere certainly worked very hard, and, on occasions when he thought that Northcliffe was going mad in money matters, he would take a firm stand. But it was rot to say that Rothermere saved the *Daily Mirror*. Rothermere, who began life as a clerk in Somerset House, was very unwilling at first to go in with Northcliffe, hesitated for some time

[1] Lady Rosabelle, widow of Lieut.-Colonel John Brand and the Earl of Rosslyn's daughter by his first wife.

[2] Reginald Nicholson (1869–1946) had been Manager of *The Times* under Northcliffe, 1911–15. Rothermere (1868–1940) was the second of the Harmsworth brothers. The other three were: Cecil (1869–1948), Under-Secretary for Foreign Affairs, 1919–22; Robert (1870–1937), Liberal M.P.; Hildebrand (1872–1929), proprietor of the *Globe*.

before accepting. Curious complex about houses; had had many; in end preferred living in hotel – restless. Like Northcliffe a heavy womaniser. Liked pictures; at one time bought many. Latterly, did not know where they all were.

Friday, 22 June 1934

Moura told me a good story of [Chaim] Weizmann, the Zionist leader, who is in London... Weizmann in 1918 had done a good deal of correspondence with Lloyd George, who wrote to him to say that he would like to see him when he next came to England. Weizmann came in end of October 1918, wrote to L.G., and was asked to luncheon on November 11th. On the day (Armistice) he assumed that the luncheon would be off. He telephoned, however, to 10 Downing Street and discovered that he was expected. He found L.G. alone, reading the Bible with tears coursing down his face. He had just ordered a trainload of supplies to be sent to Germany.

Saturday, 30 June 1934

Did not leave the office until four, went to Sports Club and had some sandwiches, then on to the Wellington where there was a rather disgusting 'bust' by the old 'topers' for the last night of its existence. Sat up till four until we had drunk up all the cellar or rather all that remained of the whisky. The cellars, furniture, etc., are to be sold.

Tuesday, 3 July 1934

Sat up late, as I suddenly received a note . . . asking for Hitler's obituary notice to be entirely revised. Lord Beaverbrook had ordered this on telephone, as he is convinced that Hitler will be assassinated. He has now turned solidly, fanatically, anti-Hitler, refers to him as Al Capone and to the Nazis as gangsters! I wrote an 'obit' of Hitler three or four months ago, perhaps a year. It was fairly favourable, Max then being not very anti! So this time I had to do the whole thing all over again – of course very anti, according to instructions and denying him any spark of genius. Yet it was my account of Hitler's platform methods which made Max alter his own methods – notably, walking straight on to the stage without an introduction and without a chairman! I expect in four months' time I shall have to do another Hitler 'obit' – perhaps several!

Friday, 6 July 1934

A hectic day. At one o'clock went to the Savoy where Warner Bros gave a luncheon for the Press to meet Leslie Howard and me in connection with the film of *British Agent*. [Michael] Curtiz, the producer, was also there. He is a Hungarian Jew like most of the film executives: Zukor, Korda, Loew, etc. Max Mildner, Warner's man over here, is also a Hungarian Jew. I sat next

Leslie Howard, who told me about the film. He thinks it is really good and that my part is first-class. All the names have been changed. I am called Stephen Locke and am unmarried. He said the first script was so bad that he nearly threw his hand in. Now, however, the story is very much improved, although there is still one scene to which the Foreign Office may object. At the luncheon Howard, Curtiz and I made speeches. I took care to dissociate myself from the picture. We had a huge spread: cocktails, champagne, cigars, etc. Mildner told me that the English censorship was not bad. He could generally get a thing through in time. Shortt,[1] however, was the devil. Generally, he was only brought in as final arbiter. When he was brought in, there was always trouble.

Thursday, 26 July 1934

Yesterday at the Russian Embassy garden party I met Woodruff,[2] the young Empire Crusader. He told me that the Empire Crusade Club was full of young opportunists who were not in the least interested in the Crusade but who were joining it purely in the hope of getting a job from Beaverbrook. They had some justification. An assistant from Barker's had been taken on as a reporter at the *Daily Express*. Peter Howard[3] was also writing for the *Sunday*. The adherence of 90 per cent of the members was purely self-interested like the adherence of the politicians to Max himself. As soon as they had a foot on the ladder of success, they left him; e.g. Paddy Hannon. Max himself must see through these things.

Early in July, Prince Louis Ferdinand had written to Lockhart:

I am writing to you, to ask you a favour. Fritzi [Prince Friedrich], my youngest brother is going to spend two weeks with the Jellicoes[4] at Cowes. He is going to leave by the end of July. I already told him, that it would be the best and only thing, if you took care of handling him, when he gets to England. With all the delicate situation he ought to be advised by you what to say to the papers, because I believe that it will not be quite easy to evade all the difficult questions they will ask him. Besides that, Fritzi has never been in England before and I do not want him only to be with the society crowd. He has a great inkling towards the social side, sports, etc., but we want that his trip be of general value for my country and family. His English could be better and perhaps there you also can influence him only to speak English. Besides that he is the most charming creature you can imagine and I am sure that you will like him. He came over to America two years ago and made

[1] Edward Shortt, K.C. 1862–1935), President of British Board of Film Censors, 1929–35, formerly Liberal M.P. and Chief Secretary for Ireland.

[2] Douglas Woodruff (*b.* 1897), then in charge of publicity for the Empire Marketing Board; later editor of the *Tablet*.

[3] (1908–64), disciple of Buchman's Moral Rearmament, wrote for *Express* until 1941.

[4] 1st Earl Jellicoe (1854–1935), Commander of the Grand Fleet at the Battle of Jutland, and his wife Florence.

a big hit there. Could you drop him a line to Prinz Friedrich, Potsdam Cecilienhof, so that he can get in touch with you?

Well Bruce, lots of luck and love from your little friend.

Tuesday, 31 July 1934

Louis Ferdinand's brother – Prince Friedrich – arrived today. I gave him a luncheon at Savoy, but owing to short notice had no time to get any guests. Friedrich brought his friend Henschel who was at Cambridge and whose grandfather was Scheffer (?), the famous German general. Friedrich is tall, good-looking, rather like Prince George, and very modest and much less American than Louis Ferdinand. He will go down here. Brendan and Michael Colefax who were my guests liked him. Friedrich told me that the Kaiser was upset by Randolph Churchill's account of his interview with him. He gave *no* interview. Randolph came to Doorn with some Dutch friends. Kaiser entertained him as private guest. Friedrich is going down to Cowes to stay with the Jellicoes.

In the evening dined with Moir and Rootes[1] at the Dorchester. Rootes, a little man with fair complexion, broad forehead and rather bald, is interesting, has quite modern views about relations between capital and labour, and believes to a considerable extent in planning. Moir says he is a bigger man in industry than Morris or Austin and is a future peer.

Monday, 6 August 1934

Violent attacks on Germany continue in the Press. This morning I wanted to do a paragraph comparing Winston (who has had about six articles in the papers during the week-end) to Dumas who once had six serials running in the Paris papers at the same time. Cudlipp, our editor, said: 'The idea is first-class, but I think you had better keep off it. The Chief (Max) will say that you are giving publicity to Winston. He hates paragraphs about Winston. He pulled me up only the other day.' I know this is true; (1) because Cudlipp does not lie; and (2) because I have heard the same thing from the little man when I was with him.

Lunched at home and in the afternoon went to Lord's to see the Lord's Schools against the Rest. Just saw the tail-end of the Lord's Schools, and then some very disappointing cricket by the Rest. Considering the time which they devote to cricket, the English public schoolboy is not very impressive. I believe that in the last thirty years the age of development is much later than it used to be. Colin McLean,[2] who is at ——'s house at Harrow (which includes most of the games cracks), tells Jean that the bigger boys use powder, put scent behind their ears, read *Vogue* and wear frightfully nancy clothes. Jean asked why the other boys did not laugh them out of it. Colin's answer was that these were the 'big shots' and the best boys at games.

[1] Willam Rootes (1874–1964), later 1st Baron, chairman of the firm that made Humber, Hillman and Singer cars.

[2] Son of Loudon McLean, who was to marry Lockhart's wife Jean.

Friday, 10 August 1934

Motored back afterwards with Leslie Hore-Belisha, Minister of Transport. He is very angry with Max who had nasty attack on him in *Express* and *Standard* recently – not because Max attacked his old friend but because of the manner of it. When Leslie was appointed Minister of Transport, *Standard* had leader saying now Ministers should cultivate Press more. Leslie called a private Press conference, offered to co-operate and suggested a joint visit to roads on Bank Holiday. Conference was held under normal conditions of ministerial conferences: i.e., information can be used but not attributed to Minister. *Express* then attacked Leslie for trying to do preliminary publicity with journalists. After his inspection trip which some forty journalists attended, *Standard* attacked him for joy-riding, called his Press show a cavalcade, and then said photography must be replaced by action!

Monday, 13 August 1934

At four-thirty went to Warner House where, alone with Max Mildner the director, I saw my film. I was to see it alone first in order to find out what my reaction was. Film has yet to pass censor. Film is not at all like book. There are one or two Americanisms which jar, especially in the Embassy scenes. But otherwise it is an entertaining picture, and the love scenes are done with great restraint. I think that provided Warner Bros put in that the characters are fictitious (as indeed they are) and that the historical accuracy has been sacrificed to make film there will be no objections.

Sunday, 19 August 1934

Finances are hopeless again. Telephone is cut off. Light and gas have not been paid. Cooper's bill is now over £20... I long to be kind, but [Jean's] attitude towards me makes any kind of meeting-ground impossible.

Prince Louis Ferdinand wrote from Bridgeport, Connecticut on 21 August 1934:

Fritzy wrote me, that you are taking wonderful care of him. Well, I knew that you would be just the right chaperon. Thousand thanks for what you are doing for the kid, whom I suppose you will have gotten to like and for your helping our family in making friends. Fritzy writes me, that he is going up to Scotland. Please keep him in your islands as long as possible. It's going to do him a lot of good. I'll return the middle or end of September and this time I am going to jump off at Plymouth and come right up to London to see you. There are a thousand and one things we have got to talk about. Please drop me a line to: Dr Louis Ferdinand, Ford Motor Co, Dearborn, Michigan.

Now lots of love and best wishes from your little Prussian friend.

Wednesday, 22 August 1934

In the evening dined at Lady Cunard's to meet Sir Thomas Beecham.

Present Prince Friedrich, Lord Moore and self. Sir Thomas is not unattractive. He is a fierce hater of politicians and shams; his *bête noire* is Sir John Reith, who he thinks is the greatest charlatan in the world. I gather that most of the Opera League Fund money which is at present being administered by Court will return eventually to music. Thousands of the original subscribers are dead or have moved their address. The latter do not bother even to notify their new address so that some £10,000 or £15,000 is sure to be left on Court's hands. In due course it will go to the opera at Sadler's Wells.

Lockhart's second book, Retreat from Glory, *which appeared in October 1934, was in proof form in August and he sent a set of proofs to Harold Nicolson, who on 26 August 1934, returned them with these comments:*

I speak only from the literary point of view. From that point of view I think this book even better than the last. It displays the uncertainty of your middle period. There is a note throughout of wistfulness, which is never stressed, and which if stressed would be Yeats-Brown. But it is there and if you try to stress it one millimetre further you will become and seem a grisly kitten. Leave it as it is. And be indifferent to the criticism it will arouse.

I am rather fussed about the effect which that criticism will, or may have upon you. You are certain to get it. Critics always approach the sequel to a resounding success in a hostile spirit. This is not due to jealousy or meanness on their part. It is due to the quite reputable circumstance that they approach a second book of this sort in a questioning spirit. 'I wonder,' they say to themselves: 'whether the success of *British Agent* was really justified?' Inevitably there is a reaction. I repeat that (in that I view the books as a sequence of psychological confessions) I myself regard this present book as a very remarkable achievement. The temptation to force the note, to alter the proportions, must have been a very strong temptation. You have resisted it. Thus you give as much space to Cattaro[1] as you do to Doorn. That is a real literary instinct, as distinct from a journalistic instinct. You are so obviously not out for news value. In the end, all serious critics will recognise this virtue on your part.

They will not recognise it at first. You must expect some very unkind reviews of this book. People will say that it is superficial, charming, undignified. They will say that you have shown a false sense of proportion by speaking of unimportant people in the same sort of terms in which you speak of important people. They will say that it is a journalistic work – which above all it is not.

You must realise that your first book was given deep significance owing to the facts that you were dealing with vital affairs, that you were very young, and that the high tragedies of death and love were your two main themes.

[1] Lockhart had been sent to Montenegro by the Anglo-Austrian Bank to sort out the problems arising from fraud by their Serbian manager, and this resulted in an idyllic interlude in Cattaro.

In this book you are dealing with less vital affairs, you were less young, you were never in danger of execution and your love affairs were mainly *Nachtlokal*. People and critics will approach the book in the glamour of the first volume. They will find that glamour lessened. And they will forget to treat the book, as a book, but will treat it as Vol. II to Vol. I. They will be disappointed at the decline from high tragedy. And they will voice that disappointment in various shapes of carping.

Eventually all this will be of no importance. I seriously believe that in the end people will come to realise that you have the real literary gift – that of telling of things as they happened and in their right proportions as these proportions appeared to you at the time. But you must expect disagreeable reviews – and I only trust that you will not be hurt by them. You are so far more sensitive than (Scots Wha' Hae, etc.) you allow yourself or other people to suppose. You underestimate your own literary gift. You must grow a great scab of indifference.

But your next volume, when you will be treating of adult conclusions, must be more serious in tone. Not that for one moment you should abandon your merry attitude towards life. Not for one moment that you should become sententious. But only that you should determine on your own attitude towards life, – what is of value and what is not – and that you should write the same tune over again but in a different key. If you can manage to do that, your three volumes will live in English literature. Of that I am quite positive.

But never try to write other than comes easily to you. Nothing could do better than your natural style. It is so elastic.

Thursday, 30 August 1934

Gave luncheon to Valentine Castlerosse and Maurice Peterson at the Savoy. Maurice sails for Egypt tomorrow. He is taking up Lampson's[1] job for three months and wants me to go out to stay with him at the Residency. He told us that when the war started he was at the Foreign Office. He was then about twenty-two and was very anxious to do more for his country than working at the office. He went round to see Basil Thomson at Scotland Yard in order to suggest that he might do some extra intelligence work in the evenings. Thomson looked at him, asked him what his qualifications were, discovered that he knew French and German, and then after some reflection suggested that he would be very useful if he could hang round West End bars in the evening and hear what foreign conversations were going on. Maurice went away sad at heart. Fortunately, he heard no more about it!

Dined with Michael Colefax in the evening. He leaves for the U.S.A. tomorrow. We went over afterwards to Leslie Howard's table and had a talk – Leslie Howard, who is now playing the title role in the *Scarlet Pimpernel*,

[1] Sir Miles Lampson (1861–1949), later Lord Killearn, High Commissioner for Egypt, 1934–6.

was with Merle Oberon who plays Lady Blakeney. She looks very Siamese-looking and is very attractive with nothing to say. Real name O'Brien. Leslie Howard seemed very devoted to her. Later, met Sieff and Mrs Sieff. Sieff is a queer type of Jew millionaire – an idealist and not a great spender and yet rather conceited intellectually.

Lockhart reported to Prince Louis Ferdinand on 5 September 1934:

Prince Friedrich has been here nearly a month now and is at present shooting in Scotland with Lord Lonsdale. He has been very popular wherever he has been, and everyone has liked him. He is indeed a very charming and so far very serious young man. He is coming back to London next week and leaves for Potsdam soon afterwards. One thing I promised you. I am certainly coming to Berlin this October if you both will be there.

Tuesday, 11 September 1934

Tommy, who has been staying at Alloa House, met Sir Harry Stonor[1] there. He is now almost stone-blind, but can play golf and the other day landed a fifteen-pound salmon in the Tay. He is a great friend of Sir Basil Zaharoff.[2] The King hates latter and objects to his using title of 'Sir', as his G.C.B., given for bringing back very valuable information from Berlin during war, is only honorary. Basil Zaharoff has probably finest gold dinner service in the world. It seats thirty people; and centrepiece is so heavy that four men are required to lift it. It was made by Boucheron to match some quaint gold salt-cellars found by Sir Basil.

Pempe Dudley Ward came in, looking rather frail after her recent operation. She kept us in fits of laughter over story of Angie Ward's lost cloth dog 'Pinkie', which she has had since she was a child. She lost it or left it in train on way back from South of France. She has slept with it every night of her life. John de Forest, who has been courting her or paying attention to her, was furious at this childishness. He said: 'Well, you'll have to throw it away on your wedding night.' 'Pinkie will be there,' replied Angie! She was in tears over its loss, went to see all the station authorities, police, etc., and cried for days. Brendan Bracken, who is in love with Pempe, sent a detective at his own expense to investigate in France.

Friday, 14 September 1934

Lunched at Sibyl's. . . Much talk about Mrs Ronnie Greville who has been at Nuremberg and who has come back full of enthusiasm for Hitler. Her influence is very strong with Simon. Her vanity is inordinate. In those countries where she is not given a special train, the local British ambassador or minister gets sacked.

[1] (1859–1939) Groom in waiting to the King.
[2] (1850–1936), munitions manufacturer, banker and philanthropist.

Friday, 21 September 1934

Had to review L.G.'s Vol. III in the Diary today and to submit it to Max. My three paras were passed without alteration. Saw Ivor Nicholson, L.G.'s publisher, at the Savoy. He tells me that L.G.'s vitality is failing a little. He is shrinking, too. Nicholson saw his doctor recently. Latter said to him: 'You will not get two volumes out of him this next year. One – perhaps!' Up to date L.G. has done wonders for a man who was supposed to be constitutionally lazy. Vol. I of the *Memoirs* was published in September 1933. Vol. IV will be published on October 26th. This means 700,000 words in about eighteen months.

Saturday, 22 September 1934

Wet and damp. Came down to Horsham by the 1.40. Before I left, Jean rang up to say that she was willing to try another period of six months together to see if things would go better. At the end of the six months she was to be free to decide.

In my talk with her mother last night my books figured largely. She said that they had in each case given Jean a *crise de nerfs* and that after reading the proofs of the new one she had nearly fainted. I replied that I was sorry and that I understood something of her feelings if not of this hysteria. I pointed out how impossible it was for me to work in this atmosphere when both Jean and she regarded my writing as a kind of garbage when my own friends were spurring me on to do more as I was making or had it in me to make a permanent contribution to English literature. I stressed the fact that I could not do my third volume unless I left Beaverbrook.

Sunday, 30 September 1934

Rose early [at Hunger Hill] and breakfasted downstairs. Went to Mass with Tommy at ten-thirty. After church went for a walk and felt better. Major Paulet[1] and his wife came to luncheon. Latter is rather terrible. He is a cousin of the Marquess of Winchester and was the War Office attendant on L.G. at the Ministry of Munitions. Ministry was first housed in a few rooms on third floor of War Office. L.G. had a great flair for picking out organisers. Picked out Riddell when he was at Ministry of Munitions. Also Eric Geddes.[2] Paulet had to engage them. Geddes, very pompous, insisted on a room for himself, one for his secretary, and one for his typist. Paulet shook his head, said there was no accommodation, and that Geddes could have only one room. 'Let's divide it into three then,' said Geddes. It was done at once. For two days Geddes sat doing nothing, an empty desk, and a stylo nearly as fat as himself, his first job was the charge of all bicycles!

[1] Major Charles Standish Paulet (1873–1953), deputy-director of supply, Ministry of Munitions, 1915–19.

[2] Sir Eric Geddes (1875–1937) became 1st Lord of the Admiralty (1917–19) and wielded the 'Geddes axe' on expenditure in 1921–2.

Monday, 1 October 1934

A quiet day with one customary annoyance. I brought back from Mary the whole inside story of Pempe Dudley Ward's engagement to play in the Bergner film of *Escape Me Never*. I was told to do it for Diary. Then I was told it was to be a news story and that Betjeman was to do it. I gave him my stuff. Not a word of it was used, and in the stuff that appeared there was a bad mistake – saying that she had left that day for Venice whereas she was not leaving till end of week (Thursday morning).

Thursday, 4 October 1934

Lunched at Lady Cunard's and sat [next] Mrs Baldwin... Mrs Baldwin was exactly like what I have always imagined her to be. She made one good remark: we were discussing who was England's greatest Queen. Choice lay between Queen Victoria and Queen Elizabeth. Mrs Baldwin calmed the storm by saying: 'Well, neither would have been a success if their roles had been reversed.' Lady Cunard told a good story of Mr Baldwin and his goodness. Mr Baldwin once remarked: 'I don't know if I'll go to Heaven, but if I ever do, it will be, I'm sure, on the train of Mrs Baldwin's dress.' Lady Cunard said: 'A very charming tribute from a man who has been married a long time – a very long time!' Good talk of old Lady Cunard about Mrs Ronnie Greville (Maggie) who is pro-Hitler and Dr Ethel Smyth, the composer, who is very poor, very deaf, and rides everywhere on a bicycle. Dr Ethel Smyth was a great suffragette and at time of suffrage campaign attacked the Royal Family. Later, met Queen Mary and had a long talk about changed times.

Sunday, 7 October 1934

After luncheon drove down to Churt to see L.G. who looked radiantly well. He wants German military books on the 1918 period, i.e. post-war reflections of German soldiers on the collapse. Was quite pro-Hitler; said he had a good programme, and obviously believes in the necessity of Radical leaders. Expressed a hope that Roosevelt would *not* go Right. Told us he had made a bet with Rothermere and Winston that there would be no war (with Rothermere) in four years and (with Winston) in six months. Had already won his Winston bet. Was prepared to bet evens on the years and odds on (decreasing of course) for every year down to ten.

Tuesday, 9 October 1934

Lunched with Randolph at Boulestin's. He told me a lot about his father and F.E. [Smith, 1st Earl of Birkenhead]. They had a quarrel in the last years of F.E.'s life. Latter had just joined the board of Tate and Lyle's sugar and in front of a lot of people at Winston's house F.E. began to pester Winston to do something for Sir Leonard Lyle, saying that he had stood down for Winston at Epping, etc. Latter statement was quite untrue, and Winston was a little sore. F.E., however, went on nagging at Winston – showing quite obviously that he wanted an allocation of shares for himself, etc. In the end Winston became angry. The quarrel was made up, but relations were never quite the same. Second volume of young Lord Birkenhead's life of his father is ready for serialisation. Is now being read by Winston and Baldwin.

In afternoon took Prince Louis to see the Prince of Wales. Prince saw him for nearly three-quarters of an hour, was very nice, told him that he was pro-German. Prince Louis talked to him about America and said that many people in America believed that the Prince did not want to be King and would step down in favour of his brother. 'That's all rot,' said our Prince.[1]

Wednesday, 10 October 1934

Randolph told me yesterday that during the Marconi crisis Winston was the go-between between L.G. and Bonar Law and carried the messages between both as to what word L.G. would accept as censure for his offence. I think 'indiscretion' was finally agreed. L.G. repaid Winston by making him Minister of Munitions in 1916 in the face of bitter Conservative opposition.[2]

Monday, 15 October 1934

Came into Edinburgh with Tom [Macgregor] at ten o'clock. Bitterly cold and wet. At eleven-thirty went to see Scott Douglas and had a long talk about my affairs. The Trustees are very severe on Jean who they consider is sinfully extravagant... There is now only £1000 in the Trust. The book *British Agent* has made up to £8700 odd. Nearly fifty per cent has gone in income-tax. Putnam's still owes us £500 on the advance for *Retreat from Glory*. There will also be some money on account of *British Agent* both from London and America at the end of this month.

Tuesday, 16 October 1934

Lunched at Huntington's. Sat next Baroness Blixen (Isak Dinesen) the author of *Seven Gothic Tales*,[3] and Ruby Lindsay (Peto that was). The Baroness is a peculiar-looking woman – very white and thin with large dark eyes. Very intense. Longs to go back to Kenya where she spent the best eighteen years of her life and where she had a love-affair with Denys Finch-

[1] Two years later the Prince, then King Edward VIII, abdicated, and his brother succeeded.

[2] There was a scandal in 1912–13 because Lloyd George, then Chancellor of the Exchequer, and other Liberal Ministers had bought shares in the American Marconi Company knowing that the British Government had accepted the Marconi tender for an 'Imperial wireless chain'. Lloyd George admitted an error of judgement, since the acceptance of the tender by the House had not, when he bought the shares, been ratified. Bonar Law was Leader of the Conservative Opposition at the time. The Liberal majority in the House prevented the Ministers being censured at all. Churchill was made Minister of Munitions in 1917, not 1916.

[3] Baroness Karen Blixen (1885–1962), who wrote under the name of Isak Dinesen. She put her African experiences into *Out of Africa* (1938).

Hatton, the big-game hunter.[1] She loves the natives and, if she goes back, will probably write in Africa.

Wednesday, 17 October 1934

Cold and wet. Lunched at Lady Cunard's. . . Sat next Mrs Ronnie Greville who talked pro-Hitler stuff with great vigour. She is a convinced pro-German and is very angry that no one from the British Embassy went to the *Partei-Tag* at Nuremberg. After all, the British Ambassador in Moscow attends the May 1st and November 7th celebrations in Moscow. She also told me that when she went to Australia a Sydney reporter made her say a lot of things she never said about Australians and emigrants to Australia. She made no reply to the Press attacks, but she never forgave. Her father left a provision in his will that she should never invest her money in Australian securities. She intends to do the same in her will.

Very good review of my book by Wyatt Tilby in the *Yorkshire Post*. A bombshell from Huntington who rang up to tell me that H. G. Wells had objected to the cherry story in my book on the grounds that it was untrue and had demanded a contradiction and the removal of the story from subsequent editions. This is pure spite and spleen on H.G.'s part . . . Story has been known to me for ages; apart from that, Philip Page, who was a member of the delegation, was actually present and gives chapter and verse for the incident.[2]

Sunday, 21 October 1934

Freda [Dudley Ward] says that, contrary to all Louis Ferdinand's remarks, Prince George is very in love with Princess Marina,[3] although at first, when he was saying that he would have to settle down and marry and Princess Marina's name was suggested to him, he did think (like Prince Louis) that she was too 'bossy'.

Tuesday, 23 October 1934

In the evening went to the first night of *Theatre Royal* at the Lyric with Sibyl. The play is American.[4] It was meant to be a skit on the Barrymore family. It was very well acted by Madge Titheradge, Marie Tempest and Laurence Olivier. It was one of the new Noël Coward productions: Wilson, Coward, Lunt and Fontanne. Laurence Olivier has a fine burlesque part as the member of this great acting family who goes to Hollywood. Went round behind stage afterwards. Sibyl is rather tiresome in these matters. She wants to talk or shake hands with anyone and everyone she has ever met. The scrum

[1] (1887–1931) 2nd son of 13th Earl of Winchilsea, killed while flying in East Africa.

[2] A harmless story in *Retreat from Glory* about H. G. Wells getting into trouble with Czech peasants for picking cherries from their trees by the roadside.

[3] Prince George (1902–42), fourth son of King George V, had announced his engagement to Princess Marina, youngest daughter of Prince Nicholas of Greece, on 5 October. He was created Duke of Kent on 12 October, and they were married on 29 November.

[4] By Edna Ferber and George Kaufman.

was stupendous. Saw and met Noël Coward who was charming to me. Said he had loved my first book and was going to take my second with him on his journey back to the States. He leaves next week.

Lockhart received a letter on 24 October 1934 from John Buchan, later Lord Tweedsmuir, the novelist, historian and Governor-General of Canada, 1935–40:

It was very good of you to send me your *Retreat from Glory*, and I read it avidly last weekend. It gave me enormous entertainment. You have invented a new kind of autobiography, a very delectable kind. It is a great thing to be a gentleman, for you manage to be self-revealing without being self-conscious! But I think it lucky that you are safely folded in the bosom of the Catholic Church, for if you had been a Buchmanite your 'sharing' would have bust up the show.

I long to talk to you about some of the things. Michael Spencer-Smith was a very old and intimate friend of mine, and his daughter Beatrice was one of our maids of honour at Holyrood.[1] I want to know more about your fishing, especially that magical stream near Munich, which somehow or other I have missed. Also about Slovenia. I was thrilled by your mention of the Krka. I once explored its lower course in a boat.

Wednesday, 24 October 1934

Lunched at Sibyl's. Present: Mrs Grenfell, Mrs Simpson,[2] Lady Ravensdale, Lady Storrs, Victor Cazalet, Ronald Storrs, Beverley Nichols, and self.

Thursday, 25 October 1934

Gave a luncheon to Sir George Clerk, Brendan Bracken, and Mr Peter Bark. Bark is to negotiate for Austria the new Austrian Reconstruction Loan. He negotiated the Austrian Loan in 1923. Now ten years after he has to do it again. A good deal of talk about war, which G.R.C. thinks is quite possible, and finally a fierce but good-humoured attack by Brendan on Montagu Norman. The talk was poor, with the honours to Brendan. G.R.C. told us an amazing story how ——, one of our younger diplomats, spent the evening in a Paris hotel on his way through from Geneva to London with Mademoiselle ——, the Slav lady who was carrying bombs for the Croat and Macedonian assassins. He met her at his usual hotel, dined with her and went out with her a lot round the town afterwards. He did *not* sleep with her. That is what made the French so suspicious. George had some difficulty in hushing matter up.

Saturday, 27 October 1934

My book continues to bring me a large correspondence: from the Kaiser,

[1] In 1933 Buchan was appointed Lord High Commissioner to the General Assembly of the Church of Scotland; this entailed regal pomp at Holyroodhouse with maids of honour.

[2] The first mention in the diary of the future Duchess of Windsor.

Lord Mersey,[1] John Buchan, etc. Kaiser's letter is marvellous – obviously written by himself and full of gratitude. Mr Belloc also wrote a very charming letter.

Monday, 29 October 1934

Came up from Coolham by the eight thirty-four and deposited my bag at 11 Montpellier Place. Jean in bed with a bad cold. She has worked like a Trojan putting my books in order. At the office Schapiro also off – ill with threatened appendicitis.

Thursday, 1 November 1934

Old Lady Horner[2] whom I sat next to at dinner last night has the four most remarkable nephews in England: Hailsham, McKenna, Freyberg V.C., and Mark Hambourg. She says in a conversation Hambourg would dominate the others! She is also grandmother to Lord Oxford and was mother-in-law to Raymond Asquith.

Friday, 16 November 1934

Lunched at the Jardin with Moura. Discussed books. H. G. Wells is going this week to Uppark, the house of Lady Fetherstonhaugh, where his mother was housekeeper sixty years ago. It was here that H.G. had his first scientific instincts aroused. He spent his days reading Plato and his nights gazing at the stars through an old telescope. This will be his first visit since he was there as a boy of seven. He attributes immense importance to his first visit as a developing influence on his life.

Monday, 3 December 1934

Lunched with Namier who has written rather a rotten review of my book. He is jealous of my 'undeserved' success compared with poor reward for his own scholarship. He is now doing a book on historical errors. Hopes to get professorship of history at Oxford. There are strong rival candidates including Feiling who is popular with Conservatives.[3]

Tuesday, 4 December 1934

Namier, with whom I lunched yesterday, is now a Tory Socialist. He thinks that capitalism is finished, but that it is important that the transition stage should be accomplished without catastrophic upheaval in order that culture may be preserved.

[1] 2nd Viscount Mersey (1872–1956), soldier and diplomat.

[2] Widow of Sir John Horner, member of the 'Souls' and close friend of Asquith – her daughter married his son. Some of the 'nephews' were nephews-in-law. Bernard Freyberg (1889–1963), later 1st Baron and Governor-General of New Zealand; Mark Hambourg (1879–1960), concert pianist born in Russia.

[3] Keith Feiling (*b.* 1884) became Chichele Professor of Modern History at Oxford in 1946. Namier was Professor of Modern History at Manchester, 1931–53. Both were subsequently knighted.

Thursday, 6 December 1934

Today, on Plummer's advice, I sent off my letter to Beaverbrook asking for two months' leave on the ground of being run down. I have almost made up my mind to resign if it is refused. This, too, in spite of being overdrawn at the bank. It is the critical moment, and if I can get a publisher to guarantee me £1500 a year for the next five years I shall take the risk.

Saturday, 8 December 1934

This morning Plummer sent for me. I am to have my ten weeks' leave on half-pay. This complicates things a little and means that I shall be obliged morally to put in another eighteen months in Fleet Street. I am to say nothing until I hear from Max. Plummer suggests that if I play my cards well further trips will not be excluded. At twelve Whelan rang up to ask if I could dine at Cherkley on Sunday. I must go.

At any rate I now get my trip. I shall probably have to fly home. Otherwise I shall not have time to do all I want which includes Federated Malay States, Port Dickson, Saigon and Angkor, and a bit of Java. If I fly back from Bangkok or Singapore I gain nearly a fortnight extra out there.

If I were to remain in Fleet Street and to keep my health, I must learn to manage my time better. I am not methodical, and Fleet Street is the hardest place to be methodical in.

Sunday, 9 December 1934

Lord Beaverbrook was very nice, told me I could go to Malaya and could write as many books as I liked. Said he liked *Retreat from Glory* and thought it was quite as good a book as first one, but for America *British Agent* was a better title. I agree.

Wednesday, 12 December 1934

A wretched day. Felt very ill after last night and as a result was able to do no work.

Lunched at Boulestin's with Michael Colefax and talked about British Gaumont who are said to be in a bad way. Beverley Baxter, the former editor of the *Express*, who is said to have been receiving £12,000 a year from British Gaumont, has gone already, and there have been 400 dismissals in the last ten days.

Thursday, 13 December 1934

Still feeling very nervy and jumpy. Lunched at Sibyl Colefax's. . . Somerset Maugham praised Harold very highly. Said he could describe a person's exterior better than any novelist. Somerset Maugham is peculiar man – has terrific inferiority complex, hates people, yet is a snob and cannot refuse a luncheon where he is to meet a countess. Life ruined by wife who is coarse and irritating. Once he was having tea in his own house with a friend, when his wife came in. Her voice downstairs irritated him so much that he hid behind the sofa and stayed there until his wife left again!

Friday, 14 December 1934

Lunched with Harold, who has just come back from the U.S.A., and Sibyl at Boulestin's. Harold is writing Dwight Morrow's[1] life and has been seeing a lot of the Lindberghs, the Morrows, the Morgans, etc. He is a little worried about his job. Morrow was not as big a man as the Americans think. On the other hand, his character is more complex than Harold thought. His chief difficulty is the suspicion of Morrow's friends. Every time he asks a pertinent question he is up against it. Only J. P. Morgan gave him an honest answer to his question: was Morrow a selfish man? 'Selfish,' said J.P., 'why he'd have murdered his own children if they'd stood in his way.'

Friday, 21 December 1934

For nearly a fortnight now I have known the real story of the Kirov murder in Russia.[2] It was an internal plot framed by the Ogpu who disliked the diminution of their power and blamed Kirov's influence with Stalin for it. Stalin's first act was to put Yagoda under arrest for twenty-four hours. Then he decided that the further detention of Yagoda or even his execution would be too damaging to Bolshevik prestige both at home and abroad. This was told to Moura by Gorky's wife whom she went to see at Vienna on her way from Moscow to Sorrento. But although the papers are full of the story now I could not get it published in my paper.

Lunched at Mrs Ronnie Greville's: Present – Lord Carisbrooke (former Prince Alexander of Battenburg),[3] Colin Davidson, General Spears, Ray Atherton, Mrs Atherton, Sonia Keppel, Lady Carisbrooke. Lord Carisbrooke button-holed me afterwards and we had a long talk about the Kaiser. He is rather anti-Kaiser, says he is a charmer but has 'this appalling vanity and this appalling streak of vulgarity'. He thinks it was a question of environment. If the Kaiser had been brought up in England, he would have been O.K. Conversely, if King Edward had been brought up in Germany, he would have been worse than the Kaiser.

Friday, 28 December 1934

Remarkable article by Rothermere, who has been seeing Hitler, on what

[1] (1873–1931) lawyer, banker and diplomat. Nicolson recorded in his diary, 26 October 1934, that Morrow 'had the mind of a super-criminal and the character of a saint. There is no doubt at all that he was a very great man.' *Diaries and Letters, 1930–9* (1966). His daughter Anne was married to Charles Lindbergh, first man to fly solo non-stop across the Atlantic.

[2] Sergei N. Kirov, one of Stalin's early close collaborators, had been assassinated on 1 December. The murder was arranged by Genrikh Yagoda, chief of the Ogpu, at Stalin's instigation. It set off the 'Great Purges' of the 1930s.

[3] The Marquess of Carisbrooke (1886–1960) was the son of Queen Victoria's youngest daughter, and thus a cousin of the Kaiser – son of her eldest daughter.

Hitler has done for Germany. There is something in it. Hitler has certainly given the Spartan spirit to Germany.

Sunday, 30 December 1934

In the evening played chess with Harry who is in a bad way with eczema and drink. He has been trying to do a cure, has been in bed for six days, and in order to stop himself drinking has been doping himself with various strong sleeping draughts . . . The result is that he feels – and looks – like death. He has not yet fixed up his finances for the trip and might easily 'chuck' at the last moment. It will be tragic if Tommy and he do not come.

Monday, 31 December 1934

Last day of a year which has been rather uneventful as far as I am concerned except for the publication of *Retreat from Glory*. In three years I have now written two books. Each has been over 120,000 words in length. Each has sold well. This, too, in addition to a yearly average of about 400,000 words in journalism.

I am fatter, lazier and definitely worse in health. My memory is defective, and I now waste more time in stupid exhausting little ways than I have ever done before. My domestic relations have not improved. My wife is more extravagant than ever, and so far from saving money as we ought to do we are actually spending more than we are receiving. I am more irritable and less insistent. My follies have been curbed by the passage of years. I am past *la grande passion*. But I am still capable of sitting in the club to one a.m. and ruining my digestion with drink. Had I more principle, I should have taken the bold course in November and left Beaverbrook instead of trying to compromise.

CHAPTER TWELVE

1935

Lockhart's visit to Malaya. Kerensky down and out. H. G. Wells on education. T. E. Lawrence dying. Prince of Wales, looking 'much coarser', with Mrs Simpson. He neglects Freda Dudley Ward. Excitement over Abyssinia. D. W. Griffith, film producer, a bore. Crown Princess of Germany on 'terrible people' in Nazi movement. Unity Mitford and Diana Guinness at Nuremberg rally. Harold Nicolson unhappy. Malcolm Muggeridge 'clever, nervous'. Kurt Hahn at German Foreign Office. Anglo-German Fellowship inaugurated. Vansittart on lack of support for sanctions against Italy.

Monday, 7 January 1935

In the evening dined at the Travellers' Club with Sir Ronald Storrs[1] who claims to be a great admirer of *Retreat from Glory*. He is thinking of writing his own autobiography and has been to see Huntington who advised him to copy my methods and do a synopsis like mine. Ronald Storrs is the son of the Dean of Rochester, has never had any money, and is careful of it now. He suffers from pernicious anaemia and has to take liver all the time. Liver – like insulin in diabetes – is not a cure. Ronald Storrs lost everything he had – all his art treasures collected in his thirty years in the East, his copy from Lawrence of *The Seven Pillars of Wisdom* and *Revolt in the Desert* with notes, etc. – in the fire at Cyprus. He lost more – he lost his reputation. He was to have left for England in two days when the fire occurred. He was being brought home secretly to be offered Bengal. The fire spoilt everything. Ronald Storrs is a little bitter. Thinks the Colonial Office a very poor show compared with the Foreign Office (it is full of jealousies and backbiters – what George Lloyd called clerks in garrets). He is a great friend of Gaselee, the Librarian of the Foreign Office, and goes to Cambridge for weekends with him. Gaselee, who is a fine scholar and has edited several Loeb classics, is first-class at his job. Vansittart told Storrs that he could produce a memo on the most difficult subject in no time. He does all kinds of odd jobs, is an expert on food and wine, and a friend of Queen Marie of Rumania whom he helped with her last autobiography. The improvement was very noticeable.

[1] Storrs (1881–1955) had been Governor of Jerusalem, 1917–26, and then of Cyprus. Instead of going to Bengal he was Governor of Northern Rhodesia, until invalided home in 1934.

Tuesday, 8 January 1935

Storrs told me a good story of Kitchener in Egypt.[1] There was a fine old Bedouin chief who while making great play of his loyalty to British was smuggling arms and munitions into Tripoli during Italo-Turkish War in 1911–12. Storrs heard of this and of course told Kitchener. By a coincidence the chief came to call on Kitchener same day. Came in full of bounce. Kitchener fixed him with that basilisk eye and said in Arabic: 'Where were you last night?' repeating it until the chief crumpled up completely. Kitchener then threatened to conscript the Bedouins who had privilege of being exempted. There was no more trouble. Allenby could never have done this.

Tuesday, 15 January 1935

Harold very amusing yesterday on Reggie Bridgeman[2] . . . Reggie Bridgeman did many foolish things at Teheran including writing a very foolish letter to Rothstein, the Bolshevist Minister, saying he could not come to his reception because His Majesty's Government very foolishly had not recognised Russia, etc. *Izvestia* published this. Final episode, however, was going to a dancing place (euphemism for brothel) disguised as Mullah. Spotted and taken back by police to Legation. Stories in papers – reported, I think, by Hodgson from Moscow, who asked if he could deny rumours that British Chargé d'Affaires had been beaten up in streets disguised as woman, etc. Curzon telegraphed out. Loraine had just arrived.[3] Not true Reggie had been beaten up. True that woman he was with was beaten up in streets. Loraine reluctant to give Reggie away. Insistance on explicit details by Curzon. Reggie dismissed. Loraine applying for him to be left for a month. Curzon agreeing if absolutely necessary and provided he was confined to his house. Reggie finally allowed to resign!

Wednesday, 16 January 1935

The other night Harold gave me full story again of Townley's dismissal.[4] When Kaiser came into Dutch territory after war, news was kept secret. Precautions taken, etc. Townley was informed officially and stupidly told his wife. She then got hold of a young British airman who had a car and made him drive her to the frontier station. She then managed to get on to the platform by insisting that she was the wife of the British Minister and had a

[1] Lord Kitchener (1850–1916), who had been Sirdar of the Egyptian Army in 1890, was consul-general there from 1911 until the outbreak of war. Storrs served as a political officer under Kitchener in Egypt and Allenby in Palestine.

[2] Reginald Francis Orlando Bridgeman (1884–1968) had been chargé d'affaires in Persia. He retired from the Foreign Office on a pension in 1923. A friend of Cocteau, he was later involved in Left-wing politics, member of British-Soviet Friendship Society and Committee for Nuclear Disarmament.

[3] Sir Percy Loraine (1880–1961), British Minister to Persia, 1921–6. Curzon was Foreign Secretary at the time.

[4] Sir Walter Beaupré Townley (1863–1945), Minister to the Netherlands, 1917–19. His wife, Lady Susan, was daughter of the 7th Earl of Albemarle.

right to the place. Then with a jeering expression she watched the Kaiser's humiliation. Whole story appeared in Dutch papers and eventually was shown to Curzon. Curzon sent for his private secretary and told him to take measures with the Dutch to ensure that lying reports of this nature should cease. Private secretary said: 'I do not think you have seen this despatch which has just arrived.' It was Townley's letter of resignation. He knew at once when the news came out that this was the last straw.

Lockhart set out for his trip to the Far East – his 'recherche du temps perdu' – on 17 January. He tells of his experiences in one of the best of his books, Return to Malaya, *published in November 1936. He travelled part of the way with Lord and Lady Rosslyn. He returned to work at the* Evening Standard *on 1 April 1935.*

Wednesday, 3 April 1933

Rather a wasted day. Tony Philpott has been appointed manager of the *Evening Standard* in succession to Plummer, who is going to the *Express* to step into Robertson's shoes eventually. Tony Philpott makes a good story. Very popular at Oxford ten years ago or so, he drank too much, got a job at Crawford's the advertising people, lost it, met Basil Murray in a pub, and was given a job in the Empire Crusade office. Continued to drink – bottle of port at luncheon favourite tipple – got ticked off by Lord Beaverbrook, desperately frightened of poverty, decided to give up smoking and drinking for one month. This was five years ago (four?). Since then has not drunk or smoked. Lives at Bath Club.

Thursday, 4 April 1935

Dined at home and went early to bed. I have been back only four days and already I feel as if I had never been away. I am slipping back, too, into all the old ways, and the difficulty of escaping from the long round of social engagements is more insoluble than ever.

Sunday, 7 April 1935

[Joseph] Conrad very good on women. Maugham as pederast, always cruel and unfair to women. Discussed literature with Michael Arlen who is a Conrad fan, put him miles above Maugham...

At Cherkley found my Lord Beaverbrook suffering from indigestion, Lord Castlerosse, eating, drinking and bubbling with good humour and lewd jokes – jester-in-chief to Lord Beaverbrook, Mike Wardell, Ruth ditto, Jean Norton and Michael Arlen. Max told us that he had lunched that day with Chipman (R. B. Bennett's doctor). Latter had told him that Bennett is fatally sick, has cardiac thrombosis, due to eating too many sweets and ices. May live for some years but doomed.

Max very keen about Joseph Patterson, owner and editor of *New York Daily News* who wrote saying England and U.S.A. should keep out of

Europe. *Express*, *Sunday Express* and *Standard* all had leaders on him. I had to find out all about him. Great things about him are: (1) that he is financially most successful journalist in U.S.A., (2) that he writes (very successfully too) his own editorials, (3) that he pays his staff best, and (4) that he *insists* on their having a five-day week. Cudlipp used all this except last which he was afraid to print. Amazing how everyone is afraid of Max.

Monday, 8 April 1935

Talk about Duke of Marlborough who has compounded with his father's creditors. . . He has also made some fuss about decorating his house for jubilee show in Carlton House Terrace. As Valentine says – 'his patriotism never flags'.[1]

Thursday, 11 April 1935

Lunched with Moir Mackenzie who gave me a long account of Sir Francis Joseph,[2] the new President of the Federation of British Industries. Began life as a railway messenger, did extra work three nights a week checking books of a local laundry, received 2*s*. 6*d*. extra a week and with this paid for his book-keeping and shorthand lessons at local Y.M.C.A. Like Citrine, Liverpool-born. Likes publicity. Will make the F.B.I. advertise. Moir, who knows Citrine well, tells me that Ramsay MacDonald sent for Citrine the other day and asked him to recommend six men from Labour side in industry for Jubilee honours. Citrine gave five and mentioned Moir as sixth. Ramsay told him that he (Ramsay) would not take a peerage but would end his days as he'd begun them, that Ishbel [his daughter] would not stay in house with him if he did. Citrine himself is to be a knight I gather. He wanted a C.H. Mrs Citrine wants the knighthood.[3]

Friday, 12 April 1935

My self-control and my nerves are worse than they have ever been before. And I come back to worry (we have again some £500 of bills) and to the necessity of working harder than ever. There is only one cure: a rigid self-discipline which in my case means abstention from alcohol and even tobacco and bread and butter, because in nothing that I like can I exercise restraint. I found this line in one of Chesterton's poems today: 'There are souls more sick of pleasure than you are sick of pain.'

To the Dorchester at seven to see Mrs Salomon, a friend of Kerensky. Kerensky is down and out; his money has come to an end; his paper has closed down. Mrs Salomon says can I get him journalistic work not so much to bring him in money (he has friends who will not let him starve) but to

[1] The 9th Duke of Marlborough had died 30 June 1934. King George V's jubilee was to be held on 6 May.

[2] (1870–1951) industrialist and ironfounder, left school at twelve.

[3] Citrine got his knighthood, but not his C.H. Mackenzie had to wait for his till 1951.

save his moral self-respect. Eighteen years ago he could have had the front page of any newspaper in the world. Today, his value is nil. *Sic transit!*

Sunday, 14 April 1935

At Cherkley I found H. G. Wells, Senator Elliot, Mike Wardell, Jean Norton and Max Beaverbrook. Conversation at dinner and after monopolised by Wells and Max. Not very good. Two chief subjects: education (to what school to send Mike's boy) and world decline or world recovery. Whole table was against public schools, Max recounting how games (organised) had ruined both his sons. Wells spoke of Dartington (two sexes – no punishments, etc.), recommended two or three years there, then four years at Royal College of Science. Some one mentioned the Navy. H.G. said: Naval education was all right provided one did not go into the Navy. There was fair science, good mathematics and some engineering. True, no biology – and biology very important, but not bad. Great drawback of all schools today – no economics in a world now dominated by economics.

Talked to H.G. after dinner about America. He thinks Roosevelt has lost ground and that there is a new movement coming from Left which may be dangerous. In U.S.A. you can talk open Communism provided you do not give it a red label. Max thinks differently, thinks America is recovering and England prosperous, laughs at idea that civilisation (in his sense) is ending and the world drifting to revolution. H.G. thinks man has lost control of his affairs.

Tuesday, 23 April 1935

In evening dined with Tommy at the Carlton Grill and then went to see Elisabeth Bergner and Pempe Dudley Ward in *Escape Me Never*. Elisabeth Bergner . . . was very good. Pempe fair. I doubt if she will ever make a great film actress. She lacks appeal and, although very beautiful, is too tall and less beautiful on screen than in real life.

Friday, 26 April 1935

Rather a wasted day. Gave luncheon at the Ivy to Maurice Peterson and Fletcher. Conversation rather poor. Fletcher suggests we should attack Air Ministry. It is a poor show – never has been good and never has had a good Air Minister. Full of discards from Army and Navy. Suggested that Fellowes[1] who was on Everest expedition would give us a lot of material.

Thursday, 2 May 1935

Lunched at Sibyl's; present: Emerald, H.G., Somerset Maugham, Brendan, Alice Obolensky, Mrs Simpson (Prince of Wales's girl), Sir Robert and Lady

[1] Air Commodore Peregrine Fellowes (1883–1955), who led an expedition to fly over Everest in 1933. The attack on slow progress in British aviation appeared three days later.

Abdy. Lot of stupid talk by Brendan and H.G. on Huey Long,[1] Ramsay, the King and the O.M. H.G. said he might be a snob but he had too much pride to take the O.M. or to belong to an order which had been given to Galsworthy and Hardy. H.G. is getting vainer every day. Saw Harold who is back from Greece.

Saturday, 11 May 1935

After tea went out shooting without much success. Early to bed. Harry in a very bad state and talking of dying. He has had a fright and has now stated his intention of going into a home again – this time Sister Agnes's. I think that at last his constitution has rebelled against his excesses. He feels bilious and sick but cannot give up his liquor. His mind is quite gone and his selfishness is unrivalled. He now keeps his own bedroom door open and makes Tommy keep hers open, too, and as he wakes her up about three times a night she gets no sleep.

Monday, 13 May 1935

Gave luncheon party to Somerset Maugham, Harold and Moura. Maugham told me that his new book is finished and that he is now going to write his autobiography – not so much the incidents of his life as his attitude towards life, towards writing, the drama, and indeed towards all the activities in which he has been engaged. He is leaving London at once, goes back to France where he is letting his villa, and will return to England in October. He does not understand how anyone can write in London.

Quite an amusing luncheon. I told them how I had saved Winston's bacon over his Jubilee articles for the *Standard*. He had described scene at Privy Council on morning after King Edward's death and not only mentioned Asquith as being present but described his entrance into the room. By an error of my own – I left Gainford's name out of a diary paragraph of Cabinet Ministers alive today who were present at succession – I had been reminded that Asquith, L.G., McKenna, etc., all were abroad at time of King Edward's death. Asquith did not get back till three days later.

Sunday, 19 May 1935

Had long talk with General [Sir Charles] Grant about Lawrence who is said to be dying now.[2] He is of illegitimate strain. His mother or grandmother was poor Scottish governess in Irish family of Chapman. Old Chapman lived with her (leaving his family) and had four children by her. Grant, who

[1] Huey Long (1893–1935), the corrupt 'Kingfish' governor of Louisiana, 1928–31, had just been murdered.

[2] T. E. Lawrence died that day as a result of a motor accident. His father was T. R. Chapman, who took the name of Lawrence to live with his governess in Oxford. T. E. Lawrence did not return to Egypt, except as part of a conference in Cairo on Arab affairs organised by Churchill in 1922. Churchill considered him a success.

was in Egypt, says that when Lawrence went back in 1923(?) Arabs had no use for him. He had no money.

Monday, 27 May 1935

Dined tonight at Sibyl Colefax's. Although I had not been warned, and, indeed, had been told to wear a short coat, I discovered that it was a large party for the Prince of Wales and Mrs Simpson. Room was divided into two tables. I sat at the Prince's table. Company very mixed. Macmullen,[1] an American journalist on *Vogue*, Alexander Korda, the film magnate, Lord Dalkeith[2] and self were men at our table. Women included Elsie Mendl, Mrs Simpson, Sibyl, Lady Dalkeith, Prince looks very lined and much coarser than he was a few years ago. He drank a good deal, joked quite a bit, followed everything Mrs Simpson said with closest interest, and was very amused by Elsie Mendl's blue hair.

After dinner we went into drawing-room where Brendan Bracken and I drew into a corner. . . Prince came over and said: 'Ah, there are the men I wish to hear,' and dragged us into his circle. Long discussion followed on foreign policy and France and Germany. Brendan very anti-German and warlike, I rather anti-French and our own foreign policy. Prince came out very strong for friendship with Germany: never heard him talk so definitely about any subject before.

Saturday, 1 June 1935

Went down to Cherkley. Present: D. W. Griffith, the film producer, who married Lilian Gish and produced *The Birth of a Nation*. Co-operated with Max, when latter was Minister of Information. . . tall with grey hair, and now rather overtaken in the cinema race. A bore. Says coloured films will not be as big a revolution as the stereoscopic and broad-strip film with screen as big as theatre stage. Could be done now, but film companies hate change – too much capital invested. Also present: [Antony] Fokker, creator of Fokker plane, a Java-born Dutchman, tubby, florid, active, great talker, doesn't drink or smoke. Made a fortune in America, but did not do as well as he ought. More Latin in type than stolidly Dutch.

Douglas,[3] a younger man, lives in California. Fair, clean-shaven, quite modest.

Both men believe in the air tremendously. Douglas no belief in fleets: says today only a few hundred miles of ocean safe from air attack. Soon there will not even be that.

Max – quite air-mad. Firing off questions at Fokker like a machine-gun!

[1] Later personal secretary to Elsie Mendl – she was a society hostess, American wife of Sir Charles Mendl, press attaché, British Embassy, Paris.

[2] (*b.* 1894) M.P. for Roxburgh, succeeded his father later that year as 8th Duke of Buccleuch.

[3] Donald W. Douglas (*b.* 1892), president of Douglas Aircraft, 1928–57, which built the various D.C.s.

Thursday, 6 June 1935

Lunched with Moura. She attacked me violently for not breaking away from Beaverbrook and for my self-indulgence and lack of courage. Said it was a scandal for me to prostitute my talents in this way. Not only were people saying that I was superficial and without principle but that I already *was* superficial, and without principle. True – *que de souvenirs! que de regrets!*

In the evening went to dine at the [Prince] Bismarcks to meet the Crown Princess of Germany, who had asked especially to see me. Tall, very stout now, and rather grand in manner but kind and good-natured. Had long talk with her afterwards. Not very pro-Hitler. Says there are some terrible people in the movement. Also that persecution of church worries her much. She was sad about the King and the Kaiser, admitted quite frankly and, indeed, unconsciously how sad she found the contrast. Here were two families related, similar – rulers of two greatest peoples. Then had come this unfortunate war. And now they – the Hohenzollerns – were more or less in exile. And here George and his wife were lucky and happy enough to be having a wonderful Jubilee.

Saturday, 8 June 1935

Last night Tommy told me a good story of Unity Mitford and Diana Guinness. Both Fascists – last year wanted to go to Nuremberg rally; couldn't get in. Saw man following them; rather frightened. Man spoke quite politely. Offered to help. Gave them card to hotel. Rooms free. Wonderful treatment. Later, met Hitler in Munich. Said, 'You must come to the rally this year as my guests.' Girls replied, 'We've been your guests already!' Going again this year.

Came down to Wilton by the 3 p.m. . . Reggie Pembroke[1] told some good stories about [the Sultan of] Johore and also about Ireland. Johore used to have diamond in his front teeth. All the girls used to try to bite it out. [Reggie] fought an election in Ireland once. Sheriff drunk at the counting. Colossal fake. All dead bodies on register polled. Reggie's agent said: 'You'll poll every name on the register, your lordship.' After election one man – a mate who had impersonated a captain at sea – was prosecuted. Reggie inclined to let him off when so many involved. 'Oh no, your lordship, it was a dirty trick. You see the mate was not only impersonating captain but was living with his wife.'

Reggie also remembers arrival of first aeroplane at manoeuvres in West Ireland in 1912. 'Glory be to God: what's that?'

'An aeroplane,' says Reggie.

'Is there anyone inside it?'

Wednesday, 12 June 1935

Lunched at the Dalkeiths. Present: Lord Delamere, and two or three

[1] 15th Earl of Pembroke (1880–1960), who lived at Wilton House.

women, whose names I did not catch. Lady Dalkeith very nice, asked me to stay with them in Scotland when I come for my Stevenson lecture. Most amusing part of conversation was re Prince of Wales's speech in favour of Germany at British Legion Meeting. Lady Dalkeith said all London was saying that I had influenced him. This – of course – after the episode the other night at Sibyl Colefax's where I defended his viewpoint against Brendan Bracken. It is quite untrue. The Prince of Wales has been playing about with this pro-German idea long before our conversation. It is a pity we had not taken it up in Stresemann's time!

Sunday, 16 June 1935

At six-thirty Hamish drove me over to Cherkley where I dined and stayed the night. Present: Richard and Jean Norton, Paul Cravath (a bore), Jimmie Dunn (another bore), Valentine, Frank Owen. Max slightly perturbed about Dorothy Cheston-Bennett's book of Arnold Bennett's letters to her. Great deal about Max and Valentine in them. Conversation reported of occasion when Arnold Bennett claimed to have come to protection of Venetia [Montagu] and Diana Cooper, because it was so bawdy. Max's theory is that Dorothy Cheston was jealous; could not go everywhere with Arnold Bennett. Arnold Bennett would tell her he was going on trip with Max – all men. Would arrive and find women. Express great surprise. Letters (with accounts of conversations, etc.) sent to keep Dorothy Cheston quiet. Arnold Bennett fond of pornography. Frightened Max and his friends by bringing pornographic (homosexual) literature from Germany. Letters poor stuff: praise of Valentine's brain; wonder at Max's wonderful memory . . . and wonderful knowledge of history. . .

Wednesday, 26 June 1935

Lunched with Harold Nicolson. He had to go over to the States about his Morrow book. Morgans had expected the book to be a eulogy not only of Morrow but of Morgans. When they learnt that the book made Morrow a hero indeed but a hero who was never very happy in Morgans, they brought pressure to bear on Mrs Morrow. Harold had to go over. He has had his way, but has toned down some of the Morgan stuff. He was firmly backed by Lindbergh, Morrow's son-in-law.

Harold, incidentally, is unhappy that at forty-eight he has no place in public life. He does not want to be a journalist. He cannot get into Parliament (he tried for Sevenoaks just now as a Tory!). He wants to go back to the Foreign Office and asked my advice how best to do it. He suggested even applying for the post of librarian! I told him to aim high – assistant under-secretary at least – and to write to George Clerk. Nicolson's people are pure Scot.

Thursday, 27 June 1935

Maurice told me last night that he drafted the Abyssinian concessions which Eden put up to Mussolini.[1] They included a strip of British Somaliland and a railway from Massawa to Mogadishu. Maurice said he drafted them as a possible suggestion without anything more than the faint hope that, if he were bluffing, Mussolini might like a way out. Eden jumped at it.

Sunday, 7 July 1935

After church went for walk in the Park. Discussed Freda Dudley Ward and the Prince of Wales. Although they had been friends for years, he has not spoken to her for over a year. Last year, when Angie Ward was being married, Freda asked Prince to wedding.[2] No answer. She then telegraphed and received very formal reply of regret. Although previously he had never missed children's birthdays, he sent no wedding present. . . . No explanation for his behaviour . . .

Monday, 15 July 1935

Lazy afternoon – too hot. In evening dined at Tommy's for bridge. Sat next Lady Mar and Kellie who very kindly asked me to stay at Alloa. She told me that ex-King of Greece is going back (after the plebiscite).[3] Seems quite confident. His recent divorce will do him no harm. It has been on the verge of publicity for years, and Greeks did not want her after Carol' streatment of his Grecian wife. Ex-Queen of Greece was or rather is Carol's sister. Queen Marie of Rumania always says: 'What did I do to deserve children like this?' Answer is: 'Never brought them up properly.'

Wednesday, 17 July 1935

Rather cooler. Lunched at Sibyl Colefax's. . . Not very exciting. Talked German with Tilly Losch,[4] who thinks very little of present Russian ballet at Covent Garden and says that Diaghilev would turn in his grave. Talked with Sibyl about Wells and Arnold Bennett. H.G. told her the other day that if he died tomorrow he would not leave £12,000. He has been very generous to his various dependants, legal and otherwise. . .

Lord Beaverbrook, Mike and Co. came back from their car-circus ride round Central Europe. Mike tells me that the Mussolini visit was a success. Mussolini was clever. He conducted the interview on his own lines and spent most of the time laughing at himself. Max was amused. Big people in Buda-

[1] Mussolini was beginning to threaten war over Abyssinia. Anthony Eden was the minister responsible for League of Nations affairs.

[2] Freda Dudley Ward had been a close friend of the Prince of Wales since 1917. Angie was her younger daughter Angela, who had married, in January 1935, Captain Robert Laycock, later Major-General Sir Robert, Chief of Combined Operations, Governor of Malta.

[3] George II of Greece (1890–1947) had lost his throne in 1923. The plebiscite in November 1938 proved favourable and he returned.

[4] Viennese danseuse and actress (*b.* 1907), married 6th Earl of Carnarvon in 1939.

pest gave him a show too. He was not impressed. Hungarians squabbled among themselves. 'This is our case,' said one. 'No, it's not,' said another.

Sunday, 28 July 1935

Rather warm and humid. Spent a very quiet morning reading. Cudlipp and Jones (of the *Evening News*) came to luncheon. Max in great form with stories of Castlerosse: how on one occasion Lady Castlerosse came to him (Max) for protection, showed her bruises. Max went for Valentine. At last Valentine, indignant, pulled up his trouser-leg, showed great bite.

Max said: 'Even this is no reason for hammering her like that.'

Valentine: 'But damn it! she wouldn't let go.'

Bathed twice. In evening Ashfield arrived. Max in terrific form dancing and singing songs: old New Brunswick songs: The Jones Brothers; 'All People That on Earth do Dwell', etc. The little man has a great sentimental streak. Jimmie Dunn tells me that his link-up with Patterson of the *New York Daily News* is not entirely politics and is kind of Anglo-American back-scratching. Patterson's father also was a Presbyterian Minister from New Brunswick!

Tuesday, 30 July 1935

In the evening dined with P. Q. Reiss to meet Amy and Jim Mollison. Dined at the Berkeley Grill. Amy and Jim are now in a difficult position. They have to live up to a certain standard and to keep up a certain showmanship. And the cash is gone and even the celebrity-value. Their end, like that of the beauty queen, will be sad. Amy is a sensible woman with her head screwed on. Jim, who writes short stories and is a cynic, is a weaker character.

Thursday, 1 August 1935

Gave a luncheon to Bernstorff, Jan Masaryk, Fletcher and Wheeler-Bennett. Bernstorff is better. He had ten inoculations for hay-fever in Berlin and one went wrong! The result was an abscess on his posterior. It had to be cut.

Conversation rather disjointed, and too many stories. Jan told several – all rather lewd. One was of Ellen Terry and Henry Irving – after *Julius Caesar*.

Irving says: 'May I see you home, Ellen?'

'Yes.'

'May I come up and have supper with you?'

'Yes.'

After supper: 'May I undress you?'

'Yes.'

How divine, how beautiful, etc. 'May I undress myself?'

'Yes.'

He does. Ellen looks down. Does not think much of what she sees. Says so.

'Ah!' says Irving. 'You are Cleopatra, Venus, all that is lovable and beautiful. But as for me I come to bury Caesar not to praise him!'

Monday, 5 August 1935

Tommy who spent Sunday with Lady Alexa Bertie, who is likely to become Lady-in-Waiting to Queen, told me good story of Princess Marina.

Queen on seeing her for first time looked at her nails (very red). 'I'm afraid the King doesn't like painted nails; can you do something about it?'

'*Your George may not, but mine does.*'

Thursday, 15 August 1935

Lunched with Willie Wiseman[1] at Savoy in Princess Ida rooms. Present: Otto Schiff, Mr. Leibeman(?), Colonel Geddes, Norman Thwaites and another. Much talk about Secret Service. Thwaites was under Wiseman in U.S.A. British collared all the German gang including Herr Dr Schider, the brilliant chemist who made the incendiary bombs. He turned King's evidence and worked afterwards for U.S.A. and for us, for Wiseman sent own formulae, etc. to England. He also gave his pals away. Dead now. Germans . . . all kept diaries – and women. Willie Wisemann told me that he thought seventy-five per cent of money he spent was wasted. Net had to be cast very wide. Was given strictest orders not to compromise himself with U.S.A. before they came in. He kept all his confidential documents in official safe marked 'Private and confidential only. Copy to American Secret Service,' so that if there were police raid or anything police would think it was O.K.!

Thursday, 29 August 1935

Times still continues to print hysterical letters from people who know nothing about foreign affairs on the iniquities of Mussolini and the necessity of sanctions, etc. The British public is never more dangerous than when it is in one of its moralising moods.

Friday, 30 August 1935

Lunched at Anthony Rothschild's: Present: Jack Churchill, Evelyn FitzGerald,[2] and a man from Schroeder's. Conversation about Abyssinia: Jack Churchill told story of inventor who came to see Winston at Admiralty.

[1] Sir William Wiseman, Bart (1885–1962), a Wall Street banker, had conducted British Intelligence in the United States in the First World War, as a member of the Purchasing Commission of the Ministry of Munitions. Lieut.-Colonel Norman Thwaites (1872–1956) had been secretary to Joseph Pulitzer for ten years before going on the special mission to the U.S.A. in 1916.

[2] Anthony de Rothschild (1887–1961) and the Hon. Evelyn FitzGerald (1874–1946) were bankers.

Plan was: trained seals with bombs attached to attack German Fleet. Seriously proposed. Winston requested by some 'big bug' to see him personally.

Also story of dinner at Embassy in Rome. Mussolini asks only British present. Arrives with cloak – fierce gesture, etc., before crowds. Once in Embassy – changes at once, rather an inferiority complex. Said to Webb Miller once: 'I began life as a journalist: maybe I'll finish as one.' Jack Churchill also told story of Winston as young man going to [Sir William] Harcourt in 1896(?) (Rosebery Government)[1] to ask his advice about politics.

Harcourt, then Chancellor of Exchequer, said: 'Certainly, my boy, go into politics, if you like; nothing ever happens.'

Winston says: 'I've been in politics nearly forty years and scarcely a day has passed without something happening.'

Tuesday, 3 September 1935

Gave luncheon to Balogh, a young Hungarian, who was employed on the Financial Committee of the League of Nations and who is now with Falk and Co.[2] Clever young man. Discussed Britain's policy or rather lack of policy in Europe. Agreed that if action should have been taken against Mussolini it ought to have been taken last December – certainly before he began sending troops to Eritrea.

Thursday, 5 September 1935

Lunched with Fitz Randolph[3] at the Park Lane. This is the first time that Germans have asked me out for some time. Randolph is a nice fellow but quite brainless. Sees Goebbels every time he goes to Berlin. Wants me to find English people to go to the *Partei-Tag* at Nuremberg. Free trips, etc., for any journalist or politician.

Friday, 6 September 1935

Maurice has been made head of the new Abyssinian Department. He tells me that Vansittart is the only strong man among the senior officials in the Foreign Office. Others are old women. Unfortunately, Van is a fanatic on the subject of Germany. He himself must be held largely responsible for the creation of Hitler. To get on in the Foreign Office you have to be one of Van's men.

Tuesday, 10 September 1935

Dined with Tommy who has come back from Scotland. She told me three good stories. One is about Portia Stanley whose French is cow-like. She was placed next King Amanullah at dinner. The King spoke no English.

[1] Actually in power March 1894 to June 1895.

[2] Thomas Balogh, later Lord Balogh and financial adviser to Socialist Government, 1964–70.

[3] Dr H. Sigismundo Sizzo Fitz Randolph was the German press attaché.

'*Avez-vous une maîtresse anglaise? Elles sont bien mieux pour les enfants.*' The other two are of the King and the Prince of Wales.

The King is going back again this year to the Hartington house near Eastbourne. Lord Hartington[1] asked H.M. if there was anything he could do to make H.M. more comfortable. After much pressing King said: 'Well, there's the bath. The water gurgles up from the bottom. I can't fill my jug when I go to get my shaving water!' Both King and Queen always pack their last little dressing-case themselves.

Prince of Wales has gone mad on gardening. Taken to it a hundred per cent like golf. Prince George wanted to bring Marina down. Prince of Wales put him off several times. At last agreed grudgingly if George would bring a scythe! George had to cut grass all afternoon!

Wednesday, 11 September 1935

Lunched today at the Travellers' with von Scherpenberg, Schacht's son-in-law.[2] He is going back to Berlin after seven-and-a-half years in London. He was worried about my paragraph on Schacht (I quoted Schacht's remark at a dinner in Berlin that 'he was going either to a monument or a scaffold') and said: 'I don't complain. I don't say that the story is not true. But if you wish to help my father-in-law as I think you do, this is not the best way to do it.' Scherpenberg is now a Nazi, but when one suggests gentle criticism he reacts. He agrees that the Allies made Hitler and thinks that even up to 1931 Germany could have been saved from Nazism.

Thursday, 12 September 1935

Fletcher worried about campaign against Vansittart. He has been asked to trace rumours. Have not heard much lately, but imagines chief anti-Van agitators are *The Times*.[3]

Friday, 13 September 1935

Opinion here is now very excited over Abyssinia.[4] There is great confusion of thought. Many wish to support the covenant at any cost believing that Mussolini is destroying the League. Others wish to support it because they believe Mussolini is threatening the existence of the British Empire; others again because they hate Fascism. The first group forget that the League committed virtual suicide the day it became legal executor of the Treaty of

[1] Later 10th Duke of Devonshire.

[2] Hilger von Scherpenberg was Second Secretary at the German Embassy. Though Schacht – then Hitler's economics minister – was sent to a concentration camp for being involved in an anti-Hitler plot, and tried for war crimes at Nuremberg, he escaped the scaffold and died in 1970 at the age of 93.

[3] *The Times*, under Geoffrey Dawson's editorship, 1929–41, was pro-appeasement. Vansittart was not.

[4] Mussolini was threatening to invade Abyssinia and the League of Nations was threatening sanctions. The home fleet was sent to Gibraltar and Britain seemed to be determined to stop Mussolini even if it meant using force.

Versailles and by that fact the tool of the victors. The second group crops up in every international crisis. The third group is the most illogical and embraces 90 per cent of the Labour Party. Its attitude would have been entirely different had Russia and not Italy been the aggressor.

Lunched with Eddie Grant. He is to marry the Herbert girl in October has not a 'bob', and has to leave Methuen's at the end of the year. He advises me to sign up with a publisher for five years against monthly advances. This is very popular nowadays, and if I wish to be free it is the best way to ensure independence. He tells me that the *Sunday Pictorial* paid £10,000 for Duff's *Haig* serial rights. *Telegraph* bid first but not enough. When Freddy Lawson finally decided to pay the £10,000, it was too late. Duff gets £5000 of this plus £5000 for the advance on the book itself. He won't make more. Two-decker memoirs do not pay nowadays. Robin came back from Aldeburgh. Dined at home and went to film.

Saturday, 14 September 1935

Lord Beaverbrook is very typical in his attitude towards the Abyssinian dispute. He is not interested in getting information. Certainly he would never consult one of his own staff. My theory is that he likes to test his own wits and his own powers of prophecy in his own papers. He takes long shots, like a punter on a horse. If they come off, he gets a kick out of it both in the personal satisfaction of having proved himself right and in being able to *épater* his own staff!

Wednesday, 18 September 1935

Malcolm Muggeridge, the author of an anti-Bolshevist book on Russia[1] and of a suppressed novel on the *Manchester Guardian*, joined us today. Clever, nervous and rather 'freakish' in appearance. Holds strong views. His arrival gives the Diary Room the appearance of an old *Manchester Guardian* office. We have Howard Spring, Thomson, Stephen Williams and Muggeridge. They are of a type in the same way that Wykehamists are.

Friday, 20 September 1935

Rex [Leeper] told me last night that foreign affairs in this country are run by Baldwin, Neville Chamberlain, Sam Hoare and Vansittart, and the greatest of these is Van.

Saturday, 21 September 1935

Saw Maurice Peterson in evening. He is very reassuring in the sense that he is convinced: (1) that sanctions will be mild; and (2) that, owing to the procedure machinery of the League being so cumbersome, it will take a long time to apply them.

[1] *Winter in Moscow* (1933). Muggeridge (*b.* 1903) was *Manchester Guardian* Moscow correspondent 1932–3. The suppressed novel was *Picture Palace*.

Went down by car to Cherkley. Present: Lady Sibell Lygon, Randolph Churchill, Valentine, Mike, Bill Brown. Much talk about Abyssinia. Winston and Randolph want strong action and are convinced that really strong action would make Mussolini climb down. Randolph says his father is fully satisfied that our fleet is completely capable of dealing with situation and that Italians would be faced with greatest surrender in history – the 200,000 men cut off in Eritrea, etc. Bill Brown is also for strong action and says that Government will lose votes if it shilly-shallies.

Saturday, 28 September 1935

Very mild and muggy. Although my throat is much better, I feel exhausted both mentally and physically. If I do not alter the whole course of my life now, I shall never do so and shall die in Fleet Street or the gutter. Were I free, I should not hesitate. I can make £1500 a year certain for the next seven years. Alone, I should not need more than £700 to do all I want.

Tuesday, 22 October 1935

At dinner last night Grigg[1] was interesting on Abyssinia. He thinks, like I do, that we have made a mess of things and that long ago we should have had a pact with Mussolini and France for North Africa. He would still let Musso be top-dog in Abyssinia. He thinks we should take strong measures to prevent any nation arming the native races of Africa. Grigg thinks our Colonial Office the worst department in Whitehall, says the present Governor of Kenya is loathed, and wonders why Lord Beaverbrook does not take up the case of the local settlers and Colonial Office. He would be on a good wicket.

Hamish told me good story of Duke of Portland who has wonderful collection of freak animals he has shot. Went to see an exhibition at Natural History Museum. Evinced great interest as one of attendants showed him white rhinoceros, pink pheasant, etc.

'We have everything,' he said, 'except a black hare.'

'Why, the Duke of Portland has a specimen?'

'Do you know him?'

'Yes,' said the Duke very slowly, 'I see him shaving every morning.'

Friday, 25 October 1935

Muggeridge is rather pro-Fascist yet stands strongly for individual liberties. Hates the big press-proprietors. Told me that Hugh Kingsmill,[2] the younger brother of Arnold Lunn, is very anti-Lunn. Also coined the phrase for Max Beaverbrook – 'Robin Badfellow'.

[1] Edward Grigg (1879–1955), later 1st Baron Altrincham, Conservative M.P., 1933–1945, had been Governor of Kenya, 1925–31.

[2] Kingsmill (1889–1949), biographer, literary collaborator with Muggeridge, dropped the surname of Lunn. His brother (*b.* 1888) was also a journalist, and was an obsessive skier.

Monday, 28 October 1935

Tommy tells me that Beecham and Lady Cunard have quarrelled. Story goes back to last winter when Emerald discovered that Beecham had another girl round the corner. There was a row. Emerald threatened never to lift a finger for opera again unless Beecham gave up his fairy. Beecham agreed. Emerald discovered recently that he had not given her up. Hence these tears.

Thursday, 31 October 1935

A poor day. Lunched with Moir, Barrington-Ward,[1] and John Brown of the Board of Trade. This last-named is now Number Two at the Board of Trade. Very foolishly (and as a result of last night) drank champagne and therefore did very little work in the afternoon.

Barrington-Ward told me a very good story about Kurt Hahn, who used to be headmaster of Salem and was turned out by Nazis. Kurt Hahn was at Oxford and was one of best speakers in English at the Union. Worked in German Foreign Office during war. Became Prince Max of Baden's secretary. Decided something wrong with German education. Started Salem. Soon four schools. Kicked out by Nazis: (1) because a Jew; and (2) because at time of some brutal Nazi murders (before Hitler came to power) made the boys resign from all Nazi associations. Now has school [Gordonstoun] at Gordon Cumming's place. Seventy or eighty boys already!

Also story of *Evening Standard* journalist: went to doctor, came back, saw editor. 'Well,' says editor, 'what does doctor say?'

'Oh, very bad. He gives me only three months.'

'Hm,' says editor, 'you'd better have tomorrow off.'

Friday, 1 November 1935

Yesterday, just before luncheon, Sir Paul Dukes[2] came to see me on a very private matter. He wears well. Clean-shaven, thin artistic hands, very dark, rather Jewish-looking, fine high forehead, hair thinning, rather bald at top of forehead. Wants to go back to Russia. Has not been there since 1919. Suggests going in disguise or rather under an assumed name. Wants to go for three months. Will write book. Also wants to capitalise his adventure by newspaper articles. In fact, wants to do what I have long had in mind if and when I leave Fleet Street.

Maurice Peterson came to luncheon at the office. He agrees with me that this general election[3] is an infernal nuisance to the foreign situation. Everything is hung up because British Government will do nothing during election campaign. Maurice holds that only value of sanctions is in the threat, i.e. the moral force. Once applied, slow in effect and doubtful whom they will

[1] R. M. Barrington-Ward (1891–1948), then assistant editor of *The Times*.

[2] Dukes (1889–1967) had been a secret agent in Russia, 1918–20.

[3] The election was to take place on 14 November; Italy had been invading Abyssinia since 3 October. The only effect so far of sanctions had been to prevent arms going to Abyssinia.

damage most. Election has coincided with most important moment of moral value of sanctions. French are becoming impatient. De Margerie said today that he could understand election was holding up things, but did not think it fair that world peace should be endangered in order to benefit a single political party in a single country!

Monday, 11 November 1935

Lunched at Sibyl Colefax's. Present: Emerald Cunard, Mrs Simpson (the Prince of Wales's girl), Mrs Vanderbilt, Mrs Otto Kahn, Sir Horace Rumbold, Orme Sargent, 'Bogey' Harris, Paul Maze (the French painter and author) and Colin Davidson. Sat between Mrs Simpson and Emerald. Conversation very stupid, Emerald trying to tease the Foreign Office boys by being violently pro-Mussolini.

Afterwards had a long talk with Maze who is intelligent and a great admirer of Conrad. He stormed against the stupidity of Englishwomen like Emerald (who is American!) and Maggie Greville, and asked if it were possible that they could have any influence. Said that when French women interfered in politics they were at least intelligent, had read books and had slept with the diplomats. And to sleep with M. Briand one had to have a certain amount of intelligence.

Friday, 15 November 1935

Lunched with Mike and met ——, a former soldier who was with Abd-el-Krim in the Riff Show and who has now joined Tom Mosley. He is full of optimism for future of Fascism in England, takes comfort from the large percentage of non-voters in the election (nearly 30 per cent) and thinks Fascism will recruit most of this. In foreign affairs favours an alliance with Germany.

Sunday, 17 November 1935

Big surprise of election is victory of A. P. Herbert at Oxford.[1] [C. R. J.] Cruttwell, his opponent, is a very unpopular don. He sent Evelyn Waugh down. Since then Evelyn Waugh has put him into all his books in the form of the most unpleasant character!

Monday, 25 November 1935

Went to see Prince Friedrich of Prussia who came over last night for the Jellicoe funeral.[2] Had to consult ex-Kaiser (who is head of the family) as well as his father. Great difficulty in getting wreath on Sunday night. Rang up a firm. Fixed everything for him. Says Nazis are losing popularity in Germany:

[1] A. P. Herbert (1890–1972), knighted 1945, had already made a name for himself as a journalist on *Punch* when he was elected as an Independent for Oxford University, a seat he was to hold until 1950.

[2] Earl Jellicoe of Scapa had died on 20 November.

not true that all the young people are pro-Nazi. Cabinet powerless except Schacht.

Wednesday, 27 November 1935

Max and Mike came back last night. They received a wonderful reception in Berlin – Mike said that no crowned head could have been better received. Max dined with Ribbentrop.[1] Foreign Office experts were told to stand by in case Max wanted information... Hitler and Max talked through former Geneva interpreter Schmidt. Mike immensely impressed by his efficiency. General Milch, Reichswehr general, transferred to Air, is the big noise. Turning out a thousand planes a week. Mike said Germans very friendly – showed everything like children showing a new toy. But conscious of their own strength – and threat behind the pride.

Saturday, 30 November 1935

Met Waldron Smithers[2] at dinner last night. Common, rather dirty. Was Neville Chamberlain's private secretary. Story of King. Last summer King could not attend levée – rheumatism – place taken by Prince of Wales. Two workmen saw him: 'Lor', Bill, I hope there ain't anything wrong with the Guv'nor.' Smithers, Kent man, told Alex Hardinge,[3] who lives near. Hardinge told King who told him this one! In war, for sake of example, went to open Parliament with two-horse carriage instead of outriders, etc. Two workmen saw him: 'Lor', Bill, see wot we've come down to. We'll be a bleeding republic next.'

Tuesday, 3 December 1935

Lunched with – or rather gave luncheon to – Fitz Randolph the Nazi press attaché. Discussed the Anglo-German Fellowship dinner to which no Press is being invited. I pointed out that this was probably a mistake. Must get a list of members.

Thursday, 5 December 1935

In the evening went to the inaugural Anglo-German Fellowship banquet at the Victoria Hotel. 250 guests. Mount Temple in chair. Poor speeches. Mount Temple[4] (who is the father of two half-Jewesses in Lady Louis

[1] Joachim von Ribbentrop (1893–1946), ex-champagne merchant, was then Hitler's adviser on foreign affairs, later ambassador to Britain, Foreign Minister, and eventually hanged at Nuremberg.

[2] Sir Waldron Smithers (1880–1954), Right-wing Conservative M.P. for Chiselhurst, 1924–45 and then for Orpington.

[3] Alexander Hardinge (1894–1960), who succeeded as 2nd Baron Hardinge of Penshurst in 1944, was assistant private secretary to the King, 1920–36, and private secretary until 1943.

[4] Wilfrid Ashley, 1st Baron Mount Temple (1867–1939), had been a Conservative M.P. until he was raised to the peerage in 1932. His first wife, Amalia Maud, was daughter of Sir Ernest Cassel. Captain A. S. Cunningham-Reid was a Conservative M.P., 1922–41 and Independent, 1942–5; he had been p.p.s. to Mount Temple.

Mountbatten and Mrs Cunningham-Reid by his first wife, Cassel's daughter) made a very indiscreet remark: 'We know Germany fought fair' – after long eulogy of traditional friendship between England and Germany – 'and I hope that in the next war – well, I mustn't say what I was going to say!' Herr von Tschammer und Osten, the Reich Sportleiter in whose honour dinner was given, was terribly long.

Friday, 13 December 1935

Dined at Sibyl's: small party to meet the Prince of Wales: Mr and Mrs Simpson, Diana Cooper, the Garvins, Harold and myself. Kenneth Lindsay[1] came in afterwards. Prince in quite good form. Had a talk with him alone (1) about foreign affairs (he is all for a square deal with Germany); and (2) about the idiotic stories in the *Express* and *Sunday Express* about the Jubilee. The King was annoyed about this.

Sunday, 15 December 1935

Bons mots on the Government crisis:[2] (1) It's stupid to send coals to Newcastle and Whores (Hoares) to Paris (Bob Boothby); (2) various jokes about the hoar-frost in Switzerland.

Monday, 16 December 1935

Dined at Stornoway. Present Sir Robert and Lady Vansittart, Mr and Mrs Rickenbacker (he was the famous American ace in the war), Brendan Bracken, Freddie Lonsdale,[3] Jean Norton. Valentine and Randolph came in afterwards.

Vansittart was in very good form and most communicative, but that idiot Brendan talked without stopping. Van's line of defence was that it was necessary for us to support sanctions in order to try system out thoroughly and to see if it would work. This was a kind of dress rehearsal for a possible bigger show in two or three years' time. They had discovered no response from other countries: you cannot have 100 per cent security on a 5 per cent support. Even French could not put oil sanctions over – not at least until they had proved to their people (i.e. by the plan) that the Italians were mad. Not a question of being afraid of Italians. But a war would cost ships (which would take four years to be replaced) and lots of money. No one would be a whit better off – England would be definitely weaker – and in two years' time she might have to face serious situation in Germany.

[1] (*b*. 1897) Independent National M.P., 1933–45, was Civil Lord of the Admiralty, 1935–7.

[2] Samuel Hoare and Pierre Laval had agreed on 9 December on proposals to hand over large parts of Abyssinia to Mussolini. Public opinion was outraged, the Cabinet was obliged to disown them, and Hoare resigned on 18 December.

[3] (1881–1954), playwright, son of a tobacconist, celebrated as author of sophisticated comedies – *The Last of Mrs Cheyney*, *Canaries Sometimes Sing*, *On Approval*, etc.

Wednesday, 18 December 1935

Dined in the House of Commons with Aneurin Bevan, A. P. Herbert and Freddie Lonsdale. Immense excitement. When we came in, we met Bob Boothby very jubilant. Government had climbed down. Baldwin had recanted and scrapped Sam Hoare. Bob loudly insistent that rank and file had won the triumph, the Junior Cabinet Ministers having ratted only at last minute. Actually what turned the day was Austen Chamberlain saying yesterday that he would go into lobby *v.* Baldwin. Freddie full of story that Vansittart had kept back information about the camel corridor from cabinet, and this gave Baldwin a let-out. Even if true, no let-out. Was in lobby when news of Sam's resignation came though on tape. Simon also there – a huge smile on his face. Went round with Freddie to Max who was all alone – depressed and licking his wounds.

Friday, 20 December 1935

In the evening drove Maurice Peterson down to Cherkley to dine. He gave me full account of crisis. Anthony Eden initiated and approved the telegram of December 10 to Sidney Barton at Addis Ababa.[2] When Vansittart and Sam Hoare came over to Paris, they came with Cabinet approval to settle points of difference between England and France with regard to the peace plan. There was (*a*) the Peterson Plan (the least generous to Italy), (*b*) the St Quentin plan; and (*c*) the further concessions Laval wished to make. Sam and Van ignored the Peterson plan, swallowed the St Quentin plan and a bit more! Van had been much influenced by a recent talk with Grandi. Latest opinion admits possibility raid of 5000 men – also air-raids – 350 miles each way.

When Hoare resigned, Lockhart wrote to him and received this reply dated 21 December 1935:

I am most grateful to you for writing me so friendly a letter. As things are, I am content to let the future decide between my critics and myself. In the meanwhile I deeply appreciate the encouragement of my many friends. Amongst those friends I am very glad to count you and to recall the times when we worked together. When I get back after a rest we must renew these associations, thinking not only of past but also of the future.

Saturday, 21 December 1935

Max gave me two pieces of news, both gleaned from Sam Hoare whom he saw today. (1) Anthony Eden submitted the plan to the Cabinet on the Monday (presumably Monday, December 9); (2) Baldwin is growing deaf.

[1] The Abyssinians were to be allowed a corridor to the sea, but not to build a railway along it. This was ridiculed by *The Times* as 'A Corridor for Camels'.

[2] Sir Sidney Barton (1876–1946) was British Minister in Abyssinia, 1929–37. Eden insisted that Haile Selassie should be told of the plan at the same time as Mussolini.

Max looks tired and ill. He is off to St Moritz on Monday. After dinner saw a film: *Thanks a Million*: musical skit on American politics. Quite amusing with one good song. Max liked it very much.

Sunday, 22 December 1935

Before luncheon Freddie Lonsdale arrived. He was rather pathetic. Told me that he was a drunkard, had wasted his life for the last three years, and now that he was going to do some work for Korda he was determined to go teetotal. It is certainly his last chance. To luncheon also came Cudlipp.

Had a rest after luncheon in an attempt to cure my cold which has now gone heavily to my head. At luncheon Max who has been seeing Sam Hoare a good bit gave his version of the crisis. Decision to scrap Hoare was arranged on Tuesday 17th. Real cause was Austen's threat to vote against Government if they persevered with plan. Sam Hoare knew nothing till mid-day Wednesday. Max says he will be back in Government as First Lord of Admiralty by February. Saw two films: *Mary Burns, Fugitive*, good gangster film, and *The Mutiny on the Bounty* – also good. Eden made Foreign Secretary – a very provocative appointment. Probably youngest foreign secretary.[1]

Monday, 23 December 1935

Lunched at Sibyl's. Sat next Mrs Rendel, whose husband, George Rendel, is head of the Eastern Department in the Foreign Office. Mrs Rendel is very anti-Vansittart, says it is complete nonsense to take the Italians seriously, and is quite confident that we are going ahead with oil and other sanctions. Fortunately, it does not seem to be the Government's intentions to push things to extremes, and Eden's promotion is mainly to win back to Baldwin the votes he lost over the brusque presentation of the plan. Drove back with Kenneth Lindsay, who leaves for Gibraltar and the Mediterranean on Saturday. He looks after docks, dockyard personnel, etc. He also does *not* think that the Government will push oil sanctions or any other sanctions to extremes.

Tuesday, 24 December 1935

Rex Leeper came to luncheon. We went over crisis together. Rex was shocked by Vansittart's volte-face – shocked and hurt, because Van was one of Rex's heroes. His account of crisis does not differ widely from ours except that he says that: (1) Anthony Eden *did* make an attempt to resign – not in the Cabinet but privately, and (2) that he initialled the telegram to the British Minister in Addis Ababa as the result of a Cabinet decision. Rex says Van will stay, that Eden's foreign policy will be cautious, aimed at (1) establishing our security and (2) restoring our good name, and that we will let Musso stew a bit in the Abyssinian juice. Rex has built up a very big department for

[1] Eden was 38.

himself in the Foreign Office, drafts most of the Foreign Secretary's speeches sees both the Foreign Secretary and Van constantly, and on that account has some jealous enemies in the Office. Discussed the British Council, and I suggested they might send me to lecture abroad.

CHAPTER THIRTEEN

1936

Beaverbrook on Kipling. John Wheeler-Bennett's life-story. Venetia Montagu caught cheating at bezique. Goebbels, 'great scholar or great criminal'. Samuel Hoare asks advice. Leeper anxious about new King, Edward VIII. Lloyd George on J. H. Thomas. Dinner with the King. Prince Louis Ferdinand 'very anti-Nazi, like the Kaiser'. Captain Kidd's treasure and the Astors. Return of Churchill predicted. Richard Tauber and his wife. Lunch with Mountbatten 'frightened of a Fascist triangle'. The King 'will marry' Mrs Simpson before July 1937. Queen Mary's view on Mrs Simpson. 'Whitehall wants King to abdicate ... altogether too irresponsible.' Vansittart prepared to give German colonies. Maugham and Godfrey Winn.

Wednesday, 1 January 1936

The New Year finds me in a desperate position: (1) health definitely bad now and partly the result of self-indulgence and the lack of will-power necessary to give diet and self-denial a chance; (2) a deficit of approximately £150 (or with outstanding bills £200) in my weekly budget and the trust money almost exhausted; (3) no attempt to economise and no sign of any desire to improve at home; (4) only 15,000 words (and poor words at that) of my new book written; (5) an atmosphere at home which excludes every kind of thought or inspiration ...

Friday, 3 January 1936

Still very muggy. Gave luncheon today at Savoy to Sir Peter Bark and M. Dimitrejvitch, president of the Yugoslav Budget Commission and also on Commission for Foreign Affairs. Says he was with me in Russia, but I do not remember him.

Gave us a long account of Yugoslav situation. Says Prince Paul realises necessity of healing Serbo-Croat differences. Dimitrejvitch has been negotiating with exiled Croats. All except Pribicevitch will be allowed back after the trial. Told us how Eden's telegram asking if Yugoslavia would stand by in event of attack on England was received by Foreign Affairs Commission at four o'clock. Categoric answer guaranteeing support sent at seven. I asked if Yugoslav army semi-mobilised or ready to start. 'Oh! No question of that. But we have agreed to let you use bases in Adriatic – Kotor, etc!'

Sunday, 5 January 1936

Pathetic story of Queen of Spain who is over here just now and who has been seeing Beatrice Pembroke. The King is brutal to her; controls all the money; allows her only £4000 a year and forbids her on pain of having her allowance cut off to see any of her children. He is behaving very badly at Rome. Reason for attitude: he hates her.

Sunday, 19 January 1936

The snow went today with a quick thaw. Went for a walk with Max and Mike and got my feet very wet. Max talked about Kipling;[1] they were great friends. Kipling was Peter's godfather, and Peter Rudyard Aitken is called after him. Max says Kipling was 'scolding' in his conversation. Very rigid in his political beliefs. Believed that good people were Conservatives; others were evil. Used to come often to Cherkley. Kipling also very rigid about Ireland. Finished with Max because Max supported Irish Treaty. Greater offence in Kipling's eyes was that Max pushed Bonar Law into supporting it.

Max very funny about Mike and me crossing his fence. He crawled through. We climbed over. A roar from Max – ruining his fence. Story about Rosebery (old Rosebery). Canadian soldiers sat on his fences. Sent for Max (who was no longer with Canadians).[2] Cursed him and Canada!

Friday, 24 January 1936

A wasted day. Gave luncheon to Muggeridge. He wants to retire to a farmhouse near Battle (which his mother-in-law will buy for him) and write his books. He will have only about £400 to do it with. But he is only thirty-two and I advised him strongly to take the risk. A cynic might have laughed at my presumption. Here am I with greater earning powers too cowardly myself to take the same decision – too selfish and too extravagant to make the decision possible.

Saturday, 25 January 1936

Felt very ill and depressed. Last night Wheeler-Bennett told me his life-story. Father went to Canada, was partner of Sir Joseph Flavelle[3] who was very unpopular in Canada and was the man whose knighthood finally made Canadian Government protest. Wheeler-Bennett *père* was partner – very rich. Had elder brother whom he liked and who died. Wheeler-Bennett was born when father was over 60. Went to Malvern. Got scholarship at Malvern. Then got shell-shocked. Zeppelin or air-raid on South Coast. Shell fell in

[1] Kipling had died the previous day.

[2] Beaverbrook had worked in various capacities for the Canadian forces before he was made Minister of Information in February 1918.

[3] Sir Joseph Flavelle (1858–1939) was a baronet, not a knight; he had been Chairman of the Imperial Munitions Board during the war and a close associate – though not partner – of Wheeler-Bennett's father.

front of him. Got stammer. Father wanted him to go into business. Wheeler-Bennett mad on history. Went to U.S.A., worked as a reporter. Began his information bureau – wrote books. Gradually father relented. Fixed up with Royal Institute. Owes much to Neill Malcolm who was almost foster-father to him...

Rested in the afternoon and in evening dined with Tommy. Hamish there. Heard about Venetia Montagu scandal. At Himley she was caught cheating at bezique – method was picking up rubbish, getting bezique knave and queen in her lap, then changing them. All London is talking about it. But so far she has not been boycotted.

Wednesday, 29 January 1936

Went to Sibyl Colefax's to luncheon. Mrs Simpson present: to meet her the Vansittarts and the Reventlows had been asked. (Reventlow is husband of Barbara Hutton, the Woolworth heiress). Neither the Vansittarts nor the Reventlows turned up. Present: Sibyl and Arthur, Mrs Simpson, Desmond MacCarthy, and Harold Nicolson. A little conversation about Poet Laureates. Desmond and Harold agreed that Tennyson in class by himself as official laureate. Poems on King's death very poor.[1] Walked home with Desmond who looks ill. He has a hard struggle to live. Says he works only when the lash is on him, or rather when his copy has to be on the table the next morning.

Thursday, 30 January 1936

After luncheon Prince Friedrich of Prussia came to see me and stayed to tea. Told me that when he heard of King's illness, he was in Berlin. At once telephoned to Doorn. Kaiser must telegraph to Sandringham. Last chance of reconciliation. Hofmarschall answered: impossible wake Kaiser – 11 p.m. – and in any case no means of telegraphing, as it was Sunday. Friedrich insisted. Telegram could be telephoned to the Hague and then sent on. Kaiser telegraphed – Queen Mary very pleased. Thanked Friedrich and gave him present to take back from King to Kaiser. Thus death-bed reconciliation. Told me King [Edward VIII] very nice – was annoyed in [funeral] procession, (1) because step of blue-jackets too slow, and (2) because not enough bands. At reception he talked with Litvinov about possibilities of big-game shooting in Russia!

Friday, 31 January 1936

Gave luncheon to Prince Hubertus Loewenstein at Boulestin's. He ... claims to represent the United opposition in Germany from the Centrum to the Socialists (he claims even some Deutsch-Nationale), and is off to the States to lecture. Thinks Goebbels is the chief Nazi genius but says that at

[1] John Masefield (1878–1967), Poet Laureate, had published 'On the Passing of George V' in *The Times* that morning. Other equally poor poems by Edmund Blunden and J. C. Squire had appeared in the special funeral issue of *The Times* the day before. The King had died on 20 January.

Freiburg, Gundolf, the great German professor and authority on Goethe, said of him: 'He will make either a great scholar or a great criminal.' School report from Jesuits was: 'We regret that we have not been able to awaken in him a consciousness for truth.'

Thursday, 6 February 1936

Today I had my luncheon with Geoffrey Faber[1] at the United Universities Club. Another partner was there. Having been prepared, I naturally expected an offer. But when it came, I was surprised. The idea is that I should do a life of King Edward for next year's Coronation. It would be a big money-maker. If I could get a new line on it, I believe it could be a big success. Faber's were also very interested in getting me out of Fleet Street and putting me on a guaranteed income for five or seven years. They suggested that I could do this with them and save the ten per cent commission to the agents. But for my overwhelming financial difficulties which wear me down, I think I could and should do this book, but it will be a race with time. I can hardly finish *Return to Malaya* before May 15th. I should only have from June 1st to February 1st in which to do King Edward.

Saturday, 8 February 1936

Beautiful sunny day, but very cold. Felt ill after last night and after an unsatisfactory morning at the office went to lunch with Muggeridge at the Jardin des Gourmets. Had a long talk with Muggeridge about his future. He is not happy and wants to get out. Thinks it is ridiculous that people like himself and me should not be consulted about anything and should have our stuff 'subbed' by some half-educated nit-wit. Well, well, he's right, and I'm always in favour of the independence, providing that it can be maintained. Discussed with Muggeridge the possibilities of the King book. He was, naturally, rather shocked at first, and thinks that I should open my mouth very wide – £5000 at least.

H. G. [Wells] is being overhauled by the doctors today. He is now very frightened about his health. He has now a new idea: youth must be brought up prepared to kill. Political reforms will never be achieved by peaceful methods, etc. He has also offered his *Anatomy of Frustration* to Constant Huntington for £400. After luncheon saw Constant and Gladys and had a talk about my book.

Monday, 10 February 1936

Saw Sam Hoare at 18 Cadogan Gardens. He looked very well. Had long talk about Foreign Affairs. Letter to *Times* of his this morning was to offer olive branch to Geoffrey Dawson and Co. who have been waging bitter feud against Sam and Van. Two people who did Sam bad turn with Baldwin were Ramsay MacDonald and Simon – the two boys who went to Stresa with the

[1] (1889–1961) knighted 1959, head of Faber & Faber, the publishers.

Abyssinian experts with them and never said a word.[1] Sam told me that at the Foreign Affairs Committee meeting Austen meant to support him – voting would have been 60 to 40 for Sam. Wild boys impressed Austen who got carried away. Sam Hoare says that Ramsay is quite 'ga-ga' now and that Austen is also very old and very *vaniteux* – always wanting to be consulted. He (Sam) is in favour of considerable reorganisation in the Foreign Office – amalgamation of consular and diplomatic services, weeding out of much personnel abroad, etc. Asked me what he ought to do (Max in favour of his coming in): Come in as friend or remain out as foe? I said 'Come in if they offer you a post. No good being a faction leader in the Conservative Party.' Baldwin very old now and getting very deaf. Hoare wants to keep talks going regularly.

Wednesday, 12 February 1936

Lunched with Eric Gillett[2] at Simpson's. He is a kind of Douglas Woodruff, was up at Oxford with Priestley and other literary 'blokes', and now is adviser to Longman's, a broadcaster on books, and a publicity expert for City firms.

In afternoon went to see Rex Leeper and had a long talk with him about foreign affairs. Rex says that the new King has not begun well – in foreign affairs at least. He would not see King Carol when, because of pro-German tendencies in Rumania, it was important to keep Carol on our side. Titulescu had to work hard to arrange that Carol's visit was a success. Carol saw Baldwin, Eden, etc., and seemed pleased. The King has also been interfering in small matters, and Rex is anxious.

Monday, 17 February 1936

In the afternoon went to see Faber who proposed £3000 advance for book on the King and a five years' contract for these years guaranteeing £1500 a year. As guarantee for continued income suggests that in the event of large profits certain percentage should be set against next book. Sounds very encouraging. Went to see M. [?Muggeridge ?Max] who agrees that the opportunity must not be lost. Agreed to give answer when I return.

Friday, 27 March 1936

In the evening went to the Dugdale's cocktail party. Her life of Balfour is coming out in the *Daily Telegraph* very soon.[3] Violet Bonham Carter, the Masseys, and a crowd of other people whom I did not know were there. Also Lewis Namier, who is violently anti-German and spends all his time fixing up jobs for German chemists and physicists in English industries in

[1] A conference between Britain, France and Italy was held at Stresa in April 1935, but the question of Abyssinia was not even raised by MacDonald and Simon.

[2] (*b.* 1893) had been professor of English Literature in Singapore, was to become a literary editor, film expert and London dramatic critic of the *Yorkshire Post*, 1960–5.

[3] Blanche ('Baffy'), wife of Edgar Dugdale, was a daughter of A. J. Balfour's brother Eustace.

order to 'disarm Germany', and Colin Coote of *The Times* . . . very pro-French.[1] Attitude of these people very dangerous – 'Public are fools and know nothing. We know Germany, and they cannot be trusted.'

Friday, 24 April 1936

Mike also tells me that Max is seriously ill and is convinced that his life is finished, that he will never be able to live in England again! He has a stone in his gall-bladder (which is apparently serious) and for some time now he has been suffering from asthma of a bronchial kind which attacks him in the evening. He is able to play golf, for instance, and has gone mad on the game. But he has a bad time in the evening, is taking oxygen, and is a bundle of nerves about himself. He leaves tomorrow for a prolonged stay in the South of France. He has never been away so often before: Switzerland before Christmas and Germany before that, Morocco since the New Year, Cannes and now Cannes again.

Monday, 27 April 1936

A hectic day. Lunched at home and in the afternoon went to see Sam Hoare. He tells me that he is coming back to the Cabinet – probably at Whitsun, but asks me not to say anything about this for the moment.[2] Further talks about the Foreign Office and about the necessity for some reform in appointments. Appointment supposed to be in hands of Secretary of State; actually controlled by small committee who pull wires for their own ultimate benefit. Succession of very bad appointments in Central Europe lately.

Tuesday, 5 May 1936

At Freddie Lonsdale's dinner on Friday night Randolph, who was teetotal, told me that since the New Year he had drunk nothing and his father had drunk no brandy. Both these examples of self-denial were the result of a bet or rather of bets made by Lord Rothermere who, I suppose, is doing a good turn in this way. Thought of F. E. [Smith, Lord Birkenhead] who gave up drink for a year for a £1000 bet, started again worse than ever at the end of the year, and died soon afterwards because his liver could not absorb the same amount as before.

Wednesday, 6 May 1936

Lunched at Sam Hoare's. Present: Mr and Mrs [L. S.] Amery, Mr and Mrs 'Bunny' Austin, Mrs Rupert Beckett,[3] Mr Young. Sat between Mrs Amery and Mrs Rupert Beckett. Mrs Amery told me that Leo Amery had a brother in Malayan Civil Service. Was ill and came home to go to sanatorium in

[1] Coote, now Sir Colin, had been an M.P., 1917–22, and was to become editor of the *Daily Telegraph* in 1950.

[2] Hoare was appointed First Lord of the Admiralty on 5 June 1936.

[3] H. W. 'Bunny' Austin (*b.* 1906) was a leading tennis-player of the 1930s. Rupert Beckett (1870–1955) was a banker, director of the Westminster Bank and chairman of the *Yorkshire Post*, his wife Muriel was a daughter of Lord Berkeley Paget.

Germany. At beginning of the war was captured. In prison met a Malay 'boy' who, overjoyed to find a white man who spoke Malay, looked after him till he died. Behaved very well; sent his things home; came and told Leo Amery all about it. Leo Amery still mountaineers; was in Bavaria last year, went up some fierce place in six hours instead of usual ten! Prepares for it; trains. Very abstemious. Does physical jerks. Walks four miles every day! Mrs Rupert Beckett very anti-Beaverbrook. Sam and I defended him. Mrs Rupert Beckett is anti, because her husband is very anti. Rupert Beckett is chief shareholder in the *Yorkshire Post*.

Friday, 8 May 1936

Lunched at Bill Aitken's rooms in Lincoln's Inn. Very nice rooms and excellent food. Present: Peter Howard, another young friend of Bill, and afterwards Panikkar, Prime Minister or Adviser to the Maharajah of Patiala.[1] Panikkar, a suave gentleman with beard and excellent, not to say rhetorical, knowledge of English, gave us a sarcastic and far from flattering account of Willingdon's, or rather Lady Willingdon's, Viceroyship. One story concerned erection of Willingdon statue outside Viceregal Lodge at Delhi (or Government buildings). Willingdon did not wish his statue to stand next to Irwin's, so he moved Hardinge's there and put his where Hardinge's had been. He was ordered by London to replace them! Sounds unlikely, but there may be a tang of truth about it. More convincing was story of squabbles about the despatch of the All-Indian test team. Trouble between Patiala and Willingdon. Patiala gave cup to All-India Cricket Club for inter-provincial competition. Message from Viceregal quarters that as 1935 was Jubilee year better call cup Willingdon Cup. Patiala pretends to agree, but gets All-Indian Cricket Club to say 'no' – cup already called Patiala Cup – cannot be changed.

Tuesday, 26 May 1936

Maurice up in arms about appointments. Charles Bentinck,[2] a quite useless diplomat who, indeed, has been laid on the shelf for years has been appointed to an important and almost critical post like Prague – merely because he has to be moved somewhere. Unbelievable. Vansittart must be held largely to blame. Maurice says he tries to keep everything in his own hands. Discussed European situation. Agreed that, whether she likes dictatorships or not, England cannot afford to be both anti-German and anti-Italian at same time. She must choose – or be friends with both! Maurice, who is now worried about the Mediterranean–Near East situation, would prefer Germany as the friend. But I am confident that Government policy, if any, will incline to patch up things with Mussolini and be suspicious of Germany.

[1] K. V. Panikkar (1895–1963) Foreign Minister of Patiala, later Indian Ambassador to France.

[2] Charles Bentinck (1895–1963) had previously been Minister to Peru and Bulgaria. In 1937 he was made Ambassador to Chile, but soon retired and took holy orders.

Thursday, 28 May 1936

I had an hour or more alone [at Cherkley] with Max who was down and dressed by nine. Max is now definitely afraid of Germany, told me that he could not come out openly in favour of Anglo-French alliance because of his position as an isolationist, but that France had his backing. Incidentally, he came back on his *laissez-passer* incident (French air-people at Le Bourget treated him badly) and told me that although he would never ask for another he would be glad to have one.

Wednesday, 10 June 1936

A hectic day. Lunched at Mrs Beckett's... Lloyd George very funny on Jimmy [Thomas], whom he described as the one unsinkable ship that Britain has ever built. Told excellent story of Jimmy and the miners. Latter had not supported Jimmy in railway strike. Miners' strike came along. Miners came to see Jimmy. All his sympathies given to them, but of course must first consult his railwaymen. Tells railwaymen – 'Boys, we must support our pals, but of course I pulled off a pretty good wages agreement for you the last time and, if you strike, you may lose that, etc., etc.' Railwaymen turned down strike. Jimmy back in his London office, lights cigar, whisky and soda. Miners come. Jimmy hides away whisky in cupboard, throws cigar out of window. Miners come in, find Jimmy with his head in hands leaning over table. 'Boys,' he says, 'me bloody heart is broke. Me boys have gone back on me!'

Two stories of Curzon. Curzon once at Pilgrims' dinner to hear American ambassador (Harvey, I think). Duke of Connaught was there. Speakers were to be: Duke, Lloyd George, Curzon and F.E. F.E. was to propose Duke of Connaught's health. F.E. never turned up. Lord Derby, chairman, pressed Curzon to undertake it. Curzon furious, but rose to his feet. Began on F.E. 'The Lord Chancellor is a man who rarely neglects a duty and never a pleasure. Tonight he has neglected both.'

Cabinet choosing or rather discussing choice of Viceroy. Several names mentioned – one rather warmly. Curzon intervenes. 'Have you considered the female element? Woman very important. The man whom you all recommend so highly has a wife. I may describe her best as a woman of colossal fortune but of calamitous appearance!'

Bee Pembroke had proposed beforehand to dislike Lloyd George. She was going to put him in his place. She was thrilled by him. When women left room, Lloyd George did not remember who she was! Went upstairs and at once went to her, talked to her about Carnarvonshire and the Angleseys, chaffed her for ratting over to Conservatism. In Carnarvon had been two big families: the Winns and the Pagets.[1] The Pagets had been Radicals; the Winns Conservative. This conversation began because Bee had teased Lloyd George about wearing 'true blue' Conservative colours. Lloyd George had on 'true blue' suit!

[1] Beatrice, Lady Pembroke, was a Paget, and sister-in-law of Bridget Paget.

Dined at Argyll House [Lady Colefax's] to meet King: Present 'Kitty' Brownlow, Duchess of Buccleuch, Lady Diana Cooper, Lady Vansittart, Mrs Artur Rubinstein and Mrs Tom Lamont and Tom Lamont, Harold, Vansittart, Artur Rubinstein, Perry Brownlow, Euan Wallace, and one or two more men. King came in rather late with Mrs Simpson – very neat in black.[1] Mrs Tom Lamont in fever because *she* was in white and other women in black. Shook hands with everyone. Said to me: 'Hello, Bruce, how are you?' Looks older and harder – a little stiffer perhaps since he became King, definitely more confidence in himself since he met Mrs Simpson. Had about five minutes talk alone with him after dinner – mostly about Germany. Told him Louis Ferdinand was coming; said he would like to see him and would try to fit him in on Friday. Otherwise not possible as he was going off on Saturday for Ascot week party at the Fort[2] and wasn't coming up except for absolutely urgent business. Said he was in favour of coming to some square deal with Germany. Position was difficult, but he hoped to be able to use his influence in right direction.

Afterwards Artur Rubinstein played to us. King sat down on little stool beside Mrs Simpson. Seemed rather bored, but stayed on.

Later, Lord Berners, Winston, Noël Coward, various other men came in (Politicians had been dining at 1900 Club where Neville Chamberlain made his speech announcing end of sanctions – 'midsummer madness') to hear music. Gerald Berners had funny story of his invitation. Sibyl rings up – 'Gerald, I particularly want you to come tonight to meet Arthur.'

Gerald: 'But I thought Arthur (Colefax who died in February) was dead.'

Sibyl: 'Oh, not my Arthur – Artur Rubinstein.'

When Rubinstein had finished, Noël Coward was asked to sing. Quite unabashed, he sat down and gave us 'Oh, Mrs Worthington, don't put your daughter on the stage,' and 'Mad Dogs and Englishmen go out in the Mid-day Sun.' King bucked up and looked quite amused. He did not leave till nearly one. Came with and left with Mrs Simpson. Quite unattended. No A.D.C. etc.

Friday, 12 June 1936

Prince Louis Ferdinand of Prussia arrived. He is on his way back from America where he stayed with Ford and Roosevelt, is going to Doorn on his way to Berlin before starting his reserve military air service on July 1st. He has already done an air training which was *soi-disant* civil but was really military. He is more American than usual this time. . . Not at all pro-Nazi, believes in internationalism, etc. Mixes with Bohemians, thinks pro-Nazi, believes in internationalism, etc. Mixes with Bohemians, thinks world will go like Russia. Says everyone in Germany is watched; corruption immense, strong undercurrent of discontent. He came to lunch at the office.

[1] In mourning for King George V.

[2] Fort Belvedere, his home, near Sunningdale, Berks.

Present: Suzanne Eisendieck, the painter, Henri Bernstein and Mlle Curie . . .[1] Louis Ferdinand, Cudlipp and Ruth [Wardell]. Bernstein, intelligent but slightly repulsive, talks English very well. Conversation not good, as too many people representing different interests present. Bernstein is a reactionary: advised me to keep an eye on Doriot,[2] former Communist and now potential Fascist. Excitement in Paris over calling out of armed guards.

Sunday, 14 June 1936

Took Prince Louis down to Cherkley by car – and had long talk on way. He is very anti-Nazi – like the Kaiser – and says the spy system in Germany today is just like the Cheka in Russia.

Tuesday, 16 June 1936

Took Prince Louis Ferdinand to lunch at Emerald Cunard's. She had rather a large party, and Prince Louis who is not so good on these occasions was rather shy. Vansittart was at the luncheon. I asked him about joining the St James's Club and he offered to put me up or second me. The Channons also present. They took Prince Louis off my hands and carried him off to the House of Commons.

Tuesday, 23 June 1936

Lunched at the Ivy restaurant with Frank Morley[3] and Faber. They want me to write a kind of modern *Treasure Island* based on the story of the Astor fortune which is roughly this. Captain Kidd's fortune was hidden in an island off coast of Massachusetts – island belonged to another American family. Astors sent a man there – collared the treasure. Proofs are found in the Astor books and bank-records. About this time sudden huge entry, unaccounted for by ordinary business transactions, to Astor's credit. Large sales of jewellery to London firm of goldsmiths! There was case in courts – settled by Astor out of court. Quite a fascinating story, but I should have to leave Fleet Street in order to undertake it.

Went to have tea with General Waters. . . He tells me that there is a deal of intrigue at Doorn. Baron Sell, the Kaiser's secretary, and the Kaiserin do not get on. Waters says that Sell tries to keep Kaiserin away from Kaiser or at least to prevent her from taking any part in politics. Waters wants me to write to Kaiserin who will arrange for me to come to Doorn again and to see the Kaiser alone!

Tuesday, 30 June 1936

Went to lunch at the Carlton with de Courcy and Wise[4] of the Imperial

[1] (1876–1953) French playwright and theatrical producer; the younger sister of Madame Joliot-Curie.

[2] Jacques Doriot (1888–1945) had just founded the Fascist 'Parti Populaire Français'. He became a leading collaborator during the war.

[3] Frank Morley, brother of Christopher Morley the American writer, was a founding director of Faber's.

[4] Kenneth de Courcy (*b.* 1909), newspaper proprietor, Secretary to the Imperial Policy Group, 1935–9.

Policy Group. They have recently been in Poland, Austria and Italy where they saw Mussolini. Mussolini was very friendly and well-disposed to make friends with Britain. Poland was, in their opinion, pro-German and would not lift a finger to help their brother Slavs, the Czechs, if they were attacked. Rather the reverse. Austria, as usual, hopeless. Both de Courcy and Wise have been to see Otto[1] and are great Ottomites. They say that he is not at all like his mother . . . and has no use for Starhemberg or Schuschnigg. Went to see Vansittart and had a long talk about various things including my proposed election to St James's Club which has had to be postponed until September as I came up too late. Van worried by German expansion ambitions and by fears lest we are too slow in building bridge to Italy.

Tuesday, 14 July 1936

Lunched at Mrs Beckett's. Present: Eddie Marsh and Lady Winifred Pennoyer, Bee Pembroke's sister. Eddie Marsh rather interesting on Jimmie Thomas to whom he had been private secretary for years. Eddie swears that Jimmie was innocent of any deliberate disclosure and has a great affection and even admiration for him.[2] Has a fund of Jimmie stories. Best was bewilderment of Jimmie's colleagues when Jimmie began talking once about the ''addock committee'. Thought he meant the herring committee and wondered what J.H.T. had to do with fishing. Jimmie was talking about an 'ad hoc' committee!

In the evening went as General Waters's guest to the Anglo-German Fellowship dinner to the Duke and Duchess of Brunswick. Large crowd; many soldiers. Mount Temple in chair, Zetland as guest, Lord Lothian, etc.[3] Kaiser's daughter looked browned and athletic. Duke who has a very guttural voice speaks English indifferently. He has, I think, some impediment in his voice. I congratulated him on text of his speech in which he told us Germany had decided to have English Rhodes scholars for German universities. He said: 'Very good speech! Could you understand this terrible voice of mine?' The Brunswicks are pro-Nazi. The Kaiser is very angry with them. He thinks that they are trying to steal his chances and his monarchical thunder by currying favours with Hitler. If anything happened to Hitler tomorrow, they might have a chance.

Thursday, 16 July 1936

Great excitement this morning. When the King was returning from the presentation of the colours ceremony in Hyde Park this morning, a man in the crowd on Constitutional Hill produced a pistol. One version says he

[1] Francis Joseph Otto, the exiled heir to the Habsburg throne of Austria.

[2] J. H. Thomas had had to resign from the Colonial Office in May 1936 because he had disclosed Budget secrets.

[3] 2nd Marquess of Zetland (1876–1961), then Secretary of State for India; 11th Marquess of Lothian (1882–1940), had been Secretary to Lloyd George 1916–21, became Ambassador to U.S.A., 1939–40.

threw it on the ground; another says that a constable or a woman struck up the man's arm and the pistol fell on the ground. A big story for the newspapers. I had to dig up all previous attempts on Queen Victoria, etc. But even at the beginning it was clear that the man was a lunatic with a grievance and out to call attention to it rather than a dangerous assassin. Lunched with Moura at the Jardin. She advises me to go to Max and tell him quite frankly that I have to finish my book before the end of September and that I must have a month's holiday. Very practical advice but not feasible.

Friday, 17 July 1936

Lunched at the Ian Hamiltons and sat between Lady Muir (Mlle Stancioff)[1] and Unity Mitford. Latter is madly pro-Nazi and will not speak to her sister Nancy because she is anti-Nazi. Lady Muir who was first or almost first lady diplomat, has just come back from Bulgaria; tells me Boris may be coming to England to shoot with the Allendales. Reads a lot. Gunther's *Inside Europe* says, 'Boris is worst-dressed King in Europe because for patriotic reasons he insists on wearing Sofia-made clothes.' King read this. Now dresses in Savile Row! Is great gardener and entomologist. In evening took Lady Muir to meet Maurice at the Ritz. She is very anti-Titulescu[2] and says he has done more than anyone to keep Bulgaria down. Dinner at home: Loudon and Lachlan McLean[3] and Mrs L'Estrange.

Wednesday, 22 July 1936

Message from Max this morning on the Spanish revolution.[4] He thinks that the rebels will succeed. We shall see. In any case I do not think that the matter is likely to be settled quickly.

Thursday, 23 July 1936

Bridget, who of course does not like Mrs Simpson, says that the King is getting tired of Emerald Cunard, that he always hated her before, and that he will hate her again.

Saturday, 25 July 1936

Went to say goodbye to Moura who leaves tomorrow for Esthonia. Discussed the new Russian constitution in the light of my yesterday's conversation with Kerensky. Moura maintains that Russia *is* going Liberal and that Russia and the democracies *do* stand together for the defence of the liberal spirit. This is only a half-truth. There is a gulf between the dictatorships which are supported by the 'haves' and the dictatorships which are maintained by the 'have-nots'. The Liberals lean more towards the have-not

[1] She was the wife of Sir Kay Muir, Bart, and daughter of a former Bulgarian Minister in London.

[2] Prime Minister of Bulgaria.

[3] Future husband of Jean Lockhart and his brother.

[4] The Army insurrection under Franco had begun on 18 July. He did not succeed in occupying Madrid until March 1939.

dictatorships. Temporarily they hold a weak balance, but when the real struggle comes they will be unequalled. Moura thinks the Right will win the civil war in Spain. So does Beaverbrook. I don't. H.G. is staying in London; he likes his new house in Regent's Park – Hanover Terrace. As pronounced by Moura it sounds like 'Hangover Terrace'. He has had five front teeth out – nothing wrong with them – just afraid they won't last as long as he intends to live.

Sunday, 26 July 1936

In the evening went to Mrs Beckett's. I was told that it was a tiny informal party (not more than six) to hear Tauber sing.[1] I found a huge party: Duchess of Portland, the Londonderrys, the Cubitts, the Pembrokes, Lady Cunard, Princess Helena Victoria,[2] Lord Anglesey, Lord Hambledon, and goodness knows who else, including Sir Thomas Beecham. At dinner sat next Lady Londonderry and Diana Napier who is Tauber's wife. Lady Londonderry very pro-German; also Lord Londonderry who had a talk with me after dinner.[3] He wants an anti-Communist front with Germany. Says Baldwin was very good in home politics but knows nothing of foreign politics – knows no geography. Party – a flop. Tauber, who did not have his own accompanist, was alarmed by Beecham's presence, and after singing a Schubert *Ständchen*, a Grieg song and 'Das Blau Himmelbett' from *Frasquita* he dried up.

Monday, 27 July 1936

Prize remark at Muriel Beckett's party last night, when after Hart-Davis[4] had accompanied Tauber, Beecham went up to take his place. Duchess of Portland in loud whisper: 'Who's that? Is that his man?' Tauber, incidentally, had sent for his proper accompanist, but he could not be found!

Emerald told me afterwards that Lady Astor has been attacking Mrs Simpson very violently – and by implication the King – in the House of Commons and elsewhere and that a member of Parliament had written to Mrs Simpson and Mrs Simpson had shown the letter to the King. Mrs Keppel in very good form. She looks rather formidable and slightly coarse. Referred to Madame Lupescu as a woman who had walked a great many miles in her youth.

In the afternoon went to see Huntington. He was very nice and gentle. Nearly everyone has let him down this autumn. We are to make a shot for

[1] Richard Tauber (1891–1948), plump, monocled Austrian tenor specialising in light opera, became a British subject after the *Anschluss*.

[2] (1870–1948) granddaughter of Queen Victoria, and daughter of Prince Christian of Schleswig-Holstein and Princess Helena Augusta Victoria.

[3] 7th Marquess of Londonderry (1878–1949), husband of Ramsay MacDonald's friend, was Air Minister (1931–5) and encouraged the development of the Hurricane and Spitfire fighter planes.

[4] Richard Hart-Davis, father of Sir Rupert.

autumn publication. It will be a strain. It means writing – revising – 40,000 words before September 30. I told him about my offers from Faber, etc. He at once began to talk again about buying me out of Fleet Street.

Wednesday, 29 July 1936

Lunched at Muriel Beckett's. Present: Princess Helena Victoria whom I sat next, Lady Chetwode, Sir Claude Schuster, Victor Cazalet. Princess Helena Victoria talked about the Kaiser; said how kind he had been to her and how she liked him. Said it was a great pity that King George and the Kaiser should have been kept apart. A little goodwill would have worked wonders. Kaiser was hurt because our Royal Family did not write at time of Kaiserin's death. King George thought of writing when Prince Henry died but did not. If the Kaiser had sent a message for King George's Jubilee, the King would have answered generously – but there was no message.

Tuesday, 11 August 1936

This morning Cudlipp came to me: 'Do you know Mrs Simpson?' I said, 'Yes,' without thinking. Next thing was a Diary paragraph for the *Evening Standard*.[1] Lord Beaverbrook's information. Every precaution to be taken to safeguard source. Cudlipp not even to tell me. Paragraph to be read by Cudlipp to him over private line. Gave luncheon to James Hilton,[2] Mrs Belloc Lowndes, and Sibyl Colefax. Hilton gets £300 a week at Hollywood. He is not supposed to do any other work. M.G.M. have bought him body and soul. He has no grouse against Hollywood. They have used him quite a lot.

Wednesday, 12 August 1936

H. G. [Wells] last night was very pessimistic about future of British Empire or rather of Britain, said we were a third-rate power and were unwilling or unable to admit it, that Britain's last great Foreign Secretary Palmerston had always backed Left, since National Government came in we had always backed Right. Now backing Fascists in Spain. Fascist Government in Spain would mean end of Gibraltar.

Sunday, 16 August 1936

Went to see Rex Leeper whom I found alone. Long talk on foreign affairs. The reason why George Clerk got Paris was because Warren Fisher, the so-called Head of the Civil Service, hates the Foreign Office, wants to reform it, and was proposing to put Leith-Ross into Van's place if Van went to Paris.[3]

[1] An innocuous-seeming mention – 'Mrs. Ernest Simpson is the former Miss Wallis Warfield and comes from Baltimore' – with no reference to Lockhart.

[2] (1900–54) author of *Lost Horizon* (1933) and *Goodbye Mr. Chips* (1934). He had settled in America in 1935.

[3] Sir Warren Fisher (1879–1948) was official Head of the Civil Service, 1919–39. Sir Frederick Leith-Ross (1887–1968) was Chief Economic Adviser to the Government 1932–46; he was never to hold any diplomatic posts.

Van stayed. This is only reason why G.R.C. got Paris. His time will be up in April. He will not be prolonged. Eden is angry with him – in spite of George's relationship with his sister.[1] When he came to Paris after March 7th,[2] saw George, asked him what French were going to say. George turned to one of his secretaries: 'Peake, I believe there was something in the *Echo de Paris*, wasn't there?' Eden was furious. General view is that G.R.C. has become lazy and doesn't care. Rex has a great idea of starting a weekly newspaper to explain the foreign situation (the dangers and the consequences) to the public. Suggests a luncheon with Eden. Wants to put my name forward as a possible editor. Van's generosity. The doctor's bills in connection with Allen Leeper's death came to £1200. Van paid one of the operations himself. Beneš, Masaryk and Titulescu raised a fund for education of child.

Monday, 17 August 1936

Incidentally, I hear that Negley, who was nearly ruined by the combination of alcohol and success, has had a wonderful cure: injections which make you vomit if you touch alcohol. Winston should have them. Rex Leeper, who admires him greatly and thinks that he is the man we need, lunched with him the other day. Although Winston has a bet with Rothermere not to touch spirits, he drank loads of beer and then after luncheon five large glasses of port. Rex thinks he will come back. Winston was hopeless [for] eight months. Now people are saying 'What a pity Winston is so unreliable, he would be a good man to have back;' tomorrow they will be saying 'Do you think it's safe to have Winston back; he'd be very good;' and the day after tomorrow: 'We must have Winston back.'

Sunday, 23 August 1936

Richard Tauber and Diana Napier (Mrs Tauber) came to luncheon – in what Tauber calls 'his old taxi'. He likes old cars – thinks new cars are a sign of new riches. She is attractive but full of nerves – never leaves him alone. 'Richard, eat this, Richard, do that.' 'Richard, you're talking too much – can't hear anyone speak for the echo of your voice.' Richard Tauber: 'Well, my sweet, we live from that echo, don't we?' He was nice – quite naïve in some ways – saying how proud he was to be singing Pagliacci – Caruso's great part – (he will also sing the prologue on first night of opening of the film – prologue not sung by Caruso or tenor but by baritone – Tauber will sing it one tone higher). Running round with his Ciné-Kodak, listening apparently sound asleep to his own songs being played on the gramophone and then waking up and saying: 'Ah, that's nice,' when a jazz tune (not sung by him!) came on. Whistling obbligato to *Ochi Chernaya*. She very talkative – rather full of dreams and clever. Her father does not like her playing the parts she

[1] Marjorie, Countess of Warwick (1887–1943), widow of the 6th Earl.

[2] Eden had become Foreign Secretary on 22 December 1935. 7 March 1936 was the date when Hitler denounced the Locarno Pact and reoccupied the Rhineland.

does – will not see her playing what he calls 'prostitutes'. 'Can't they get real ones for those roles?' Fantastic salaries of film-stars: Marlene Dietrich is getting £60,000 free of tax for her new British film. Gertrude Lawrence, however, gets only £200 a week because the bosses know she is hard up.

In the afternoon drove over to Lloyd George's with the Taubers, Tommy, and Muriel Beckett. Gorgeous weather, but too many cars and people on the road. Superb view from Churt. L.G. has built a new room on to his tea and cinema room with St David in stained glass. New room is where old loggia was. Mural painting in tea-room by John Churchill. Fine picture by Winston of Mimizan in L.G.'s library. Tauber very comic running after L.G. with his Ciné-Kodak.

L.G. cut some white heather for us. Talked of Parliament and of Spain Good on Spain; thinks Government will win and is prepared to bet. Deplores people (knowing nothing about it) taking violent sides. Very dangerous. Six months ago half-a-dozen war causes – diplomacy trying to get them out of way – now out of blue, more or less, comes Spain.

Reminded him of his first salmon caught on the Ewe (Gairloch, Flowerdale House) about this time in 1921. Important event, because it was time of Irish troubles and L.G. called first and only British Cabinet meeting held North of Tweed. Held at Inverness in Town Hall on September 7th, 1921. Treaty signed in December. Muriel Beckett has the photograph of L.G. discussing meeting with the King and The Mackintosh at Moy Hall. Muriel told L.G. the King had had this picture a few months before he died. She had sent it for him to sign. L.G.'s speeches six months before the election had been so bad that she had asked the King not to sign! 'That was an awful mess you made, L.G.,' she said. Back like a flash came the answer: 'Not as big a mess as your Prime Minister landed us all in six months after.'

Wednesday, 26 August 1936

Lunched with or rather gave luncheon to Fitz Randolph at Boulestin's. He tells me that Ribbentrop is not likely to arrive before October 15, (1) because of the lateness of the King's return, and (2) because of difficulties of re-equipping the house for a married ambassador. The two great rival champagne brands will now be represented at the Embassy by Frau von Ribbentrop and Frau von Wenninger (Henckel and Kupferberg). The two women are friends. Ribbentrop will give German champagne; the Fuehrer likes his ambassadors to get as much as possible from Germany!

Fitz Randolph says that Germany is willing to discuss disarmament at any moment; only the disarmament must be general and not one-sided. Disarmament is a very sore point with Germans; they do not forget the failures of the previous disarmament conferences or of the attempts to keep them unarmed by armed neighbours. Great excitement in the afternoon over alleged war-scare speech by Stalin on wireless. *Evening News* had it exclusive. I spent all the afternoon in trying to trace its source without success.

Thursday, 27 August 1936

In afternoon Namier came to see me in a state of great indignation about our complete surrender to the terrorists in Palestine. He says that Arabs are openly rejoicing at first step towards creation of Arab Federation and that we have agreed to stop Jewish immigration and to give an amnesty to terrorists. Namier says that we can hold Palestine only with the Jews. Arab nationalists are anti-British and anti-French. Nationalist leader said to Jewish leaders: You can have 6,000,000 Jews in Palestine if you will come in with us to drive out French and British.

Friday, 28 August 1936

Last night Namier told me that Jack Wheeler-Bennett's *Hindenburg* was the best book written for a long time – brilliantly done and very valuable. Jack, always a neurotic, had had a nervous breakdown and was still in the U.S.A. . . . Namier told me that one of Jewish leaders had seen Mussolini a few years ago. Musso had said: 'Your Zionist state will never come to anything under Britain. You would be better under an Italian mandate: *Quant aux Arabes, moi, je m'en chargerai.*'

Tuesday, 15 September 1936

Lunched at home and in afternoon worked on my book. In the evening went to dine at Tony Rothschild's. Present: 'Cardie' Montagu, Stoppard who is on the still-stand [?] Committee for Germany, and Tony. Discussion on Baldwin: 'Cardie' defended him on historical grounds. As things have turned out, a stronger man might have led us into irreparable disaster. Generally agreed that prevailing spirit of this country just now is peace at any price – the old Danegeld spirit – buy them off, even with colonies! Tony Rothschild is not a Baldwin admirer. . .

Went on to 'Slip In' and stayed up till four dancing. A foolish performance which counteracted most of my hard work on Saturday and Sunday. As I have two more dinners this week, I had better take Rothenstein's advice in future:

'Long hair, shabby clothes, even affectation, may protect an artist from idle, or so-called fashionable, people. When an artist goes into their world, he risks his pride and his integrity. Better remain unwashed than be wasted on fools; better spend his evenings in cafés than waste them on lionising hostesses.'

Thursday, 17 September 1936

Gave luncheon at the Ivy to Negley Farson, Stefan Litauer,[2] Rex Leeper and self. Negley looked older. He has had a bad time: After his success with *The Way of a Transgressor* he went off the deep end with drink. Came home or rather back to England last March, went into a nursing home and had the

[1] (1892–1959) journalist and diplomat, Chief London Correspondent of Polish Telegraph Agency.

Dent cure: injections which are supposed to make you violently sick if you touch alcohol again. Went back to Yugoslavia, got well – too well, felt good and went off to Vienna to get material for his novel. Cure broke down. Negley was sick at first, but being sick didn't spoil his taste for alcohol!

Rex says England will get her national spirit back, will become strong morally, will grow alive to the danger, and will re-establish strength of democratic principles – whereas dictators will fail one day and leave no successors.

In the evening went to the Tauber concert at Covent Garden with Mrs Beckett. With her Evelyn FitzGerald and her daughter; Lady Delamere. Concert – a financial success and therefore triumph for Mrs Beckett. Tauber – very good in his Viennese stuff, but rather a trick voice than a great voice. Supper afterwards at Savoy in private room. Sat next Tauber's doctor (Howard) and his wife. . . Fabulous entry of Marlene Dietrich with Douglas [Fairbanks] junior. Everyone silent – eyelashes three inches long. Hard cruel face; hideous arms.

Sunday, 20 September 1936

At five-thirty went to see Sibyl Colefax who is in Empire Nursing Home. Found Aldous Huxley there and on this occasion rather liked him. He is certainly amazingly erudite. Told us about French cure for drink: something like twilight sleep and chloral which puts you under and makes you peculiarly susceptible to hypnotic influence. The effect remains after the hypnosis. Been very successful. Possibilities immense for dictators, etc., Russian confessions. Also told us of this place near Paris where highbrows (literary and scientific) meet to discuss *décades*. Told us of Blum's[1] Brains Trust – author of *L'Humanisme Economique*. Aldous Huxley had been at Peace Conference at Brussels – failure – too many people. Cannot have very effective meeting over twelve: not for nothing limit fixed on twelve apostles.

Sibyl's story of Goering and Lindbergh which she heard from Harold. Lindberg went to dine with Goering and Frau Goering. The General in white uniform. Conversation difficult. Lindbergh: 'You keep a lion, don't you?' Goering: 'Lioness.' She comes in, plays with Goering, finally makes water – a great puddle; Goering, embarrassed, tries to stop her, gets wet, has to leave room, comes down in plus-fours.

Thursday, 24 September 1936

Mike is very much impressed by his friendship with 'Dicky' Mountbatten who is in the Admiralty Intelligence. He tells Mike that the Admiralty has absolute proof of the existence of a secret treaty between Italy, Germany and Franco whereby Italy is to receive Balearics and Ceuta and Germany the Canary Islands in return for their help. Mike wanted me to write this up in a

[1] Léon Blum (1872–1950) had become French Socialist Prime Minister in May.

signed article. I had the greatest difficulty in persuading him that no intelligence reports can be taken at more than twenty per cent of truth, and that secret treaties, etc., are the kind of thing intelligence officers keep supplying all the year round. Finally agreed to write an article on Spain in conjunction with Rex [Fletcher]. Went to see Rex who tells me Admiralty Intelligence is particularly bad, no grey matter in it, and that Troup,[1] head of D.N.I., however good he may be as a sailor, is an absolute child about intelligence.

Kerensky very interesting on France and Russia. Says reason for plot in Russia was existence of pro-German group in army.[2] Kerensky, says 'You will see in six months' time pro-German group will be heard of again.' Rex rather agrees. Army is coming more and more to fore. As transition proceeds, Stalin and even Voroshilov may go. Hitler anti-Russian – but German General Staff not. Rex says Winston is making great recovery in Conservative Party – Many regard him as only 'P.M.' in a crisis.

Sunday, 4 October 1936

Summer time ends – another winter before me and how I hate the English winter. There will not be many more for me now.[3] This last year has brought a great change in my health, and there has not been a single week during which I have felt really well.

Wednesday, 7 October 1936

Lunched at office with 'Dicky' Mountbatten . . . very interesting on Spain. He is very frightened of a Fascist triangle and thinks it will be very bad for us. He would prefer a Left victory in Spain – even Communist.

Tuesday, 27 October 1936

Most of conversation about King and Mrs Simpson. General view is that he will marry her before July. Lord Anglesey has bet £50 to this effect. Lord Kemsley told me that his peerage title was signed both by King George and present King. King George died soon after peerage was conferred.

Thursday, 29 October 1936

Went to luncheon with the Noel Charleses[4] at Quinto's (Arlington House). Did not feel too well after last night. Present: Johnny Mulholland, a cinema star whose name I did not catch, Oliver Messel, and self.[5] Talk, as usual, mostly about the King and Mrs Simpson. Mulholland gave us interesting

[1] Admiral James Troup (*b.* 1883), Director of Naval Intelligence, 1935–9.

[2] Zinoviev and Kamenev had been sentenced to death on 25 August in the first trial of Stalin's purge.

[3] There were to be thirty-four more winters for him.

[4] Sir Noel Charles, Bart (*b.* 1891), at this time Counsellor, Brussels; later High Commissioner to Italy, 1944–7; and Ambassador to Turkey, 1949–51.

[5] Hon. John Mulholland (1892–1948), son of 2nd Baron Dunleath, banker and company director. Messel (*b.* 1904), theatrical designer, uncle of Lord Snowdon.

account of headlines, etc., in the American Press. Everyone in this circle is convinced that the King will marry her. Only doubt is whether he will do so before the Coronation or wait until afterwards.

Monday, 2 November 1936

Moir, just back from Canada and the U.S.A., in great form. Says Canadians talk of only three things: the King and Mrs Simpson, the coming war, and what their salary is going to be next year. The feeling about Mrs Simpson is very strong; stronger still about the King and his bagpipe jazz and changing the fashion at Balmoral. Hector McKinnon,[1] one of the leading Canadian officials, told Moir: 'He can have fifty mistresses for all we care, but let him keep his blasted hands off Scotland.' Moir came home with Walter Citrine. The two men are old friends. Walter has always been a loyalist. He is shocked, says: 'King is well paid to do his job; if he does not do it, he will have to make way for someone else!' Moir says Lord Lothian who also arrived with him says King will marry her before Coronation.

Tuesday, 3 November 1936

Brendan red-hot on the King and Mrs Simpson. Suggests that someone should put down question to Home Secretary in the House to ask if he will bar the entry into England of such newspapers as the *New York Times*, *New York Herald-Tribune*, *Chicago Tribune*, etc., for spreading base and false rumours about the King. Sir John Simon would then go to Baldwin. Latter would say: these papers are true; they are respectable; they are important and friendly to England. He would have to go to the King, and the King would have to take notice. Latter condition is not certain, but this would be most dignified line of action.

Friday, 13 November 1936

More gossip (well-informed gossip) about the King and Mrs Simpson. He will marry her before the Coronation; she will be made Duchess of Lancaster as soon as the decree absolute is through. People like Lord Derby, Lord Salisbury, etc., are very opposed, but will do nothing. Lord Derby would have been Prime Minister if he had had one ounce of courage.[2] He has not one pennyweight to tackle King. Queen [Mary] is supposed to have said: 'I don't like it, but the one thing that I have always feared for David is drink. I was afraid it would ruin him or make him a laughing-stock. And she (Mrs Simpson) has been a sane influence in that respect. And this is important.'

Friday, 20 November 1936

After luncheon much gossip, as usual, about Mrs Simpson. Latest news is

[1] Hector Brown McKinnon (*b.* 1890), Chairman of Canadian Tariff Board.

[2] 17th Earl of Derby (1865–1948), had been Conservative Secretary for War, 1922–4, but never held any higher office.

that when she saw Queen last week Queen warned her she was destroying crown of Britain, Mrs Simpson replied she realised danger, had no intention of marrying the King, but that difficult to leave him as he threatened suicide, etc.![1] George IV, apparently, did same in case of Mrs Fitzherbert. Sat on a dagger – or used leeches – but was found in small pool of blood!

Sunday, 22 November 1936

A day of fog and gloom. Immense excitement yesterday in the office. Exactly a week ago Lord Beaverbrook left for Canada and U.S.A. 'for a long time'. He wrote an article of farewell to the nation saying this and adding that 'this was his first holiday for sixteen years'. Much else about what he was going to do – and what the *Express* was to do in his absence! . . It is true that this was Lord Beaverbrook's sixteenth attempt to take a holiday in one year and that we know his little idiosyncrasies, but this time we all gave him at least two months. Hence our laughter mingled with dismay this morning when *Express* announced Lord Beaverbrook was cured and was returning to England by same boat as he went over on – the *Bremen*![2]

Monday, 23 November 1936

Busy day. Ronnie Knox told good story last night. In Lord Salisbury's time trouble somewhere in East.

Salisbury said: 'Suppose better send gunboat.'

Commander sent for; received by Salisbury. 'What am I to do if natives do not yield to threat?'

Salisbury hummed: 'I'm afraid nothing to do but get up steam and leave.'

Commander arrived. Local opinion divided – most people afraid. Sultan, still obdurate, sends Vizier; asks: 'What is alternative if we do not agree your demands?'

Commander replies. 'Then I am afraid that very reluctantly I shall have to carry out second part of my orders!'

Saturday, 28 November 1936

Much colder. A wasted day. Read André Gide's *Retour de l'U.R.S.S.* – poor stuff of an intellectual who does not know where he stands, but it has caused a political sensation in France, because Gide, who made the principal oration at Gorky's funeral,[3] was supposed to have become a hundred per cent Communist, and this book is more anti than pro. Moura tells good story of Gide at Gorky's funeral. While Gide was delivering his speech, Stalin turned to Alexei Tolstoy: 'Who's that?' Tolstoy replied: 'That's Gide. He's our great

[1] But see below, page 360.

[2] Beaverbrook was returning at the request of the King who wished to consult him on the proposal that he should make a morganatic marriage with Mrs Simpson (see Brian Inglis, *Abdication*, 1966, pp. 271ff). The *Bremen* was a German liner.

[3] Gorky had died on 18 June, just before the Zinoviev trial began. There were later rumours that he had been murdered by Yagoda or by Stalin.

conquest. He's the leading writer of France and he's ours!' 'H'm,' said Stalin; 'I never trust these French fellows.'

Wednesday, 2 December 1936

Lunched as guest of Fitz Randolph at Carlton. Guests included A. J. Cummings, who was full of Bishop of Bradford's attack on King yesterday and of organised comment of provincial Press.[1] Says we shall soon be up against situation like time of Charles I and we shall have to choose between King and Parliament.

Thursday, 3 December 1936

King's crisis now public property. House of Commons said to be unanimous against marriage. But one thing certain. For weeks M.P.s have been saying that whole country is seething about King's conduct and Mrs Simpson and that they (the Members) were being deluged with letters from their constituents. Probably true; but letters came from Mrs Rector and Mrs Town Councillor. It is now quite clear that ninety per cent of country had never heard of Mrs Simpson. Now there will be – for moment at least – a reaction in favour of King, and it will be amazing if people like Beaver, Winston, etc., do not try to exploit this against Baldwin.

Lunched in the City at the Rothschilds – talked of nothing but the King. One man – a Stern – just back from Paris said everyone had been saying England only country in world without crisis and now we had worst of lot. I was optimistic – said if quickly settled people would say – how marvellous – in any other country revolution – here people settle everything over week-end. Spoke to Rex Leeper. Gather that Whitehall wants King to abdicate in any case – altogether too irresponsible.

Friday, 4 December 1936

Forces are now beginning to align themselves. Lord Beaverbrook has been rather slow in making up his mind, but now he is beginning to see his chance of using the King issue to beat Baldwin with. We are becoming more royal than the royalists. Mike showed me some unctuous messages from Beaverbrook transmitted on his dictaphone. They were pro-King and anti-Baldwin.

[1] Alfred Blunt (1879–1957), Bishop of Bradford, 1931–55, did not exactly make an attack. What he said (see Peart-Binns, *Blunt*, Bradford, 1969) in an address to his diocesan conference on the previous day was: 'I ask you to commend him to God's grace which he will so abundantly need, as we all need it – for the King is a man like ourselves – if he is to do his duty faithfully. We hope that he is aware of his need. Some of us wish that he gave more positive signs of his awareness.' Blunt later said that when he wrote his address in October he had never heard of Mrs Simpson. He did so in November, but decided not to alter his address.

There was no 'organised' comment. All the papers, including *The Times*, reported the Bishop's address; only the *Yorkshire Post*, *Manchester Guardian* and *Birmingham Post* carried leader comment. The first paper to print the address was the *Bradford Telegraph and Argus*.

They called attention to fact that Lyons, Australian Premier was R.C. and therefore prejudiced, that country was in favour of King marrying and therefore against Baldwin's interference (main point, of course) and that Mike must use his judgement but that 'right and justice must be done to King'. Mike laughed like mad at last line and said: 'I suppose you'll put that down in your diary.' Leslie Marsh, who edits the Diary, takes different line: 'I see Beaver and Rothermere are supporting King. That means the poor devil is sunk.'

Lunched with Harold and Sibyl Colefax at Boulestin's. Harold says bulk of House and of serious people in City and Whitehall want King to go anyway; too irresponsible and now his prestige damaged. Sibyl says Mrs Simpson had no idea until few days ago that the King was really serious in his intention to marry her. This accords ill with Sibyl's other story that Mrs Simpson wanted to leave him and clear out, but that King threatened to quit, to follow her, and even to commit suicide! Mike himself is furious at Max's indecision, wants to come out for King, says we could organise huge demonstration – and doubtless sell 2,000,000 copies of *Evening Standard*!

Saturday, 5 December 1936

The situation this morning is that the deadlock is complete. The King refuses to give up intention of marrying Mrs Simpson. The Cabinet refuse to introduce special legislation to enable him to marry her without her being Queen. Beaver, Winston, Rothermere now openly on King's side – even to encouraging him to marry Mrs Simpson – against Baldwin. Very important that crisis should be speedily settled. Otherwise, country will be split from top to bottom.

Sunday, 6 December 1936

Cabinet meetings both this morning and this evening; crowds before Buckingham Palace and in Downing Street cheering the King, but no change in the situation, which I believe is a complete deadlock, in the sense that Government refuse to bring in special legislation to enable King to marry Mrs Simpson morganatically, and King refuses to give up idea of marrying her. It is significant that pro-King demonstrations are being worked up mainly by Beaverbrook and Rothermere, Baldwin's two principal enemies. Tommy, who knows King well and would die for him, is afraid for him, knowing that he is irresponsible and nearly a mental case.

Monday, 7 December 1936

Van came, at my suggestion, to luncheon. Only Mike, Cudlipp and myself present. He spoke very well, slightly nervously, but without any frills or any attempt to speak *ex cathedra*. Is not afraid of European war over Spain – geographically not the point Germany would choose for an explosion – but thinks situation very serious in that internal situation in Germany is worse than people realise and that rather than lose prestige at home Hitler and Nazis may risk a foreign adventure. Not perhaps very likely to come soon; tolerably certain that army chiefs do not think Germany is ready yet. Army went into last war on a 6 to 4 chance; they lost. Now they want odds of 5 to 1 in their favour. Britain should make herself strong enough to prevent these odds from ever becoming anything like 5 to 1 on Germany. Mike was much impressed by Van's exposé.

Van, incidentally, said he was quite prepared to give Germany colonies if this would bring peace. Is afraid however that concession would do little good. While Germany continues to upset her financial and domestic economy by wild spending on armaments colonies would make no difference, and within four weeks Hitler would require another success to bolster up his prestige, and there would be more demands and more threats.

Thursday, 10 December 1936

Abdication Day. The crisis has ended with the end which I had always predicted. The King will not give up his woman. He is, I believe, suffering from *dementia erotica*. He is not a strong man. To have resisted the pressure which has been brought to bear on him must have meant that he was completely obsessed by one thought. We had a hectic morning. We have taken the wrong line from the beginning, and today Cudlipp, the editor, and I both wanted to close the ranks and welcome the new King. Mike Wardell agreed. But not my Lord Beaverbrook. I do not think his pro-King attitude was entirely inspired by his anti-Baldwinism. I think the King 'got' him, and the little man, taken up for the first time by royalty, saw himself as a crusader defending his monarch when men of better blood had 'ratted'. Effect, however, has been bad. Ninety per cent of intelligent public regard the Beaverbrook–Rothermere campaign on King's behalf as mischievous and irresponsible anti-Baldwinism. Winston is tarred with the same brush and has lost ground, and de Margerie at French Embassy is worried by Winston's loss of ground. Baldwin is right up again.

Friday, 11 December 1936

Lunched at Anthony Rothschild's. . . City relieved that Edward has gone. Anthony Rothschild quoted his brother who had said: 'If anyone had said that years ago that a King of England had abdicated and on same afternoon there had been boom on Stock Exchange (as there was yesterday, and prices higher again today) he would have been qualified for a lunatic asylum.'

Monday, 14 December 1936

Spent most of the morning writing a paragraph attacking the Archbishop of Canterbury. In his broadcast last night he not only rebuked the ex-King but called on the nation to rebuke the ex-King's friends.[1] The people who

[1] The passage from Cosmo Gordon Lang's broadcast referred to here read: 'Even more

were closest to him during his reign were: Duff and Diana Cooper, Duke and Duchess of Sutherland, Lord and Lady Brownlow, Euan and Barbara Wallace, Mr and Mrs Fitzgerald, Lord Dudley, Duke and Duchess of Marlborough. Not heavy-weights, but certainly no more deserving of Archbishop's rebuke than ninety per cent of population! In the end Max turned down the paragraph. Lunched in the office and listened to Mike on the King. Mike is an old loyalist and tries to justify the attitude we took during the crisis.

Sunday, 20 December 1936

An idle day. Barbara Wilson has a good story about Vansittart and the King. After his broadcast last Friday the King sent for Vansittart. Lady Van went with him and, feeling sorry for the King, took a travelling rug with her as a present. When they arrived at Fort Belvedere, Lady Van remained in car. Van went in. King Edward was calm and smiling. In the corner was the Duke of Kent his eyes swollen and red with crying. Van gave the rug from Lady Van. King asked where she was and was told in car. Went out to say good-bye to her. Composure was perfect.

Monday, 21 December 1936

Tommy hears: (1) that the King – King Edward that is – has St Vitus's dance very badly; and (2) that Mrs Simpson has no intention of marrying him.

Tuesday, 22 December 1936

Maugham has had relations with women (after all, he married and had a daughter). One was ——. She has a hold on him still. One reason is that because of his homosexual nervosity he could not perform alone. The liaison was *à trois*. The third was Godfrey Winn! Maugham . . . is a man who has tried everything: drugs, etc., but has an iron self-discipline and is now master of himself. He is a man of method. No matter who is staying with him, he works every day from ten to one and during this time no one must disturb him.

Monday, 28 December 1936

Yesterday's lovely weather changed again to fog and rain. Mike Wardell, who has been spending the weekend with Perry Brownlow, gave me his good stories of King Edward's abdication. King, on eve of departure for France, sent for Crisp, his valet. 'We're going abroad, Crisp. What about the

strange and sad it is that he should have sought his happiness in a manner inconsistent with the Christian principles of marriage, and within a social circle whose standards and ways of life are alien to all the best instincts and traditions of his people. Let those who belong to this circle stand rebuked by the judgement of the nation which had loved King Edward.' But the Archbishop praised his 'most genuine care for the poor, the suffering, the unemployed; his years of eager service both at home and across the seas'.

luggage?' Crisp hesitated. He was married, didn't want to go. King saw at once. 'Never mind, I'll get you a job here.' Rings up his brother. 'Bertie, what about my valet – he's best authority on medals and decorations in the world.' King went without valet. Crisp now with King George VI. Same with junior piper. King Edward wanted him to come to Austria for a month. Piper stammered. 'I've a large family, sir. They'd be shocked.'

CHAPTER FOURTEEN

1937

Defence problems 'depressing'. Duke of Kent divorce rumours. Visit to King Boris of Bulgaria, and King Carol of Rumania. Reports to F.O. Bertrand de Jouvenel. Churchill's braces removed by conjurer. Vansittart on British 'folly'. Did ex-King Edward VIII pay his income tax? Leeper notes 'new wave of pro-Germanism'. Lockhart resigns from *Evening Standard.* Beaverbrook in the bath. Max Aitken, junior, does tricks in his aeroplane. Muggeridge returns. Leslie Hore-Belisha on rearmament. A. P. Herbert on feeling ill before a speech. Mrs Jones, the 'Mrs Simpson of Greece'.

Tuesday, 5 January 1937

Lunched with Chenevix-Trench[1] at Simpson's and discussed defence problems. Very depressing. He says very little is being done and nothing for defence from air attack. He thinks our decline is at the flood and that we shall deserve all we get. Inertia in high quarters is complete. Tragedy is that there are always so many plausible reasons for doing nothing. This was the curse of the weak commander during the war.

Monday, 18 January 1937

Stormy, rain with light intervals. On Saturday *Evening Standard* Diary carried story of rumours of Duke of Kent's divorce in connection with his visit to phrenologist in Fleet Street with Mrs 'Bill' Allen, formerly Paula Gelliebrand later Casa Maury. Story, of course, was published with view to denying it – but actually to make it public. Yesterday *Sunday Express* repeated it with screaming headlines. Today, 'Bill' Allen has letter in *Times* complaining against this persecution and threatening certain individuals who have grown rich on ruthless exploitation of people's private lives with horse-whipping. I wonder how many people will connect me with this story, and how am I, short of statement in *Times*, to explain: (1) that I had nothing to do with it; and (2) that I was in bed with influenza when it appeared.

Monday, 15 February 1937

Still very seedy with a 'flu' cold. On Saturday I had a letter from Jean saying

[1] Colonel Lawrence Chenevix-Trench (1883–1958), A.Q.M.G., Northern Command India, 1933–7.

that she had left the house and intended to marry Loudon McLean and wanted me to divorce her.

On 29 January 1937, Lockhart had left for Central Europe. He reached Sofia, the capital of Bulgaria, in mid-February.

Tuesday, 16 February 1937

Another glorious day: cold but clear with bright sunshine. At eleven twenty set out in Legation car for Palace – yellow building (used formerly to be residence of Turkish Pasha – now rebuilt) in centre town. Bulgarian flag flying. A few sentries at entrance gate and inside. Go up stairs into rather dark and dingy waiting-room with toy cannon on table. Talk French and Russian to King's secretary. At eleven-thirty bell rings and I am shown through another ante-room into King's study. King Boris comes to door to meet me, shakes hands effusively. He is short – shorter than I am, slightly built, rather bald, dark with small black moustache, a pleasant smile and attractive eyes. He has a prominent nose. He is dressed in short black coat and striped trousers and is rather pale. He has, like me, a 'flu' cold. He has a habit of stroking his long nose with his first finger and thumb. Room is quite big and oblong-shaped. King's table – big – is at end of room opposite entrance.

Writing desk covered with large photo frames of family and relations. Wall immediately behind (high room) covered with pictures. Immediately behind King's seat is a fine portrait of Prince Alexander of Battenberg (very like Admiral Louis Battenberg)[1] and beneath is photogravure of Congress of Berlin 1879 which split up Bulgaria!

After a few questions about myself, King began to expand and to expound his views. Pleased with Yugoslav–Bulgarian Pact and with [Milan] Stojadinovitch [Yugoslav Prime Minister]. Things thinks will improve. I mentioned frontier difficulties and no bridge on Danube. Yes, bridge would be a great help. Things must be done in small stages – recreate confidence. Balkans behaving well just now – better than most of Europe. Hoped extend pact, but must be signs of goodwill from others. Bulgaria had lost ground – three wars in fifty years – all ended badly – had suffered most cruelly in Great War. Could not expect the beggar always to give and the rich neighbour to get. Greece and Rumania difficult – with Greece first. Bulgars poorest people in Europe – ripe for Communists, but inherently sound, full of common sense. Stopped on brink of precipice. Trouble was Bulgaria had gone too fast. He, Boris, was a king made by revolution. His father, Tsar Ferdinand, he said, 'although I ought not to say it, was a very clever man. He had a long nose, we have all long noses' (stroking his own). 'He saw whole odium of defeat would need a victim. Took it on himself and went.' Saved throne for his son. At least, saved it so far. 'You never know how it will end.'

[1] Prince Alexander of Battenberg (1857–93) had been Prince of Bulgaria, 1879–86; he was father of Admiral Louis Battenberg (1st Marquess of Milford Haven) and grandfather of Earl Mountbatten of Burma (*b.* 1900).

This is partly true. Certain Bulgarians say: this dynasty associated with disaster brought nothing but tragedy to Bulgaria. Queen expected to have a child in May; all hoping for boy. Went to German doctor – same as Crown Prince of Italy – before Princess was born. Since 1918 Bulgaria had gone through three revolutions; peasants, intelligentsia and *coup d'état*. King gave me graphic account of Velcheff coup of 19th May. Said he might have lost both his throne and head. Described scene in French how new government came into his room to limit his powers – perhaps remove him. Saw new head of government had Velcheff in his pocket. Everything decided but no Minister for War. Picked out one man among them. 'You must have Minister for War: you had better take it, General.' Discussions went on all through night. Since then King has ruled without Parliament. Does not like idea of military dictatorship too much. Says to me, stroking nose: 'Have I the head of a dictator!' Has modified his régime twice.

I said I had heard régime unpopular with parties, popular with country which had had good harvest. 'So is it,' he said, 'another good harvest and we shall be all right.' Nevertheless, may have to fall back on military – praised Lukoff, Minister of War, aged forty-eight. I said Bulgars were Scots Slavs. Loud in praise of Scotland – loves it – sees great affinity Bulgaria.

King Boris told me that before he made his *coup d'état* (i.e. dispensed with Parliament) he made tour abroad to assure himself that there would be no trouble from outside. Saw the Duce. Went to Balmoral saw King George and Ramsay MacDonald. Both pressed him, especially MacDonald, to go back at once and not to lose time!

Lockhart also visited Rumania, and its capital, Bucharest.

Thursday, 18 February 1937

Felt a little better: sunshine accompanied by strong thaw. In morning Matlescu who runs Anglo-Rumanian Society and another Rumanian journalist came to see me. Discussed 'Iron Guard'. Strength growing. Ninety per cent of students. Mysticism mixed with certain amount of gangsterism: religious and ascetic. Kneel to take oath to forswear human love and earthly pleasures and dedicate life to service of country. Many secret sympathisers. Relations with King: no desire as yet to oust King. Latter clever enough to keep Iron Guard in check.

Saturday, 20 February 1937

At three Legation car came to fetch me and took me to the royal palace for my interview with King Carol. Much grander than Sofia but less atmosphere. Met by lackeys and ushered into a very modern lift and taken upstairs, where I waited a few minutes. In lift again, and taken by A.D.C. in uniform up another flight and straight along corridor – apparently unguarded – to King's room. Big square room, heavily carpeted, big table against one wall. Carol quite fair, blue-eyed, dressed in uniform of some greeny-blue colour as our Air Force with rows of order ribbons, smoking cigarette in holder (chain-wise) came forward, shook hands, sat down. Speaks very good English. I congratulated him on accepting patronage of Anglo-Rumanian Society. He began at once to expatiate on necessity of improving Anglo-Rumanian relations. Hoped to pay private visit to England soon. Actually, was coming when King George died, and again when Edward abdicated. Has strong views about Englishmen's indifference to Rumania. Said he realised Hungarians very successful propagandists with English upper classes – gave English good time, spoke English, liked the same things: sport, shooting, gentleman's life. Spoke to me very frankly about Bulgarian–Yugoslav pact, said he was in favour of better relations between neighbours. Then got on to inclusion of Bulgaria in Balkan League. I said I was sure English would like it – and also Italians – necessary counteraction to Germany going south. Rather sticky. Inclined to agree. Said, owing to Titulescu [former Foreign Minister], Italian relations had not been as good as might have been, but were improving. Nevertheless, bringing Bulgaria in would mean concessions – probably by Greece in Aegean. And he was against revision. Once begun, no one knew where it would stop. Possibly true, but not very encouraging. Discussed Beneš's plan for Little Entente and French Pact. Quite frank on this. Said Rumania must be very careful: certain advantage to Rumania if she could have her frontier (on Russian side) guaranteed by France. Russia, however, will not sign any pact involving her army in assistance against Germany. In hopes of good relations with Russia – but no Russian interference and no Russian armies through Rumania. (Here in Rumania Communism not tolerated.) Attitude re Little Entente same as Yugoslavia's. I said in plain words this means if Czechoslovakia attacked by Germany, you won't help. If at same time Hungary has a cut [at] Slovakia, you would step in. He said: 'You have defined position exactly.' Does not think, however, that Germany intends to march into Czechoslovakia. Kept me three-quarters of an hour – talked of sport, etc. Not so forthcoming as Boris, but talks carefully and intelligently.

From Royal Palace went to other palace to see Queen Marie:[1] in big grounds on top of hill. Fine staircase. Very good-looking A.D.C. general – might pass for Englishman. Shown into almost religious-looking Byzantine room overlooking grounds with old Byzantine fireplace. On fireplace a cross with clock in centre (first I've seen); on tables china figures of animals, tigers, rabbits, penguins, etc. Taken by general to Marie's private sitting-room or boudoir: she looks old now, but traces of beauty very evident. Graceful, outspoken, perfect English. Talked of Colonel Boyle whom she liked very much. Said she had been blamed for rating him too highly under emotions

[1] Granddaughter of Queen Victoria, married Ferdinand, who became King of Rumania in 1914. King Carol was their eldest son. She wrote *The Story of My Life* (3 vols., 1934–5).

of war, but Boyle a big man. I agreed. Talked of Russia; said Rumanian peasants not Bolshevist: too practical and slightly cynical in attitude towards life. Sat in chair opposite me – small table between – kind of divan – alongside with tiger-skin cover. Two pekinese – reminded me of Millie, Duchess of Sutherland, a little. A good deal about King Edward whom she liked – and from King Edward very easily to King Carol. Asked me how I found him – I praised his intelligence. She said 'Yes; his failures were moral.' Referred to Carol's Mrs Simpson [Madame Lupescu). Said he didn't listen to her. She [Queen Marie] was not quite so strict perhaps as Queen Mary, but on these matters her views were the same. Said Carol had inferiority complex with English but hoped he would go to England soon.

Spoke of Iron Guard – had the young people – people also afraid of Russia, Germany doing much, Britain nothing. Rumanians ('my Rumanians') not very consistent. Told me about her books – new one *Some More Chapters From My Life*. Couldn't write everything up to date because of Carol. Also six articles on Coronation – done for Edward – now had to be revised. Told me she was only European who, Americans said, had stood fatigue of American lecture tour, done everything, etc., without turning hair.

Tuesday, 23 February 1937

My trip is drawing to a close. By tomorrow evening I shall have visited score capitals, delivered dozen lectures of an hour each, made as many speeches, given goodness knows how many interviews, seen scores of politicians, attended numerous luncheons, teas, and dinners in my honour, and travelled some 4000 miles!

Sunday, 28 February 1937

Reached London at five and went home to a changed house, Jean having taken away with her many knick-knacks and pieces of furniture.

Thursday, 11 March 1937

Rang up the lawyers to make an appointment about my divorce. I am to see Mr Stormonth Darling on Monday. It is an unsavoury business, and I am much distressed, (1) by the manner in which Jean is making a broadcast of it to her friends; and (2) by the bills she has left unpaid and the gear she has taken out of the house. However, I suppose that even in these matters least said soonest mended. As far as I can make out, it will take me weeks and months of economy to get straight, and in April there is three months' rent due and Robin's fees to pay. In mood of despair went to Harrod's and ordered thirty-five pounds of furniture (sheets, rugs, tablecloths, etc.) to replace what Jean has taken away.

Friday, 12 March 1937

A strenuous day. Lunched with Moura Budberg at the Jardin. She had heard about Jean's departure and divorce plans from Nata Ramsden,[1] and the story has lost nothing in the telling. I cannot think what Jean can mean. She rang up Schapiro [his secretary] the other day and told her . . . her lawyers were busily reading my books when she went to see them. This kind of thing is both undignified and dangerous.

At three-fifteen went to see Charles Bridge at the British Council headquarters and had a long talk about propaganda in Europe. The Council receives £30,000 from the Government. This is fantastically little in comparison with what other countries spend. Last year France spent over £1,250,000. Incidentally, Moura told me that Alexei Tolstoy, who arrived today for the Congress of Friendship with U.S.S.R., is terrified. He [says he] has a Cheka man following him wherever he goes.

Sunday, 14 March 1937

Did no work on my political report[2] for the Foreign Office, although it is important and Rex will arrange for me to see Eden. I was, however, too ill and too weak-willed to command the necessary energy. This inertia is the chief penalty for all excesses of the flesh.

Friday, 19 March 1937

Lunched at the Ivy with Robert de St Jean to meet Bertrand de Jouvenel,[3] son of the former French ambassador, high commissioner (Syria), senator, etc. Robert de St Jean is very nice and gentle. Bertrand de Jouvenel is attractive but volatile. He changes his political allegiances every two months. There was only one thing on which we were agreed. It is essential to bring Italy into line with France and Britain in order to safeguard peace. With Italy, France can defend integrity of Czechoslovakia; that is to say, she can tell Germany she will regard an invasion as a *casus belli*. Without Italy she cannot do this, and Germany knows this. We cannot afford to be anti-Italian and anti-German at the same time. Yet a mass of ignorant people who know nothing about foreign affairs go on reviling Italians and Mussolini. Only this morning Foreign Office rang up to ask why we had played up Dean of Winchester's speech in which he had compared Mussolini to the mad Emperor Antiochus. I agreed, but told Rex he should go to the Dean of Winchester and not us.

Neither Roland de Margerie nor St Jean thinks very much of de Jouvenel. Margerie says he is unreliable and untrustworthy. At present he is pro-Fascist, pro-Hitler, pro-Italian, pro-Franco (in various degrees of pro) and thinks that sooner or later in France this issue will be decided by machine-guns. The right will win, but the issue will be bloody.

[1] Wife of Charles Ramsden, retired diplomat, Overseas Director of Federation of British Industries. [2] Resulting from his tour of Central and South-East Europe.

[3] Political philosopher, author of *Sovereignty*, *The Pure Theory of Politics*, etc.

Monday, 22 March 1937

Lunched at Sibyl Colefax's new house (19 Lord North Street) – small but decorative. Met Ormsby-Gore for first time – quite pleasant but rather pedantic.[1] Also present Sir John Maffey,[2] Harold, and Duchess of Westminster who told me good story about Winston. He was staying at Eaton for Grand National. The Duke and the famous Italian conjuror present – the man who can empty your pockets without your knowing. He took Winston's braces off. He was furious and retired upstairs in a dudgeon.

Wednesday, 31 March 1937

Gave luncheon to Rex at St James's and discussed his trip to Central Europe. He told me that he had been offered the post of private secretary to Eden and also head of Central Department after Wigram's death, but had preferred to stay where he was. He was now more or less general adviser to Secretary of State. He told me that Eden was sore with Beaverbrook Press. His effort to get Eden to see me had failed for moment. Eden's private secretary had asked if Leeper insisted on this interview, and Rex said in the circumstances better leave it alone for a bit.

Thursday, 1 April 1937

After luncheon went to Foreign Office where I had nearly an hour with Vansittart. He is very worried indeed about two situations – especially about British attitude towards Italy, which has put Anglo-Italian relations back to where they were at height of Abyssinian crisis. Apart from folly of having made the impossible come true, i.e. the bringing of Italy and Germany together, we insist by violent language on welding them together. Visitor from Mars hearing our talk and reading our Press, might assume we were most bellicose nation in world. Yet all this is talk – most dangerous talk – from nation not ready to fight and not wanting to fight. Wants me to write at once to Beaverbrook – will see him as soon as he returns. Wants Government to act – say something – intends to speak to Baldwin. Vansittart is a hundred per cent right, but Government will do nothing.

Friday, 9 April 1937

After luncheon went to see Godfrey Thomas [formerly the Prince of Wales's private secretary] about the Duke of Windsor's income tax. Lord Beaverbrook, who poses as a friend of the Duke, has sent Cudlipp a memorandum suggesting some paragraphs on King's income tax. Basis of story is following: During war or just after it when Bonar Law was Chancellor,

[1] (1885–1964) Secretary of State for the Colonies, became 4th Baron Harlech in 1938.

[2] Maffey, 1st Baron Rugby (1877–1969) was Permanent Under-Secretary of State for Colonies, 1933–7, and U.K. Representative to Eire, 1939–49.

King George V sent £500,000 to Exchequer. Regarded by King as a gift to Treasury, and by Treasury as an income tax payment. Suggestion is that Kings are slack about payment of tax. Lord Beaverbrook puts forward idea that we should ask who pays tax on £25,000 for Duke of Windsor – King George VI or the Duke, or is there some special arrangement. We should bring out that King Edward VIII was very extravagant – i.e. implying did not pay his tax – and that he is supposed to have settled £500,000 on Mrs Simpson and that Mrs Simpson has now returned it. Of course the paragraphs are to go in 'Londoner's Diary'! ! !

Sunday, 11 April 1937

Lunched at 18 Eaton Square to meet Lord and Lady St Levan[1] who had been with Tommy and Harry on their world cruise. Both very old. Lady St Levan was Lady Warwick's bridesmaid. Lady Warwick was also at luncheon – still rather a wonderful old girl with her mind quite alert in spite of the fact that she is blind in one eye and that she has difficulty in getting out of her chair once she has sat down (on account of her bulk). She ate a man-and-a-half's meal! Went for a walk with Tommy and made a string of new resolutions which I broke on the same evening.

Monday, 19 April 1937

Grannie Turner rang up to talk about Robin and his desire to be bought out of the Navy.[2] He has talked so much about Aldous Huxley and Dick Sheppard[3] to his term officer and other people at Dartmouth that he not to be made a cadet captain. This is a pity. I had hoped that he would be and that the extra responsibility would bring out what is good in him. Grannie says that his mind is in a complete muddle . . . I was sarcastic and unnecessarily unkind about the inevitable results of his having been spoilt and over-praised by two women. For this I felt ashamed and depressed. I am worried about the boy.

Friday, 14 May 1937

Lunched at the Anthony Chaplins'[4] in Trafalgar Square to meet Princess Marthe Bibesco next whom I sat. She has aged and is no longer beautiful but is intelligent. We discussed King Carol. She is pro-Carol and anti-Queen Marie and wants us to realise Carol's importance and intelligence. He has an inferiority complex with regard to England, wants to conquer it and would

[1] 2nd Baron St Levan (1857–1940), formerly commander of Grenadier Guards.

[2] His eyesight was poor, and since he did not wish to become an Engineer Officer or a Paymaster, he was given the option of leaving the Navy.

[3] Very Rev. H. R. L. Sheppard (1880–1937), Canon of St Paul's, Chaplain to the King, founded the Peace Pledge Union in 1936.

[4] (*b.* 1906) zoologist and musician, became 3rd Viscount Chaplin 1949.

like to come here. I told her that I agreed entirely and had already told Van so. She thinks that here we all harp too much on Titulescu. Titulescu was good up to a point but stayed too long and thought himself indispensable. He is not likely to come back soon – perhaps never. I agreed again. The mistake made by people who think themselves indispensable is to forget that death intervenes – death and age! Other guests included Emerald Cunard, young Ladbrooke. Emerald, who drove me back into Mayfair, very bitter about Mrs Simpson whom she blames for the abdication. She, Emerald, is sure that the Duke of Windsor has not yet lived with Mrs Simpson, and that he worships her as a virginal saint. I doubt this. I agree that since he met her he has taken no decision without consulting her.[2]

Friday, 21 May 1937

Last night Sibyl Colefax talked to me at supper for over an hour about Mrs Simpson, whom of course she knew better than anyone. Said that up to the last almost Mrs Simpson thought that she was in command of the situation and could do what she liked with the King. She never thought that he would abdicate. She did not want to be Queen . . . She wanted to go to U.S.A. for a while recently. King, or rather Duke of Windsor threatened to follow her by next boat. On night before Bishop of Bradford's attack last autumn, King Edward, Sibyl, Wallis and Edward Stanley at cinema. King in rollicking form: 'Sibyl must give a dinner for us at Christmas.' Within a week Mrs Simpson was out of country, and within a fortnight King was off his throne.

Thursday, 27 May 1937

Walked down to Foreign Office with Rex who talked to me very confidentially about Baldwin and Eden. Said Baldwin had been worse than a failure in foreign politics and was a sly drifter. We were now face to face with new wave of pro-Germanism, idea being pal up with Germany and then put Italy in her place. Rex says – and I think rightly – wrong way. We cannot satisfy Germany. If we make our relations with Italy worse, Germany sits back and laughs . . . Rex says that Eden is as weak as water and is entirely swayed by the home political situation and feeling in constituencies.[3]

Wednesday, 2 June 1937

Mrs Lesser[3] and Tommy came to see me. We discussed getting out of Fleet Street. Both strongly recommend me to do so. It is really a question of £ *s. d.* Apart from an annual income, I need about £1500–£2000 in cash: (1) in

[1] The King had been made Duke of Windsor as soon as he arrived in France on 12 December 1936. The Coronation of George VI took place on 12 May 1937, and the Duke and Mrs Simpson were to be married on 3 June in France.

[2] But see Leeper's revised opinion on 14 October 1937.

[3] The married name of Lockhart's secretary, Miss Schapiro.

order to pay off moneylender and outstanding bills, say £700, (2) to clear my income tax, say, £800, and (3) to set up cottage, say £200.

Friday, 4 June 1937

Decided now to leave Fleet Street even if I starve. Mrs Lesser, Tommy and Rufus [his brother], not to mention the doctors, are emphatic that this is the right decision and that to remain in Fleet Street is collapse within a year or two. Sent Mrs Lesser to see Huntington with a view to getting some guarantee for my books for two or three years. She came back to say that Huntington would see me through and would arrange a guaranteed income.

Sunday, 6 June 1937

At twelve Huntington came to see me and we had a long discussion on my decision to leave Fleet Street. He pointed out that Beaverbrook would be sure to think that I intended to go to another newspaper, and that I wanted first to have a holiday at his expense. I said that I was through with daily journalism and Fleet Street for ever and was prepared to sign anything to that effect. Huntington is enthusiastic, says that had I been a man of great foresight and sound commercial instinct I could not have chosen a better moment. He compares my move to taking silk. I hope he is right. At any rate, I shall feel happier and more self-respect on £400 a year in the country and writing what I want to write than being a slave in Fleet Street on £3000 a year.

Lockhart took the plunge on 7 June 1937.

This was a nerve-racking day. I went to the office in the morning, did my work on the Diary and arranged to see Wardell after luncheon. At 1.25, however, he was called forth to a meeting on newsprint at the *Express* and I had to talk to him while he changed from his country clothes into City clothes in the little room in his flat above the office.

It was very difficult, of course, in these circumstances to talk to anyone who is trying to do five things at once. I told him that I would have to leave because I had reached an age when it would no longer be possible for me to recover my health and remain on in Fleet Street at the same time.

He was not very surprised or wholly unsympathetic. He took the line, however, that I was a sick man and that of course in two months' time would probably change my mind. The best plan therefore was to take two months' holiday and to come back to the question after that period. I told him quite frankly that I had expected that, but that my mind was made up and there was no possibility of my changing it. I told him that I was going to see Lord Beaverbrook, and he advised me to tell Lord Beaverbrook that I had already spoken to him. . .

At five in the afternoon I took a car and motored down to Cherkley, Lord

Beaverbrook having told me that he would be back at six. I arrived punctually at six to find that he had just gone out to play golf and would not be back until after seven. I sat on the front. Cherkley was very beautiful in spite of all the building that was taking place there. The peace of it was very wonderful. No house to be seen from the terrace at the back for miles and miles, and the view is one of the finest of the South of England, and the peace of the place was really very wonderful. On the right the Italian garden with a circular glade of trees. At the back showing a white cross; at the right-hand corner of the Italian garden clusters of laburnum trees hanging over the wall. And I sat there tired, having forgotten all I wanted to say, when suddenly at ten minutes to eight Lord Beaverbrook came dashing in, took me upstairs, asked me what the whole question was about, and here again I had to speak to him while he was undressing and having his bath.

He undressed completely naked, showed me his little body, brown as that of a Balinese, proud of it, from sunbathing. He too was not entirely surprised or wholly unsympathetic, although it was quite obvious that he did not want me to go. He made the same point that Wardell made that I was a sick man, and that he was not going to take the decision of a sick man, and that I must have two months' holiday, and that at the end of that time I must take up the question again. I again repeated that whatever he might think I could assure him that I would not change my mind. He left it at that.

We went downstairs. He spoke to Wardell on the telephone made some arrangements with him on the telephone from which I concluded that I was to have my outstanding debt cancelled of the original £1000 which I understood he had given me when I joined the paper, and that I would have two months' salary free for a holiday.

He advised me to go to Karlsbad, and afterwards we left the matter where it was.

What the whole thing really amounts to is that I have been given two months' holiday and the option of taking up my job again when I come back. If I do not I imagine that will be all I shall receive. Not particularly generous treatment, but one that is slightly better than nothing at all.

After dinner I went back by car to London. It was a very clear night. Cool and not too hot, and I felt extraordinarily exhilarated. The sense of freedom was very wonderful, and as soon as I got into my house I wanted to get in touch with the people like Tommy who had supported me in this difficult decision. It was, however, after eleven o'clock and the only person I could get hold of was my doctor, David McMyn, who really advised this course of action, not only recently but twelve months ago. He, too, was pleased. I also found a letter from Constant Huntington saying how good a decision it would be and hoping that I would make it resolutely and successfully.

That ended a very exciting day in my life. I shall be fifty on September 2 of this year, and at fifty I start my last career as an independent author.[1]

[1] This was to be by no means his 'last career'.

Tuesday, 8 June 1937

Saw Mike this morning and arranged that Saturday, June 12, should be my last day at the office. On August 12 I must write to Max and Mike to say that I have not changed my mind. I told Mike that I was prepared to lay any money that I would not. He told me that he had cancelled my debt to the *Standard* of £90 which was very nice of him. I shall have little enough money for betting or anything else. I have the barest minimum to get out with, and hanging over my head is the wretched loan of £400 which I took in April from the money-lender. I have already paid £60 interest on it in two months, and the capital must be repaid at once if I am not to be ruined. But how! Gave luncheon to Harold at Boulestin's. He was delighted by my decision, and we had a good talk about books, etc. *Small Talk* has gone very well.

Thursday, 10 June 1937

When I was having my talk with Max at Cherkley on Monday about leaving Fleet Street, we were walking on grass terrace. Aeroplane came over, dipped, did tricks. It was young Max. Beaverbrook said: 'Damn that boy,' but there were tears of pride and sorrow in his eyes.

Friday, 11 June 1937

My last day at the office, and a very hot one too. Lunched there with Mike, Cudlipp and Muggeridge. Dramatic exit. Muggeridge left us a year ago, loathing journalism and determined to live in a cottage in the country on his books. Now, just at the moment when I am going out to do the same thing, he has had to come back, having been too unsuccessful to make a living. It is true that owing to his wife's serious operation (gall stones) he has had heavy unexpected expenses and that he hates Fleet Street as much as ever and is determined to leave it again in two months. We discussed the Battye[1] disappearance case, journalism and the merits of a country life *v.* city life. Cudlipp thinks I am sure to come back to Fleet Street. I told him that I was prepared to bet £100 against it. Mike confessed to me that he too was suffering from nervous indigestion and would soon be like me.

Went to see Randolph who has also been engaged for Diary and hopes to succeed me as chief Diary writer. Told me story of wedding at Château de Candé [Duke of Windsor and Mrs Simpson], how he offered to give Valentine the story and how Valentine was so enraged at Randolph being a guest and his not being one, that he walked away. Randolph only frock-coat present! *vide* photos in *Bystander*.

[1] Diana Battye, daughter of Captain Percy Battye, disappeared from the house of Viscountess Long on Tuesday, 1 June 1937. She had apparently been receiving anonymous letters and had been attacked by a man with a razor. She was found early on the morning of 9 June near Regent's Park. She was 'ill, in a distressed condition, and apparently suffering from loss of memory'. Doctors diagnosed 'severe nervous strain'. There was no evidence that she had been kidnapped.

Saturday, 12 June 1937

My first day's freedom – not very wisely spent. Cashed cheque for £10 and spent most of it on (1) new hat, (2) a case for bottles (hairwash, etc.) and a travelling book-case! Lunched with Tommy who is chained to the house by Harry's illness after his drunken fall.

Monday, 14 June 1937

In the morning saw Popkin, my income-tax expert.[1] I shall have to find some £900 by August 1st. The actual figure is £876. But for my carelessness in signing returns and thereby forfeiting my claim for rebate, I should have not only to pay nothing but also to receive £400 back from the tax authorities.

After Popkin I saw Prince Bibesco[2] and discussed a book on Balkans with special reference to Rumania. We agreed, (1) that I must have absolutely free hand and every facility to see things in Rumania and (2) that I should receive half the guarantee (£1000) down and the other half on completion of the manuscript. He is to let me know as soon as he returns to Bucharest.

Wednesday, 16 June 1937

After luncheon went to see Sir Robert Vansittart and told him my plans to leave Fleet Street and also to become a specialist in foreign affairs. He was very nice and said that he would give me all the help he could. He was interesting on the pro-German feeling in Cabinet. He fears that, as usual, we shall talk vaguely of coming to terms with Germany, latter will respond and think they are going to get something. Then will come the bill – bill we cannot pay. And when we do not pay, there will be the same revulsion of feeling in Germany as there was in 1914, when, contrary to their expectations, we came in. Hymn of hate was result.

Monday, 19 July 1937

A satisfactory letter from Huntington about my contract. His proposals seem acceptable, and if all goes well I should be able to exist in comfort in the country and compelled by necessity to avoid London, and this is exactly what I want. My father, however, sends disturbing news. For weeks he has been writing (and indeed himself proposing that it should be carried out at once) about a loan of £500 on my patrimony. This loan is essential to my new start, otherwise I am doomed from the beginning. Now from Sedbergh where, doubtless, he has come under Rufus's influence, he writes saying, 'I hope that you will not need a loan from me.'

[1] Percy A. Popkin (*d.* 1960), doyen of income-tax experts; his first client was Anna May Wong.

[2] Prince Antoine Bibesco (1878–1951), Rumanian diplomat and author, married to Asquith's daughter Elizabeth.

Wednesday, 28 July 1937

Received from London[1] my Greek Testament. The Greek reading that I have done up here in the mornings has certainly helped my Greek. I find that I can read my Testament now far more easily than before – in fact, almost with facility. If I persevere – and I enjoy my Xenophon and Herodotus – I do not see why I should not be able to read Greek as easily as I do Dutch.

Friday, 30 July 1937

Howard Spring writes enviously of me and also of Carl Fallas, the *Evening Standard* reporter, who without a penny chucked journalism in order to write books. His second book [*Down the Proud Stream*] has just been taken as the *Evening Standard* Book of the Month. Spring says he does not know why he does not follow our example. Then he gives a reason – or what he supposes is the reason – two boys to educate.

Friday, 6 August 1937

I had another shock today when I read in the *Daily Mail* that Mr and Mrs Sacheverell Sitwell had been invited to Rumania as guests of the Government in September. I hope that this does not mean that Prince Bibesco has let me down. It would be not unlike the Rumanians. I understood from him that as far as I was concerned the whole thing was fixed. I must write to him at once.

Tuesday, 10 August 1937

Today, too, I sent off my final letters of resignation to Beaverbrook and Wardell. I said much the same thing in each letter: that I should be fifty on September 2, that the strain of the job was becoming too much for me, that I was already the oldest man on the editorial staff, and that as there is only one rule in journalism – that a man must hold his job by his own efficiency – I was merely taking a decision which would be forced on me in a year or two's time.

Monday, 6 September 1937

A letter from Miss Foyle asking me to speak at a literary luncheon at which famous correspondents will speak of how they made their best scoops. Refused. There are no 'famous' correspondents and most scoops are 'fakes'.

Wednesday, 8 September 1937

Another letter from Tommy who is being driven off her head by Harry and is quite unable to make a decision. He is apparently drinking harder than ever, is incapable of making a bean and of doing anything for himself. Tommy has even to bath him now in case he slips in the bath.

[1] He was on holiday in Scotland.

Monday, 13 September 1937

Mike's letter was shattering. After telling me that Lord Beaverbrook had insisted on my salary being paid up to the end of September, he went on: 'I've had the most bitter and miserable August. On the last day of July, Ruth came to me and said she loved Hugh Seeley and wished to marry him. So the divorce takes place next month I think. Like a wandering Jew I go back where I was in the autumn of 1927 – just ten years ago.' I am sad because I liked them both... I am also relieved and touched by Lord Beaverbrook's generosity which is noble. It will make a big difference to me especially if I husband my resources.

Friday, 1 October 1937

At eight, having had several gins, I went to the Écu de France where I was to give dinner to Freda [his sister], Rupert [his brother] and Sylvia. Here we had more cocktails, red wine and brandy and my bill came to nearly £4. It was the more expensive because what might have been a very pleasant evening was spoilt by excess of alcohol. I remember little of the conversation. At eleven we said good-night, and very foolishly I went back to the club where I sat up till nearly 2 a.m. By now the damage was done, and I then went by myself to the 'Slip-In' where I danced, drank and spent money till 8 a.m. My bill came to £15. At least I signed a cheque for that amount. I have now been ten days in London. During these ten days I have cashed £45 in cheques. I have not paid yet for my week's board at Georgian House. Most of this money – indeed, practically all of it, has gone on alcohol, food and taxis. It is an appalling record after three months' rest in Scotland.

Saturday, 2 October 1937

A day of ghastly depression. Dull and muggy. Wandered about the streets in a taxi from ten till eleven-thirty visiting chemists' shops for pick-me-ups and Bentley's in Swallow Street for oysters and champagne cocktails. Came home to my flat in Georgian House before noon and after ringing up 18 Eaton Square to ask how Tommy Rosslyn was went to bed. Slept fitfully till seven when I awoke with a splitting headache and a general sense of malaise in mind and body. Had a bath, packed a bag, and went off to the Sports Club where I dined. Then, too lazy or too ill to go by train, I hired a car and drove down to Wellington College to the hotel. Took a liver pill and went to bed at 10.45. My moral and physical dégringolade since I returned to London surprises even myself. Obviously, I must get out of London as soon as I can, not merely to economise and repair the ravages to my purse, but also to recover my equilibrium of mind. As a start, I must have two or three quiet days here at Wellington. There are one or two people whom I must see in London: Vansittart, Rex Leeper, Harold, Baxter, Mike, but they can be seen from the country. Then I must make my programme: Sweden, Norway, broadcast, *Times* exhibition, etc., and in the spring tour Balkans. I fear my

South American trip with Tommy is a dream. Still more I feel that with Harry it will be a failure. I hate that man more and more every day. He is murdering Tommy by slow torture, and no one can do anything.

Sunday, 3 October 1937

In the evening the sourness of my stomach began to subside, and my mind became more tranquil and reflective. It is a miracle which has been proved scores of times. As soon as I sleep two nights in the country, my mind becomes active and I begin to think and to create. As soon as I have been two days in London, I am anaethetised mentally and physically by petrol fumes. And then as an escape come the alcohol and the tobacco.

Thursday, 7 October 1937

Warm and muggy. Another black-out for me as far as work was concerned. Felt very ill and jumpy and, as soon as I got up, went off to Bentley's where I had nine oysters, half a lobster and two glasses of 'black velvet'. Then to club where I had two or three drinks before luncheon. Work was out of the question and, after going to see Tommy, I made up my mind to go to bed and recover my health and my sanity. Instead, I went back to the club at 5.30 just to have one drink to steady my nerves. Sat down with Taylor at 5.30, was joined by Reid-Kerr, and drank 'pink gins' till 8.30. Then dinner and more drinks. Finally we were joined by Morley and various outsiders whom I do not like. The conversation became heated and inarticulate. In other words, everyone made a fool of himself. This was one of the worst days in my life, and at present I cannot afford to waste twelve hours. Every day that I stay in London sees the rapid diminution of my tiny capital. Yet I cannot leave London until I have finished my proof and seen various people like Vansittart, Leeper, Wardell, Baxter, etc.

Monday, 11 October 1937

At 1.15 gave luncheon party at Boulestin's to Willie Maugham, Moura and Harold. Cost me with tips just over £5 10*s* which is for me now a week's living! Maugham, dressed in soft shirt with coloured soft collar to match – monocle with gold rim, which he uses seldom. In good form, but Maugham told me afterwards that Harold had irritated him: (1) by asking him to receive a young French journalist (female) (this Maugham hates), and (2) by making rather a facetious remark about Maugham's nephew [Robin] who is the apple of his eye. Maugham is going to India to see temples in the south – is worried because he has been told he ought to go first to see Viceroy (right thing to do) and he doesn't want to go out of his way to Delhi!

Wednesday, 13 October 1937

Freddie Lonsdale very funny last night. Arrived just as we were discussing his new play, which he has now really finished. Gilbert Miller says it will be a great success and will be remembered when *The Last of Mrs Cheyney* is dead and buried. Freddie quite changed. Says he doesn't care a damn for money or fame; he has recovered his self-respect. Looked well; talked volubly; behaved like a child: 'We dramatists' – 'by gad, good dramatists are rare.' Drank tomato juice – drunker on success and tomato juice than ever he used to be on champagne! Said when he really went back to work, nearly went mad. Couldn't write a line for a fortnight!

Thursday, 14 October 1937

Corrected proofs and at 1.30 gave luncheon to Rex Leeper at the St James's. Discussed my future in journalism; he will help and thinks I ought to go back to foreign affairs quickly. He also promised to ring up Bridge [of the British Council] to advise him to help me in my Balkan tour.

Rex is very pessimistic about our policy of continual surrender; thinks that when the Germans see us knuckling down to Mussolini they will begin to imitate his methods. Rex is in favour of making a stand – calling the bluff, in fact – and of occupying Minorca with the French. But says nothing will happen. Eden is the only member of the Cabinet with any 'guts'. The others, especially Chamberlain are surrenderers, and in any case are terrified of Bolshevism (Rex says counter-revolution is now the danger in Russia). Sam Hoare is among these. Rex says quite a strong pro-German feeling among certain Conservatives. Duke and Duchess of Kent are strong in German camp.

Friday, 15 October 1937

Slept in the afternoon, neglecting my proofs and in the evening gave dinner to Maurice Peterson at the Savoy. Drank a lot of brandy, went on with him to Romano's and had more drink. By the time Maurice went, I was set for a night. I went on to the 'Slip-In', stayed there till dawn and breakfast, and then, having paid a bill of £12, went home *via* Heppel's [chemists] at 7.30 a.m. The whole evening counting the dinner must have cost me £16. My month in London has cost me, I reckon, £120 – and of this about £60 has been thrown away. In other words, my passage money for a trip to almost anywhere in Europe: Turkey, Greece, etc.

Sunday, 24 October 1937

At Victoria ran into Leslie Hore-Belisha. He congratulated me on having left Fleet Street; said it was a foul job and gave a man no time to think. Advised me never to write for newspapers. Praised Max for his energy, but said: (1) no man who had any self-respect could work for a 'big chief' because such work allowed him no independent judgement, and (2) no man who had any belief in things of the spirit could work for a man who held views like Max's. Said politics was nearly as bad, that rearmament was progressing, but that much remained to be done.

Wednesday, 27 October 1937

Rested in the afternoon and, being run-down went off to Heppel's in Piccadilly (near hotel) for a pick-me-up. Found A. P. Herbert sitting calmly on a chair and smoking his pipe and sipping a pick-me-up (American cocktail bitter). He was hatless. We had a ten minutes' conversation on literature. He told me that his Divorce Bill[1] had taken up a tremendous lot of his time with the result that he had done little writing and had earned no money. He was going up to Scotland very soon to open National Book Council show. Discussed speaking. I told him how ill I always felt before a speech. He said he was just the same, and no practice made any difference. Quoted Austen who had spoken in House of Commons often. Never got up without feeling his knees rock!

Tuesday, 2 November 1937

Gave luncheon to Rex Leeper at the St James's and had a long talk about foreign affairs. Rex is now Eden's closest adviser after Vansittart and writes his speeches. He wrote Eden's big speech of yesterday.[2] Rex thinks that Italy and Germany have no intention of going to war at present. They know that they could not stand a long war. But they think that we are yielding. Therefore they are determined to get what they can by beating the big stick. Our policy should be firm and non-committal. We should say as little as we can till we are stronger. Unfortunately Cabinet is weak. Rex very annoyed by foolish correspondence in *The Times* by people (who do not know foreign affairs) on subject of German colonies. Does no good. Merely excites Germans.

Rex now admits that Franco will probably win but that the end is not so near as the Italians think. Rex is now very busy. He has at last succeeded in getting the B.B.C. to take up the broadcasts in foreign languages. He has to superintend these. Says that Reith who is an obstructionist used to treat him (Rex) like dirt. Now when he sees Rex he is, like most bullies, subservient and crawling. Rex has also arranged cheap rates for Agency (Reuter) cables. In return he has established a gentleman's agreement that Foreign Office can exercise a discretionary control over cables. He was very confiding – like Van is. Said real secret of discretion was to know to whom you could be indiscreet! Doubtful.

Sunday, 7 November 1937

Two of the greatest evils in British social life are venereal disease and the Press. One reason is that they cannot command the services of first-class men. No young medical student who has any hopes of success dreams of taking up

[1] Matrimonial Causes Act, 1937.

[2] Chamberlain, the Prime Minister, was ill, and Eden spoke out against the dictators in his speech in the debate on the King's Speech.

venereal disease' because there is a social stigma on 'pox-doctors'. For same reason no decent man goes into journalism.

Wednesday, 17 November 1937

Went to British Council to arrange Scandinavian trip, then to *Standard* to lunch with Wardell and arrange for articles, diary, etc., on Scandinavian trip. Mike told me good story: when he was engaged to Ruth Wardell, he was in Paris. Saw lovely woman. Was told she was a widow – a Mrs Jones. Last week in Quaglino's saw well-dressed woman sitting with King of Greece [George II]. Looked – recognised Mrs Jones. She is the Mrs Simpson of Greece. When King Edward VIII and Mrs Simpson went on yacht *Nahlin* cruise to Dalmatia, Greek islands, etc. [in August 1936], Mrs Jones and King of Greece formed a *partie carrée* with them when they met. Duke of Windsor, incidentally, is very angry with his own family – especially for withholding the title H.R.H. from Duchess. Tommy who was spending weekend with the Westmorlands at Lyegrove [Badminton] had talk with ——. He told her Buckingham Palace had had to stop Duke of Windsor ringing King up every day. He answers telephone himself.

Sunday, 21 November 1937

After concert went to St James's to see Bernstorff. Talked or hour and half. Bernstorff's conclusions are: Hitler megalomaniac, mystic, sod – plays no part in administration, spends his time with toy blocks of new cities, but holds régime together; good at playing off his subordinates. Clash between Goering and Goebbels – latter responsible for anti-British policy. Bernstorff wants us to bring Goering to London.

Monday, 22 November 1937

Lunched with Moura at the Jardin. Ate and drank too much. She has just returned from Esthonia and is full of forebodings about Russia. She says Litvinov is now in trouble and that he may be the next to go. I doubt this, but nothing would surprise me today. Since Gorky's death and especially since Yagoda's arrest, she has been herself completely cut off by Bolsheviks...

In afternoon went to see Rex and Clifford Norton at Foreign Office. Rex is worried about Russia and also about Czechoslovakia. Told him about Bernstorff and Goering, also of German view of Edward, Duke of Windsor. Germans still believe he will come back as social-equalising King, will inaugurate English form of Fascism and alliance with Germany.

During November and December, Lockhart visited Holland, Denmark, Norway, Sweden on a lecture tour. He was back in England before Christmas.

Monday, 20 December 1937

At 5.30 p.m. to Rex Leeper at Foreign Office to report on my trip. Told

Rex what Colijn[1] and other neutrals had said: that we should make our peace with Germany. Rex said: 'For God's sake don't put that into your *Times* articles. They'll bless you and you'll do only harm. I'm all for peace with Germany. But Germany's terms are: return of colonies and a free hand in Central Europe. This means getting complete control of Central and South-East Europe. In two or three years she would be so strong that she could do what she liked. No need to yield to bluff and bluster. Beneath outward show of strength in Italy and Germany many weaknesses. Beneath outward weakness of Britain much hidden strength.'

Rex has been lecturing to Staff College on 'Press and Public Opinion' and 'The European Situation'. He is to send these to me. He thinks influence of Press pernicious abroad but exaggerated here. Government can do anything with public opinion provided it does not offend against two canons: (1) Must do nothing discreditable, i.e. to lower prestige public expects from British Government, and (2) must not imperil safety of Empire. Rex told me our Ministers at Stockholm and Oslo had written to say my lecture had been most successful ever held.

Tuesday, 21 December 1937

To Savoy to give luncheon to George Clerk who is now suffering a little from the vanished pomp of the ex-ambassador.[2] Sore with Eden and with Oliver Harvey, Eden's Private Secretary whom George recommended. Sore at being removed under age rule from Paris at age of 63 and being replaced by Phipps who is only eleven months younger. Sorest of all at Foreign Office behaviour. When King Leopold of Belgium came over recently, George who was ambassador in Brussels before Paris was asked to the Buckingham Palace show, and also to the Belgian ambassador's small show. Eden gave dinner-party at Foreign Office, George not asked, although Granville, who had been ambassador twelve years before, was!

[1] Hendrikus Colijn (1869–1944), Netherlands Prime Minister, 1925–6, 1933–9.
[2] He had been British Ambassador in Paris, 1934–7.

CHAPTER FIFTEEN

1938

Vansittart becomes Diplomatic Adviser, talks of going into politics. Lockhart's father at eighty has mania for dancing. Visit to Bulgaria, Rumania, Czechoslovakia. Ward Price's warning to Czechs. Prince Louis Ferdinand in Berlin. Sir Nevile Henderson 'very anti-Eden'. Lord Halifax's 'intelligent questions'. 'Korda is a crook'. McCabe and O'Reilly, Australian cricketers. 'A bad night'. A Foreign Office job in case of war, but Leeper says 'we shall give in'. Chamberlain flies to Munich. Czech errors of omission. Political Intelligence Department to be revived. Returns to *Evening Standard* for three months. Masaryk shattered. Letter from Lady Diana Cooper. Duke of Windsor says in another world war 'victory would go only to Communism'. Orde Wingate bores Beaverbrook. At Buckingham Palace for reception to King Carol. Joseph Kennedy pro-Chamberlain. Death of Karel Čapek.

Tuesday, 11 January 1938

Miserable and depressed about Tommy who is very ill, either physically or mentally, and probably both. It is a terrible tragedy. She is being slowly murdered by Harry, who (bar the Rosslyn charm) is the worst man I have ever known. At the same time Harry has now become an obsession to her. She is afraid to leave him alone in case she comes home to find him dead. Only two days ago he fell full length on the floor, having crashed in a drunken stumble. She also worries because she believes that Harry worries because, having gambled away all Tommy's private means, he has left or will leave Tommy and her children disgracefully badly off. Harry's mind is too senile to worry about anything. But Tommy will also lose affection of her children, who will not forgive her for letting Harry squander everything.

Wednesday, 12 January 1938

At twelve went to the British Council to see Lloyd.[1] He sails for South Africa tomorrow and at last minute had to put me off. Had long talk with Charles Bridge instead. He is very pro-Lloyd and says Lloyd has done already tremendous lot to make the Government move. Most of reforms which I suggested last March have been adopted. Honours are to be given to secretaries of local Anglo-Societies abroad. Maurois is to get a K.B.E. Uggla is to

[1] Lord Lloyd (1879–1941), former High Commissioner for Egypt, was chairman of the British Council, 1937–40.

be given something and I hope Matlescu. There is also to be a co-ordinating committee for all propaganda, broadcasting etc., and Vansittart is to take part in this. Bridge told me Lloyd is worried lest Van's promotion to be Diplomatic Adviser should turn out a polite kick-upstairs and refuses to accept Rex Leeper's assurance that Van will make a huge job of it. Personally I feel like Lloyd.[1] British Council has also appointed young [E. D. 'Toby'] O'Brien who has been doing Peterborough of *Daily Telegraph* as Press Officer.

Thursday, 13 January 1938

At five went to see Rex Leeper at Foreign Office. He told me story of Vansittart's promotion. Rex thinks Prime Minister was responsible. Van is regarded as pro-French – and excitable. Has enemies among pro-Germans in Cabinet. Like all strong men he sometimes differs from Eden, and that is embarrassing to Eden. Chamberlain finds Eden also a little excitable, wants to calm things down, made this compromise. Van himself did not regard it as promotion – talked to Rex of resigning and going into politics. Rex begged him carry on, make new job big (as he can do). Civil servant (even as big as Van) is only big so long as he remains in Civil Service. Van will stay. Rex gave me a letter which Van had left for me – very friendly.

Sunday, 16 January 1938

In the evening went for a short walk with Rupert [his younger brother] and discussed arrangements for [their father] R.B.L.'s eightieth birthday. Although in some respects his mind is wonderfully clear, he is alarmingly childish in other respects, e.g., his passion for dancing (Rupert says that he is now going up to London once a week in order to dance) and his vanity about his singing. Ever since he has read my book with the gibe about his singing, he has been doing his best to persuade us that he had a tremendous success as a singer when young. This would not be so bad if only he were not persuaded that he still has a wonderful voice. Today his voice is like an old crow's. He cannot keep in tune. Yet he sings daily at the pitch of his voice so that even in winter all the neighbours hear! It is very sad, because one can do nothing. It is equally sad to know that one day (perhaps even already) one will be like that oneself.

Another tour of Europe began on 30 January, and in February he arrived once more in Bulgaria.

Thursday, 24 February 1938

Fine but rather cold. Felt a little squeamish after two calomels. At 11.45 Maurice[2] sent me off from Legation in big car. Received by Boris to the second. In same room as last year. Came forward to meet me. 'My dear

[1] Lloyd and Lockhart were correct.

[2] Peterson was now British Minister in Sofia.

friend, etc., etc.' Sat in same chairs; they have been there for years and were used by his father. Likes to dramatise himself. Last time the *coup d'état*. Today, the dismissal of General Conkoff for intriguing with the political 'out-of-works'. Said he should have acted sooner but liked him. Case where Boris the friend interfered with Boris the King. In the same chair sat O'Beirne when he had his last audience with Ferdinand to present ultimatum.[1] Boris present on stool opposite. Ferdinand, Edward VII, Leopold II – cousins – clever – too clever – all suspicious of each other. Duke of York (George V) shared his father's dislike of Ferdinand. There was some scene at Lisbon. (Small picture of George V as young man produced from table.) Boris very pro-English – even defended Press. Admired Stojadinovitch, because kept down military league and church. When Stojadinovitch, was having his difficulties with the Concordat, Boris said he felt repercussion here.

Sunday, 27 February 1938

Caught 1.20 to Bucharest – Rex Hoare sent car to meet me at Giurgin – five minutes late. Arrived at Legation at four. Long talk with Rex who gave me account of crisis: pusillanimity of Titulescu, collapse of Iron Guard (three leaders bumped off or shot by ricochet by guards who fired at tyres of car which refused stop). Strong man: Antonescu – in reserve job before – rude about Madame Lupescu – taken in Goga government strong man – squashed Guard. Carol and Jews – very sensitive about public opinion abroad. Goga and Rex on Jews. Goga violent attack on French – one Minister Jew. Rex thought fit remind him own Minister of War [Hore-Belisha] also Jew. Quite different. In England Jew gets to top by merit. In France he is put there by whole conspiracy of other Jews.

He travelled on to Prague.

Thursday, 17 March 1938

At twelve went to see Beneš. Lovely view from Hradčany. Had to wait several minutes. Little man came over to door to meet me. Rather wan little smile. Aged considerably since last year. Looked tired and admitted that he was. On table in ante-room a life of *Hugh Lane and His Pictures* – numbered edition beautifully bound – with inscription by Cosgrave.[2] Beneš still hopeful – making best of things – but obviously anxious – his nerves, however, are good.[3]

[1] H. J. O'Beirne was the British diplomat who brought the ultimatum from Russia to Tsar Ferdinand in 1915 which precipitated war between Bulgaria and the Allies.

[2] Sir Hugh Lane (1875–1915), Irish art-collector, drowned on the *Lusitania*, intended to leave 39 French Impressionists to the National Gallery of Ireland, but as the codicil was unwitnessed they went to London and became a *cause célèbre*. W. T. Cosgrave (1880–1965) had been president of the Executive Council of the Free State.

[3] Germany had invaded Austria the week before, and was threatening Czechoslovakia.

Friday, 18 March 1938

At five to Karel Čapek's... Twenty people – deputies of Czech socialists, professors, editors, painters, representatives of Foreign Office. Subjected to bombardment about England's intentions, but on whole attitude calm and very determined. Karel may go to England for first night of his *Power and Glory*. Then Kupka got me into corner and told me following story: On Thursday Ward Price went to Foreign Office, asked for interview with Beneš, said he was Hitler's friend and could tell President what Hitler's intentions were. President would not see him. Ward Price, annoyed, said pity, as he could tell no one else. Kupka then delegated to take him out. Posed as great anti-Bolshevik and Hitler admirer. Filled Ward Price up and finished up with him at Sekt at 7 a.m. Gist of Ward Price's views: Hitler coming here. Will demand autonomy for Deutsche Boehmen, withdrawal of Czech troops from frontier, Slovakia to Hungary, Bohemia and Moravia remain independent but in orbit of German influence. Czechs must acquiesce. Small nation must think small. Schuschnigg had nearly caused European War by deceiving Hitler. Czechs go down history as race saved Europe from war. Beneš or Hodža[1] go Berlin arrange this at once. Only hope. If fought, annihilated. Foolish madness suppose anyone help them. England not able fight a war – decadent. Germany invincible. Dined at Legation. Told Newton.[2] This report given to Beneš and Knoffe(?) at 9 a.m. today. Newton who lunched with Ward Price today able to confirm substantially true.

Lockhart travelled on to Berlin.

Monday, 21 March 1938

Another superb day. In morning Prince Louis Ferdinand came to the Esplanade to breakfast with me and stayed an hour. He has little sympathy with the Nazis and does not hesitate to say so, although he is careful to modulate his voice. For me it was a curious situation to be in. Here was I more or less talking with, or rather listening to sedition by, the grandson of the Kaiser in the former capital of the Hohenzollerns. Also discussed very frankly marriage and his approaching wedding with Grand Duchess Kyra, daughter of Grand Duke Michael . . . a marriage which has pleased his grandfather!

To luncheon with Ogilvie-Forbes[3] at his house in West Berlin. Present Professor Meyer who is the leading authority on the history of Scottish Catholicism, one of his Scottish pupils, and a Catholic priest. None of them a Nazi. Walked back through a very dusty Tiergarten and dustier streets where I had a long talk to Nevile Henderson.[4] He was just recovering from 'flu' and had a huge fire, central heating, and himself two waistcoats. Very

[1] Milan Hodža (1878–1944), Czech Prime Minister, 1935–8.

[2] Basil Newton, British Minister to Prague, 1937–8.

[3] Sir George Ogilvie-Forbes (1891–1954), Counsellor at the British Embassy.

[4] Sir Nevile Henderson (1882–1942), British Ambassador in Berlin, 1937–9. Eden had

anti-Eden ('If Eden had stayed, we should have had a European war') and very anti-ideologists as a whole. In favour of making the Czechs give way. Says cannot possibly go to war over Sudeten Germans. If we won (which was more than doubtful), we should have to settle the problem again. Why not settle it without a war? Showed me cigarette case given him by Queen Marie [of Yugoslavia] after King Alexander's death. He was King Alexander's best friend and loves him and hopes he will become a hero to his country. Told me reason why Prince Paul was not very popular – he was not a man! True enough perhaps.

Tuesday, 22 March 1938

At 12.30 went to 11 Unter den Linden – the former Nederland Palais and now the Haus-Ministerium of the Hohenzollerns – to meet Prince Louis Ferdinand and his bride. Princess Kyra late – and we had to race to Potsdam to be in time for luncheon. Prince Louis drove us in open car . . . and averaged about 80 miles an hour! Not pleasant for me who was in back-seat. Cecilienhof – originally summer-pavilion and most children born in Marmor-palais close by – unpretentious – attractive – like English country-house. Crown Princess very nice. Small household party – Crown Princess, Princess Cecilie (very sweet), Louis Ferdinand, Princess Kyra, Countess Tolstoy (Russian friend of Princess Kyra), and Herr von Radowitz, ex-diplomat who, after war, became a successful lawyer. Conversation guarded. Not pro-Nazi. At same time quite pleased with Hitler's successes, and not much sympathy with the Jews. In evening dinner at Bernstorff's; present Pinsent of Treasury, Ogilvie-Forbes, Prittwitz, former German ambassador to Washington, and a young Dutchman. The Dutchman full of alarms. Hitler would next take Czechoslovakia, which would be dismembered. Hungary would get Slovakia, etc., etc. Then Germany all powerful. What could countries like Holland and Denmark do? Prittwitz very nice and gentle – disapproves of Nazi diplomatic methods and obviously very afraid of war. Bernstorff said not an intellectual German in Berlin who did not believe Fuehrer was mad.

Thursday, 24 March 1938

Duller but still amazingly warm. In morning went to see Louis Lochner, head of American Associated Press in Berlin, in the Zimmerstrasse. Been in Berlin for years, pro the German people and German life, married to a German; not a Nazi. Very pessimistic, thinks war inevitable. Believes that the machine is now running away with the Fuehrer who himself is in a state of semi-permanent exaltation. Considers that Henderson, who as half-a-Fascist

---

resigned on 20 February because Chamberlain had gone behind his back in making approaches to Mussolini, and had been succeeded by Lord Halifax.

and a keen game-shot gets on well with Goering, is fooled by him. True, Hitler sincere in fanatical sense; true, has said Germany does not want minorities, but already Nazis are calling Prague a German city with the oldest German university. Also repeating old German saying that you can drive from Regensburg to Black Sea in a cart and sleep every night in a German village. Who is safe? The Italians in Trieste? Where will it end? Berlin–Bagdad again. No limit to Hitler's visions. Might make peace with England if could drive from station to Buckingham Palace with King George beside him!

Thursday, 31 March 1938

At twelve to Alex Cadogan at Foreign Office.[1] He is level-headed; does not think very much of Russia, and obviously hopes by trying now to relieve tension to build up our own strength and to win back nations which we have lost. . . At five to Sam Hoare in House of Commons. Hour's talk. He has seen Jan Masaryk, counselled caution and even adoption Federal system. Very anti-Eden and anti-Winston.

Friday, 1 April 1938

In evening gave dinner to Rex Leeper at the St James and had a long talk about the European situation. He does not like changes in personnel at Foreign Office, says Alex Cadogan does not take same interest in News Department and all propaganda work which Rex has built up. Also told me that in skeleton measures decided for propaganda in wartime (perhaps Ministry of Information) Rex is not to be the man. He does not want to be Number Two. We agree pretty well on general line of policy. Rex, who used to write Eden's speeches and saw him at breakfast nearly every day, is now writing Halifax's. I recognised him in last two speeches.

Monday, 4 April 1938

Went to luncheon with the Oliver Stanleys at 58 Romney Street. He looks well but has been ill with inflammation of the gall-bladder. Very small luncheon arranged for me to meet Lord Halifax. I liked him. He is tall with high forehead, is gentle and not awe-inspiring, yet has considerable dignity and gives one an impression of great intellectual honesty with considerable scholarship and a fine intellect. He would make a very fine judge. All the conversation was about Central Europe. (Oliver Stanley had asked me in order to provide some counter-arguments to Winston's scheme of the 'grand alliance' against Germany and also against Ward Price.) Halifax asked many intelligent questions. His own most interesting contributions were: (1) that in his conversation with Hitler he had not formed the impression that the Fuehrer would be an easy person to deal with or that he would keep

[1] Sir Alexander Cadogan (1884–1968) succeeded Vansittart as Permanent Under-Secretary of State, January 1938 and remained in the post until February 1946.

any promise; and (2) that during last few years we had 'lectured' everybody too much.

Tuesday, 5 April 1938

Went to club where I received message to ring up Sam Hoare. He wanted to see me before I saw Van this afternoon. Went to Home Office at 12.50. Nothing very serious. All that Sam wanted was to suggest I should tell story of Hoare-Laval Pact in my book[1] – i.e. to justify him, since events (papers today give details of new Anglo–Italian agreement) are now swinging his way. Sam never leaves a stone unturned which may help his chances of the Prime Ministership.

Lunched at Boulestin's with Louis Gillet, Godfrey Nicholson and Harold. Harold who was sitting close to Commander Bower during yesterday's scene in House of Commons when Shinwell smacked Bower's face, said he was amazed at Bower's restraint and told him so. 'You don't hit a man like that,' said Bower (who is big and an ex-boxing champion). 'You get a fox-terrier to bite him.' . . .[2]

Saw Van who talked to me very freely about situation. He has no use for Nevile Henderson whom he regards as greatest menace. Saw Rex for a minute.

Saturday, 9 April 1938

A fortnight since I came home – on Monday four weeks since I left Zagreb. . . And, as far as I am concerned, the moral *dégringolade* has been depressing. During this last week I have drunk more than ever before in my life and I seem to have lost all control. Altogether England makes a deplorable impression on me: everyone whining and uneasy about future, yet strangely inactive. Within last twenty-four hours I have heard Anthony Rothschild say that he doubted if the people of this country had the will-power left to defend themselves, and Vernon Bartlett say that, if in order to combat the dictators we had to use or adopt some of their methods, he thought he would probably prefer to join Peace Pledge and not fight at all. 'Greater Germany' day in Austria. Hitler in Vienna – fanatical speech on his Mission. People here call it hysteria – perhaps true but not so depressing as knowledge that here in Conservative Party chief candidate for Chamberlain's successorship is Inskip.[3]

[1] *Guns or Butter*, published later that year.

[2] Emanuel Shinwell, Labour M.P. for Seaham, was incensed that R. A. Butler had spoken of Franco's 'Government' in Spain, although it was not yet officially recognised and called his explanations 'humbug', 'hypocrisy' and 'half-truths'. Commander R. T. Bower, M.P. for Cleveland, then said to Shinwell 'Go back to Poland!' Shinwell, born in the East End of London in 1884, was even more incensed and slapped his face.

[3] Sir Thomas Inskip (1876–1947), later Viscount Caldecote, Minister for Co-ordination of Defence, 1936–9, and responsible for British rearmament.

Monday, 11 April 1938

Lunched at White's with Mike, Perry Brownlow, Duff Cooper and Anthony Winn. Duff's stock is low – made indiscreet speech and received letter from Chamberlain. Luckily for him, Eden's resignation coincided – two resignations not possible. Duff remained... In evening, dinner Sibyl's sat next to Mrs Neville Chamberlain – picturesque – like a piece of Meissen or Dresden china – long talk with Jan with whom I went home. His attitude: for God's sake let us know what you intend to do.

Tuesday, 12 April 1938

Article by Frank Owen in *Evening Standard*: 'No war in Europe'. Obviously written by Lord Beaverbrook.

Wednesday, 29 June 1938

Also a long letter from Tania [a friend he had made on his tour] to tell me that she has been unable to keep her good resolutions, has fallen in love with a Russian colleague, is presumably living with him, and is going to marry him. And so passes a romantic dream without its fairy-tale ending.

Friday, 29 July 1938

Major Bell[1] ... made a film of the *Daily Express* at work which Zukor presented to Beaverbrook. Bell made Beaverbrook come into the picture. After a show of protest Max agreed, made up his face or let it be made up, and of course thoroughly enjoyed the fun. Bell was shocked at the conditions in which journalists had to work. Said theatre and music-hall bosses were often blamed for 'sweating' the girls in their employ, keeping them for hours in foul atmosphere, etc. But conditions paradise compared with those of journalists. No factory owner would dare to house his workmen so badly!

Bell also told me quite out of the blue that Castlerosse was the most expensive of all the London journalists. I asked him what he meant. He said he wants the most and insists on getting it for everything he puts in his Log about a show or an actress. I told Bell that if this were true Beaverbrook would be furious.

Saturday, 30 July 1938

One part of my nature tugs me towards the intellectual side of life; the other to the lusts and joys of sport and good living. The latter have spoilt my mind and ruined my faculties.

Friday, 12 August 1938

Still, I should be able to finish the whole book within ten days. What am I to do then? Hang about London doing nothing? Begin my lectures? Write

[1] Oliver Bell (1898–1952), head of the London Casino, formerly a director of Paramount, of which Adolph Zukor was chairman.

articles? I shall have to make some extra money. Perhaps I should do another European tour, see Kemsley, and write a series of articles for the *Sunday Times* or the *Telegraph*. Or do another British Council Tour.

Tuesday, 16 August 1938

At 12.30 went to see Sir Robert Vansittart at the Foreign Office. Found him very pessimistic and, as usual, much concerned at the ignorance, lack of preparedness, and generally too comfortable attitude of most people in this country. Blamed Beaverbrook and Rothermere, whom I hear regarded as the chief exponents of 'my money for my time' philosophy, for misleading the people. Thinks that the crisis in Germany over Czechoslovakia will come soon and does not believe that a real settlement is possible. Can come in two ways. Sudeten Deutsche (and this means Berlin) may refuse Czech terms – then internal troubles, Germany walks in to restore order, etc. Secondly, Sudeten may accept Czech terms if they convey large enough measure of autonomy, then in a few months when they have neutralised the Czech state they may declare for *Anschluss*. In any case Germany intends to reduce Czechoslovakia to vassal state. If she is allowed to do this, she will go on – Rumania, Yugoslavia, etc., etc. Britain will be second-class power.

At three to Jan Masaryk, pessimistic but not so gloomy as Van. Says Czechs will go as far as possible but not to state-within-state status. In extremes they will fight. Said he had spent weekend with Eden who said difference between Baldwin and Chamberlain this: both thought foreigners 'dagos' – Baldwin said, 'Don't understand them – don't want to have anything to do with them. Anthony, this is your affair.' Chamberlain same attitude, but tries to run his own foreign policy.

Tuesday, 23 August 1938

Last night Bayliss-Smith, who is a leading chartered accountant and represents the creditors in some of the big cinema financial messes in this country, says the cinema industry here has cost the banks and insurance companies about £4,000,000. Most of this lost by Jews – like Korda and Max Schacht. Latter already lost a packet for German Government before Hitler. Has now done same here. In Bayliss-Smith's opinion, and he would not say so lightly, Korda is a much worse man than Schacht. Schacht is just a slick Jew who sees financial moves ahead of the other fellow. Korda is a crook and, according to Bayliss-Smith, an evil man.

Monday, 29 August 1938

At eleven a.m. Mike Wardell rang up. The situation was very serious. Next ten days would be critical.[1] War and peace were in the balance. Would I go to Europe for the *Standard* at once: aeroplanes, big money, daily Lockhart column on Europe? Last week when I saw Vansittart who is always

[1] Germany had mobilised on 12 August.

pessimistic I told Mike. Mike was then very optimistic. Today, he was far more pessimistic than Van. Why? I discovered. He had spent the weekend at Cherkley. Prouvert of the *Paris-Soir* had also been there. Performance had been like a mad-house; Max and Prouvert both hopping out and the telephone ringing every two minutes!

Impossible for me to accept Mike's offer but decided to go up to London. Went up by 4.11. Stayed at 18 Eaton Square. Went to see Mike at his new house in 22 Gayfare Street (Rob Hudson's house). Had a talk about affairs, told him I could not go abroad just now, discussed possibility of my coming to *Standard* from October to December. I am to take up matter with him in three weeks' time.

Friday, 2 September 1938

Rang up the Czech Legation to have some names checked for my book: spoke to Jan Masaryk who said that the news was slightly better. Henlein had been to see Hitler 'who had shown interest in the Sudeten leader's report and had agreed with his point of view'. Two days ago Jan said that Henlein was for negotiations and a settlement.

Wednesday, 7 September 1938

Today, the results of the Diplomatic and Consular exams published in *The Times*. Young ——, son of —— (who Maurice says and I know is a fool), passed in. Maurice says that in spite of the democratisation of the diplomatic examination there is still a certain amount of 'wangling'. This is done through the preliminary oral examination which takes place weeks or months before the exam. For this 300 marks (out of total of 1200) are given. Last year or two years ago young ——, ——'s son, passed in. Twelve vacancies, a record number, were available. —— passed in twelfth. He was given full marks (a record, I believe) for the oral!

Arrived at Club at 7.30 and was just going up to dine when I ran into Jim Foley, and Stan McCabe and Bill O'Reilly, the Australian cricketers. The beginning of a bad night. Went first to Oddenino's where we drank gins till after eleven. Then to Piccadilly to dine and then to 'Slip In'. Spent £20! Stan told me Australian teams left Australia when Hitler was about to seize Austria. They were afraid war would stop them. Now Hitler was about to seize Czechoslovakia as they were going back.

Tuesday, 13 September 1938

Rang up Jan Gerke[1] at the Czech Legation in order to check various Czech spellings. Jan was very pessimistic. Things were moving very rapidly. So far from having a pacifying effect, Hitler's speech of yesterday had aggravated the situation. Henlein had become more provocative and was now

[1] Czech Press Attaché, later a senior executive in Marks and Spencer.

demanding self-determination. The country was on the verge of civil war. The Czechs had seized Nazi written instructions ordering the Sudeten to provoke trouble and chaos by rioting and by firing shots, etc.

German pressure on Czechoslovakia continued and many thought that war was imminent.

Wednesday, 14 September 1938

At 4.30 p.m. to Foreign Office to see Rex Leeper. . . Rex told me that I was sure to get some kind of job with or through the Foreign Office if and when the war started. Even if I went to Beaverbrook's in October and war started then, I could rely on the Foreign Office overriding any claims of the Press Lord! Rex, however, said there would be no war – at least not at present. I said: 'You are an optimist.' He replied: 'No, a fatalist.'

He went on to say that we should give in. This country would have to pull itself together and would have to change or go under. If we wanted a leader, we'd have to scour the lunatic asylums. In a game of diplomatic poker what chance had three lily-livered men (Chamberlain, Simon and Hoare) against a lunatic like Hitler?

On to Putnam's. Huntington told me that on previous night Italian Chargé [d'Affaires] had dined at his house, had almost broken down, and had said: 'If there is war, it is the end of all that I have stood for. Europe will go Bolshevik.' He is an educated but convinced Fascist.

Thursday, 15 September 1938

Another fine day after last night's drizzle. Papers full of Chamberlain's dramatic departure (he is nearly seventy and made his first flight to Munich this morning).

At seven p.m. was rung up by Wardell. Would I write an article on Chamberlain and Czechoslovakia and the suggested plebiscite? Rang up Jan Gerke and also Jan Masaryk and discussed the various possibilities of solution. Czechs do not want plebiscite, which might make a jigsaw puzzle of this territory; nor will they accept self-determination, which (1) will destroy the historic frontiers of Bohemia; and (2) will hand over to the Germans all their expensive fortifications.

Both Jan Masaryk and Gerke are very suspicious of Chamberlain's visit. They fear – and it is a natural fear – that, if peace is to be achieved, it will be made at their expense. This, I feel sure, is not only true but inevitable. The Czechs are to blame (1) for not having made concessions earlier; and (2) for not having realised the improbability of Britain risking a world war for Czechoslovakia. France and Britain are to blame for allowing the situation to drift and for leading the Czechs up the garden almost to the last, so that if there is no war Czechs will have to surrender and make far worse terms than they could have achieved six months ago – not to say six years.

Friday, 16 September 1938

Fine weather continues; but air cooler and sky more clouded. Rose at 7.45 and at 8 a.m. began to dictate my article on 'Chamberlain and Czechoslovakia' to the *Evening Standard* telephonist. Spent the rest of the morning in the house telephoning and being telephoned to by Mike Wardell who wanted to (and did) make changes in my article as the news altered from hour to hour. London or rather Fleet Street was excited by Chamberlain's unexpectedly early return (he flew back today), and the journalists were full of rumours: Hitler had given Chamberlain a kick in the pants. The situation was worse than ever. Hitler would be satisfied with nothing less than secession. Chamberlain would probably not go back to Germany. In the end my article was cut, and the pro-Czech parts toned down. I did not see it myself, but I am told that even the truncated form was not too bad.

Rang up de Margerie who told me that all the rumours were without foundation (including story that Daladier[1] was coming to London) because no one in Foreign Office or Quai d'Orsay knew anything and could not know anything until Chamberlain returned. All these rumours were guesswork based on Chamberlain's sudden return. Did nothing else all day. At a moment like this it is difficult to concentrate on ordinary correspondence. Yet this is the only thing to do. In the afternoon went for a picnic in the heather country near the Duke of Wellington's monument.

Saturday, 17 September 1938

Letter . . . from Christina Foyle. [She] wants me to write a book of 80,000 words for the Right Book Club. Must consult Huntington and also find out what such a book will bring in. Another difficulty is the term 'Right' Book Club. I should not write a book by choice either for the 'Right' or for the 'Left' Book Club. Played golf with Robin. In the afternoon played croquet and slacked. In the evening dreary family bridge till eleven.

Listened in to the news. No new complications today, although there is no improvement in the situation. It seems clear that Hitler is determined to incorporate the bulk of the Sudeten Germans in the Reich, and that the Czechs will resist a plebiscite. Runciman[2] came back from Prague to report to the Cabinet. The King is not returning to Scotland, but is spending the weekend near London. MM. Daladier and Bonnet[3] arrive in London tomorrow. I see no issue except war or a peace at Czechoslovakia's expense. The Left papers – the *New Statesman* and *Time and Tide* – are already accusing Chamberlain of surrender. At the same time both in France and Britain voices are being raised to say that Czechoslovakia is not worth a war. After sitting on the fence for a week, Beaverbrook has leader in *Evening Standard*

[1] Édouard Daladier (1884–1972) had been French Prime Minister since April.

[2] Viscount Runciman (1870–1949) had been sent by the British Government to Prague to 'mediate' between Czechs and Germans. He recommended 'self-determination' for the Sudeten Germans.

[3] Georges Bonnet (*b.* 1889), French Foreign Minister, 1938–9.

today: 'This is no concern of ours; keep out.' Robin does not want war – in fact, wants peace at any price. I expect that there are many young men like him.

Monday, 19 September 1938

During day plan of French and British Governments for Czechoslovakia became more or less known. Cabinet sat with French Ministers Daladier and Bonnet till midnight. Full agreement in end and plan approved today by both Cabinets. It apparently involves giving Sudeten areas with 80 per cent majority to Hitler without a plebiscite. Czechoslovakia is to have her new frontiers guaranteed by Britain, Italy, France, Rumania, Poland, etc. The Czechs will not like it. Osusky was in tears when he left the Quai d'Orsay, having just been told terms by Bonnet. 'If ever a man has been condemned to death without a trial, I am that man,' he said. Rupert and Sylvia who call themselves Left-wingers are indignant at the betrayal – indignant and bellicose. Two days ago they were dreading war and terribly depressed. I imagine that in all the discussions one thought prevailed: was Europe to be plunged into war in order to keep 3,000,000 Germans in and under Czechoslovakia against her will?

Tuesday, 20 September 1938

Went into St James's Club where I saw Valentine Castlerosse, Evelyn FitzGerald and Perry Brownlow. Perry is ashamed of our settlement. Evelyn is pleased. Val Castlerosse is delighted. He has recently been to Czechoslovakia (Karlsbad) with Joe Schenk and is rather anti-Czech – he calls them an unpopular race. . . He predicts a great wave of anti-Semitism in England, because the Jews are trying to push us into war. I feel, however, that the country is ashamed – and rightly so.

Wednesday, 21 September 1938

Went to Bumpus where I met Wilson (J. G.)[1] and for the first time his daughter Kitty who looks after the fiction. He told me that, although the crisis and, indeed, all 1938, has been bad for trade, Bumpus are down only £500 on a turnover of £25,000. His reason is that in times of crisis English people become serious, go to ground a bit and read more.

Sunday, 25 September 1938

Found St Ronan's in a state of gloom with the shadow of war hanging over it. Freda here; she has been seeing Margaret Runciman now Mrs [King-Farlow] who has been seeing her father. Runciman liked Hodža very much but found Beneš intransigent and over-logical. Took the line that the Czechs had not maltreated the German minority, but that there had been a lot of

[1] (1876–1963) manager of the once-famous Oxford Street bookshop, soon to become the G.O.M. of the British book trade.

unnecessary pin-pricks – an accumulation of pin-pricks, he called it. Found letters from Rex Hoare and Cynthia Cheetham. Rex wrote: 'Are you sorry for the Czechs? My feelings are mixed but are dominated by a craven reluctance to see the end of the world.' My own are the same. Cynthia writes to praise my article saying that it was the first that she had seen which did justice to the Czechs. 'You and I,' she writes, 'are the only pro-Czechs in London.' I suppose she is speaking of London society. Freda and Rupert's friends are violently anti-Nazi.

Monday, 26 September 1938

The news is grave. France, Britain and Czechoslovakia do not accept the Hitler memorandum. Like two meteors travelling through space, the two forces in Europe are now moving on a collision line and the final catastrophe seems inevitable. Trenches were being dug in Hyde Park today; anti-aircraft Territorials were called up. Parliament is to meet on Wednesday.

At eight Hitler addressed a frenzied crowd in the Sportpalast in Berlin. We listened in to Rupert's little set and heard very clearly. It was a violent speech – delivered in a raucous, ranting voice. His violent denunciation of Beneš was like the raving of a lunatic. There was no trace of conciliation in his speech. He did not entirely bar the door to peace. He gave the Czechs until October 1st to hand over the Sudeten areas which he has fixed in his memorandum. After the 9.40 news Harold Nicolson spoke on the events of the week. He was bitter and sarcastic about Germany. Defined the issue as two problems: (1) The Germans wanted their compatriots in the Sudetenlands; they could have them; (2) they wanted to destroy the independence of Czechoslovakia; that they could not be allowed to do.

Tuesday, 27 September 1938

Stopped at St James's Club and found message from Foreign Office. 'Very urgent.' Rang up Rex Leeper but could get only Christopher Warner. Foreign Office are starting or reviving the Political Intelligence Department of the Great War and want me to take over Russia. Harold Nicolson is to be asked to do Central and South-Eastern Europe. The offer is for the duration of the war!

Listened in to the Chamberlain broadcast at No. 18 Eaton Square. He sounded tired. He certainly gave an impression of great sincerity, but there is no denying that he is an unimpressive speaker. He used one reference which will be interpreted in Germany as a justification of Ribbentrop's insistence that 'we will never fight for Czechoslovakia'. He said 'however much we may admire a gallant little country, it is a very serious thing to commit the people of the British Empire to fighting for it'.

Wednesday, 28 September 1938

Dull and warm. Rose early and telephoned to Rex Leeper who gave me more details of my war job. Pay would be only £600 a year free of tax – impossible give more to anyone. But Foreign Office recognised it was too small for people like Harold and me. We should be allowed to write. Was to have gone down to Ovington to stay with Rex Hoare. But as situation looked blacker than ever decided to go down for day only. Met at Winchester by Rex and drove to Ovington – not far from Tichborne – where his brother has a large house and a very pretty stretch of the Itchen. Rex is pessimistic. Like me he thinks that the wheels of mobilisation have moved so fast and so far towards war that they cannot be reversed. Joan Hoare still believes in a last-minute miracle. She is a pacifist and puts 3,000,000 living Germans against 20,000,000 who must die to keep them in Czechoslovakia.

Friday, 30 September 1938

At 12.15 went down to the *Standard* to pick up Wardell and go to Marlborough Club to lunch with him. Fixed up terms of my temporary agreement. I am back on old terms, shall do Diary and page sevens, and also keep an eye on young Goulding and train him on in foreign politics. Mike very bitter about Beaverbrook whose interference, he says, makes it quite impossible to produce a good *Evening Standard*, as our *Evening Standard* readers dislike most of things which Lord Beaverbrook likes and tries to do. At luncheon met Godfrey Thomas and Commander Elliot – latter looked nice and is now Assistant Secretary to Imperial Defence Committee.

After luncheon to Beaverbrook who . . . predicts (1) a great hullabaloo next week about the sham of peace, (2) the end of the Russian–French–Czech alliances for ever, and (3) an immense rearmament campaign.

In evening farewell dinner to Jim Foley at Sports Club. About thirty guests. Too much to drink. Sat up till three and by then was too lit up to go to bed. On to 'Slip-In' by myself. Stayed there till 8.30 a.m., drank 11 bottles of champagne, and spent nearly £20.

Sunday, 2 October 1938

Duff Cooper has resigned. His friends say 'Duffie did it' by mobilising the fleet and that the Navy was ready to the last pin.[1] His enemies, like Beaverbrook, say he was a failure at the War Office, never went to his office at the Admiralty, and was going to be sidetracked anyway. Harold Nicolson speaking yesterday attacked Chamberlain for neglecting the advice of his experts like Van who was consistently right and listening to Sir Horace Wilson 'whose advice was never inconvenient'. Clear now that Labour will regard the triumph as a surrender – but also clear to me that man in street will be immensely relieved and grateful to Chamberlain. As pictures of Four-Power Conference were shown on the screen there was some booing – but

[1] Duff Cooper resigned as First Lord of the Admiralty over the Munich Agreement concluded on 29 September between Chamberlain, Daladier and Hitler, which handed the Sudeten lands over to Germany.

also some cheering – of Hitler and Mussolini – there was much cheering of Chamberlain but also a few shouts of 'What is your peace worth?' and 'How long?'

Monday, 3 October 1938

My first day back in Fleet Street; a hectic one too, for I arrived at office at 9.45 a.m. and did not leave it until 7.15 p.m. Great disorganisation in office; Frank Owen is acting editor in place of Thompson who has been sacked. Staff do not know yet. Owen is erratic and has no sense of time or organisation...

Wrote Page Seven on Duff Cooper and rang up Eddie Grant, who is or was his best friend, to ask for story. There was a party for Eddie's twenty-first birthday. Duff there – all went on to Empire. Duff very tight and very truculent – not allowed in – made scene – arrested and taken to Vine Street – his pals fixed things with sergeant also very nice: 'Leave him here till 1 a.m., they're generally all right by then.'

Duff wasn't. When released mistook policeman for Empire commissionaire and told him to go and fetch his coat and hat. Nearly knocked him down when he did not move.

Chamberlain, Duff and Eden spoke on the crisis. My impression is that Chamberlain has the country behind him on this issue of peace or war and Labour are afraid of being angled into a position in which, if there is an election, they may be represented as the Party desiring war.

Tuesday, 4 October 1938

In the afternoon went to see Roland de Margerie who told me that every Frenchman felt ashamed and humiliated. Poland last Friday had kicked the British and French ambassadors down the stairs (Beck refused to see Kennard and Noël!),[1] and there had been almost no protest in British Press. Poles were like the ghouls who in former centuries crawled the battlefields to kill and rob the wounded. Diplomatic activity transferred to Rome. Mussolini may do something with Hungary and Yugoslavia.

To Jan Masaryk – a sad and painful experience. He is shattered; his eyes are sunk; he looks ten years older; talked slowly as if making great effort to control himself. 'Your people have finished us – let me down. You advised us to mobilise; then you told us to give up our defences – and now we cannot defend ourselves against any brigand. I am ruined – must sell these houses to get money to pay for my staff – this is too big a Legation for a vassal state. Country needs £250,000,000 to be refloated.'

Thursday, 6 October 1938

At 3.30 to Van... Profoundly pessimistic. Wants re-trebled rearmament

[1] Colonel Joseph Beck was the Polish Foreign Minister; Sir Howard Kennard and M. Noël were the British and French Ambassadors. Poland had demanded Teschen from the Czechs on 1 October.

and economic aid for Balkans to keep them neutral. Thinks Government will not do much. Said: 'I have been right all through – and that is fatal.' Thinks the surrender may have ultimate effect on Franco-British relations. Met Culverwell, the West Bristol M.P.,[1] who is going tomorrow on month's tour to Sudetenland . . . very rich – has yacht. Pro-German but suspicious of Nazi Germany. At 9 to Stornoway: Aneurin Bevin, Frank Owen, Mike, Brendan, Mr Justice and Lady Langton.[2] Sat next Langton. Simon and Rowlatt.[3] Latter very fine brain – but no good at exposition. Simon beautifully lucid – makes job easy for judge. Simon not popular at Bar – egocentric – cold, always considers himself first – gives nothing to his fellow-man. Langton plays off 5 at golf. Was under Winston at Ministry of Munitions – sent to Coventry settle big strike. Thompson in *Mail* – attacked Langton – unknown – useless – Winston sent for Northcliffe – asked him: 'Do you want win war?' Then waved papers before him. Northcliffe sent Thompson to Ministry – never to put anything without Winston's O.K.

R.H.B.L. received a letter from Lady Diana Cooper, dated 5 October 1938:

Thank you so much for your article about Duff. It gave a true and delightful picture of the past, and showed your attitude of friendship and admiration which was nice for me to read.

I only cavil at the paragraph that tells of how poorly equipped he left the army. I can only tell you that the Government (P.M.s two of them) never meant there to *be* an army, not that it should be equipped with armaments. Many were the frustrated interviews with Neville, some-time Chancellor, some-time Prime Minister during Duff's tenure. The money was never given out. What meagre equipment there is today is due to three years! struggle of Duff's.

I meant this to be only a letter of thanks for the article, and the typist has lost her head in the welter of Czech letters – and made it untidy and inaccurate. Anyway it was a nice write up.

Yours
Diana C.

Friday, 7 October 1938

Letter from Diana Cooper – very sweet and nice – about the article on Duff, but cavilling a little at the paragraph on Duff's period at the War Office. I knew that this would hurt. But what was I to say? The instructions given to me were far more anti-Duff, and I toned them down. But what is the good of explaining? Also letters from Vansittart – very nice about the new book[4] – and from Moir who is really enthusiastic and predicts great success.

[1] Cyril Tom Culverwell (1895–1963), Unionist M.P., 1938–45.

[2] Sir George Langton, K.C. (1881–1942), judge of the High Court, Director of Labour, Ministry of Munitions, 1916–18.

[3] John Rowlatt (1898–1956), one of Parliamentary counsel to the Treasury from 1937, later Q.C. and knighted. Sir John Simon was then Chancellor of the Exchequer.

[4] *Guns or Butter.*

Saturday, 8 October 1938

A fine morning; in the afternoon and evening rain and squalls. A week ago German troops marched into Czechoslovakia after hurried Four-Power Agreement. Today, a week later, there is not much left of Munich or, indeed, of Godesberg [agreements]. Czechoslovakia is reduced to a province.

Monday, 10 October 1938

Sir John Anderson is being tipped as successor to Sir Thomas Inskip – his record is remarkable.[1] He came back from Bengal at end of 1937. Within less than a year he has been elected to Parliament, appointed to Privy Council, made a director of Vickers, a director of Midland Bank, a director of Imperial Chemicals, and refused the chairmanship of Imperial Airways.

Tuesday, 11 October 1938

In evening dined at Anthony Rothschild's: long talk in White's. He told me of German offers to buy Witkowitz steel works [in Moravia] (now an island in sea of Germans) – formerly Austrian Rothschilds owned 51 per cent, Gutmann 49. Gutmanns were in trouble over slump – sold more to Rothschilds – Witkowitz have big Admiralty orders. Tony is very anti-Chamberlain and has written to his local Conservative association refusing to subscribe to party funds for Chamberlain candidate.

Wednesday, 12 October 1938

Then to Jan Gerke who as a Sudeten loyal to Czechs is in a very difficult position. Wants a job here either with Reuter's or in the Intelligence. Tells me that the son of W., an old Austrian deputy and the first Nazi, is an officer in the British Army (naturalised before war) and is supplying information to Germany! Showed me a confidential report (given to H.M.G. on August 8) which stated exactly what would happen in Czechoslovakia. Beneš, he says, is now in as great danger from Czechs as from Germans.

Saturday, 15 October 1938

In evening to Cherkley; Jack Warner (of Warner Bros) and his wife, 'Scatters' Wilson, Mike, Frank Owen, Brendan Bracken, and young man-secretary with Warners. Jack Warner – neat, dapper, fairly thickset Jew – bald, pleasant smile. Wife – Jewess – very dark – almost dusky skin. Much talk of our unpreparedness. Max says our military advisers stated Czech Maginot line no good – no guns, etc. – corruption. Hore-Belisha told him we had 3000 anti-aircraft [guns] – we had 300! He also told us how *Daily Express*, Manchester, had secured interview with De Valera – interview was anti-British Empire. Max took it out of Manchester edition – all other editions

[1] In fact Inskip was succeeded as Minister of Co-ordination of Defence by Admiral of the Fleet Lord Chatfield (1873–1967). Anderson (1882–1958), later Lord Waverley, became Lord Privy Seal. Inskip went to the Colonial Office in January 1939.

– ten minutes before going to press – papers late – De Valera furious – probably propaganda for his own country, where he is having difficulty with his own Leftists for being too pro-British! Sat up far too late – 2 a.m. This has been my worst week since I came back to London. In order to conquer London one must train like a boxer or a professional footballer.

Sunday, 16 October 1938

Feeling ill and suffering from indigestion. Except for a four-mile walk in the afternoon [at Cherkley] with Brendan Bracken and Frank Owen, stayed indoors all day and listened to an orgy of talk. Max, Brendan, Frank Owen, etc., gave terrible figures of our unpreparedness – no guns, no turrets, etc., etc.

Max told us that Duff Cooper had to leave War Office because he took view that in event of war we must send expeditionary force abroad.[1] Chamberlain was opposed. Last December or early this year Simon made cut of £200,000,000 in our defence programme; said (or was told by Treasury) that the country could not stand it.

Brendan Bracken, who accompanied Duff Cooper on yacht (Admiralty) to Baltic, full of praise of Tommy Troubridge,[2] British naval attaché in Berlin – says he is splendid, direct, forceful.

Wrote some paras on Lord Stanley who died (aged 44) in early hours of this morning. Brendan says that the estate will have to pay huge death duties because Lord Derby had made over bulk of his property to Edward Stanley.

In evening watched films in Max's little theatre including two by 'March of Time' which are banned in this country by our censorship. One is a League of Nations film; the other a Gibraltar film. Both are anti-dictator and pro-British. The League film is very pro-Eden, very anti-dictator (Musso and Hitler are called men of war), and slightly anti-Chamberlain. No reason, however, for banning them except that they are political. If you admit thin end of wedge of politics in films, no knowing where you'd be able to stop. Sat up late again. An exhausting weekend.

Monday, 17 October 1938

Worked all morning in office. Gave luncheon to Rex Leeper at the St James's. He looks much older since the crisis, is tired, and is worried about his own position and, indeed, that of Foreign Office. Chamberlain today does his own foreign policy (with Horace Wilson), and Foreign Office have a tag: 'If at first you can't concede, fly, fly, fly, again.' Rex who sees Anthony Eden regularly says Eden had wonderful reception in Wales. Eden is fed up with Parliament and the Parliamentary reshuffle of jobs among the old dul-

[1] Duff Cooper had been succeeded at the War Office by Leslie Hore-Belisha on 28 May 1937. He then went to the Admiralty, from which he had just resigned.

[2] Captain Thomas Troubridge (1895–1949), later knighted, vice-admiral and Fifth Sea Lord.

lards; thinks country is fed up with Parliament and the politicians. Rex says he is disgusted with Sam Hoare's behaviour over the crisis and that so is Seton-Watson.[1] Rex also told me that he tried very hard to persuade the Government to appoint me as assistant to Runciman when latter was sent on his mission to Czechoslovakia. Decided, however, that it would be too dangerous, as I knew too much! In other words, Germans would object to me as biased in favour of Czechs! My book goes well. On Thursday of last week we reprinted 5000 after initial edition of 10,000, and today we are reprinting 5000 more, making 20,000 in all.

Tuesday, 18 October 1938

Another pleasant day although slightly muggy. Tired and disinclined to work. Spent most of the morning writing paragraphs about Lord Chatfield who Beaver says is to be stopped from going to India and to be given Inskip's job as Minister of Co-ordination. In the evening had long talk with Allen of the Air Ministry. He says Chatfield will be bad appointment – almost impossible for a man, even if superhuman, from one service to dominate all three. Only man for job Winston – and he won't get it. Allen is also against Ministry of Supplies – too much centralisation already and months wasted in explaining schemes to different central authorities. Lack of powers of democracies. The laying of a telephone cable, vital to defence scheme, delayed for five months seven days because an urban council refused to have a road dug up.

Lunched with Moir Mackenzie at the Ivy. He is close friend of Horace Wilson – Wilson told him that when Chamberlain was ill in summer, Sam Hoare and Simon, both with ambitions to succeed him, hovered round him like vultures, anxious to be in at the kill and suspicious of each other. They impeded his recovery.

Lockhart received a very friendly letter from the Duke of Windsor on 19 October thanking him for an inscribed copy of Guns or Butter, *and saying that he felt very strongly that Chamberlain should be applauded for his efforts to avoid war, which would destroy both the democracies and the totalitarian states 'and victory go only to communism'.*

Wednesday, 19 October 1938

At seven to George Clerk at 60 South Audley Street. He gave me a very graphic account of Kemal Atatürk who is dying in Constantinople. Kemal used to drink too much – especially *raki* (white and same as arrack) – occasionally got 'muzzy' – but was never the debaucher of the 'Grey Wolf' legend. Spoke no English – began with foreign diplomats with interpreter. Then if interested broke into quite good French – but language German –

[1] Professor R. W. Seton-Watson (1879–1951), distinguished authority on Central European and Balkan history and affairs, later a colleague of Lockhart in the Political Intelligence Department.

quarrelled over military matters with Liman von Sanders – and was 'stellenbosched' and sent to train division near Chanak[1] – hence his chance to surprise British at landing. Anti-Italian – and at first anti-British – not so much because of war and pro-Greek policy as for occupation of Constantinople and deportations of Turks to Malta.

Thursday, 20 October 1938

Got to office at 10.15 and worked till 1.15 when I came West to give luncheon to Dick Shanks at the Mirabelle Restaurant. Dick looks heavy and is, I am sure, drinking far too much. He is depressed about his work, says he will write no more books, and is heavily in debt. Indeed, the income tax people have a bankruptcy writ against him. He is now on verge of joining the *Mail* at £3000 a year as leader-writer, has seen Esmond Harmsworth, and is waiting now for answer. Told me that Toulson, who was 'axed' from *Standard* in my time, has made success of his life. Is the local postmaster, coal-merchant, baker, etc. of little village in Wiltshire, has done well. His business now worth £7000 or so. In addition, Toulson all his life put every penny he could save into endowment policies. Many now falling due – he thus has security for future.

Friday, 21 October 1938

Had long talk with Alec Cadogan who is pro-Chamberlain, sorry for the Czechs, and rather critical of Beneš.[2] He thinks that (1) there was no truth in story that Chamberlain had all the cards in his hands in September, (2) we are paying for past mistakes, etc., that we should have made concessions ten–fifteen years ago to Stresemann, Brüning, etc. – especially at time of Disarmament Conference, and (3) we destroyed Stresemann and Brüning and made Hitler.

He also says no use Halifax wringing his hands and writing pretty speeches deploring the rule of force. Every German will tell you that from 1918 to 1932 the rule of force was in operation against them. Alec Cadogan said that both in Geneva and in the Foreign Office he tried very hard for concessions to Germany, but was frustrated by those same people who are now wanting to go to war with the man their policy created! He thinks we must stop talking about past now and go forward, rearm, try out appeasement policy. He is not without hope.

Saturday, 22 October 1938

At 10.30 a.m. rang up Jan Masaryk for news of Beneš who is said to be going to Switzerland for a rest. Jan told me privately that he expected Beneš

[1] General Otto Liman von Sanders was the German commander of the Fifth Turkish Army in the Dardanelles. To be 'stellenbosched' was to be relegated to a less important military post – like Stellenbosch, Cape of Good Hope, which was used as a dumping-ground for incompetents.

[2] Beneš had resigned on 5 October.

in London soon on his way through to the U.S.A., but begged me not to say a word until Beneš had actually left Czechoslovakia; otherwise, his life might be endangered. Of course I promised, and Jan said he would give me first news on Monday or Tuesday. An hour later Beneš had arrived with his wife and a secretary at Croydon. Jan knew only a few minutes after he had spoken to me and was late at the aerodrome. Beneš is ill and is living in strict secrecy at a friend's house in the country. Jan said he was in danger not only from Germans, but also from Czechs . . . who were now blaming him for what had happened. Had to write a news story on Beneš and also wait at office till three to discuss with Mike and Blackburn[1] terms to be offered to Beneš for (1) one article, and (2) for six articles – exclusive and to start on Monday. There is little chance of Beneš doing anything just now – and I told Mike this. He replied that in six months Beneš would have no value. His present value was for one article of 1200 words on 'What I feel about it' £250 – for six articles in final form to start on Monday (1000–1200 words each) = £1000!

Sunday, 23 October 1938

Talked to Jan Masaryk by phone. Beneš will do nothing in way of writing just now. Very seedy and run-down. Suffering from giddy fits. Unlikely to be able to leave for U.S.A. for at least two months. His arrival more or less surprise to Jan.

Monday, 24 October 1938

Curious story of rumour. Randolph Churchill rang me up the other day. He'd heard on absolute authority. High member of Lord Halifax's immediate staff had told him that many young members of Foreign Office disliked policy of His Majesty's Government and criticised it both in and out of Foreign Office. Halifax had ordered inquiry. There was to be a purge. Spoke to Christopher Warner. Story had been going about since Eden's resignation. Quite untrue. True that in times of crisis circular often went round telling people they must be careful what they say.

Thursday, 27 October 1938

He [Beaverbrook] wanted to have a 'crack' at Lloyd George . . . for his mischievous speech [yesterday] championing the Czechs and saying we had handed over little democratic state wrapped in Union Jack and Tricolour to a ruthless dictator. There was magnificent attack on Lloyd George for inconsistency. In July of this year he was attacking Beneš in the *Daily Telegraph* calling him grasping, and saying because of his greed and cunning Allies were induced to give recognition to 'polyglot and incoherent state with hundreds of thousands of discontented Magyars and millions of Sudeten Germans'. Truth is Lloyd George was virtually opposed to Beneš since Genoa

[1] Thomas Blackburn, who was to become Joint Chairman of Beaverbrook Newspapers, 1955–68, knighted 1968.

Conference when he was unable to induce Beneš to side with him against French on issue of recognition of and pact with Russia. Curiously enough, too, in the official life of Goering only English statesman singled out for praise was Lloyd George 'who had the decency to admit' (presumably on his hurried visit) 'that the Nazis had saved Europe from Communism!' Amazing record in inconsistency.

Gave luncheon to Christopher Warner at Boulestin's. He is pessimistic; thinks that Britain has two choices: (1) to rearm on a vast national effort, and this will mean nationalisation of industry and coal, etc. – in fact, end of capitalism, or (2) to resign gracefully from Europe and from any lead, and arm sufficiently to protect our Empire. Back to office in afternoon. In evening took George R. Clerk to Scott's, Victoria Palace (*Me and My Gal*)[1] and Savoy. Told me he'd been at Chatham House [Royal Society of International Affairs] for Committee meeting – Toynbee had read most pessimistic paper against dictators. He, G.R.C., had protested. He is pro-Chamberlain.

Saturday, 29 October 1938

At twelve noon to the Ritz to see Princess Marthe Bibesco and to talk about Carol and Rumania. She told me that Rex Hoare was given some papers by Queen Marie (like the Ponsonby Letters) and that these papers contain the mother's attacks on the King. Carol knows about this arrangement. Princess Bibesco thinks it would be a fine gesture on our part if we were to hand the papers back during his visit. She also hopes that someone like the Pembrokes will ask him to shoot so that he can see something of English country life.

Sunday, 30 October 1938

Then at 8.45 to the Anthony Rothschilds' to dinner. Present: Brendan Bracken, Korda and Princess Bibesco. (*She says she spells it with an o.*)[2] Conversation pessimistic and anti-German, with Brendan in the role of Cassandra and, in the presence of foreigners, very naughtily *défaitiste*. One Funk in the German Cabinet, and twenty-two in the British! Chamberlain would give away the whole empire, etc.! Anthony Rothschild believes that out of this crisis will come a rejuvenation of England. He agrees with me no use cursing and blaming; at same time he is against the frightful complacency of the Chamberlainites and wants a strong line. He is afraid that Chamberlain does not mean to rearm. Princess Bibesco says Carol wants England to send ships to Constantia, Sea of Marmara, etc. Have big influence.

Wednesday, 2 November 1938

At 1.30 to luncheon with the Cadogans. Present: American ambassador

[1] Lupino Lane's show, which had already had more than 500 performances and included the famous song and dance 'The Lambeth Walk'.

[2] Lockhart had earlier spelt it Bibescu.

and Mrs Kennedy, Lord Plymouth, Lady George Cholmondeley,[1] Lord and Lady Harlech. . . Had short talk with Alec Cadogan about Carol's visit and the letters given by Queen Marie to Rex Hoare. I gather that Alec Cadogan is very cautious. He is quite willing that Lady Leconfield should ask Carol to Petworth, but does not wish her to say the Foreign Office asked her to do it. Returning Queen Marie's letters to Carol will not be easy; for, apparently, the letters compromise other people who might be adversely affected. Talked with Lady George Cholmondley who is pro-Chamberlain; also with Lady Harlech who is very anti-Nazi. . . Lord Plymouth is another very cautious bird – not very impressive. Took the line: What did the Czechs think France or we could have done for them?

Thursday, 3 November 1938

Fine day; much warmer. Letter from Rex Leeper (official) asking me to confirm the verbal arrangement made with him during crisis week: namely, that in the event of war I agree to give my services to the Foreign Office for the duration and will undertake to superintend Russia and Russian affairs in the Political Intelligence Department. Harold is to do Central Europe; Sir Frederick Whyte America. Our salaries are limited (by the Treasury of course) to £600! I shall accept again. What else can I do unless I am sent on some foreign mission?

Lunched at Sibyl Colefax's – a very 'grand' party with the Duke and Duchess of Devonshire, the Duchess of Rutland, Mr and Mrs Ogilvie (new B.B.C. chief),[2] Somerset Maugham, and H. A. L. Fisher. Had talk with Fisher while walked with him from 19 [Lord] North Street to Athenaeum. He does not like what has happened but does not disapprove of what Chamberlain did. Thinks that we have to recognise new situation. Spoke of Ireland. He drafted the Home Rule Bill.

Saturday, 5 November 1938

Fortunately, I was able to get Dimancescu, the Rumanian attaché, on the telephone, and he gave me some very good notes on Prince Michael, the son of King Carol, which I was able to add to my own. News to me was the story that every night after dinner Carol and Michael sit down and play duets on two pianos. Debussy is their favourite. Lunched at 18 Eaton Square and then went with Tommy to the Zoo and for a walk in Regent's Park. In Zoo saw a 'red brocket', a kind of antelope from Dutch Guiana – *Mazama americana* – reminded me of Lord Brocket.

[1] Joseph Kennedy (1888–1969), American Ambassador, 1938–40, father of President Kennedy. 2nd Earl of Plymouth (1889–1943), Parliamentary Under-Secretary Foreign Office, 1936–9. Diana, wife of Lord George Cholmondeley.

[2] Frederick Ogilvie (1893–1949) had succeeded Reith as Director-General of the B.B.C.

Monday, 7 November 1938

In morning met Robertson of *Daily Express* who looked very well. Told me Beaverbrook was now unlikely to go abroad or to U.S.A., because he was enjoying himself too much here. In Baldwin's time people (Ministers) were afraid to go to see him. Now he has Sam Hoare, Belisha, etc., on his doorstep, and Chamberlain's speeches read like *Daily Express* leaders.

Tuesday, 8 November 1938

Dull and warm. A hectic day. Lunched with the Sieffs to meet Captain Wingate,[1] the Palestine Lawrence. Medium-height, fair, gaunt features, parts hair wrong way, firm mouth, queer sunken eyes with almost fanatical look in them. A nephew of Sirdar – a Scottish family from Ayrshire. Came to Palestine two-and-a-half years ago as first class interpreter in Arabic – learnt Hebrew since. Now pro-Jew – wants to arm Jewish force – let in immigrants – soon deal with problem – thinks nothing of Arab strength or Arab danger – very down on our administration – he himself has organised (with official connivance) band of 150 (mostly young Jews), has done in more Arabs than all the official troops, and has kept order unaided in large tract of territory. Like Lawrence – good at disguise. Goes into Arab places like Damascus disguised as Jewish doctor.

Wednesday, 9 November 1938

Lunched at the Ritz with Rumanian Minister Grigorcea (known as 'The White Slug') who was giving 'show' for Press in connection with King Carol's visit. Curious show and precedence comic. On Grigorcea's right sat young O'Brien, formerly of the *Daily Telegraph* and now of British Council, and on his left Victor Gordon-Lennox.[2] Opposite Minister sat Matila Ghyku, Counsellor. On his right Baxter (*Sunday Times*) and on his left Denkin of *Times*. Berry Brothers right on top! I sat beside ——, Counsellor, whom I used to know in Prague in 1920–1. In those days a dashing Don Juan, and at a ball at the American Legation some girl complained that —— had been pushing his penis into her while dancing! ——was had on mat, said nonsense – only his house-key which he produced – very large. Now sedate and serious bourgeois. Fat and married to a rich wife!

At six took Captain Wingate to see Lord Beaverbrook. A flop – Wingate did his 'stuff' again but not nearly so well as yesterday. Lord Beaverbrook was bored, and when he told Wingate that he had heard other people argue the Arab case just as sincerely as Wingate had pled the Jew case, Wingate was rude. Those people didn't know. His press was inaccurate. 'Everything

[1] Orde Charles Wingate (1903–44), later major-general and leader of the Chindit force in Burma, was then on the intelligence staff, Palestine, where he organised Jewish night squads. His uncle, the Sirdar (Commander-in-Chief) Egypt and Governor-General of the Sudan, 1899–1916, was Sir Reginald Wingate (1861–1953).

[2] (*b.* 1897) *Daily Telegraph* journalist, had been on 'Peterborough' column.

depended on whose side God was!' Beaverbrook was annoyed and will now hunt Wingate down.

At 12.30 a.m. took Frank Owen, Tom Driberg and Michael Foot[1] to Sports Club. Huge talk on Russia, with Tom Driberg and Michael Foot violently pro-Communist and Frank anti!

Thursday, 10 November 1938

Today received (for first time) an invitation to Buckingham Palace for next Wednesday's party to King Carol. Lord Chamberlain's office not very smart on the divorce lists. Invitation issued to Mr and Mrs Bruce Lockhart![2] Lunched at Sibyl's... Talked to Mrs Cronin [wife of novelist, A. J. Cronin] who comes from Lanarkshire. Said she liked *My Scottish Youth* best of my books. Told me that her husband had no great difficulty in getting his royalties from Germany; did it through an agent. Also talked to Lady Rodd whom I sat next. Very pro-German and anti-Czech.

Walked to House of Commons with Leslie [Hore-Belisha] and discussed Wingate. As I thought, Lord Beaverbrook *is* now pursuing him in ministerial quarters. Leslie, as a Jew, is pro-Wingate but a little worried. He told me that General Ironside had spoken highly of him. At six went to Mrs Adams (Vyvyan)[3] at Gloucester Gate to have preliminary talk about my television broadcast on November 21. Met Horrabin, the Labour geographer – tall, fair, pleasant and, I should think, efficient. Talk not so difficult as I thought. We have to show several maps, but I do not wish to confine myself to frontiers and can really give an informative talk about Rumania.

Saturday, 12 November 1938

In the evening to Cherkley with Wardell and Bracken. At dinner Sir John Anderson, the new A.R.P. [Air Raid Precautions] chief... Sir John Anderson, pompous and platitudinous and very conceited. Hard to believe that he is the great man who is to put our affairs in order. Made me say at once: 'Well, we've lost the next war.' May be good organiser, but a smug and wrong type of Scot. Lord Beaverbrook told us Madame Lupescu was coming with Carol to London. I said I did not believe it, and he replied that he had had letter from Lord Halifax to that effect. Beaverbrook also said: Chamberlain should fight election in January on appeasement but should have a row with Hitler a fortnight before in order to win votes, as Baldwin did with Italy before last election. Then having won we had Hoare–Laval Pact.

Tuesday, 15 November 1938

Long letter from Robin with amusing account of Cambridge 'rags' on

[1] (*b.* 1913) Assistant Editor *Tribune*, later Acting Editor *Evening Standard*, 1942; Left-wing Labour M.P. 1945–55, 1960–.

[2] Lockhart was divorced earlier in the year.

[3] Mary Adams, producer B.B.C. television, 1936–9.

Guy Fawkes Day and on Armistice Day when nearly £3000 was collected for ex-service wounded. Undergratuates dressed up as Chamberlain, Stalin, Hitler, Mussolini, and signed treaties on toilet paper. There was a raffle of Major Attlee's 'pants'.

Went round to club and sat up latish talking to [Thomas] Waddington who is now a full-time brigadier in charge of territorials. Says not only would we not have gone to war in crisis, but could not go to war now. The army has nothing, and the organisation is chaotic.

Wednesday, 16 November 1938

In the afternoon went to Moss Bros to hire breeches, stockings and pumps for tonight's reception at Buckingham Palace in honour of King Carol. Signed copies of my book for the Book Society and sent an autographed copy to King Carol who has good sense of humour. On the destroyer yesterday he took out his cigarette case, offered cigarettes to officers, and then said: 'Now, tell that to Bruce Lockhart.' (This because I had criticised him in my book for not offering cigarettes to his visitors.) Saw first criticism in American paper of *Guns or Butter – New Yorker*. Short and not very favourable. Said, too, that I 'was vastly impressed by Nazi Germany'. Does not look so far as if book would go well in U.S.A.

In evening dined with Harold at Savoy and went on to Buckingham Palace. Not very impressive – but quite well done. Shook hands with Queen and had very good view of royal entry.

Monday, 21 November 1938

Dull, some rain, colder. A busy day spoilt by sitting up too late. In morning young Max Aitken ran up. He had been to Paris to persuade Duke of Windsor to write for Beaverbrook Press: either book to be serialised or series of articles. H.R.H. apparently was prepared to play with the idea, provided that I should write the book for him. Young Max is prepared to send me to Paris; is coming to see me tomorrow. Lunched at the Oliver Stanleys. Present: Alec Hardinge and wife, Teddy Jessel and wife, Lady Reading, – Brocklehurst. Gathered from Hardinge, Carol's visit went off quite well, but that he (Carol) is not very popular in Court circles. Apparently he behaved badly at funeral in sense that he made adverse remarks about King George V to the person attached to him. Hardinge did not like Urdureanu. Lady Maureen Stanley is going to Balkans to lecture for British Council.

Lady Reading praised John Anderson who, she says, is pompous but more efficient than he sounds or looks. Gets things done. His staff told him A.R.P. pamphlet would take six weeks. He said 'one'. It was done. Did my television broadcast on Rumania. Longish job. Rehearsal at Alexandra Palace from 5 to 7.30. The broadcast at 9.40. Went off quite well, I think. Back to club at 11.15. Stupidly sat up late. Peter Eckersley[1] came in; is going to Paris with

[1] (1892–1963) Consultant radio engineer.

Chamberlain to see French Air Chiefs. Says German Air Force is short of engines. Have been disappointed in Diesel. Have no bombers as fast as ours. Loud in his praise of Harold Balfour,[1] who was air ace in war – more victories than Goering. Has been three months in present job. Has flown solo every type we have including Spitfire and Hurricane.

Tuesday, 29 November 1938

Gave luncheon at Boulestin to Willie Maugham, Jan Masaryk, Harold Nicolson. Jan – semi-jovial and semi-cynical – rather better about Chamberlain. Told us had today received order from Legation. Beneš better but does realise how strong is feeling against him in Czechoslovakia. Irene Ravensdale and Thelma Cazalet are raising testimonial for him. Jan, who goes to U.S.A. on 30 December, is to be chief speaker at International Jewish Conference in Washington. Has about £35,000 in Czechoslovakia; is afraid it will be confiscated, especially if he says word against new order.

Maugham told us good story. Years ago on cruise met rich American Jew who regards Maugham as God. Maugham once able do him service. Met him on way to Russia (on secret service) *via* Siberia – Yank had big holding of roubles – wanted information. Maugham afraid in official position – sent telegram 'Rachel very ill recovery impossible.' Yank sold – made £200,000. Said must give Maugham something – gave him fine box of cigars! Repaid however. Later, Maugham gave him £2000 to invest (Yank is broker) – now worth £30,000. In afternoon with Tommy to cinema for hour and half.

Wednesday, 30 November 1938

At 4 to American Embassy or rather Chancery – Grosvenor Square – fine offices. Saw Kennedy for twenty minutes – keen, cocksure, began with nothing, got to Harvard. His hero was Huntington's brother who was great athlete. Asked him if I would have rough time lecturing in U.S.A. and in recommending necessity of understanding with dictator countries. Said 'no'; told me he was going to U.S.A. on Saturday to tell his Government the facts: England could do nothing else except Munich – no longer able to dictate to world – her glory gone – war would have been lost – France not only not wants to fight – unable to fight them (as present position shows). Americans crazy – a hundred per cent isolationist – yet telling England what to do – did they think England's defeat or collapse of Europe would help them? Very pro-Chamberlain.

Thursday, 1 December 1938

Randolph Churchill came back to [*Evening Standard*] office. Gave us one good joke about the Duke of Windsor: 'Why has Duchess of Windsor no

[1] (*b.* 1897) Parliamentary Under-Secretary for Air, 1938–44, later Baron Balfour of Inchrye.

child yet?' 'Ah, you see, the Duke is air-minded but not heir-conditioned.' Gave luncheon to Moir Mackenzie who told me that Sir Horace Wilson was sore that his (the Chamberlain) policy of appeasement was being torpedoed by wild talk both here and in U.S.A. Was not finished yet.

Saturday, 3 December 1938

Before luncheon went with Randolph Churchill to Brooks's Club and had two cocktails. Discussed Winston and his splendid 'in war resolution, in defeat defiance, in victory magnanimity, and in peace goodwill'. Randolph said Winston practised it from first moment. In November 1918 wanted to send food-ships to Germany, was opposed to continuance of blockade. Amazing energy – now over 60. On August 1st began new book on English-speaking races, set himself task of 1000 words a day. Crisis came – very active – speeches – articles. Yet has not only kept to but exceeded schedule. On December 1 – 122 days – has written 136,000.

Gave luncheon to Rex Leeper at the St James's Club and discussed my lecture tour in the U.S.A. Rex not able to help very much, but advises keeping off current politics as far as possible and dealing with war of ideas in Europe. Rex is anti-Chamberlain, thinks Chamberlain is unable to see any one else's point of view, told me Chamberlain had said that Foreign Office were hopeless, because always tried to make simplest problem complicated! . .

In afternoon wrote preface to D. J. Hall's *Romanian Furrow*. In evening dined at club and discussed Franco-British air-relations with Peter Eckersley, who has been over in France seeing French air people. Their view is: France cannot maintain huge army (also for us) and huge air force – we must do air. Eckersley pointed out that for 1939–40 we are spending on air alone more than France on all her defences – and we have expensive navy as well.

Tuesday, 6 December 1938

Ribbentrop arrived in Paris to sign the Franco-German declaration. Wrote two paragraphs telling how exactly twenty years ago Ribbentrop set out to Paris on very different errand. Then a poor ex-cavalry officer; wanted to get (and did get) Pomméry agency for Germany. Rose to fame on foam of champagne. For some years sold French champagne to German Jews. Married Fräulein Henkell, etc. Went in early with Hitler. Served him well; told him England would not fight. Now on top of world – even above Goering. At least he, and not Goering, forms with Goebbels and Hitler the Nazi triumvirate honoured with nicknames at Eton, where boys of Lower School call them 'Hit, Rib and Gob'. Paragraphs were sent over to Max, who turned them down as too cruel!

Thursday, 8 December 1938

Gave luncheon for Goulding to meet Fitz Randolph at the Carlton Grill.

Conversation not easy, and Fitz Randolph himself very reticent; expressed regret that tension could not be relieved, admitted that Nazis had made some mistakes, but said more and more Germans getting the impression that English wished to fight a preventive war before Germany became too strong. Quoted Duff Cooper's Paris speech (which was provocative!) and Malcolm MacDonald's statement in House yesterday on Colonies. This will, of course, produce outburst in Berlin.

Saw Bernstorff for a moment. He arrived last night. Says, internally and externally, everything in Germany is boiling up for crisis in spring. Hitler wants a war against anyone; wants to use the new toy which he has created. Many Germans are now saying Britain is the Erzfeind [Arch enemy]. Hitler does *not* like Chamberlain because latter prevented him from enjoying his *Excursionskrieg* into Prague. Feeling in Party is divided as follows: Goebbels, Himmler, Ribbentrop against Goering. Latter at moment not quite so strong. Goering was furious about the Jewish pogrom. Nevertheless, took him a week to get one of his own non-Aryan protegées out of prison or detention. Pirow, South African Minister [of Defence], in London again. Saw King and Chamberlain and renewed his statement of 'almost unqualified anxiety'.

Saturday, 10 December 1938

At Wilton. Much talk about the Windsors. Most people here opposed to Windsors coming back.

Story of the Queen. Someone said to her, Duchess of Windsor had done much for Duke – stopped him drinking – no more pouches under his eyes. 'Yes,' said Queen, 'who has the lines under his eyes now?' David Herbert very amusing on his stay at the Kent's when news came in that the Duke of Gloucester had broken collar-bone hunting just after return from holiday – Kent who has been working hard has to go to Norway for Queen's funeral: 'Damn you, Harry; eighteenth time you've fallen off – why can't you stick to croquet.' Queen Mary also displeased: 'Told Harry not to hunt until Aunt Maud buried.'

Talk with Hambleden[1] on Penguins and Gollancz. He is against both.

After dinner long talk with Duke of Alba.[2] Talks perfect English – reactionary – says Franco will restore monarchy at once. Good on Spanish history and on obstinacy of Spaniards. Took Rome two hundred years to conquer Spain – and Spain had her revenge. Gave Rome – Seneca, Martial, Trajan, Hadrian, etc.

Sunday, 11 December 1938

Taw-taw Gilmour[3] who is friend of Queen's asked her if Windsors coming

[1] W. H. Smith, 3rd Viscount Hambleden (1903–1948), head of the bookselling chain.

[2] FitzJames Stuart, 17th Duke of Alba (1878–1953), was to be Franco's Ambassador to Britain 1939–45. He was descended from an illegitimate son of James II.

[3] Mrs John Little Gilmour, Lady-in-Waiting to the Queen.

to England: 'No, certainly not; wouldn't receive her if she did. Quite untrue that matter was discussed with Mr Chamberlain in Paris; was never mentioned.'

Taw-taw Gilmour: 'May I mention this?'

'Certainly.'

Long talks with Duke of Alba who has been in sling from synovitis, hitting golf-ball into bunker. Talks very well. Looks like a Stuart – Stuart head and eyes, courageous – faced troubles – called 'Comrade Stuart' by Socialists – fine knowledge of history and the arts – his house in Madrid destroyed – his pictures God knows where – in Valencia, he thinks.

Daudet's description of Daladier: *a bull with a snail's horns*. Later, a long talk with Simon Rodney who told me curious stories about big business. Not long ago Nuffield's head manager came to him and said: 'Bound to tell you I have been approached by another firm.' Nuffield said: 'Lord Austin, I suppose?' 'Yes.' 'Well, you can go at once.' Man was getting £50,000 a year. According to Simon, McKenna – gangster, gambling banker – ought to have been out of the Midland long ago.[1]

Friday, 23 December 1938

At 12.45 went to say goodbye to Jan Masaryk – an emotional farewell. He goes to U.S.A. on December 30 – will speak twelve times – mainly on and for Jews. His father was great champion of Jews – therefore Jan is too. But when I asked his advice how to help Geduldiger, Pollak, Nembroch, Pik, etc., who had appealed to me – he raged.

'God,' he says, 'that's the difference between you and me and them. We are sick for an hour if we have to ask someone for a tenner; these people you mention are all richer than we'll ever be. I've had a fellow in here for a fortnight; he's got over £30,000 over here – he's going to start a Czech restaurant. He's been in here five times a day to worry me, when people are starving – parents in concentration camps. Finally, I told him: "You get out and keep out – or I'll telephone to Sam Hoare to have you deported".'

Jan is not very bitter – sore . . . about Lord Maugham,[2] and especially Runciman hobnobbing with aristocracy. Pleased with *Times* quote on him: other diplomats are Excellencies; Mr So-and-So – Jan to everyone 'Jan Masaryk'. Jan says – 'Pays to be kind. I was sore with them in crisis – Now I can say nothing!' Said to me: 'I won't forget – you've been a good friend to me and my country.' Interesting on Beneš: many admirers including me – but he has no friends, no sense of humour, doesn't know how to deal with people. Two years ago: 'I (Jan) could have arranged everything with Goering – Beneš couldn't see it, wouldn't have it.'

[1] Reginald McKenna (1863–1943), who had been Chancellor of the Exchequer in 1916, was now Chairman of the Midland Bank at the age of 75.

[2] (1866–1958), Lord Chancellor, who maintained in the House of Lords that we had given the Czechs all the help they could reasonably expect.

Tuesday, 27 December 1938

Karel Čapek died of pneumonia in Prague. He would have been forty-nine on January 9th. Of all Czechs he attracted me most. He stood for nearly everything I stand for. He was the disciple and interpreter of Masaryk. He believed in the small nations, felt that they had to be more efficient than big powers to survive, hated and loathed war. Two years ago, we had a very gay party at his house in Prague. His wife, Olga Scheinpflugova, an actress and a poet, thought he was like me. We planned a tour of Scotland together. Last March he was overwhelmed by the pending tragedy to his country. He knew then. Pneumonia may have been the cause of his death, but I dare swear he died because everything for which he had lived had been outraged and strangled.

ACKNOWLEDGEMENTS

My first thanks go to Sir Max Aitken, Bart, who on my advice purchased the diaries of Sir Robert Bruce Lockhart, thus following the policy of his father, Lord Beaverbrook, in forming a remarkable collection of political and private papers.

I have had the greatest help from Sir Robert's son, Robin Bruce Lockhart, in my editing and annotating; and he has also let me see a great many letters, some of which are included in these volumes, as well providing many illustrations. Lady Bruce Lockhart has enlightened me on many points about her husband's war-time and subsequent career and I am most grateful to her.

For permission to quote letters to Bruce Lockhart I am grateful to Prince Louis Ferdinand of Prussia; Lady Diana Cooper; Sir Rupert Hart-Davis (Hugh Walpole); The London School of Economics and Political Science (Lord and Lady Passfield); Nigel Nicolson (Harold Nicolson); Lady Tweedsmuir (John Buchan).

Among the many people who have cleared up knotty points or helped me with their memories I should like to thank Sir John Wheeler-Bennett, Sir Rupert Hart-Davis, Gregory Macdonald, Gerald Pawle, A. J. P. Taylor, Mrs Joan Saunders, C. J. Child, Admiral Sir Norman Denning, George Malcolm Thomson and, of the staff of Messrs. Macmillan, Alan D. Maclean, Richard Garnett and Miss Caroline Hobhouse.

To a succession of typists who have struggled with Bruce Lockhart's handwriting I raise my hat.

KENNETH YOUNG

LIST OF FAMILIAR NAMES

Bertie: Duke of York, later George VI
Bloggs: Betty Baldwin
Blossom: Mary Freeman-Thomas, Viscountess Ratendone
Blum: R. D. Blumenfeld
Brendan: Brendan Bracken
Bridget: Lady Bridget Paget
Buck: Lord De La Warr
Constant: Constant Huntington of Putnam
David: Edward VIII
Diana: Lady Diana Cooper
Diana: Lady De La Warr
Doris: Lady Castlerosse
Duff: Alfred Duff Cooper
F. E.: F. E. Smith, 1st Earl of Birkenhead
Frank: Arthur Francis Aveling
G. R. C.: Sir George Clerk
Hamish: J. A. W. St Clair Erskine, son of 'Tommy'
Harold: Harold Nicolson
Harry: 5th Earl of Rosslyn
Hickie: Captain William Hicks
Hugo: 11th Earl of Wemyss
Jean: Jean Bruce Lockhart (1st wife)
Jean: Mrs Jean Norton
Jill: unidentified girl friend
Jix: Sir William Joynson-Hicks
Kitty: Katherine, Lady Brownlow
L. G.: Lloyd George
Laura: Laura, Lady Lovat
Loughie: Lord Loughborough
Mary: Mary St Clair Erskine (later Dunn) daughter of 'Tommy'
Maurice: Sir Maurice Peterson
Max: Lord Beaverbrook
Max, Little Max: Sir Max Aitken
Mike: Michael Wardell
Millie: Millicent, Duchess of Sutherland
Moir: Moir Mackenzie
Moura: Baroness Budberg
Negley: Negley Farson
Nigs: Inigo Freeman-Thomas, Viscount Ratendone
Pam: Pamela Chichester (later Wrench)
Perry: Peregrine, 6th Baron Brownlow
Pip: Rupert Bruce Lockhart (brother)
Ramsay: Ramsay MacDonald
Randolph: Randolph Churchill
Rex: Sir Reginald Leeper
Robin: R. N. Bruce Lockhart (son)
Rufus: J. H. Bruce Lockhart (brother)
Tom: Sir Oswald Mosley
Tom: Tom Macgregor (uncle)
Tommy: Vera Mary, Countess of Rosslyn
Tootie: Arnold, Count de Bendern
Valentine: Viscount Castlerosse
Van: Sir Robert Vansittart

INDEX